This is Poetry

Ollie O' Gallaghan

GW00949911

Brian Forristal & Billy Ramsell

FORUM PUBLICATIONS LTD.

Published by
Forum Publications Ltd
Unit 1703, Euro Business Park,
Little Island, Cork
Tel: (021) 4232268 | Fax: (01) 6335347
www.forum-publications.com

ISBN: 978-1-906565-53-4

ACKNOWLEDGEMENTS

Poems by Seamus Heaney are reproduced by kind permission of Faber and Faber Ltd; Poems by Eileán Ní Chuilleanáin are reproduced by kind permission of the Gallery Press, Loughcrew, Oldcastle, Co. Meath, Ireland. Poems by Sylvia Plath are reproduced by kind permission of Faber and Faber Ltd; Poems by W. B. Yeats are reproduced by kind permission of Henry Holt and Company; Poems by Paula Meehan are reproduced by kind permission of Dedalus Press.

Contents

Poetry Notes

Rhyme

Rhyme Schemes

Since time immemorial, rhyme has been deeply associated with poetry. The poem's rhyme scheme describes how rhymes are arranged in each stanza. When we describe a rhyme scheme, we refer to lines that rhyme with one another by the same letter.

In 'Inversnaid' by Gerard Manley Hopkins, for example, the first line of each stanza rhymes with the second line, while the third line rhymes with the fourth. We say, therefore, that the poem has an AABB rhyme scheme:

This darksome burn, horseback brown A

His rollrock highroad roaring down, A

In coop and in comb the fleece of his foam B

Flutes and low to the lake falls home. B

In 'Design' by Robert Frost, the first 8 lines follow an ABBA rhyme scheme:

I found a dimpled spider, fat and white, A

On a white heal-all, holding up a moth B

Like a white piece of rigid satin cloth - B

Assorted characters of death and blight A

Mixed ready to begin the morning right A

Like the ingredients of a witches' broth -B

A snow-drop spider, a flower like froth B

And dead wings carried like a paper kite. A

Half-rhyme

An important technique to watch out for is half-rhyme. This is where two lines end in words that almost rhyme.

In 'The Harvest Bow' by Seamus Heaney, for example, the poet rhymes 'peace' with 'device'.

Emily Dickinson makes use of half-rhyme in 'There's a certain Slant of light'. In the final stanza, the poet rhymes 'listens' and 'Distance'.

Metaphor and Simile

Metaphors and similes are incredibly common in poetry, and many poems owe their most vivid and memorable moments to these techniques.

A metaphor is when one thing is compared to something else. A simile is very similar to a metaphor in that it also compares one thing to something else. The big difference is that it uses the words 'like' or 'as'.

Each of the following phrases compares the hurler D.J. Carey to a lion:

- 'D.J. was like a lion in attack.'
- 'D.J. played as if he were a lion in attack.'
- 'D.J. was a lion in attack.'

The first two comparisons are similes because they use the words 'like' or 'as'. The third comparison is a metaphor because it does not feature the words 'like' or 'as'. Very often a metaphor is referred to as a 'strong' or 'direct' comparison, while a simile is referred to as a 'weak' or 'indirect' comparison. As a general rule, similes tend to occur more often than metaphors, especially in modern poetry.

Consider the following phrases, and in the case of each say whether it is a metaphor or a simile:

- *'The words are shadows'* **(Eavan Boland)**
- *'One tree is yellow as butter'* **(Eavan Boland)**
- *Suspicion climbed all over her face, like a kitten, but not so playfully'* **(Raymond Chandler)**
- *'A leaping tongue of bloom'* **(Robert Frost)**
- *'Love set you going like a fat gold watch'* **(Sylvia Plath)**
- *''a dump of rocks/ Leftover soldiers from old, messy wars'* **(Sylvia Plath)**
- *''The mists are … Souls'* **(Sylvia Plath)**
- *''He stumbles on like a rumour of war'* **(Eavan Boland)**
- *''My red filaments burn and stand, a hand of wires'* **(Sylvia Plath)**
- *'I thought of London spread out in the sun/ Its postal districts packed like squares of wheat'* **(Philip Larkin)**
- *''The sky is a torn sail'* **(Adrienne Rich)**

Personification

This is a technique whereby an inanimate object is described as if it had the qualities of a living thing.

In 'Mirror', for example, Plath personifies the mirror, presenting it as a thinking being, a character with thoughts, ideas and emotions. The poem endows the mirror with human traits such as truthfulness, faithfulness and jealousy.

Glossary of Poetry
Ideas & Terms

Hyperbole

This is where we deliberately exaggerate to make a point. For example:

- These books weigh a ton. (These books are heavy.)
- I could sleep for a year. (I could sleep for a long time.)
- The path went on forever. (The path was very long.)
- I'm doing a million things right now. (I'm busy.)
- I could eat a horse. (I'm hungry.)

Metonymy

This is a technique whereby we describe something without mentioning the thing itself; instead, we mention something closely associated with it.

For example, we use the phrase 'White House', to refer to the President of the US and his advisors, or 'Hollywood' to refer to the film industry.

Synecdoche

When we use this technique, we identify some-thing by referring to a part of the thing instead of naming the thing itself.

A good example is the phrase 'All hands on deck'. In this instance, the sailors are identified by a part of their bodies, i.e. their hands. Similarly, we might use the word 'wheels' to refer to a car or 'head' to refer to cattle.

Sound Effects

One of the features that most distinguishes poetry from ordinary language is its 'musical' quality. Much of this 'word music' is generated by assonance, alliteration and onomatopoeia.

Alliteration

Alliteration occurs when a number of words in close proximity start with the same sound.

We see this in the repeated 'h' sounds in line 3 of 'The Lake Isle of Innisfree' by Yeats: 'will I have there, a hive for the honey-bee'.

Alliteration also occurs in line 2 of Hopkins's 'Spring', with the repeated 'w' and 'l' sounds: 'When weeds, in wheels, shoot long and lovely and lush'.

Assonance

Assonance occurs when a number of words in close proximity have similar vowel sounds.

Emily Dickinson uses assonance in 'I felt a Funeral, in my Brain'. In line 18, she uses repeated 'o' sounds: 'I dropped down, and down'. A similar repetition of the 'o' sound is evident in lines 10 to 11: 'across my Soul/ With those same Boots'.

Onomatopoeia

Onomatopoeia occurs when a word or a group of words sounds like the noise it describes. Examples of onomatopoeic words include buzz, murmur and clang. It features in 'Lake Isle of Innisfree' by Yeats. In the phrase, 'noon a purple glow,/ And evening full of the linnet's wings', we can almost hear the fluttering sound of song-birds' wings.

Onomatopoeia is also a feature of 'The Forge' by Seamus Heaney. In the phrase, 'hiss when a new shoe toughens in water', we can almost hear the sound of the red-hot iron being dipped into the cooling water.

Euphony and Cacophony

Euphony and cacophony are also important concepts. Euphony can be defined as any pleasing or agreeable combination of sounds. Cacophony, meanwhile, is a harsh, jarring or discordant combination of sounds.

Euphony features in 'The Arrival of the Bee Box' by Sylvia Plath in lines 32 to 36, where the repeated broad vowel sounds in 'source of honey', 'moon suit' and 'funeral veil' create a pleasant musical effect.

Cacophony features in 'A Constable Calls' by Seamus Heaney. The repeated hard 'b', 'd', 'p' and 't' sounds in the lines 'With its buttoned flap, the braid cord/ Looped into the revolver butt' create a harsh verbal effect suited to the tough and rigid material of the constable's gun.

Other Useful Poetic Terms

Allegory A story in which the characters and events are symbols that stand for ideas about human life or for a political or historical situation.

Allusion Where a poem makes reference to another poem or text.

Anaphora The repetition of words or phrases at the beginning of lines.

Antithesis A figure of speech in which words and phrases with opposite meanings are balanced against each other. An example of antithesis is 'To err is human, to forgive, divine'.

Ballad A poem that tells a story. Ballads are traditionally rhymed ABAB.

Beat The rhythmic or musical quality of a poem. In metrical verse, this is determined by the regular pattern of stressed and unstressed syllables.

Couplet A unit comprising of two lines.

Elegy Poem written to lament the dead.

Ellipsis The omission of words whose absence does not impede the reader's ability to understand the expression.

Enjambment When a single sentence is spread across two or more lines of verse.

Form The structural components of a poem, e.g. stanza pattern, metre, syllable count – as opposed to the content.

Free verse Verse without formal metre or rhyme patterns.

Imagery The mental pictures created by a piece of writing.

Internal rhyme Rhyme that occurs within a single line of verse. Also refers to rhyme between internal phrases across multiple lines.

Irony The expression of one's meaning by using language that normally signifies the opposite.

Neologism The coining of new words.

Oxymoron Figure of speech containing two seemingly contradictory expressions, e.g. a happy funeral.

Paradox Seemingly absurd or contradictory statement which, on closer examination, reveals an important truth, e.g. Wordsworth's 'The child is father of the man'.

Pathetic Fallacy Occurs when human emotions or behaviours are attributed to the natural world.

Pun A humorous way of using a word or phrase so that more than one meaning is suggested. For example: 'She's a skilful pilot whose career has really taken off.'

Quatrain A stanza comprising of four lines.

Refrain A line or phrase that recurs throughout a poem – especially at the end of stanzas.

Sonnet A fourteen, line poem, usually in iambic pentameters. Typically, it consists of an octave (eight lines) and a sestet (six lines). Usually, the octave presents or outlines a problem, situation or dilemma. The sestet meditates on this issue or attempts to resolve it. There is usually a 'volta', a turn or change in tone or outlook, that occurs between the octave and the sestet.

- Italian or Petrarchan Sonnet The sonnet was originated by the Italian poet Guittone of Arezzo and then popularised by Petrarch (1304-74). The term 'sonnet' derives from the Italian for 'little song'. The Italian sonnet has the following rhyme scheme: ABBA ABBA CDE CDE.

- Shakespearean or English Sonnet: The Shakespearean or English sonnet employs an ABAB CDCD EFEF GG rhyme scheme. Essentially, therefore, it consists of three quatrains and a final couplet. Sometimes the volta or change of direction only occurs in the last two lines.

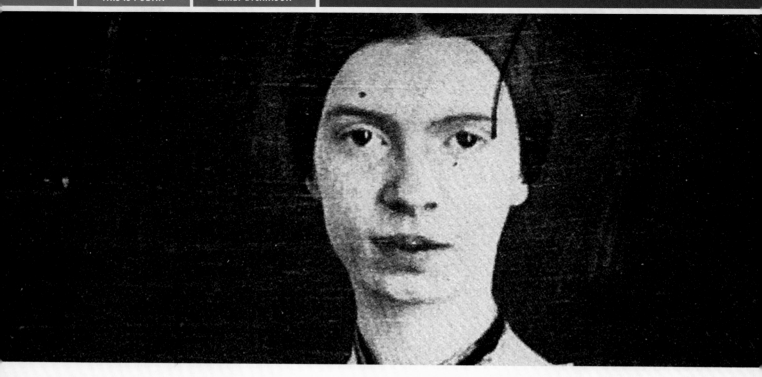

Emily Dickinson

Emily Dickinson was born in December 1830 in Amherst, Massachusetts. She had an older brother, Austin, and a younger sister, Lavinia. Her family had long been prominent in politics and local government. She was raised in 'Homestead', a mansion built by her grandfather on Amherst's main street. Her father, Edward, was a busy lawyer and a politician who served in the US Congress in Washington. He provided a comfortable, thought not extremely wealthy, upbringing.

Dickinson, at her father's insistence, enjoyed a first-class education. (Not all girls of the period, we must remember, were afforded such an opportunity). She first attended the local primary school – a two-room building that can still be seen on Amherst's Pleasant Street. Then in 1840, at the age of ten, she began her studies in Amherst Academy, a secondary college that had only begun to admit girls two years earlier.

Dickinson would spend seven years at the Academy, studying such subjects as history, literature and Latin. She was also introduced to botany, the study of plants, which became a life-long passion. Dickinson, in later years, loved to garden and developed an extraordinary collection of pressed flowers. She would often include pressed flowers with her letters, and her work is marked by many botanical reverences. Her last years in the Academy were marked by a close friendship with Leonard Humphrey, the Academy's popular young principal, who was only five years her senior.

Dickinson's fascination with the written word began to deepen in 1848, when she was 18 years old. It was around this time, scholars believe, that Dickinson began writing poetry in earnest. She became friends with Benjamin Franklin Newton, a young lawyer who worked with her father. It was Newton who introduced her to the latest trends in literature and poetry, lending her works by Wordsworth, Keats and Longfellow, and introducing her to the writings of Ralph Waldo Emerson, the great American poet, philosopher and nature writer. Emerson would prove an indispensable influence for Dickinson; his writings, she declared, had 'touched a Secret Spring' within her. His influence is especially palpable in 'I taste a liquor never brewed'.

Dickinson, having completed her education, lived the life of an ordinary young woman of the day. Her family's circumstances meant she had no need to work outside the home. Instead, she baked for the family and took care of various household chores. She enjoyed the social life of Amherst, attending concerts, festivals and other social events. 'Amherst is alive with fun this winter', she wrote in one of her letters, 'Oh, a very great town this is!'

Gradually, however, Dickinson began to confine herself more and more to the family home, where she lived with her mother and her sister Lavinia, who was also unmarried. This process began in the mid-1850's, when she was around twenty-five years old. By the early 1860's she had withdrawn almost entirely from social life. By 1866, when she thirty-six years old, Dickinson was effectively a recluse. She seldom left 'Homestead' and preferred to speak to visitors from behind a door rather than face to face. It was around this time, too, that she began to dress only in white clothing. Her

"I have a brother and sister; my mother does not care for thought, and father, too busy with his briefs to notice what we do. He buys me many books, but begs me not to read them, because he fears they joggle the mind."

family respected Emily's choice of a contemplative life: 'She had to think – she was the only one of us who had that to do'.

Scholars have long debated the cause of this retreat from the outside world. Her mother's ill-health was certainly a factor. In the mid-1850s, Dickinson's mother became ill, and would go on to suffer from a variety of chronic ailments that left her bedridden for almost thirty years. Dickinson took on the responsibility of being her mother's primary carer, a role that required her to stay in and around the family home. Dickinson, it must be noted, had always been sensitive and melancholic, aspects of her personality that became more pronounced throughout her twenties and thirties. She was also deeply shaken by the deaths of several friends; Leonard Humphrey, her former principal at Amherst College, passed away from 'brain congestion', and Benjamin Franklin Newton, her literary mentor, died from tuberculosis at only twenty-three years of age.

What's undeniable, however, is that Dickinson's seclusion brought with it an extraordinary surge of creativity. Between 1858 and 1866, she produced nearly 800 poems, which were carefully edited, rewritten and stitched into little booklets known as 'facsicles'. These poems – distinguished by a unique use of syntax, phrasing and punctuation – display an extraordinary originality. Dickinson's unconventional style is startling today and would have been utterly shocking to the tastes of American readers in the 1860s.

Dickinson, though highly reclusive, wasn't completely shut off from the outside world. From time to time, she received friends and relatives who came to visit her at Amherst. Through letter-writing, she kept in touch with a range of correspondents. Her letters – which at times rival her poems in their brilliant use of language – reveal her to be witty, energetic and curious about the world around her. There are moments, too, when she reveals herself to be highly practical and insightful about the quirks of human behaviour.

One of Dickinson's correspondents was the newspaper editor Samuel Bowles, who facilitated her first appearance in print,

publishing a number of her poems in the Springfield Republican. Another was the well-known writer Thomas Wentworth Higginson, who was disconcerted by her unconventional poetics and suggested that she 'regularise' the poems. Dickinson flatly refused his advice. Despite this disagreement, Dickinson remained friendly with Higginson for the rest of her life, valuing his advice and encouragement. They met face to face for the first time in 1870, eight years after beginning their correspondence.

In 1874 Dickinson's father passed away. Shortly after that, Dickinson's mother suffered a stroke, rendering her more dependent than ever on the poet's care and attention. Dickinson continued to write, though less prolifically. The poems from this period appear less carefully edited and were written on loose pages rather than stitched into 'facsicles'.

Dickinson's later years were marked by a close relationship with Otis Lord, an elderly judge from the nearby town of Salem. It's believed that in 1877, when Lord's wife died, this relationship blossomed into a romance, though one largely conducted through the medium of letters. The bulk of their correspondence, alas, has been destroyed. But their few surviving letters reveal an intense affection, one that endured until Lord's death in 1884.

Dickinson herself fell ill with Bright's disease in November 1885 and died on 15 May 1886. She was fifty-five years old. After the poet's death, a locked chest containing nearly 1,800 poems and fragments, some stitched into 'facsicles', hundreds of others written on loose sheets, was discovered. Fewer than a dozen had been published in Dickinson's lifetime.

In 1890, four years after her death, Dickinson's first collection of poetry was published. The volume's editors 'regularised' her unusual punctuation and 'normalised' much of her unique phraseology. The book, featuring 115 poems, proved a literary sensation, and Dickinson has never since been out of print. It was only in 1955, however, that an unedited version of her work appeared, one that preserves her unique style in all its eccentricity, force and power.

'Hope' is the thing with feathers –

'Hope' is the thing with feathers –
That perches in the soul –
And sings the tune without the words –
And never stops – at all –

And sweetest – in the Gale – is heard –   [5]
And sore must be the storm –
That could abash the little Bird
That kept so many warm –

I've heard it in the chillest land –
And on the strangest Sea –   [10]
Yet – never – in Extremity,
It asked a crumb – of me.

Annotations

[5] *Gale:* a very strong wind

[6] *sore:* severe, extreme

[7] *abash:* rattle, disconcert, to cause to feel ill at ease

Tease It Out

1. The poet presents life as a journey that we must each undertake. What different places does she imagine travelling through or across in the third stanza? What times or periods in life do you think these places represent?

2. In the second stanza, what sorts of weather conditions does the poet imagine encountering on this journey? Again, what sorts of experiences or moments do you imagine these represent?

3. The poet imagines 'Hope' accompanying her on this long and sometimes very arduous journey. How does she characterise 'Hope' in the opening stanza? What features or attributes does she ascribe to it?

4. Where does the poet imagine that 'Hope' is located? How does she describe the manner in which it abides there? How do you imagine or picture what the poet describes?

5. Based on the description given in the opening stanza, do you think that hope is something that has always been with us and will never leave us? Or do you think that hope is something that comes and goes? Give reasons for your answers.

6. The poet says that hope 'sings the tune without the words'. What sort of 'tune' do you imagine hope singing? What two adjectives do you think might best describe this tune?

7. When is Hope's tune 'sweetest … heard'? Why do you think the tune sounds sweetest at these times?

8. The poet says that it would have to be a severe or 'sore' storm to 'abash' this 'little Bird'. What does the word 'abash' mean? What do you think the 'storm' represents?

9. Why do you think this is 'the tune without the words'? Consider the following possibilities and rank them in order of likelihood:
   - The tune has no words.
   - Hope is described as a bird and, therefore, is incapable of singing words.
   - The tune has words, but the bird chooses not to sing them because the effect is then more powerful.

10. Which of the following statements do you think best captures what the poet is saying in lines 6 and 7?
    - There are no occasions or circumstances that could damage our sense of hope.
    - Hope is vulnerable when it comes to particularly severe times in life.
    Give a reason for your answer.

11. In line 8, what effect or impact is hope said to have on 'so many' people? Describe in your own words what you think the poet has in mind here?

12. The poet describes being in the 'chillest land' and 'on the strangest Sea'. Describe in your own words the different landscapes and seascapes she has in mind. What do you think these different locations represent?

13. The poet describes being 'in Extremity'. Is this 'Extremity' the 'chillest land' and 'strangest Sea', or do you think the poet has an even more remote and inhospitable place in mind? Give a reason for your answer.

14. What does the poet say that hope asks for in return for all it does for her? Why do you think hope acts or behaves in this manner?

Exam Prep

1. **Personal Response:** The poet ascribes a number of characteristics to 'Hope'. Consider the following adjectives and rank them in order of their suitability for describing 'Hope', giving reasons for your decisions:
   - Constant
   - Changeable
   - Fragile
   - Brave
   - Universal
   - Necessary
   - Selfless
   - Foolish

2. **Class Discussion:** Out of all the creatures in the animal kingdom, why do you think Dickinson chose a bird to represent 'Hope'? What attributes does a songbird share with hope, if any?

3. **Theme Talk:** 'The poem suggests that hope and suffering are symbiotic; that one cannot exist without the other.' Do you agree or disagree with this statement? Write a few paragraphs in response.

Language Lab

1. 'By describing 'Hope' as a 'little Bird', Dickinson gives life to an abstract concept.' Write a few paragraphs in response to this statement.

2. Many Dickinson poems end in a dash, but 'Hope is the thing with feathers' ends in a full stop. What is the effect of this full stop on the closing lines? In your opinion, would a dash have been more or less effective here? Explain your answer.

3. Why do you think Dickinson refers to 'the thing with feathers' instead of using its more familiar name?

4. The poem features a number of metaphors. Can you say what metaphors the poet uses or suggests for the following:
   - Hope
   - Difficult circumstances in life
   - Periods of intense loneliness and hardship
   - Our individual lives

There's a certain Slant of light

There's a certain Slant of light,
Winter Afternoons –
That oppresses, like the Heft
Of Cathedral Tunes –

Heavenly Hurt, it gives us –   [5]
We can find no scar,
But internal difference,
Where the Meanings, are –

None may teach it – Any –
'Tis the seal Despair –   [10]
An imperial affliction
Sent us of the Air –

When it comes, the Landscape listens –
Shadows – hold their breath –
When it goes, 'tis like the Distance   [15]
On the look of Death –

Annotations
[3] *Heft:* weight
[10] *seal:* an official stamp, often associated with a king or other royal personage; the
Biblical Book of Revelation features a scroll bound with seven seals. The opening of each seal
signals a terrifying or cataclysmic event.
[11] *imperial:* having to do with an empire or emperor

Tease It Out

1. Identify two separate meanings of the word 'certain'. Would you agree that both meanings might be relevant here?
2. Which meaning of the word 'Slant' does the poet have in mind here? Rank the following options in order of plausibility:
   • A trait or quality
   • A tendency of someone or something to behave in a particular fashion
   • The angle at which something moves or is positioned
   • Crooked or untrustworthy
3. **Class Discussion:** Consider the poet's portrayal of the light on winter afternoons:
   • In what sense might the light on 'Winter Afternoons' be said to differ from that at other times of the year?
   • Pick three adjectives that might describe the quality of such winter light?
   • Can you see why someone might find such light oppressive or depressing?
4. What type of music do you think of when you hear the term 'Cathedral Tunes'?
5. Would you agree that it's fair to describe such music as having 'Heft', as being weighty and somehow oppressive?
6. Do you think the poet enjoys attending church and listening to the music that accompanies religious services? Give a reason for your answer.
7. The oppressive winter light causes no physical or external damage to those it falls upon. Which phrase indicates this?
8. 'Where the Meanings, are': what aspect of human nature is being referred to here?
9. What impact does the winter light have on this aspect of our selves?
10. Which phrase indicates that the light operates almost like an airborne disease?
11. Which phrase indicates that the light has a merciless, implacable quality?
12. **Class Discussion:** According to the poet, the light cannot be taught. What might the poet like to 'teach' the winter light? Does the light listen to those it falls upon?
13. What two entities are personified in lines 13 and 14?
14. Describe in your own words the impact that, according to the poet, the winter light has on the landscape when it appears.
15. The departure of this light brings a great relief. What simile does the poet use to describe this? Is it an effective one in your opinion?

Exam Prep

1. **Personal Response:** Pick three adjectives that in your opinion best describe the atmosphere of this poem. In each case, write three or four sentences explaining your choice.
2. **Class Discussion:** 'This poem presents a very negative view of religion, with God as a cruel emperor in heaven sending down an 'imperial affliction' to punish his subjects'. Do you agree with this reading?
3. **Theme Talk:** 'This poem is a powerful study of depression. It shows how when we're in a depressive state, even light, something we usually associate with hope and optimism, strikes us as cruel and oppressive'. Write a paragraph in response to this statement.
4. **Exam Prep:** 'Emily Dickinson's original approach to poetry results in startling and thought-provoking moments in her work'. Write a short essay in response to this statement, making reference to this poem and at least two others on the course.

Language Lab

1. **Class Discussion:** In the Bible's Book of Revelation, seven seals are broken, each revealing or prophesying a judgement or apocalyptic event. Would you agree that Dickinson refers to or adapts these Bible verses in her poem?
2. Consider the phrase 'Heavenly Hurt' and pair with the person beside you to answer the following questions:
   • Does the light bring 'Heavenly Hurt' because it has been sent down from Heaven by God?
   • Does the light bring 'Heavenly Hurt' because it drifts down from the sky, often referred to as the heavens?
   • What's an oxymoron? Why might this phrase be considered an oxymoron?

I felt a Funeral, in my Brain

I felt a Funeral, in my Brain,
And Mourners to and fro
Kept treading – treading – till it seemed
That Sense was breaking through –

And when they all were seated,   [5]
A Service, like a Drum –
Kept beating – beating – till I thought
My mind was going numb –

And then I heard them lift a Box
And creak across my Soul   [10]
With those same Boots of Lead, again,
Then Space – began to toll,

As all the Heavens were a Bell,
And Being, but an Ear,
And I, and Silence, some strange Race,   [15]
Wrecked, solitary, here –

And then a Plank in Reason, broke,
And I dropped down, and down –
And hit a World, at every plunge,
And Finished knowing – then –   [20]

Annotations

[3] *treading:* walking on, pressing down or crushing with the feet

[6] *Service:* a formal ceremony, often religious in nature

[12] *toll:* to sound a bell with a slow, uniform succession of strokes as a signal or announcement

Tease It Out

1. The poet feels a funeral occurring inside her own brain. What does this suggest about her mental state? Rank the following statements in order of plausibility:
   • She is no longer in control of her own mental state.
   • She feels as if her mind is being invaded.
   • She feels as if she's having a nervous breakdown.
   • She is actually quite relaxed and curious about this strange psychological experience.
2. The funeral service proper has yet to begin. What are the mourners doing as they wait?
3. Suggest why the poet repeats the word 'treading' in line 3.
4. The poet can hear and feel the events taking place inside her own head. But can she see them? Give a reason for your answer.
5. **Class Discussion:** The speaker says that 'Sense' was 'breaking through'. What does the word 'Sense' signify in this particular context? Do you think that this 'breaking through' represents greater mental clarity or a loss of such clarity?
6. The funeral proper is called to order. What do the mourners do?
7. The poet compares the sound of the service to that of a drum. Is she suggesting a) that someone was hitting a drum throughout the ceremony or b) that the voice of the minister had a percussive drum-like quality?
8. How does the poet convey that the sound of the service was both intense and monotonous? If possible, identify two phrases or images that enable her to do this.
9. Consider the phrase: 'My mind was going numb'. Write two or three sentences describing your impression of such numbness. Do you think of it as a pleasant or unpleasant mental state? Could it possibly be both?

10. What sound does the speaker hear as the mourners walk?
11. This ringing sound experienced by the speaker is so intense that it seems to emanate from the 'Heavens' themselves. Is she referring to a) outer space b) the afterlife or c) something else?
12. This sound is so intense that everything on Earth has no choice but to listen to it. Which line conveys this?
13. The poet suggests that she and 'Silence' are closely related, are members of the same 'Race'. What does this suggest about her attitude towards noise and bustle?
14. The poet describes herself as 'Wrecked'. Can you think of at least two different meanings for this word? How might these different meanings be relevant here?
15. What does the speaker mean by 'Reason' in line 17?
16. The poet depicts herself falling down some kind of chute or shaft. What kind of mental state or event does this represent?
17. Does she plummet directly downwards, or does she collide against the sides of the shaft as she falls? Give a reason for your answer.
18. The poem ends with the speaker saying that she 'Finished knowing'. What does the poet mean by this? Rank the following statements in order of plausibility:
   • She acquired some specific knowledge at this moment.
   • She gained some general insight and self-awareness at this moment.
   • Her ability to know or understand ceased at this moment.

Exam Prep

1. **Personal Response:** Would you agree that there's a sense of relief or release at the poem's conclusion? Give a reason for your answer.
2. **Class Discussion:** Based on your reading of the poem, do you think 'brain', 'mind' and 'soul' mean different things to the poet? Or does she use these terms interchangeably?
3. **Theme Talk:** 'This poem provides a powerful portrayal of a mind at the end of its tether'. Write two paragraphs in response to this statement.
4. **Exam Prep:** 'Dickinson's use of an innovative style to explore intense experiences can both intrigue and confuse'. Discuss this statement, supporting your answer with reference to 'I felt a Funeral' and two other poems on your course.

Language Lab

1. Consider the poet's use of the terms 'brain', 'mind' and 'soul'. Write one or two sentences describing your understanding of each concept.
2. Line 10 features a most unusual comparison, as the poet likens her soul to a floor on which the mourners walk. What kind of surface do you visualise?

A Bird, came down the Walk –

A Bird, came down the Walk –
He did not know I saw –
He bit an Angle Worm in halves
And ate the fellow, raw,

And then, he drank a Dew   [5]
From a convenient Grass –
And then hopped sidewise to the Wall
To let a Beetle pass –

He glanced with rapid eyes,
That hurried all abroad –   [10]
They looked like frightened Beads, I thought –
He stirred his Velvet Head –

Like one in danger, Cautious,
I offered him a Crumb,
And he unrolled his feathers,   [15]
And rowed him softer Home –

Than Oars divide the Ocean,
Too silver for a seam,
Or Butterflies, off Banks of Noon,
Leap, plashless as they swim.   [20]

Annotations
[3] *Angle Worm:* earthworm
[20] *plashless:* smoothly; fluidly; without splashing

Tease It Out

1. Watch Video 6, which is a trailer for the TV series *Emily*.
   - Mention three things it suggests about Dickinson's life.
   - Mention three things it suggests about her personality.
   - Did this portrayal fit with your own mental image of the poet?
2. Is there anything surprising or unusual about the phrase 'A Bird, came down the Walk'? Which two worlds are colliding within this phrase?
3. Lines 3 to 4: Do you find the image of the 'Angleworm' being eaten 'raw' to be violent and disturbing or lighthearted? Give a reason for your answer.
4. In stanza 1, do you think the bird is aware that he's being observed? Give a reason for your answer.
5. What do you understand by the phrase 'a convenient Grass'? How can grass be said to be convenient?
6. Lines 7 to 8: Do you think the bird really hops aside 'To let a Beetle pass'? What sort of behaviour is the speaker ascribing to the bird here?
7. How is the bird's fear and alertness suggested in stanza 3? What do you think he is on the lookout for?
8. To what sort of materials does the speaker compare the bird's eyes and head? What does this suggest about her feelings towards the bird?
9. How does the speaker attempt to make contact with the bird? Why do you think she wants to do this?
10. Consider the questions below on your own for five minutes and jot down some ideas. Then compare notes with the person beside you. Finally, share your ideas with the class.
    - In line 13, who is being described as being 'in danger' and 'Cautious' – the speaker or the bird?
    - Is it possible that both the speaker and the bird are feeling 'Cautious' at this moment?
    - What reason has the speaker to feel 'Cautious' when she meets the bird? How might the bird be 'in danger' from the speaker?
11. Why might the bird's feathers be said to be 'unrolled'? How do you picture this?
12. What 'Home' do you think the bird is returning to in line 16? Is there a broader meaning to the word 'Home' in this context?
13. Which action does the speaker say the bird's flight is 'softer' than?
14. Line 20: What does the poet mean when she suggests that the bird does not leave a 'seam' in his wake as he flies? What does this suggest about the manner of the bird's flight?
15. In lines 15 to 20, the poet makes two comparisons between flight and travelling on water. Describe these two comparisons in your own words. Do you think these are apt comparisons? Why or why not?
16. The poet compares the bird's flight to that of butterflies. What similarities are there between these two images? What differences are there?

Exam Prep

1. **Personal Response:** Do you think the poem focuses more on the danger of nature or on the beauty of nature? Is there equal emphasis on both? Support your answer with reference to the poem.
2. **Class Discussion:** How would you characterise the tone of this poem? Is it serious or lighthearted? Is it strange or familiar? Does the tone shift from stanza to stanza?
3. **Theme Talk:** What does the poem suggest about humanity's place within nature? Support your answer with reference to the poem.
4. **Exam Prep:** 'Time and again, Dickinson shows a remarkable facility for zooming in on the small details of nature.' Discuss this statement with reference to 'A Bird, came down the Walk' and at least two other poems on your course.

Language Lab

1. As in many of her poems, Dickinson uses personification to describe an animal. What human characteristics does she ascribe to the bird? Explain your answer.
2. Consider the word 'plashless'. Could this be considered an example of onomatopoeia? Give a reason for your answer.
3. Suggest an alternative title for this poem and explain your choice.

I heard a Fly buzz – when I died –

I heard a Fly buzz – when I died –
The Stillness in the Room
Was like the Stillness in the Air –
Between the Heaves of Storm –

The Eyes around – had wrung them dry –   [5]
And Breaths were gathering firm
For that last Onset – when the King
Be witnessed – in the Room –

I willed my Keepsakes – Signed away
What portion of me be   [10]
Assignable – and then it was
There interposed a Fly –

With Blue – uncertain – stumbling Buzz –
Between the light – and me –
And then the Windows failed – and then   [15]
I could not see to see –

Annotations

[4] *Heaves:* forceful, violent impacts

[6] *gathering firm:* preparing, readying

[7] *Onset:* attack, the beginning of something unpleasant

[9] *Keepsakes:* small items kept in memory of a person, place or event

[11] *Assignable:* transferable; capable of being given to another person

[12] *interposed:* placed between two people or objects

Tease It Out

1. List the different associations you have with flies. Is every association negative? Can you think of any positive traits we associate with these ubiquitous creatures?
2. 'I heard a Fly buzz – when I died'. This poem is spoken by someone who has already died. Can you think of any other poem, story or film you've come across that features a dead narrator?
3. As the speaker lay dying, the atmosphere in the room was very 'Still'. Do you think this was a pleasant stillness or a tense and uncomfortable one? Give a reason for your answer.
4. This stillness was only temporary. Describe in your own words the simile used to convey this?
5. What sounds and movements do you think might have preceded this stillness?
6. What sounds and movements will bring it to an end?
7. The speaker's relatives were present in the room and had been weeping a great deal. What metaphor is used to convey this? Is it an effective one in your opinion?
8. The relatives held their breaths. In fact they scarcely dared to breathe at all. How does the speaker convey this? What does it suggest about the relatives' mood?
9. The speaker braces herself for the 'last Onset' or attack of her illness. What will happen to her when this last assault on her mind and body finally occurs?
10. The speaker's relatives expected that a 'King' would be present at the moment of her death. What or whom does this King represent? Is it Jesus? Is it an angel? Or is it Death itself? Give a reason for your answer.
11. **Class Discussion:** The speaker's relatives believed that this 'King' would be 'witnessed' in the room. Do they expect that the King will be physically visible? Or do they imagine that the King will make its presence felt in a more subtle manner?
12. What practical action does the speaker take before she dies?
13. The speaker refers to 'Keepsakes'. What kind of possessions does this term suggest to you? Do you imagine small items of sentimental value, larger goods like pieces of furniture or financial assets such as stocks and bonds? Give a reason for your answer.
14. The speaker says that one part of her is 'assignable', which implies that one part of her, presumably, is not. Which part of her might not be 'assignable' in this way? Give a reason for your answer.
15. Describe in your own words the manner in which the fly moved.
16. The fly positioned itself between the speaker and the 'light'. What verb is used to convey this?
17. **Group Discussion:** 'The Windows failed'. In small groups, try to work out what the speaker means by this:
    • Is the speaker referring to the actual windows in the room? If so, how might these be said to fail?
    • Or is the speaker referring to her own eyes? If so, how might these be said to fail?

Exam Prep

1. **Personal Response:** In your opinion, was the speaker ready to die when the moment of her death arrived? Refer to the poem in support of your answer.
2. **Class Discussion:** Would you agree that the speaker was hallucinating at the poem's conclusion? Consider this question in small groups, giving reasons for your answer.
3. **Theme Talk:** Would you agree that the speaker intended the moment of her death to be a solemn and peaceful one? What reduces the solemnity of this moment?
4. **Exam Prep:** 'Dickinson's poetry is a powerful exploration of the workings of the mind'. Discuss this statement in relation to this poem and at least two others on the course.

Language Lab

1. 'Given that it is concerned with death, this is a surprisingly light-hearted poem'. Would you agree that the tone of this poem is somewhat playful? Write a paragraph in response, identifying two or three phrases that support your point of view.
2. What is the literary device known as synesthesia? Can you find an example in this poem?
3. The speaker says that the fly comes between her and the light, blocking it out.: What source of 'light', precisely, is the speaker referring to here?
    • Is she referring to the ordinary light of this world? What might it mean for the fly to block out this light source?
    • Or is she referring to the holy glow of the afterlife, which she glimpses (or thinks she glimpses) as she drifts towards death? What might it mean for the fly to block out this light source?

The Soul has Bandaged moments –

The Soul has Bandaged moments –
When too appalled to stir –
She feels some ghastly Fright come up
And stop to look at her –

Salute her, with long fingers –   [5]
Caress her freezing hair –
Sip, Goblin, from the very lips
The Lover – hovered – o'er –
Unworthy, that a thought so mean
Accost a Theme – so – fair –   [10]

The soul has moments of escape –
When bursting all the doors –
She dances like a Bomb, abroad,
And swings opon the Hours,

As do the Bee – delirious borne –   [15]
Long Dungeoned from his Rose –
Touch Liberty – then know no more –
But Noon, and Paradise

The Soul's retaken moments –
When, Felon led along,   [20]
With shackles on the plumed feet,
And staples, in the song,

The Horror welcomes her, again,
These, are not brayed of Tongue –

Annotations
[2] *appalled:* horrified, terrified, dismayed
[3] *ghastly:* horrifying, terrifying
[3] *Fright:* monstrous, goblin-like creature that personifies negative emotion
[9] *mean:* inferior in quality; nasty or malicious
[10] *Accost:* harrass, interfere with
[10] *Theme:* concept or idea; tune or melody
[13] *abroad:* outside, out and about
[15] *delirious:* in a state of wild excitement or ecstasy
[16] *Dungeoned from:* kept away from, excluded from
[20] *Felon:* a person who has committed a serious crime
[21] *shackles:* metal restraints connected by a chain
[21] *plumed:* decorated with long conspicuous feathers
[22] *staples:* metal fastening devices
[24] *brayed:* spoken of loudly or widely

Tease It Out

1. What sort of mental state do you think the first two lines of the poem describe? What do you think has given rise to this state of mind?
2. Does the term 'bandaged' suggest that the trauma is ongoing or that it has ended? Give a reason for your answer.
3. The speaker says that in the wake of what has happened, the soul is 'too appalled to stir'. What does it mean to be 'appalled'? What different meanings of the word might be relevant here?
4. The poet personifies her negative emotions, characterising them as a 'Goblin', or 'ghastly Fright', that 'come[s] up' and 'look[s] at her. How does this creature behave towards the soul? How does the soul react or respond?
5. The Goblin is said to 'Sip' from the soul's lips. What do you imagine the Goblin doing here? What does the term 'Sip' suggest about the manner in which this is done?
6. The Goblin's behaviour in line 7 is contrasted with the 'Lover' in line 8. Who or what do you imagine the 'Lover' represents? How does the Lover's behaviour compare and contrast with that of the Goblin's?
7. What sort of 'thought', do you think, can damage or tarnish the speaker's idea of romantic love? Why might such thoughts be 'Unworthy' of this kind of love?
8. What sort of image does 'swings upon the Hours' bring to mind? What do you think the poet is suggesting here about the soul's attitude to time and routine when it is feeling so ecstatically happy?
9. Lines 15 to 18: The poet compares her soul's circumstances to a bee that has been 'Long Dungeoned from his Rose'. Why do you think the bee has been kept from visiting the flower it desires? What circumstances, do you think, make it possible for the bee to finally visit the flower again?
10. How does the poet characterise the manner in which the bee flies to the flower that it loves? What does this suggest about the bee's state of mind at this moment?
11. When the bee finally reaches the rose, it is said to 'Touch Liberty'. What sort of 'Liberty' do you think it experiences? From what is it free now that it has arrived at the flower it has been longing to visit?
12. Why do you think the soul's 'feet' are described as 'plumed'? What special ability does this suggest that the soul possesses?
13. The poet says that the 'Horror' is ready to greet the soul when it finally reaches the cell or dungeon. What do you think this 'Horror' represents? Do you think that the 'Horror' and the 'Goblin' are one and the same thing? Give reasons for your answer.

Exam Prep

1. **Personal Response:** Do you think the speaker has realistic expectations when it comes to love, or is she too idealistic? Support your answer with reference to the poem.
2. **Class Discussion:** What sort of person do you think the poem describes? Do you think that this person is experiencing a healthy range of emotions or do you think that there is something extreme or manic about their mood swings? Give reasons for your answer?
2. **Exam Prep:** 'Dickinson is a poet of hope and despair'. Discuss this statement in relation to this poem and two others on the course.

Language Lab

1. The poet says that these terrible moments are not 'brayed of Tongue'. What do you think it means to 'bray' about something? Why would someone not wish to 'bray' about the kind of experience described in these lines? What would prevent them from doing so?
2. 'She dances like a Bomb'. What does this unusual comparison suggest about the manner in which the soul dances? Does it suggest energy and excitement, or is there a sense of danger and destruction evident here? Give reasons for your answer.

I could bring You Jewels – had I a mind to

I could bring You Jewels – had I a mind to –
But You have enough – of those –
I could bring You Odors from St Domingo –
Colors – from Vera Cruz –

Berries of the Bahamas – have I –   [5]
But this little Blaze
Flickering to itself – in the Meadow –
Suits Me – more than those –

Never a Fellow matched this Topaz –
And his Emerald Swing –   [10]
Dower itself – for Bobadilo –
Better – Could I bring?

Annotations

[3] *Odors:* odours, aromas

[3] *St Domingo:* a Caribbean island

[4] *Vera Cruz:* a Mexican port

[9] *Topaz:* a yellow gem; yellowish-brown in colour

[10] *Emerald:* a green gem, dark green in colour

[11] *Dower:* dowry, money or property brought by a woman to her husband at marriage

[11] *Bobadilo:* Francisco de Bobadilla (died in 1502). He was the Spanish governor of Santo Domingo and reputed to be the richest man in the world.

Tease It Out

1. Watch Video 7, which provides a virtual tour of Homestead, the house where Dickinson spent her adult life. Based on your viewing of the video, pick three adjectives that, in your opinion, best describe the poet's personality.
2. **Get in Gear:** Look up St Domingo, Vera Cruz and the Bahamas on Google Maps. Write a short paragraph describing each location, saying which one you would most like to visit?
3. Who do you imagine the speaker of this poem to be? Who do you imagine he or she is addressing?
4. Is it significant that the word 'You' is capitalised in lines 1 and 3? What does this suggest about the importance of this 'You' to the poet?
5. What do you think might be meant by the 'Colors' referenced in line 4?
6. Why do you think the speaker rejects the idea of sending gems, perfumes, fruit and other traditional gifts?
7. What is the 'Blaze' referred to in line 7? Where is it burning?
8. The 'Blaze' is described as 'Flickering to itself'. What sort of mood does this convey?
9. The 'Blaze' contains a 'Topaz' and an 'Emerald Swing'. What might these refer to?
10. What is the 'Dower' referenced in line 11? Why might the poet consider the 'Blaze' to be a suitable 'Dower'?
11. The speaker asks a question at the end of the poem. Rewrite this question in your own words. What effect does this question have on the poem's ending? Does it convey uncertainty or something else?

Exam Prep

1. **Class Discussion:** Compare and contrast St Domingo, Vera Cruz and the Bahamas with the location where the speaker finds her 'little Blaze'. How do these locations differ? What does it say about the poet that she would rather bring a gift from the nearby 'Meadow' than one from an exotic destination?
2. **Theme Talk:** 'For Dickinson, the beauty of nature surpasses anything man-made.' Discuss this statement with reference to this poem and at least one other on your course.
3. **Exam Prep:** 'Dickinson isn't all about death and depression. She can also be a playful and witty poet.' Discuss this statement with reference to 'I could bring You Jewels' , 'I taste a liquor never brewed' and 'A Certain Slant of Light'.

Language Lab

1. In your opinion, could this be described as a love poem? Support your answer with reference to the text.
2. Can you find any examples of hyperbole, or deliberate exaggeration, in the poem?
3. Pick out a phrase from the poem that strikes you as particularly memorable and say why you like it.
4. How would you characterise the overall tone of the poem?

A narrow Fellow in the Grass

A narrow Fellow in the Grass
Occasionally rides –
You may have met Him? Did you not
His notice sudden is –

The Grass divides as with a Comb,   [5]
A spotted Shaft is seen –
And then it closes at your Feet
And opens further on –

He likes a Boggy Acre –
A Floor too cool for Corn –   [10]
But when a Boy and Barefoot –
I more than once at Noon

Have passed I thought a Whip lash
Unbraiding in the Sun
When stooping to secure it   [15]
It wrinkled And was gone –

Several of Nature's People
I know, and they know me
I feel for them a transport
Of Cordiality   [20]

But never met this Fellow
Attended or alone
Without a tighter Breathing
And Zero at the Bone.

Annotations

[5] *as with a Comb:* as if it had been brushed with a comb

[6] *Shaft:* *l*ong, narrow pole-shaped object or part of an object

[10] *Floor:* ground, surface of the earth

[13] *Whip lash:* a whip, used in farming, especially to control livestock

[14] *Unbraiding:* unravelling, uncurling

[15] *stooping:* bending

[15] *secure:* claim, pick up

[17] *Several of Nature's People:* different creatures or animals

[19] *transport:* an overwhelmingly strong emotion

[20] *Cordiality:* affection, kindness, friendship

[22] *Attended or alone:* in the company of others or by myself

Tease It Out

1. **Get in Gear:** Can you think of any famous snakes in literature, pop culture or religion? What function do these snakes serve in their respective narratives? What do they represent?
2. **Class Discussion:** 'But when a Boy and Barefoot': this poem, unusually for Dickinson, features a male speaker. It's easy to imagine that the speaker is based on one of the farmhands who worked in her home at Amherst. Why do you think Dickinson might have chosen to take on a male persona in this poem?
3. Consider the term 'Fellow'. Would you consider it a respectful or disrespectful form of address? What does it suggest about the farmhand's attitude to the snake?
4. 'You may have met Him'. Who do you imagine the farmhand is speaking to in this line? Is he addressing the reader directly? Or are we eavesdropping on a conversation between the farm-boy and some other local person?
5. What does the verb 'ride' suggest about the snake's movement through the grass? Consider the following possible meanings of 'ride' and rank them in order of plausibility:
   * The snake's movement is like that of a gentleman in a horse-drawn carriage.
   * As he moves, the snake exhibits the speed and grace of a jockey on a thoroughbred horse.

* The snake covers a large area in a short period of time.
* To journey on the surface of the grasses, supported by the blades of grass themselves.

6. The snake is excellent at concealing itself and can appear very suddenly. Which phrase conveys this?
7. What is the 'Shaft' referred to in line 6? Is the farm-boy able to study this shaft when it appears, or is it visible for only an instant?
8. 'The Grass divides as with a Comb'. Describe in your own words how the snake affects the grass it crawls through.
9. Describe in your own words the snake's preferred environment.
10. The farmhand recalls how in his younger days he came across an object lying in a field. What did he think this object was?
11. What happened when he bent to pick up this object?
12. The farmhand refers to 'Nature's People'. Who or what is he referring to? What poetic technique is being used here?
13. Which phrase suggests that the farmhand spends a great deal of time outdoors and is familiar with animals and their ways?
14. What physical reaction does the speaker experience whenever he glimpses a snake gliding through the grass? Which phrase suggests that the speaker experiences a chill on such occasions?

Exam Prep

1. **Personal Response:** Write a paragraph describing the farmhand's lifestyle as depicted in this poem. Do you think Dickinson would have pitied such a farmhand for his tough working conditions or envied him for his freedom ?
2. **Class Discussion:** Which phrases suggest that the farmhand respects the snake? Which phrases suggest that he fears and mistrusts this creature? Do you think the speaker considers the snake to be one of 'Nature's People'? Give a reason for your answer.
3. **Theme Talk:** 'The farmhand regards the snake not only as dangerous and threatening, but also as noble and even beautiful in its colouring and movement'. Write a brief paragraph in response to this statement.
4. **Exam prep:** Dickinson, in one of her letters, wrote: 'and so I sing, as the Boy does by the Burying Ground – because I am afraid –'. Would you agree that fear rather than hope is the dominant emotion in her poetry? In your answer, refer to this poem and at least two other poems on your course.

Language Lab

1. Why do you think Dickinson uses so many 's' sounds throughout the poem? Do you find this appropriate to the subject of the poem? What sort of atmosphere does it create?
2. The poet uses male pronouns to describe the snake throughout the poem, but refers to the snake as 'it' in stanzas 2 and 3. What, in your opinion, might be the reason behind this shift? Does it affect how we view the snake?
3. List all the nouns that the poet uses to describe the snake. Why, in your opinion, is the word 'snake' never used?
4. Discuss the phrase 'Zero at the Bone', highlighting in particular all the possible meanings of the word 'Zero'. Do you find this to be an effective or memorable phrase? Explain your answer.

I taste a liquor never brewed –

I taste a liquor never brewed –
From Tankards scooped in Pearl –
Not all the Vats upon the Rhine
Yield such an Alcohol!

Inebriate of Air – am I –   [5]
And Debauchee of Dew –
Reeling – thro endless summer days –
From inns of molten Blue –

When 'Landlords' turn the drunken Bee
Out of the Foxglove's door –   [10]
When Butterflies – renounce – their 'drams' –
I shall but drink the more!

Till Seraphs swing their snowy Hats –
And Saints – to windows run –
To see the little Tippler   [15]
Leaning against the – Sun!

Annotations

liquor: alcoholic drink

[2] *Tankards:* cylindrical drinking cups

[2] *scooped in:* filled with

[3] *Vats:* vessels for storing liquid

[3] *Rhine:* The region around the River Rhine in Germany is famous for the production of alcoholic beverages.

[5] *Inebriate:* someone who is drunk

[6] *Debauchee:* someone completely devoted to drinking alcohol

[8] *Molten:* vivid, having a burning intensity

[9] *Landlords:* publicans, innkeepers

[10] *Foxglove:* Common wildflowers known for their purple hue

[11] *renounce:* give up, promise to abstain from

[11] *drams:* small measures of liquor

[13] *Seraphs:* a type of angel

[15] *Tippler:* a drinker

Tease It Out

1. What substance does this speaker 'taste'?
2. Which phrase indicates that this substance is naturally occurring and didn't have to be created?
3. What is a paradox? In what sense could the phrase 'a liquor never brewed' be considered a paradox?
4. With what type of alcoholic beverage do we associate the Rhine region?
5. Explain in your own words how lines 3 and 4 convey the potency of the liquor that the speaker drinks.
6. Explain in your own words what the terms 'Inebriate' and 'Debauchee' mean.
7. What has made the speaker inebriated? What has made her debauched?
8. Describe in your own words the nature of the speaker's movement as she travels through these 'endless summer days'.
9. Consider the phrases 'Tankards scooped in Pearl' and 'inns of molten Blue'. Is the speaker referring to actual pubs and drinking mugs? Or does it make more sense to view these terms as metaphors? Give a reason for your answer.
10. What substance do bees usually consume? Where has this particular bee been drinking? What impact has such consumption had?
11. With what type of establishment might you associate a landlord? Who or what might be the landlord of the Foxglove?
12. What does the landlord do to the drunken bee?
13. What does the term 'dram' mean? What substance might make up the drams enjoyed by butterflies?
14. Describe in your own words the personification that occurs in line 11.
15. Would you agree that there's a sense of playfulness and humour in these lines? Give a reason for your answer.
16. Will the speaker be deterred by the fates of the bee and the butterfly?
17. **Class Discussion:** How does line 13 suggest that the speaker will continue to be intoxicated by nature until she dies?
18. What are 'Seraphs'? What do the Seraphs do to celebrate in line 13?
19. What does the term 'Saints' mean, as it is used in line 14? What are the saints eager to see?
20. What is the setting for this last stanza?
21. Comment on the phrase 'little Tippler'. What does this suggest about the speaker?
22. How does the last line suggest that the speaker is exhausted from her exertions?
23. **Class Discussion:** What is meant by the poem's last line? In what sense could the speaker be 'Leaning' against the sun? Consider the following possibilities and rank them in order of plausibility:
    • The speaker is leaning against a fence at the end of the day while the sun goes down behind her.
    • The speaker has died and ascended to heaven.
    • The speaker is leaning against a mirror in which the sun is reflected.

Exam Prep

1. **Personal Response:** 'This poem emphasises Dickinson's ability to get 'high on life', to be rendered almost intoxicated by the delights of summer'. Think of an occasion that filled you with exhilaration and excitement and write two paragraphs recounting your experience.
2. **Class Discussion:** Read the poem again carefully. Who or what is speaking in this poem? Is it a human, an insect or a bird? Does it make sense to think of the speaker as sometimes human and on other occasions non-human?
3. **Theme Talk:** Describe in your own words the view of nature put forward in this poem. Is it a realistic view, in your opinion? Give a reason for your answer.
4. **Exam Prep:** 'Dickinson can be playful at times, but each of her poems has its serious side'. Discuss this statement in relation to at least three of the poems on your course.

Language Lab

1. Identify two examples each of assonance and alliteration in this poem.
2. What is the literary device known as a conceit? Explain how Dickinson uses a conceit relating to alcohol in the poem's first twelve lines.
3. Would you agree that there are several moments of hyperbole or deliberate exaggeration in this poem? If so, identify them.
4. List the poetic devices used by Dickinson in both 'I taste a liquor never brewed' and 'I could bring You Jewels'. How do these poetic devices contribute to the meaning and atmosphere of each poem?

After great pain,
a formal feeling comes –

After great pain, a formal feeling comes –
The Nerves sit ceremonious, like Tombs –
The stiff Heart questions 'was it He, that bore',
And 'Yesterday, or Centuries before?'

The Feet, mechanical, go round –   [5]
A Wooden way
Of Ground, or Air, or Ought –
Regardless grown,
A Quartz contentment, like a stone –

This is the Hour of Lead –   [10]
Remembered, if outlived,
As Freezing persons, recollect the Snow –
First – Chill – then Stupor – then the letting go –

Annotations

[1] *formal:* marked by elaborate ceremony, obedient to convention, adhering to rules or constraints

[2] *ceremonious:* behaving in an extremely formal and polite manner

[3] *bore:* suffered, endured

[7] *Ought:* anything

[8] *Regardless:* unmindful, heedless

[9] *Quartz:* resembling the hard, transparent mineral of that name

[9] *contentment:* a state of happiness and satisfaction

[11] *outlived:* survived

[13] *Stupor:* a state of near-unconsciousness

Tease It Out

1. Consider the term 'Nerves'. What is the scientific meaning of this term? We sometimes use the term 'nerves' in a more casual or everyday sense. Can you think of one such usage?

2. The speaker describes how her nerves 'sit'. Does this suggest that her mind is in an alert, active state or a drowsy, passive one?

3. In lines 3 and 4 the speaker personifies her heart:
   • The speaker's heart recently 'bore' or carried a great burden. What does this burden refer to?
   • Is the heart presented as male or female?
   • What has made her heart feel 'stiff'?
   • Is her heart sure about when this ordeal occurred?
   • Is her heart even sure that this ordeal occurred at all?

4. What does this personification suggest about the speaker's mental state? Rank the following adjectives in order of plausibility as descriptions of that mental state: she is a) exhausted b) confused c) numb d) empty e) relaxed

5. 'The Feet … go round'. The speaker finds herself walking around in circles again and again. What this does strange behaviour suggest about her mental state?

6. The speaker declares that she walks in a 'mechanical' and 'Wooden' manner. Can you think of three other adjectives that might describe this kind of movement?

7. 'The speaker feels compelled to keep walking. She would keep doing so even if the ground disappeared in front of her'. Can you identify two separate words or phrases that support this view?

8. **Class Discussion:** The speaker says that she experiences a form of 'contentment'. What do we mean when we say that someone is content? Is contentment the same as happiness? Do you think it's fair to describe the speaker, in this instance, as being in a happy state of mind?

9. 'A Quartz contentment, like a stone'. Consider the following adjectives, each of which we might associate with 'Quartz' and 'stone':
   • Cold   • Unfeeling   • Precious
   • Hard   • Indestructible   • Beautiful
   Which of these adjectives seems most appropriate to the 'contentment' experienced by the speaker? Rank them in order of plausibility.

10. **Class Discussion:** The element lead has many associations in the popular imagination. List at least three of these.

11. The speaker describes her post-traumatic period as the 'Hour of Lead'. What does this suggest about her thoughts and emotions in the wake of the great pain that she has experienced?

12. The poet describes people 'Freezing' in the snows of an arctic environment. What three different stages do these 'Freezing persons' experience as they freeze to death? Write a sentence or two saying what you understand by each of these terms.

13. What do you understand by the phrase 'the letting go'? Are there a number of different things that the poet could mean here?

Exam Prep

1. **Personal Response:** 'The strangest thing about this poem is that the speaker finds a strange contentment in her numbness, the freedom of no longer caring, or thinking or feeling'. Do you agree with this statement? Write a short paragraph outlining your response.

2. **Class Discussion:** How will the speaker remember this post-traumatic period when she looks back on it? Is the speaker certain that she will actually survive or 'outlive' this difficult period in her life?

3. **Theme Talk:** 'This poem is a powerful study of post-traumatic stress, of the numbness and fatigue experienced in the wake of terrible trauma'. Write a few sentences in response to this statement.

Language Lab

1. How would you describe the atmosphere of the poem? What words and images capture or convey this atmosphere?

2. Consider the different references to stones, timber and metal in the poem. Why do you think the poet included these? What does each suggest about her emotional and physical condition?

3. Identify as many instances of personification as you can in the poem. In each case, say what is being personified and which human attributes have been assigned to non-human creatures or objects.

John Donne

When we look at the world today, we see how religious differences cause tension everywhere from the Middle East to Northern Ireland. In 1572, when John Donne was born, things were little different. Both his parents were Roman Catholics, which made life difficult for them in an England that had recently converted to the Protestant religion. Catholicism was illegal, and those who remained loyal to the Catholic faith were subject to punishments including fines and imprisonment. Catholics found guilty of treason were liable to be executed in a particularly grisly manner. Several members of Donne's extended family were exiled or executed because of their loyalty to the Roman Catholic faith. The poet later asserted that no other family had 'suffered more in their persons and fortunes' for following Catholicism.

Donne was born in 1572, the son of a successful London merchant (also called John Donne) who died when he was only four years old. His mother, Elizabeth Heywood, came from a prominent and well-connected family. She did not long remain a widow, marrying Dr John Syminges only a few months after her husband's death. We don't know what the young poet made of this quickly acquired stepfather. Infant mortality was incredibly high in those days; though Donne had five siblings, only three of them made it to adulthood. It's clear that the young Donne possessed an extraordinary intellect, enrolling in Hart Hall at Oxford

University when he was only eleven years old. He studied for six years – first at Oxford and later at Cambridge – but was unable to obtain a degree. To graduate, each student had to sign an Oath of Supremacy acknowledging the reigning monarch as Supreme Governor of the Church of England. Donne, loyal to the Pope and Catholicism, was unwilling to do this.

Donne was an ambitious young man and was keen to pursue some kind of political or diplomatic career. Like many budding politicians – then as now – he chose to study law and attended a number of legal schools around London. In the 1590s, London was buzzing. A growing and thriving metropolis, it was the centre of England's commercial, literary and intellectual life. Donne, in his late teens and early twenties, naturally responded to the excitement of the city. He enjoyed a colourful social life and earned a reputation as a womaniser. One friend described him as 'a great visitor of ladies, a great frequenter of plays, a great writer of conceited verses'. (In this instance, 'conceited' means intellectually complicated and ingenious.)

Religion continued to be a major issue. England was at war with Catholic Spain. The English government began to crack down even harder on its Catholic subjects, terrified that they might serve as agents of the Spanish enemy. It was in this climate that Donne's

"No man is an island, entire of itself; every man is a piece of the continent, a part of the main ... Any man's death diminishes me, because I am involved in mankind, and therefore never send to know for whom the bells tolls; it tolls for thee."

brother, Henry, was arrested for harbouring a Catholic priest. He contracted bubonic plague while incarcerated and died. (The priest, William Harrington, suffered an even worse fate, being hung, drawn and quartered.)

Donne, then, was faced with a major dilemma. Remaining loyal to Catholicism meant sacrificing any hopes of a successful career. However, it was equally difficult for him to contemplate abandoning the faith for which three generations of his family had suffered. Finally in 1595, following his brother's death, Donne succumbed to religious pressure and relinquished the Catholic faith. Over the next few years, Donne travelled widely. While we don't have the specifics of his 'grand tour', we do know that he visited France, Italy and Spain, returning home 'perfect in their languages'. This we must remember was at a time when few Englishmen travelled further than the next town. He also participated in several naval expeditions, fighting under Sir Walter Raleigh and the Earl of Essex. He saw battle against the Spanish navy at Cadiz in 1596 and in the Azores in 1597.

Donne's service on these voyages stood to him. He befriended a shipmate named Egerton, who recommended Donne to his father. On his return to England, Donne ended up working as private secretary for Sir Thomas Egerton, the Lord Keeper of the Great Seal of England and one of the highest-ranking officials in the English government. Sir Thomas was impressed by Donne and was influential in helping the young poet become Member of Parliament for Brackley in 1601. Now aged twenty-nine, Donne appeared to have every prospect of winning fortune and distinction – until he fell in love.

Egerton had been acting as guardian to Anne More, whose father, Sir George More, was also a high ranking government figure. Donne and Anne fell in love, and were married without the consent of either father or guardian. Sir George was furious about their secret marriage and had Donne thrown into prison. He was released after a number of weeks and used his legal training to have the validity of his marriage upheld. He was, however, dismissed from his position as Egerton's secretary and, under the circumstances, was unlikely to find another employer.

Donne and his seventeen-year-old wife moved to the town of Pryford, in Surrey, where the ambitious young poet must have deeply felt his exile from the bustle of the capital and its centres of power. Donne was extremely poor during these years. He repeatedly tried and failed to gain stable employment and was forced to eke out a living by practising law whenever he could. The family's financial situation wasn't improved by the fact that Anne gave birth to twelve children over sixteen years. With so many mouths to feed, there were moments when Donne despaired and even contemplated suicide. Indeed, if it hadn't been for Anne More's cousin Sir Francis Wolley, who provided the poet and his growing family with living quarters, Donne's circumstances would have been truly desperate.

Through it all, however, Donne continued to write poetry. His poems weren't formally printed but were circulated through 'coteries', informal circles of literary gentlemen. The brilliance and originality of his verse won him the admiration of lords, courtiers and even the king himself. One nobleman, Sir Robert Drury, became Donne's patron and benefactor, providing financial assistance when he needed it most. With Drury he undertook his final trip abroad, travelling through France and the Low Countries in 1611. It's generally believed that 'Sweetest Love, I do not go' and 'A Valediction: Forbidding Mourning' were prompted by this trip.

In 1615, under pressure from King James, Donne gave up his political ambitions and was ordained. The king was quick to make him an honorary Doctor of Divinity at Cambridge. But just as Donne's fortunes seemed to be improving, Anne Donne died. She passed away on 15 August 1617, aged thirty-three, after their twelfth child was stillborn. According to Donne's friend Izaak Walton, Donne was thereafter 'crucified to the world'.

He continued to write poetry, notably his 'Holy Sonnets', but the time for love poems was over. In 1620 he returned to London, where he was appointed Dean of Saint Paul's, an incredibly prestigious post that he held until his death. In this last period of his life Donne achieved the distinction he had desired for so long, becoming the most eminent preacher of his generation. He died, aged fifty-nine, on 31 March 1631. The first edition of his poems was printed two years later. For some 250 years, Donne's reputation as a poet was uncertain, though he always had admiring readers. It was only in the 20th century that he became acknowledged as one of the major English poets.

Song: Go and catch a falling star

Go and catch a falling star,
   Get with child a mandrake root,
Tell me where all past years are,
   Or who cleft the devil's foot,
Teach me to hear mermaids singing,   [5]
Or to keep off envy's stinging,
      And find
      What wind
Serves to advance an honest mind.

If thou be'st born to strange sights,   [10]
   Things invisible to see,
Ride ten thousand days and nights,
   Till age snow white hairs on thee,
Thou, when thou return'st, wilt tell me,
All strange wonders that befell thee,   [15]
      And swear,
      No where
Lives a woman true, and fair.

If thou find'st one, let me know,
   Such a pilgrimage were sweet;   [20]
Yet do not, I would not go,
   Though at next door we might meet;
Though she were true, when you met her,
And last, till you write your letter,
      Yet she   [25]
      Will be
False, ere I come, to two, or three.

Annotations

[2] *get with child:* impregnate

[2] *mandrake root:* a poisonous plant whose forked root resembles the lower half of the human body

[4] *cleft:* split, divided in two

[4] *the devil's foot:* the Devil's foot was believed to be shaped like a goat's hoof, with a 'cleft' or divide in the middle

[5] *mermaids singing:* the song of the mermaid was believed to enchant sailors and lure them to their death upon the rocks

[6] *envy's stinging:* the mental pain and torment of envy

[9] *advance:* benefit

[10] *If thou be'st born to strange sights:* If you have the gift or ability to see strange sights

[15] *befell thee:* happened to you

[18] *true:* faithful

[18] *fair:* beautiful

[20] *pilgrimage:* arduous physical and spiritual journey

[27] *False:* unfaithful

[27] *False, ere I come, to two, or three:* The poet is saying that the woman will have been unfaithful two or three times before he arrives.

Tease It Out

Stanza 1

1. Watch Video 8, which features a reading of the poem by actor Richard Burton. Pick out three words or phrases to which he gives particular emphasis while he reads. Identify one place where he speeds up his reading and one place where he slows down.

2. The poet mentions a number of feats and tasks:
   - What is the scientific name for the phenomenon known as 'falling stars'?
   - The poet instructs the reader, somewhat bizarrely, to impregnate a plant. Suggest why he chose a 'mandrake root' rather than some other species of plant or flower.
   - Does the question in line 3 make any sense? Come up with the best and most imaginative answer you possibly can to this question.
   - **Group Discussion:** Who or what might be responsible for the devil's feet having a cloven appearance, like a goat's hooves? Working as a group, can you come up with two or three suggestions? Is it possible to know for sure?
   - 'Teach me to hear mermaids singing'. Write a short story with this title. The story can be as realistic or unrealistic as you like.

3. What does the term 'stinging' suggest about the experience of envy? Do you think the poet believes it's possible to 'avoid or 'keep off' this negative emotion?

4. Would you agree that all the tasks mentioned above or by the poet are impossible or even nonsensical? Write a paragraph explaining your answer.

5. Finally, the poet asks us to find a circumstance that allows honest people to get ahead in life. What metaphor, related to ships and sailing, does he use to make this point?

6. **Class Discussion:** 'By lumping this last task in with the other nonsensical ones, the poet presents a very cynical view of the world'. Does the class as a whole agree with this assessment?

Stanza 2

7. The poet imagines a woman who is both 'true, and fair'. What do you understand by each of these characteristics?

8. The poet imagines a man on horseback heading off to explore the world:
   - **True or false:** This rider would have strange, almost supernatural, abilities.
   - For how long would this rider explore the world?
   - What sign of aging would he display by the end of his journey?
   - What would he tell the poet about when he returned?

9. According to the poet, is the rider likely to encounter any woman who is both true and fair?

Stanza 3

10. In the unlikely event that the rider meets a true and fair woman, he must inform the poet. How will the rider do this?

11. The poet would set off immediately to meet such a woman. What does the term 'pilgrimage' suggest about this journey?

12. The poet then changes his mind about undertaking such a 'pilgrimage'. Which phrase indicates this?

13. How would such a woman behave while the poet was on his way to meet her?

Exam Prep

1. **Personal Response:** What view of women and and femininity is presented in this poem? Write a few paragraphs outlining your own impression.

2. **Class Discussion:** 'Donne is a hateful and misogynistic poet'. Discuss this statement as a class, referring to the present poem and at least two others.

3. **Exam Prep:** 'In Donne's poetry women are alternately celebrated for their perfection and damned for their insincerity, and sometimes both in the same poem'. Write an essay discussing Donne's view of women, referring to this poem and three others on your course.

Language Lab

1. **True or false:** The poet wouldn't go as far as next door in order to meet such a woman.

2. Donne's poetry is known for its outrageous claims and demands. Read the poem carefully. Identify three claims and three demands and state why each might be decribed as outrageous.

3. Which of the following terms best describe your reaction to the poem's opening stanza? Rank them in order:
   - Witty • Playful • Imaginative
   - Silly • Over-the-top • Irrelevant

4. 'This poem isn't meant to be taken too seriously. It's more a quip or a witticism than a genuine statement about women and the world'. Write a

The Flea

Mark but this flea, and mark in this,
How little that which thou deniest me is;
It sucked me first, and now sucks thee,
And in this flea our two bloods mingled be;
Thou know'st that this cannot be said   [5]
A sin, nor shame, nor loss of maidenhead,
    Yet this enjoys before it woo,
     And pampered swells with one blood made of two,
     And this, alas, is more than we would do.

Oh stay, three lives in one flea spare,   [10]
Where we almost, nay more than married are.
This flea is you and I, and this
Our marriage bed, and marriage temple is;
Though parents grudge, and you, we're met,
And cloistered in these living walls of jet.   [15]
    Though use make you apt to kill me,
     Let not to that, self-murder added be,
     And sacrilege, three sins in killing three.

Cruel and sudden, hast thou since
Purpled thy nail in blood of innocence?   [20]
Wherein could this flea guilty be,
Except in that drop which it sucked from thee?
Yet thou triumph'st, and say'st that thou
Find'st not thy self, nor me the weaker now;
    'Tis true; then learn how false, fears be: [25]
     Just so much honour, when thou yield'st to me,
     Will waste, as this flea's death took life from thee.

Annotations

[1] *Mark:* note, notice

[6] *maidenhead:* virginity

[7] *woo:* courts and marries

[8] *pampered swell:* indulged, completely satisfied, lavishly treated

[10] *stay:* stop, refrain from action

[11] *nay:* no

[14] *we're met:* we are together or joined

[15] *cloistered:* being secluded in or confined to a monastery

[15] *jet:* black; a polished, black gemstone

[16] *apt:* have a tendency

[17] *self-murder:* suicide

[18] *sacrilege:* the destruction or violation of a sacred place

[20] *Purpled thy nail in blood of innocence:* The woman has swatted and killed the flea.

[27] *waste:* waste away, disappear

Tease It Out

Stanza 1

1. Watch Video 9, which features a dramatised reading of 'The Flea'. Identify two emotions displayed by the female actor throughout the piece and two emotions displayed by the male actor. Did you find the performance effective or silly and over-the-top?

2. The woman is 'denying' the speaker some 'little' thing ('How little that which thou deny'st me is'). What is this little thing she refuses to give him?

3. What has the flea done to both the speaker and the woman?

4. What, according to the poet, is now mingled inside the flea's body?

5. **Class Discussion:** 'A sin, nor shame, nor loss of maidenhead'. What does this line suggest about the woman's reasons for denying the speaker?

6. The speaker asks the lady to 'mark' or pay attention to the flea. What lesson does he want her to learn from the flea's behaviour?

7. Why might the flea be described as 'pampered'?

8. 'And this, alas, is more than we would do'. What does the flea do that the speaker and the woman do not?

Stanza 2

9. The woman is about to do something, but the poet asks her to 'stay', or stop. What is she about to do?

10. By killing the flea, the woman will take 'three lives'. Who, according to the poet, will she kill?

11. The speaker suggests that he and the woman have become 'married' despite the objections of the woman herself and of her parents ('Though parents grudge, and you'). How and where have they become husband and wife?

12. What two striking metaphors does the speaker use to describe the flea in line 15?

13. What are the 'living walls of jet'? What has been 'cloistered' within them?

14. According to the speaker, what three sins will the woman commit if she kills the flea?

Stanza 3

15. At the beginning of stanza 3, we learn that the woman has taken action. What has she done?

16. What effect has this had on her fingernail?

17. According to the speaker, did the flea deserve this treatment?

18. Why does the woman claim to have triumphed in their argument or debate?

19. **Class Discussion:** The woman's action. according to the speaker, has disproved her fears. Working as a class, restate the speaker's argument in your own words.

20. How much honour, according to the speaker, will 'waste' or drain from the woman if she yields to his advances?

Exam Prep

1. **Personal Response:** "The Flea' has been described as a poem of seduction. Yet no woman could possibly be seduced by all this talk about a blood-sucking insect.' Do you agree with this opinion?

2. **Class Discussion:** Many critics have suggested that 'The Flea' is a poem of the head rather than of the heart, that it is designed to impress Donne's male readers with its clever comparisons rather than to win the affection of a lover. Do you agree?

3. **Theme Talk:** 'The Flea' is often compared to 'The Dream'. What similarities are there between the poet's situation in the two poems? Which of them do you think is most effective as a love poem? 'The Flea' can be contrasted with 'The Anniversary'. Can you identify two major differences between that poem and this?

4. **Exam Prep:** 'John Donne is a poet who celebrates love in all its aspects: sexual, emotional and spiritual'. Write an essay in response to this statement in which you mention 'The Flea' and at least three other poems on the course.

Language Lab

1. 'Use' or habit has made the woman 'apt' or expert at killing the poet. Can you suggest how the woman, in the poet's opinion, has been killing him slowly?

2. Each stanza of the poem introduces a different argument. Summarise each one in your own words. Which one do you find most convincing and which one least convincing?

3. **Group Discussion:** Discuss the poem as a group and identify as many metaphors as you can. How many of these might be described as 'conceits' or extended metaphors?

The Dream

Dear love, for nothing less than thee
Would I have broke this happy dream;
      It was a theme
For reason, much too strong for fantasy,
Therefore thou waked'st me wisely; yet   [5]
My dream thou brok'st not, but continued'st it.
Thou art so true that thoughts of thee suffice,
To make dreams truths, and fables histories;
Enter these arms, for since thou thought'st it best,
Not to dream all my dream, let's act the rest.   [10]

As lightning, or a taper's light,
Thine eyes, and not thy noise waked me;
      Yet I thought thee
(For thou lovest truth) an angel, at first sight;
But when I saw thou sawest my heart,   [15]
And knew'st my thoughts, beyond an angel's art,
When thou knew'st what I dreamt, when thou knew'st when
Excess of joy would wake me, and cam'st then,
I must confess, it could not choose but be
Profane, to think thee any thing but thee.   [20]

Coming and staying showed thee, thee,
But rising makes me doubt, that now
      Thou art not thou.
That love is weak where fear's as strong as he;
'Tis not all spirit, pure and brave,   [25]
If mixture it of fear, shame, honour, have;
Perchance as torches, which must ready be,
Men light and put out, so thou deal'st with me;
Thou cam'st to kindle, goest to come; then I
Will dream that hope again, but else would die.   [30]

Annotations

[3-4] *a theme/ For reason:* The dream was about something that should happen in reality, not fantasy.

[6] *brok'st:* broke

[7] *so true:* so real

[8] *make ... fables histories:* make fictitious tales reality

[11] *taper's light:* light from a candle

[16] *beyond an angel's art:* beyond the capabilities of an angel (Only God can see into the hearts of humans.)

[19] *it could not choose but be:* it would only be

[20] *Profane:* irreverent

[20] *to think thee any thing but thee:* to think of you as being anything but who you really are

[21] *show'd thee, thee:* showed the real you

[27] *Perchance:* perhaps

[27] *torches, which must ready be:* Torches were lit and extinguished so that it would be easier to light them when needed.

[28] *Men light:* Men get aroused

[29] *goest to come:* leave with the intention of returning

[30] *die:* 'to die' can also mean to reach sexual climax

Tease It Out

1. The poet is in bed. He was asleep and having a dream. Describe in your own words what the poet has been dreaming about.
2. The poet says that his lover came into the bedroom and woke him up. What does he say was just about to happen in his dream the moment he awoke? What lines in the poem tell us this?
3. **Class Discussion:** Donne says that his lover has 'brok'st not, but continued'st' his dream. How might her presence in the bedroom be a continuation of the dream he has been having?
4. Donne believes that his lover woke him deliberately. What, does he say, were her intentions or motivations for waking him? What lines in the poem tell us this?
5. 'Thine eyes, and not thy noise wak'd me'. To what does the poet compare his lover's eyes? How did his lover's eyes wake him up?
6. Donne says that he first thought his lover was an angel when he woke. But he quickly realised that she wasn't an angel because his lover managed to do something that is 'beyond an angel's art'. Explain in your own words what the lover can do that angels cannot.
7. 'Thou art so true'. What does the poet mean by this? Consider the following options:
   - His lover's existence or presence is so real that it cannot be doubted.
   - His lover is very honest and would never say anything false.
   - His lover is faithful in her love for the poet and would never betray him.
8. Create a two-columned table. One column will be headed 'Real', and the other 'Unreal'. Now place each of the following into one or both columns and give a reason for your decision:
   - Dreams • Fables • Histories • Angels
   - The poet's lover's presence in the room.
   - The love that the poet feels for his beloved.
   - The love that the poet's lover has for him.
9. 'Coming and staying show'd thee, thee'. The poet says that entering the bedroom and staying revealed something about his lover. What does he say her presence showed?
10. However, the poet's lover is not in the room. He gets up, and she is not there. Her absence tells him that 'now,/ Thou are not thou'. Consider the following and say which you think is the most relevant or correct:
    - She is not present. The poet was mistaken in thinking she was ever in the room.
    - She is not sincere in her love for him. Her absence shows that her feelings are false.
    - Not staying in the room is out of character for her. She is not being herself, or being true to herself, when she behaves like this.
11. What does the poet 'hope' has happened at the end of the poem? What does he hope his lover has done or is doing?

Exam Prep

1. **Personal Response:** How would you characterise the poet's descriptions of his lover in the first two stanzas? Do you think he is being sincere, or is he merely flattering his lover in order to get what he wants?
2. **Class Discussion:** The poet says that true love ought to be 'all spirit'. What do you think he means by this? Is he being hypocritical in making demands of his lover if this is what he truly believes? Give a reason for your answer.
3. **Theme Talk:** Donne associates love with being 'true', honourable and 'pure'. What do you think he means by each of these qualities? Based on your reading of this and other poems by Donne on the course, does the poet believe that men and women ought to be held to the same standard when it comes to love?
4. **Exam Prep:** 'Donne uses startling imagery and wit in his exploration of relationships'. Write a response to this statement, making reference to 'The Dream' and three other poems on the course.

Language Lab

1. How would you characterise the poet's tone and mood in the first two stanzas? How does his tone and mood change in the third stanza? What has happened to bring about this change?
2. Outline in your own words the argument that the poet puts forward in the opening stanza to convince his lover to come to bed with him. Do you think that the poet's argument is reasonable or crazy? Give a reason for your answer.
3. Donne uses a number of interesting comparisons in the poem. In what way does he say that a man's passion and arousal is similar to a 'torch' or candle? Explain in your own words the comparison he makes and say whether you think it is an effective one.

The Sun Rising

Busy old fool, unruly sun,
      Why dost thou thus,
Through windows, and through curtains call on us?
Must to thy motions lovers' seasons run?
      Saucy pedantic wretch, go chide   [5]
      Late school boys and sour prentices,
   Go tell court huntsmen that the king will ride,
   Call country ants to harvest offices;
Love, all alike, no season knows nor clime,
Nor hours, days, months, which are the rags of time.   [10]

      Thy beams, so reverend and strong
      Why shouldst thou think?
I could eclipse and cloud them with a wink,
But that I would not lose her sight so long;
      If her eyes have not blinded thine,   [15]
      Look, and tomorrow late, tell me,
   Whether both th' Indias of spice and mine
   Be where thou left'st them, or lie here with me.
Ask for those kings whom thou saw'st yesterday,
And thou shalt hear, All here in one bed lay.   [20]

      She's all states, and all princes, I,
      Nothing else is.
Princes do but play us; compared to this,
All honour's mimic; all wealth alchemy.
      Thou, sun, art half as happy as we,   [25]
      In that the world's contracted thus.
   Thine age asks ease, and since thy duties be
   To warm the world, that's done in warming us.
Shine here to us, and thou art everywhere;
This bed thy center is, these walls, thy sphere.   [30]

Annotations

[1] *unruly:* disruptive, disorderly

[5] *saucy:* cheeky, brazen

[5] *pedantic:* very fussy and excessively concerned with minor detail

[5] *wretch:* miserable creature

[5] *chide:* scold

[6] *prentices:* apprentices

[8] *country ants:* farmers, those working in fields

[9] *all alike:* always the same, unchanging

[9] *clime:* climate

[17] *both th'Indias:* the East and West Indies

[17] *mine:* gold mines

[23] *play:* pretend, imitate

[24] *mimic:* imitation

[24] *alchemy:* false, not real. Alchemy was the medieval forerunner of chemistry, concerned particularly with attempts to convert less valuable metals into gold.

[27] *Thine age asks ease:* Your advanced years require that you take it easy.

Tease It Out

Stanza 1

1. Beams of sunlight are entering the poet's bedroom. Which phrases indicate this?

2. Is he happy that the sun has come to 'call' on him in this manner? Give a reason for your answer.

3. The poet lists other people whom the sun should bother instead:
   - Why are the schoolboys he mentions in need of chiding?
   - What does the term 'sour' suggest about the apprentices' mood? Why might they feel this way?
   - What rather insulting metaphor does he use to describe the peasants in the countryside? What 'offices' or tasks does he imagine them performing?
   - Describe in your own words why the court huntsmen have a busy day ahead of them.

4. **Class Discussion:** What does it mean to be pedantic? What according to the poet is the sun being pedantic about on this particular morning?

Stanza 2

5. The sun believes that its beams of sunlight are extremely powerful. Which phrase suggests this?

6. Does the poet agree with sun's assessment of its power?

7. The poet believes that he could 'eclipse' and 'cloud' these beams of light. How can he do this? Why is he reluctant to do so?

8. According to the poet, what is capable of blinding the sun itself?

9. The poet uses the conceit of states and princes to describe the relationship.
   - The poet compares his lover to all the _____ in the world. He compares himself, meanwhile, to all the _____ in the world. (Fill in the blanks.)
   - Will the islands of the East and West Indies be where the sun 'left' or last saw them' as it travelled around the earth? Where will they be instead?
   - What will the sun 'hear', according to the poet, if it asks about the kings of various lands around the world?
   - What does this conceit suggest about the poet's view of the relationship?

Stanza 3

10. Donne produces a typically weird and wonderful argument, declaring that his bedroom is now the whole world:
    - Which phrase indicates that the world has shrunk?
    - Which phrase indicates that nothing exists outside the bedroom?
    - What according to Donne is now at the centre of the world?
    - What now marks the limits of the world?

Exam Prep

1. **Personal Response:** 'This is yet another poem where Donne focuses on showing off his intellect rather than on expressing genuine emotion'. Do you agree? Write a paragraph or two in response.

2. **Class Discussion:** Consider the following lines: 'compared to this, /All honour's mimic, all wealth alchemy'.
   - What does the term 'honour' mean in this context?
   - How does the poet suggest the worthlessness of conventional wealth?
   - What do these lines suggest about the value the poet places on his current relationship?
   - Can you think of any songs that make a similar point about love?

3. **Exam Prep:** 'The poetry of John Donne contains wit as well as wisdom'. Discuss this statement in relation to 'The Sun Rising' along with at least two other poems on your course.

Language Lab

1. Donne's tendency for making outrageous and unlikely claims is especially evident in 'The Sun Rising'. Can you identify one such claim from each of the poem's three stanzas?

2. 'The Sun Rising' is well known for its personification of the sun:
   - Describe the device known as personification in your own words.
   - Consider the following terms: busy, fool, wretch, call, chide, saucy, old, unruly. Which are verbs, which are adjectives and which are nouns?
   - What does each term suggest about the personality of the sun as the poet perceives it?
   - Mention two things that Donne imagines the sun doing in stanza 2.
   - How does stanza 3 add to this personification?
   - The sun is usually thought of as powerful and magnificent. Does Donne's personification fit with this view? Give a reason for your answer.

Song: Sweetest love, I do not go

Sweetest love, I do not go
    For weariness of thee,
Nor in hope the world can show
    A fitter love for me;
        But since that I   [5]
Must die at last, 'tis best
To use myself in jest
        Thus by feign'd deaths to die.

Yesternight the sun went hence,
    And yet is here today;   [10]
He hath no desire nor sense,
    Nor half so short a way:
        Then fear not me,
But believe that I shall make
Speedier journeys, since I take   [15]
        More wings and spurs than he.

O how feeble is man's power,
    That if good fortune fall,
Cannot add another hour,
    Nor a lost hour recall!   [20]
        But come bad chance,
And we join to it our strength,
And we teach it art and length,
        Itself o'er us to advance.

When thou sigh'st, thou sigh'st not wind, [25]
    But sigh'st my soul away;
When thou weep'st, unkindly kind,
    My life's blood doth decay.
        It cannot be
That thou lov'st me, as thou say'st,   [30]
If in thine my life thou waste,
        That art the best of me.

Let not thy divining heart
    Forethink me any ill;
Destiny may take thy part,   [35]
    And may thy fears fulfil;
        But think that we
Are but turn'd aside to sleep;
They who one another keep
        Alive, ne'er parted be.   [40]

Annotations

[2] *weariness:* discomfort, dislike, mistrust

[4] *fitter:* better, more appropriate

[6-8] *'tis best/ To use myself in jest, / Thus by feign'd deaths to die:* The poet considers his departure good preparation for the ultimate end (death).

[8] *feign'd:* fake

[9] *Yesternight:* last night

[21] *But come bad chance ... length:* We succumb to misfortune, which allows it to grow stronger; our misery in the face of bad situations simply begets more misery.

[31] *waste:* lay waste to, destroy

[33] *divining:* intuitive, predictive

[34] *Forethink:* predict, anticipate

Tease It Out

Stanza 1

1. In the opening four lines the poet reassures his wife that he has not fallen out of love with her. Describe in your own words the specific claims that he makes.
2. The poet refers to a 'feign'd' or fake death. How might his departure be considered such a fake death? What do death and such a departure have in common?
3. 'But since that I/ Must die at last'. According to the poet, how should he and his wife prepare for his eventual death?
4. **Class Discussion:** 'To use myself in jest': What does the poet mean by this phrase? Try to describe his meaning in your own words.

Stanza 2

5. What did the sun do last night? What did it do this morning?
6. What does the poet suggest about the sun in line 11? Does this strike you as a reasonable claim?
7. 'Nor half so short a way'. Which journey is shorter, that of the poet or that of the sun? Explain your answer.
8. In lines 15 and 16 the poet uses the metaphor of 'wings' and 'spurs', saying these will allow him to make 'speedier journeys' than the sun. What do these 'wings' and 'spurs' represent?

Stanza 3

9. In lines 17 to 20, the poet laments that man's 'power is feeble', that human beings are incapable of changing certain things. According to the poet, what aspects of our existence are we powerless over?

10. What are we incapable of doing on those occasions when we experience good fortune?
11. What does the poet say about the 'lost hours' of good fortune that are now in the past?
12. What do you understand by the expression 'bad chance'? According to lines 22 to 24, how do we facilitate such misfortune when it arises in our lives?

Stanza 4

13. According to the poet, his wife isn't sighing wind or air. What does he suggest she is actually sighing?
14. What substance, according to the poet, drains away with every tear she cries?
15. What consequences, according to stanza 4, will the wife's grief have for the poet's health?
16. The poet suggests that his wife may not really love him after all. Why does he suggest this? Do you think he really means this?

Stanza 5

17. In lines 33 to 36, the poet asks his wife to avoid thinking in a particular fashion. What kind of thoughts does he ask her to avoid?
18. Why does he ask her to do this? Would you agree that the poet is superstitious? Give a reason for your answer.
19. How does he ask his wife to think of their separation?
20. Why, according to lines 39 to 40, can he and his wife never be truly parted?

Exam Prep

1. **Class Discussion:** In this poem, Donne uses several different arguments to comfort his lover. List them. Which did the class find most effective? Which did the class find least effective?
2. **Personal Response:** Imagine your boyfriend or girlfriend was leaving you for a long trip abroad and tried to make you feel better by saying the kinds of things that Donne says in this poem. How would you feel?
3. **Theme Talk:** 'Donne's poem is little more than a guilt-trip. He tries to make his partner feel guilty about crying over his departure so he doesn't have to face the reality of the pain he's causing her.' Do you agree with this statement? Write three or four paragraphs outlining your response.
4. **Exam Prep:** Donne wrote that 'to know and feel all this and not have the words to express it makes a human a grave of his own thoughts.' Write an essay describing three concepts or emotions that Donne knew, felt and expressed.

Language Lab

1. In this poem, Donne makes a number of deliberately exaggerated comparisons. Identify as many as you can. Which do you think are witty, over the top, or just plain silly?
2. 'That art the best of me'. Describe in your own words what the poet means by this movingly simple statement.
3. The poet refers to his wife as 'unkindly kind'. What does he mean by this seemingly contradictory statement? How can his wife's behaviour be simultaneously both kind and unkind?
4. **Class Discussion:** This poem is described as a 'Song'. What song-like qualities does it have? Do you think it would work as lyrics to a modern day piece of music? Can you think of any recent songs that articulate a similar sentiment?

A Valediction: Forbidding Mourning

As virtuous men pass mildly away,
   And whisper to their souls to go,
Whilst some of their sad friends do say
   The breath goes now, and some say, No:

So let us melt, and make no noise,   [5]
   No tear-floods, nor sigh-tempests move;
'Twere profanation of our joys
   To tell the laity our love.

Moving of the earth brings harms and fears,
   Men reckon what it did, and meant;   [10]
But trepidation of the spheres,
   Though greater far, is innocent.

Dull sublunary lovers' love
   (Whose soul is sense) cannot admit
Absence, because it doth remove   [15]
   Those things which elemented it.

But we, by a love so much refined,
   That our selves know not what it is,
Inter-assured of the mind,
   Care less, eyes, lips, and hands to miss.   [20]

Our two souls therefore, which are one,
   Though I must go, endure not yet
A breach, but an expansion,
   Like gold to airy thinness beat.

If they be two, they are two so   [25]
   As stiff twin compasses are two;
Thy soul, the fixed foot, makes no show
   To move, but doth, if the other do.

And though it in the centre sit,
   Yet when the other far doth roam,   [30]
It leans and hearkens after it,
   And grows erect, as that comes home.

Such wilt thou be to me, who must,
   Like the other foot, obliquely run;
Thy firmness makes my circle just,   [35]
   And makes me end where I begun.

Annotations

Valediction: farewell; a poem of farewell

[1] *virtuous men:* men who have not led sinful lives

[1] *pass mildly:* die in a calm manner

[6] *No tear-floods, nor sigh-tempests:* no floods of tears or heavy, mournful sighs

[7] *profanation:* a defilement or desecration

[8] *laity:* ordinary people

[9] *Moving of the earth:* an earthquake

[10] *reckon what it did, and meant:* consider the damage and significance

[12] *innocent:* harmless

[13] *sublunary:* earthly, and therefore prone to change

[14] *Whose soul is sense:* who rely on physical, sensual contact

[16] *elemented:* constituted

[19] *Inter-assured of the mind:* confident in the understanding that their love is not just a physical thing

[23] *breach:* break, separation

[24] *Like gold to airy thinness beat:* like gold beaten to a sheet of such incredible thinness that it resembles air

[26] *twin compasses:* two arms of a mathematical compass used for drawing circles

[31] *hearkens:* listens for

[34] *obliquely:* in a slanting direction, not straight

Tease It Out

1. The poet is about to embark on a lengthy trip to Europe. He tells his wife that they should 'melt' apart. What does this term suggest about the manner in which he would like them to part?

2. Donne uses the image of a virtuous man on his deathbed to illustrate how he would like he and his wife to behave as they separate.
   - Which phrase does he use to suggest that such men die in a very peaceful manner?
   - **True or false:** The virtuous man desperately clings to his soul, not wishing it to leave his body.
   - Why are the friends who stand by his bedside unsure whether the moment of death has arrived?

3. To what does the poet compare tears and deep, mournful sighs in line 6?

4. What effect, according to the poet, would any public show of grief have on their love?

5. The poet uses religious terms to suggest that their love is something special and sacred. Identify these terms and explain them in your own words.

6. The poet describes how people react and respond when earthquakes occur? What impact does he say such events have on peoples' lives?

7. The poet says that a tremor or disturbance of planets in outer space has no impact on human lives. What word or phrase indicates this?

8. **True or false:** The shaking or tremor of the planets is of less significance than earthquakes.

9. The poet characterises the love that most couples share as 'Dull' and 'sublunary'. Describe in your own words what each of these terms suggests or implies.

10. **Class Discussion:** What 'elements' constitute the love that most couples share? Which one is most important to these peoples' relationship?

11. Donne says that he and his wife share a love 'so much refined':
    - What does the term 'refined' suggest about the nature or quality of their love?
    - **True or false:** Donne and his wife are capable of comprehending the nature of their love.
    - How does Donne convey the fact that their love is more than just physical?

12. Donne argues that he and his wife share the one soul. If this is the case, what will happen to this soul as he journeys away from his wife?

13. Fill in the blanks in the following sentences. The poet uses an ingenious mathematical conceit, declaring that their souls are joined together like the two legs of a compass. The wife's soul is compared to the _____ leg of the compass. The poet's soul, meanwhile, is compared to the _____ leg. The fixed leg _____ as the moving leg _____. This suggests how the wife will long for her husband while he is gone. The fixed leg remains at the _____ of the arc traced by the moving leg. This suggests how the poet's wife will remain at the forefront of his mind as he _____. Once the circle has been traced, the two legs are recombined. This suggests how _____.

Exam Prep

1. **Personal Response:** Compare the poem's opening lines with those of 'Sweetest love, I do not go'. How does the poet's style of address differ? Which poem do you find more convincing?

2. **Class Discussion:** 'But we, by a love so much refined'. Discuss the way in which the poet distinguishes the love that he and his wife share from the love that others experience. Do you think he is being honest about what matters most to his wife and himself?

3. **Theme Talk:** 'Donne is a great poet of sex and seduction, but his poems also deal with romantic love and the ups and downs of married life'. Discuss this statement in relation to 'A Valediction' along with at least two other poems on your course.

4. **Exam Prep:** 'John Donne's poetry is cold and unfeeling. It's all about ingenious metaphors rather than genuine emotion'. Write an essay in response to this statement, making reference to at least four poems on your course.

Language Lab

1. Donne uses a typically inventive simile when he compares the 'expansion' of their single soul to gold that is beaten to an 'airy thinness'. What does this simile suggest about their relationship as the poet journeys ever further away??

2. **Class Discussion:** Donne suggests that when most people part, it is as if an earthquake has occured, but when he and his wife part it it is like a disruption of the planets. What point is he trying to make with this analogy? Would you consider this to be a reasonable or a crazy argument?

3. Donne is well known as a poet of paradox and contradiction. Do you find it paradoxical when Donne, having characterised the couple's love as 'so refined', then says that their parting should cause no grief or disturbance?

The Anniversary

All kings, and all their favourites,
   All glory of honours, beauties, wits,
The sun itself, which makes times, as they pass,
Is elder by a year now than it was
When thou and I first one another saw: [5]
All other things to their destruction draw,
   Only our love hath no decay;
This no tomorrow hath, nor yesterday,
Running it never runs from us away,
But truly keeps his first, last, everlasting day.   [10]

   Two graves must hide thine and my corse;
   If one might, death were no divorce.
Alas, as well as other princes, we
(Who prince enough in one another be)
Must leave at last in death, these eyes, and ears,   [15]
Oft fed with true oaths, and with sweet salt tears;
   But souls where nothing dwells but love
(All other thoughts being inmates) then shall prove
This, or a love increased there above,
When bodies to their graves, souls from their graves remove.   [20]

   And then we shall be throughly blessed;
   But we no more than all the rest.
Here upon earth, we're kings, and none but we
Can be such kings, nor of such subjects be;
Who is so safe as we, where none can do   [25]
Treason to us, except one of us two?
   True and false fears let us refrain,
Let us love nobly, and live, and add again
Years and years unto years, till we attain
To write threescore: this is the second of our reign.   [30]

Annotations

[1] *favourites:* lords or courtiers especially favoured by a king

[2] *wits:* people known for their intelligence

[6] *all other things ... draw:* everything is drawn towards destruction

[11] *corse:* corpse

[16] *Oft:* often

[19] *there above:* in heaven

[20] *remove:* depart, leave

[26] *Treason:* betrayal

[27] *refrain:* control, restrain, hold back

[30] *threescore:* sixty

Tease It Out

1. Read the first stanza carefully. When did the poet and his lover see each other for the first time?
2. **Class Discussion:** Think about the phrase 'glory of honours'. What does it bring to mind? Is the poet talking about physical objects or about something more abstract?
3. Why might 'wits', 'beauties' and 'favourites' command the envy and admiration of those around them?
4. We use the sun's movements to regulate our concept of time. Which lines indicate this?
5. What has happened to all these things – even the sun itself – in the year since the poet and his lover first met?
6. What makes the love between the speaker and his partner different from everything else in the world?
7. 'Running it never runs from us away.' What is the 'it' referred to in this line? What do you visualise or imagine here?
8. **Class Discussion:** In lines 9 to 10, Donne makes a typically outrageous claim about the nature of love. What does he suggest? Is he speaking literally or metaphorically?
9. The poet and his lover must be buried in two separate graves. Why do you think this is?
10. How might death be considered a form of divorce?
11. Under what circumstances would the poet consider death not to constitute divorce?
12. The poet and his lover must leave behind their bodies when they die. Which lines indicate this?
13. According to line 20, what happens to our souls when our bodies are laid in the ground?
14. In heaven, the souls of the poet and his lover will be free to continue their relationship. They will, he says, be 'thoroughly blessed'. Yet the speaker does not appear to be fully satisfied with this arrangement. Why is this?
15. The poet considers himself and his lover to be exceptionally 'safe'. Why is this?
16. The poet mentions the possibility of 'treason'. What does he have in mind here? Do you think he comes across as someone who is secure in his relationship?
17. The poet mentions fears that are 'true' and 'false'. What 'false' fears does he have in mind here? What might be an example of a 'true' fear that concerns him?
18. 'Let us love nobly, and live'. In the poem's final four lines, the speaker advises his lover with regard to how they should live and continue their relationship. Summarise this philosophy in a few lines.
19. According to the poem's final line, for how long does the poet envisage their relationship lasting?

Exam Prep

1. **Personal Response:** Do you think 'The Anniversary' is successful as a love poem? Many of Donne's critics have suggested that his verse lacks passion and romance. Would you describe 'The Anniversary' as a passionate poem or an intellectual one?
2. **Class Discussion:** The poem presents several different conceptions of what an 'everlasting love' might be. Think about these. Which of them do you find most realistic?
3. **Theme Talk:** 'This is a poem that begins with disgust at change but moves towards embracing our changing, living world with all its joys and challenges'. Write a paragraph in response to this statement.
4. **Exam Prep:** 'Donne writes about emotional, sexual and spiritual matters in a manner that is suited to his time but not to ours'. Write an essay in response to this statement, making reference to at least four poems on your course.

Language Lab

1. Donne uses a typically inventive metaphor when he compares himself and his lover to both kings and subjects. What does this metaphor suggest about his view of their relationship?
2. **Class Discussion:** According to the poet, why are souls more suited to love than bodies?
3. Donne is a poet famous for his conceits or extended metaphors. Identify a conceit in this poem. Say whether or not you think it is effective and why.
4. Donne is known for his weird and wonderful arguments. In 'The Anniversary', each stanza represents a different argument with regard to love. Summarise each argument in a few lines. Which argument did you find most convincing?

Batter my heart

Batter my heart, three-personed God, for you
As yet but knock, breathe, shine, and seek to mend;
That I may rise and stand, o'erthrow me, and bend
Your force to break, blow, burn, and make me new.
I, like an usurped town to another due,   [5]
Labour to admit you, but oh, to no end!
Reason, your viceroy in me, me should defend,
But is captived, and proves weak or untrue.
Yet dearly I love you, and would be loved fain,
But am betrothed unto your enemy;   [10]
Divorce me, untie or break that knot again,
Take me to you, imprison me, for I,
Except you enthral me, never shall be free,
Nor ever chaste, except you ravish me.

Annotations

[5] *usurped:* wrongfully seized; captured

[7] *viceroy:* governor of a country, province or colony, ruling as the representative of a sovereign

[8] *captived:* captured, held captive

[9] *fain:* gladly

[10] *betrothed:* engaged

[13] *enthral:* capture, enslave

[14] *chaste:* virginal, pure, refraining from sexual intercourse

[14] *ravish:* to seize and carry away by force, to rape or violate, to overwhelm with emotion; to enrapture

Tease It Out

Line 1 to 4

1. **Class Discussion:** Consider the phrase 'Batter my heart':
   - What Christian idea does the term 'three-personed' refer to?
   - What kind of action is suggested by the verb 'batter'?
   - Is this choice of verb surprising in the context of a religious poem?
   - Is the poet referring to the actual, physical heart or to something more abstract?

2. God has been seeking to 'mend' the poet. Can you suggest what these efforts by God might have consisted of?

3. The poet instead wants to be completely remade by God. Which phrase indicates this?

4. Which phrase suggests that such re-making will require a great effort on God's part?

5. Contrast the verbs 'knock, breathe, shine' with the verbs 'break, blow, burn'. Which set of verbs is more aggressive? Give a reason for your answer.

6. **Class Discussion:** These lines are influenced by pottery. There is a sense in which Donne compares God to a potter and himself to a defective vase. Can you identify words and phrases that support this view?

Lines 5 to 8

7. The poet compares himself to a town that has been 'usurped' or captured. Tease out this conceit or extended metaphor by filling in the gaps below:
   - The town owes its loyalty to its rightful lord, just as the poet owes his loyalty to _____.
   - But the town has been taken over by a foreign power, just as the poet's life has been taken over by _____.
   - The townspeople struggle to expel the foreign power and re-admit their rightful lord. The poet, similarly, struggles to _____ and _____.
   - The town's rightful lord appointed a 'viceroy' to 'defend' it on his behalf. _____, similarly, gave the poet the faculty of _____ with which to _____.

Lines 9 to 14

8. The poet presents his feelings towards God in what might be described as romantic terms. What phrase indicates this?

9. Who or what is god's 'enemy'? Which does the term 'betrothed' suggest about the poet's relationship with this enemy?

10. **True or false:** The poet calls on God to break up this relationship.

11. **Class Discussion:** The poet calls on God to 'imprison' him. What action on God's part is being imagined here?

Exam Prep

1. **Personal Response:** Donne's poetry is known for its outrageous claims and demands. In this poem, for instance, he calls on God to 'make [him] new'. In what sense does Donne wants to be re-invented? In what sense would his life be altered by this remaking?

2. **Class Discussion:** The poet mentions the faculty of 'reason':
   - As a class, list three or four terms you might associate with this faculty.
   - What role did the poet expect 'reason' to play in his life?
   - Why, according to the poet, did reason fail to play this role?

3. **Theme Talk:** 'Donne always thinks of himself as special, even when it comes to sinning. He insists the normal path to redemption isn't good enough for him; he requires special treatment'. Write a short essay in response to this statement, referring to 'Batter my Heart' and the other Holy Sonnets on the course.

Language Lab

1. Donne is poet well known for paradox and contradiction:
   - Which phrase indicates that the poet wants God to enslave him?
   - The poet claims there is only one way he can find freedom. What is this?
   - The term 'ravish' has multiple meanings. Which do you think is most relevant to line 14?
   - Describe in your own words why lines 13 and 14 are examples of the literary device known as paradox.

2. What three words would you use to describe the poem's tone? Are you surprised that someone would use such a tone when addressing God?

3. In the Bible, the nation of Israel, when it sinned against God, was compared to a defective piece of pottery, to a captured town and to a woman trapped in an adulterous relationship. Suggest how these images might have influenced Donne's poem.

Thou hast made me

Thou hast made me, and shall thy work decay?
Repair me now, for now mine end doth haste,
I run to death, and death meets me as fast,
And all my pleasures are like yesterday;
I dare not move my dim eyes any way,   [5]
Despair behind, and death before doth cast
Such terror, and my feebled flesh doth waste
By sin in it, which it towards hell doth weigh.
Only thou art above, and when towards thee
By thy leave I can look, I rise again;   [10]
But our old subtle foe so tempteth me,
That not one hour I can myself sustain;
Thy grace may wing me to prevent his art,
And thou like adamant draw mine iron heart.

Annotations

[2] *doth:* does

[2] *haste:* hurry

[7] *feebled:* enfeebled, weakened, decayed

[8] *weigh:* lean, droop

[10] *leave:* permission

[11] *tempteth:* tempts

[14] *adamant:* legendary stone said to have magnetic powers

Tease It Out

1. **Class Discussion:** Consider the 'work' mentioned in line 1:
   - Does this term refer to the poet's soul, to his body or to both?
   - Who is responsible for this 'work'?
   - What has happened to this work in recent years?
   - What action does the poet want God to undertake with regard to this work?
   - When must this task be undertaken?
   - Why is this a matter of some urgency for the poet?
2. What fast-approaching event is mentioned in line 3?
3. Which phrase suggests that the poet's 'pleasures' are a thing of the past? Suggest at least three different activities the poet might have in mind here.
4. The poet describes his eyes as being 'dim'? Is he referring a) to his power of vision, b) to the appearance of his eyes or c) to both?
5. Donne uses a conceit or extended metaphor to describe his predicament, declaring that he is unable to look in any direction:
   - What does the poet 'see' when he looks back? What does this suggest about his attitude towards the past?
   - What does the poet 'see' when he looks ahead? How does this prospect make him feel?
   - What is described as being below the poet? What weighs or drags him downwards?
   - Who or what is described as being 'above' the poet? Is it easy for the poet to look upwards? What kind of activity or behaviour would this looking upwards involve?
6. **Class Discussion:** Consider the phrase 'I rise again'. In what sense is the poet 'rising' at such moments? Is he referring to his body, his soul or his emotions?
7. What does line 6 suggest about the poet's physical condition? According to the poet, what causes this malaise?
8. The poet claims that he cannot 'sustain' himself for even an hour. What does he mean by this? Who or what prevents him from doing so?
9. **Class Discussion:** What do you understand by the idea of God's 'grace'? What impact will this 'grace' have on the poet's life? What metaphor does he use to describe this impact?
10. Read the poem's final line carefully:
    - Who or what is compared to a piece of iron?
    - Who or what is compared to a magnet?
    - What does the poet envisage the magnet doing?
    - What activity or outcome is suggested by this metaphor?

Exam Prep

1. **Personal Response:** Do you think it is accurate to describe 'Thou hast made me' as a kind of prayer? What features might set it apart from more conventional prayers?
2. **Class Discussion:** Discuss the following questions with your classmates, then write your own response to each one:
   - Is Donne a poet of the intellect rather than of the emotions?
   - Which emotion comes across most clearly in this poem? Is it fear, rage, self-disgust, desperation or something else entirely?
   - What view of God emerges from this poem? Does He come across as gentle and forgiving or as stern and vengeful?
3. **Theme Talk:** This poem is often compared to 'Batter my heart'. Do you think there is a similar attitude to religion in these poems? Which of them do you prefer? Give a reason for your answer.
4. **Exam Prep:** 'Donne presents a bleak and unappealing view of religion and spirituality'. Write an essay in response to this statement in which you refer to this poem and also to 'The Anniversary', 'Batter my heart' and 'A Valediction'.

Language Lab

1. How would you describe the poet's tone in 'Thou hast made me'? Does he address God in a haughty fashion or a humble one? Refer to specific words and phrases in your answer.
2. Consider the phrase 'old subtle foe'. What impression of the devil is created by this phrase? According to the poem, what is the devil's' art'? Which phrase indicates that the devil is exceptionally gifted at this art?
3. Try to identify each of the metaphors used by Donne in this poem. Which metaphor do you think is most effective? Give a reason for your choice.

At the round earth's imagined corners

At the round earth's imagined corners, blow
Your trumpets, angels, and arise, arise
From death, you numberless infinities
Of souls, and to your scattered bodies go;
All whom the flood did, and fire shall o'erthrow,   [5]
All whom war, dearth, age, agues, tyrannies,
Despair, law, chance, hath slain, and you whose eyes
Shall behold God and never taste death's woe.
But let them sleep, Lord, and me mourn a space,
For if above all these my sins abound,   [10]
'Tis late to ask abundance of thy grace
When we are there; here on this lowly ground
Teach me how to repent; for that's as good
As if thou hadst sealed my pardon with thy blood.

Annotations

The description of the angels at the earth's 'corners' comes from the Book of Revelation, the final book of the New Testament, which contains an account of how the world will end: 'And after these things I saw four angels standing on the four corners of the earth'.

[5] *fire:* the fire that will accompany the world's end

[6] *dearth:* famine; poverty

[6] *agues:* fevers or illnesses

[6] *tyrannies:* cruel, oppressive regimes

[7] *hath slain:* has killed

[8] *and never taste death's woe:* those who are free of sin and still alive when God appears on the Day of Judgement; these people will go straight to heaven without dying.

[9] *a space:* for a short time

[10] *my sins abound:* My sins are even more plentiful.

[11] *abundance of thy grace:* God's generous blessing or forgiveness

[14] *sealed my pardon:* guaranteed my forgiveness

Tease It Out

1. A vast number of people have lived and died since the beginning of the world. Which phrase indicates this?
2. The 'flood' killed many people. To which biblical story is the poet referring?
3. Describe in your own words three other causes of death described by the poet.
4. **Class Discussion:** Where have the souls of these dead people been residing?
5. Which phrase suggests that their bodily remains are to be found all over the world?
6. How will angels signal that the end of the world has come?
7. What will the souls of the dead do at this moment?
8. **Class Discussion:** Some people will still be living when the angelic trumpets sound and the end of the world arrives.
   - According to Donne, will these people ever experience death?
   - Suggest what will happen to these bodies and souls now that the world has ended.
   - Which phrase indicates that these individuals will experience God in a special way?
9. In the first eight lines, the poet is eager for the end of the world to come. What phrases indicate this? Can you suggest why he is so eager?
10. In which line does the poet change his mind about wanting this to happen?
11. The poet considers himself to be a truly terrible sinner. Which phrase indicates this?
12. **True of false:** When the world ends it will be too late to seek forgiveness for his sins.
13. What do you understand by the term 'lowly ground'?
14. What does the poet want to accomplish while he is still on this 'lowly ground'?

Exam Prep

1. **Personal Response:** Write a few lines describing your understanding of the term 'repent'. Why must Donne be taught how to do this? Rank the following in order of plausibility:
   - Donne knows little about Christianity and requires special instruction.
   - Donne is asking God to grant him resolve and mental fortitude.
   - Donne is a special person who requires God to enter his life in a special way.
2. **Class Discussion:** 'Donne presents a very bleak view of religion, one obsessed with sin, death and damnation'. Discuss this statement as a class, referring to the three Holy Sonnets on your course.
3. **Exam Prep:** Write an introduction to the poetry of John Donne aimed at Transition Year students. You should mention two poems that focus on spirituality and two poems that focus on romantic and sexual love. Don't forget to mention Donne's use of metaphor and other literary devices.

Language Lab

1. Donne is well known as a poet of paradox and contradiction.
   - Would you agree that the poem's opening line contains such a contradiction?
   - What common expression is referred to in this line?
   - Search for images of 17th-century maps of the world. Can you suggest how these might have influenced this line?
2. Donne's poetry is known for its outrageous claims and demands. Read the poem carefully. Identify one such claim and one such demand, and state why each might be decribed as outrageous.
3. The poem's conclusion features a typically inventive simile. Repentence is compared to a legal document sealed with Christ's own blood. Come up with three similes of your own that compare an abstract concept (such as victory, sorrow, desire) to a physical object.

Seamus Heaney

Seamus Heaney was born on 13 April 1939, the eldest of nine children. He grew up on the family farm, Mossbawn, near Castledawson in County Derry. His father, Patrick, worked as a cattle dealer as well as a farmer. Patrick was a man of few words, while Heaney's mother, Margaret, was articulate and outspoken. Heaney inherited both of these traits, and believed this to be fundamental to the 'quarrel with himself' from which his poetry arises.

At age twelve, Heaney won a scholarship to St Columb's College, a Catholic boarding school in Derry city. Heaney's family, meanwhile, moved from Mossbawn to the nearby village of Bellaghy. Though they left the farm where Heaney was reared in 1953, Mossbawn looms large in his work, and rural County Derry is the 'country of the mind' where much of his poetry is grounded.

While Heaney was studying at St Columb's, his brother Christopher was killed in a road accident at the age of four. Christopher's death had a profound effect on the young Heaney, and he would write extensively about it in later years, most notably in his famous poem 'Mid-Term Break'.

In 1957, Heaney left school and began studying English literature at Queen's University Belfast. During his college years, he developed an interest in poetry particularly that of Ted Hughes. He graduated in 1961 with a first class honours degree and went on to teacher training college at St Joseph's in Belfast.

While on teaching placement, Heaney met the writer Michael McLaverty, who became a mentor to the young poet, introducing Heaney to the work of Patrick Kavanagh and encouraging him to publish his work. After graduating from St Joseph's, Heaney became a lecturer there in 1963. Under the guidance of the poet Philip Hobsbaum, he joined a writing workshop with Derek Mahon, Michael Longley and others.

In 1965 Heaney married Marie Devlin, a teacher from Co. Tyrone. The following year, just before Marie gave birth to Michael, the first of their three children, Heaney's first collection of poetry was published. *Death of a Naturalist* dealt primarily with Heaney's childhood experiences of growing up in rural County Derry. It won several awards, including the Geoffrey Faber Prize. Heaney's reputation grew, and he was appointed a lecturer in Modern English Literature at Queen's that same year.

Another son, Christopher, was born in 1968. Heaney's second collection, *Door into the Dark*, was published in 1969. Including such key poems as 'The Forge' and 'Bogland', the collection was

"My poetry journey into the wilderness of language was a journey where each point of arrival turned out to be a stepping stone rather than a destination."

well-received, being selected as the Poetry Book Society Choice for the year. In 1970 he taught for a year at the University of California, Berkeley, before returning to Belfast.

In 1972 Heaney published *Wintering Out*, in which he continued his exploration of landscape, and in particular boglands, in poems such as 'The Tollund Man'. He resigned his lectureship at Queen's University and moved his family to Glanmore, County Wicklow. By moving to Wicklow he wanted, as he put it later, 'to put the practice of poetry more deliberately at the centre of my life'. He also wanted to escape the pressures he felt as a Catholic writer working in the North: 'In the late sixties and early seventies the world was changing for the Catholic imagination. I felt I was compromising some part of myself by staying in a situation where socially and, indeed, imaginatively, there were pressures against regarding the moment as critical. Going to the South was perhaps emblematic for me and was certainly so for some of the people I knew. To the Unionists it looked like a betrayal of the Northern thing.'

For the next three years, Heaney made his living as a full-time writer. Then, in 1975, he resumed lecturing at Carysfort, a teacher-training college in Dublin. Heaney moved to Sandymount, Dublin, shortly afterwards, and it remained his home for the rest of his life. The same year, 1975, also saw the publication of *North*, arguably his most political collection, which juxtaposes imagery of bog bodies and *Vikings* with violence in Northern Ireland. The book won the W.H. Smith Award and the Duff Cooper Memorial Prize, and was a Poetry Book Society Choice. 'The Skunk' and 'Harvest Bow' were among the poems included in *Field Work* (1979), and his first volume of *Selected Poems* followed in 1980.

When Aosdána was formed in 1981 to honour important Irish artists, Heaney was one of the first artists to be made a member. That same year, Heaney left his lectureship at Carysfort to become a visiting professor at Harvard University. In 1984 he was elected Boylston Professor of Rhetoric and Oratory at Harvard. *Station Island*, his sixth volume of poetry was published in the same year. Heaney's mother, Margaret, died in 1984, and his father, Patrick, passed away in 1986. The loss of both parents within two years affected Heaney deeply. He explored his grief in the sonnet cycle 'Clearances', which appeared in the 1987 collection *The Haw Lantern*. In 1989, Heaney was elected professor of poetry at Oxford, a position which he held until 1994. Throughout this period, he continued to divide his time between Ireland and the United States. *Seeing Things* (1991), his ninth collection of poetry, included such poems as 'The Pitchfork' and 'Lightenings'.

Heaney was awarded the Nobel Prize for Literature in 1995 for what the Nobel committee described as 'works of lyrical beauty and ethical depth, which exalt everyday miracles and the living past.' He was the fourth Irishman to receive the honour, after William Butler Yeats, George Bernard Shaw and Samuel Beckett. His 1996 collection, *The Spirit Level*, which includes the poem 'Postscript', won the Whitbread Book of the Year Award, as did his 1999 translation of *Beowulf*.

In 2003, the Seamus Heaney Centre for Poetry was opened in Queen's University Belfast. Today, it houses the Heaney Media Centre – a record of all his writings, TV and radio appearances – and also serves as a creative writing school for postgraduate students.

In August 2006, Heaney suffered a stroke, from which he recovered. That same year, his collection *District and Circle*, which includes 'Tate's Avenue', won the T.S. Eliot Prize. In 2008, the poet Dennis O'Driscoll published *Stepping Stones*, a series of interviews with Heaney. This interview series is the closest thing to an autobiography that Heaney ever published.

Heaney's twelfth and final collection, *Human Chain*, was published in 2010. It was inspired in part by his stroke and was critically acclaimed, winning the Forward Poetry Prize. In 2011, Heaney donated his personal literary papers to the National Library of Ireland.

On 30 August 2013, Heaney died in hospital after a short illness. He was seventy-four years old. His funeral Mass was held in Donnybrook, Dublin, and was broadcast live on RTE. He was buried in his home village of Bellaghy, County Derry, in the same graveyard as his parents and brother Christopher. His epitaph is taken from his poem 'The Gravel Walks' and reads, 'Walk On Air Against Your Better Judgement'.

The Forge

All I know is a door into the dark.
Outside, old axles and iron hoops rusting;
Inside, the hammered anvil's short-pitched ring,
The unpredictable fantail of sparks
Or hiss when a new shoe toughens in water.   [5]
The anvil must be somewhere in the centre,
Horned as a unicorn, at one end square,
Set there immoveable: an altar
Where he expends himself in shape and music.
Sometimes, leather-aproned, hairs in his nose,   [10]
He leans out on the jamb, recalls a clatter
Of hoofs where traffic is flashing in rows;
Then grunts and goes in, with a slam and flick
To beat real iron out, to work the bellows.

Annotations

Forge: a blacksmith's workshop

[2] *axles*: shafts on a vehicle to which the wheels are fitted

[3] *anvil*: a heavy block of iron with a smooth face on which heated metals are hammered into desired shapes

[4] *fantail of sparks*: the clash of metal on metal produces sparks that radiate out from the anvil

[5] *shoe:* horseshoe

[5] *toughens in water:* heating metal makes it softer and easier to manipulate. It must then be cooled rapidly so that it hardens and retains its new shape.

[7] *horned:* The traditional anvil is pointed at one end. The pointed end is known as the 'horn' or 'beak' and is used for bending and shaping the heated metal.

[9] *expends himself:* uses all his energy

[10] *jamb*: vertical side of a door frame

[12] *bellows*: a tool used for blowing air into a fire

Tease It Out

1. Watch Video 12 of a blacksmith at work in Bunratty Castle, Co. Clare. Then answer the following questions:
   - What is he making?
   - Name the different pieces of equipment he uses.
   - Choose three adjectives that best describe the sounds of the forge and three adjectives that best describe the colours and visuals of the forge.
2. The poet has never actually been inside the forge. Which phrase indicates this? Do you think the poet finds this 'door into the dark' fascinating or intimidating or a mixture of both? Explain your answer.
3. What can the poet see outside the door of the forge?
4. Has the blacksmith been based here for a long time or is this a relatively new business? Give a reason for your answer.
5. What one sight can the poet make out when he peers through the forge's door? What might cause this phenomenon? Suggest why it appears at 'unpredictable' intervals.

6. The blacksmith's labour produces two sounds that can be heard outside the forge. What qualities does each sound possess? What activity is responsible for each one?
7. Why according to the poet does the blacksmith place freshly fashioned horseshoes in cold water? Can you describe the scientific process at work here?
8. The poet imagines the blacksmith's anvil. In what part of the forge does he envisage it being located?
9. The poet mentions two aspects of the anvil's shape, as he imagines it. What are these? Which verb suggests that the blacksmith's work leaves him exhausted?
10. What can the blacksmith see passing by outside his forge? What used to travel along this roadway years ago?
11. What implication might this change have for the blacksmith and his livelihood?
12. Read line 13 carefully. What three things does the blacksmith do before returning to his forge? What does his behaviour suggest about his attitude to modernity and the changes in society he has witnessed?

Exam Prep

1. **Class Discussion:** 'This is a great poem of imagination. The poet himself never crosses the door into the darkness of the blacksmith's workspace. Only his imagination makes this transition'. Identify two other poems by Heaney where the power of imagination is celebrated.
2. **Theme Talk:** Think about the questions below on your own for a few minutes. Then compare your ideas with those of the person beside you. Together, formulate answers, supporting your conclusions with evidence from the poem.
   - The poet describes the blacksmith's craft as one of 'shape and music'. In what way do the blacksmith's endeavours involve shaping various items?
   - How might they produce music of a kind?
   - In what way does poetry also involve shape and music?
   - What hints are there that the poet holds the blacksmith and his craft in high esteem?
3. **Exam Prep:** Throughout his work, Heaney shows a captivation with the symbols of a traditional way of life that is fast disappearing in our modern world'. Discuss this statement with reference to 'The Forge' and at least one other poem on your course.

Language Lab

1. 'The Forge' is an example of the sonnet form.
   - Can you identify two aspects of this form in the poem?
   - The sonnet has long been associated with love poetry. Would you agree that 'The Forge' can be described as a love poem of sorts?
   - Can you suggest why Heaney chose this tightly structured form for a celebration of the blacksmith's craft?
2. Heaney's work is known for its exquisite verbal music. Can you identify two examples each of alliteration and assonance within this poem? Can you identify any lines that mimic the sound of the blacksmith's labour?

Bogland
for T.P. Flanagan

We have no prairies
To slice a big sun at evening –
Everywhere the eye concedes to
Encroaching horizon,

Is wooed into the cyclops' eye   [5]
Of a tarn. Our unfenced country
Is bog that keeps crusting
Between the sights of the sun.

They've taken the skeleton
Of the Great Irish Elk   [10]
Out of the peat, set it up,
An astounding crate full of air.

Butter sunk under
More than a hundred years
Was recovered salty and white.   [15]
The ground itself is kind, black butter

Melting and opening underfoot,
Missing its last definition
By millions of years.
They'll never dig coal here,   [20]

Only the waterlogged trunks
Of great firs, soft as pulp.
Our pioneers keep striking
Inwards and downwards,

Every layer they strip   [25]
Seems camped on before.
The bogholes might be Atlantic seepage.
The wet centre is bottomless.

Annotations

[1] *prairie*: an extensive stretch of flat land without trees, especially in North America

[3] *concedes*: gives way to

[4] *Encroaching* intruding, pushing in upon

[5] *wooed*: lured, seduced

[5] *cyclops*: a one-eyed giant from Greek mythology

[6] *tarn*: small mountain lake

[10] *the Great Irish Elk*: extinct species of giant deer; Heaney's neighbours dug the skeleton of one from a bog when he was a child.

[12] *crate full of air*: refers to the Elk's huge skeleton

[13] *butter*: In the past people would preserve butter by storing it in peat bogs. Sometimes containers of butter were forgotten about and only discovered hundreds or thousands of years later.

[18] *definition*: meaning or significance; having a definite shape or outline

[22] *pulp*: a soft, wet, shapeless mass of material

[23] *pioneer*: person who is among the first to explore or settle a new country or area

[6] *Atlantic seepage*: The poet imagines that water from the Atlantic seeps through the bedrock of the country and up through the bog's layers until it reaches the surface.

Tease It Out

1. The poem draws an interesting contrast between the Irish landscape and the American prairie. Draw a Venn diagram, labelling one circle 'The American prairie' and the other 'The Irish landscape'. Now categorise the following adjectives, placing those that correspond with *both* categories in the centre where the circles overlap.
   - expansive • varied • soft • beautiful
   - unfenced • rugged • featureless
   - mutable • flat • awe-inspiring
2. What metaphor is used to describe the sun setting on the American prairies?
3. In Ireland, according to the poet, one can rarely see very far into the distance. Which line suggests this?
4. The poet says that one's eye is 'wooed' by the tarns that are a feature of the Irish landscape. What does the term 'wooed' suggest about the appearance of these tarns?
5. How does the poet describe the cycle of day and night in line 8? What does he say happens to the surface of the bog 'Between the sights of the sun'?
6. To what does the poet compare the texture of the bog in lines 16 to 17?
7. **Class Discussion:** Why do you think the poet describes the boggy ground as 'kind'?
8. The poet makes reference to the bog's incredible powers of preservation. What items or things does he describe emerging intact from the bog? State why each discovery was remarkable.
9. Which phrase suggests that the bog will never settle into a final and definite shape?
10. The poet mentions 'pioneers', 19th-century explorers who journeyed across the prairies, charting the new lands of America. He suggests that in Ireland we have our own 'pioneers' who 'keep striking/ Inwards and downwards'.
11. **True or false:** The poet suggests that there might be no end to this voyage of discovery into the bogs.
12. Consider the following questions on your own for five minutes:
13. What sort of people does the poet have in mind here?
14. What sort of activity involves going 'Inwards and downwards'?
15. In what way might these people be compared with the American pioneers?
16. Now pair with the person next to you and compare answers. Can you agree on your answers?

Exam Prep

1. **Personal Response:** 'Inwards and downwards'. Do you think that these terms might be applied to the Irish race and their outlook on life? Give reasons for your answer.
2. **Class Discussion:** The bog is made up of layers that when stripped away reveal more layers beneath. What do you think the poet means when he says that 'Every layer ... Seems camped on before'? What does the word 'camped' suggest about the nature of each occupation of the land?
3. **Theme Talk:** 'Bogland', like many of Heaney's poems, is concerned with the process of memory, presenting the bog as the collected memory of the Irish race. Write a paragraph in response to this statement.

Language Lab

1. The poem features a number of fine metaphors. In each case, state what is being described, what it is being compared to, and what the comparison suggests about it.
   - 'We have no prairies/ To slice a big sun at evening'
   - 'the cyclops' eye/ Of a tarn'
   - 'An astounding crate full of air'
   - 'The ground itself is kind, black butter'
2. The poem makes repeated references to the wet, soggy texture of the bog. Identify as many references as you can. Would you agree that the poet identifies a special kind of beauty in these descriptions of the bog? Give reasons for your answer.
3. Describe the poet's use of alliteration and assonance in lines 3 to 6.

The Tollund Man

I
Some day I will go to Aarhus
To see his peat-brown head,
The mild pods of his eyelids,
His pointed skin cap.

In the flat country nearby   [5]
Where they dug him out,
His last gruel of winter seeds
Caked in his stomach,

Naked except for
The cap, noose and girdle,   [10]
I will stand a long time.
Bridegroom to the goddess,

She tightened her torc on him
And opened her fen,
Those dark juices working   [15]
Him to a saint's kept body,

Trove of the turfcutters'
Honeycombed workings.
Now his stained face
Reposes at Aarhus.   [20]

II
I could risk blasphemy,
Consecrate the cauldron bog
Our holy ground and pray
Him to make germinate

The scattered, ambushed   [25]
Flesh of labourers,
Stockinged corpses
Laid out in the farmyards,

Tell-tale skin and teeth
Flecking the sleepers   [30]
Of four young brothers, trailed
For miles along the lines.

III
Something of his sad freedom
As he rode the tumbril
Should come to me, driving,   [35]
Saying the names

Tollund, Grauballe, Nebelgard,
Watching the pointing hands
Of country people,
Not knowing their tongue.   [40]

Out there in Jutland
In the old man-killing parishes
I will feel lost,
Unhappy and at home.

Annotations

Tollund Man: the well-preserved body of a man who lived during the fourth century BC. He was found in 1950 on the Jutland Peninsula in Denmark, buried in a peat bog near the village of Tollund. He was discovered with a pointed leather cap on his head, a belt or 'girdle' around his waist and a noose around his neck. He'd been hanged, and afterward his body was carefully placed in the bog. It's believed he died as a human sacrifice in an ancient fertility rite.

[1] ***Aarhus:*** city in Denmark (the Tollund Man is on display near here at a museum in Silkeborg)

[13] ***torc:*** a collar or necklace consisting of a twisted narrow band, in this case the rope around the Tollund Man's neck

[14] ***fen:*** boggy land

[16] ***saint's kept body:*** reference to the Catholic belief that saints' bodies do not decompose after death

[17] ***Trove:*** treasure found hidden in the earth

[17] ***turfcutters:*** men who cut the turf from the bogs

[18] ***Honeycombed working:*** describes how sods of turf are arranged carefully in stacks; they have a geometric pattern like the cells in a beehive

[22] ***Consecrate:*** to make or declare sacred

[22-25] ***I could…pray/ Him:*** The poet considers praying to the Tollund Man as if he were a God or saint.

[22] ***cauldron bog:*** The poet likens the bog to a pot used to brew or mix magic potions, suggesting the bog's almost magical ability to preserve bodies.

[24] ***to make germinate:*** cause to grow or sprout, cause to develop or flourish. The poet wishes the Tollund Man could somehow germinate those who died during Ireland's troubled past.

[25-26] ***scattered, ambushed flesh:*** refers to a group of farm labourers who were taken by surprise and shot during Ireland's War of Independence (1919-1921). Their flesh is described as 'scattered', suggesting that they were blown to bits by gunfire.

[27] ***Stockinged:*** wearing nightclothes. Heaney recalls a photograph in Tom Barry's book *Guerrilla Days in Ireland*. The photograph depicts a family who were dragged from their beds and shot during Ireland's War of Independence.

[30] ***sleepers:*** wooden beams supporting the rails on a railway track

[31] ***four young brothers:*** reference to the killing of four Catholic brothers by Protestant paramilitaries. Their bodies had been trailed along the railway line.

[34] ***tumbril:*** two-wheeled, open cart

[37] ***Tollund, Grauballe, Nebelgard:*** Sites on the Jutland Peninsula in Denmark where bog bodies were discovered

Tease It Out

Section I

1. How does the poet characterise the colour of the Tollund Man's head? Why is the head this colour?

2. The poet describes the Tollund Man's eyelids as 'mild pods'. Are the Tollund Man's eyes open or shut? Why do you think the poet compares the eyelids to pods? What do 'pods' normally contain? Why do you think he describes the pods as 'mild'?

3. What was the Tollund Man wearing?

4. What was around the Tollund Man's neck? What does this tell us about the manner in which he died?

5. What did the Tollund Man eat before he died?

6. Who discovered the Tollund Man? What work were they doing when they came across the body?

7. Heaney compares the stacked turf to honeycomb. Is it an effective comparison in your opinion?

8. The Tollund Man was killed as a sacrifice to a goddess of earth and fertility.
   - The goddess's servants strangled him. Which phrase indicates this?
   - Her servants then placed him in the 'fen' or bog. Which phrase indicates this?
   - Would you agree that there is an element of personification in these lines?
   - What impact does the bog's liquid have on the Tollund Man's body?
   - Heaney compares the Tollund Man to a saint. Is there more than one way in which this comparison might be valid?
   - Heaney compares the noose to a 'torc'. How does this suggest that the Tollund Man's death was a kind of honour?

Section II

9. The poet mentions three violent incidents from Ireland's troubled history.
   - He describes 'labourers' who were ambushed'. Which phrase indicates that their bodies were shot to bits?
   - He describes a murdered family. Which phrase indicates they were taken from their beds and shot?
   - He describes the murder of 'four young brothers'. What happened to their bodies after they were killed?

10. The poet imagines praying to the Tollund Man. Describe in your own words what he asks the Tollund Man to do.

11. Write three or four words or phrases that come to mind when you think of the word 'cauldron'. How many of these phrases fit the bog as Heaney describes it in this poem?

12. **Class Discussion:** Heaney wants the corpses of these victims to 'germinate'. What precisely do you imagine happening here?

13. Heaney thinks of the bog as a consecrated or sacred place. Does he really believe this or is it merely a flight of fancy?

14. What is 'blasphemy'? Can you suggest why such thoughts might 'risk blasphemy'?

15. **Class Discussion:** Contrast the manner in which the Tollund Man's body was treated after he died with the bodies of the victims Heaney describes in lines 25 to 32.

Section III

16. How was the Tollund Man transported to his death?

17. Why might the Tollund Man have experienced a sense of 'freedom' as well as sorrow as he made this final journey?

18. The poet imagines going to Denmark to see the Tollund Man. How does he imagine feeling as he drives through the Danish countryside?

19. The poet imagines stopping for directions:
    - Mention the three places he wants to visit.
    - Does the poet speak Danish? Give a reason for your answer.
    - How would the local people direct him?

20. The Danish landscape, according to the poet, consists of 'man-killing parishes'. What killings is he imagining? How might the phrase 'man-killing parishes' be applied to Ireland?

21. **Class Discussion**: The poet imagines himself feeling 'lost,/ Unhappy and at home'. Suggest a reason for each of these emotional states. Do you think there is something paradoxical about feeling simultaneously 'lost' and 'at home'?

Language Lab

1. 'Trove of the turfcutters'/ Honeycombed workings'.
   These lines are richly poetic. Write a short
   paragraph discussing the poet's use of assonance,
   alliteration and metaphor, and state what effect
   or impact each device has. Can you identify other
   instances of assonance, alliteration and metaphor in
   the poem?
2. 'Tell-tale skin and teeth/ Flecking the sleepers'.
   Discuss the poet's use of cacophony in these lines.
   Where in the poem can you find examples of
   euphony?
3. How would you characterise the mood and
   atmosphere of the third section of the poem? What
   is it that creates or determines this mood and
   atmosphere?

Exam Prep

1. **Personal Response:** Discuss the following
   questions in small groups and come up with a
   personal response to each one:
   - Is the poet angry and outraged at the thought of
     the Tollund Man being sacrificed by members
     of his own community?
   - Is it possible that Heaney viewed the Tollund
     Man's death as necessary and, even, as an
     honour? Is it possible that the Tollund Man, too,
     felt this way about his own passing?
   - The poet is clearly fascinated and inspired by
     the Tollund Man. Offer two or three reasons
     why this is the case.
2. **Class Discussion:** 'The poem highlights how
   violence and religion inevitably go hand-in-hand,
   in patterns that can be seen across many centuries'.
   Discuss this statement as a class.
3. **Theme Talk:** Consider Heaney's prayer to the
   Tollund Man in Section II. What does this suggest
   about the possibility of salvaging something positive
   from Ireland's long history of conflict? Is this a
   realistic hope in your opinion?
4. **Exam Prep:** 'Heaney uses fresh and imaginative
   language to bring the past and the present crashing
   together'. Write a short essay in response to this
   statement, making reference to 'The Tollund Man'
   and at least three other poems on your course.

Sunlight

There was a sunlit absence.
The helmeted pump in the yard
heated its iron,
water honeyed

in the slung bucket   [5]
and the sun stood
like a griddle cooling
against the wall

of each long afternoon.
So, her hands scuffled   [10]
over the bakeboard,
the reddening stove

sent its plaque of heat
against her where she stood
in a floury apron   [15]
by the window.

Now she dusts the board
with a goose's wing,
now sits, broad-lapped,
with whitened nails   [20]

and measling shins:
here is a space
again, the scone rising
to the tick of two clocks.

And here is love   [25]
like a tinsmith's scoop
sunk past its gleam
in the meal-bin.

Annotations

[2] *helmeted pump:* The protective iron cladding on the pump resembled a helmet, especially the bulbous part on the top.

[4] *honeyed:* Sunlight lends the water a golden appearance resembling honey.

[5] *slung:* describes how the bucket's handle is hung from the top of the pump so it can be filled

[7] *griddle:* a circular, flat iron plate that is heated and used for cooking food

[10] *scuffled:* describes how her fingers interlocked and rubbed against one another as she kneaded the dough

[11] *bakeboard:* a wooden board on which dough is kneaded and rolled

[13] *plaque of heat:* The poet imagines heat emanating from the oven door in an intangible plaque or square of warmth.

[18] *goose's wing:* a feather used as a duster

[20] *measling:* having or developing red spots

[22] *scone:* a loaf of brown bread

[26] *tinsmith's scoop:* a scoop or spoon made of tin

[28] *meal-bin:* a container for storing flour or animal feed

Tease It Out

1. Where is the poem set? What time of year do you imagine it is? Give a reason for your answer.
2. Heaney introduces the figure of his aunt in stanza 3. What is the aunt doing? What does the word 'scuffled' suggest about the way she works?
3. The speaker describes his aunt as 'broad-lapped'. What does this suggest about her, and about the speaker's perception of her? Is she maternal or girlish, strong or dainty? Explain your answer.
4. Consider the poet's description of the yard outside the kitchen in the first two stanzas. From what vantage point do you imagine the yard is being viewed?
5. Describe in your own words the effect that the sunlight has on the pump and the water coming out of it.
6. To what does the poet compare the sun in Stanza 2? What similarities can this item be said to have to the sun?
7. Consider the phrase 'the wall// of each long afternoon.' What 'wall' can the sun be said to be 'cooling/ against' on a long afternoon? What does the word 'wall' suggest about the force of the afternoon's heat?
8. What does the speaker's aunt use to clean up after her work?
9. Why do you think that the tinsmith's scoop, symbolising love, is 'sunk past its gleam'? Pair with a classmate and consider the following possibilities, ranking them in order of likelihood:
   - The love between them is 'sunk past its gleam' because it's past its best.
   - The scoop represents how firmly this familial love is embedded in both of them.
   - The love between them is 'sunk past its gleam' because although they don't verbalise it with fancy words ('gleam'), they both still know it's there.
10. The speaker notes three ways in which his aunt's work has temporarily altered her appearance. Describe each in your own words.
11. Line 22: 'here is a space'. What does it say about the poet's aunt that she only allows herself to sit down after the scones are put in the oven and the workspace cleared up?
12. Line 24: 'to the tick of two clocks.' Why do you think the poet specifically mentions two clocks? What might the two clocks ticking in harmony together symbolise?

Exam Prep

1. **Personal Response:** Write a short poem or text describing a treasured memory from your own childhood, one that you find yourself returning to from time to time.
2. **Class Discussion:** 'There was a sunlit absence'. Who or what do you think is absent from this scene? Does Heaney present this absence in a positive or a negative light?
3. **Theme Talk:** 'In several of his poems, Heaney celebrates ordinary, everyday physical work and the quiet mastery of older men and women'. Discuss this statement with reference to 'Sunlight' and at least two other poems on your course.
4. **Exam Prep:** 'In Heaney's work, familial love is often unspoken. If love is expressed at all, it's usually through gestures rather than words'. Do you agree with this statement? Write a short essay in response, referring to 'Sunlight' and at least three other poems on your course.

Language Lab

1. 'Heaney presents the pump as a 'helmeted' soldier protecting the safety of the household'. Do you find this statement plausible or utterly fanciful? Explain your answer.
2. Heaney compares the heat that emerges from the heating oven to a 'plaque'. Do you find this to be an effective metaphor? Can you identify another moment in the poem where Heaney compares heat to a tangible, solid structure?
3. Do you find the images of the cast-iron water pump, goose-wing duster, tinsmith's scoop and meal-bin to be striking images, or are they humble and everyday? What do you think Heaney saw in them that led him to highlight them in the poem?

A Constable Calls

His bicycle stood at the window-sill,
The rubber cowl of a mud-splasher
Skirting the front mudguard,
Its fat black handlegrips

Heating in sunlight, the 'spud' [5]
Of the dynamo gleaming and cocked back,
The pedal treads hanging relieved
Of the boot of the law.

His cap was upside down
On the floor, next his chair. [10]
The line of its pressure ran like a bevel
In his slightly sweating hair.

He had unstrapped
The heavy ledger, and my father
Was making tillage returns [15]
In acres, roods, and perches.

Arithmetic and fear.
I sat staring at the polished holster
With its buttoned flap, the braid cord
Looped into the revolver butt. [20]

'Any other root crops?
Mangolds? Marrowstems? Anything like that?'
'No.' But was there not a line
Of turnips where the seed ran out

In the potato field? I assumed [25]
Small guilts and sat
Imagining the black hole in the barracks.
He stood up, shifted the baton-case

Further round on his belt,
Closed the domesday book, [30]
Fitted his cap back with two hands,
And looked at me as he said goodbye.

A shadow bobbed in the window.
He was snapping the carrier spring
Over the ledger. His boot pushed off [35]
And the bicycle ticked, ticked, ticked.

Annotations

[2] *cowl:* hood-shaped covering

[2] *mud-splasher:* cover draped over or around the mudguard

[5] *spud:* The dynamo is bulbous or egg-shaped. To the young poet it resembles a potato.

[6] *dynamo:* small generator fitted to a bicycle to produce electricity for its lights

[7] *pedal treads:* the upper surface of the pedal, on which the foot is placed

[11] *bevel:* ridge or indentation

[14] *ledger:* accounts book in which the constable records the tillage returns

[15] *making tillage returns:* calculating the tax liability arising from the production of different crops

[16] *roods:* a measure of land area, equal to a quarter of an acre

[16] *perches:* another measurement of land

[22] *Mangolds:* a variety of beet

[22] *Marrowstems:* a root vegetable, also known as kale

[28] *baton-case:* The constable is armed not only with a revolver but also with a type of club known as a baton.

[30] *domesday book:* Heaney compares the constable's ledger to the record of a survey of the lands of England made by William the Conqueror in 1086.

Tease It Out

1. The speaker says that 'my father/ Was making tillage returns'.
   - What are tillage returns? How are these returns measured?
   - Where does the constable record this information?
   - The constable, as an agent of the state, has been sent to gather this data. Why might it be of value to the government?
   - Do you think this is a routine visit, or something out of the ordinary?
2. Where does the constable park his bicycle?
3. The constable has one item of equipment in particular that fascinates the young poet. What is it?
4. Line 17 describes an atmosphere of 'fear'. In your opinion, who or what is generating this fear? Consider the following possibilities and rank them in order of likelihood:
   - The child is afraid.
   - The child detects fear coming from his father.
   - The constable is nervous.
   - The line refers to a broader fear in society.
5. What last question does the constable ask before he leaves? According to the young poet, does his father answer truthfully?
6. What information does the father conceal? Why do you think he wants to conceal this from the constable?
7. 'No' is the only word spoken by the father that is quoted in the poem. What does this suggest about his attitude to the constable?
8. Look up the word 'assume' and write down its different meanings. Which meaning is intended here? Is it possible that more than one meaning is intended?
9. Consider the word 'small'. Did the young poet think this was a small matter at the time, or did he consider it a big deal? Give a reason for your answer.
10. What did the young poet fear might happen to him because of his part in this minor deception?
11. Has the young poet actually seen the barracks, or is he imagining it?
12. List the different things that the constable does as he prepares to leave the house.
13. 'And looked at me as he said goodbye': What kind of look do you imagine the constable giving the poet as he departs? Is it affectionate, suspicious or indifferent?
14. What did the poet imagine was on the constable's mind when he 'looked at [him]'?

Exam Prep

1. **Personal Resonse:** Heaney is a poet well known for his ability to capture a child's point of view. Can you identify three or four phrases or lines in the poem where a child's outlook and concerns are accurately conveyed?
2. **Class Discussion:** Watch Video 13, which depicts a series of events that took place twenty years after those described in this poem. What is ticking at the conclusion of the poem? What other devices are known for producing a ticking sound? Do these lines anticipate the Troubles depicted in the video?
3. **Exam Prep:** 'Heaney uses vivid imagery to explore both positive and negative emotional states'. Write a short essay in response to this statement, making reference to 'A Constable Calls' and at least two other poems on your course.

Language Lab

1. Working in pairs, look closely at lines 2 to 8 and discuss the different features of the bicycle. When you think you have a good understanding of what the poet is describing, attempt to sketch the bicycle that the constable rides.
2. The constable is associated with an almost oppressive weight. Find three or four phrases that support this.
3. Based on your reading of the poem, write a paragraph describing your impression of the constable's appearance and demeanour

The Skunk

Up, black, striped and damasked like the chasuble
At a funeral Mass, the skunk's tail
Paraded the skunk. Night after night
I expected her like a visitor.

The refrigerator whinnied into silence.   [5]
My desk light softened beyond the verandah.
Small oranges loomed in the orange tree.
I began to be tense as a voyeur.

After eleven years I was composing
Love-letters again, broaching the word 'wife'   [10]
Like a stored cask, as if its slender vowel
Had mutated into the night earth and air

Of California. The beautiful, useless
Tang of eucalyptus spelt your absence.
The aftermath of a mouthful of wine   [15]
Was like inhaling you off a cold pillow.

And there she was, the intent and glamorous,
Ordinary, mysterious skunk,
Mythologised, demythologised,
Snuffing the boards five feet beyond me.   [20]

It all came back to me last night, stirred
By the sootfall of your things at bedtime,
Your head-down, tail-up hunt in a bottom drawer
For the black plunge-line nightdress.

Annotations

[1] *damasked:* wearing or covered in a patterned fabric

[1] *chasuble:* sleeveless vestment worn by a priest;

[2] *At a funeral Mass:* When conducting funerals, priests wear black and white chasubles.

[3] *Paraded the skunk:* the skunk's tail seems to be leading the skunk rather than the other way around

[5] *whinnied:* produced a soft, high sound like the neighing of a horse

[6] *verandah:* a large open porch

[8] *voyeur:* person who gains pleasure and excitement from watching others

[10] *broaching:* mentioning a subject; piercing a cask in order to draw out the liquid within

[11] *cask:* a small wooden barrel in which beverages mature over a number of years

[12] *mutated:* to change; in linguistics, a mutation is a change in the sound of a vowel

[14] *eucalyptus:* a type of gum tree with aromatic leaves

[20] *Snuffing:* the sniffing sounds made by an animal as it investigates an object's scent

[21] *stirred:* aroused, excited

[22] *sootfall:* the soft sound of soot falling down the inside of a chimney

[24] *plunge-line:* garment with a low, revealing neckline

Tease It Out

1. How often does the poet see the skunk?
2. Based on your reading of the first stanza, do you think the poet looked forward to seeing this 'visitor', actively disliked its visits or was indifferent to them? Give a reason for your answer.
3. Can his desk light illuminate much of the yard outside? What species of tree grows there?
4. What is the poet's mental state as he waits for the skunk's arrival?
5. The poet claims that he hadn't written his wife any love letters over the previous eleven years. Can you suggest two different reasons why this might have been the case?
6. The poet describes how the 'Tang' or scent of the eucalyptus trees seems almost to communicate with him. What does it 'spell' out or remind him of?
7. The poet remembers 'inhaling' his wife's scent. From what surface did he breathe it in? Do you think his wife was present when he did this?
8. What taste, now that he's far away from her in California, reminds him of this aroma?
9. What phrase indicates the suddenness with which the skunk makes its appearance in the poet's yard?
10. Consider the adjectives 'ordinary', 'mysterious', 'intent' and 'glamorous'. Working in pairs, describe in your own words what each suggests about the skunk's demeanour and behaviour. Is it possible for something to be both 'ordinary' and 'mysterious' at the same time?
11. What does the skunk do to the boards of the poet's veranda?
12. At this moment, how far is the skunk from the poet's writing desk?
13. This final stanza takes place some years after the poet's stay in California. Which phrase indicates this jump forward in time?
14. What are the 'things' referred to in line 22?
15. What kind of sound does soot make when it falls down a chimney? What reminds the poet of this sound now?
16. The poet describes how he's 'stirred' by the sound he's hearing. What do you think he means by this?
17. What is his wife looking for in the bottom drawer?
18. 'It all came back to me'. Why do you think this incident reminds the poet of his stay in California?

Exam Prep

1. **Personal Response:** The poet clearly misses his wife while he's in California. List the different ways in which he expresses this.
2. **Class Discussion:** 'Like much of Heaney's work, 'The Skunk' is very much concerned with the process of memory, and highlights no less than four different layers of remembering'. Discuss this statement as a class.
3. **Theme Talk:** Would you agree that there's a sense in which the poet has taken his wife ever so slightly for granted, and that he only appreciates how wonderful she is when he's far away from her?
4. **Exam Prep:** 'Heaney makes extraordinary use of language in order to explore love of different kinds'. Write a short essay in response to this statement, making reference to 'The Skunk' and three other poems on your course.

Language Lab

1. Consider the verb 'parade'. What does it suggest about the manner in which the skunk moved? Does it creep about stealthily or strut in a confident and carefree fashion?
2. In a most unusual metaphor, the poet compares the word 'wife' to a cask or barrel of wine. Break into pairs and answer the following questions:
   - Is he thinking of a new vintage or an aged one? Give a reason for your answer.
   - How does one broach a cask of wine? (Google it!)
   - How might one 'broach' a 'word'?
   - The poet imagines this vowel spreading into the 'night earth and air' like the scent from a just-broached barrel. What does this suggest about his feelings towards his absent wife?
3. Suggest a reason why the poet assumes the skunk is female. Could there be more than one reason for this assumption?

The Harvest Bow

As you plaited the harvest bow
You implicated the mellowed silence in you
In wheat that does not rust
But brightens as it tightens twist by twist
Into a knowable corona,   [5]
A throwaway love-knot of straw.

Hands that aged round ashplants and cane sticks
And lapped the spurs on a lifetime of gamecocks
Harked to their gift and worked with fine intent
Until your fingers moved somnambulant: [10]
I tell and finger it like braille,
Gleaning the unsaid off the palpable,

And if I spy into its golden loops
I see us walk between the railway slopes
Into an evening of long grass and midges,   [15]
Blue smoke straight up, old beds and ploughs in hedges,
An auction notice on an outhouse wall –
You with a harvest bow in your lapel,

Me with the fishing rod, already homesick
For the big lift of these evenings, as your stick   [20]
Whacking the tips off weeds and bushes
Beats out of time, and beats, but flushes
Nothing: that original townland
Still tongue-tied in the straw tied by your hand.

The end of art is peace   [25]
Could be the motto of this frail device
That I have pinned up on our deal dresser –
Like a drawn snare
Slipped lately by the spirit of the corn
Yet burnished by its passage, and still warm.   [30]

Annotations

Harvest Bow: a small bow that was traditionally woven from fresh straw at harvest time; sometimes worn like a badge

[2] *implicated … the silence:* conveyed or suggested the father's near silence; interwove this silence with the strands of straw; suggested that this silence might have been involved in something unpleasant or harmful

[2] *mellowed silence:* suggests that the father's temperment has grown more calm and relaxed with age

[4] *brightens as it tightens:* tightening the straw dries it out and prevents it from rotting so it retains its golden colour

[5] *corona:* a circle of light; a crown or crown-like structure

[7] *ashplants:* walking sticks made from ash

[7] *cane sticks:* walking canes

[8] *lapped the spurs:* spurs are the sharp protrusions of bone at the sides of a rooster's claws. These were 'lapped' or covered with pieces of cloth in order to prevent injury

[8] *game cocks:* a type of rooster bred for fighting

[9] *Harked:* listened; responded

[10] *somnambulant:* as if sleepwalking; the father's fingers moved with an absentminded ease.

[11] *braille:* a system of writing in which words are read by touch

[12] *Gleaning:* to obtain information; to reap or gather

[12] *palpable:* tangible, capable of being touched

[18] *lapel:* the fold on each side of a coat or jacket just below the collar

[22] *flushes:* beating bushes to scare out birds

[25] *The end of art is peace:* a quote from the 19th-century English poet Coventry Patmore

[26] *device:* a mechanism; a symbol; a ploy or strategy

[27] *dresser:* a piece of furniture used for displaying kitchenware

[28] *snare:* a trap made from loops of chords or ropes

[30] *burnished:* polished

Tease It Out

1. The poet describes his father making a harvest bow. From what substance is it manufactured?
2. Consider the words 'plaited', 'tightens' and 'twists'. What do they suggest about the process by which the bow was created?
3. **Class Discussion:** The poet describes the bow as 'knowable'. What does he learn or know through contemplating the harvest bow? Is this knowledge gained by touching it, by looking at it or through both senses? Give a reason for your answer.
4. A 'corona' can be defined as a) the glow around the edge of the sun or b) a crown or crown-like structure. Which definition do you think Heaney has in mind here? Do you think both definitions could be relevant? Give a reason for your answer.
5. Which word suggests that the harvest bow wasn't intended to last for a very long time, that it was created as a disposable piece of decoration?
6. The bow is described as a 'love-knot' or love token. For whom, do you think this token of love was intended?
7. Throughout his life, the poet's father handled 'ashplants' and 'cane sticks'. Suggest several different uses that the father, as a farmer, might have made of these implements.
8. Roosters and cockerels are born with 'spurs' of bone that protrude from their claws. What do you think the word 'lapped' means in the context of these spurs? Suggest why farmers might carry out such a procedure on their male poultry.
9. Consider the questions below on your own for five minutes and jot down some ideas. Then compare notes with the person beside you. Finally, share your ideas with the class.
    - Which phrase suggests that in making the harvest bow, the father is responding to some impulse, talent or calling that lay deep within his psyche?
    - Which phrase suggests that the poet's father initially worked with intense concentration?
    - Which phrase suggests that after a while the father didn't even need to concentrate anymore, that his fingers seemed to be moving automatically?
10. The poet remembers taking a stroll with his father. At what time of day did this take place?
11. Identify three hints that suggest that this walk took place at harvest time, towards the end of summer or in early autumn.
12. Which phrase indicates that it was a still and windless evening? What indications are there that this was a rural, farming environment?
13. What was the poet carrying?
14. What was the father doing as they walked along the country road?
15. Did the rhythm of his stick match the rhythm of their footsteps?
16. **Class Discussion:** What other meaning might the phrase 'out of time' have? What does it suggest about the father and his ways in the modern world?
17. The father, we're told, 'flushes nothing' as he beats the bushes with his stick. What might he have been attempting to flush or scare from the hedgerows?
18. The poet has kept one of the bows made by his father. Where exactly in his house has he positioned it?
19. 'The end of art is peace'. Write a few lines describing what you understand by this statement.
20. The poet declares that this phrase could be the 'motto' of the harvest bow. What does this suggest about his attitude towards this object?

Exam Prep

1. **Personal Response:** The poet suggests that certain things were 'unsaid' between himself and his father. Suggest two different topics or areas of conversation they might have avoided. Would you agree that such reluctance or difficulty in communication is relatively common among Irish fathers and sons?
2. **Class Response:** Would you agree that the memory depicted in stanzas 4 and 5 is presented in an especially vivid fashion? What images or details create this effect?
3. **Exam Prep:** 'Heaney's poetry can be dense and challenging but always has human emotion at its core'. Write a short essay in response to this statement.

Language Lab

1. Consider the phrase 'big lift'. What does it suggest about the evening sky? Have you personally ever experienced the optical illusion that makes the sky seem bigger or higher at certain times of the year?
2. Using a simile, the poet compares the harvest bow to a snare used for trapping animals. Is this a valid or accurate visual comparison in your opinion? Give a reason for your answer.
3. What, according to the poet, has recently been trapped by this snare? Has this object or entity managed to escape? What two traces has it left on the bow?

The Underground

There we were in the vaulted tunnel running,
You in your going-away coat speeding ahead
And me, me then like a fleet god gaining
Upon you before you turned to a reed

Or some new white flower japped with crimson   [5]
As the coat flapped wild and button after button
Sprang off and fell in a trail
Between the Underground and the Albert Hall.

Honeymooning, mooning around, late for the Proms,
Our echoes die in that corridor and now   [10]
I come as Hansel came on the moonlit stones
Retracing the path back, lifting the buttons

To end up in a draughty lamplit station
After the trains have gone, the wet track
Bared and tensed as I am, all attention   [15]
For your step following and damned if I look back.

Annotations

The Underground: London's underground rail network

[1] *vaulted:* having a high, arched ceiling

[2] *going-away coat:* part of the outfit worn by a bride when leaving her wedding reception to go on honeymoon

[3] *fleet:* quick, speedy

[3] *god:* refers to the Greek god Pan, who was known, among other things, for his great sexual appetite

[4] *before you turned to a reed:* Syrinx was a beautiful young nymph who fled Pan's sexual advances. As Pan was about to catch her, she prayed to the gods for help. They responded by transforming her into a reed, thereby allowing her to escape Pan's clutches.

[4] *japped:* spattered or stained

[8] *the Albert Hall:* a concert hall in South Kensington, London

[9] *mooning around:* to move around or spend time without any clear purpose

[9] *the Proms:* a series of classical music concerts presented each summer by the BBC

[11] *Hansel:* In the famous fairytale, Hansel and Gretel are abandoned by their father deep in the forest. As they are led through the woods, however, Hansel leaves a trail of white pebbles behind him. This allows them to retrace their steps and find their way home.

[16] *damned if I look back:* a reference to the Greek myth of Orpheus and Eurydice. When Eurydice died, her husband, Orpheus, freed her from the underworld on the condition that he could not look back at his wife until they reached the earth. Just as they were about to return to the land of the living, Orpheus glanced back. Eurydice vanished, and Orpheus lost her forever.

Tease It Out

1. The poet remembers the honeymoon he took with his wife. Which city did they visit?
2. The couple are 'running' through an underground station. Suggest two or three reasons why they might be in such a hurry.
3. The wife is running ahead of the husband. Which phrase indicates this?
4. What happened to the buttons of the coat as the couple moved through the city streets?
5. Towards what venue were they headed, and what event were they due to attend there?
6. 'Our echoes die in that corridor'. What corridor is the poet referring to? Is it the Underground station, a tunnel leading from the station or a corridor in the concert venue? Give a reason for your answer.
7. The poet finds himself walking the cobbled streets of the city. Which phrase indicates that darkness has fallen and it is now night-time?
8. Is the poet alone? Give a reason for your answer.
9. What does he use to retrace his steps back to the station?
10. To which fairytale character does he compare himself?
11. Which phrase indicates that the trains have stopped running for the night?
12. The poet describes himself as being 'Bared and tensed'. What does this suggest about his state of mind as he moves through the empty station? How do we usually use the word 'bared'? What might its use in this context suggest about the poet's feelings of vulnerability?
13. '[Y]our step following'. Who do you think was walking behind the poet?
14. Which phrase indicates the poet's intense focus on the sound of this person's steps?
15. [D]amned if I look back'. Why do you think the poet was unwilling to look behind at the person following him? In what other ways do we use the word 'damned'? How might they be relevant in this context?

Exam Prep

1. **Personal Response:** 'The poem's opening ten lines capture the energy and excitement of young love'. Write a paragraph in response to this statement.
2. **Class Discussion:** Read about the myth of Orpheus and Eurydice. In what ways does the last stanza of the poem resemble this myth? In what ways does it differ?
3. **Exam Prep:** 'Heaney's poetry portrays the ups and downs of relationships'. Discuss this statement in relation to this poem and to 'The Skunk' and 'Tate's Avenue'.

Language Lab

1. **Class Discussion:** The last six lines of the poem present a dreamlike scenario where the poet walks through the streets and the Underground station, followed by his wife. He listens intently for her every step behind him, but like Orpheus he believes that if he looks back something terrible will happen. Rank the following possibilities in order of likelihood:
   - The poet has fallen out of love with his wife.
   - The poet worries that she has fallen out of love with him.
   - One of them is moving to another country, forcing them to have a long-distance relationship.
2. Pick three words that best capture the atmosphere of a) the poem's first nine lines and b) its second nine lines. Would you agree that these two sections of the poem represent very different moments in a relationship?

The Pitchfork

Of all implements, the pitchfork was the one
That came near to an imagined perfection:
When he tightened his raised hand and aimed with it,
It felt like a javelin, accurate and light.

So whether he played the warrior or the athlete   [5]
Or worked in earnest in the chaff and sweat,
He loved its grain of tapering, dark-flecked ash
Grown satiny from its own natural polish.

Riveted steel, turned timber, burnish, grain,
Smoothness, straightness, roundness, length and sheen.   [10]
Sweat-cured, sharpened, balanced, tested, fitted.
The springiness, the clip and dart of it.

And then when he thought of probes that reached the farthest,
He would see the shaft of a pitchfork sailing past
Evenly, imperturbably through space,   [15]
Its prongs starlit and absolutely soundless –

But has learned at last to follow that simple lead
Past its own aim, out to an other side
Where perfection – or nearness to it – is imagined
Not in the aiming but the opening hand.   [20]

Annotations

[4] *javelin:* a light spear designed to be thrown, now used mainly in athletics

[6] *in earnest:* in a serious manner, with determination

[6] *chaff:* the husks or outer shells of seeds; they are separated from the seeds themselves through the process known as winnowing.

[7] *tapering:* gradually becoming thinner towards one end

[8] *satiny:* smooth and silky to the touch

[9] *Riveted:* A rivet is a metal bolt or pin; in this instance, rivets bind the pitchfork's metal teeth to its wooden handle.

[9] *burnish:* polish

[11] *cured:* hardened by means of a chemical process

[15] *imperturbably:* steadily, calmly, in an untroubled fashion

Tease It Out

1. 'The farmer thinks of his pitchfork as a perfect implement'. Is this statement true or false? Write a few lines explaining your answer.
2. The farmer makes believe that the pitchfork is a javelin. What does he do with the pitchfork during these moments?
3. The farmer, of course, also uses the pitchfork 'in earnest', for serious work. Based on your reading of the poem, can you determine what task he performs with it?
4. From what type of wood is the pitchfork's handle manufactured?
5. From what substance are the fork's prongs manufactured? How are they secured to its handle?
6. Consider the words 'satiny', 'burnish', 'smoothness' and 'sheen'. What feature of the pitchfork do they emphasise?
7. How is wood usually cured? What effect does this produce? (Google it!) How has the pitchfork's handle been cured?
8. Which words or phrases suggest that the farmer cares for and maintains this implement?
9. Which words suggest the pitchfork handles well and is fit for purpose?
10. The farmer compares his pitchfork to a technological wonder? Does this comparison surprise you? What visual similarities might exist between these two very different objects?
11. What illuminates these reaches of space, as the farmer imagines them? What acoustic conditions does he imagine prevailing here? Is this scientifically accurate?
12. **Class Discussion:** Who or what has 'learned' to follow a 'simple lead'? What do you understand by the term to 'follow your own lead'? How might this phrase apply to the trajectory of a space probe or a pitchfork?
13. According to the poet, the probe travels 'Past its own aim'? Has it a) overshot and missed its target or b) travelled farther than was ever intended or envisaged? Give a reason for your answer.
14. The poet refers to 'an other side' in line 18. Where might this 'other side' be located?
15. Think about throwing a ball or a javelin. What associations do the phrases 'aiming hand' and 'opening hand' have for you? How might 'perfection' be imagined in each of these? Which is most important to get right?

Exam Prep

1. **Personal Response:** Think of an object or item that you consider to be efficient and well designed. Write a few paragraphs describing its features and explaining why it is fit for purpose.
2. **Class Discussion:** Discuss the following statements as a class:
   - Perfection, according to the poet, can only be 'imagined'. It can never actually be attained.
   - The farmer finds something approaching perfection in the pitchfork, an implement superbly suited to its purpose.
   - What kind of 'perfection' might be associated with the 'aiming hand'? What form of 'perfection' might be associated with the 'opening hand'?
3. **Exam Prep:** 'Heaney is a poet who discovers the marvellous in the past, present and future'. Write a short essay in response to this statement, making reference to 'The Pitchfork', 'Lightenings VIII' and 'The Forge'.

Language Lab

1. 'The rich detail and imagery in this poem is a source of pleasure for the reader'. Would you agree with this statement? Explain your answer.
2. Discuss the use of punctuation in 'The Pitchfork'. Over the course of this poem, commas gradually give way to dashes. What effect do the dashes have on the pace and rhythm of the final two stanzas?
3. Would you agree that the poem's closing lines refer back to the opening stanza? What effect does this have on the tone and atmosphere of the poem?

Lightenings VIII

The annals say: when the monks of Clonmacnoise
Were all at prayers inside the oratory
A ship appeared above them in the air.

The anchor dragged along behind so deep
It hooked itself into the altar rails   [5]
And then, as the big hull rocked to a standstill,

A crewman shinned and grappled down the rope
And struggled to release it. But in vain.
'This man can't bear our life here and will drown,'

The abbot said, 'unless we help him.' So   [10]
They did, the freed ship sailed, and the man climbed back
Out of the marvellous as he had known it.

Annotations
Lightening: becoming brighter, becoming less heavy
[1] *annals:* historical records that note each year's significant events. Annals were maintained by the monasteries of medieval Ireland.
[1] *Clonmacnoise:* monastery situated in County Offaly on the River Shannon, founded in the sixth century AD
[2] *oratory:* small chapel
[6] *hull:* the main body of a ship including the bottom, sides and deck
[7] *shinned:* to shin or 'shinny' is to climb a rope by gripping it with the arms and legs
[10] *abbot:* the head of a monastery

Tease It Out

1. **Class Discussion:** Who is the 'you' referred to in this poem? Is the speaker addressing a specific person, such as a friend or acquaintance? Or is it possible that he's even addressing himself?
2. What trip does the speaker recommend in the opening lines?
3. When, according to the speaker, is the best time to visit this location?
4. Read lines 5 to 7, where the speaker remembers or visualises driving along the Clare coastline. What can be seen on each side of the car as he drives by?
5. Is the ocean calm or stormy, or somewhere in between?
6. What causes the appearance of 'glitter' on its surface?
7. Which phrase indicates that this is a rough and rugged landscape?
8. What colour is the lake that the poet passes by? What might have lent it this shade?
9. What might be responsible for roughing up and ruffling the feathers of the swans?
10. Which human emotion does the speaker attribute to the swans? Have you ever personally observed swans at rest on water? If so, would you agree that this description seems accurate and appropriate?
11. Describe in your own words the three different ways the swans position their heads. Why might their heads be 'Tucked'? What might they be 'busy' doing 'underwater'?
12. The speaker imagines himself as 'A hurry' that various things pass through. Consider this unusual turn of phrase. What does it suggest about the pace at which the speaker is travelling through this beautiful landscape? What does it suggest about the manner in which most of us live our lives?
13. Line 15 describes the wind's impact on the speaker's car as he drives along the coast. Is the wind closer in force to a mild breeze or a howling gale? Does its impact on the car make the speaker uneasy or is he quite comfortable?
14. What does it mean for a bolt of lightning to be 'earthed'? What device is used in this process and how does it work?
15. The poet compares the floating swans to such 'earthed' lightning. Do you find this metaphor an effective one? What does it suggest about the swans' appearance?

Exam Prep

1. **Personal Response:** "Some time make the time' is not only the opening phrase but also the most important message of this poem. It's a work that urges us to find a space for beauty and contemplation amid the stresses and strains of modern life'. Write a paragraph in response to this statement.
2. **Class Discussion:** "Postscript' is an ode to driving, capturing how settling into a long car journey can be a pleasantly meditative experience, allowing both expected and unfamiliar thoughts to pass through the mind'. Would you agree with this interpretation of the poem's conclusion? Give a reason.
3. **Exam Prep:** 'Heaney's poetry consistently reminds us of the world's strangeness and beauty'. Write an essay in response to this statement in which you refer to 'Postscript' and at least three other poems on the course.

Language Lab

1. **Class Discussion:** The speaker claims that the wind and light are 'working off each other'. Does this suggest that these forces are working together, or are they in conflict? How is it possible for these two intangible elements to interact at all? How do you visualise the effect they have on the landscape and on the surface of the ocean?
2. What does the speaker mean by the phrase 'You are neither here nor there'? Consider the following possibilities and rank them in order of likelihood:
   - He is referring to the car journey: he's between his starting point and his destination.
   - The scene before him is so magical that he feels suspended between the real world and a mysterious, dreamlike world.
   - The speaker, because he's sealed within a car, is somehow both present and not present in the landscape that surrounds him.
   - He is referring to the contrast between the 'wild' ocean and the more tranquil lake.

Tate's Avenue

Not the brown and fawn car rug, that first one
Spread on sand by the sea but breathing land-breaths,
Its vestal folds unfolded, its comfort zone
Edged with a fringe of sepia-coloured wool tails.

Not the one scraggy with crusts and eggshells   [5]
And olive stones and cheese and salami rinds
Laid out by the torrents of the Guadalquivir
Where we got drunk before the corrida.

Instead, again, it's locked-park Sunday Belfast,
A walled back yard, the dust-bins high and silent   [10]
As a page is turned, a finger twirls warm hair
And nothing gives on the rug or the ground beneath it.

I lay at my length and felt the lumpy earth,
Keen-sensed more than ever through discomfort,
But never shifted off the plaid square once.   [15]
When we moved I had your measure and you had mine.

Annotations

Tate's Avenue: a street in Belfast

[1] *fawn:* a light brown colour

[3] *vestal:* virginal; chaste, pure

[4] *sepia:* a dark reddish-brown colour

[5] *scraggy:* untidy

[6] *salami rinds:* Salami is a type of cured sausage; the rinds are the coarse skins or casings in which the sausage
meat is contained.

[7] *Guadalquivir:* a river in southern Spain

[8] *corrida:* bullfight

[9] *locked-park:* In Northern Ireland, public parks were closed on Sundays for religious reasons.

[10] *high:* suggests that the bins were piled high with rubbish; also suggests they were emitting an unpleasant smell

[12] *nothing gives:* describes ground which has no 'give' or softness; also a slang term suggesting that nothing is happening, that no progress is being made

[16] *I had your measure:* I understood you; I had a clear sense of your feelings and intentions.

Tease It Out

1. Read the first stanza and answer the following questions:
   * Why does the poet describe this rug as the 'first rug'?
   * Where was this rug stowed when not in use?
   * Which phrase suggests that the rug emits a stale or musty odour, especially in comparison with the freshness of the sea air?
   * The rug is described as 'vestal'. What does this suggest about the relationship between the poet and his wife during the period when they owned this rug?
2. What event was the poet due to attend after their picnic of Spanish delicacies. Does their trip strike you as a typical Spanish holiday? Give a reason for your answer.
3. 'In Stanza 2, the popping language captures the excitement that the poet must have felt as he experienced the smells and tastes of Spain'. Identify three examples of assonance or alliteration in these lines.
4. Does it surprise you that in Belfast public parks were once locked on Sundays? Google the reason for this policy. When was it abolished?
5. **Class Discussion:** Did the event Heaney remembered in stanzas 3 and 4 take place:
   * before the poet and his wife had got together?
   * shortly after they had got together as a couple?
   * a relatively long time before they had got together as a couple?

6. With no access to the parks, where, on this particular Sunday, did the poet and his future wife decide to sit out and enjoy the warm weather?
7. Does this strike you as a pleasant or unpleasant location? Give a reason for your answer.
8. What was the poet's future wife doing as she lay on the rug?
9. The poet lay down on the rug beside his future wife. Which   phrase indicates that his whole body was pressed against   hers?
10. What response, if any, did his future wife give to the poet lying down beside her? What response do you think the poet might have been hoping for?
11. Which phrases indicate that the poet was physically uncomfortable as he lay on the rug? Did this discomfort cause him to move? Why do you think this was?
12. The poet describes how he was 'Keen-sensed' at this moment. Suggest two different reasons why his senses might have heightened as he lay beside his future wife.
13. What does the phrase 'to have someone's measure' mean? What had the poet and his future wife learned about each other's feelings by the time they finally moved from the rug? How had this knowledge been conveyed?

Exam Prep

1. **Personal Response:** 'In this poem, Heaney flicks through the memories in his mind, as though he were scrolling through an internal Instagram account.' Does this strike you as a reasonable summary of the poem? Give a reason for your answer.
2. **Theme Talk:** 'Perhaps more than anything else, this poem captures the intense excitement of a budding relationship, of that moment when you suspect, but are not certain, that the object of your affection likes you back'. Write a paragraph in response to this statement.
3. **Exam Prep:** 'Memory in all its forms plays a key role in Heaney's work'. Discuss this statement in relation to 'Tate's Avenue', 'Bogland' and 'The Harvest Bow'.

Language Lab

1. In this poem, the poet considers three different memories. Break into groups of four. Place a large sheet of paper on your table and divide it into a placemat. On your section of the placemat, jot down everything that occurs to you in response to the questions below. Share your ideas with the group, writing in the centre the answers you can all agree on.
   * Which memory has the most pleasant setting? Which has the most unpleasant setting?
   * Which phrase suggests that the third memory is the one the poet holds most dear?
   * Which phrases suggest that the other memories are rejected or passed over in its favour?
   * Which phrase suggests that the poet returns to this memory again and again?
   * Suggest why this memory might be so important to him.

Gerard Manley Hopkins

Hopkins was born in Stratford, Essex, on 28 July 1844, to a wealthy and cultured family. His father was a businessman and diplomat who dabbled in literature, writing books and articles on a variety of subjects, including several books of poetry. His mother, Catherine, was the daughter of a physician and was noted for her love of philosophy and literature. Hopkins, it seems, had a relatively happy childhood. His education began at home and was influenced by his father's literary interests.

Hopkins attended the prestigious Highgate School, in London, where he received a classical Victorian education, focusing on subjects such as history, Greek and Latin. He was a reasonably sociable and outgoing boy, one who by all accounts got on quite well with his fellow schoolmates. Though Hopkins was slight and physically unimposing, he was surprisingly tough and athletic, managing to hold his own on the vicious playing pitches of a Victorian public school.

However, there were signs that he was not an average schoolboy. Even at Highgate, he began to exhibit a strong inclination towards an ascetic or self-punishing lifestyle, a quality that in later life would lead him to pursue a vocation as a Jesuit priest. On one occasion, he theorised that people consumed more liquids than they needed and, to prove himself right, abstained from drinking water and other liquids for three days before he began to suffer from dehydration. He also exhibited a stubborn nature that often caused him to run afoul of the school authorities, and he was once whipped and threatened with expulsion. However, it was also at Highgate that Hopkins's poetic instincts began to stir, and he won a prize for writing a long poem called 'The Escorial'.

After school, Hopkins went to Oxford University, where he continued to write poetry. Though he could be stubborn, touchy and arrogant, he was popular with his fellow students and enjoyed the university's social life, especially boating with friends on the River Cherwell.

At the time, Oxford was buzzing with theological debate. Many young students of an artistic bent, including Hopkins, were unhappy with their own Protestant religion. They were also unwilling to contemplate the possibility of atheism. Beguiled by what they regarded as the drama and mystery of the Mass and confession, many of these Protestant men found themselves drawn to the Catholic religion. They regarded Catholic rituals as a kind of theatre, and Catholicism's rich symbolism appealed to their artistic nature. Hopkins, it seems, was attracted to Catholicism not only because of its symbolism and mystery but also because of its rigour and severity. He eventually took the leap and converted to the Catholic faith in 1866, at the age of twenty-two.

"No doubt my poetry errs on the side of oddness ... But as air, melody, is what strikes me most of all in music, and design in painting, so design, pattern, or what I am in the habit of calling inscape is what I above all aim at in poetry."

Having graduated from Oxford, Hopkins taught for nine months at the Oratory school founded by John Henry Newman, one of England's leading Catholics. While there he decided to become a priest. His decision to join the Jesuit order – known as the 'spiritual army' of the Church – shows his desire for rigorous order and soldierly discipline.

Hopkins entered the Jesuit novitiate in 1868 and burned his youthful verses, determining 'to write no more, as not belonging to my profession'. Life as a Jesuit was incredibly demanding and austere – an endless succession of fasting, praying and penance. Throughout this time Hopkins studied at Manresa House, which is the Jesuit school in London, and also at Stonyhurst, near Blackburn in Lancashire.

Hopkins' health was consistently poor, however, and the order sent him to St Bueno's in Wales to recuperate. The period in Wales was one of the happiest in Hopkins's life. He fell in love with the Welsh countryside, and – prompted by the rector at St Bueno's – began writing poetry again. Many of Hopkins's best-known poems date from this period, including 'Spring', 'The Windhover' and 'God's Grandeur'.

Until 1875, Hopkins kept a journal recording his vivid responses to nature and working out his original philosophical theory, 'inscape', which emphasised the individuality of every natural thing. To Hopkins, each sensuous impression had its own elusive 'selfness', each scene was to him a 'sweet especial scene'. As Hopkins scholar Norman H. MacKenzie has written, 'inscape is not a superficial appearance; rather, it is the expression of the inner core of individuality, perceived in moments of insight by an onlooker who is in full harmony with the being he was observing'. For Hopkins, then, as Robert Bernard Martin has pointed out, the experience of beauty was largely a perception of the uniqueness of what he saw.

From 1877 onwards, Hopkins spent much of his time in the bleak slums of industrialised northern Britain. He spent several periods at Stonyhurst, a few months in Glasgow and a particularly dismal time in Liverpool. The bleakness of urban industrialised life did not agree with Hopkins, and he struggled to find inspiration for his poetry ('Felix Randal' – written during his Liverpool period – was inspired by the death of one of his parishioners).

In 1884, the Jesuits moved Hopkins to Dublin to teach at the newly formed Catholic university. This was a particularly unhappy period in Hopkins's life. He felt out of place in Ireland, deeply missing the friends and acquaintances he had left behind in Britain. To him, the Irish seemed an alien and incomprehensible race, and he found it difficult to relate to his students and colleagues, and indeed to Dublin life in general. His Irish co-workers, for their part, didn't know what to make of this intense and eccentric Englishman who had been thrust into their midst. He despised the grimy slums that had overtaken the once grand city, and to make matters worse, he was massively overworked at the university.

Under these conditions, Hopkins' physical health became very poor. His mental well-being also deteriorated, and he was overcome by feelings of depression, frustration and religious doubt. Hopkins's 'terrible sonnets' – including 'No worst, there is none' and 'I wake and feel the fell of dark' – stem from this bleak period. As one critic put it, he was a 'sensitive, over-scrupulous and unusual man who had been formed with too little capacity for human happiness'. Hopkins spent five years in Dublin, until his poor health, exacerbated by the filth and squalor of the city, finally got the better of him. He died, harassed and exhausted, from typhoid fever in 1889. His last words were 'I am so happy, I am so happy'.

Apart from a few minor poems scattered in periodicals, Hopkins was not published during his own lifetime. (Although some of his friends urged him to publish his poems, Hopkins continually resisted.) After Hopkins's death, his friend and fellow poet, Robert Bridges, whom Hopkins had met at Oxford, began to publish a few of his poems in anthologies. In 1918, Bridges – then the poet laureate – arranged for the first collected edition of Hopkins's poetry to be published. However, it was not until 1930, when a second edition was issued, that Hopkins's work was properly recognised as one of the most original, powerful, and influential literary accomplishments of his century.

God's Grandeur

The world is charged with the grandeur of God.
  It will flame out, like shining from shook foil;
  It gathers to a greatness, like the ooze of oil
Crushed. Why do men then now not reck his rod?
Generations have trod, have trod, have trod;   [5]
  And all is seared with trade; bleared, smeared with toil;
  And wears man's smudge and shares man's smell: the soil
Is bare now, nor can foot feel, being shod.

And for all this, nature is never spent;
  There lives the dearest freshness deep down things;   [10]
And though the last lights off the black West went
  Oh, morning, at the brown brink eastward, springs –
Because the Holy Ghost over the bent
  World broods with warm breast and with ah! bright wings.

Annotations
[1] *charged:* suggests the charge of an electrical current
[2] *grandeur:* splendour, majesty
[2] *foil:* very thin sheets of metal
[3-4] *oil/ crushed:* suggests the crushing of olives to produce olive oil
[4] *reck:* acknowledge, recognise, pay heed to
[6] *seared:* parched, dry
[6] *trade:* commercial and industrial activity
[6] *bleared:* blurred, reddened
[6] *smeared:* soiled, tarnished
[8] *shod:* fitted or wearing shoes
[9] *spent:* exhausted, used up, expended
[12] *brink:* edge, precipice
[14] *broods:* suggests how birds sit on eggs to warm them and encourage them to hatch

Tease It Out

1. The opening lines describe how God's 'grandeur' emanates from the world to be enjoyed by human beings:
   - It flames from the world like light reflected from a metalic surface. Which phrase indicates this?
   - **True or false:** God's grandeur oozes from the world like oil from an olive press.
   - There are times, Hopkins says, when God's grandeur 'gathers to a greatness'. Can you think of one or two natural sights where different aspects of creation combine to create something truly grand?
2. The poet refers to a 'rod' that is wielded by God:
   - What kind of rod do you visualise: a shepherd's crook, a sceptre of authority or a stick of punishment? Give a reason for your answer.
   - Would you agree that the rod is an effective symbol of God's authority? Give a reason for your answer.
   - According to Hopkins, do people nowadays respect God's authority? Did people do so in the past?
   - **Class Discussion:** This seems to both surprise and distress the poet. Based on your reading of the first four lines, suggest a reason for his horrified reaction.
3. Hopkins focuses on the environmental effects of industry and commerce:
   - Is this destructive behaviour a new phenomenon or has it been going on for a long time?
   - **Group Discussion:** What aspect of human industry might leave the environment 'seared'? What industrial activity might leave it 'bleared'? What might leave it 'smeared'?
   - Hopkins laments that much of the earth's 'soil/ Is bare now'. Mention three activities that might have left the soil exposed.
   - Why do you think the poet repeats the phrase 'have trod' in line 5? What effect does this repetition have?
4. Hopkins laments the fact that human beings now wear shoes. Why does he lament this fact? Rank the following in order of plausibility:
   - Bare feet provide physical contact with the earth and therefore greater empathy with the natural world.
   - Wearing shoes is bad for one's posture.
   - Shoes symbolise the unnatural and artificial nature of our industrial age.
5. **Group Discussion:** Hopkins refers to a 'dearest freshness' that exists within 'things':
   - Where does this 'freshness' reside?
   - Who or what might have put it there?
   - Is this 'freshness' to be found in every aspect of the natural world, or only in certain aspects?
   - According to line 7, what impact does this 'freshness' have on the natural world?
6. How does the poet describe the presence of the Holy Ghost in the world? What does the word 'brood' call to mind?

Exam Prep

1. **Personal Response:** Consider Hopkins' depiction of the sunrise:
   - What are the 'last lights' referred to by Hopkins in line 11?
   - What colour, according to Hopkins, is the sky just as dawn is about to break?
   - 'For Hopkins, the endless cycle of sunset and sunrise symbolises nature's ability to renew itself'. Write a paragraph in response to this statement.
2. **Class Discussion:** The poem was written around the time of the Industrial Revolution, when cities were growing and many factories were being built. Do you think that the poet's view of man's relationship with the world is still relevant today? Do you think that this can be read as an environmentalist poem before its time?
3. **Theme Talk:** The poem presents two different aspects of God: the Father and the Holy Ghost. With what symbols or images is each aspect associated? Which aspect is presented as most benevolent in your opinion?

Language Lab

1. Read the poem aloud. Would you agree that lines 11 and 12 create an unusual rhythmic effect? In the opinion of the class, is the verbal music that 'sprung rhythm' creates pleasant or unpleasant?
2. **Class Discussion:** Hopkins is fond of using words with several different meanings. Discuss the different meanings of the word 'charged'. Which meaning, according to the class, is most relevant to line 1?
3. Hopkins has a tendency to use nouns as verbs and verbs as nouns. Can you identify an instance of this in line 2?
4. Can you complete the following statements by filling in the gaps? The Holy Spirit, in an inventive metaphor, is compared to a _____ . The _____ is compared to an unhatched egg. The _____ protects and preserves the _____, just as a hen protects the egg she broods over.

As Kingfishers Catch Fire, Dragonflies Draw Flame

As kingfishers catch fire, dragonflies draw flame;
   As tumbled over rim in roundy wells
   Stones ring; like each tucked string tells, each hung bell's
Bow swung finds tongue to fling out broad its name;
Each mortal thing does one thing and the same: [5]
   Deals out that being indoors each one dwells;
   Selves – goes itself; *myself* it speaks and spells,
Crying *What I do is me: for that I came.*

Í say more: the just man justices;
   Keeps gráce: that keeps all his goings graces;   [10]
Acts in God's eye what in God's eye he is –
   Chríst. For Christ plays in ten thousand places,
Lovely in limbs, and lovely in eyes not his
   To the Father through the features of men's faces.

Annotations

[1] *As:* just as, similar to how

[1] *kingfishers:* small, brightly coloured birds, known for their expertise at catching fish

[1] *catch fire:* to receive or be struck by; to snatch or snare; to go up in flames

[1] *draw:* to attract; to create a picture of; to pull out of oneself

[2] *as tumbles over rim...stones:* stones that have been thrown over the rim or edge of a well

[2] *roundy wells:* a well with a circular rim

[3] *tucked:* plucked

[3] *each hung bell's:* Bells are typically 'hung' or suspended in the tower of a church or other building.

[3] *Bow:* the part of a bell that's struck is known as a 'bow' or 'soundbow', the part that does the striking is known as the clapper.

[4] *finds tongue:* finds the mean to express itself

[4] *fling out broad:* describes how the sound is transmitted far and wide

[6] *Deals out:* expresses

[6] *that being indoors:* that which exists inside of something

[7] *Selves:* Hopkins creates a new verb, to 'self', which means to express one's truest and deepest nature.

[7] *goes itself:* does its own thing, expresses itself

[8] *for that I came:* Tthat's why I exist; that's why I entered the world

[9] *justices:* lives a just life; acts in a just manner

[10] *Keeps gráce:* lives in accordance with God's law and stays free of sin

[10] *keeps all his goings graces:* ensures that all his actions ('goings') are good and righteous deeds ('graces')

Tease It Out

1. **Class Discussion:** What does Hopkins mean when he says the kingfishers 'catch fire'? Rank the following in order of plausibility:
   - The kingfishers are being set alight, and will soon go up in flames.
   - The fire is a metonym or alternative name for the glinting fish the birds pluck from the stream.
   - The phrase describes how the kingfishers' feathers catch and reflect the sunlight.
2. **Class Discussion:** Hopkins is well known for using words that have several different meanings. Consider the different meanings of the word 'draw' as used in line 1. Which is most relevant in the opinion of the class?
3. What is an adjective? The entire phrase 'tumbled over rim in roundy wells' could be thought of as a single adjective. What object or set of objects does it describe?
4. What is happening to the stones in lines 2 to 3? What kind of sound do they produce when this happens?
5. The poet describes the ringing of church bells:
   - What is the bell's 'bow'? When might this bow be 'swung'? Who might swing it?
   - **Class Discussion:** Each bell's ringing sound is described as its 'name'. What does this suggest about the quality of the sound that each bell produces?
   - How does Hopkins indicate that the sound of a bell expressing its 'name' can cover a great distance?
6. **Class Discussion:** According to line 6, something dwells 'indoors' or within each aspect of God's creation. What does Hopkins have in mind here?
7. Every single creature, according to Hopkins, 'Deals out' or expresses something. Describe in your own words what it expresses.
8. Line 8 suggests that every aspect of God's creation has a purpose. What do you understand this purpose to be?
9. **Class Discussion:** Everything the 'just man' does, according to Hopkins, must be a kind of 'grace'. Suggest two or three types of behaviour that might be considered such a 'grace'.
10. Hopkins refers to the concept of the Holy Trinity, whereby God is considered to have three aspects: the Father, the Son (Christ), and the Holy Spirit:
    - The just man, by acting in a Christ-like manner, actually makes Christ present in the world. Which lines and phrases indicate this?
    - Christ, according to Hopkins, is actually visible in the physical appearance of 'just' men. What physical features does Hopkins mention in this regard?
    - **True or false:** Christ can be present in many places at once.
    - How does God the father react to the sight of the Son being made present in such a fashion?
    - The third aspect of the trinity, the Holy Spirit, isn't actually mentioned in this poem. Can you find a poem by Hopkins where it does receive a mention?

Exam Prep

1. **Personal Response:** 'Each mortal thing does one thing and the same'. The different aspects of God's creation are extremely diverse. But they are all similar in one important sense. How do we make sense of this paradox or apparent contradiction?
2. **Class Discussion:** 'Each creature and object reveals God's glory by simply being itself. But human beings must act in a particular way if they want to reveal such glory'. Discuss this statement as a class.
3. **Theme Talk:** This poem, like 'The Windhover' and 'I wake and feel the fell of dark', makes explicit reference to Christ. Write three paragraphs describing the differences in these poems' respective portrayals of Christ.
4. **Exam Prep:** This poem is often compared to 'God's Grandeur'. Write one paragraph describing a few similarities between the two poems, and another commenting on the differences.

Language Lab

1. In line 7, Hopkins uses the noun 'self' as a verb. What might it mean to 'self'? What kind of behaviour does this freshly coined verb suggest? Can you identify another example of a noun being used as a verb in line 9?
2. **Class Discussion:** Hopkins often uses a profusion of assonance and alliteration in an attempt to capture an object's 'inscape' or unique essence. Discuss how this technique is applied to the kingfisher, the stone and the bell.
3. The phrase 'keeps all his goings graces' is an example of Hopkin's tendency towards compression – the omission of what he regards as inessential words. Rewrite the phrase in your own words.
4. Watch Video 15, which features a reading and discussion of the poem. Did you find the choice of images that accompaied the reading appropriate? What did you enjoy most about the presenter's interpretation of the poem?

Spring

Nothing is so beautiful as Spring –
   When weeds, in wheels, shoot long and lovely and lush;
   Thrush's eggs look little low heavens, and thrush
Through the echoing timber does so rinse and wring
The ear, it strikes like lightnings to hear him sing;   [5]
   The glassy peartree leaves and blooms, they brush
   The descending blue; that blue is all in a rush
With richness; the racing lambs too have fair their fling.

What is all this juice and all this joy?
   A strain of the earth's sweet being in the beginning   [10]
In Eden garden. – Have, get, before it cloy,

Before it cloud, Christ, lord, and sour with sinning,
   Innocent mind and Mayday in girl and boy,
Most, O maid's child, thy choice and worthy the winning.

Annotations

[4] *wring:* to twist or squeeze (as with a damp cloth)

[11] *cloy:* to become distasteful or sickening

[13] *Mayday:* the first day of May, traditionally associated with the Virgin Mary

[14] *maid's child*: Jesus, who was born of a maid or virgin

Tease It Out

1. **Class Discussion:** Take a moment to visualise weeds or wildflowers. Which parts of such plants might resemble the hub of a wheel, the spokes of a wheel and/or the rim of a wheel, respectively?
2. **True or false:** Hopkins finds the growth of these 'weeds' upsetting and irritating.
3. Google an image of a thrush's eggs. What colour are they? What kind of patterns can typically be seen on their shells?
4. Hopkins compares these eggs to miniature skies. Is this an effective comparison in your opinion? Give a reason for your answer.
5. According to the poet, the thrush's singing has a cleansing and revitalising effect on the mind. What words and phrases does he use to suggest this?
6. What very imaginative simile is used to describe the thrush's singing? What does this suggest about the poet's response to this sound?
7. The pear-tree, according to Hopkins, is 'glassy'. Is he referring to a) the tree's bark or b) the tree's leaves or c) the tree's fruit? Give a reason for your answer.
8. Which phrases indicate that the sky is a particularly intense shade of blue? Which phrases indicate that to Hopkins this blue possessed a liquid, flowing quality?
9. The lambs, according to Hopkins, are having a 'fling'. What do you think he means by this? Rank the following in order of plausibility:

   - The lambs are throwing or flinging themselves around the meadow.
   - The lambs seem relaxed and liberated as they roam about the meadow.
   - The lambs are conducting a series of love affairs with one another.

10. The countryside in springtime, according to Hopkins, can be compared to the biblical Garden of Eden.
    - Can you suggest two features that these seemingly very different settings have in common?
    - Which phrase indicates that the Garden of Eden existed very far back in humanity's history?
    - What does the phrase 'sweet being' suggest about the nature of the world during that long-ago period?
    - The beauty of springtime only hints at the beauty of 'Eden garden'. Which phrase indicates this?
11. According to Hopkins, what will cause each child's 'innocent mind' to 'cloud' and 'sour'?
12. Why does Hopkins refer to Christ as the 'maid's child'? Who is the 'maid' in question?
13. **Class Discussion:** Hopkins calls on Christ to 'get' and 'have' the children of the world before their innocence can be destroyed in such a fashion.
    - How might Christ claim the children?
    - Is Hopkins referring to any specific religious ceremony or practice?
    - Does Hopkins think that all children are worthy of being claimed by Christ?

Exam Prep

1. **Personal Response:** 'Hopkins's writing skilfully captures the freshness, newness and energy of the springtime.' Write a paragraph or two in response to this statement, in which you refer to at least two different techniques deployed by Hopkins throughout the poem.
2. **Class Discussion:** The sonnet's sestet begins with the question, 'What is all this juice and joy?' Do you think that it provides an answer to this question? If so, what is it?
3. **Exam Prep:** 'Hopkins pushes language to its limits in his efforts to reveal God's presence in the world around him'. Write a short essay discussing this statement in light of 'Spring' and two other poems on your course.

Language Lab

1. In line 6 Hopkins uses two nouns as verbs. Can you identify them? What do they suggest about the pear tree's appearance in springtime?
2. Hopkins is a poet of compression, one who is more than happy to omit what he regards as inessential words. Can you identify an example of this tendency in the poem's opening six lines?
3. 'Hopkins often uses assonance and alliteration in an attempt to capture an object's 'inscape' or unique essence'. Can you identify two separate instances of such inscaping in 'Spring'?
4. Hopkins is also known for his tendency to use long and complicated sentences that stretch across several lines of verse. Can you identify one such sentence in 'Spring'? Try to rewrite the sentence in your own words.

Pied Beauty

Glory be to God for dappled things –
   For skies of couple-colour as a brinded cow;
   For rose-moles all in stipple upon trout that swim;
Fresh-firecoal chestnut-falls; finches' wings;
   Landscape plotted and pieced – fold, fallow, and plough;   [5]
   And all trades, their gear and tackle and trim.

All things counter, original, spare, strange;
   Whatever is fickle, freckled (who knows how?)
   With swift, slow; sweet, sour; adazzle, dim;
He fathers-forth whose beauty is past change: [10]
   Praise Him.

Annotations

Pied: having a patchy or patchwork appearance

[1] *dappled:* speckled, potted

[2] *brinded:* marked with streaks or patches; usually suggests something that is grey or brown in colour

[3] *rose-moles:* marks on the scales of trout that resemble roses

[3] *stipple:* dot or speckle

[4] *firecoal:* a lump of coal that is partially burnt and reddened

[4] *chestnut-falls:* chestnuts that have fallen and cracked open, revealing their reddish brown interiors

[5] *fold:* a field that encloses animals

[5] *fallow*: land that is left idle so that the soil can replenish itself

[6] *trades*: occupations, areas of human activity

[6] *gear, tackle:* the equipment used by people who practise particular trades

[6] *trim:* suggests the clothing worn by members of a particular trade; also suggests the decoratiove element associated with the work of certain trades

[7] *spare:* unique, one-off

[8] *fickle:* prone to change

[9] *adazzle:* glittering, gleaming

Tease It Out

1. **Class Discussion:** Hopkins compares the couple-colour of the skies to a cow with a 'brinded' hide, a comparison that has been described as both ingenious and ridiculous:
   - In the class's opinion, does the term 'couple-colour' describe a cloudy sky or a sky exhibiting two different shades of blue?
   - What aspect of the sky's appearance might resemble the streaks on the 'brinded' cow's hide?
   - Which literary device is used to make this comparison?
   - Is it an effective or reasonable comparison in your opinion?
2. To what does Hopkins compare the moles or markings that can be found on a trout's skin?
3. Which word or phrase indicates that trouts tend to have a great deal of such markings?
4. Hopkins compares chestnuts to burning coals:
   - **True or false:** The chestnuts that he is visualising have been split open.
   - Which aspect of the chestnut resembles the black part of a burning coal?
   - Which aspect of the chestnut resembles the reddened parts of such a coal?
5. **True or false:** The landscape when viewed from above resembles a patchwork combined from various fields or plots.
6. What is happening in fields that are used as a 'fold'? Why might a farmer leave a field 'fallow' for a year or two? What has happened to the third type of field mentioned by Hopkins?
7. Some of the phenomena mentioned by Hopkins have a 'pied' or patchwork appearance. Some have a dappled or speckled appearance. Which is true of the finch's wings?
8. Lines 7 and 8 feature no fewer than six different adjectives:
   - Which adjectives suggest objects that are unusual or very rare?
   - Which adjective might suggest objects that exhibit contradictory characteristics at the same time?
   - Which adjectives suggest objects that change from moment to moment?
9. Hopkins finds God's creative powers mysterious and incomprehensible. Which phrase indicates this?
10. **Group Discussion:** Can you think of something, naturally occurring or manmade, that is capable of being both 'swift' and 'slow', something that is both 'sweet' and 'sour', and something that is both 'bright' and 'dim'?

Exam Prep

1. **Personal Response:** Think of a landscape you find especially attractive or appealing. Write a descriptive paragraph in which you outline its most distinctive features.
2. **Class Discussion:** Consider the term 'trades' as used in line 6:
   - Can you suggest at least three different activities that Hopkins might have in mind?
   - According to Hopkins, the materials associated with these trades have a 'pied' or dappled appearance. Can you think of an example of such material?
   - Can you identify two other poems by Hopkins in which trades are mentioned? Does Hopkins always present trade in a positive light?
   - Would you agree that there are some aspects of human activity that he approves of and some that he disapproves of?
3. **Theme Talk:** 'God creates a world that is constantly altering but is Himself utterly unchanging'. Write a paragraph discussing this statement. Do you think it's reasonable to describe 'Pied Beauty' as a prayer? In what ways might it differ from a more conventional prayer?
4. **Exam Prep:** 'For Hopkins, the role of the poet is to show how God is reflected in nature.' Do you agree with this statement? Support your answer with reference to at least three poems on your course.

Language Lab

1. 'Pied Beauty' is written in a form that Hopkins christened the 'curtal sonnet'. In what ways does it resemble a conventional sonnet? In what ways does it differ?
2. Hopkins is a poet of compression, one who regularly leaves out words he deems to be unnecessary. Would you agree that 'Fresh-firecoal chestnut-falls' is an example of such compression? Attempt to rewrite this phrase at is it might have been written by a more conventional poet.
3. Hopkins in line 10 uses a noun as a verb, a common technique of his. What is the noun in question? What action does it suggest in this instance?
4. Hopkins is also known for coining new words or compound words. Can you identify one such coinage in line 2?

The Windhover

To Christ our Lord

I caught this morning morning's minion, king-
   dom of daylight's dauphin, dapple-dawn-drawn Falcon, in his riding
   Of the rolling level underneath him steady air, and striding
High there, how he rung upon the rein of a wimpling wing
In his ecstasy! then off, off forth on swing,   [5]
   As a skate's heel sweeps smooth on a bow-bend: the hurl and gliding
   Rebuffed the big wind. My heart in hiding
Stirred for a bird, – the achieve of, the mastery of the thing!

Brute beauty and valour and act, oh, air, pride, plume, here
   Buckle! AND the fire that breaks from thee then, a billion   [10]
Times told lovelier, more dangerous, O my chevalier!

No wonder of it: shéer plód makes plough down sillion
   Shine, and blue-bleak embers, ah my dear,
Fall, gall themselves, and gash gold-vermilion.

Annotations

Windhover: a falcon

[1] ***I caught:*** I saw; I caught sight of

[1] ***minion:*** a favourite or highly-regarded servant

[2] ***dauphin:*** a prince, especially a king's eldest son

[2] ***dapple:*** to speckle, to mark with many tiny spots of diverse colour

[2] ***dawn-drawn:*** attracted by the dawn, painted or revealed by first light of morning

[4] ***wimpling:*** rippling; undulating

[5] ***then off:*** off it went

[5] ***forth on a swing:*** moving in an arc or swinging motion

[6] ***skate's heel:*** an ice skate

[6] ***bow-bend:*** describes how the skater executes a u-turn, a long undulating curve

[7] ***rebuffed:*** rejected in a contemptuous manner

[8] ***stirred:*** experienced powerful emotions

[9] ***Brute:*** fierce, brutal

[9] ***Buckle:*** to break or collapse; to combine several different things in a single gesture; also
suggests the buckling involved in the donning of armour

[9] ***valour:*** courage in the face of battle

[11] ***my chevalier:*** my mounted knight, my champion or representative in battle

[12] ***shéer plód:*** sheer hard work or plodding labour

[12] ***sillion:*** freshly ploughed

[14] ***gall themselves:*** chafe or cut themselves

[14] ***gash gold-vermilion:*** bleed or release sparks that are gold or red in colour

Tease It Out

1. **Class Discussion:** 'Morning' is presented as a king, and 'Daylight' as a kingdom. What role, metaphorically speaking, does the falcon play in this domain? What does this metaphor suggest about Hopkins's attitude to the bird?
2. Hopkins describes the falcon's 'riding/ Of the … air' and how it goes 'striding/ High there'. What do the verbs 'riding' and 'striding' suggest about the falcon's movement?
3. Consider the phrase 'rolling level underneath him steady':
   • What is an adjective? Could this entire phrase be regarded as a single adjective?
   • What does this phrase suggest about the air beneath the bird?
   • In what sense might this phrase be considered paradoxical or contradictory?
4. Hopkins describes how the falcon 'rung' through the air. Does this suggest that the bird was a) travelling in a straight line b) circling or c) moving in a criss-cross fashion?
5. What metaphor is used to describe the falcon's wing? With what sport or activity might we associate this item? Would you agree that it reinforces our sense of the bird's power and majesty?
6. **Class Discussion:** To Hopkins, the falcon seemed to be experiencing nothing less than 'Ecstasy'. Why do you think Hopkins came to this conclusion? What aspects of the bird's movement and demeanour gave him this impression?
7. The falcon suddenly flies off on a swinging arc over the landscape. Which phrase describes this?
8. To what sport or activity does the poet compare its flight? What does the comparison suggest about the bird's movements?
9. **Class Discussion:** The poet tells us that his heart has been 'in hiding'. What does this phrase suggest about his mental state?
10. What effect does seeing the falcon in flight have upon the poet's 'heart'?
11. The poet associates the falcon with achievement ('achieve') and 'mastery'. What is it that the falcon achieves on this particular morning? What kind of 'mastery' does it display?
12. **True or false:** The falcon is not only a beautiful creature but also a ferocious one.
13. The 'big wind' is presented as the falcon's enemy. It offers the falcon some kind of truce or deal. Does the falcon accept this offer?
14. Consider the term 'Buckle'. How does it suggest that the falcon was ultimately broken or defeated by the wind?
15. **Class Discussion:** 'The falcon takes on and ultimately loses to an almost undefeatable foe, rather than besting a lesser foe. In doing so, it exhibits a remarkable level of courage, ferocity and beauty'. Discuss this statement as a class.
16. According to Hopkins, soil can only shine when it has been broken open by being ploughed. Can you envisage why 'sillion', or freshly ploughed land, might be said to 'shine'?
17. What does Hopkins mean when he says that an ember galls itself? What colour sparks come from an ember when this happens?

Exam Prep

1. **Personal Response:** Hopkins addresses the falcon as his 'chevalier'. What does this suggest about his attitude to the bird? What does it suggest about the bird's effect upon his mental state?
2. **Class Discussion:** It is 'No wonder', according to Hopkins, that in defeat the falcon exhibited its greatest strength and beauty. How do the images of the 'sillion' and the 'embers' help him to make this point?
3. **Theme Talk:** 'The falcon is broken by the wind, just as Christ was broken on the cross. But in defeat both achieved an extraordinary victory of sorts'. In what sense might the falcon serve as a symbol or metaphor for Christ himself? Consider the following words and phrases in your answer: 'Brute beauty', 'Valour', 'Buckle'.
4. **Exam Prep:** 'This poem follows the pattern of many of Hopkins' sonnets, in that a sensuous experience or description leads to a set of moral reflections.' Discuss this statement with reference to three poems on your course.

Language Lab

1. Hopkins compares both falcon and Christ to a medieval knight riding into battle. Can you identify at least four different words and phrases that suggest this comparison? In what sense does Christ act as the poet's champion or representative?
2. **Class Discussion:** Hopkins declares that a fire comes bursting from the falcon as it buckles. Can you suggest which aspect of the falcon's appearance is referred to here? In what sense might a metaphorical fire have also come bursting forth from Christ as he hung dying upon the cross?
3. 'Hopkins uses inscaping, a profusion of assonance and alliteration in order to capture an object's essence'. Consider the phrase 'dapple-dawn-drawn' in light of this statement.
4. Watch Video 16, which features 'The Windhover' set to music and sung by Lorcán Mac Mathúna. Do you think that Hopkins's lines lend themselves well to such a performance? Give a reason for your answer.

Inversnaid

This darksome burn, horseback brown,
His rollrock highroad roaring down,
In coop and in comb the fleece of his foam
Flutes and low to the lake falls home.

A windpuff-bonnet of fáwn-fróth   [5]
Turns and twindles over the broth
Of a pool so pitchblack, féll-frówning,
It rounds and rounds Despair to drowning.

Degged with dew, dappled with dew
Are the groins of the braes that the brook treads through,   [10]
Wiry heathpacks, flitches of fern,
And the beadbonny ash that sits over the burn.

What would the world be, once bereft
Of wet and of wilderness? Let them be left,
O let them be left, wildness and wet;   [15]
Long live the weeds and the wilderness yet.

Annotations

Inversnaid: a village near the shores of Loch Lomond in the Scottish Highlands

[1] *darksome:* dark, sombre

[1] *burn:* small stream

[3] *coop:* 'enclosed hollow' (definition from Hopkins' notebook)

[3] *comb:* rippling stretch of water

[4] *Flutes:* brings to mind both the musical instrument and a long-stemmed glass

[5] *bonnet:* hat

[5] *fáwn-fróth:* the fawn-coloured foam that is sometimes generated by the motion of water in streams and rivers

[6] *twindles:* a mixture of 'twists', 'twitches' and 'dwindles'

[7] *féll:* evil, dark and menacing

[9] *Degged:* sprinkled (Scots dialect)

[10] *braes:* steep banks or hillsides (Scots dialect)

[11] *heathpacks:* clumps of heather

[11] *flitches:* strands, branches

[12] *beadbonny:* one of the many phrases Hopkins invented, with 'bonny' meaning beautiful and 'bead' possibly a reference to berries

Tease It Out

1. The poet describes a 'burn' or stream running down the mountain:
   - What colour is the stream's water?
   - What does the verb 'roaring' suggest about the water's movement?
   - Consider the phrase 'rollrock highroad'. What does this suggest about the course of the stream?
   - At what stages of its journey does the stream produce foam?
   - What metaphor does Hopkins use to describe this foam?
   - What is the stream's 'home'?

2. The stream encounters a hollow on its journey downhill and forms a little swirling pool:
   - The poet finds this miniature whirlpool somewhat sinister or depressing. Which words and phrases convey this response?
   - **Class Discussion:** The poet uses the word 'drowning' in connection with this little pool. Is he speaking literally or metaphorically? What thoughts or emotions is he trying to convey?
   - Consider the words 'Turns' and 'twindles'. What do they suggest about the movement of the water on the surface of this pool?

   - In line 5, what metaphors are used to describe the froth that forms on the pool's surface?

3. Hopkins focuses on the stream's 'braes', the steep hillsides down which it flows.:
   - What phrase indicates that the stream sprays or splashes these braes?
   - Would you agree that for Hopkins this creates a pleasant visual effect? Give a reason for your answer.
   - **True or false:** The heather that grows on the hillsides is soft to the touch.
   - How does Hopkins indicate that berries are growing on the ash tree?

4. Hopkins turns his mind to environmental concerns:
   - **True or false:** He feels that without wild streams like this one the world would be a desolate place.
   - What hope or prayer does he express?
   - **Class Discussion:** What is the effect of repetition in these lines?
   - What does the word 'weeds' refer to in the poem's last line? Would you agree that Hopkins is using this word in a somewhat unusual way?

Exam Prep

1. **Personal Response:** Would you agree that the mood or tone of this piece shifts several times? Can you identify where the tone is happy and full of celebration, and where it is darker and more anxious?

2. **Class Discussion:** 'This is the only poem on the course where Hopkin doesn't mention God. It is also the only poem that isn't a sonnet of some kind. Furthermore, it is the weakest poem by Hopkins on the course'. Discuss this statement as a class.

3. **Theme Talk:** In your opinion, is Hopkins despairing or hopeful about the future of nature in this poem? In what ways is the poem's attitude to the environment similar to that expressed in 'God's Grandeur'? In what ways is it different?

4. **Exam Prep:** 'Hopkins uses extraordinary language to explore both the highs and lows of human existence'. Write a short essay in response to this statement in which you discuss at least four different poems by Hopkins.

Language Lab

1. Describe what you understand by the technique that Hopkins called 'inscape'. Can you suggest why the phrase 'a pool so pitchblack, féll-frówning' might be considered an example of this technique?

2. Working in small groups, try to identify each of the words or compound words that Hopkins invents throughout this poem. Then try to come up with three new coinages of your own.

3. Hopkins is known for using nouns as verbs, and verbs as nouns. Can you identify an example of this tendency in line 4? What does it suggest about the movement of the water?

4. The phrase 'rollrock highroad roaring down' is an example of 'sprung rhythm'. Can you suggest how this unusual rhythmic effect captures the stream's downhill motion?

Felix Randal

Felix Randal the farrier, O is he dead then? my duty all ended,
Who have watched his mould of man, big-boned and hardy-handsome
Pining, pining, till time when reason rambled in it and some
Fatal four disorders, fleshed there, all contended?

Sickness broke him. Impatient, he cursed at first, but mended   [5]
Being anointed and all; though a heavenlier heart began some
Months earlier, since I had our sweet reprieve and ransom
Tendered to him. Ah well, God rest him all road ever he offended!

This seeing the sick endears them to us, us too it endears.
My tongue had taught thee comfort, touch had quenched thy tears,   [10]
Thy tears that touched my heart, child, Felix, poor Felix Randal;

How far from then forethought of, all thy more boisterous years,
When thou at the random grim forge, powerful amidst peers,
Didst fettle for the great grey drayhorse his bright and battering sandal!

Annotations

[1] *farrier:* a blacksmith

[3] *pining:* wasting away

[4] *contended:* fought, struggled, competed

[5] *mended:* changed his ways, altered his attitude towards God

[6] *anointed:* rubbed with oil as part of a religious ceremony; in this instance refers to the last rites administered to the dying by a Catholic priest

[6] *and all:* and all that, and so on (dialect expression)

[7] *sweet reprieve and ransom:* Holy Communion

[8] *tendered:* administered

[8] *all road:* in any event (dialect expression)

[9] *endears:* causes a feeling of fondness or love

[10] *quenched:* extinguished, quelled

[12] *forethought of:* imagined in advance, anticipated

[12] *boisterous:* lively, energetic

[13] *random:* made from rough uneven stones

[13] *forge:* a blacksmith's workshop

[14] *fettle:* fix

[14] *drayhorse:* a work horse used to pull ploughs, carts, etc.

[14] *sandal:* horseshoe

Tease It Out

1. The poet says his duty is 'all ended'. Can you suggest what duties Hopkins, as a priest, might have had towards Felix?
2. Hopkins describes how he has 'watched' Felix:
   - What does the verb 'watched' suggest about their relationship? Do you think it was a close one?
   - What were Felix's physical characteristics before he became ill? Describe them in your own words.
   - What does the repetition of the term 'pining' suggest about Felix's decline?
3. Felix's illness had a terrible impact on his mental health. Which phrase indicates this? Rewrite it in your own words.
4. How many different disorders or ailments did Felix suffer from? Which phrase indicates that Felix was locked in a battle with these various illnesses?
5. What was Felix's attitude towards God when he first became ill? What effect did his receiving the sacrament of Holy Communion have on his attitude?
6. Which phrase suggests that Hopkins gave Felix the last rites on his deathbed?
7. According to Hopkins, these last rites 'mended' Felix. What do you think he means by this?
8. What prayer does Hopkins say for the recently deceased Felix?
9. One of a priest's duties is tending to the sick. What effect does this duty have on the sick person? What effect does it have on the priest?
10. Mention two ways in which Hopkins attempted to comfort Felix.
11. **Group Discussion:** Can you suggest some of the things he might have said in his efforts to console this sick and dying man?
12. Why do you think the poet refers to Felix as a 'child'? What might this suggest about the nature of their relationship?
13. In the poem's final lines, where is Felix depicted at work? What task does the poet imagine him performing?
14. Which phrase indicates that Felix's physicality made him stand out from other workers?
15. What do you understand the poet to mean when he refers to Felix's 'more boisterous years'?
16. **True or false:** Felix, even during those 'boisterous years', had a sense that he would one day become extremely ill.

Exam Prep

1. **Personal Response:** Do you think a religious person would get more from this poem than someone with no religious beliefs? Give a reason for your answer.
2. **Class Discussion:** 'This poem highlights how quickly and suddenly health and good looks can be snatched away.' Write a paragraph outlining your response to this statement. Would you agree that there are two different portrayals of Felix in this poem? How do you think Felix would like to be remembered?
3. **Theme Talk:** Both 'Felix Randal' and 'No worst, there is none' deal with the notion of religious doubt. Write a couple of paragraphs describing one similarity and one difference in their respective approaches to this theme.
4. **Exam Prep:** 'Hopkins's innovative style displays his struggle with what he believes to be fundamental truths'. Write a short essay in response to this statement in which you discuss at least four different poems by Hopkins.

Language Lab

1. The phrases 'till time when', 'fleshed there' and 'ever he offended' are all examples of how Hopkins compresses language. Rewrite each phrase in your own words.
2. Hopkins uses inscape, a profusion of assonance and alliteration, to capture the essence of a sight or object. Would you agree that inscape features in the poem's final lines where Hopkins describes Felix at work? Write a paragraph outlining your answer.
3. The poem was written while Hopkins was working in Lancashire. Can you identify the different colloquial expressions Hopkins uses throughout the piece?
4. Which phrase indicates that communion saves us from sin and damnation?
5. **Class Discussion:** In what circumstances might a ransom be paid? In what sense might communion be regarded as a ransom?

No worst, there is none

No worst, there is none. Pitched past pitch of grief,
More pangs will, schooled at forepangs, wilder wring.
Comforter, where, where is your comforting?
Mary, mother of us, where is your relief?
My cries heave, herds-long; huddle in a main, a chief   [5]
Woe, world-sorrow; on an age-old anvil wince and sing –
Then lull, then leave off. Fury had shrieked 'No ling-
ering! Let me be fell: force I must be brief.'
O the mind, mind has mountains; cliffs of fall
Frightful, sheer, no-man-fathomed. Hold them cheap   [10]
May who ne'er hung there. Nor does long our small
Durance deal with that steep or deep. Here! creep,
Wretch, under a comfort serves in a whirlwind: all
Life death does end and each day dies with sleep.

Annotations

[1] Pitched: thrown or cast; set at a particular pitch or tone; covered in tar; erected, as in a tent or camp

[1] pitch: an extreme height or depth; a musical note or tone; a tar-like substance; a defined patch or piece of ground

[2] pangs: a burst or spasm of pain

[2] schooled: educated, taught

[2] forepangs: earlier pangs

[2] wring: squeeze, twist, torture

[3] Comforter: Jesus Christ

[4] Mary: Mary, Mother of Jesus

[6] wince: grimace or hiss in pain

[7] Fury: In Greek mythology, the Furies were demons who relentlessly persecuted their prey.

[8] force: perforce, of necessity, it is essential

[8] fell: evil or ferocious

[8] I must be brief: I must permit no pause or delay

[9-10] of fall/ Frightful: having a terrifying drop

[10] sheer: almost completely vertical

[10] no-man-fathomed: depths that have not been explored or reached by any human being

[12] Durance: endurance

[13] Wretch: an unfortunate or unhappy person

Tease It Out

1. As a class, consider the terms 'pitch' and 'pitched' as used in the poem's opening line:
   - Hopkins is fond of using words that have multiple meanings. Which meaning of 'pitch', in the opinion of the class, is most relevant to line 1?
   - **Class Discussion:** Bearing the above answer in mind, what do you think Hopkins means by the 'pitch of grief'?
   - What might it mean to be 'past' this pitch? Would you agree that this phrase suggests an extreme emotional state?
   - **True or false:** Hopkins takes comfort in the fact that at least things can't get any worse, in the knowledge that he has hit rock bottom.
2. 'Each pang that Hopkins experiences learns and adapts from the pangs that have come before it'. Discuss this statement as a class. What does this suggest about the nature of Hopkins's suffering?
3. The poet cries out for 'relief'. Do you think he has spiritual, physical or psychological relief in mind here? Support your answer with reference to the text.
4. Which lines or phrases indicate that the poet feels abandoned by God?
5. Hopkins describes how his cries 'heave' from him. What does this suggest about the state or movement of his body?
6. Hopkins, in a startling metaphor, compares his cries to cattle. Which words and phrases suggest this? What does this comparison suggest about his self-image and his state of mind?

7. Class Discussion: 'Hopkins is confronted with a variety of problems, but he has one over-riding concern'. What, according to the class, is this 'chief woe'? Which phrase indicates that this issue confronts not only Hopkins but all of mankind?
8. In a most unusual metaphor, Hopkins declares that he produces his cries while he is beaten on an anvil. What might the anvil represent? Who or what, metaphorically speaking, is responsible for wielding the hammer that strikes the poor poet again and again?
9. Which line indicates that the poet enjoys a brief moment of relief or respite?
10. What is a Fury? What does Hopkins intend the Fury to symbolise or personify? Describe in your own words what the Fury demands.
11. In the sonnet's sestet, Hopkins depicts his mind as a physical landscape:
    - **True or false:** Hopkins depicts himself hanging from a cliff.
    - **True or false:** The cliff in question has a gentle slope and is easy to hold on to.
    - **True or false:** The cliff is above a ravine so deep that nobody could ever measure it.
12. 'The image of the 'whirlwind' suggests a state of psychological frenzy'. Suggest two or three different thoughts that might be swirling around the poet's mind.
13. What two forms of 'comfort' does Hopkins offer to miserable wretches like himself who suffer in such a mental whirlwind?

Exam Prep

1. **Personal Response:** Would you agree that 'No worst there is none', while impressive in its use of language, is a difficult poem to like? Do you think that the poem's last lines are effective as a form of consolation?
2. **Class Discussion:** Hopkins doesn't specify the precise causes of the anguish he is experiencing. Working as a class, rank the following potential causes in order of plausibility: exhaustion and overwork; doubts about God; depression; regrets; ill-health.
3. **Theme Talk:** In line 12 Hopkins refers to things that are 'steep' and 'deep'. What aspects of mental life does he have in mind here? Do human beings, according to Hopkins, have the endurance to deal with these aspects of human psychology?
4. **Exam Prep:** 'Hopkins uses his unique style to address the themes of both faith and doubt'. Write a short essay in response to this statement in which you discuss at least four different poems by Hopkins.

Language Lab

1. 'Hopkins unusual rhythmic effects – which he described as 'sprung rhythm' – can produce a pleasant verbal music. In this poem, however, they produce a jolting, jarring soundscape'. Write a paragraph in response to this statement. Can you identify two or three lines or phrases in the poem where such a jarring musical effect is evident?
2. **Class Discussion:** Note how the word 'ling-/ering' is split over two lines. What effect does this splitting have? Can you identify any other unusual uses of punctuation in the poem?
3. Hopkins suggests that certain people won't take his account of suffering all that seriously. Why will such people 'Hold' his words 'cheap'?
4. **Group Discussion:** The phrase 'Hold them cheap/ May who ne'er hung there' is a classic example of how Hopkins squeezes and compresses language. Together, write a couple of lines in which you try to 'unpack' this phrase.

I wake and feel the fell of dark

I wake and feel the fell of dark, not day.
What hours, O what black hours we have spent
This night! what sights you, heart, saw; ways you went!
And more must, in yet longer light's delay.
  With witness I speak this. But where I say   [5]
Hours I mean years, mean life. And my lament
Is cries countless, cries like dead letters sent
To dearest him that lives alas! away.

  I am gall, I am heartburn. God's most deep decree
Bitter would have me taste: my taste was me;   [10]
Bones built in me, flesh filled, blood brimmed the curse.
  Selfyeast of spirit a dull dough sours. I see
The lost are like this, and their scourge to be
As I am mine, their sweating selves; but worse.

Annotations

[1] *fell:* wickedness or ferocity, the skin or hide of an animal, a large barren field or moor

[5] *with witness:* from personal experience

[6] *my lament/ Is cries countless:* My lament consists of countless individual cries.

[7] *dead letters:* letters that cannot be delivered because the recipient has moved away

[8] *dearest him:* Christ

[9] *gall:* a bitter fluid secreted by the liver

[9] *heartburn:* a burning sensation caused by excess stomach acid

[9] *decree:* official order or ruling

[11] *brimmed:* filled to the brim

[11] *the curse:* Hopkins refers to his own body as a curse.

[12] *Selfyeast:* coined by Hopkins from the words 'self' and 'yeast'. Yeast is what causes bread to rise.

[12] *a dull dough sours:* Bad dough spoils the yeast, preventing the bread from rising.

[13] *The lost:* may refer to those who've been damned to an eternity in hell; may also describe those without religious faith

[13] *scourge:* a whip or lash used for punishment or torture, a source of suffering or affliction

Tease It Out

1.	The poet wakes in the middle of the night:
	- The poet realises that it is still night-time. What emotions do you think he experiences when he realises this? Does he feel relief, dismay, surprise or dread?
	- The poet presents the 'dark' as a tangible substance, as something that he can 'feel'. What does this suggest his about his state of mind?
	- The term 'fell' has several different meanings. Which do you think is most relevant to line 1? Give a reason for your choice.
2.	What phrase indicates that the poet has been longing for morning to come? Does he feel that morning will soon arrive?
3.	The poet describes how over the course of the night his 'heart' has seen various sights and travelled various 'ways':
	- Are these 'sights' and 'ways' pleasant or unpleasant? Give a reason for your answer.
	- **Class Discussion:** What aspects of the poet's mental state might these 'sights' and 'ways' represent?
	- **Class Discussion:** What aspect of the poet does the 'heart' represent'?
4.	The poet claims to be familiar with mental suffering:
	- His experience, he claims, entitles him to speak with some authority about such suffering. Which phrase suggests this?
	- True or false: Each hour of this terrible night seems to drag on for an incredibly long time.
5.	**Group Discussion:** Consider the phrase 'cries countless'. What does it suggest about the poet's lament?
6.	To whom has the poet been addressing his 'cries'? Is this person accessible to the poet? Suggest why this might be the case?
7.	What very inventive metaphor does the poet use to describe his 'cries' for help? What does it suggest about the response they have been receiving?
8.	The poet experiences an overwhelming sense of bitterness. Which phrases indicate this?
9.	**Class Discussion:** Does this bitterness refer to a specific problem the poet is experiencing in his mouth, throat or stomach? Could it refer instead to a more general physical discomfort, or might it be a metaphorical bitterness that represents mental anguish?
10.	**True or false:** The poet feels that God actually wants him to experience such bitterness. What does this suggest about his attitude towards God on this particular night?
11.	The poet imagines his body forming around his soul. What three different stages of this process does he describe?
12.	The poet compares himself to the 'lost'. Which group of people does he have in mind?
13.	Both the poet and the 'lost' are described as having 'sweating selves'. Suggest why the lost might be thought of as 'sweating'. What does the fact that the poet is sweating suggest about his mental and physical state on this long night?
14.	**True or false:** The poet feels that his plight is actually worse than that endured by the 'lost'. Suggest why he comes to this conclusion.

Exam Prep

1.	**Personal Response:** Consider the phrase 'My taste was me'. What does it suggest about the poet's attitude to his physical self? Does he come across as someone comfortable in his own body?
2.	**Theme Talk:** This poem is very much a 'lament'. But what precisely is causing the poet's extraordinary anguish? Working in pairs, suggest three different issues the poet might be facing.
3.	**Exam Prep:** What attitude towards God is evident in this poem? Would you agree that it is a more negative attitude than that expressed in 'The Windhover' or 'God's Grandeur'? Contrast the poet's 'lament' in this poem with his 'plea' in 'Thou are indeed just, Lord'. In which of these 'terrible sonnets' does Hopkins most clearly doubt God's goodness?

Language Lab

1.	Hopkins often achieves compression and energy by leaving out certain words. Would you agree that 'more must, in yet longer light's delay' and Bones built in me, flesh filled' are examples of such compression? Attempt to rewrite these phrases in your own words.
2.	Hopkins uses inscape, a profusion of assonance and alliteration, to capture the essence of a sight or object. Would you agree that inscape features in the poem's opening lines where Hopkins attempts to capture the essence of the darkness that confronts him on awakening? Write a paragraph outlining your answer.
3.	The poet uses a most unusual baking metaphor to describe the relationship between soul and body. What ingredient is the body compared to? What ingredient is the soul compared to? What impact, according to Hopkins, does the body have on the soul?

Thou art indeed just, Lord

Justus quidem tu es, Domine, si disputem tecum: verumtamen
justa loquar ad te: Quare via impiorum prosperatur? &c. (Jerem xii 1)

Thou art indeed just, Lord, if I contend
With thee; but, sir, so what I plead is just.
Why do sinners' ways prosper? and why must
Disappointment all I endeavour end?

Wert thou my enemy, O thou my friend,   [5]
How wouldst thou worse, I wonder, than thou dost
Defeat, thwart me? Oh, the sots and thralls of lust
Do in spare hours more thrive than I that spend,

Sir, life upon thy cause. See, banks and brakes
Now, leavèd how thick! lacèd they are again   [10]
With fretty chervil, look, and fresh wind shakes

Them; birds build – but not I build; no, but strain,
Time's eunuch, and not breed one work that wakes.
Mine, O thou lord of life, send my roots rain.

Annotations

This poem's epigraph comes from the Book of Jeremiah, and can be translated as follows:
You are righteous, O LORD, when I bring a case before you. Yet I would speak with you about your justice:
Why does the way of the wicked prosper? Why do all the faithless live at ease?

[1] *contend:* debate, argue
[2] *plead:* make a case; present and argue for a position; make an emotional appeal
[3] *prosper:* succeed, thrive, flourish
[4] *all I endeavour:* all I attempt
[7] *thwart:* frustrate, prevent
[7] *sots ... of lust:* those who are addicted to lustful thoughts and actions
[7] *thralls:* those who are hypnotised, enthralled or enslaved by lust
[8] *spend:* expend, exhaust, wear out
[9] *brakes:* a thicket, a patch of ground overgrown with bushes and brambles
[11] *fretty:* having an interlaced pattern or design
[11] *chervil:* a type of herb
[13] *eunuch:* a man who has been castrated

Tease It Out

1. In the opening lines Hopkins sets out to 'contend' or take issue with God:
   - 'This poem uses the formal language of the courtroom or the tribunal'. Can you identify any terms or phrases that might be appropriate in such a setting? `
   - **True or false:** According to the poet, sinners typically suffer for their wrongdoings and seldom get ahead in life.
   - According to lines 3 to 4, do the poet's various projects and ambitions typically end in success or failure?

2. The poet considers his relationship with God:
   - **Class Discussion:** The poet complains that God 'defeat[s]' and 'thwart[s]' him. Suggest two ways in which the poet's hopes might be foiled and frustrated.
   - Do you think the poet is right to blame God for these setbacks?
   - The poet 'wonder[s]' how God would treat him if God were actually his enemy. Does he think that God would treat him any differently?

3. Consider the phrase 'sots and thralls of lust':
   - What kind of people does this highly expressive phrase refer to?
   - According to the poet, sinners seem to 'thrive' without making an effort. Which phrase conveys this?

   - What 'cause' does the poet 'spend' his life serving? Does the verb 'spend' have more than one meaning in this context?

4. Hopkins refers to riverbanks and 'brakes' or thickets:
   - Which phrases indicates that these 'banks and brakes' experience a lush and abundant growth?
   - Are the banks and brakes permanently fertile? Or do they also experience periods of barrenness? Support your answer with reference to the text.
   - What are the birds doing in line 12? What contrast is drawn between the activity of the birds and the life of the poet?

5. The poet claims that he is unable to 'breed one work that wakes':
   - What different types of 'work' might he be referring to here? Which phrase indicates that the poet makes a great effort to bring his various works to completion?
   - What might be the difference between a work that 'wakes' and a work that doesn't wake?
   - Class Discussion: Comment on the poet's choice of the verb 'breed' in line 13. What does it suggest about the poet's relationship with the various works that he produces (or attempts to produce)?

Exam Prep

1. **Personal Response:** Consider the poem's conclusion:
   - What does the poet, metaphorically speaking, have in mind when he refers to his 'roots'?
   - What does the poet ask God to do in the final line? What changes in Hopkins's life are represented by this image?
   - 'The banks and brakes experience freshness and rebirth but Hopkins never does'. Write a paragraph in response to this statement.

2. **Theme Talk:** 'This poem deals with one of the oldest themes in Christian thought, asking why, if God is good, is the world such an unjust and terrible place'. Write a paragraph or two in response to this statement.

3. **Exam Prep:** 'Hopkins uses remarkable language and images culled from the natural world in order to explore man's relationship with God'. Write a short essay in response to this statement in which you discuss this poem and at least three others by Hopkins that feature on your course.

Language Lab

1. Write a short story entitled 'Why do sinners' ways prosper?'

2. **Class Discussion:** Consider the phrase 'Time's eunuch':
   - What might this mean in the context of Hopkins's life choices and vocation?
   - What has he denied himself by choosing such a path?
   - How do you imagine Hopkins felt about such self-denial when he wrote this poem?
   - Do you think that in this poem Hopkins secretly envies the 'sots and thralls of lust'?

   In each case, support your answer with reference to the text.

3. **Class Discussion:** As a class, consider the tone of 'Thou art indeed just, lord'. Would you have an actor read it aloud in a tone of anger, frustration, bafflement, humility or despair? Would you agree that the tone changes over the course of the poem? Would you agree that its tone differs from that of the other 'terrible sonnets' on the course?

Paula Meehan

The eldest of six children, Paula Meehan was born in a working-class community in Dublin's inner-city tenements in 1955. With its rich heritage of storytelling and song, that community played a vital early part in the process that led Meehan to embrace the life of a poet. A dramatic change took place in 1968, when Meehan's neighbourhood was scheduled for development, and the local people were moved to the Dublin suburb of Finglas. Witnessing the break-up of her original, close-knit community was an important early experience that subsequently informed her attitude to poetry and art. Between 1972 and 1977, Meehan studied English, History and Classical Civilization at Trinity College Dublin. While she was studying at Trinity, she became actively involved in street theatre, beginning as a costuming assistant before moving on to become a dramatist.

Between 1981 and 1983, Meehan studied for an MFA (Master of Fine Arts) degree at Eastern Washington University in the United States. While attending Eastern Washington, she participated in writing workshops with some famous American writers. Among them was the poet and environmental activist Gary Snyder, who became a major influence on Meehan's thinking and writing. Meehan found herself especially drawn to Snyder's concern for nature, to his emphasis on the importance of communities and to the discipline that stemmed from his Zen

Buddhist spiritual practice. In Snyder's understanding of the poet as a sort of dreamer and spiritual hero for the tribe, Meehan found an important conception of poetry that would underpin her resistance to aspects of Irish culture that she thought were harmful and oppressive. It's important to note that the influence of Snyder and other American writers didn't simply replace Meehan's earlier Irish inspirations. What really happened was far more interesting: American themes and influences fused with Meehan's highly original take on Irish culture to produce something new and unique. During her time in Washington, Meehan began to compose the poems that would feature in her first two collections, *Return and No Blame* (1984) and *Reading the Sky* (1986). Even in the first of these collections, Meehan's trademark blend of lyric poetry and more dramatic forms was already evident.

In Meehan's next two collections, *The Man Who Was Marked by Winter* (1991) and *Pillow Talk* (1994), the inner-city-Dublin and American settings and themes of the first two volumes were joined by reflections on life in County Leitrim, where she lived between 1985 and 1989. Meehan's original focus on her native Dublin was revived when she moved back there in 1990, living first in the city's Merrion Square and subsequently in the north Dublin suburb of Baldoyle. In the poetry written between 1990

> **"There are poems that tell stories but there are also poems that just give you a moment of vision or transcendence or colour even, or just an image that you can carry around with you. Two lines. Two lines can save a life, I believe it."**

and the end of the twenty-first century's first decade, Meehan chronicled the dramatic changes that took place in Dublin, particularly during the period when a boom in property prices gave rise to intensive building and redevelopment. We can see Meehan's often critical and sorrowful attitude to these changes in such poems as 'Death of a Field' , which is set in a suburban building site and laments the harmful effects of the boom years on local communities.

Another form of oppression that became a major theme for Meehan is the subjugation and silencing of women's voices by Ireland's religious and secular authorities. Although she could draw inspiration from the powerful women poets who had emerged in Ireland during the 1980s and 1990s, Meehan once again followed a distinctive and original path in her poetic response to the oppression of women. For one thing, Meehan is less interested in private reflections on women's lives than she is in creating a form of public poetry that will resist the systemic oppression that restricts those lives. In 'The Statue of the Virgin at Granard Speaks,' for example, Meehan is consciously intervening in public debates about the status of women and commenting on Ireland's political and legislative battles about contraception, divorce and abortion. In doing so, she is not only reflecting the influence of socially conscious poets from America and elsewhere but also placing herself in the tradition of the pre-Christian Irish bards, whose poetry had as much of a social function as it had a purely aesthetic or literary one.

In addition to her six collections of poetry, Meehan has written plays for both adult and young audiences. She has also authored *Music for Dogs*, a series of three radio plays that address the tragic subject of suicide during Ireland's boom years. Meehan's poetry has been translated into many languages, and she has been awarded numerous literary prizes, including the Butler Literary Award for Poetry, the Marten Toonder Award for Literature, the PPI Award for Radio Drama and the Denis Devlin Award. The famous folk singer Christy Moore is among the musicians who have set her poetry to music. This process of collaboration with other art forms has consistently played an important part in Meehan's artistic life, and she has frequently worked with dancers, visual artists and film makers. Meehan's commitment to social justice and communal values has inspired her to lead writers' workshops in communities, prisons and recovery programmes.

In February 2012, Meehan and her fellow poet and life partner, Theo Dorgan, co-hosted 'The Old Triangle – A Celebration for the Benefit of the Irish Penal Reform Trust' at the Abbey Theatre in Dublin. This event reflected Meehan's intense belief in the need for penal reform and for greater awareness of the issues confronting prisoners in Ireland today. Meehan has also acted as a mentor to emerging poets both within and beyond the universities.

Meehan has been publicly acknowledged by being elected as a member of Aosdána, an association of artists whose work is deemed to have made a particularly important contribution to the creative arts in Ireland. From 2013 to 2016, she served as Ireland Professor of Poetry, a position created following the award of the Nobel Prize for Literature to Seamus Heaney in 1995. In October 2020, a collections of Meehan's selected poetry was published under the title *As If By Magic*.

Buying Winkles

My mother would spare me sixpence and say,
'Hurry up now and don't be talking to strange
men on the way.' I'd dash from the ghosts
on the stairs where the bulb had blown
out into Gardiner Street, all relief.   [5]
A bonus if the moon was in the strip of sky
between the tall houses, or stars out,
but even in rain I was happy – the winkles
would be wet and glisten blue like little
night skies themselves. I'd hold the tanner tight   [10]
and jump every crack in the pavement,
I'd wave up to women at sills or those
lingering in doorways and weave a glad path through
men heading out for the night.

She'd be sitting outside the Rosebowl Bar   [15]
on an orange-crate, a pram loaded
with pails of winkles before her.
When the bar doors swung open they'd leak
the smell of men together with drink
and I'd see light in golden mirrors.   [20]
I envied each soul in the hot interior.

I'd ask her again to show me the right way
to do it. She'd take a pin from her shawl –
'Open the eyelid. So. Stick it in
till you feel a grip, then slither him out.   [25]
Gently, mind.' The sweetest extra winkle
that brought the sea to me.
'Tell yer Ma I picked them fresh this morning.'

I'd bear the newspaper twists
bulging fat with winkles   [30]
proudly home, like torches.

Annotations
Winkles: a species of edible sea snail

Tease It Out

1. What advice would the poet's mother give her before allowing her out to buy the winkles?
2. How does Meehan convey the fact that the winkles were a luxury that her family could rarely afford?
3. What did the young poet imagine dwelt in the stairwell leading down to the street? Why was this part of the building so dark?
4. Why would she experience a sense of 'relief' when she reached the street?
5. Why would the young poet only see a 'strip of sky' when she looked up?
6. What term does Meehan use to suggest that seeing the moon or the stars on these occasions afforded her additional pleasure?
7. Describe in your own words the effect that the rain would have on the appearance of the winkles? What simile does the poet use to describe the appearance of the wet winkles?
8. Why do you think the young poet jumped 'every crack' in the pavement?
9. The poet recalls how she would 'wave up' to the women in her neighbourhood.
   - Where would these women be located?
   - What do you imagine the women were doing?
   - Do you think these women were familiar to the poet? Give a reason for your answer.
10. Where was the woman selling the winkles located? What kind of premises was she outside?
11. Describe what the young poet would see and smell each time the bar door swung open.
12. Which line suggests that the poet would be feeling the cold as she waited to buy the winkles?
13. **Class Discussion:** The young poet would ask the woman to show her 'again' the 'right way' to extract the winkle from its shell. Why did she do this? Consider the following and say which you think is most likely:
    - She could never remember how to do this.
    - It takes great skill to do this and was very difficult for the young poet.
    - She knew if she asked, she would get to eat the winkle.
    - She just wanted to spend more time out on the evening streets.
14. Describe in your own words the method used to extract the winkle from its shell.
15. How does the poet convey the fact that she would return home with a great quantity of winkles?
16. How would the young poet be feeling as she walked back home? What do you think made her feel this way?

Exam Prep

1. **Personal Response:** Can you recall an occasion when you were young and were asked to do something that made you feel important? Describe the task that you were given and the feelings that you experienced when doing it.
2. **Class Discussion:** What impression does the poem give us of the men that lived in the neighbourhood?
3. **Theme Talk:** 'Although Meehan's poetry vividly documents the hardships of growing up in an impoverished neighbourhood, her poems are never gloomy'. Discuss this statement with reference to 'Buying Winkles' and two other poems on your course.
4. **Exam Prep:** 'Meehan's poetry presents us with a cast of memorable women who possess powerful personalities and great character'. Write a short essay in response to this statement, referring to 'Buying Winkles' and two other poems on your course.

Language Lab

1. How does this poem capture and convey a childlike view of the world? Which words and phrases best illustrate this?
2. **Class Discussion:** Meehan describes how she would carry the packages of winkles home 'like torches'. Why do you think she makes this comparison? What does this simile tell us about the young poet's feelings as she made her way home?
3. 'Meehan's poetry provides us with wonderful snapshots of Dublin over the last seventy years'. Discuss this statement with reference to 'Buying Winkles' and two other poems on your course.

The Pattern

Little has come down to me of hers,
a sewing machine, a wedding band,
a clutch of photos, the sting of her hand
across my face in one of our wars

when we had grown bitter and apart.   [5]
Some say that's the fate of the eldest daughter.
I wish now she'd lasted till after
I'd grown up. We might have made a new start

as women without tags like *mother, wife,*
sister, daughter, taken our chance from there.   [10]
At forty-two she headed for god knows where.
I've never gone back to visit her grave.

       *

First she'd scrub the floor with Sunlight soap,
an arm reach at a time. When her knees grew sore
she'd break for a cup of tea, then start again   [15]
at the door with lavender polish. The smell
would percolate back through the flat to us,
her brood banished to the bedroom.

As she buffed the wax to a high shine
did she catch her own face coming clear?   [20]
Did she net a glimmer of her true self?
Did her mirror tell what mine tells me?

I have her shrug and go on
knowing history has brought her to her knees.
She'd call us in and let us skate around   [25]
in our socks. We'd grow solemn as planets
in an intricate orbit about her.

       *

She bending over crimson cloth,
the younger kids are long in bed.
Late summer, cold enough for a fire,   [30]
she works by fading light
to remake an old dress for me.
It's first day back at school tomorrow.

       *

Annotations
[17] *percolate:* to filter through the air
[18] *brood:* a family of young birds or animals
[19] *buffed:* polished

'Pure lambswool - Plenty of wear in it yet.
You know I wore this when I went out with your Da.   [35]
I was supposed to be down in a friend's house,
your Granda caught us at the corner.
He dragged me in by the hair – it was long as yours then –
in front of the whole street.
He called your Da every name under the sun,   [40]
cornerboy, lout; I needn't tell you
what he called me. He shoved my whole head
under the kitchen tap, took a scrubbing brush
and carbolic soap and in ice-cold water he scrubbed
every spick of lipstick and mascara off my face.   [45]
Christ but he was a right tyrant, your Granda.
It'll be over my dead body anyone harms a hair of your head.'

                              *

She must have stayed up half the night
to finish the dress. I found it airing at the fire,
three new copybooks on the table and a bright   [50]
bronze nib, St Christopher strung on a silver wire,

as if I were embarking on a perilous journey
to uncharted realms. I wore that dress
with little grace. To me it spelt poverty,
the stigma of the second hand. I grew enough to pass   [55]

it on by Christmas to the next in line. I was sizing
up the world beyond our flat patch by patch
daily after school, and fitting each surprising
city street to city square to diamond. I'd watch

the Liffey for hours pulsing to the sea   [60]
and the coming and going of ships,
certain that one day it would carry me
to Zanzibar, Bombay, the Land of the Ethiops.

                              *

There's a photo of her taken in the Phoenix Park
alone on a bench surrounded by roses   [65]
as if she had been born to formal gardens.
She stares out as if unaware
that any human hand held the camera, wrapped
entirely in her own shadow, the world beyond her
already a dream, already lost. She's   [70]
eight months pregnant. Her last child.

                              *

Her steel needles sparked and clacked,
the only other sound a settling coal
or her sporadic mutter
at a hard place in the pattern.   [75]
She favoured sensible shades:
Moss Green, Mustard, Beige.

I dreamt a robe of a colour
so pure it became a word.

Sometimes I'd have to kneel   [80]
an hour before her by the fire,
a skein around my outstretched hands,
while she rolled wool into balls.
If I swam like a kite too high
amongst the shadows on the ceiling   [85]
or flew like a fish in the pools
of pulsing light, she'd reel me firmly
home, she'd land me at her knees.

Tongues of flame in her dark eye
she'd say, 'One of these days I must   [90]
teach you to follow a pattern.'

Annotations

[41] cornerboy: a young man who hangs around on
street corners looking for trouble; a mild term of abuse

[44] carbolic soap: a type of soap made from
carbolic acid. It's known for its abrasive qualities.

[51]nib: the tip of a fountain pen

[51] St Christopher: the patron saint of travellers

[55] stigma: a mark of disgrace

[63] Zanzibar: an island off the coast of east Africa

[63] Bombay: the Indian city known today as
Mumbai

[63] Land of the Ethiops: Ethiopia

[74] sporadic: occasional

[82] skein: a loosely coiled and knotted length of
wool

[89] Tongues of flame: the *Acts of The Apostles*
describes how at Pentecost 'tongues of flame',
descended from heaven and landed on the twelve
apostles, granting them special powers, including the
ability to speak in all known languages

Tease It Out

Lines 1 to 12

1. What physical sensation does the poet recall? Can you suggest why this sensation lingered so visibly in the poet's memory?
2. **Class Discussion:** The poet presents the memory of this sensation as an heirloom she inherited. In what way is it different to the other heirlooms mentioned by the poet? In what ways is it similar?
3. The poet describes the relationship with her mother during her late teens and early twenties. Rank the following in order of plausibility:
   - She and her mother were best friends.
   - They were close, but they argued.
   - They had a love/hate relationship.
   - They were completely estranged.
   - They rarely conversed, and when they did it led to terrible arguments.
4. What age was the mother when she died?
5. What does the poet wish for?
6. **True or false:** The poet frequently visits her mother's grave. What does this suggest about her feelings towards her dead mother?

Lines 13 to 27

7. The poet remembers her mother polishing the floor of the family's flat on Sean MacDermott Street.
   - What hints do we get that the flat was a small one?
   - Which phrases indicate that the mother went about this task in a systematic manner?
   - Which phrases indicate that the mother was a hard worker who set out to perform the task well?
   - Where were the children while the mother performed the task?
8. **Class Discussion:** 'Did her mirror tell what mine tells me?' Suggest the thoughts and feelings the adult poet experiences when she looks in the mirror.
9. Did the mother study her reflection in a similar fashion? Does the poet know this for sure?
10. The poet describes how she and her siblings would skate around the room in a 'solemn' fashion. Does this choice of adjective surprise you? Give a reason for your answer.
11. The mother played a central role in the lives of her children. What comparison does the poet use to describe this? Is it a metaphor or a simile. Is it an effective comparison in your opinion?

Lines 34 to 63

12. Consider the phrase 'bending over crimson cloth'. What does this suggest about the manner in which the mother went about her work?
13. **True or false:** The mother was casual with her possessions and frequently threw things out.
14. The mother recalls when she herself wore the red dress. Describe what she was doing at the time.
15. Describe in your own words how the poet's grandfather punished the mother. Can you suggest why the grandfather was so angry? Does his reaction strike you as reasonable?
16. **True or false:** It took little effort for the mother to complete the alterations on the dress.
17. **Class Discussion:** Consider the term 'grace' in line 54. Does this suggest a) gratitude, b) physical deportment or c) something else entirely? Why did the poet react to the dress in this manner?
18. Which phrases suggest that the young poet explored the 'world beyond [the] flat' in a deliberate and systematic manner?
19. **Group Discussion:** The poet would spend hours watching the river. Working in pairs, suggest two or three topics she might think about while she watched the river flow.

Lines 64 to 71

20. The mother seemed unaware that 'any human hand held the camera'. Does this suggest a) that the mother is exhibiting great poise and self-confidence or b) that she is distracted and distressed.
21. Consider lines 68 to 69 and rank the following in order of plausibility:
    - The mother seems self-reliant and independent.
    - The mother seems troubled and depressed.
    - The mother's natural appearance in the photo is due to the photographer's skill.
22. Consider the poet's choice of the word 'wrapped' in these lines. Is it an effective one in your opinion? How does it relate to the poem's other images, especially those that relate to clothing?
23. **Class Discussion:** [T]he world beyond her/ already a dream, already lost'. Does this suggest the mother was a) a mindful person who lived in the moment, b) someone who resented lost opportunities or c) someone who is happy to live within the limits of their own area.

Lines 72 to 91

24. The poet describes her mother knitting by the fireside.
    - What sounds would be audible during these knitting sessions?
    - What indicates that the mother worked with intense concentration?
    - Suggest why the mother's needles 'sparked'.
    - **True or false:** The mother improvised a lot, adding stitches in an almost random fashion.
25. The poet also recalls helping her mother convert a 'skein', or hunk, of wool into neat balls.
    - What position would the poet have to take up during this procedure?
    - How would she have to hold the skein of wool?
    - What indicates that she frequently lost concentration?
    - How did her mother react when she did so?
26. How did the young poet imagine interacting with the shadows on the ceiling?
27. The flames from the hearth were reflected in the polished floor. What metaphor does the poet use to describe this?
28. How did she imagine interacting with these reflections?
29. Comment on the poet's use of the verbs 'swim' and 'fly' in this passage. Does this surprise you? What does this suggest about her imagination when she was a child?

Exam Prep

1. **Personal Response:** Meehan paints a very vivid portrait of her mother in this poem. Pick out two or three lines that indicate the following:
   - The mother was a diligent worker.
   - She was fiercely protective.
   - She tried to do the best for her family.
   - She had an angry side.

   Which of the above characteristics are associated with the 'Tongues of flame' that the poet sees in her mother's eyes?

   Is the mother, overall, presented as a strong and powerful woman or as a vulnerable one? Give a reason for your answer.
2. **Class Discussion:** Consider the following phrase for a moment: 'I dreamt a robe of a colour/ so pure'.
   - What do you visualise when you read these lines?
   - Would you agree that they are difficult to visualise precisely?
   - What do they suggest about the young poet's imagination?
   - Can you find two other phrases that suggest that even as a young person Meehan was evolving into a creative artist?
   - 'Knitting, like poetry, is presented as a creative act'. Can you identify any passages that support this claim?
3. **Theme Talk:** 'Meehan's concern with social justice is evident in this poem, as she descibes how her mother had been brought 'to her knees' by a society that denied her freedom and opportunity'. Write a short essay in response to this statement.
4. **Exam Prep:** Meehan has described how poetry 'can be a tool for excavation'. Discuss how Meehan's own poetry excavates the past, making reference to 'The Pattern', 'Cora, Auntie' and 'Hearth Lesson'.

Language Lab

1. The poet imagines herself and her mother meeting as 'women without tags'.
   - Is the poet suggesting that society views women only in terms of their family roles rather than as individuals?
   - Is the poet suggesting that relations with her mother would become easier when she 'grew up' and no longer depended on her as a provider?
   - Would you agree that men are 'tagged' in a similar fashion by society?
2. 'One of these days I must/ teach you to follow a pattern'.
   - What does this suggest about the young poet's personality?
   - Which of Meehan's poems can be said to follow a pattern? Which have a freer and looser quality?
   - 'This poem presents each family as a pattern in which traits and characteristics are repeated across the generations'. Write a short essay in response to this statement.
3. Watch Video 21, which features a reading of the poem by the poet herself.
   - Mention three things we learn about the poet's mother from the introduction to the reading.
   - Pick out two or three words or phrases that Meehan particularly emphasises as she reads.
   - During which section of the poem did the poet's reading become most emotional? Give a reason for your answer.

The Statue of the Virgin at Granard Speaks

It can be bitter here at times like this,
November wind sweeping across the border.
Its seeds of ice would cut you to the quick.
The whole town tucked up safe and dreaming,
even wild things gone to earth, and I   [5]
stuck up here in this grotto, without as much as
star or planet to ease my vigil.

The howling won't let up. Trees
cavort in agony as if they would be free
and take off — ghost voyagers   [10]
on the wind that carries intimations
of garrison towns, walled cities, ghetto lanes
where men hunt each other and invoke
the various names of God as blessing
on their death tactics, their night manoeuvres.   [15]
Closer to home the wind sails over
dying lakes. I hear fish drowning.
I taste the stagnant water mingled
with turf smoke from outlying farms.

They call me Mary — Blessed, Holy, Virgin.   [20]
They fit me to a myth of a man crucified:
the scourging and the falling, and the falling again,
the thorny crown, the hammer blow of iron
into wrist and ankle, the sacred bleeding heart.
They name me Mother of all this grief   [25]
though mated to no mortal man.
They kneel before me and their prayers
fly up like sparks from a bonfire
that blaze a moment, then wink out.

It can be lovely here at times. Springtime,   [30]
early summer. Girls in Communion frocks
pale rivals to the riot in the hedgerows
of cow parsley and haw blossom, the perfume
from every rushy acre that's left for hay
when the light swings longer with the sun's push north. [35]

Or the grace of a midsummer wedding
when the earth herself calls out for coupling
and I would break loose of my stony robes,
pure blue, pure white, as if they had robbed
a child's sky for their colour. My being   [40]
cries out to be incarnate, incarnate,
maculate and tousled in a honeyed bed.

Annotations

Granard: a town in County Longford. The statue is located in a grotto on the outskirts of the town

[7] *vigil:* a period of keeping awake during the time usually spent asleep, especially to keep watch or pray

[9] *cavort:* jump or dance around excitedly

[10] *ghost voyagers:* the statue imagines the trees being carried through the night by the wind

[11] *intimations:* indications; hints; communications

[12] *ghetto:* an impoverished part of the city, often occupied by a minority group

[18] *stagnant water:* water that has an unpleasant odour due to having no current or flow

[37] *coupling:* sexual intercourse

[41] *incarnate:* made flesh; having a human form or body

[42] *maculate:* stained; imperfect; sexual. The Virgin Mary is usually thought of as being immaculate, as being stainless, perfect and asexual

[42] *tousled:* caressed

[43] *pageantry:* elaborate display or ceremony

[45] *scud:* to move fast in a straight line as if driven by the wind

[46] *windfalls:* fruit that has fallen from a tree's branches

[50] *All Soul's Night:* In the Catholic Church this is a day of remembrance for all the faithful who have passed away. It is celebrated annually on 2 November.

Even an autumn burial can work its own pageantry.
The hedges heavy with the burden of fruiting
crab, sloe, berry, hip; clouds scud east   [45]
pear scented, windfalls secret in long
orchard grasses, and some old soul is lowered
to his kin. Death is just another harvest
scripted to the season's play.

But on this All Souls' Night there is   [50]
no respite from the keening of the wind.
I would not be amazed if every corpse came risen
from the graveyard to join in exaltation with the gale,
a cacophony of bone imploring sky for judgement
and release from being the conscience of the town.   [55]

On a night like this I remember the child
who came with fifteen summers to her name,
and she lay down alone at my feet
without midwife or doctor or friend to hold her hand
and she pushed her secret out into the night,   [60]
far from the town tucked up in little scandals,
bargains struck, words broken, prayers, promises,
and though she cried out to me in extremis
I did not move,
I didn't lift a finger to help her,   [65]
I didn't intercede with heaven,
nor whisper the charmed word in God's ear.

On a night like this I number the days to the solstice
and the turn back to the light.
                              O sun,   [70]
centre of our foolish dance,
burning heart of stone,
molten mother of us all,
hear me and have pity.

Annotations

[51] *keening:* wailing

[53] *exultation:* a state of elation or exhuberance

[56] *I remember the child:* refers to the tragic death of Ann Lovett, a 15-year-old schoolgirl from Granard. Ann had become pregnant but had managed to keep the pregnancy secret from her family and friends. On 31 January 1984, knowing her baby was coming, she went to the grotto alone to give birth. Ann was discovered by some fellow school children, who noticed her schoolbag while passing the grotto. By then Ann's baby was already dead, and Ann passed away some hours later. The story became a national scandal and greatly influenced the debate on women, sexuality and pregnancy in Irish life. The story of Ann's death played a huge part in a critically important national debate on women giving birth outside marriage

[63] *in extremis:* at the point of death

[68] *solstice:* refers to 21 December, the shortest day of the year, when the sun appears furthest from the equator

Tease It Out

The weather on All Soul's Night

1. The statue describes the wind on this particular November evening.
   - The wind carries particles of ice and sleet. Which line indicates this?
   - How does the statue characterise the sound of the wind? Is this sound constant or intermittent?
   - What impact does the wind have on the nearby trees? What poetic device is used to describe this?
   - What can the statue taste when the wind blows into her mouth?

2. On this night, the statue is the only person or creature exposed to these terrible conditions. Which lines or phrases indicate this?

3. In lines 50 to 55, the statue suggests that the wind is loud enough to wake the dead:
   - This suggestion might be considered an example of what poetic device?
   - Which term suggests that this exceptionally loud wind has a mournful quality?
   - Why is this image appropriate to the night in which the poem is set?
   - **True or false:** The risen corpses of the dead will move quietly through the land.
   - What does the statue imagine that these risen bodies would demand?

Intimations from the North

4. It's time to refresh your knowledge of Irish history and geography:
   - How is the term 'garrison town' used in the context of Irish history?
   - Name one 'garrison town' in the northern part of the island.
   - Name one city in the northern part of the island that still has its city walls.
   - Which phrases indicate that violent acts are carried out each night in these towns and cities?

5. Describe in your own words how the statue learns about these violent acts.

6. **Class Discussion:** '[I]nvoke/ the various names of God'. Discuss the Northern Ireland Troubles as a class. What role did religion play in this terrible conflict?

The statue's view of Christianity

7. What startling simile does the statue use to describe the prayers of the local people?

8. What does this comparison suggest about the statue's attitude to these prayers? Rank the following in order of plausibility:
   - Awe
   - Admiration
   - Pity and contempt
   - Puzzlement

9. **Class Discussion:** 'They call me Mary'. How does the statue feel about being addressed in such a fashion? Does she respond with puzzlement, pride, indifference or something else entirely?

10. What visitors – real or imagined – come to the statue's grotto in spring, summer, autumn and winter? What does this suggest about the role of the Catholic faith in Irish society?

11. The statue mentions different forms of suffering associated with the crucifixion. Describe each one in your own words.

12. The statue refers to the crucifixion as a 'myth'. Which different meanings of the word 'myth' might be relevant here?

13. The statue seems to view Catholicism as a religion that focuses on misery and sorrow. Which phrases support this?

The changing seasons

14. This poem features a great deal of imagery related to the seasons and the sun.
    - Consider the term 'riot'. What does this suggest about the wildflowers that fill the hedges in spring and early summer?
    - **True or false:** The whiteness of the wildflowers is less intense than that of the Communion frocks.
    - According to the statue, is the smell from rush-covered fields pleasant or unpleasant?
    - What use will farmers make of these fields later in the year?
    - What causes the hedges to be weighed down in autumn?
    - In autumn, the scent of fruit hangs in the air. Which phrase indicates this?

15. **Class Discussion:** In summer, according to the statue, what does the earth itself want people to do? Which two poetic devices might be said to feature here? (Hint: they both start with a 'p').

The death of Ann Lovett

16. The statue remembers the tragic death of Ann Lovett in 1984.
    - What age was Ann when she so tragically passed away?
    - Did Ann have any assistance or medical attention while she was giving birth?
    - Suggest why Ann might have 'cried out' to the statue at this moment. What did the statue represent to her?

Language Lab

1. Read lines 38 to 42 carefully and answer the following questions:
   - In what sense does the statue want to break free? Is this possible?
   - What comparison does she use to describe the colour of her robes? Is this a simile or a metaphor?
   - The statue would like to become a living, breathing human being. Which words and phrases indicate this?
   - What activity would the statue like to engage in once it has attained human embodiment?
2. The statue presents a very spiritual view of nature.
   - Over the years the statue has watched funerals taking place. Does it feel any grief or sorrow for the people who have died?
   - **True or false:** The statue presents the earth itself as a goddess. Give a reason for your answer.
   - Describe in your own words why the statue is looking forward to 21 December.
   - To whom or what does the statue pray at the close of the poem?
   - Does she present this entity as male or female?
   - What does she ask this entity to do? Do you find this request surprising? Give a reason for your answer.
   - **Class Discussion:** 'There is something pagan or almost pre-Christian in how the statue presents the changing of the seasons'. Discuss this statement as a class.
3. Watch Video 22, which is the first part of a documentary about the tragic death of Ann Lovett.
   - Mention three things you learned about Irish society in the 1980s.
   - Has Irish society changed completely since that time?
   - Are any aspects of Irish society still the same?

Exam Prep

1. **Class Discussion:** The statue refers to various 'scandals' that have occurred in Granard.
   - Can you suggest two or three topics that these scandals might relate to?
   - According to the statue, are these scandals important in the greater scheme of things?
   - How do the local townspeople attempt to deal with these scandals? Do you get the impression they are dealt with openly and honestly?
2. **Personal Response:** Consider the phrase 'she pushed her secret out into the night'.
   - What literary device is being used here? (Hint: It starts with an 'm' but isn't a metaphor).
   - What does the phrase suggest about how Ann behaved during her pregnancy? What does it suggest about the nature of the society in which she lived?
   - List two or three emotions you experienced while reading the statue's account of Ann's tragic passing.
   - 'There is a terrible irony in Ann's decision to give birth at the grotto'. Discuss this statement in small groups. Then write a paragraph outlining your own personal response.
3. **Theme Talk:** 'This poem presents a very negative view of the Catholic religion'. Write a short essay in reponse to this statement. Consider the statue's statements about the Troubles in Northern Ireland, about the crucifixion and about the local peoples' prayers. Also consider the statue's response to Ann's prayers and cries.
4. **Exam Prep:** 'Again and again in her poetry, Meehan gives voice to the voiceless, to those who have been failed and forgotten by society at large'. Discuss this statement in relation to the present poem and to three others on the course.

Cora, Auntie

Staring Death down
with a bottle of morphine in one hand,
a bottle of Jameson in the other;

laughing at Death –
love unconditional keeping her just this side   [5]
of the threshold

as her body withered
and her eyes grew darker and stranger
as her hair grew back after chemo

thick and curly as when she was a girl;   [10]
always a girl in her glance
teasing Death – humour a lance

she tilted at Death.
Scourge of Croydon tram drivers and High Street dossers
on her motorised invalid scooter   [15]

that last year;
bearing the pain,
not crucifixion but glory

in her voice.
Old skin, bag of bones,   [20]
grinning back at the rictus of Death:

always a girl in her name-
Cora, maiden, from the Greek Κορη,
promising blossom, summer, the scent of thyme.

Sequin: she is standing on the kitchen table.   [25]
She is nearly twenty-one.
It is nineteen sixty-one.

They are sewing red sequins, the women,
to the hem of her white satin dress
as she moves slowly round and round.   [30]

Sequins red as berries.
red as the lips of maidens,
red as blood on the snow

in Child's old ballads,
as red as this pen   [35]
on this white paper

Annotations

[2] *morphine:* a narcotic drug, obtained from opium, that's used to relieve pain

[3] *Jameson:* a brand of whiskey

[5] *love unconditional:* unconditional love

[9] *chemo:* chemotherapy

[12] *humour a lance:* humour was a lance

[13] *tilted at:* aimed at; attacked with a lance while on horseback

[14] *Scourge:* menace

[14] *Croydon:* an area of south London

[14] *dossers:* idle people; people who sleep rough

[23] *Κορη:* can mean girl, maiden or daughter. In the latter sense it came to be an alternate name given to the Greek goddess Persephone to denote her being the daughter of Demeter, the sister and consort of the chief Greek god, Zeus. (Zeus was Persephone's father.)

[25] *Sequin:* a small piece of shiny coloured metal foil or plastic, usually round, used to decorate garments; an ancient coin of Italy and Turkey

[34] *Child's old ballads:* The Child Ballads are 305 traditional ballads from England and Scotland, and their American variants, anthologised by Francis James Child during the second half of the 19th century.

[46] *taking the boat to England:* emigrating to England

[65] *coinage:* coins that have been standardised for use as currency; a brand new word or phrase created by an author

I've snatched from the chaos
to cast these lines
at my own kitchen table –

Cora, Marie, Jacinta, my aunties,   [40]
Helena, my mother, Mary, my grandmother –
the light of those stars

only reaching me now.
I orbit the table I can barely see over.
I am under it singing.   [45]

She was weeks from taking the boat to England.
Dust on the mantelpiece,
dust on the cards she left behind:

a black cat swinging in a silver horseshoe,
a giant key to the door,   [50]
emblems of luck, of access.

All that year I hunted sequins:
roaming the house I found them
in cracks and crannies,

in the pillowcase,   [55]
under the stairs,
in a hole in the lino,

in a split in the sofa,
in a tear in the armchair
in the home of the shy mouse.   [60]

With odd beads and single earrings,
a broken charm bracelet, a glittering pin,
I gathered them into a tin box

which I open now in memory –
the coinage, the sudden glamour   [65]
of an emigrant soul.

Tease It Out

Lines 1 to 24

1. The poet mentions 'love unconditional':
- For whom do we usually feel unconditional love?
- Who do you imagine was giving the aunt such love?
- How does the poet convey that it was such love that was keeping the aunt alive at this point?

2. What surprised the poet about the aunt's hair when it grew back after her chemotherapy?

3. **Class Discussion:** The poet describes how in her final year she heard '[N]ot crucifixion but glory// in her [aunt's] voice'. What does this tell us about the manner in which the aunt bore the great pain and suffering in her final years?

4. Where was the aunt living at this stage in her life? Which line makes this clear?

5. How did the aunt get around the city streets? What indication are we given that she was rather reckless and careless with the handling of this device?

6. '[G]rinning back at the rictus of Death'. What sort of facial expression does 'rictus' suggest? Which emotions does it suggest that the personified Death experienced when it came face to face with the poet's aunt? What does this line suggest about the aunt's attitude towards death?

7. The poet contemplates the aunt's name. What does she say that the name Cora means? What associations does the Greek form of the name Cora have?

8. **Class Discussion:** Based on your reading of lines 1 to 24, does the poet think that her aunt's name suit her?

Lines 25 to 51

9. The poet recalls a moment from 1961 when her aunt was 'nearly twenty-one'.
- Why is the aunt 'standing on the kitchen table'?
- Do you think that this is happening in the aunt's house or in the young poet's house? Give a reason for your answer.
- Who are the 'women' who have gathered around the aunt? What are these women doing?
- **True or false:** The aunt remains completely still while the women go about their work.

10. Do you think it was traditional to have such sequins sewn into the hem of a wedding dress or do you think that this was something that Cora just wanted to do? Give a reason for your answer.

11. Lines 36 to 39: The poet shifts to the present moment, where she is at her own kitchen table writing this very poem. Where is she seated? What colour pen is she using to write the poem? What colour paper is she writing on?

12. What is it that the poet has 'snatched from the chaos'? Is it a moment from her hectic life, or is it some paper that she has retrieved from the mess of her kitchen?

13. The poet thinks of her three aunties, her mother and her grandmother. She compares them to stars whose 'light' is only now 'reaching' her. What do you think she means by this? Rank the following in order of plausibility:
- These women always seemed so remote from her in terms of age and life experience, but now she can relate to them.
- The poet only now realises how important and special these women were.
- These women never cared about her.

14. Lines 44 to 45: The poet returns to the occasion in 1961 when the sequins were being sewn onto the hem of Cora's wedding dress. How does the poet convey that she was a very young child at this time? What does she remember doing while the women were gathered around the kitchen table?

15. 'She was weeks from taking the boat to England'. Why do you think Cora moved to England around this time?

16. **Class Discussion:** The poet recalls the cards that Cora received in the weeks leading up to her move to England. What sorts of images or pictures were on the front of these cards? What was the purpose of these cards, and what sort of messages do you think they contained?

Lines 52 to 63

17. Did the young poet go in search of sequins around the house, or did she come across them by accident? Which word or phrase indicates this?

18. List the different places in the house where the poet found sequins.

19. What else did the young poet find as she searched for the sequins?

20. Where did the poet store the things she found? Why do you think she wanted to keep these items?

21. **Class Discussion:** Why do you think the poet refers to the items kept in the tin box as 'coinage'?

22. Whose soul is the poet referring to in the poem's last lines? Why do you think she uses the term 'emigrant' to describe this soul? Do you think there are a number of ways of interpreting this? Give a reason for your answer.

Exam Prep

1. **Personal Response:** The first twenty-one lines detail the manner in which Cora responded to and coped with the fact that she was close to death. List the different ways in which Cora dealt with this uncomfortable truth. Do you think that the aunt was genuinely fearless, or do you think she was just pretending to be? Give a reason for your answer.

2. **Class Discussion:** What three adjectives would you use to describe the poet's aunt, based on your reading of the poem? What do you think Meehan most admired about Cora?

3. **Theme Talk:** 'Meehan's poetry documents the formative role that strong female relatives played in her young life'. Write a short essay discussing this statement, making reference to 'Cora, Auntie' and at least two other poems on your course.

4. **Exam Prep:** 'Meehan's poetry wonderfully captures the the ups and downs, the joys and heartbreaks, of family life'. Discuss this statement with reference to 'Cora, Auntie' and at least two other poems on the course.

Language Lab

1. Consider the poem's title. Why do you think the poet used 'Cora, Auntie' as opposed to 'Auntie Cora'? Give a reason for your answer.

2. The poet imagines the aunt as a kind of gunslinger in the opening lines.
   - What is the aunt armed with?
   - Who is her enemy?
   - What immediate impression do these opening lines give us of the aunt?

3. What other metaphors does the poet use to describe the aunt's attitude to death? Describe them in your own words and say which you found to be the most effective and memorable.

4. The poet uses four similes to describe the vivid red colour of the sequins that were being sewn into the hem of the aunt's wedding dress. What are the four comparisons that she makes?

5. Meehan describes the 'sudden glamour' of the sequins in the tin box. What do you think these found sequins represent or symbolise for the poet? What does she think of when she sees them?

The Exact Moment
I Became a Poet
for Kay Foran

was in 1963 when Miss Shannon
rapping the duster on the easel's peg
half obscured by a cloud of chalk

said *Attend to your books girls,*
or mark my words, you'll end up   [5]
in the sewing factory.

It wasn't just that some of the girls'
mothers worked in the sewing factory
or even that my own aunt did,

and many neighbours, but   [10]
that those words 'end up' robbed
the labour of its dignity.

Not that I knew it then,
not in those words – labour, dignity.
That's all back construction.   [15]

making sense; allowing also
the teacher was right
and no one knows it like I do myself.

But: I saw them; mothers, aunts and neighbours
trussed like chickens   [20]
on a conveyor belt,

getting sewn up the way my granny
sewed the sage and onion stuffing
in the birds.

Words could pluck you,   [25]
leave you naked,
your lovely shiny feathers all gone.

Annotations
[2] *easel:* used for holding the blackboard in place
[20] *trussed:* having your legs and arms tied together

Tease It Out

1. How did Miss Shannon attempt to get the attention of the girls in her class?
2. Why for a moment or two was Miss Shannon difficult to see?
3. What advice did Miss Shannon give the girls?
4. What would happen to the girls, according to Miss Shannon, if they failed to follow this advice?
5. Why might Miss Shannon's words have made some of the girls feel awkward or embarrassed?
6. Did the poet herself experience such feelings? Give a reason for your answer.
7. **Class Discussion:** What does the word 'dignity' mean? What does it mean for labour to possess dignity? Would you agree that all jobs, when done well, possess dignity of a sort?
8. **True or false:** The young poet felt that work in the sewing factory possessed no such dignity.
9. Use the phrase 'end up' in three separate sentences. Does it suggest a good or a bad outcome?
10. Can you suggest why this phrase, as the young poet saw it, made work in the sewing factory seem undignified?
11. 'the teacher was right/ and no one knows it like I do myself'. In what sense, according to the poet, was Miss Shannon 'right' in her assessment of the sewing factory? Suggest how the poet came to this conclusion.
12. 'But: I saw them'. The poet's imagination runs away with her, and she is struck by an intensely vivid daydream:
    * Who does the poet see, and where are these individuals?
    * The poet describes how these individuals have been 'trussed up'. What do you visualise here?
    * Describe in your own words what is happening to these poor 'trussed up' individuals.

Exam Prep

1. **Personal Response:** Pick an occasion from your time in primary school that stands out in your memory. Write a poem or short prose piece in which you describe that 'exact moment' in as much detail as possible.
2. **Theme Talk:** Meehan is well known for her depictions of childhood:
    * What do you understand by the term 'back construction' as Meehan uses it in this poem?
    * Compare this poem to 'Buying Winkles' and 'Hearth Lessons'. Which poem in your opinion most vividly captures the mentality of childhood?
3. **Class Discussion:** Consider the poem's title. What was so special about this moment in the classroom? In what sense did the young poet's understanding of language change on that day in 1963? In what sense did she become a poet at that very moment?
4. **Exam Prep:** 'Meehan is nothing if not outspoken when it comes to issues of poverty and social justice'. Write an essay responding to this statement in which you reference this poem and two others on the course.

Language Lab

1. The young poet realised for the first time that words are extremely powerful and can cause great psychological harm. What metaphor is used to describe this harm? Is it an effective one in your opinion?
2. Meehan is known for her playful, witty approach to the poetry. Is this playfulness in evidence in her depiction of the 'trussed up' mothers, aunts and neighbours? Or is this an image of pure horror? Give a reason for your answer.

My Father Perceived as a Vision of St Francis

for Brendan Kennelly

It was the piebald horse in next door's garden
frightened me out of a dream
with her drawn whinny. I was back
in the boxroom of the house,
my brother's room now,   [5]
full of ties and sweaters and secrets.
Bottles chinked on the doorstep,
the first bus pulled up to the stop.
The rest of the house slept

except for my father. I heard   [10]
him rake the ash from the grate,
plug in the kettle, hum a snatch of a tune.
Then he unlocked the back door
and stepped out into the garden.

Autumn was nearly done, the first frost   [15]
whitened the slates of the estate.
He was older than I had reckoned,
his hair completely silver,
and for the first time I saw the stoop
of his shoulder, saw that   [20]
his leg was stiff. What's he at?
So early and still stars in the west?

They came then: birds
of every size, shape, colour; they came
from the hedges and shrubs,   [25]
from eaves and garden sheds,

from the industrial estate, outlying fields,
from Dubber Cross they came
and the ditched of the North Road.
The garden was a pandemonium   [30]
when my father threw up his hands
and tossed the crumbs to the air. The sun
cleared O'Reilly's chimney
and he was suddenly radiant,
a perfect vision of St Francis,   [35]
made whole, made young again,
in a Finglas garden.

Annotations
St Francis: St Francis of Assissi (1182-1226)
was an Italian monk, mystic and preacher.
Known for his intense bond with animals
and the natural world, he is Italy's patron
saint and one of the most venerated figues in
Christianity
[1] *piebald:* having irregular patches of
black and white
[4] *boxroom:* small room used for storage
or as a bedroom
[30] *pandemonium:* chaos; uproar
[34] *radiant:* shining; glowing

Tease It Out

1. Watch Video 23, which is a scene from *Brother Sun, Sister Moon*.
   - Who has St Francis come to visit, and what does he want?
   - Do Francis and his followers seem to fit in in this location? Give a reason for your answer.
   - Pick three adjectives that best describe your impression of St Francis's personality.
2. The poet has returned for a brief stay at her family home in Finglas.
   - Which room of the house is she staying in?
   - Who normally sleeps in this room nowadays?
   - What items of clothing are scattered around the room?
   - What secret items might the room's normal occupier have hidden in there?
3. What sound woke the poet from her dream?
4. What other two sounds does she hear as she lies in bed?
5. What indications do we get that it is still very early in the morning?
6. The poet listens to her father downstairs. What does she hear him doing?
7. The poet looks out an upstair's window. What are the weather conditions like outside?
8. **True of false:** It is so early that stars are still visible in the sky?
9. The poet is suddenly struck by the fact that her father is growing older. Mention three aspects of his appearance and demeanour that she finds startling.
10. Suddenly, the garden starts to fill with birds:
    - **True or false:** The birds all belong to a single species.
    - The poet imagines that the birds have travelled from all around the locality. Mention three locations that she thinks of.
    - What did the father toss into the air once the birds had assembled?
    - How did the birds respond to this event?
11. **Class Discussion:** How do we know that the father does this every morning?
12. What object has been blocking the light of the rising sun?
13. The poet's father seemed very different when the sunlight finally struck him. Pick out three phrases that suggest this.
14. What does the comparison with St Francis suggest about the poet's father at this moment? Rank the following in order of plausibility:
    - He seemed like a kindly and gentle person.
    - He seemed like someone with a close kinship with the natural world.
    - He seemed like a mystical figure, one capable of triggering miraclulous events.
    - He seemed like an extremely holy and moral person.
    - He seemed capable of persuading, leading and influencing others.

Exam Prep

1. **Personal Response:** Describe the birds in as much detail as you can imagine them. What emotions do you imagine you would feel if such a flock of birds descended on your garden?
2. **Class Discussion:** 'All too often we fail to see close even family members for who they really are'.
   - Might this statement be applied to both family members mentioned in this poem?
   - Mention two ways in which the poet is surprised by her father on this particular morning.
   - Do you agree that at the end of the poem, the poet sees her father as he really is? Give a reason for your answer.
3. **Theme Talk:** 'Meehan uses her unique poetic style to explore the highs and lows of family relationships'. Discuss this statement in relation to this poem and two others on your course.
4. **Exam Prep:** 'Meehan has a uniquely spiritual view of the natural world'. Write a short essay discussing this topic.

Language Lab

1. **Class Discussion:** Take a moment to consider the poem's title:
   - How is the term 'vision' used in the context of religion?
   - Are 'visions' the same as hallucinations or do they reveal a deeper reality about the world?
   - In what sense is the poet's experience similar to such a religious 'vision'? In what sense is it different?
   - Is the poet's father really transformed at this moment, or does this transformation only occur in the poet's perception?
2. Meehan is a poet who makes skilful use of repetition in her poetry. Discuss this statement with reference to this poem and to 'Death of a Field' and 'Prayer for the Children of Longing'.

Hearth Lesson

Either phrase will bring it back —
money to burn, burning a hole in your pocket.

I am crouched by the fire
in the flat in Seán MacDermott Street
while Zeus and Hera battle it out.   [5]

for his every thunderbolt
she had the killing glance;
she'll see his fancyman
and raise him the Cosmo Snooker Hall;
he'll see her 'the only way you get any   [10]
attention around here is if you neigh';
he'll raise her airs and graces
or the mental state of her siblings
every last one of them.

I'm net, umpire, and court; most balls   [15]
are lobbed over my head.
Even then I can judge it's better
than brooding and silence and the particular hell of the unsaid,
of 'tell your mother…' ' ask your father…'.

Even then I can tell it was money,   [20]
the lack of it day after day,
at the root of the bitter words
but nothing prepared us one teatime
when he handed up his wages.

She straightened each rumpled pound note, then   [25]
a weariness come suddenly over her,
she threw the lot in the fire.

The flames were blue and pink and green,
a marvellous sight, an alchemical scene.
'It's not enough,' she stated simply.   [30]

The flames sheered from cinder to chimney breast
like trapped exotic birds;
the shadows jumped floor to ceiling, and she'd
had the last, the astonishing, word.

Annotations

[5] *Zeus and Hera:* in Greek mythology Zeus and his wife Hera were the king and queen of the gods and rulers of Mount Olympus. Many legends recount their tempestuous relationship

[8-9] *see … raise:* terms used in the game of poker. To 'see' is to match the amount being gambled by another player. To 'raise' is to increase the amount being gambled.

[8] *fancyman:* a married woman's male lover or a man with whom she flirts

[29] *alchemical:* relating to alchemy, which was the medieval forerunner of chemistry and focused on transforming one substance into another and on finding universal cures and chemical means of ensuring unending life

[31] *sheered:* swerved

[31] *chimney breast:* portion of a chimney which projects forward from a wall to accommodate a fireplace

Tease It Out

1. Where did the young poet frequently find herself during the arguments between her parents?
2. What posture did the young poet adopt at these moments? What does this suggest about her emotional state as the argument raged above her?
3. **Class Discussion:** 'The poet's reference to Zeus and Hera is playful and amusing, but it also highlights the feelings of dread and powerlessness she felt during these rows'. Discuss this statement as a class.
4. What do the terms 'see' and 'raise' mean in the context of poker and similar card games? What does Meehan's use of these terms suggest about the arguments between her parents?
5. Working in pairs, answer the following questions:
   - What do you understand by the terms 'fancyman' and 'airs and graces'? What is the father suggesting about the mother when he uses these terms?
   - Which phrase indicates that the father, in the opinion of the mother, spent too much time and money betting on horses?
   - Mention another of the father's pastimes that met with the mother's disapproval.
   - Which phrase indicates that the father, as the mother saw it, paid the mother very little attention?
6. What sporting metaphor does the poet use to describe the argument between her parents? Is it an effective one in your opinion?

7. Which phrase indicates that the young poet didn't understand much of what was said in these arguments? Do you think this was deliberate on the parents' part?
8. **True or false:** The poet preferred her parents' arguments to the periods when they silently ignored one another.
9. The poet describes how the father handed up his wages each week.
   - **True or false:** The father was paid by cheque.
   - What use do you imagine the mother made of this money?
   - Do you get the impression the father always handed over the entirety of his wages? Give a reason for your answer.
10. What did the mother do with the wages one day at teatime?
11. '[N]othing prepared us'. Can you suggest why the family were so surprised by this gesture?
12. Describe the mother's demeanour as she did this. What mental or emotional state did it exhibit?
13. Why does the poet view this gesture as part of the argument between her parents? Why does she view it as the winning move in this argumentative game, the one to which there can be no response?

Exam Prep

1. **Theme Talk:** Meehan writes frequently about the theme of poverty and hardship. Consider the phrase 'It's not enough' in this regard.
   - Is the mother referring only to money here?
   - Would you agree that this demeans the father's role as worker and provider?
   - Do you think this was deliberate on the mother's part?
   - In what sense is this gesture a self-defeating one?
   - 'The gesture is born of frustration and desperation'. Write a paragraph in response to this statement.
2. **Exam Prep:** 'Meehan uses her unique style to explore the positive and negative aspects of human existence'. Write a short essay in response to this statement.

Language Lab

1. **Personal Response:** 'Either phrase will bring it back'. Can you suggest why these phrases are linked in the poet's mind to this particular set of memories? Can you a recall a time when your own memory was triggered by an overheard phrase, a scent or a piece of music? Write a paragraph describing your experience.
2. **Class Discussion:** 'Meehan's use of the present tense renders her memories immediate and vivid for the reader'. Discuss this statement as a class.
3. What impact did the burning notes have on the colour of the flames? What simile does Meehan use to describe the action of the flames at that moment? What other literary device is used in this passage?
4. Do you think the flames really behaved in this fashion, or is it just in the poet's memory?

Prayer for the Children of Longing

*A poem commissioned by the community of Dublin's north inner city for the
lighting of the Christmas tree in Buckingham Street, to remember their
children who died from drug use.*

Great tree from the far northern forest
Still rich with the sap of the forest
Here at the heart of winter
Here at the heart of the city

Grant us the clarity of ice   [5]
The comfort of snow
The cool memory of trees
Grant us the forest's silence
The snow's breathless quiet

For one moment to freeze   [10]
The scream, the siren, the knock on the door
The needle in its track
The knife in the back

In that silence let us hear
The song of the children of longing   [15]
In that silence let us catch
The breath of the children of longing

The echo of their voices through the city streets
The streets that defeated them
That brought them to their knees   [20]
The streets that couldn't shelter them
That spellbound them in alleyways
The streets that blew their minds
That led them astray, out of reach of our saving
The streets that gave them visions and dreams   [25]
That promised them everything
That delivered nothing
The streets that broke their backs
The streets that we brought them home to

Let their names be the wind through the branches   [30]
Let their names be the song of the river
Let their names be the holiest prayers

Under the starlight, under the moonlight
In the light of this tree

Here at the heart of winter   [35]
Here at the heart of the city

Annotations

[12] *track:* track mark, a scar created by
continuously injecting a needle into the same
point in the body over and over again

Tease It Out

I

1. This entire poem is addressed to the 'Great Tree' on Buckingham Street. What is the name for the literary device by which a poet addressses an inanimate object?
2. The tree grew in a 'far northern forest'. Is the poet referring to a) The Northside of Dublin, b) Northern Ireland or c) a country in Northern Europe.
3. How do we learn from the poet that the Christmas tree was only recently cut down?
4. The poet asks the tree to 'Grant' the community a moment of stillness and serenity.
5. The poet asks the tree to 'freeze' life, or at least certain aspects of life.
   - Line 11 describes three events associated with a murder. Describe each of these events in your own words.
   - What aspect of drug abuse is referred to in line 12?
   - What kind of crime is referred to in line 13?

II

6. **Class Discussion:** The poet refers to the young victims of drug use as 'the children of longing'. What did these young people long for? Is it possible that they longed for more than one thing?
7. The poet imagines it might be possible to hear these young victims. In what sense might the 'children of longing' be present, despite the fact that they have passed on?
8. **Class Discussion:** Metonymy occurs when we substitue something associated with a concept for the concept itself. What concept is the term 'streets' being substituted for?
9. The street's 'broke' these young victims in both body and spirit. Identify three phrases that suggest this.
10. What do the phrases 'spellbound' and 'blew their minds' suggest about the nature of drug addiction?
11. The 'streets', according to the poet, promised these young victims 'everything'. Can you suggest two or three specific promises the 'streets' might have made? Did any of these promises come true?
12. The relatives of these young victims felt guilty about their untimely deaths. Which phrases indicate this?

III

13. The moment is approaching when the 'Great tree' will be illuminated.
    - Which phrases indicate that it is a cloudless night?
    - Which words or phrases, according to the poet, do those assembled now utter?
    - These words should be spoken like the 'holiest prayers'. What kind of speaking and tone of voice do you think the poet has in mind?
14. What does the poet imagine hearing in the wind and in the sound of the river? What does this suggest about how the young victims are remembered by those who love them?

Exam Prep

1. **Personal Response:** Imagine you were at the event where the poet read this poem aloud for the first time. Write a diary entry describing your experience.
2. **Class Discussion:** 'In life, these young victims were confined to the streets of the inner city. In death, however, the poet wishes them beauty and free movement'. Discuss this statement as a class.
3. **Theme Talk:** 'Meehan presents nature as if it were a mystical, almost conscious entity that surrounds and nourishes human beings'. Write a short essay responding to this statement in whcih you compare this poem to 'Death of a Field' and 'My Father Perceived as a Vision of St Francis'.
4. **Exam Prep:** 'Meehan is a poet of social justice, someone who again and again speaks out on behalf of those who have been forgotten'. Write a short essay discussing this statement, making reference to this poem and three others on your course.

Language Lab

1. Consider the following common features of prayers and say which are present in the poem:
   - Asking for a grant, blessing or favour
   - Repetition
   - Admitting your faults and asking for help to do better
   - Praise
2. **Class Discussion:** Let's focus on the poet's depiction of the northern forest.
   - Consider the phrase 'clarity of ice'. Would you agree that the word 'clarity' has two different meanings here?
   - What might these woodland trees remember? Why do you think these memories might be described as 'cool'?
   - In what sense might snow, often considered to be a cold and unforgiving feature of the landscape, provide a form of comfort?

Death of a Field

The field itself is lost the morning it becomes a site
When the Notice goes up: Fingal County Council – 44 houses

The memory of the field is lost with the loss of its herbs

Though the woodpigeons in the willow
The finches in what's left of the hawthorn hedge   [5]
And the wagtail in the elder
Sing on their hungry summer song

The magpies sound like flying castanets

And the memory of the field disappears with its flora:
Who can know the yearning of yarrow   [10]
Or the plight of the scarlet pimpernel
Whose true colour is orange?

And the end of the field is the end of the hidey holes
Where first smokes, first tokes, first gropes
Were had to the scentless mayweed   [15]

The end of the field as we know it is the start of the estate
The site to be planted with houses each two or three bedroom
Nest of sorrow and chemical, cargo of joy

The end of dandelion is the start of Flash
The end of dock is the start of Pledge   [20]
The end of teazel is the start of Ariel
The end of primrose is the start of Brillo
The end of thistle is the start of Bounce
The end of sloe is the start of Oxyaction
The end of herb robert is the start of Brasso   [25]
The end of eyebright is the start of Persil

Who amongst us is able to number the end of grasses
To number the losses of each seeding head?

I'll walk out once
Barefoot under the moon to know the field   [30]
Through the soles of my feet to hear
The myriad leaf lives green and singing
The million million cycles of being in wing

That – before the field become solely map memory
In some archive of some architect's screen   [35]
I might possess it or it possess me
Through its night dew, its moon white caul
Its slick and shine and its profligacy
In every wingbeat in every beat of time

Annotations

[3] *castanets:* small wooden percussion intruments that produce a clacking sound

[9] *flora:* plantlife

[10] *yarrow:* a wildflower

[11] *scarlet pimpernel:* a wildflower

[14] *tokes:* inhalations from a marijuana cigarette

[14] *first gropes:* earliest, somewhat awkward sexual experiences

[15] *mayweed:* a wildflower

[28] *seeding head:* describes how the top, flowering part of a plant transforms into a dry cluster of seeds

[32] *myriad:* countless

[37] *caul:* a membrane or covering

[38] *profligacy:* extravagance; plentifulness; wastefulness

Tease It Out

1. A planning notice has been placed at a field near the poet's home. What does the Local Authority have planned for this site?
2. **Class Discussion:** According to the poet, 'the field is lost' the moment this notice is posted. How can the field be 'lost' before any construction has taken place?
3. The field, according to the poet, has a memory all of its own. What kind of things do you think the field might remember?
4. Where, according to the poet, do its memories reside? What causes its memories to be erased?
5. Describe, in your own words, the literary device known as personification. In what way is the field being personified in these lines?
6. **True or false:** The death of the field will cause the birds in the locality to stop singing.
7. **Class Discussion:** The birds' song is described as 'hungry'. Suggest what the birds might be hungering for. Why might such hunger lead to their constant singing?
8. Take a moment to visualise the 'hidey holes' referred to in line 13:
   - Write two or three sentences describing these little hideaways as you imagine them.
   - Which members of the community made use of these spaces?
   - Describe in your own words the activities that took place in them.
9. **True or false:** The poet views the arrival of the estate in a completely negative light. Give a reason for your answer.
10. **Group Discussion:** Read lines 19 to 26 carefully. Then, working in small groups, attempt to answer the following questions:
    - How many of the products or brand names do you recognise?
    - How many of the herbs or wildflowers would you recognise if you saw them growing wild?
    - What impact will the arrival of the estate have on local biodiversity?
    - What impact will the arrival of the estate have on soil and on the water table?
11. How does the poet intend to say goodbye to the field? At what time of day or night will she do this? What will she be wearing on her feet when she does so?
12. The field will live on as a 'map memory'. Where, according to the poet, will this memory reside? Does this thought bring the poet any comfort? Give a reason for your answer.
13. Consider the term 'profligacy'. What does it suggest about the kind of growth the poet has witnessed in the field over the years?
14. Every second spent barefoot in the field will be filled with sensation. How does the poet convey this?

Exam Prep

1. **Personal Response:** Discuss the following questions as a class:
   - The poet maintains that she will 'know' the field better by walking across it barefoot. Can you suggest why this might be the case?
   - 'I might possess it or it possess me'. In what ways might the poet possess the field? In what ways might she be possessed?
   Then, drawing on the discussion, write your own response to each question in your copybook.
2. **Class Discussion:** Meehan is a poet well known for her concern for social justice. In what sense might 'Death of a Field' be said to share this concern?
3. **Theme Talk:** 'In this poem Meehan emphasises the extraordinary richness and diversity of growth that can be found in even a modest patch of ground'. Identify at least four words or phrases that support this statement.
4. **Exam Prep:** 'Meehan's poetry emphasises an intense, almost spiritual bond between nature and human beings'. Write a short essay responding to this statement in which you discuss 'Death of a Field' and at least one other poem on the course.

Language Lab

1. 'Death of a Field', like many of Meehan's poems, is rich in metaphor and simile:
   - What very inventive simile is used to describe the sound of the magpies' singing?
   - In what sense might the 'night dew' that covers the field resemble a 'caul'? Is this an effective comparison in your opinion?
2. 'Death of a Field' has been described as an outpouring of emotion:
   - How many punctuation marks can you identify in the poem? How might the lack of punctuation contribute to this outpouring?
   - Identify two emotions that in your opinion the poet is attempting to convey. What is a litany? In what sense might lines 19 to 26 be described as a litany?
   - Litanies are associated with prayer. Is it reasonable to describe this poem as a kind of prayer? To whom or what might the poet be praying?
   - Would you agree that the poem increases in intensity towards its conclusion?

Them Ducks Died for Ireland

'6 of our waterfowl were killed or shot, 7 of the garden seats broken and about 300 shrubs destroyed'.
- Park Superintendent in his report on the damage to
St Stephen's Green, during the Easter Rising 1916

Time slides slowly down the sash window
puddling in light on oaken boards. The Green
is a great lung, exhaling like breath on the pane
the seasons' turn, sunset and moonset, the ebb and flow

of stars. And once made mirror to smoke and fire,   [5]
a Republic's destiny in a Countess' stride,
the bloodprice both summons and antidote to pride.
When we've licked the wounds of history, wounds of war,

we'll salute the stretcher-bearer, the nurse in white,
the ones who pick up the pieces, who endure,   [10]
who live at the edge, and die there and are known

by this archival footnote read by fading light;
fragile as a breathmark on the windowpane or the gesture
of commemorating heroes in bronze and stone.

Annotations

This poem comes from Meehan's series 'Six Sycamores', which was commissioned by the Office of Public Works to celebrate the opening in 2001 of the Link Building near St Stephen's Green in Dublin. Meehan set out to write about Georgian Dublin and its multiple, conflicting histories. During her research for this project, she visited the Irish Architectural Archive where she discovered the Park Superintendent's report which serves as the poem's epigraph.

[1] *sash window:* window made up of two moveable panes or panels

[2] *The Green:* St Stephen's Green

[6] *Countess:* Countess Constance Markievicz (1867–1927). She was born into the aristocratic Anglo-Irish Gore-Booth family in County Sligo. In 1900 she married Polish aristocrat and artist Casimir Dunin Markievicz. She was the only female leader in the 1916 Rising and, along with Michael Mallin, commanded the Rebel position on St Stephen's Green. After the Rising, she served as a minister in the First Dáil, becoming the first woman in Europe to attain such a position.

[9] *stretcher-bearer:* St Stephen's Green served as a field hospital during the Rising

Tease It Out

1. The poet's breath forms a mist on the window of the Office of Public Works. Which phrase indicates this? The Green, too, exhales. What features of the Green might be responsible for this 'exhaling'?
2. **True or false:** According to the poet, the Green exhales differently depending on the time of day and time of year.
3. What feature of the Green might be compared to a 'mirror'?
4. The poet remembers a time when this 'mirror' reflected smoke and fire. What historical event was responsible for this effect?
5. **Class Discussion:**
   - Consider the verb 'stride'. What does it suggest about the manner in which the Countess walked across the Green?
   - Consider the phrase 'Republic's destiny'. Does it suggest that the fate of the fledgling Irish Republic was a) already determined or b) very much in the balance?
   - **True or false:** The poet suggests that the actions and choices of the Countess are central to the outcome of the Rising.
6. An independent Irish Republic could only be established through war and bloodshed. Which phrase indicates this?
7. **Class Discussion:** Consider the phrase 'summons and antidote to pride'.
   - The word pride has several different meanings. Is it possible that more than one meaning is being referred to here?
   - Whose 'pride' does the poet have in mind?
   - In what sense might this 'pride' be both a 'summons' and an 'antidote'?
8. Consider those who 'pick up the pieces' after an event like the Easter Rising. What kind of work do you imagine them doing?
9. These people, along with nurses and stretcher-bearers, 'live at the edge'. But at the 'edge' of what exactly? What does this phrase suggest about their role in history?
10. Which phrase suggests that these people at the 'edge', no less than heroes like the Countess, exhibit strength and courage?
11. The poet is reading a note she found in an archive.
    - What does it say?
    - Who wrote it?
    - Is this person also one of those who '[picked] up the pieces'?

Exam Prep

1. **Personal Response:** The poem's opening lines depict time as if it were a physical substance. What precisely do you visualise when you read these lines? Is it an effective comparison in your opinion? What do these lines suggest about the nature of time's passage?
2. **Class Discussion:** 'Some heroes are commemerated by statue, others are recalled only in long lost footnotes, but all will be forgotten in due time'. Discuss this statement as a class.
3. **Theme Talk:** 'Meehan's poetry celebrates the strength and power of ordinary women as well as the strength and power of those recorded in the history books'. Discuss this statement in relation to 'Them Ducks', 'Cora, Auntie' and 'The Pattern'.
4. **Exam Prep:** 'Paula Meehan uses her uniquely playful style to explore topics of great importance'. Write an essay in response to this statement, referring to 'Them Ducks' and at least three other poems on your course.

Language Lab

1. **Class Discussion:** The poet compares St Stephen's Green to a 'great lung' at the centre of the city.
   - Is this comparison a metaphor or a simile?
   - In what sense might the Green be said to function like a lung?
   - In this an effective comparison in your opinion?
2. This poem comes from what the poet has described as 'a series of sonnets interspersed with what I would hear as living voices, snatches of conversation out of the flux of the city'. Consider the title of the poem.
   - Who do you imagine speaking these words?
   - Would you agree that they differ in tone from the poem itself?
   - How does the title relate to the theme of the poem as you understand it?
3. Which features of the sonnet form can you identify in this poem?
4. Meehan described how she adopted this form in order to 'mirror the incredibly beautiful Georgian structures around St Stephen's Green'. As a class, discuss this formal choice.

Eiléan Ní Chuilleanáin

Eiléan Ní Chuilleanáin was born in Cork city in 1942 into a literary household. Her mother, Eilís Dillon, was a novelist who wrote over fifty books for children, with bestsellers such as *The Lost Island* remaining in print for decades. Her father, Cormac O'Cuilleanáin, was professor of Irish at UCC. Her siblings, too, grew up to be highly cultured people; her sister Máire was a violinist with the London Philharmonic, while her brother Cormac is a professor and writes novels under the pen name Cormac Millar. This artistic tradition has continued with the younger generations of the family; Ní Chuilleanáin's niece is the novelist Léan Cullinan.

As well as literary ties, there are also strong Republican connections in Ní Chuilleanáin's family. The poet has described herself as 'a Gaelic-speaking female papist whose direct and indirect ancestors, men and women, on both sides, were committed to detaching Ireland from the British Empire.' Her mother was the niece of Joseph Mary Plunkett, one of the executed leaders of the 1916 Rising.

Ní Chuilleanáin's father, meanwhile, was active in the War of Independence, a fact commemorated by the poet in 'On Lacking the Killer Instinct': 'I have a story which my father told me about running away from the Black and Tans when he was, I suppose,

about twenty or twenty-one. I was trying to connect that with my memories of his final illness. He had described to me what it felt like running away from this lorry, and he ran into a house and the lorry came and pulled up alongside the house. He had bolted into the kitchen and he saw a towel and some water. He picked up the towel and put it up to his face and looked as bleary eyed as he could. And they looked around the kitchen and those there said they hadn't seen anybody and the lorry went on. He said he never felt so well in his life as when he was running, so I've been trying to put that into a poem.'

Ní Chuilleanáin studied English and History at UCC, and she received an MA in English in 1964. She won a scholarship to the prestigious Lady Margaret Hall at Oxford University to study Renaissance Literature. She became a junior lecturer in the School of English at Trinity College Dublin in 1966, teaching medieval and Renaissance literature. This was the beginning of a long and distinguished career at Trinity. In 1972, she published her first collection of poetry, *Acts and Monuments*, which went on to win the Patrick Kavanagh Award the following year.

In 1975, Ní Chuilleanáin founded the literary journal *Cyphers* with fellow poets Macdara Woods, Leland Bardwell and Pearse Hutchinson. The journal sprang from a weekly poetry event

"A really serious use of language is a public good.... We need to know the things that language can do and studying literature is one of the ways to find that out."

that the four writers ran in Sinnotts pub on South King Street, Dublin. It was named after Ní Chuilleanáin's cat, Cypher, who was in turn named for a series of poems by Macdara Woods. One of the journal's early patrons was Katherine Kavanagh, widow of the poet Patrick Kavanagh. She also taught Ní Chuilleanáin how to keep proper financial accounts, something which Ní Chuilleanáin credits as crucial to the journal's survival. *Cyphers* is still published today and is one of Ireland's longest-running literary periodicals. Ní Chuilleanáin married her co-editor and fellow poet Macdara Woods in 1978; they have one son together, Niall.

In all, Ní Chuilleanáin has published ten collections of poetry, including *Site of Ambush* (1975), *The Second Voyage* (1977), *The Rose Geranium* (1981), *The Magdalen Sermon* (1989), *The Brazen Serpent* (1994), *The Girl Who Married the Reindeer* (2001) and *The Sun-Fish* (2009). Her *Selected Poems* was published in 2008. Ní Chuilleanáin's poetry often focuses on religion, mythology and folklore. This interest is evident in several of the poems on the course – for example, 'Following' and 'The Second Voyage'. 'To Niall Woods and Xenya Ostrovskaia …' contains several allusions to Irish and Russian folk tales, and also to the Bible's Book of Ruth.

Ní Chuilleanáin has won many prestigious prizes throughout her career. Her collection, *The Sun-Fish*, won Canada's Griffin Poetry Prize, one of the most respected and financially rewarding ($75,000) poetry prizes in the world. She was awarded the O'Shaughnessy Poetry Award in 1992 by the Irish American Cultural Institute, which called her 'among the very best poets of her generation'. *The Magdalen Sermon* was also shortlisted for the Irish Times/Aer Lingus Poetry Prize and the European Literature Prize.

In addition to her poetry, Ní Chuilleanáin taught at Trinity College, progressing to become a Fellow and Dean of the Faculty of Arts. She has described how her academic and artistic careers interweave: 'There is always the rhythm of the academic year. There would always be a time around June when I would start pulling together bits of things I have written during the winter and I know I can get a bit of extra time.' She specialised in Renaissance literature, studying and teaching writers such as John Donne, another poet featured on this course. She retired

as a senior lecturer in 2011, but continues to contribute to the college in the areas of Renaissance literature, medieval literature, literary translation and comparative literature.

From the beginning, language and translation have been central to Ní Chuilleanáin's view of the world. It is hardly surprising, therefore, that one of the poems on this course is entitled 'Translation'. Ní Chuilleanáin speaks and translates from Irish, Italian, French and Latin. In 1999, along with renowned poet Medbh McGuckian, she translated Nuala Ní Dhomhnaill's *The Water Horse* from Irish to English to critical acclaim. In 2005, she was asked to translate the work of the Romanian poet Ileana Malancioiu by using cribs, or 'intermediate translations', in the English language. Instead, she learned Romanian and did the job from scratch: 'Because I have good Italian and Romanian isn't that different, I hoped it would be easy enough. And it was just when I was starting working as Dean, and I found that administration was driving me crazy. Learning a language was so different.... It was using a completely different part of my brain.'

For many years she and Macdara Woods spent long periods in Umbria in central Italy. As she puts it: 'We had been renting a house from Italian friends since 1980. Then in the late 1980s we thought we'd like a place that would be ours. We have spent long periods there: a year in 1992–3, and several months in most other years.' Ní Chuilleanáin feels that these spells in Umbria nourished her creativity: 'Often I write when I am in Italy. I travel a certain amount and I find I get ideas when I travel. You can't really sit in an airport, for instance, correcting papers. Well you can, but it's much nicer to be sitting in an airport writing poetry.'

As well as continuing to co-edit *Cyphers*, Ní Chuilleanáin has served as editor of *Poetry Ireland Review*. She has also edited several academic texts, including *Irish Women: Image and Achievement*, *The Wilde Legacy* (essays about Oscar Wilde and his family) and several volumes on the art and science of translation. Ní Chuilleanáin is a member of Aosdána, having been elected in 1996. She divides her time between Ireland and Italy.

Lucina Shynning in Silence of the Nicht

Moon shining in silence of the night
The heaven being all full of stars
I was reading my book in a ruin
By a sour candle, without roast meat or music
Strong drink or a shield from the air   [5]
Blowing in the crazed window, and I felt
Moonlight on my head, clear after three days' rain.

I washed in cold water; it was orange, channelled down bogs
Dipped between cresses.
The bats flew through my room where I slept safely.   [10]
Sheep stared at me when I woke.

Behind me the waves of darkness lay, the plague
Of mice, plague of beetles
Crawling out of the spines of books,
Plague shadowing pale faces with clay   [15]
The disease of the moon gone astray.

In the desert I relaxed, amazed
As the mosaic beasts on the chapel floor
When Cromwell had departed, and they saw
The sky growing through the hole in the roof.   [20]

Sheepdogs embraced me; the grasshopper
Returned with lark and bee.
I looked down between hedges of high thorn and saw
The hare, absorbed, sitting still
In the middle of the track; I heard   [25]
Again the chirp of the stream running.

Annotations
Lucina Schynning in Silence of the Nicht: the opening line of the poem 'The Birth of Antichrist' by the 15th-century Scottish poet William Dunbar, in which the speaker dreams of a battle between the forces of good and evil
[9] ***cresses:*** small green plants
[17] ***desert:*** a term deriving from the Irish *díseart*. Refers to an isolated place where a hermit might retreat from the world. Sometimes abbeys and castles would be built on these sites.
[18] ***mosaic:*** a picture or pattern produced by arranging together small pieces of stone, tile or glass
[19] ***Cromwell:*** Oliver Cromwell (1599–1658), an English military and political leader who invaded Ireland in 1649 and became infamous for massacres that his troops carried out in Drogheda and Wexford.

Tease It Out

1. The poet is sleeping alone in a ruined castle at the edge of Cork city:
   - The poet imagines long-ago feasts that might have taken place here. What three things does she imagine those attending the feast to have enjoyed?
   - Does the poet herself have such comforts?
   - Consider the phrase 'crazed window'. What does it suggest about the wind on this particular night?
   - Is the roof of the castle still intact? Give a reason for your answer.
   - What book is the poet reading while in the abbey? How does it reflect her situation?
2. The poet bathes in an outdoor pool or stream. What colour is the water? What has given it this colour?
3. Did the poet feel secure while she slept in this ruined building?
4. What animal was in the room with her when she awoke?
5. The poet's father is dying in hospital.
   - What does the phrase 'waves of darkness' suggest about her emotional response to this development?
   - What three different kinds of 'plague' does the poet mention?
   - What do these thoughts of disease and infestation suggest about her state of mind?
   - Which phrase indicates that these bleak thoughts and mental images were suggested by a book she has read over the years?
6. The moon is thought to sometimes regulate the human psyche. What does the phrase 'disease of the moon gone astray' suggest about the poet's psyche on this particular evening?
7. In the winter of 1649, Cromwell's men occupied many buildings in the vicinity of Cork city, including this particular castle.
   - What damage did they do to the chapel of the castle before they departed?
   - Can you suggest why they might have done this?
   - How is the chapel floor decorated?
   - How does the poet personify this decoration?
8. What impact does being in this 'desert' have on the poet's state of mind?
9. Which phrases suggest that the poet feels a sense of oneness with the natural world?
10. Which phrases suggest that the poet is looking at the natural world in a new way?
11. **Class Discussion:** Where is the hare sitting? How is it behaving? In what sense might the poet consider the hare as a source of inspiration?

Exam Prep

1. **Personal Response:** Try to envisage the castle and the 'desert' Ní Chuilleanáin describes in this poem. Do you think you could feel 'relaxed' and 'amazed' in such an environment? Give a reason for your answer.
2. **Class Discussion:** 'The poet feels cleansed and restored having cast off all human comforts and got back to nature'. Discuss this statement as a class.
3. **Theme Talk:** 'In Ní Chuilleanáin's poetry, nature, and thoughts of nature, provide solace in even the bleakest moments'. Write a paragraph in which you discuss 'Lucina Schynning' and 'The Second Voyage' in light of this statement.

Language Lab

1. 'Ní Chuilleanáin uses strange and startling imagery to convey a troubled state of mind'. Write a paragraph in response to this statement.
2. **Class Discussion:** Ní Chuilleanáin took her title and opening lines from a poem by William Dunbar. Why do you think these phrases from Dunbar spoke to her at this particular moment in her life?
3. How would you describe or characterise the atmosphere in the first eleven lines of the poem? Which images in particular contribute to or generate this particular atmosphere? Would you agree that there is a shift in atmosphere towards the end of the poem?
4. Would you classify this poem overall as optimistic or pessimistic? Give a reason for your answer.

The Second Voyage

Odysseus rested on his oar and saw
The ruffled foreheads of the waves
Crocodiling and mincing past; he rammed
The oar between their jaws and looked down
In the simmering sea where scribbles of weed defined [5]
Uncertain depth, and the slim fishes progressed
In fatal formation, and thought
If there was a single
Streak of decency in these waves now, they'd be ridged
Pocked and dented with the battering they've had, [10]
And we could name them as Adam named the beasts,
Saluting a new one with dismay, or a notorious one
With admiration; they'd notice us passing
And rejoice at our shipwreck, but these
Have less character than sheep and need more patience. [15]

I know what I'll do he said;
I'll park my ship in the crook of a long pier
(And I'll take you with me he said to the oar)
I'll face the rising ground and walk away
From tidal waters, up riverbeds [20]
Where herons parcel out the miles of stream,
Over gaps in the hills, through warm
Silent valleys, and when I meet a farmer
Bold enough to look me in the eye
With 'where are you off to with that long [25]
Winnowing fan over your shoulder?'
There I will stand still
And I'll plant you for a gatepost or a hitching-post
And leave as for a tidemark. I can go back
And organise my house then. [30]

But the profound
Unfenced valleys of the ocean still held him;
He had only the oar to make them keep their distance;
The sea was still frying under the ship's side.
He considered the water-lilies, and thought about fountains [35]
Spraying as wide as willows in empty squares,
The sugarstick of water clattering into the kettle,
The flat lakes bisecting the rushes. He remembered spiders and frogs
Housekeeping at the roadside in brown trickles floored with mud,
Horsetroughs, the black canal, pale swans at dark; [40]
His face grew damp with tears that tasted
Like his own sweat or the insults of the sea.

Annotations

[1] *Odysseus:* hero of Greek mythology, who fought in the epic Trojan War and was known for his cleverness and cunning. Homer's epic poem The *Odyssey* describes his ten-year journey home from that conflict.

[2] *ruffled:* resembling lacy frilly material, or hair through which hands have been run

[3] *mincing:* walking in an exaggeratedly dainty manner

[5] *simmering:* agitated, heated almost to boiling point, filled with pent-up emotion

[11] *as Adam named the beasts:* In the Bible, Adam, as the first human being, was given the task of choosing a name for each species of animal.

[17] *crook:* bend, angle

[21] *parcel out:* share, divide among themselves

[26] *Winnowing fan:* an implement used by farmers to separate wheat from chaff

[28] *hitching-post:* a post used for tethering a horse

[29] *tide mark:* the sea's water will mark the oar's wood, indicating the tide's highest point

[31] *profound:* deep

[37] *sugarstick:* confectionery like a stick of rock or candy cane

[38] *bisecting:* cutting in half

Tease It Out

1. Google the mythical character of Odysseus and answer the following questions:
   - What was the name of his island home?
   - How long did he spend fighting in the Trojan War?
   - How long did it take him to get home after the war concluded?
   - Mention one of the adventures he experienced during his journey home.
2. In this poem, Odysseus is alone. What do you think might have happened to his crew?
3. What kind of vessel do you imagine him to be sailing? Are there clues in the poem as to the nature of this craft?
4. What does the term 'simmering' suggest about the ocean's surface? Is it calm or choppy and disturbed?
5. Mention two things that Odysseus can perceive when he looks into the water's depths.
6. Odysseus claims that the waves lack 'decency'. Why is this?
7. Group Discussion: Work in small groups to answer the following questions.
   - In what sense does Odysseus want to be like the biblical character of Adam?
   - How would Odysseus react?
   - How would such waves react to his present predicament?
   - Is any of this possible? Give a reason for your answer.
8. What do Odysseus' thoughts about the waves suggest about his mental state? Rank the following in order of plausibility:
   - Isolation has driven him insane. He now thinks that waves have minds and lives of their own.
   - He is extremely bored and indulges in a flight of fancy to pass the time.
   - His years of voyaging by sea have left him with an irrational resentment of the ocean.
9. To who or what is Odysseus speaking in the second stanza? What does this suggest about his mental state?
10. Describe in your own words where he imagines leaving his boat.
11. Mention three things he imagines seeing as he journeys inland. Who does he imagine meeting? What indicates that this person has never seen the ocean?
12. What does he imagine doing with the oar? To what use would the oar be put by the local people after Odysseus himself departs?
13. Odysseus snaps out of his daydream about a journey inland. Which phrase conveys the terrible reality of his current situation?
14. Which phrase indicates that Odysseus has been sailing for so long that he now hates water in all its forms?
15. Does he think that water can ever be escaped? How does he respond to this realisation?

Exam Prep

1. **Personal Response:** Odysseus is one of the great heroes of Greek mythology. However, is the figure in this poem a heroic one? Do you think that the Odysseus presented here is still the same soldier who set out for Troy all those years ago? In each case, give a reason for your answer.
2. **Class Discussion:** 'This poem is a powerful study of isolation and its effects on a human being's mental state'. Write two paragraphs in response to this statement in which you reference specific lines and phrases.
3. **Theme Talk:** 'Odysseus, like many figures in Ní Chuilleanáin's poetry, is ultimately motivated by devotion to his family'. Write a paragraph in which you agree or disagree with this statement.

Language Lab

1. Odysseus imagines meeting a farmer as he journeys inland.
   - For what would the farmer mistake his oar?
   - A prophet had told Odysseus that only when such a mistake occurred would he be able to return home and live in peace. Which phrase indicates this?
   - Is such a mistake ever likely to occur? Give a reason for your answer.
2. Lines 35 to 40 mention no fewer than eight instances of water. List them in your own words. How many similes or metaphors can you identify in these lines?
3. Why do you think the poem is called 'The Second Voyage'? What might have been Odysseus's first voyage?
4. Watch Video 25, which shows how Odysseus has been represented in literature, art, and cinema over the ages. How does Ní Chuilleanáin's portrayal of Odysseus compare? Why do you think the poet was drawn to Odysseus? What is it about this character that she finds most fascinating? Give a reason for your answer.

137

Deaths and Engines

We came down above the houses
In a stiff curve, and
At the edge of Paris airport
Saw an empty tunnel
–The back half of a plane, black   [5]
On the snow, nobody near it,
Tubular, burnt-out and frozen.

When we faced again
The snow-white runways in the dark
No sound came over   [10]
The loudspeakers, except the sighs
Of the lonely pilot.

The cold of metal wings is contagious:
Soon you will need wings of your own,
Cornered in the angle where   [15]
Time and life like a knife and fork
Cross, and the lifeline in your palm
Breaks, and the curve of an aeroplane's track
Meets the straight skyline.

The images of relief: [20]
Hospital pyjamas, screens round a bed
A man with a bloody face
Sitting up in bed, conversing cheerfully
Through cut lips:
These will fail you some time.   [25]

You will find yourself alone
Accelerating down a blind
Alley, too late to stop
And know how light your death is;
You will be scattered like wreckage,   [30]
The pieces every one a different shape
Will spin and lodge in the hearts
Of all who love you.

Annotations

[7] **Tubular:** long, round, and hollow like a tube

[15] **Cornered:** trapped

[17] **lifeline:** in palm-reading, a person's lifeline is thought to suggest their health and vitality. It can also predict how long a person will live.

[27-28] **blind/ Alley:** a dead end, a cul-de-sac

[32] **lodge:** become fixed or embedded

Tease It Out

1. The poet recalls landing in Paris airport:
   - How does she describe the plane's trajectory on its final approach?
   - The wrecked plane had been on fire. Which phrases indicate this?
   - Had this fire occured recently? Give a reason for your answer.
   - What metaphor does the poet use to describe the back half of the wrecked plane?
2. The poet recalls sitting onboard the return flight to Ireland just before take-off:
   - What are the weather conditions like?
   - What would you expect to hear over the plane's 'loudspeakers' before take-off?
   - What does the poet claim to have heard instead? Did she really hear this?
   - What does this suggest about her state of mind just before take-off?
3. The poet, as she sits on the runway, finds herself imagining being onboard a plane that is about to crash:
   - Where is the 'curve' of the plane's trajectory taking it?
   - Which phrase suggests that the poet would be trapped and utterly powerless at such a moment?
   - **Class Discussion:** What is suggested by the crossing of life and time?
   - Suggest why we might need 'wings of [our] own' at such a moment.
4. As she sits on the runway, the poet thinks about 'images of relief'.
   - What three images does she mention?
   - Why might each of these images be associated with 'relief'?
   - What indicates that the man 'Sitting up in bed' has been through an ordeal?
   - **Class Discussion:** The poet suggests that these images will eventually 'fail'. Is she saying that a) these images will no longer have a calming effect or b) that everyone eventually finds themselves beyond medical care?
5. The poet thinks of how each of us must eventually face the moment of our death:
   - In what sense will each of us be 'alone' at this moment?
   - **Class Discussion:** All deaths, according to the poet, can be compared to a car accelerating into a wall. Does this claim strike the class as a reasonable one?
   - What extraordinary metaphor is used to describe the effects of our deaths on those who love us?
   - The poet describes death as very 'light'. Does this suggest a) that no human life matters very much or b) that dying is easy?

Exam Prep

1. **Personal Response:** 'This poem provides an everyday moment of panic that many people, even experienced flyers, can experience before a plane takes off'. Write a paragraph in response to this statement.
2. **Class Discussion:** Consider the poem's title. In what different ways are the ideas of engines and of death combined in the poet's mind? What attitude towards machines and technology does the poem display?
3. **Theme Talk:** 'In 'Deaths and Engines' the poet approaches the reality of death with a mixture of fear and acceptance'. Write a paragraph in response to this statement?

Language Lab

1. The poet says that the 'cold of metal wings is contagious'. What do you think the 'metal wings' represent? Rank the following in the order you consider most relevant:
   - When we touch metal objects, we feel cold.
   - There is something lifeless and soulless about metal objects. When we are close to them we feel lifeless and souless too.
   - There is something particularly lifeless or sinister about aeroplanes which makes us feel inhuman.
2. **Class Discussion:** Comment on the poet's use of pronouns. What does the use of the pronoun 'you' imply about her understanding of death? Who might the pronoun 'we' refer to in the poem's opening lines? Does she ever use the pronoun 'I'?

Street

He fell in love with the butcher's daughter
When he saw her passing by in her white trousers
Dangling a knife on a ring at her belt.
He stared at the dark shining drops on the paving-stones.

One day he followed her   [5]
Down the slanting lane at the back of the shambles.
A door stood half-open
And the stairs were brushed and clean,
Her shoes paired on the bottom step,
Each tread marked with the red crescent   [10]
Her bare heels left, fading to faintest at the top.

Annotations
[6] *shambles:* slaughterhouse
[11] *crescent:* a half-moon shape

Tease It Out

1. What colour clothing did the young woman wear?
2. What did she carry on her belt?
3. What substance did she leave behind her as she walked along the street?
4. What indicates that the young woman works in her father's business?
5. Which phrase indicates that the man saw the young woman on a regular basis?
6. What did he decide to do 'one day'?
7. **Class Discussion:** Was this a spontaneous decision or a pre-meditated one?
8. Suggest why the young woman might live and/or work near the shambles.
9. 'A door stood half-open'. Does this door lead to the woman's home or her place of work, or both?
10. What items does she leave at the door?
11. What mark does she leave on each step of the stairway?
12. Describe in your own words how these marks were created?
13. Suggest why these marks were 'faintest at the top'.

Exam Prep

1. **Personal Response:** The poem ends with the man looking in the 'half-open door':
    - What do you imagine might have happened next?
    - Pick three emotions that he might have experienced while he stood there.
    - What is your opinion of the man's behaviour?
2. **Class Discussion:** 'Even familiar streets and familiar people contain mysteries, hidden lives we only occasionally glimpse'. Discuss this statement as a class in relation to 'Street' and other poems by Ní Chuilleanáin.
3. **Theme Talk:** 'Ní Chuilleanáin's poetry explores love in all its forms'. Do you think it is fair to refer to 'Street' as a love poem? What sort of love does it describe?
4. **Exam Prep:** 'Ní Chuilleanáin presents us with narratives or stories that are tantalisingly incomplete, giving glimpses into the lives of others and leaving us wondering what happens next'. Write an essay in response to this statement, making reference to 'Street' and at least three other poems on your course.

Language Lab

1. What impression do you get of the butcher's daughter from the hints provided in the poem? Are we given any indications as to her lifestyle and personality?
2. How would you describe the atmosphere of this poem? Does the atmosphere change as the poem progresses? Give a reason for your answer.
3. This short poem contains a series of striking and memorable images? Identify two images that you found particularly vivid and interesting, and give a reason for your selection.

141

Fireman's Lift

I was standing beside you looking up
Through the big tree of the cupola
Where the church splits wide open to admit
Celestial choirs, the fall-out of brightness.

The Virgin was spiralling to heaven,   [5]
Hauled up in stages. Past mist and shining,
Teams of angelic arms were heaving,
Supporting, crowding her, and we stepped

Back, as the painter longed to
While his arm swept in the large strokes.   [10]
We saw the work entire, and how the light

Melted and faded bodies so that
Loose feet and elbows and staring eyes
Floated in the wide stone petticoat
Clear and free as weeds.   [15]

This is what love sees, that angle:
The crick in the branch loaded with fruit,
A jaw defining itself, a shoulder yoked,

The back making itself a roof
The legs a bridge, the hands   [20]
A crane and a cradle.

Their heads bowed over to reflect on her
Fair face and hair so like their own
As she passed through their hands. We saw them
Lifting her, the pillars of their arms   [25]

(Her face a capital leaning into an arch)
As the muscles clung and shifted
For a final purchase together
Under her weight as she came to the edge of the cloud.

Parma 1963-Dublin 1994

Annotations

Fireman's Lift: a technique allowing one person to carry another; the carried person is placed across the shoulders of the carrier.

[2] *cupola:* dome, in this case that of Parma Cathedral. The ceiling of the dome features a massive fresco by the Italian painter Correggio (1489-1534).

[3] *church splits wide open:* a metaphor for the intensely realistic light depicted in the painting

[4] *Celestial choirs:* groups of angels depicted in the painting

[5] *Virgin was spiralling to heaven:* The painting depicts the miracle of the Assumption, the ascension of the Virgin Mary, body and soul, into heaven at the conclusion of her earthly existence.

[8-9] *we stepped // Back:* The poet and her mother visited the cathedral in 1963.

[9] *as the painter longed to:* Correggio

[14] *petticoat:* a woman's underskirt, a metaphor for the church's dome

[17] *crick:* a cramp or spasm caused by muscular strain

[22] *Their heads bowed:* refers to the angels

[28] *purchase:* grip

Tease It Out

1. The poet is 'standing beside' her mother.
   - The poet compares the cathedral's dome, or 'cupola', to a 'big tree'. What visual similarity might there be between these two very different things?
   - The poet claims to be looking 'through' the cupola. Is this really happening? Which is she attempting to convey here?
   - In lines 3 and 4, what metaphor is used to describe the extraordinary light in Correggio's painting?
   - What are the angels doing? What phrases indicate the great physical effort they're expending?
   - The Virgin travels upwards 'in stages'. What is the reason for this gradual progress?
2. '[H]is arm swept in the large strokes'. This phrase describes the artist at work. What image or impression of Correggio does it create?
3. What, according to the poet, did the painter long to do while he worked on the mural? Why do you think he might have longed to do this? Is such a desire possible to satisfy?

4. The poet focuses on the angels depicted in the mural:
   - How do the angels use their backs, legs and hands to help the Virgin upwards? Describe in your own words the actions that they take.
   - What type of harness is a yoke? How do you imagine a shoulder being 'yoked' as part of such an effort?
   - 'A jaw defining itself'. What is happening to increase the definition of this angel's features?
   - According to line 12, what effect does the light in the painting have on the angels' bodies?
   - How do the angels react to the Virgin as she passes 'through their hands' on her journey?
5. Do the Virgin and the angels look the same? Give a reason for your answer.
6. What is the final 'purchase' referred to at the end of the poem? Could the word 'purchase' have more than one meaning here?
7. Where is the Virgin at the poem's conclusion? What is about to happen to her now?

Exam Prep

1. **Personal Response:** This poem remembers the poet's mother and was written shortly after her death. Do you think the mother's presence and personality are felt throughout the poem? Give a reason for your answer.
2. **Class Discussion:** 'The crick in the branch loaded with fruit'. Consider a branch that's straining and suffering under the weight of the fruit it has produced. Would you agree that this serves as a powerful symbol for the hard work of loving, helping and supporting those around us?
3. **Theme Talk:** 'This poem celebrates art more than religion.' Write a paragraph either agreeing or disagreeing with this statement. Having considered the poem carefully, do you imagine Ní Chuilleanáin to be a particularly religious person?
4. **Exam Prep:** 'Ní Chuilleanáin uses inventive language to stimulate both our thoughts and our emotions'. Write a short essay in response to this statement, making reference to this poem and three others on your course.

Language Lab

1. What is the fireman's lift and when is it used? Why do you think the poet chose this title for her poem? Is it a surprising title? Is it an appropriate one? Give reasons for your answers.
2. Google Correggio's fresco 'Assumption of the Virgin'. Is the poem accurate in its portrayal of the mural? Would you agree that the poet captured the spirit of the painting? Refer to specific lines of the poem in your answer.
3. The angels' eyes, feet and elbows are described as 'Loose' elements that 'Floated' within the painting. Try to visualise what Ní Chuilleanáin is depicting here. Write a couple of lines that describe it in your own words.

All For You

Once beyond the gate of the strange stableyard, we dismount.
The donkey walks on, straight in at a wide door
And sticks his head in a manger.

The great staircase of the hall slouches back,
Sprawling between warm wings. It is for you.   [5]
As the steps wind and warp
Among the vaults, their thick ribs part; the doors
Of guardroom, chapel, storeroom
Swing wide and the breath of ovens
Flows out, the rage of brushwood,   [10]
The roots torn out and butchered.

It is for you, the dry fragrance of tea-chests
The tins shining in ranks, the ten-pound jars
Rich with shrivelled fruit. Where better to lie down
And sleep, along the labelled shelves,   [15]
With the key still in your pocket?

Annotations

[3] *manger:* a trough from which animals feed

[4] *slouches:* reclines, leans back

[5] *Sprawling:* spreading out over a large area in an untidy or irregular way

[5] *wings:* sections of the house

[6] *wind and warp:* twist and turn

[7] *vaults:* underground rooms used for storage; arched roofs

[7] *ribs:* arches of masonry which form the framework on which a vaulted ceiling rests

[8] *guardroom:* room where guards or soldiers are stationed

[10] *brushwood:* small pieces of wood that have broken off trees and bushes

[13] *ranks:* neat rows

Tease It Out

1. The speaker has arrived at the stableyard of a large house:
   - Is she travelling alone?
   - By what means did she travel here?
   - **Class Discussion:** Has she ever been in this house before?
   - Are there any signs that her arrival was expected?
2. Describe the entrance hall's staircase in your own words.
3. What indications are there that this home is very large and very grand?
4. The speaker and her companion enter the building's 'vaults'. Where do you imagine these vaults are located?
5. What are the vaults' 'thick ribs', as referred to in line 7?
6. What indicates that the vaults are an extensive maze of rooms and passageways?
7. What metaphor is used to describe the heat emanating from the ovens?
8. What type of fuel do the ovens burn?
9. List the different items contained in the storeroom.
10. Where does the speaker suggest her companion should sleep?
11. **Class Discussion:** The speaker mentions a 'key' possessed by her companion. What in your opinion might this key unlock?
12. Write a paragraph describing how you imagine the key came to be in the companion's possession.
13. **Group Discussion:** Do you think it's strange that the speaker and her companion encounter no one else as they venture through the stableyard and mansion? Suggest different reasons why no one else seems to be present.

Exam Prep

1. **Personal Response:** What in your opinion is the nature of the relationship between the speaker and her companion? Does the fact that they're both riding on a single donkey suggest anything about their ages and the relationship that might exist between them?
2. **Class Discussion:** Consider the phrase 'It is for you.'
   - Is the speaker addressing a) her companion, b) herself, c) the reader or d) someone else entirely?
   - What does the term 'It' refer to?
   - Suggest why Ní Chuilleanáin chose to repeat this particular phrase.
3. **Theme Talk:** Ní Chuilleanáin has described 'All For You' as a love poem of sorts. Which lines and phrases, in your opinion, most effectively convey this emotion? In what ways does 'All For You' differ from a typical love poem?
4. **Exam Prep:** 'Ní Chuilleanáin presents us with segments of mysterious stories that leave us both enchanted and disturbed'. Write an essay in response to this statement, making reference to 'All For You' and three other poems on your course.

Language Lab

1. Watch Video 24, in which Ní Chuilleanáin reads and speaks about 'All For You'.
   - What provided Ní Chuilleanáin's original spark of inspiration for the poem?
   - **Class Discussion:** To what extent is the house in the poem the same house in which Ní Chuilleanáin herself grew up?
   - What effect did Ní Chuilleanáin wish to convey through her depiction of the house's ovens?
   - What trope common to many fairy tales does Ní Chuilleanáin refer to in the video?
   - Do you agree that the description of the doors 'Of guardroom, chapel, storeroom' contributes to this fairy tale atmosphere?
2. 'This poem conjures a most mysterious atmosphere, depicting a house that has endless passageways, rooms of every conceivable function and secrets that will not easily be discovered'. Write a paragraph in response to this statement.

Following

So she follows the trail of her father's coat through the fair
Shouldering past beasts packed solid as books,
And the dealing men nearly as slow to give way –
A block of a belly, a back like a mountain,
A shifting elbow like a plumber's bend –   [5]
When she catches a glimpse of a shirt-cuff, a handkerchief,
Then the hard brim of his hat, skimming along,

Until she is tracing light footsteps
Across the shivering bog by starlight,
The dead corpse risen from the wakehouse   [10]
Gliding before her in a white habit.
The ground is forested with gesturing trunks,
Hands of women dragging needles,
Half-choked heads in the water of cuttings,   [15]
Mouths that roar like the noise of the fair day.

She comes to where he is seated
With whiskey poured out in two glasses
In a library where the light is clean,
His clothes all finely laundered,   [20]
Ironed facings and linings.
The smooth foxed leaf has been hidden
In a forest of fine shufflings,
The square of white linen
That held three drops   [25]
Of her heart's blood is shelved
Between the gatherings
That go to make a book –
The crushed flowers among the pages crack
The spine open, push the bindings apart.   [30]

Annotations

[3] *dealing men:* men buying and selling animals

[5] *plumber's bend:* a curved piece of pipe used in plumbing

[7] *skimming:* moving quickly and lightly

[10] *wakehouse:* a house that is in mourning, holding a wake for a family member who has passed away

[11] *habit:* a long, loose garment worn by a member of a religious order

[15] *cuttings:* holes in the bog where turf has been removed

[16] *fair day:* a day when the people of a town gather to buy and sell animals, goods and other produce

[21] *facings:* pieces of fabric at the edges of a garment

[22] *foxed leaf:* a page of a book where one corner has been turned down

[23] *fine shufflings:* papers shuffled on a desk

[27] *gatherings:* a group of sheets of paper folded in half; a number of gatherings are bound together to produce a finished book.

[31] *spine:* the back portion of a book's cover, which is visible when the book is shelved

[31] *bindings:* the glue or stitching that holds the pages of a book together

Tease It Out

1. A young woman is at a cattle fair when she sees (or thinks she sees) her recently deceased father:
   - What simile does she use to describe the manner in which the cattle are packed together?
   - The men that are buying and selling cattle are all physically imposing. Which phrases suggest this?
   - **True or false:** She finds it easy to make her way through these 'dealing men'.
   - Can she see her father clearly through the crowd?
   - What does the term 'skimming' suggest about the manner in which the father moves?
2. The young woman leaves the fair and follows her father (or the ghost of her father) across a bog:
   - Which phrase indicates that she follows him through the night?
   - Which phrase indicates that it is very cold?
   - The ground of the bog's surface is covered with 'trunks'. Do you visualise the trunks of trees or the torsos of human bodies?
   - The bog's surface also features strangely disembodied hands. What are these hands doing?
   - What bizarre sight does the young woman see in the holes created by turf-cutting? What sound issues from these holes?
   - She encounters a zombie-like entity 'risen from the wakehouse'. What is it wearing?
   - **True or false:** This entity is present for her entire journey across the bog.
3. The young woman finally catches up with her father in what seems to be some sort of library:
   - Which phrase indicates that the father expects the young woman's arrival?
   - **Class Discussion:** One particular page (one 'foxed leaf') has been hidden in the shuffled papers on the father's desk. What do you think might have been written on this page?
   - What marks can be seen on the piece of 'white linen'?
   - Where has this piece of linen been stashed away?
   - One book in the library has 'crushed flowers' pressed between its pages. What effect do the flowers have on this volume?

Exam Prep

1. **Personal Response:** What does the evidence in the poem suggest about the answers to the following questions:
   - Did Ní Chuilleanáin and her own father have a close relationship?
   - How did the poet and her father bond?
   - Did she find her father's passing easy to come to terms with?
2. **Class Discussion:** The symbolism at the conclusion of the poem is mysterious and open to interpretation. What, in the opinion of the class, is represented by the 'foxed leaf', the 'square of white linen' and the 'crushed flowers'?
3. **Theme Talk:** 'Ní Chuilleanáin presents us with gapped and fractured narratives that invite the reader to fill in the missing pieces'. Discuss this statement in relation to 'Following', 'Street', 'All For You' and 'The Second Voyage'.
4. **Exam Prep:** 'Ní Chuilleanáin's demanding subject matter and formidable style is challenging but ultimately highly rewarding'. In response to this statement, write an essay in which you make reference to 'Following' and three other poems on the course.

Language Lab

1. The term 'Following' has several different meanings. Which is most appropriate to your understanding of the poem?
2. The father is a stylish and meticulous dresser. Which phrases indicate this? What other hints do we get about his lifestyle, interests and personality?
3. 'The "dealing men" are heavy and crude, while the father is light and refined'. Write a paragraph in response to this statement.
4. **Class Discussion:** 'In fairy tales, as in dreams, characters think nothing of suddenly shifting from one environment to a very different one. When they reach the new location, though, they often find that their arrival there is expected'. To what extent does this statement apply to 'Following'? Could it apply to any other poem by Ní Chuilleanáin on the course?
5. Is 'Following' best described as a ghost story or a fairy tale? Give a reason for your answer.

Kilcash
From the Irish, c. 1800

What will we do now for timber
With the last of the woods laid low –
No word of Kilcash nor its household,
Their bell is silenced now,
Where the lady lived with such honour, [5]
No woman so heaped with praise,
Earls came across oceans to see her
And heard the sweet words of Mass.

It's the cause of my long affliction
To see your neat gates knocked down, [10]
The long walks affording no shade now
And the avenue overgrown,
The fine house that kept out the weather,
Its people depressed and tamed;
And their names with the faithful departed, [15]
The Bishop and Lady Iveagh!

The geese and the ducks' commotion,
The eagle's shout, are no more,
The roar of the bees gone silent,
Their wax and their honey store [20]
Deserted. Now at evening
The musical birds are stilled
And the cuckoo is dumb in the treetops
That sang lullaby to the world.

Even the deer and the hunters [25]
That follow the mountain way
Look down upon us with pity,
The house that was famed in its day;
The smooth wide lawn is all broken,
No shelter from wind and rain; [30]
The paddock has turned to a dairy
Where the fine creatures grazed.

Mist hangs low on the branches
No sunlight can sweep aside,
Darkness falls among daylight [35]
And the streams are all run dry;
No hazel, no holly or berry,
Bare naked rocks and cold;
The forest park is leafless
And all the game gone wild. [40]

And now the worst of our troubles:
She has followed the prince of the Gaels –
He has borne off the gentle maiden,
Summoned to France and to Spain.
Her company laments her [45]
That she fed with silver and gold:
One who never preyed on the people
But was the poor souls' friend.

My prayer to Mary and Jesus
She may come safe home to us here [50]
To dancing and rejoicing
To fiddling and bonfire
That our ancestors' house will rise up,
Kilcash built up anew
And from now to the end of the story [55]
May it never again be laid low.

Annotations

Kilcash: 'Kilcash' is translated from an Irish poem written in the 18th century, a time when the country was under English domination. The original has been set to music and is still a well-known song. At this time, Kilcash, near Clonmel, County Tipperary, was the site of a great castle and estate. The poem remembers Margaret Butler, also known as Lady Iveagh, who had been Lady of Kilcash Castle. She protected the people of Kilcash and the surrounding area from the worst excesses of English rule.

[1] *What will we do now for timber:* After Lady Iveagh's death, the estate of Kilcash fell into the hands of the British government. Its woods were chopped down and their timber exported to England.

[8] *the sweet words of Mass:* At this time, the Catholic religion was banned in Ireland. Masses and other religious services could only be conducted in secret.

[15] *the faithful departed:* a phrase from the Catholic Mass that describes those who've passed away while remaining loyal to the Catholic faith

[31] *paddock:* horses' enclosure

[40] *game:* animals hunted for sport or food

[42] *prince of the Gaels:* Irish chieftains who fled to Europe

[43] *the gentle maiden:* refers to the concept of Irish freedom

[55] *the end of the story:* the end of time

Tease It Out

1. What has happened to the woodlands of Kilcash?
2. Why is there now 'No word' of Kilcash's former owners? What do you think has happened to them?
3. 'Their bell is silenced now'. What do you think was the purpose of this bell? Why has it now been silenced?
4. Why did earls come 'across oceans' to visit Kilcash?
5. What clues do we get in the second stanza about how the Kilcash estate looked in its prime?
6. What has happened to its gates and avenues?
7. Why might the walks through the estate now be unshaded?
8. What effect have these developments had on the poet's state of mind?
9. Why do you think the people of Kilcash are 'depressed and tamed'? Who has tamed them?
10. List the different birds mentioned in Stanza 3. Describe the sound that each one makes.
11. According to the poet, these sounds are 'no more' to be heard in Kilcash. Is this because the birds have left the estate? Or are they still present but refusing to sing? Support your answer with reference to the text.
12. What happened to the estate's beehives?
13. Who, according to the speaker, looks down on Kilcash 'with pity'? Does it surprise you that these figures would feel pity for the people of the estate and the surrounding area? Explain your answer.

14. What has happened to the 'smooth wide lawn'? What do you think has permitted this damage to occur?
15. What animals once grazed on the estate's paddock? What grazes there now? Why has this change occurred?
16. In Stanza 6, the poet mentions three strange phenomena that have occurred in and around the estate.
    - Describe each one in your own words.
    - Would you characterise these descriptions as realistic or outlandish?
    - Would you agree that they describe the poet's state of mind rather than the physical reality of the estate?
17. Who or what is the 'gentle maiden' referred to in the sixth stanza?
18. In line 45, to whom does the word 'company' efer?
19. The poet believes that a free Ireland was a happy and prosperous Ireland. Which lines and phrases convey this?
20. Describe in your own words what the poet prays for in the final stanza.
21. What would be the reaction of Ireland's people if this prayer were granted?
22. What is her hope for Kilcash house?
23. What, in this context, do you understand by the phrase 'the end of the story'?

Exam Prep

1. **Personal Response:** What impression do you get of Lady Iveagh from reading the poem's opening stanzas? Write a brief description of this formidible woman in your own words.
2. **Class Discussion:** Why might the speaker associate 'the sweet words of Mass' with Kilcash? Does it surprise you that Mass might have been said in a castle rather than in a church? Is there a historical explanation for this?
3. **Class Discussion:** The speaker says that Kilcash will 'rise up' once more. Did this actually happen? What is the status of Kilcash today?
4. **Exam Prep:** 'Ní Chuilleanáin explores both the past and the present, using language that is both intriguing and disturbing'. Write a short essay in reponse to this statement, making reference to 'Kilcash' and three other poems on your course.

Language Lab

1. Stanza 6 features a great deal of personification:
    - Who is the 'prince of the Gaels'? Is more than one person being referred to here?
    - The prince has 'borne off' or carried away the 'gentle maiden'. Where have they gone?
    - What historical event or events is being referred to here?
    - Why do you think the speaker refers to this series of events as 'the worst of our troubles'?
    - What did the 'gentle maiden' once give to her 'company'?
    - What does this suggest about the poet's view of Ireland before these disastrous events?

Translation
for the reburial of the Magdalenes

The soil frayed and sifted evens the score –
There are women here from every county,
Just as there were in the laundry.

White light blinded and bleached out
The high relief of a glance, where steam danced   [5]
Around stone drains and giggled and slipped across water.

Assist them now, ridges under the veil, shifting,
Searching for their parents, their names,
The edges of words grinding against nature,

As if, when water sank between the rotten teeth   [10]
Of soap, and every grasp seemed melted, one voice
Had begun, rising above the shuffle and hum

Until every pocket in her skull blared with the note –
Allow us now to hear it, sharp as an infant's cry
While the grass takes root, while the steam rises: [15]

> Washed clean of idiom • the baked crust
> Of words that made my temporary name •
> A parasite that grew in me • that spell
> Lifted • I lie in earth sifted to dust •
> Let the bunched keys I bore slacken and fall •   [20]
> I rise and forget • a cloud over my time.

Annotations

Translation: converting words or text from one language into another; altering or transforming; transfering remains from one grave to another.

Magdalenes: inmates of asylums run by the Catholic Church for so-called 'fallen' women. These operated throughout Ireland in the 19th and 20th centuries. Inmates were required to work unpaid in the laundries attached to the asylums. The asylums initially focused on reforming prostitutes. However, their remit gradually expanded to include women and girls who were sexually promiscuous, who became pregnant before marriage or who simply proved troublesome to their parents. Such women were confined to the asylums against their will. The last Magdalene laundry closed in 1996.

reburial: In 1993, builders discovered a mass grave containing the bodies of 155 inmates in the grounds of a Dublin convent. These remains were cremated and reburied in Glasnevin cemetery. This poem was written for and read out at the reburial cemetery.

[1] *frayed:* loosened or pulled apart

[1] *sifted:* sieved

[1] *evens the score:* smoothes out marks and indentations; restores justice and balance

[16] *idiom:* a person's unique and individual manner of speaking; a person's or community's natural manner of speaking or expression

[18] *parasite:* a creature that lives inside another creature, usually at its host's expense

[20] *slacken:* loosen

Tease It Out

1. The poet depicts the scene in Glasnevin cemetery:
   - Which phrase indicates that the gravediggers have been busy?
   - **True or false:** Only women from the Dublin area were committed to this particular laundry.
   - Consider the term 'score' in line 1. Would you agree that more than one meaning of this term might be relevant here?

2. The poet describes the laundry where the inmates worked:
   - **Class Discussion:** Consider the phrase 'high relief of a glance'. What feature of the laundry is the poet referring to here?
   - What happened to this image over a number of years?
   - What other physical feature of the laundry is mentioned?
   - Which poetic device is used to describe the behaviour of steam in the laundry room? (Hint: it starts with a 'p'!)
   - In Stanza four, what indications are we given of the harsh conditions that existed in the laundry?
   - What metaphor is used to describe the worn bars of soap with which the Magdalenes laboured?

3. The poet focuses on the reburied inmates:
   - They are described as 'ridges under the veil'. Under what veil do they now reside?
   - The poet describes how their remains go 'shifting' through the soil of the cemetery. What are they searching for?
   - In what sense might these women have been deprived of their names? Is there more than one sense in which this might be true?

4. Consider the phrase 'As if … one voice/ Had begun':
   - What does the poet imagine happening in the laundry all those years ago?
   - 'Allow us now to hear it'. What does the poet imagine her audience hearing? Does she mean this in a literal or in a metaphorical sense?
   - Which phrase indicates that the Magdalene felt liberated and empowered by her outburst?
   - What does the poet imagine issuing from the Magdalenes' freshly dug grave? Is this image realistic or fantastical?

5. The poem's last six lines seem to be spoken by one of the inmates:
   - In line 16, the Magdalene mentions the language that was used to control and diminish her. What three metaphors are used to describe this oppressive language?
   - **Class Discussion:** The inmate says that she was given a 'temporary name'. What does this suggest about life in the laundry?
   - The Magdalene claims that now she has been 'washed clean' of this oppressive language. How might this have happened?
   - 'I rise and forget'. Is the poet referring to the afterlife here, to the Magdalene's soul or spirit? Or can we interpret this phrase in a broader sense?
   - Which image suggests that Ireland will be haunted by this scandal for a long time to come?

Exam Prep

1. **Personal Response:** Words can harm us just as badly as violence or confinement'. Write three paragraphs discussing 'Translation' in light of this statement.

2. **Class Discussion:** Ní Chuilleanáin suggests that we can somehow 'hear' the Magdalenes and calls on us to 'Assist them now'. But how is this possible? What does the poem call on us to do in this regard?

3. **Theme Talk:** 'Ní Chuilleanáin is a poet who often proceeds by way of image rather than through story or argument.' Compare and contrast 'Translation' with 'Following' in light of this statement.

4. **Exam Prep:** 'Ní Chuilleanáin tells fascinating stories, often examining themes that are relevant to contemporary Ireland, in a style that is both beautiful and mysterious.' Write a short essay in response to this statement, making reference to 'Translation' and three other poems.

Language Lab

1. Look up the word 'Translation' in your dictionary. What different meanings does it have? Is 'Translation' an appropriate title for this poem? Consider the various references to language in the poem before you answer.

2. This poem uses many images associated with laundry and with washing. Identify as many as you can. Choose the one you consider most memorable or effective and explain your choice.

3. Imagine you were present during the reburial ceremony for which Ní Chuilleanáin wrote the poem. Write a diary entry recording your experiences.

The Bend in the Road

This is the place where the child
Felt sick in the car and they pulled over
And waited in the shadow of a house.
A tall tree like a cat's tail waited too.
They opened the windows and breathed   [5]
Easily, while nothing moved. Then he was better.

Over twelve years it has become the place
Where you were sick one day on the way to the lake.
You are taller now than us.
The tree is taller, the house is quite covered in   [10]
With green creeper, and the bend
In the road is as silent as ever it was on that day.

Piled high, wrapped lightly, like the one cumulus cloud
In a perfect sky, softly packed like the air,
Is all that went on in those years, the absences,   [15]
The faces never long absent from thought,
The bodies alive then and the airy space they took up
When we saw them wrapped and sealed by sickness
Guessing the piled weight of sleep
We knew they could not carry for long;   [20]
This is the place of their presence: in the tree, in the air.

Annotations
[11] *green creeper:* plants that grow up and along the walls of a house
[13] *cumulus:* dense white fluffy cloud

Tease It Out

1. The first six lines describe an occasion when the poet and her family were on a trip to 'the lake':
   - Why did they have to pull over and stop?
   - How does the poet convey the fact that the nearby house was very large?
   - Did the poet and her family get out of the car, or did they remain in the car?
   - How does the poet describe the nearby tree? To what does she compare its shape? Describe in your own words how you picture or imagine this tree.
   - **Class Discussion:** '[W]hile nothing moved'. Is the poet decribing a) the weather conditions on this day, b) the quietness of the road or c) the family's behaviour as they sat in the car?
   - What sort of road do you imagine this to be? Is it a rural or an urban road? Give a reason for your answer.
2. The poet recalls this moment twelve years later:
   - How do the family now refer to or characterise the place where they had to stop?
   - What changes have taken place over the 'twelve years' since they stopped along this road?
   - What does the poet say has not changed about the place?
3. The poet compares 'all that went on' over this twelve-year period to a cloud in the sky:
   - Describe in your own words the sky and the cloud that the poet imagines.
   - To what do you think the 'absences' might be a reference? Is the poet describing friends and relatives who have passed away, or is she referring to those who live far away and seldom get a chance to visit? Give a reason for your answer.
   - **True or false:** The poet seldom thinks about these people.
   - How does the poet characterise the manner in which 'sickness' can take hold of us? What metaphor does she use to describe this?
   - The poet speaks of the 'weight of sleep'. Why do you think she describes sleep as something heavy and burdensome to those who are very sick?

Exam Prep

1. **Personal Response:** Can you think of a particular location or place that you associate with feelings of peace and calm? Write a poem or prose piece in which you describe the features and atmosphere of this place.
2. **Class Discussion:** Why do you think this particular place has remained important or significant to the poet? Do you think it was the beauty and serenity of the location that caught her imagination, or do you think it reminds her of a time in her life when she was very content and happy?
3. **Theme Talk:** "The Bend in the Road' is a wonderful celebration of the importance of family and shared experiences'. Write a paragraph in response to this statement.
4. **Exam Prep:** 'Ní Chuilleanáin uses images from the natural world to explore complex emotional states.' Discuss this statement making reference to 'The Bend in the Road' and at least two other poems on your course.

Language Lab

1. 'The poem's title describes not only the road where the poet and her family stopped but also serves as a metaphor for the manner in which we can never be sure of what the future holds'. Write a paragraph in response to this statement.
2. Discuss the different references to weight and weightlessness that feature in the poem. What different things does the poet describe as having little or no weight? What does the poet describe as heavy or burdensome?
3. How would you characterise the poem's atmosphere? Is there a change in atmosphere at any point?

On Lacking the Killer Instinct

One hare, absorbed, sitting still,
Right in the grassy middle of the track,
I met when I fled up into the hills, that time
My father was dying in a hospital –
I see her suddenly again, borne back   [5]
By the morning paper's prize photograph:
Two greyhounds tumbling over, absurdly gross,
While the hare shoots off to the left, her bright eye
Full not only of speed and fear
But surely in the moment a glad power,   [10]

Like my father's, running from a lorry-load of soldiers
In nineteen twenty-one, nineteen years old, never
Such gladness, he said, cornering in the narrow road
Between high hedges, in summer dusk.
The hare   [15]
Like him should never have been coursed,
But, clever, she gets off; another day
She'll fool the stupid dogs, double back
On her own scent, downhill, and choose her time
To spring away out of the frame, all while   [20]
The pack is labouring up.
The lorry was growling
And he was clever, he saw a house
And risked an open kitchen door. The soldiers
Found six people in a country kitchen, one   [25]
Drying his face, dazed-looking, the towel
Half covering his face. The lorry left,
The people let him sleep there, he came out
Into a blissful dawn. Should he have chanced that door?
If the sheltering house had been burned down, what good   [30]
Could all his bright running have done
For those that harboured him?
And I should not
Have run away, but I went back to the city
Next morning, washed in brown bog water, and   [35]
I thought about the hare, in her hour of ease.

Annotations

Killer Instinct: a ruthless determination to win or achieve one's goals

[1] ***absorbed:*** engrossed, in a state of focus or concentration

[5] ***borne back***: carried back, reminded

[11] ***gross:*** large or oversized; also brutish or oafish

[12] ***nineteen twenty-one:*** during the Irish War of Independence

[13] ***cornering:*** taking a corner at speed

[16] ***coursed:*** pursued

[21] ***labouring up:*** struggling up

Tease It Out

1. The poet remembers a time when she 'fled up into the hills'.
   - What terrible event was she trying to get away from?
   - Where was the hare sitting when the poet encountered it? Did the poet's arrival cause it to move?
   - Consider the term 'absorbed'. What does it suggest about the hare's appearance and demeanour?
   - Do you think these events took place a long time ago or in the relatively recent past? Give a reason for your answer.
   - Would you agree that the poet still feels guilty because she fled into the hills? Is she right to feel this way? Give a reason for your answer.
2. 'I see her suddenly again'. What reminds the poet of these long-ago events?
3. Working in small groups, consider the poet's description of the 'prize photograph':
   - Which phrase indicates that the greyhounds look ridiculous to the poet?
   - Which phrase indicates that the hare has escaped their clutches?
   - Which phrase indicates the hare's alertness and quickness of thought?
   - **Class Discussion:** The poet also detects a look of 'glad power' in the hare's eye. How could the hare possibly feel gladness at such a trying time? And where does its sense of 'power' come from?
   - Do you think the poet approves of the sport of hare coursing? Give a reason for your answer.

- **Class Discussion:** Consider the phrase 'spring away out of the frame'. What 'frame' is being referred to here? Where is the hare springing from? And where is it springing to?
4. What conflict was taking place in Ireland during 1921?
5. What age was the poet's father in the summer of that year?
6. **Class Discussion:** Based on your reading of the poem, do you think the poet's father was involved in the conflict? Or was he an innocent bystander? What words and phrases led the class to its conclusion?
7. The poet's father found himself pursued by a 'lorry-load of soldiers'.
   - Consider the verb 'cornering'. What does it suggest about the manner in which the poet's father was moving?
   - What emotion did the poet's father feel as he was being pursued? Does this surprise you?
   - Where did the father go in an effort to evade his pursuers?
   - What effort did the father make to disguise his appearance?
   - The poet says her father's strategy was risky. According to lines 29 to 32, what might have gone wrong?
8. Consider the phrase 'blissful dawn'. What does it suggest about the father's emotions when he left the farmhouse?

Exam Prep

1. **Personal Response:** The poet describes how she found herself thinking about the hare after she 'went back to the city'. Did the memory of the hare bring her a) calmness and comfort or, b) a sense of nostalgia or c) feelings of anxiety and insecurity?
2. **Class Discussion:** 'This poem deals with the strange reality that we often feel most alive in stressful situations, when our very lives are under threat.' Would you agree?
3. **Theme Talk:** The 'killer instinct' has been defined as 'a ruthless determination to survive, succeed or win'. Which figures in the poem display such an instinct? Which lack it? Did the poet herself display such a mentality when her father was dying?
4. **Exam Prep:** 'Ní Chuilleanáin, ultimately, is a love poet. She uses rich and inventive language to explore love in all its forms'. Write an essay in response to this statement in which you make reference to 'On Lacking the Killer Instinct' and three other poems on the course.

Language Lab

1. **Class Discussion:** The poet describes how she stripped off and washed herself in a stream filled with water from the bogs. What might have motivated this rather unusual behavior?
2. 'The poet draws a parallel between the pursuit of her father and the pursuit of the hare'. Write a paragraph in response to this statement.
3. Imagine you are the poet's father. Write a diary entry describing the events of that night in 1921 from your own point of view.
4. 'In this poem Ní Chuilleaáin weaves several very different threads of narrative into a coherent whole'. List the different narrative threads that feature in this poem. Then write at least two paragraphs responding to this statement.

To Niall Woods and Xenya Ostrovskaia, married in Dublin on 9 September 2009

When you look out across the fields
And you both see the same star
Pitching its tent on the point of the steeple —
That is the time to set out on your journey,
With half a loaf and your mother's blessing.   [5]

Leave behind the places that you knew:
All that you leave behind you will find once more,
You will find it in the stories;
The sleeping beauty in her high tower
With her talking cat asleep   [10]
Solid beside her feet — you will see her again.

When the cat wakes up he will speak in Irish and Russian
And every night he will tell you a different tale
About the firebird that stole the golden apples,
Gone every morning out of the emperor's garden,   [15]
And about the King of Ireland's Son and the Enchanter's Daughter.

The story the cat does not know is the Book of Ruth
And I have not time to tell you how she fared
When she went out at night and she was afraid,
In the beginning of the barley harvest,   [20]
Or how she trusted to strangers and stood by her word:
You will have to trust me, she lived happily ever after.

Annotations

Niall Woods: the poet's son

Xenya Ostrovskaia: the poet's daughter-in-law

[5] *With half a loaf and your mother's blessing:* reference to the English folktale 'The Red Ettin'

[14] *firebird that stole the golden apples:* reference to the Russian fairy tale 'Tsarevitch Ivan, the Firebird and the Grey Wolf'

[16] *King of Ireland's Son and the Enchanter's Daughter:* reference to the Irish folktale 'Fedelma, the Enchanter's Daughter'

[17] *Book of Ruth:* The Book of Ruth features in the Old Testament of the Bible. Ruth lived in the land of Moab. When her husband died, she made the following promise to her mother-in-law Naomi: 'Wherever you go, I will go; wherever you lodge, I will lodge; your people shall be my people, and your God my God'. Naomi decided to return to her native land of Israel. Ruth, true to word, went with her. They settled near Bethlehem, where Ruth found work helping with the harvest. At first Ruth found Israel to be a strange and alienating environment. But she eventually found love and happiness in her new home.

[19] *When she went out at night:* One evening Ruth ventured out to the household of a man named Boaz in the hope that he would take her as his wife. After a number of complications, she and Boaz were happily married.

Tease It Out

1. The poem tells the story of two lovers who set out to find one another:
   - The lovers set out at the same time, each from his or her community. What signals that their respective journeys must commence?
   - Do you get the impression that the lovers have met before?
   - Do you get the impression that their communities are close together or far apart? Give a reason for your answer.
   - Do their mothers approve or disapprove of these journeys?
2. Each of the lovers takes 'half a loaf' on his or her journey. Why do think they do this? Rank the following in order of plausibility:
   - Both couples came from very poor households and half a loaf of bread was the only provisions they could afford for their journey.
   - They knew their journey would be a short one and that they didn't need much food.
   - The two half-loaves symbolise how the lovers are destined to be together. It's only by combining with one another that they can be truly whole.
3. Which phrase indicates that the lovers, once they find each other, will set up home in a new community, somewhere in between their respective homelands?
4. What role, according to the poet, will stories play for the lovers as they begin their new life together?
5. Where, according to the poet, does Sleeping Beauty lie as she slumbers?
6. What is unusual about Sleeping Beauty's cat?
7. **Class Discussion:** 'You will see her again'. What does this suggest about the relationship between the couple's story and the tale of Sleeping Beauty? Can you suggest when the couple might have encountered the Sleeping Beauty story for the first time?
8. The talking cat steps out of the lovers' storybook and into their real lives. How do you think the couple responded to this extraordinary event? Suggest three adjectives that might describe their reaction.
9. What two languages does the talking cat speak?
10. What will the talking cat do for the lovers every evening?
11. **Group Discussion:** Research the story of the 'Emperor and the Firebird' and the story of the 'King of Ireland's Son and the Enchanter's Daughter'.
    - Working as a group, write a paragraph for each story in which you summarise its main events.
    - Can you identify one similarity and one difference between the two stories?
    - The talking cat will tell the couple many stories. Why do you think the poet chose to focus on these two?
    - How do they relate to the couple's situation?

Exam Prep

1. **Personal Response:** 'This poem highlights both the excitement and the challenges of leaving one's family and homeland in order to start a new life elsewhere. It also emphasises how stories allow us to retain a link to our homelands even when we are far away'. Write a paragraph in response to this statement.
2. **Class Discussion:** 'You will have to trust me'. How would you characterise the poet's response to the fact that her son is embarking on a new life? Discuss this question as a class.
3. **Theme Talk:** 'Like Ruth, lovers must not only keep their word but also learn to trust the word of others'. Write a paragraph in response to this statement.
4. **Exam Prep:** 'Ní Chuilleanáin's poetry explores family in all its forms'. Write a short essay in reponse to this statement, making reference to the present poem and three other poems on your course.

Language Lab

1. The poet steps into her story and addresses its characters directly. What biblical story does she tell them?
2. **Class Discussion:** According to the poet, the story of Ruth is the only story unknown to the talking cat. Can you suggest why this might be the case? Does it tell us something about the special nature of this particular tale? Or is the cat's ignorance of this story simply a quirky detail?
3. Which phrase indicates that Ruth found Israel's people strange and unsettling at first? Did she manage to overcome these feelings?
4. To what extent are the couple in the poet's skillfully woven fairy story the same as the real-life Niall and Xenya? Can you identify one similarity between the real couple and the fictional one? Can you identify one major difference? How do you think Niall and Xenya must have felt when they read this poem?

Sylvia Plath

Sylvia Plath was born in Boston, Massachusetts in October 1932. Her father, Otto Plath, was a professor of entomology, the study of insects, and published an important scientific book entitled *Bumblebees and Their Ways* (His specialisation may well have influenced Plath's later interest in bee-keeping and poems such as 'The Arrival of the Bee Box'.) Plath seems to have had a happy childhood, and from the beginning it was clear that she was extremely bright and academically gifted. When she was eight years old, however, her father developed diabetes and died from complications during a surgery to amputate his foot. Plath experienced a loss of faith as a result of this tragedy.

Plath's interest in literature began at an early age, and she published her first poem in the Boston Herald when she was just eight years old. At high school, Plath excelled academically and by then had set her sights on becoming a writer. She devoted much of her spare time to reading and to writing poems and stories, a number of which were published in the school magazine. It was around this time that Plath's application to enroll in a creative-writing class conducted by the Irish writer Frank O'Connor was rejected. The rejection sent her into a black depression. She underwent a course of electroconvulsive therapy, attempted suicide by overdosing on sleeping pills, and spent several months thereafter in a psychiatric institution. Plath recovered from this

setback, however, and returned to Smith College, from which she graduated in 1955. As usual, her academic performance was exceptional, and earned her a two-year Fulbright scholarship to Cambridge University.

Plath loved Cambridge but continued to endure bouts of depression and self-loathing. In January 1956 she met Ted Hughes, a young poet who shared her hunger for literary success. The two fell in love and were married four months later. The young couple spent 1957–59 in the US. Plath taught for a while at Smith College and later did part-time secretarial work.

Plath's marriage to Hughes was turbulent. She struggled with depression and fits of writer's block, but continued to produce powerful poetry, including 'The Times Are Tidy' and 'Black Rook in Rainy Weather'. In 1959, she attended a writing class with the highly respected American poet Robert Lowell and, with Hughes, spent time at the famous artists' colony at Yaddo in New York State. These two developments that greatly contributed to her maturation as a writer.

Plath and Hughes returned to England at the end of 1959 and moved to London, where Plath gave birth to her first child, Frieda. *The Colossus*, Plath's first collection, comprising some

> **"And by the way, everything in life is writable about if you have the outgoing guts to do it, and the imagination to improvise. The worst enemy to creativity is self-doubt."**

forty poems – was published in 1960. This included such works 'The Times are Tidy' and 'Black Rook in Rainy Weather'. The British scholar, Bernard Bergonzi, described it as an 'outstanding technical accomplishment'.

In the autumn of 1961, the family relocated to what Plath described as her 'dream house' in the Devon countryside. Here, the couple wrote and shared the responsibility of looking after their baby daughter. Many of Plath's most important poems were written in Devon. That autumn she wrote 'Finisterre' and 'Mirror'. The following spring brought 'Elm' and 'Pheasant'.

Plath gave birth to a second child, Nicholas, in January 1962, but by that summer her marriage had started to collapse. Hughes became involved with another woman. Plath's anguish at this development is evident in 'Poppies in July'. The two separated that autumn, leaving Plath alone in Devon with her two children. This was an extremely difficult period in Plath's life and she became profoundly depressed. She continued to write powerful poetry, however, including 'The Arrival of the Bee Box'.

There was a marked change in Plath's output after her split from Hughes. In the aftermath of their separation, Plath penned dozens of poems that were ripe with anger and inexorable sadness. In December, Plath left behind the isolation of Devon and returned to London with her children. Her famous, semi-autobiographical novel, *The Bell Jar*, which offers a fictionalised retelling of a brief period that she spent working at *Mademoiselle* magazine's office in New York City, was published in 1963. However, the strain

of a failed marriage and the weariness of a lifelong battle with depression simply became too much for Plath. In February 1963 – just a month after *The Bell Jar* was published – Plath took her own life. She was thirty years old.

Ariel, Plath's most celebrated collection – and arguably on which her literary status largely rests – was not published until 1965, two years after her death. It featured pieces that would go on to become some of Plath's best-known poems, such as 'Poppies in July', 'Elm' and 'Morning Song'. *Ariel* received rave reviews, partly because it offered a powerful insight into Plath's darkening depression and despair.

For many readers, the poetry of Sylvia Plath will always be overshadowed by the tragedy of her suicide. It is tempting to view Plath's work as a protracted suicide note, a record of her psychological and spiritual decline. Much of Plath's mental anguish stemmed from the fear that her poetic gifts would desert her, that she would never again feel sufficiently inspired to write another poem. It is perhaps ironic, therefore, that she produced the majority of her most famous poems when she was at her lowest psychological ebb.

Plath had continued to write until the very end. 'Child', for example, was written on 28 January, just two weeks before her death. She was buried in the church of St Thomas the Apostle in Heptonstall, Yorkshire, and her headstone is inscribed with the phrase, 'Even amidst fierce flames/ The golden lotus can be planted'.

The Times Are Tidy

Unlucky the hero born
In this province of the stuck record
Where the most watchful cooks go jobless
And the mayor's rôtisserie turns
Round of its own accord.   [5]

There's no career in the venture
Of riding against the lizard,
Himself withered these latter-days
To leaf-size from lack of action:
History's beaten the hazard.   [10]

The last crone got burnt up
More than eight decades back
With the love-hot herb, the talking cat,
But the children are better for it,
The cow milks cream an inch thick.   [15]

Annotations

[4] *rôtisserie:* a cooking appliance with a rotating spit for roasting meat

[6] *venture:* a dangerous or risky undertaking

[8] *latter-days:* recent times

[10] *hazard:* threat, danger

[11] *crone:* ugly or unpleasant old woman; here meaning a witch

[13] *love-hot herb:* a herb used by the crone to produce a love potion

[13] *talking cat:* Witches were thought to be accompanied by intelligent animals known as familiars.

Tease It Out

1. Do you know what happens to a vinyl record when the record player's needle sticks in one of its grooves?
2. The province where the poet lives is likened to such a stuck record. Does this suggest a) it is a place of chaos and uncertainty, b) it is a place where nothing ever changes or c) it is a place where people really like music?
3. What do you understand by the term watchfulness? Why might watchfulness be a desirable trait for a cook?
4. The mayor of the province has a new gadget. Briefly describe in your own words what it is and what it does.
5. Can you suggest why gadgets like this might leave even the most watchful cooks 'jobless'?
6. What mythical fire-breathing creature might be described as a type of lizard?
7. In the past, brave young men made their 'careers' by taking on this creature. Based on your knowledge of fairy tales, can you suggest two or three different ways in which these warriors might have been rewarded.

8. Do you value of the province still value such heroism? Are warriors still motivated to 'ride against' the creature? In each case give a reason for your answer.
9. Describe in your own words what has happened to the creature as a result.
10. When did the province's last witch or 'crone' disappear? Who or what was the witch's companion?
11. Based on line 13, what kind of components did the witch use to make her potions?
12. Why did the people of the province burn the witch? Rank the following possible reasons in order of plausibility:
    - Her love potions were proving problematic.
    - They felt she was negatively effecting the province's children.
    - They felt she was negatively effecting the province's cattle.
13. Which phrase indicates that the province is a wealthy one, a place where people want for nothing?

Exam Prep

1. **Class Discussion:** In small groups, consider the poem's title. Mention three features you might associate with a historical period that is 'tidy'. Mention three features you might associate with times that are untidy. Are we, in present-day Ireland, living through tidy or untidy times?
2. **Personal Response:** Consider the following questions and write down your response to each:
   - Why were witches burned? Can you identify at least one alleged real-life witch who suffered such treatment?
   - What values or ideals does the witch in this poem represent?
   - What does the absence of the witch suggest about 1950s America?
   - Does the poet really believe that children are 'better off' in a society without such values?
3. **Theme Talk:** 'The poet laments that all the great threats or 'hazards' have been diminished by time's passage. There are no more epic battles to be fought'. Write a paragraph responding to the poem in light of this statement.

Language Lab

1. **Class Discussion:** This poem is a satire on 1950s America (A satire is a poem which sets out to ridicule the follies and shortcomings of a person or a society). Can you identify which lines and phrases suggest each of the following aspects of American society?
   - America's enemies are believed to be diminished or defeated.
   - America is a place that no longer values heroism.
   - Technology and automation are having a negative effect.
   - America is wealthy.
   - America is a safe place.
   - However, that safety comes at the price of boredom
2. Watch Video 26, which is titled ' Living the American Dream'. How would you characterise the lifestyle that the video showcases? What does the video suggest brings fulfillment and happiness in life? Do you think that it was this kind of life that Plath is criticising in 'The Times Are Tidy'?

Black Rook in Rainy Weather

On the stiff twig up there
Hunches a wet black rook
Arranging and rearranging its feathers in the rain.
I do not expect a miracle
Or an accident   [5]

To set the sight on fire
In my eye, nor seek
Any more in the desultory weather some design,
But let spotted leaves fall as they fall,
Without ceremony, or portent.   [10]

Although, I admit, I desire,
Occasionally, some backtalk
From the mute sky, I can't honestly complain:
A certain minor light may still
Leap incandescent   [15]

Out of kitchen table or chair
As if a celestial burning took
Possession of the most obtuse objects now and then –
Thus hallowing an interval
Otherwise inconsequent   [20]

By bestowing largesse, honor,
One might say love. At any rate, I now walk
Wary (for it could happen
Even in this dull, ruinous landscape); skeptical,
Yet politic; ignorant   [25]

Of whatever angel may choose to flare
Suddenly at my elbow. I only know that a rook
Ordering its black feathers can so shine
As to seize my senses, haul
My eyelids up, and grant
                                                                 [30]
A brief respite from fear
Of total neutrality. With luck,
Trekking stubborn through this season
Of fatigue, I shall
Patch together a content   [35]

Of sorts. Miracles occur,
If you care to call those spasmodic
Tricks of radiance miracles. The wait's begun again,
The long wait for the angel,
For that rare, random descent.   [40]

Annotations

Rook: a type of crow

[8] *desultory:* lacking enthusiasm or purpose

[10] *portent:* omen, a sign of things to come

[15] *incandescent:* glowing, incredibly bright

[18] *obtuse:* physically blunt or lacking sharp edges; stupid or slow to understand

[19] *hallowing:* making holy or sacred

[19] *interval:* a period of time

[20] *inconsequent:* unimportant

[21] *largesse:* generosity

[23] *wary:* cautious

[25] *politic:* prudent, crafty

[31] *respite:* a period of relief

[37] *spasmodic:* fitful, occasional, unpredictable

Tease It Out

1. Read the first two stanzas carefully. Describe in your own words the landscape through which the speaker is walking.
2. What time of year is it? What is the weather like?
3. Why do you think the leaves are described as 'spotted'? Could the spots that mark them be caused by more than one thing?
4. Where is the rook situated? What is it doing?
5. **Class Discussion:** In lines 3 to 18, the speaker uses three different metaphors to describe poetic inspiration:
   - She refers to something that would 'set the sight on fire/ In [her] eye'.
   - She refers to backtalk coming from the sky.
   - She refers to an 'incandescent' light that might 'leap' out of ordinary objects.
   Which of these strikes you as the most imaginative? Which makes most sense to you? Which strikes you as the least logical or reasonable?
6. The speaker also describes inspiration as a 'miracle' or 'accident'. Take each of these words and write down five other words associated with it. What does your list suggest about poetic inspiration as the speaker has presented it?

7. Based on your reading of lines 1 to 13, does the speaker expect such a 'miracle' or 'accident' to occur as she walks through this landscape?
8. The speaker walks 'wary' through the landscape. What is the reason for this wariness? What does she think 'could happen' at any moment?
9. **Group Discussion:** Consider the words 'skeptical' and 'politic'. What do these terms mean? What do they suggest about the speaker's attitude to the possibility of inspiration in this 'dull' place?
10. According to the speaker, this experience staves off the threat of 'total neutrality'. What do you think she means by 'total neutrality'? What kind of mental state is being referred to here? Do you think it is a pleasant or unpleasant one?
11. Read stanza 7 carefully and pick three words that, in your opinion, best describe the speaker's state of mind as she 'treks' along.
12. What do you think is the 'content' that the speaker aims to patch together?
13. 'The wait's begun again'. What is the speaker waiting for?

Exam Prep

1. **Personal Response:** Sylvia Plath viewed the ability to write poetry as being essential to her mental well-being. She once said, 'I don't think I could live without it. It's like water or bread, or something absolutely essential to me'. Identify three instances where the poem communicates this view.
2. **Theme Talk:** The theme of order and chaos is one that recurs throughout Plath's poetry. Would you agree that the poem presents the world as a place of randomness and chaos? The poem has a hidden rhyme scheme. Can you identify it? What does this suggest about the place of order in the world around us?
3. **Exam Prep:** 'In Plath's poetry, nature is both a source of terror and inspiration'. In response to this statement, write a short essay in which you discuss three poems by Plath on the course.

Language Lab

1. **Vivid Imagery:** 'This poem is structured around the opposition between heat and light, on one hand, and coldness and darkness, on the other'. Discuss this issue with your group and write a few lines listing where these opposites appear throughout the course of the poem.
2. Try to describe in your own words what the speaker perceives happening to the 'obtuse objects' in lines 14 and 20. Do you consider this an effective metaphor for poetic inspiration?
3. What effect does this 'celestial burning' have on periods of time that would otherwise be 'inconsequent' or totally unimportant?
4. The speaker claims to have been granted 'largesse', 'honor' and 'love' during such moments. What does this suggest about her attitude towards poetic inspiration?

Morning Song

Love set you going like a fat gold watch.
The midwife slapped your footsoles, and your bald cry
Took its place among the elements.

Our voices echo, magnifying your arrival. New statue.
In a drafty museum, your nakedness   [5]
Shadows our safety. We stand round blankly as walls.

I'm no more your mother
Than the cloud that distils a mirror to reflect its own slow
Effacement at the wind's hand.

All night your moth-breath   [10]
Flickers among the flat pink roses. I wake to listen:
A far sea moves in my ear.

One cry, and I stumble from bed, cow-heavy and floral
In my Victorian nightgown.
Your mouth opens clean as a cat's. The window square [15]

Whitens and swallows its dull stars. And now you try
Your handful of notes;
The clear vowels rise like balloons.

Annotations

[8] *distil:* to purify a liquid by heating it and condensing the resulting vapour; to extract the essence of something

[9] *effacement:* the process of being erased or obliterated

[14] *Victorian:* associated with the Victorian era of the late 19th century; in this context, old-fashioned and unglamorous

Tease It Out

1. The poet says that it was 'Love' that 'set' the baby going. What kind of love do you think the poet has in mind here?
2. The poet likens her newborn child to a 'fat gold watch'. What do you think she is seeking to convey with this comparison? Consider the following and say which you think is most accurate:
   * The child is very special and valuable.
   * The child is like a finely crafted mechanism that, once created, can run by itself.
   * The child is just another object in the world for which the poet has no special feeling.
3. The poet and her husband find themselves saying the same things over and over. Which phrase indicates this?
4. The poet compares her new baby to a 'New statue'. Does this suggest:
   * that the baby is hardly moving.
   * that she regards the baby as a magnificent work of art.
   * that she regards the baby as something alien and inhuman?
5. Does the term 'drafty museum' refer to a) the poet's house, b) a hospital ward or c) the world as a whole? Give a reason for your answer.
6. The child's vulnerability follows the parent's everywhere - they can never switch off from their duty of care to this new being. Which phrase suggests this?
7. Might we understand this phrase in different ways? What does this line as a whole suggest about the feelings of the parents at this moment in time?
8. Lines 7 to 9: The poet compares herself to a raincloud and her child to a puddle that the raincloud produces.
   * According to the poet, does the raincloud have any special relationship with the puddle?
   * What does this suggest about the poet's attitude towards her new baby?
   * How does the puddle register or display the disappearance of the raincloud?
   * How might a child be said to record the 'effacement' of its parents?
9. What pattern is on the child's bed clothes?
10. How does the poet convey the fact that she is hyper-alert and highly responsive to her child's needs?
11. The poet is awoken early in the morning to tend to her child. Which phrase indicates this?
12. The child is still getting used to expressing itself, using its mouth, its throat and vocal chords. Which phrase indicates this?
13. What does the adjective 'clear' in line 18 suggest about the poet's attitude to her newborn child?

Exam Prep

1. **Class Discussion:** The poet uses a number of non-human comparisons in order to describe her new baby. List them. What does each one suggest about her attitude towards her newborn child?
2. **Theme Talk:** Write a short essay on the depiction of femininity and motherhood in 'Morning Song'. Consider the following points:
   * The impact of pregnancy on her body and appearance.
   * The new responsibilities of motherhood.
   * The impact of parenthood on her relationship with her husband.
   * The sense that her new baby is a strange, unknowable being.
3. **Exam Prep:** 'Plath makes effective use of language to explore her personal experiences of suffering and to provide occasional glimpses of the redemptive power of love'. Write an essay in response to this statement, making reference to 'Morning Song' and at least two other poems on your course.

Language Lab

1. **Class Discussion:** 'Morning Song' is rich in simile and metaphor:
   * 'We stand around blankly as walls'. Is this a simile or metaphor? What does this suggest about the couple's attitude to their child's arrival?
   * 'A far sea moves in my ear'. What sound is being described here? How might this sound bear comparison to the noises of the ocean?
   * 'The clear vowels rise like balloons'. Is this a simile or metaphor? What are the main features and behaviours of a balloon? Which of these might be applicable to the sounds produced by an infant?
2. How does the poet describe the morning's arrival? Explain in your own words the image that she uses. Is this an example of metaphor, personification or something else entirely? Explain your answer.

Mirror

I am silver and exact. I have no preconceptions.
Whatever I see I swallow immediately
Just as it is, unmisted by love or dislike.
I am not cruel, only truthful –
The eye of a little god, four-cornered.   [5]
Most of the time I meditate on the opposite wall.
It is pink, with speckles. I have looked at it so long
I think it is a part of my heart. But it flickers.
Faces and darkness separate us over and over.

Now I am a lake. A woman bends over me,   [10]
Searching my reaches for what she really is.
Then she turns to those liars, the candles or the moon.
I see her back, and reflect it faithfully.
She rewards me with tears and an agitation of hands.
I am important to her. She comes and goes.   [15]
Each morning it is her face that replaces the darkness.
In me she has drowned a young girl, and in me an old woman
Rises toward her day after day, like a terrible fish.

Annotations

[1] *exact:* precise; to obtain or demand something from someone

[1] *preconceptions:* opinions formed before having relevant knowledge or experience

[3] *unmisted:* clear, not blurred in any way

[14] *agitation of hands:* hands that are wrung or twisted due to stress or anxiety

Tease It Out

Stanza 1

1. **Class Discussion:** What does the mirror mean by the word 'exact'? Do you think more than one meaning of this word might be intended here?
2. The mirror emphasises how it reflects an accurate and unbiased image of anyone who looks into it. Which words and phrases convey this message?
3. The mirror says that it 'swallows' whatever it sees. What do you think it means by this? Do you think it is fair to say that in this context the word 'swallow' has negative or sinister connotations?
4. **Class Discussion:** In line 5, the mirror describes itself as a kind of god-like being. In what sense might mirrors be said to function like gods in our everyday lives?
5. Write a short paragraph describing in your own words the mirror's feelings towards the speckled wall.
6. What repeatedly 'separates' the mirror from the wall?

Stanza 2

7. The mirror compares itself to a lake. Do you think this is a good or accurate comparison? What similarities, if any, are there between a mirror and a lake?
8. The mirror's owner is described as 'searching' in the mirror. What is she searching for? Are these lines literal or metaphorical? Write a short paragraph describing the woman's behaviour in your own words.
9. What do lines 13 and 14 suggest about the mirror's relationship with its owner? In what tone of voice do you imagine these lines being spoken? Are they sad or angry, pleading or sarcastic?
10. What does line 14 suggest about the owner's state of mind? Pick three words that, in your opinion, best describe her mental state and in each case give reasons for your choice.
11. The mirror claims it is 'important' to the woman. In what ways might a mirror be important to an individual? Consider here psychological as well as purely practical factors.
12. Line 16 suggests that the opposite is also true: that the woman is also important to the mirror. How does it do this?

Exam Prep

1. **Personal Response:** Imagine you are the woman in the poem. Write a few lines describing your daily routine, your mental state and your attitude towards the mirror.
2. **Class Discussion:** 'This poem highlights the special challenges faced by women in modern society'. Discuss this statement as a class.
3. **Theme Talk:** 'Plath's obsession with death comes across in the final two lines'. Write a paragraph responding to this statement.
4. **Exam Prep:** 'Plath's poetry is distinguished by its extraordinary portrayal of mental anguish'. Discuss this statement in relation to 'Mirror' and two other poems on your course.

Language Lab

1. **Class Discussion:** This poem is unusual in that it is spoken by an inanimate object.
   - What is the technical term for this poetic technique?
   - Do you think the use of this literary device is successful or silly in 'Mirror'? Give a reason for your answer.
   - Do you imagine the mirror as a male or female character? Or do you think of it as somehow 'gender neutral'? Why?
   - The mirror stresses that it is 'not cruel'. Based on your reading of the first stanza, do you think this is a fair statement?
   - In what sense could the poem's form be said to resemble a mirror?
2. Pick out two different images from the poem. In the case of each image, say whether or not you think it is convincing and effective.

Finisterre

This was the land's end: the last fingers, knuckled and rheumatic,
Cramped on nothing. Black
Admonitory cliffs, and the sea exploding
With no bottom, or anything on the other side of it,
Whitened by the faces of the drowned.　　　　　　　　　　[5]
Now it is only gloomy, a dump of rocks –
Leftover soldiers from old, messy wars.
The sea cannons into their ear, but they don't budge.
Other rocks hide their grudges under the water.　　　　　[10]

The cliffs are edged with trefoils, stars and bells
Such as fingers might embroider, close to death,
Almost too small for the mists to bother with.
The mists are part of the ancient paraphernalia –
Souls, rolled in the doom-noise of the sea.　　　　　　　[15]
They bruise the rocks out of existence, then resurrect them.
They go up without hope, like sighs.
I walk among them, and they stuff my mouth with cotton.
When they free me, I am beaded with tears.

Our Lady of the Shipwrecked is striding toward the horizon,　[20]
Her marble skirts blown back in two pink wings.
A marble sailor kneels at her foot distractedly, and at his foot
A peasant woman in black
Is praying to the monument of the sailor praying.
Our Lady of the Shipwrecked is three times life size,　　　[25]
Her lips sweet with divinity.
She does not hear what the sailor or the peasant is saying –
She is in love with the beautiful formlessness of the sea.

Gull-colored laces flap in the sea drafts
Beside the postcard stalls.　　　　　　　　　　　　　　　[30]
The peasants anchor them with conches. One is told:
'These are the pretty trinkets the sea hides,
Little shells made up into necklaces and toy ladies.
They do not come from the Bay of the Dead down there,
But from another place, tropical and blue,　　　　　　　　[35]
We have never been to.
These are our crêpes. Eat them before they blow cold.'

Annotations

Finisterre: a region in the far edge of Brittany in north-western France. The name comes from the Latin 'finis terræ', meaning 'end of the earth'.

[1] *rheumatic:* suffering from rheumatism; stiff and immobile

[3] *Admonitory:* giving a warning

[11] *trefoils:* a three-leafed plant, such as clover

[14] *paraphernalia:* equipment, apparatus, miscellaneous items

[20] *Our Lady of the Shipwrecked:* a large statue of the Virgin Mary is located on Pointe du Raz, a headland in the Finistère region

[26] *divinity:* holiness

[31] *conches:* large snail-shaped sea shells

[32] *trinkets:* a small ornament or item of jewellery that is of little value

[34] *Bay of the Dead:* the bay overlooked by the cliffs of Finistère

[37] *crêpes:* a light, thin pancake, especially popular in the Brittany region

Tease It Out

1. What metaphor is used to describe the rocky outcrops of Finisterre?
2. **True or false:** The cliffs are presented as pleasant and inviting.
3. What literary device is used in line 4? (Hint: it starts with a 'h').
4. Which phrase indicates that the water is dark and opaque rather than shimmering and transparent?
5. Flowers grow around the cliff edge. Which phrases indicate their intricate and complex patterns? Which phrases indicate their weakness and fragility?
6. **Group Discussion:** What metaphor is used to describe the mists that drift up from the sea? Is it an effective one?
7. What happens to the speaker when she enters the mist?
8. **Group Discussion:** Why does the speaker claim to be beaded with tears when she exits the mist? Is this phrase open to more than one interpretation?
9. **Group Discussion:** Carefully reread the lines about Our Lady. What poetic device does Plath use in her depiction of this inanimate object?
10. 'Her lips sweet with divinity'. What does this suggest about the statue's facial expression?
11. Who is praying at the monument?
12. Why, according to the speaker, does Our Lady of the Shipwrecked ignore these prayers?
13. The speaker visits nearby 'postcard stalls' where little trinkets are for sale. How are these fragile souvenirs created?
14. Where do the shells used in their manufacture originate?
15. How do the peasants prevent these objects from blowing away in the 'sea drafts'?
17. What type of food do the peasants offer the speaker?

Exam Prep

1. **Personal Response:** While composing 'Finisterre', Plath was deeply concerned about the possibility of a global nuclear conflict. How does this concern colour her description of the personal experience of visiting Finisterre?
2. **Class Discussion:** Consider again Plath's description of the peasant woman and the statue. What does this suggest about Plath's attitude towards religion? Does the poem suggest that Plath believes in God? Does it suggest that she regards religion as a positive force in the world?
3. **Theme Talk:** 'In 'Finisterre', Plath uses the physical description of a landscape to illustrate her internal mental anguish'. Write a paragraph in response to this statement.
4. **Exam Prep:** 'Plath uses astonishingly vivid visual writing to explore not only the themes of death and oblivion but also that of hope'. Write a short essay in response to this statement, making reference to 'Finisterre' and two other poems on your course.

Language Lab

1. 'Finisterre', like much of Plath's poetry, is marked by its vivid and disturbing imagery.
   - What metaphor is used to describe the small rocks that protrude through the water's surface?
   - Consider the words 'cannons' and 'exploding'. What do they suggest about the manner in which the waves roll in?
   - 'Other rocks hide their grudges under the water'. What does the use of the word 'grudges' suggest about these rocks' physical features and the danger they might pose?
   - In the opening stanza, what do you think the poet means by 'wars'? Identify all the words, phrases and images she uses that are associated with war and combat.
2. Can you identify any other poems where Plath describes or mentions the sea? State in each case whether the sea is presented as a positive or negative presence.

Pheasant

You said you would kill it this morning.
Do not kill it. It startles me still,
The jut of that odd, dark head, pacing

Through the uncut grass on the elm's hill.
It is something to own a pheasant,   [5]
Or just to be visited at all.

I am not mystical: it isn't
As if I thought it had a spirit.
It is simply in its element.

That gives it a kingliness, a right.   [10]
The print of its big foot last winter,
The tail-track, on the snow in our court –

The wonder of it, in that pallor,
Through crosshatch of sparrow and starling.
Is it its rareness, then? It is rare.   [15]

But a dozen would be worth having,
A hundred, on that hill – green and red,
Crossing and recrossing: a fine thing!

It is such a good shape, so vivid.
It's a little cornucopia.   [20]
It unclaps, brown as a leaf, and loud,

Settles in the elm, and is easy.
It was sunning in the narcissi.
I trespass stupidly. Let be, let be.

Annotations

[3] *jut:* a point that protrudes or sticks out

[4] *elm's hill:* This poem was written at Court Green, in Devon, where Plath lived with her husband Ted Hughes between August 1961 and December 1962. There was a large elm tree on a hill at the back of the property.

[7] *mystical:* inclined towards spiritual or supernatural beliefs

[9] *in its element:* where it belongs

[11] *print:* snow print

[12] *tail-track:* track made by the pheasant's tail as it dragged across the snow

[12] *court:* courtyard of the property

[13] *pallor:* whiteness

[14] *crosshatch of sparrow and starling:* criss-cross pattern produced by these birds' feet in the snow

[20] *cornucopia:* an extravagant abundance, a symbol of plenty that consisted of a goat's horn overflowing with produce

[21] *unclaps:* describes how the pheasant collapses or folds its tail feathers

[23] *narcissi:* plural of narcissus, a species of white and yellow flower

Tease It Out

1. The poet and her husband have owned the pheasant for at least a number of months. Which lines in the poem tell us this?
2. What does the poet's husband intend to do with the pheasant 'this morning'? Can you suggest why he might want to take this action?
3. It seems that the pheasant spends much of its time on a hill behind the poet's house. Read the poem carefully. Can you mention three different features of this hillside?
4. What do we learn about the following features of the pheasant's appearance? In each case refer to a line or phrase from the poem:
   - The motion of the pheasant's head when it walks
   - The size of its feet
   - The colour of its tail feathers when they're up
   - The colour of its tail feathers when they're down
5. **True or false:** Say whether each of the following statements is true or false:
   - The poet is a spiritual person and feels that the pheasant has a soul or consciousness like that of a human being.
   - The poet feels it would be pointless to have more than one pheasant.
   - The poet has got used to the pheasant and no longer really notices it.

6. What is a cornucopia? Which of the pheasant's features does this unusual term refer to?
7. What do we mean when we say that something or someone is 'in its element'? Where, according to the poet, is the pheasant in its element?
8. **Group Discussion:** 'The pheasant is so confident and regal that it can seem as if this bird, rather then the poet herself, is the real owner of the house and its gardens'. Working in small groups, try to find at least four different phrases that support this statement.
9. 'Do not kill it'. Why does the poet want the pheasant to live? Rank the following in order of plausibility:
   - She is impressed by its 'kingliness', by its regal demeanour.
   - She gets a sense of pride or accomplishment from owning this bird.
   - She thinks it has a soul.
   - She's aware that this is a rare species.
   - She is overwhelmed by its physical beauty.
   - She doesn't really enjoy eating roast pheasant.
10. **Class Discussion:** 'Let be, let be'. To whom is the poet talking here? Can you suggest why this phrase is repeated?

Exam Prep

1. **Personal Response:** 'It is something… just to be visited at all'. Would you agree that these lines suggest the poet's sense of loneliness and inadequacy? Give a reason for your answer. Are there any other phrases that suggest such negative feelings?
2. **Class Discussion:** Are there any hints about the nature and status of the poet's relationship? Do she and her husband seem at odds, or are they living in perfect harmony?
3. **Theme Talk:** 'The poet finds the pheasant to be not only a beautiful but also an alien and somehow overbearing presence'. Write a paragraph in response to this statement.
4. **Exam Prep:** 'Plath's provocative imagery serves to highlight the intense emotions expressed in her poetry'. Write a short essay in response to this statement, making reference to 'Pheasant', 'Elm' and 'Finisterre'.

Language Lab

1. **Vivid Imagery:** Plath's gift for exquisite imagery is evident in lines 11 to 15?
   - In what part of the property did the pheasant's tracks appear?
   - What was the weather like?
   - Were they the only tracks visible that morning?
   - Describe in your own words the poet's reaction to this sight.

Elm

I know the bottom, she says. I know it with my great tap root:
It is what you fear.
I do not fear it: I have been there.

Is it the sea you hear in me,
Its dissatisfactions?   [5]
Or the voice of nothing, that was your madness?

Love is a shadow.
How you lie and cry after it
Listen: these are its hooves: it has gone off, like a horse.

All night I shall gallop thus, impetuously,   [10]
Till your head is a stone, your pillow a little turf,
Echoing, echoing.

Or shall I bring you the sound of poisons?
This is rain now, this big hush.
And this is the fruit of it: tin-white, like arsenic.   [15]

I have suffered the atrocity of sunsets.
Scorched to the root
My red filaments burn and stand, a hand of wires.

Now I break up in pieces that fly about like clubs.
A wind of such violence   [20]
Will tolerate no bystanding: I must shriek.

The moon, also, is merciless: she would drag me
Cruelly, being barren.
Her radiance scathes me. Or perhaps I have caught her.

I let her go. I let her go   [25]
Diminished and flat, as after radical surgery.
How your bad dreams possess and endow me.

I am inhabited by a cry.
Nightly it flaps out
Looking, with its hooks, for something to love.   [30]

I am terrified by this dark thing
That sleeps in me;
All day I feel its soft, feathery turnings, its malignity.

Clouds pass and disperse.
Are those the faces of love, those pale irretrievables?   [35]
Is it for such I agitate my heart?

I am incapable of more knowledge.
What is this, this face
So murderous in its strangle of branches?–

Its snaky acids hiss.   [40]
It petrifies the will. These are the isolate, slow faults
That kill, that kill, that kill.

Annotations

[1] *tap root:* a central root that grows vertically downwards and provides a tree with much of its nourishment

[10] *impetuously:* rashly, impulsively

[15] *arsenic:* a lethal poison, often in the form of a white powder

[18] *filaments:* slender threads or fibres

[24] *radiance:* brightness

[24] *scathe:* to harm or injure

[26] *radical surgery:* surgery that removes or restructures part of the body

[27] *endow:* to give something a quality or asset

[33] *malignity:* evil, wickedness, malice

[35] *irretrievables:* things that can never be regained

[36] *agitate:* trouble, bother

Tease It Out

1. **Group Discussion:** What does the elm tree mean when it says this root 'knows the bottom'? Can this be understood in more than one way?
2. The elm declares that it's producing a sound similar to the sea. What is happening to the elm to make it produce such a sound?
3. 'Love is a shadow'. What does this phrase suggest about the elm's attitude towards love?
4. What do lines 7 to 9 suggest about the poet's present difficulties?
5. Lines 10 to 12: The elm produces a galloping sound. How exactly is this sound produced? What does it suggest about the woman's love life? What effect, according to the elm, will this sound have on the woman's state of mind?
6. In Stanza 5, the elm describes how it has been tortured by a particular type of rain. Describe this rainfall and its consequences in your own words.
7. What impact have 'sunsets' had on the elm tree? What terrible events from history do these 'sunsets' recall?
8. What causes the elm tree to 'break up in pieces'?
9. What two torments does the moon visit upon the elm tree? Why, according to the elm tree, does the moon act in such a cruel manner?
10. 'Diminished and flat'. Is this phrase used to describe the moon or the elm tree? Give a reason for your answer.
11. The elm and the woman seem to share a strange psychic link or connection. Which phrase suggests this?
12. What does the elm's depiction of the clouds suggest about the nature of love and romance?
13. 'I am incapable of more knowledge'. What mental state does this phrase suggest? Pick three adjectives that best describe it.
14. The poem's final lines describe a 'face' that seems to appear among the elm's branches. What are the physical features of this face? What impact does it have on the speaker?

Exam Prep

1. **Personal Response:** 'This poem has elements of a horror or fantasy story, featuring a bizarre 'psychic link' between a woman and an elm tree growing in her garden.' Did you find this aspect of the poem engaging or silly and over-the-top? Give a reason for your answer.
2. **Class Discussion:** When Plath was composing 'Elm', she was very concerned about the possibility of a nuclear conflict between the Soviet Union and the United States. How is this fear evident in the poem?
3. **Theme Talk:** The poem's final lines refer to various 'faults' or failings. Write a short essay on the theme of inadequacy as it features in 'Elm' and two other poems by Plath.

Language Lab

1. 'Elm' is an intensely visual poem and contains many powerful images. Identify one image from the poem that you found memorable or vivid, and explain why you found it compelling.
2. In 'Elm', Plath's mastery of sound effects is at its greatest. Read the poem again and identify one example of each of the following: assonance, alliteration, cacophony, rhyme and repetition. Say how each contributes to the poem's mood, atmosphere or meaning.
3. Would you agree that the poem's last three stanzas seem to be spoken by the woman rather than by the elm tree? Give a reason for your answer.

The Arrival of the Beebox

I ordered this, this clean wood box
Square as a chair and almost too heavy to lift.
I would say it was the coffin of a midget
Or a square baby
Were there not such a din in it.   [5]

The box is locked, it is dangerous.
I have to live with it overnight
And I can't keep away from it.
There are no windows, so I can't see what is in there.
There is only a little grid, no exit.   [10]

I put my eye to the grid.
It is dark, dark,
With the swarmy feeling of African hands
Minute and shrunk for export,
Black on black, angrily clambering.   [15]

How can I let them out?
It is the noise that appals me most of all,
The unintelligible syllables.
It is like a Roman mob,
Small, taken one by one, but my god, together!   [20]

I lay my ear to furious Latin.
I am not a Caesar.
I have simply ordered a box of maniacs.
They can be sent back.
They can die, I need feed them nothing, I am the owner.   [25]

I wonder how hungry they are.
I wonder if they would forget me
If I just undid the locks and stood back and turned into a tree.
There is the laburnum, its blond colonnades,
And the petticoats of the cherry.   [30]

They might ignore me immediately
In my moon suit and funeral veil.
I am no source of honey
So why should they turn on me?
Tomorrow I will be sweet God, I will set them free.   [35]

The box is only temporary.

Annotations

[5] *din:* loud noise

[13] *swarmy:* moving in a vast and irregular mass

[13] *African hands:* refers to African slaves desperately reaching up towards the metal grille above the cramped hold in which they are kept while being transported by ship

[14] *shrunk for exports:* Like shrunken versions of African slaves on slave ships, the black bees have been crammed into tight spaces so that they can be transported.

[18] *unintelligible:* impossible to understand

[19] *Roman mob:* angry citizens could threaten even the rule of the Emperor himself

[21] *Latin:* language spoken in the ancient Roman Empire

[22] *Caesar:* title used by Roman Emperors

[29] *laburnum:* a tree with yellow flowers

[29] *colonnade:* a row of evenly spaced trees

[30] *petticoat:* a woman's undergarment, a skirt worn under another skirt or dress

[32] *moon suit and funeral veil:* refers to a beekeeper's protective clothing

Tease It Out

1. 'I ordered this'. Based on your reading of stanzas 1 and 2, describe the speaker's initial response to the box's arrival. Is she delighted, worried, horrified or perhaps even surprised at her own decision?
2. What metaphor does the speaker use to describe the beebox in lines 3 to 4? What does this suggest about her attitude towards the box?
3. The speaker describes the box as 'dangerous'. What dangers might the box or its contents pose to her?
4. **Class Discussion:** The speaker, however, is unable to 'keep away from it'. Why do you think this is?
5. Which line indicates that the speaker can't immediately get rid of the box?
6. **True or false:** The speaker can clearly make out the inside of the box.
7. What most striking and unusual comparison does she use to describe the bees' appearance through the grid?
8. Pick two words that in your opinion best describe the speaker's reaction to the sound emanating from the box.
9. What historical comparison does the speaker use to describe the bees and their buzzing?
10. To the speaker the bees resemble 'maniacs'. What associations does the term 'maniac' have for you? Write down three other words that come to mind.
11. 'How can I let them out?' Why do you think the speaker is reluctant to release the bees? What options does she feel she has in relation to this box, which frightens her so much?
12. What transformation does the speaker imagine in lines 28 to 30?
13. 'They might ignore me'. Why does she feel the bees won't 'turn on' her if she releases them?
14. What does she finally decide to do with the box and the bees it contains?

Exam Prep

1. **Class Discussion:** Plath once said: 'I believe that one should be able to control and manipulate experiences, even the most terrific, like madness, being tortured, this sort of experience, and one should be able to manipulate these experiences with an informed and an intelligent mind'. Do you think it's fair to say that this poem is about confronting and mastering one's fears? Discuss this question as a class.
2. **Theme Talk:** 'Plath's obsession with death and oblivion is once again on display in this poem. She envisages herself slipping away from this human life, transforming into a tree, wearing a funeral veil like a mourner or a 'moon suit' like an astronaut ready to depart this world'. Do you agree with this reading? Give reasons for your answer.
3. **Exam Prep:** Write a short essay discussing how effectively Plath uses a range of images to develop her themes and add drama to her poetry. In your answer refer to 'The Arrival of the Beebox' and three other poems on the course.

Language Lab

1. Like much of Plath's best work, this poem is intensely visual. Identify two images from the poem that struck you as vivid or memorable, and say why.
2. It has often been suggested that in this poem the beebox functions as a symbol or metaphor for the poet's own mind. Do you think this is a reasonable view? What features of the box might be said to resemble or represent the human mind's deepest aspects?
3. Watch Video 27, in which Iseult Gillespie discusses why she thinks you should read Sylvia Plath. What is it about Plath's poetry that Gillespie finds most interesting? Do you agree with her interpretation of Plath's work, based on your reading of the poems on your course?

Poppies in July

Little poppies, little hell flames,
Do you do no harm?
You flicker. I cannot touch you.

I put my hands among the flames. Nothing burns.
And it exhausts me to watch you   [5]
Flickering like that, wrinkly and clear red, like the skin of a mouth.

A mouth just bloodied.
Little bloody skirts!
There are fumes that I cannot touch.

Where are your opiates, your nauseous capsules?   [10]
If I could bleed, or sleep! –
If my mouth could marry a hurt like that!

Or your liquors seep to me, in this glass capsule,
Dulling and stilling.

But colorless. Colorless.   [15]

Annotations
[10] *opiates:* a family of highly addictive drugs derived from opium, which is in turn derived from the opium poppy
[10] *nauseous:* causing nausea
[10] *capsules:* refers to the poppy's seed pods; the milky fluid that seeps from these pods is used to produce opium.
[13] *liquors:* intoxicating drinks

Tease It Out

1. **Class Discussion:** What would you expect from a poem titled 'Poppies in July'? What sort of imagery and atmosphere does the title suggest to you?
2. The poet addresses the flowers, speaking directly to them. How would you characterise or describe her tone in the first two lines. Consider the following and say which seems most accurate:
   - She is being humorous.
   - She is angry and upset.
   - She is being objective and factual.
   - She is being hysterical.
3. The poet compares the flowers to 'little hell flames'?
   - What does this suggest about the colour of the poppies?
   - What does it suggest about the manner in which the flowers move?
   - What does the comparison suggest about the poet's state of mind?
4. 'I cannot touch you'. What is the poet trying to touch here? Is it the flowers, or is she trying to touch the flames that she associates with the flowers? Give a reason for your answer.
5. 'Nothing burns'. Do you think the poet is relieved or disappointed that this is the case? Give a reason for your answer.
6. What effect does looking at the poppies have upon the poet?
7. What simile does the poet use to describe the poppies in lines 6 to 7? What metaphor does she use in line 8?
8. The poet would like to indulge in narcotics that are derived from poppies. Which lines indicate this?
9. What does the term 'liquors' suggest about the poet's attitude towards these narcotics?
10. What does the term 'seeps' suggest about the manner in which they will enter her body?
11. What effect will these 'liquors' have on her, according to line 14?
12. Does the term 'colorless' refer to a) the opiates, b) the poet herself or c) the manner in which the poet will perceive the world once the opiates have taken effect?
13. What does this desire for colourlessness suggest about the poet's state of mind?

Exam Prep

1. **Personal Response:** Based on your reading of the poem, what do you think is causing the poet the greatest amount of distress? Rank the following in the order you consider most relevant:
   - She feels numb and exhausted.
   - She feels that her relationship with her husband is not working.
   - She feels overwhelmed by the demands of her life and the world around her.
2. **Class Discussion:** 'The poet is trapped in a state of unfeeling numbness and can see only two ways out: a narcotic slumber or intense physical pain'. Discuss this statement as a class. Does it fit with the class's reading of the poem?
3. **Exam Prep:** 'The poetry of Sylvia Plath is intense, deeply personal and quite disturbing'. Write a short essay in response to this statement, making reference to 'Poppies in July' and two other poems on the course.

Language Lab

1. Poppies have long been used as a symbol of sleep, peace and death. How are these symbolic associations evident in Plath's poem?
2. The poem features a number of instances of euphony and cacophony. Identify two instances of each and say how they contribute to the poem's mood and atmosphere.
3. The poet uses the term 'marry' when she describes being hit in the mouth. What does this suggest about her personal life?
4. The poet imagines herself being placed inside a 'glass capsule'. What fairy tale does this call to mind? What does it suggest about the poet's state of mind?
5. **Class Discussion:** 'In this poem, Plath exhibits an almost masochistic desire to experience pain'. Discuss this statement as a class. Identify two lines or phrases in the poem that support this statement and two lines or phrases that can be used against it.

Child

Your clear eye is the one absolutely beautiful thing.
I want to fill it with color and ducks,
The zoo of the new

Whose names you meditate –
April snowdrop, Indian pipe,   [5]
Little

Stalk without wrinkle,
Pool in which images
Should be grand and classical

Not this troublous   [10]
Wringing of hands, this dark
Ceiling without a star.

Annotations

[5] *April snowdrop:* white flower that blossoms in late spring

[5] *Indian pipe:* plant native to temperate regions of Asia and America

[10] *troublous:* agitated

[11] *wringing of hands:* clasping and twisting of hands, indicating anxiety and distress

Tease It Out

1. The poet describes her child's eye as 'clear' in the opening line. What do you think she means by this? Consider the following and say which you think are relevant:
   - The child's eye is clear in colour and complexion.
   - The child's eye sees everything clearly, undistorted by thought and experience.
   - The child's eye is the one thing the poet knows and understands completely.
2. To the poet, there is nothing more innocent than a child. Which phrase indicates this?
3. To a child, everything around it is a source of wonder and excitement. Which phrase indicates this?
4. The poet would like to show her child many beautiful and wonderful things. List three of the things she mentions.
5. **Class Discussion:** How do children respond when they learn the names of new items and objects? In what sense might this behaviour resemble a form of meditation?
6. Consider the phrase 'Little// Stalk without wrinkle'. Is the poet describing the child herself or something she would like to show the child? Give a reason for your answer.
7. The poet compares the child's eye to a 'pool'. Is this an effective comparison in your opinion?
8. The poet wants the child to only experience things that are 'grand' and 'classical'. Take a moment to consider these terms? Can you mention two things you consider to be 'grand' and two things you consider to be 'classical'?
9. What phrase indicates that the poet is in a distressed state of mind?
10. Is the poet capable of showing the child all the things she would like to? Give a reason for your answer.

Exam Prep

1. **Personal Response:** 'Child' was written in the final weeks of Plath's life, when she was suffering from the depression that would ultimately lead to her suicide. What does the poem suggest is causing her the most anguish? Can you find any hope in this poem?
2. **Theme Talk:** Plath's poetry is very frank when dealing with the demands and difficulties of motherhood. Write a paragraph in response to this statement, in which you discuss 'Child' and 'Morning Song'.
3. **Exam Prep:** 'Feelings of mental anguish and inadequacy are central to Plath's poetry'. Discuss this statement in relation to 'Child' and three other poems on the course.

Language Lab

1. The poet uses objects or images from the natural world to convey a sense of beauty and innocence. Identify three such images and say what each might represent or symbolise for the poet.
2. 'Colour and light, and the absence of colour and light, play a significant part in this poem'. Write a short paragraph in response to this statement.
3. How would you characterise the tone of this poem? Would you agree that the tone and atmosphere shift in the poem's final stanza?
4. Consider the phrase 'dark/ Ceiling without a star'. Do you think this refers to the poet's house, the poet's state of mind or both? Give a reason for your answer.

William Butler Yeats

William Butler Yeats was born into an Anglo-Irish family in Sandymount, Dublin, on 13 June 1865. When Yeats was a child, his father, John Butler Yeats, gave up a career in law and moved the family to London to pursue his passion for painting. Although talented, John Butler Yeats was never able to make painting pay, and the family struggled financially.

In 1872, when William was seven, the family travelled to Sligo for a summer holiday, staying with his mother's family. The holiday lasted the best part of two and a half years and proved to be a vital experience for Yeats. He fell in love with the landscape and listened intently to the servants' stories of fairies. From an early age, Yeats was fascinated by both Irish legends and the occult. These memories and stories of Sligo were to remain with the poet for the rest of his life.

Back in England, Yeats struggled at school. He was considered to be 'very poor in spelling', a weakness that persisted throughout his poetic career. It was in science that he excelled. While reading his son's school report, John remarked that William would be 'a man of science; it is great to be a man of science'.

In 1880 the family moved back to Dublin, settling first in Harold's Cross and later in Howth. Yeats didn't fare any better in school in Dublin, but spent a lot of time at his father's nearby studio, where he met many of the city's artists and writers. John Butler Yeats

constantly encouraged his children to pursue ideas, philosophy and art. The entire family was highly artistic; William's brother Jack went on to become a famous painter, while his sisters Elizabeth and Susan were active in the arts and crafts world.

After finishing school in 1883, Yeats attended the Metropolitan School of Art in Dublin, now the National College of Art and Design. By then, Yeats had been writing poetry for a few years, beginning in his late teens. His early work was strongly influenced by Percy Bysshe Shelley, William Blake and other Romantic poets. His first published poem, 'The Island of Statues', appeared in the Dublin University Review in 1885.

Despite their Anglo-Irish background, Yeats' parents were broadly supportive of Irish nationalism. Yeats, in turn, was passionate about the Irish cause. In 1885, he met the Fenian activist John O'Leary, whose romanticised view of the nation struck a chord with him. O'Leary's twenty years of imprisonment and exile, his sense of patriotism, and his devotion to cultural rather than militant nationalism all held an attraction for the young Yeats. O'Leary embodied a sense of an older, romantic Ireland, one that was ancient and mysterious. Yeats termed this 'indomitable Irishry'. He would later lament O'Leary in the poem 'September 1913': 'Romantic Ireland's dead and gone,/ It's with O'Leary in the grave'.

The Yeats family moved back to London in 1887, where Yeats continued to write in earnest. In 1888, he wrote one of his most famous poems, 'The Lake Isle of Innisfree'. When this poem

"The creations of a great writer are little more than the moods and passions of his own heart, given surnames and Christian names, and sent to walk the earth."

was published in the *National Observer* in 1890, it received critical acclaim and brought Yeats' work to national attention. His first collection, *The Wanderings of Oisin and Other Poems*, was published in 1889. It drew heavily on Irish mythology and dealt with one of Yeats's most common themes: the tension between a life of action and a life of contemplation.

Yeats met the heiress and Irish nationalist Maud Gonne in 1889 when she visited the family home. He was immediately struck by Maud, and his unrequited longing for her would provide him with the inspiration for a lifetime of great love poetry. He proposed to Gonne four times and was refused on each occasion, partly because Gonne believed that Yeats's unrequited love for her inspired his greatest poetry. Gonne went on to marry the republican icon John MacBride in 1903. The marriage soon fell apart, and though Gonne did have a fleeting romance with Yeats in 1908, it never became the committed relationship he hoped for.

In 1890, Yeats joined the Order of the Golden Dawn, a secret society with initiation rites, rituals and other occult practices. His membership of this society was reflective of his lifelong interest in mysticism and the supernatural. Yeats attended séances and read widely in the mystical literature of other belief systems, such as Buddhism and Judaism. He was fascinated by the ritual and mystery of the supernatural, something which also fuelled his interest in Irish legends. That sense of ceremony and symbolic importance in the revelation of truth never left Yeats and permeates his poetry.

In 1896, Yeats met Lady Augusta Gregory, and her estate at Coole Park in Galway was to become a summer retreat for Yeats for many years. Lady Gregory encouraged Yeats's nationalism and his playwriting. Together with other writers such as J.M. Synge and Sean O'Casey, Yeats and Gregory were instrumental in founding the movement known as the Irish Literary Revival. In 1899, they established the Irish Literary Theatre for the purpose of performing Irish and Celtic plays. This led in turn to the foundation of the Abbey Theatre in 1904. Yeats' play *Cathleen Ní Houlihan*, starring Maud Gonne, was performed on the opening night.

Yeats proposed to Maud Gonne one last time in 1916, soon after John MacBride was executed for his part in the 1916 Rising. When Maud refused him, Yeats proposed to her daughter, twenty-one-year-old Iseult Gonne. When Iseult also turned him down, Yeats eventually married twenty-five-year-old Bertha Georgie Hyde-Lees at the age of fifty-one. Georgie was involved in much of Yeats's writing, and like her husband was interested in the occult. With Georgie, Yeats wrote numerous poems using an experimental process called 'automatic writing'. Georgie considered herself a medium and claimed to channel the messages of spirits in the form of symbols. Together they produced hundreds of pages' worth of poetic material, eventually published in the 1925 book *A Vision*.

The couple bought a Norman castle, Thoor Ballylee, from Lady Gregory sometime in 1916 or 1917. Their first-born, Anne, arrived in 1919, the same year that Yeats published his seventh collection of poetry, *The Wild Swans at Coole*. Their second child, Michael, was born in 1921 while the family was living in Oxford.

Yeats was appointed to the first Senate of the Irish Free State in 1922, and was reappointed for a second time in 1925. In 1923, Yeats was awarded the Nobel Prize for Literature, becoming the first Irish person to achieve that honour. The Nobel Committee remarked on his 'inspired poetry, which in a highly artistic form gives expression to the spirit of a whole nation.' Yeats could not help but associate his win with Ireland's recently-won independence, saying: 'I consider that this honour has come to me less as an individual than as a representative of Irish literature; it is part of Europe's welcome to the Free State.'

Despite ill health, Yeats remained a prolific writer. After reportedly going through an operation that restored his libido, Yeats had several affairs with younger women in his later years, among them the actress Margot Ruddock and the novelist Ethel Mannin. He died in the town of Menton in the south of France in 1939, aged seventy-three. He was initially buried nearby in Roquebrune, before being exhumed in 1948 to be brought back to Drumcliff, County Sligo. His epitaph is taken from the last lines of one of his final poems 'Under Ben Bulben': 'Cast a cold Eye/ On Life, on Death./ Horseman, pass by!'

The Lake Isle of Innisfree

I will arise and go now, and go to Innisfree,
And a small cabin build there, of clay and wattles made;
Nine bean-rows will I have there, a hive for the honey-bee,
And live alone in the bee-loud glade.

And I shall have some peace there, for peace comes dropping slow,   [5]
Dropping from the veils of the morning to where the cricket sings;
There midnight's all a glimmer, and noon a purple glow,
And evening full of the linnet's wings.

I will arise and go now, for always night and day
I hear lake water lapping with low sounds by the shore;   [10]
While I stand on the roadway, or on the pavements grey,
I hear it in the deep heart's core.

Annotations

Innisfree: a tiny uninhabited island on Lough Gill, County Sligo

[2] *Clay and wattles:* refers to an ancient construction technique known as 'wattle and daub', whereby clay is smeared over a frame of interwoven branches

[7] *a purple glow:* Innisfree comes from the Irish *Inis Fraoich*, which means 'island of heather'. Here Yeats imagines the purple heather glowing in the noon sunlight.

[8] *linnet's wings:* a linnet is a type of finch, typically brown and red-breasted

Tease It Out

1. The poet declares his intention to go and live on Innisfree. Is this a spontaneous decision or something he's been thinking about for a long time? Give a reason for your answer.
2. What ancient building process will the poet use to construct his cabin on Innisfree? Describe it in your own words.
3. The poet imagines living a self-sufficient life on the island. What different foodstuffs does he imagine growing in order to feed himself?
4. What metaphor does the poet use to describe the mist that drifts across the island each morning? Is it an effective one in your opinion?
5. Which word or phrase describes the effect of starlight as it's reflected in the waters around the island?
6. What sound fills the island as evening comes?
7. Google the Irish language origins of the name Innisfree? What does this suggest about the purple glow that fills the island each noon?
8. What sound does the poet claim to hear 'night and day'?
9. Consider his description of this sound. Do you think he finds it a pleasant one? Do you think it bothers him that he 'always' hears this sound, seemingly everywhere he goes?
10. Is he really hearing this sound or does he experience it only in his own imagination?
11. What aspect of the mind or self is suggested by the phrase 'deep heart's core'?
12. In what sort of environment is the poet at this moment? Is he happy to be where he is?

Exam Prep

1. **Personal Response:** Take a moment to visualise your own perfect getaway. It could be a real place or an imaginary one. Write a poem or a short prose piece in which you describe its most important features.
2. **Class Discussion:** The poet states three times that he will 'go' and live on Innisfree. Do you think the poet is serious about changing his life in this way or is he merely trying to convince himself that he's actually capable of such a radical move? Do you think the poet is prepared for the challenges of living a solitary, self-sufficient lifestyle?
3. **Theme Talk:** 'Innisfree is a real place, but it's also an idea, a state of mind that the speaker can access any time'. Do you agree with this statement? Write a few paragraphs in response.
4. **Exam Prep:** 'Yeats's poetry is driven by a tension between the real world in which he lives and an ideal world that he imagines'. Write a short essay in response to this statement, referring to 'Lake Isle' and at least two other poems on your course.

Language Lab

1. 'In Stanza 2, peace is depicted almost as a physical substance, 'dropping' like dew from veils of mist onto the grasses'. Do you agree with this interpretation? Write a few sentences in response.
2. 'The Lake Isle of Innisfree' uses repetition to great effect. In particular, the phrase 'I will arise and go now' has great power when repeated in the final stanza. Suggest how the meaning and tone of this line changes between Stanza 1 and Stanza 3.
3. This poem makes extensive use of assonance and alliteration to create a beguiling verbal music, such as in line 3: 'Nine bean-rows will I have there, a hive for the honey-bee'. Can you identify another example of assonance and another example of alliteration in the poem?
4. 'And I shall have some peace there'. Identify three words or phrases that emphasise the island's soothing tranquillity. Is the impression he creates of the island a realistic one, in your opinion?

September 1913

What need you, being come to sense,
But fumble in a greasy till
And add the halfpence to the pence
And prayer to shivering prayer, until
You have dried the marrow from the bone;   [5]
For men were born to pray and save:
Romantic Ireland's dead and gone,
It's with O'Leary in the grave.

Yet they were of a different kind,
The names that stilled your childish play,   [10]
They have gone about the world like wind,
But little time had they to pray
For whom the hangman's rope was spun,
And what, God help us, could they save?
Romantic Ireland's dead and gone,   [15]
It's with O'Leary in the grave.

Was it for this the wild geese spread
The grey wing upon every tide;
For this that all that blood was shed,
For this Edward Fitzgerald died,   [20]
And Robert Emmet and Wolfe Tone,
All that delirium of the brave?
Romantic Ireland's dead and gone,
It's with O'Leary in the grave.

Yet could we turn the years again,   [25]
And call those exiles as they were
In all their loneliness and pain,
You'd cry, 'Some woman's yellow hair
Has maddened every mother's son':
They weighed so lightly what they gave.   [30]
But let them be, they're dead and gone,
They're with O'Leary in the grave.

Annotations

[1] *being come to sense:* having achieved wisdom

[7] *Romantic:* passionate and idealistic; creative and imaginative; open to risk and adventure

[8] *O'Leary:* John O'Leary (1830–1907) was an Irish patriot and a mentor to Yeats

[10] *stilled:* silenced, brought to a stop

[17] *the wild geese:* Irish soldiers who left the country, often after defeat in rebellion against English rule, and served in continental European armies during the 16th, 17th and 18th centuries

[20] *Edward Fitzgerald:* (1763–1798) Irish patriot and leading figure in the United Irishmen, who fought against British rule in Ireland. Died in captivity

[21] *Robert Emmet:* (1778–1803) Irish patriot who was executed after leading an rebellion against British rule in 1803.

[21] *Wolfe Tone:* (1763–1798) Irish patriot and leader of the 1798 rebellion against British rule in Ireland. Died in captivity

[22] *delirium:* madness, condition in which one is overcome by excessive emotion

[28] *Some woman's yellow hair:* This can be read as a personification of Ireland and/or as an illusion to Yeats's beloved Maude Gonne.

Tease It Out

1. This poem is addressed to the leading businessmen of Dublin. Which phrase indicates that in Yeats's opinion, these are a mean-spirited, miserly lot?
2. Which phrase indicates that these people pray a lot?
3. Consider the phrase 'prayer to shivering prayer'. Does it suggest that
   - These people pray in churches that are cold and draughty.
   - They pray out of fear rather than true spiritual devotion.
   - They count their prayers, adding them up like coins.
4. According to line 6, what are the twin purposes of human existence and the only things the middle classes need to do?
5. Consider the poem's tone in these lines. Is it sarcastic or sincere?
6. Google the Fenian John O'Leary. What political goals did he strive for and what did his efforts cost him?
7. **Class Discussion:** Yeats associates O'Leary with a 'Romantic' vision of Ireland. What does the word 'Romantic' mean in this context?
8. How do the values embodied by O'Leary differ from those of the businessmen, as depicted in this stanza?
9. Yeats imagines these captains of industry playing as children. What, according to the poet, would interrupt their childhood games?

10. Yeats describes the great heroes of Irish history, declaring that 'They have gone about the world like wind'. Which of the following statements best sums up his meaning?
    - The heroes' names have travelled around the world, as their fame grew and word of their deeds spread.
    - The heroes themselves have travelled around the world because they were exiled from Ireland.
11. Which phrase indicates that these heroes were more interested in revolution than religion?
12. Which phrase indicates that in Yeats's opinion they were destined to die as soon as they embraced the cause of Irish freedom?
13. Does the poet feel that heroes like Emmet and Tone would be delighted with or horrified by the Ireland of 1913?
14. The poet imagines somehow calling these heroes back from the past. What image does he use to describe this feat of time travel?
15. According to Yeats, how would the businessmen who now run Ireland react to these heroes, if the heroes were summonsed and turned up in 1913.
16. Consider line 30. What did the heroes give for Ireland? According to the poet, what was their attitude to this great sacrifice they were making?
17. 'But let them be'. The poet eventually decides it's better not to 'call' these heroes from the past. Why do you think he makes this choice?

Exam Prep

1. **Personal Response:** Try to identify the three main criticisms Yeats makes of Ireland in 'September 1913'. Express each one in your own words. How many of these criticisms might equally be applied to the Ireland of today?
2. **Class Discussion:** Consider the questions below on your own for five minutes and jot down some ideas. Then compare your notes with those of the person beside you. Finally, share your ideas with the class.
   - Why does Yeats refer to the heroes as 'exiles'?
   - Might they have been exiled in more than one way?
   - Why might they have experienced 'loneliness'?
   - Why might they have experienced 'pain'?
3. **Theme Talk:** Consider Yeats's use of the term 'delirium'. Would you agree that Yeats's portrayal of these patriots isn't an entirely positive one?
4. **Exam Prep:** 'Yeats is both enticed and repelled by political violence'. Write a resonse to this statement, making reference to 'September 1913' and at least two other poems on your course.

Language Lab

1. Picture someone with his or her hands in a dirty, greasy till, fumbling to pick up a few coins. Write a few sentences describing precisely what you visualise. Is it a pleasant or an unpleasant image?
2. Who is the yellow-haired woman referred to in line 28? Is this an actual woman the heroes might have known when they were alive? Or is this woman a symbol or metaphor of some kind? Could it be a mixture of both?
3. **Class Discussion:** 'Until/ You have dried the marrow from the bone'. What precisely do we visualise happening here? What kind of approach to living does this image of a dried-up bone suggest?

The Wild Swans at Coole

The trees are in their autumn beauty,
The woodland paths are dry,
Under the October twilight the water
Mirrors a still sky;
Upon the brimming water among the stones   [5]
Are nine-and-fifty swans.

The nineteenth autumn has come upon me
Since I first made my count;
I saw, before I had well finished,
All suddenly mount   [10]
And scatter wheeling in great broken rings
Upon their clamorous wings.

I have looked upon those brilliant creatures,
And now my heart is sore.
All's changed since I, hearing at twilight,   [15]
The first time on this shore,
The bell-beat of their wings above my head,
Trod with a lighter tread.

Unwearied still, lover by lover,
They paddle in the cold   [20]
Companionable streams or climb the air;
Their hearts have not grown old;
Passion or conquest, wander where they will,
Attend upon them still.

But now they drift on the still water,   [25]
Mysterious, beautiful;
Among what rushes will they build,
By what lake's edge or pool
Delight men's eyes when I awake some day
To find they have flown away?   [30]

Annotations

Coole: Coole Park, near Gort in County Galway. Was the home of Yeats's friend, Lady Gregory, whom he visited often

[10] *mount:* take to the air

[11] *wheeling:* flying in wide circles or curves

[12] *clamorous:* noisy

[13] *brilliant:* bright, magnificent

[21] *Companionable streams:* streams where the swans can be togther

[23] *Passion or conquest:* Yeats personifies these qualities, suggesting that they follow the swans wherever they go.

Tease It Out

1. What time of the year is it, and what time of day?
2. Through what type of landscape is the poet walking? What has the weather been like?
3. The water on the lake is very calm. Which word or phrase indicates this? What does the word 'brimming' suggest about the level of water in the lake?
4. The poet describes the water 'among the stones'. How do you visualise this? Are the stones on the bank, or scattered across the lake surface?
5. How many swans are swimming on the lake, according to the poet?
6. This is not the first time the poet has counted the swans in this particular lake. How long ago did he first count them?
7. Back then, the poet saw the swans 'suddenly mount'. What process is he describing here? How do we usually use the verb 'mount'? What does the poet imagine the swans mounting?
8. What does the word 'wheeling' suggest about the swans' motion as they took flight?
9. The swans' wings made a great ruckus as they ascended. Which word suggests this?
10. What feature of the swans' appearance is suggested by the adjective 'brilliant'?
11. How does contemplating these 'brilliant' creatures make the poet feel? Pick two adjectives that best describe his mood or state of mind as he looks at the swans.
12. The poet declares that nineteen years ago he 'Trod with a lighter tread'. Why does he not move as lightly now? Is this a reference to mental changes or physical changes or both?
13. 'Their hearts have not grown old'. What does this suggest about the swans' mental vibrancy and vitality?
14. The poet imagines the swans being engaged in a series of long-term, loving relationships. Which phrase indicates this?
15. The swans, according to the poet, are capable of romantic 'Passion' and sexual 'conquest'. Does he believe that this capacity will ever diminish?
16. The poet imagines the swans leaving the lake at some future time. Where does he imagine them going once they leave? What does he imagine them doing there?
17. The poet imagines other people in these locations watching the swans. How will they react to the sight of these creatures?
18. Lines 29 to 30: The poet imagines himself looking on the empty lake after the swans have left. How do you imagine he will feel when that moment comes?

Exam Prep

1. **Personal Response:** In this poem, the poet grapples with the effects of reaching middle age. What does each of the following suggest about the stage of life in which the poet finds himself: the time of day, the time of year, the fullness of the lake, a sore heart, a heavy tread?
2. **Theme Talk:** The poet anticipates old age, which is associated with the departure of the swans. What does this image suggest about old age, as the middle-aged Yeats imagines it?
3. **Group Discussion:** The poet compares and contrasts himself with the swans throughout the poem. Form a group with three classmates. Draw two overlapping circles, labelling one 'The Poet' and the other 'The Swans'. Now categorise the following descriptions, placing those that are relevant to both in the area where the two circles overlap:

   - Imposing
   - Strong-willed
   - Untiring
   - Passionate
   - Free
   - Contented
   - Physically powerful
   - Self-pitying
   - Physically tired
   - Ageing

4. **Exam Prep:** 'Yeats uses powerful imagery to explore the harsh realities of ageing and death'. Discuss this statement in relation to this poem and to 'An Acre of Grass' and 'Sailing to Byzantium'.

Language Lab

1. How would you characterise the atmosphere of the woodland lake the poem describes? Pick out three adjectives that in your opinion best describe this setting, and in each instance support your choice with a quotation from the poem.
2. Alliteration occurs when two words in close proximity begin with the same sound, for example the 't' sound in 'Trod with a lighter tread'. Can you find two other examples of alliteration in this poem?
3. Identify three words that are repeated throughout the poem. What effect does this repetition have?
4. Consider the phrase 'Unwearied still, lover by lover'. For Yeats, the swans almost seem to be immortal, creatures somehow immune to time and change. Would you agree with this statement? Does Yeats really think that swans have such immunity? Or is he speaking in a symbolic or metaphorical fashion?

An Irish Airman Foresees His Death

I know that I shall meet my fate
Somewhere among the clouds above;
Those that I fight I do not hate,
Those that I guard I do not love;
My country is Kiltartan Cross,   [5]
My countrymen Kiltartan's poor,
No likely end could bring them loss
Or leave them happier than before.
Nor law, nor duty bade me fight,
Nor public men, nor cheering crowds,   [10]
A lonely impulse of delight
Drove to this tumult in the clouds;
I balanced all, brought all to mind,
The years to come seemed waste of breath,
A waste of breath the years behind   [15]
In balance with this life, this death.

Annotations

An Irish Airman: The poem is spoken by an Irish pilot serving with the British forces during the First World War (1914-18). It was inspired by Major Robert Gregory, the son of Yeats's great friend Lady Gregory. Major Robert served with distinction in the Royal Flying Corps before being shot down and killed on a combat mission in Italy in 1918.

[3] ***Those that I fight:*** Germany and its allies

[4] ***Those that I guard:*** the British people; the air force in which the airman serves is dedicated to their defence.

[5] ***Kiltartan Cross:*** a crossroads near Lady Gregory's home in Gort, Co. Galway

[9] ***Nor law, nor duty:*** As an Irish person, the airman is under no legal or moral obligation to fight for Britain.

[10] ***public men:*** politicians

[12] ***tumult:*** a state of confusion or disorder

Tease It Out

1. The speaker anticipates the moment of his death. What kind of death do you think he is imagining? Where does he imagine this taking place?
2. What does the word 'fate' suggest about his death?
3. How does the airman feel about those he is fighting? Why do you think he feels this way?
4. 'Those that I guard I do not love'. In which country's military is the airman serving? Why doesn't he love this country or its people?
5. Where is the airman from? What does he tell us about his native village?
6. **True or false:** The outcome of the war will have a great impact on the airman's 'countrymen'?
7. The airman mentions four different reasons why an individual might join the military. Explain each one in your own words.
8. **Class Discussion:** The airman finds delight in flying and in aerial combat. Can you suggest why these activities might bring him pleasure and excitement?
9. The airman's impulse to fly is a 'lonely' one. What do you think he means by 'lonely'? Consider the following possibilities and rank them in order of likelihood, giving reasons for your decisions:
   - He arrived at his decision alone, without consulting with others.

   - It's the only impulse affecting him.
   - Not many people share the impulse to fly, making it a lonely vocation.
   - He is alone in the cockpit and can only rely on himself.
   - He is motivated by a desire to ascend into the clouds alone, leaving the busy world of people behind.
10. What does the word 'tumult' suggest about the nature of aerial combat?
11. 'I balanced all'. What does this suggest about the process that was involved in the speaker's decision to join the air force? Do you think it took him long to reach his decision?
12. The speaker feels that his life prior to becoming a fighter pilot was pointless; life only really began when he became a fighter pilot. Which phrase captures this?
13. **True or false:** The airman is excited by the prospect of life after the war.
14. **Group Discussion:** Break into pairs and discuss the following statements:
    - The speaker feels that this dramatic, exciting death will make up for the boredom and the pointlessness of his existence up until then.
    - The speaker feels that this pointless death is a fitting end for his pointless life.
    - Which statement best captures the last line of the poem?

Exam Prep

1. **Personal Response:** Would you agree that the speaker is indifferent to the outcome of the war? If given the choice between going home and fighting for the other side, which do you think he would choose? Explain your answer.
2. **Class Discussion:** 'The speaker of the poem is essentially a thrill seeker; he has no other motivation for getting involved in the war'. Do you agree with this statement? Support your answer with lines or phrases from the poem.
3. **Theme Talk:** 'The speaker feels he has nothing but hatred and contempt for ordinary life and longs to die in order to escape it'. Write a paragraph agreeing or disagreeing with this statement. Support your answer with reference to the poem.
4. **Exam Prep:** 'Yeats, in both his life and work, exhibited great admiration for men of action'. Write a short essay in response to this statement, making reference to this poem and two other poems on your course.

Language Lab

1. 'Anaphora' is a literary device in which words at the beginning of lines or phrases are repeated. Can you identify any examples in this poem? What effect does this give?
2. Identify the rhyme scheme of this poem.
3. This is a very rhythmic poem. Is there any connection between this rhythmic effect and the relentless mechanical rhythm of an airplane's engine? What does this rhythm suggest about the airman's state of mind?
4. 'A lonely impulse of delight'. Do you think of impulses as being hard or easy to resist? Is an impulse like an addiction or a desire, or is it more like a whim? Explain your answer.

Easter 1916

I have met them at close of day
Coming with vivid faces
From counter or desk among grey
Eighteenth-century houses.
I have passed with a nod of the head   [5]
Or polite meaningless words,
Or have lingered awhile and said
Polite meaningless words,
And thought before I had done
Of a mocking tale or a gibe   [10]
To please a companion
Around the fire at the club,
Being certain that they and I
But lived where motley is worn:
All changed, changed utterly: [15]
A terrible beauty is born.

That woman's days were spent
In ignorant good-will,
Her nights in argument
Until her voice grew shrill.   [20]
What voice more sweet than hers
When, young and beautiful,
She rode to harriers?
This man had kept a school
And rode our wingèd horse;   [25]
This other his helper and friend
Was coming into his force;
He might have won fame in the end,
So sensitive his nature seemed,
So daring and sweet his thought.   [30]
This other man I had Dreamed
A drunken, vainglorious lout.
He had done most bitter wrong
To some who are near my heart,
Yet I number him in the song;   [35]
He, too, has resigned his part
In the casual comedy;
He, too, has been changed in his turn,
Transformed utterly:
A terrible beauty is born.   [40]

Annotations

Easter 1916: refers to the Easter Rising, a rebellion by about 700 Irish volunteers against British rule in Ireland. The Rising lasted six days, and sixteen of its leaders were executed in the aftermath.

[1] *I have met them:* Yeats knew several leaders of the Rising and would have met them regularly on the streets of Dublin

[10] *gibe:* an insulting remark

[12] *club:* a gentleman's club

[14] *motley:* clothing created by combining patches of many different colours; traditionally worn by the court jester

[17] *That woman:* Countess Constance Markievicz (1867–1927), a leader of the Rising

[20] *shrill:* piercing, sharp

[23] *rode to harriers:* participated in a hunt with horses and hounds

[24] *This man:* Patrick Pearse (1879–1916), a leader of the Rising and one of those executed

[25] *wingèd horse:* Pegasus, a mythological winged horse and symbol of poetry

[26] *This other:* Thomas MacDonagh (1878–1916), a leader of the Rising

[27] *Was coming into his force:* Yeats feels that MacDonagh was coming into his own as a writer when he died.

[31] *This other man:* Major John MacBride (1868–1916), a participant in the Rising and one of those executed
vainglorious: excessively vain, proud and boastful

[33-34] *He had done … heart:* MacBride was married to Maud Gonne, the woman Yeats loved, and allegedly mistreated her throughout their marriage.

Hearts with one purpose alone
Through summer and winter seem
Enchanted to a stone
To trouble the living stream.
The horse that comes from the road,   [45]
The rider, the birds that range
From cloud to tumbling cloud,
Minute by minute they change;
A shadow of cloud on the stream
Changes minute by minute;   [50]
A horse-hoof slides on the brim,
And a horse plashes within it;
The long-legged moor-hens dive,
And hens to moor-cocks call;
Minute by minute they live: [55]
The stone's in the midst of all.

Too long a sacrifice
Can make a stone of the heart.
O when may it suffice?
That is Heaven's part, our part   [60]
To murmur name upon name,
As a mother names her child
When sleep at last has come
On limbs that had run wild.
What is it but nightfall?   [65]
No, no, not night but death;
Was it needless death after all?
For England may keep faith
For all that is done and said.
We know their dream; enough   [70]
To know they Dreamd and are dead;
And what if excess of love
Bewildered them till they died?
I write it out in a verse –
MacDonagh and MacBride   [75]
And Connolly and Pearse
Now and in time to be,
Wherever green is worn,
Are changed, changed utterly:
A terrible beauty is born.   [80]

[43] *Enchanted to a stone:* made stone-like, transformed into a stone

[46] *range:* wander, roam

[51] *slides on the brim:* slips at the edge of the stream

[52] *plashes:* splashes

[68] *England may keep faith:* In 1914 the British government had promised to grant Ireland 'Home Rule', a measure of independence. This promise had been put on hold for the duration of the First World War. Yeats considers the possibility that it might still be kept.

[76] *Connolly:* James Connolly (1870–1916), socialist and trade union organiser who was among the executed 1916 leaders

Tease It Out

Lines 1 to 35

1. Watch Video 33 and explain in your own words why the Rising happened. What did those who organised it hope to achieve?

2. Yeats would run into nationalist revolutionaries on the streets of Dublin. At what time would these encounters typically occur?

3. Where do you imagine these revolutionaries worked during the day?

4. **True or false:** Yeats was always eager to stop and chat with the revolutionaries when he met them.

5. The poet thought the revolutionaries were rather ridiculous. Which phrase indicates this?

6. The poet describes how he would attend a 'club'.
   - What sort of establishment do you imagine this was?
   - What does the poet imagine sharing with his companions there?
   - Do you think the revolutionaries would attend such an establishment?

7. What is 'motley' and who typically wears it? What is Yeats suggesting about Ireland when he describes it as a place 'where motley is worn'?

8. The first part of the poem ends with the poet stating that 'All changed, changed utterly'. What do you think has changed, and what was it that brought about this change?

Lines 17 to 40

9. How has Constance Markievicz been spending her nights? What impact does this have on her voice?

10. What does the phrase 'ignorant good-will' suggest about the poet's attitude towards Markievicz's political beliefs?

11. Yeats knew Markievicz personally when she was younger. What activities does he recall her being involved in?

12. Lines 24 to 25 describe the rebel leader Padraig Pearse. What was his profession?

13. **Class Discussion:** Yeats associates Pearse with a 'winged horse'. Does this symbolise Pearse's career as a) a poet, b) a revolutionary soldier or c) a journalist?

14. Yeats expresses a high opinion of Thomas MacDonagh's abilities as a poet and thinker in lines 29 to 30. How does he convey this?

15. Lines 31 to 34: How does Yeats characterise Major John MacBride?

16. **True or false:** Yeats has no personal reason to dislike MacBride.

17. **Class Discussion:** MacBride and the other leaders have left the 'casual comedy'. Does this phrase refer to a) human existence in general, b) life in Ireland or c) something else entirely?

Lines 41 to 56

18. Consider the scene the poet paints in lines 45 to 54:
    - List everything that the horse and its rider do.
    - Where, according to Yeats, do the birds 'range' or wander?
    - **True or false:** The shadow or reflection of the cloud is unchanging.
    - What behaviour is exhibited by the moorcocks and hens?

19. 'Minute by minute they change'. Would you agree that this scene presents the natural world as a place of constant change?

20. How does the stone differ from everything else depicted in the scene?

21. Yeats compares life itself to such a body of water, describing it as a 'living stream'. What does this suggest about his view of human existence?

22. Fanatical people, meanwhile, are compared to unbudging pieces of stone. What does this suggest about an obsessive or fanatical mindset?

23. **Class Discussion:** What impact do fanatical people have on the 'living stream' of human existence?

Lines 57 to 80

24. The revolutionaries, according to Yeats, sacrificed much in their devotion to the cause of Irish freedom. Suggest two or three things they may have sacrificed?

25. What impact did this sacrifice have on their psyches?

26. **True or false:** People who have devoted themselves to a cause always know when they have sacrificed enough.

27. For a moment the poet denies to himself that the revolutionary leaders are actually dead. Which phrase indicates this? Can he maintain this self-deception?

28. The poet worries that the deaths of the rebel leaders might have been needless. What political outcome might render their actions redundant?

29. 'We know their dream'.
    - What was the rebel leaders' 'dream'?
    - Who is the 'We' referred to in this line?
    - How do these people now 'know' or understand the dream of the rebel leaders?

30. **Class Discussion:** Yeats describes how the rebel leaders were 'Bewildered' by an 'excess of love'. What did the rebel leaders 'love'? In what sense might this have 'Bewildered' them?

Exam Prep

1. **Group Discussion:** The poet describes how 'All [has] changed, changed utterly' in Ireland since the Rising. Based on your knowledge of the period, can you suggest two ways in which the country has changed? Do you think that Yeats was pleased with these changes?

2. **Group Discussion:** What does Yeats mean when he says that the rebel leaders have been 'Transformed utterly'? Rank the following in order of possibility:
   - They will be regarded as figures of hate for bringing destruction to Dublin.
   - They once were living, but are now dead
   - They have undergone a career change, swopping the life of a shopkeeper or school teacher for that of a military leader.
   - They have been transformed in the national imagination from obsessives and oddballs into figures of heroism and majesty

   Do you think this transformation applies to the leaders who survived as well as to those who were executed?

3. **Class Discussion:** 'Yeats thought that Irish society was being in permanent decline'. Is this statement true of 'Easter 1916'. You might also compare the poem to 'September 1913' and 'Under Ben Bulben'.

4. **Theme Talk:** Yeats regards reborn Irish patriotism as a thing of 'terrible beauty'.
   - The phrase 'terrible beauty' is an example of what literary device? (Hint: It starts with an 'o').
   - In what sense might it be terrifying? In what sense might it be beautiful?
   - How are the rebel leaders similar to the businessmen satirised in 'September 1913'? How are they different?
   - The rebel leaders, like the heroes in 'September 1913', are presented as somewhat crazed. Identify two phrases from each poem that supports this claim.
   - Compare the treatment of patriotism in this poem with 'The Stare's Nest by my Window'.

5. **Exam Prep:** 'As a poet, Yeats is both horrified and facinated by war, violence and social upheaval'. Write a response to this in which you discuss 'Easter 1916' and two other poems.

Language Lab

1. **Personal Response:** The poem is full of uncertainty and doubt. Create a two-column table. Label the first column 'Things the poet is sure of' and label the second column 'Things the poet is unsure of'. Now read through the poem and identify five things the poet is sure of and five things that belong in each column.

2. In lines 60 to 63, Yeats focuses on an image of a mother and her sleeping child.
   - What has the child been doing all day?
   - What has happened to the child now?
   - How does the mother comfort the child?
   - In what sense do the rebel leaders resemble the child?
   - The Irish people, according to Yeats, must behave like the child's mother. What exactly does he want the Irish people to do?

3. What do you understand by the phrase 'Wherever green is worn'? Rank the following in order of plausibility:
   - The poet is referring to the St. Patrick's day parades.
   - The poet is referring to matches involving Ireland's national team.
   - The poet is referring to parades by the Irish army.
   - The poet is referring to any occasion where Irish people around the world take pride in their country.

The Second Coming

Turning and turning in the widening gyre
The falcon cannot hear the falconer;
Things fall apart; the centre cannot hold;
Mere anarchy is loosed upon the world,
The blood-dimmed tide is loosed, and everywhere   [5]
The ceremony of innocence is drowned;
The best lack all conviction, while the worst
Are full of passionate intensity.
Surely some revelation is at hand;

Surely the Second Coming is at hand.   [10]
The Second Coming! Hardly are those words out
When a vast image out of Spiritus Mundi
Troubles my sight: somewhere in sands of the desert
A shape with lion body and the head of a man,
A gaze blank and pitiless as the sun,   [15]
Is moving its slow thighs, while all about it
Reel shadows of the indignant desert birds.
The darkness drops again; but now I know
That twenty centuries of stony sleep
Were vexed to nightmare by a rocking cradle,   [20]
And what rough beast, its hour come round at last,
Slouches towards Bethlehem to be born?

Annotations

The Second Coming: The poem's title refers to the Christian belief that Jesus will return to Earth at some time in the future. Yeats's poem is not Christian in its outlook, however. It adapts the term 'Second Coming' to describe the appearance, or reappearance, of a terrifying beast.

[1] *gyre:* a spiral or a cone; describes the shape traced by the falcon's flight-path as it soars upwards and away from the falconer

[2] *falconer:* In the sport of falconry a hunter, known as a falconer, uses trained birds of prey to pursue small birds and animals.

[4] *anarchy:* disorder, chaos, the collapse of political authority

[5] *blood-dimmed tide:* The fast-moving and powerful currents of history have been allowed to flow freely; they are so bloody that the water is no longer transparent.

[6] *ceremony of innocence:* refers not to a specific practice or ritual, but to a formal and ordered approach to living

[7] *lack all conviction:* lack firmly-held beliefs

[9] *some revelation is at hand:* Something striking and important is about to be revealed or disclosed.

[12] *Spiritus Mundi:* a Latin term meaning 'world spirit'; a vast universal mind or consciousness that contains the memory of everything experienced by mankind. Yeats believed that at certain moments poets and writers could tap into this supernatural consciousness. It would fill them with extraordinary inspiration, providing them with symbols and images for their writing

[17] *indignant:* annoyed, angry, irritated

[20] *vexed to nightmare:* (The beast's slumber becomes) agitated until it experiences a nightmare.

[22] *Bethlehem:* Yeats imagines the beast entering the world where Jesus was born two thousand years ago.

Tease It Out

1. Watch Video 34. Based on your viewing of this video, what topics do you anticipate will be tackled by 'The Second Coming'?
2. What is the sport of falconry? Write a few lines describing this activity in your own words.
3. The poem describes a falcon whose flight path takes it spiralling upwards and outwards away from its falconer. Which words and phrases indicate this?
4. How, according to the poet, does a falconer normally direct the falcon?
5. Is the falcon responding to the falconer's directions on this occasion? Why or why not?
6. The poet believes that sensible, balanced political opinion is being replaced by views that are extreme and unreasonable. Which phrase suggests this?
7. Which phrase suggests that in the poet's opinion the world is becoming a chaotic and unstable place?
8. Consider the phrase 'is loosed'. Does it suggest that this unwanted change is occurring quickly or slowly?
9. The poet imagines a rising tide of water. What has happened to this tide to make it 'dim'?
10. **Class Discussion:** Consider the phrase 'ceremony of innocence':
    - Does it suggest a particular ceremony or something more general and symbolic?
    - What impact does the rising tide have on this ceremony?
    - What does this suggest about the state of the world as the poet sees it?
11. According to the poet, what is the attitude or demeanour of good people in these terrible times? Meanwhile, how are wicked, immoral people behaving?
12. The poet feels that sóme great upheaval, possibly even the end of the world as we know it, is fast approaching. Which phrases indicate this?
13. **Class Discussion:** Consider the phrase 'vast image'. Do you think the poet is dreaming, day-dreaming or perhaps even hallucinating? Give a reason for your answer.
14. Is the poet thrilled or terrified by this image? Support your answer with reference to the poem.
15. The poet describes the creature he witnesses in this 'image'. Where is it located? What mythical monster does it resemble?
16. Which phrase indicates the end of the poet's dream or vision?
17. For how many years has the creature been sleeping?
18. Which phrase indicates that the creature rouses itself only slowly from its slumber, twitching gradually into wakefulness?
19. Where is the creature headed? What will happen when it reaches its destination?

Exam Prep

1. **Personal Response:** This is one of Yeats's most quoted poems, featuring in everything from political speeches to the lyrics of death metal songs. Can you suggest why such a seemingly strange text would have such broad appeal?
2. **Class Discussion:** 'Yeats's poetry laments the end of a particular innocence, the decline of the Anglo-Irish class and the social order they were associated with'. Discuss this statement with reference to 'The Second Coming', 'Under Ben Bulben' and 'In Memory'.
3. **Theme Talk:** 'Yeats's poetry reveals a complex attitude towards war, violence and social upheaval'. Compare and contrast the various treatments of this topic in 'The Second Coming', 'Politics' and 'Easter 1916'.
4. **Exam Prep:** 'Yeats's poetry speaks with great clarity to our present moment'. Discuss this statement with reference to 'The Second Coming' and two other poems on the course.

Language Lab

1. Yeats had a number of occult beliefs. How many references to such beliefs can you find in the poem?
2. Yeats imagines this terrifying creature being 'born' in Bethlehem. What precisely does he mean by this? Consider the following options and, working in pairs, rank them in the order you consider most accurate or appropriate:
    - The 'rough beast' will physically enter the world; a vast lion-bodied creature will actually appear in Bethlehem.
    - The 'rough beast' is about to enter the world in the form of new born human being, an individual whose life will change the world and have terrible consequences for the rest of humanity.
    - The rough beast is a metaphor, symbolising a sequence of traumatic events that will leave the world altered forever.
3. What simile does the poet use to describe the way the creature looks at him? What does this suggest about the creature's temperament?

Sailing to Byzantium

I

That is no country for old men. The young
In one another's arms, birds in the trees,
– Those dying generations – at their song,
The salmon-falls, the mackerel-crowded seas,
Fish, flesh, or fowl, commend all summer long   [5]
Whatever is begotten, born, and dies.
Caught in that sensual music all neglect
Monuments of unageing intellect.

II

An aged man is but a paltry thing,
A tattered coat upon a stick, unless   [10]
Soul clap its hands and sing, and louder sing
For every tatter in its mortal dress,
Nor is there singing school but studying
Monuments of its own magnificence;
And therefore I have sailed the seas and come   [15]
To the holy city of Byzantium.

III

O sages standing in God's holy fire
As in the gold mosaic of a wall,
Come from the holy fire, perne in a gyre,
And be the singing-masters of my soul.   [20]
Consume my heart away; sick with desire
And fastened to a dying animal
It knows not what it is; and gather me
Into the artifice of eternity.

IV

Once out of nature I shall never take   [25]
My bodily form from any natural thing,
But such a form as Grecian goldsmiths make
Of hammered gold and gold enamelling
To keep a drowsy Emperor awake;
Or set upon a golden bough to sing   [30]
To lords and ladies of Byzantium
Of what is past, or passing, or to come.

Annotations

Byzantium: an ancient city, renamed Constantinople in 330 AD and known today as Istanbul; it was the capital of an empire and a great centre of art and learning.

[4] *salmon-falls:* waterfalls over which salmon leap as they swim up-river to spawn

[5] *commend:* praise, celebrate, glorify

[6] *begotten:* conceived

[8] *Monuments:* landmark achievements and permanent objects; creations that will outlast us

[9] *paltry:* pitiful, insignificant

[12] *mortal dress:* the soul's 'clothing', i.e. the body

[17] *sages:* men revered for their profound wisdom

[18] *mosaic:* a picture produced by arranging together small pieces of stone, metal or glass

[19] *perne in a gyre:* Yeats believed that time is a stream that spirals in a 'gyre' or clockwise direction. He imagines the sages 'perning' or moving in a counter-clockwise direction, as if they were swimming against time's current.

[24] *artifice:* workmanship; ingenuity; a cunning strategem

[27] *Grecian:* relating to Greece. Byzantium was a Greek-speaking city

[28] *enamelling:* varnish, decorative paint

[30] *a golden bough:* In an explanatory note on the poem, Yeats writes that in the Imperial Palace in Byzantium there was 'a tree made of gold and silver, and artificial birds that sang'.

Tease It Out

Stanza 1

1. Line 6 mentions three stages in the cycle of life. Describe each one in your own words.
2. The poet regards the summer as a time of fertility and sexuality.
   - What happens to shoals of mackerel at this time of year?
   - What indicates that it is mating season for the birds?
   - What journey do the salmon make?
   - For human beings too, summer is regarded as a time of passion and sexuality. Which phrase indicates this?
3. **Class Discussion:** These creatures through their actions 'commend' the cycle of life. Discuss this statement as a class.
4. The poet himself feels incapable of commending this cycle. Suggest why this might be the case.

Stanza 2

5. **True or false:** The poet is quite comfortable with the reality of bodily ageing.
6. What metaphor does the poet use to describe his ageing body?
7. What do you understand by the term 'mortal dress'? Who or what is wearing this dress?
8. The poet imagines the soul responding with joy to the body's decline. Which phrase indicates this?
9. **Group Discussion:** Can you suggest why the soul might respond to old age in such a fashion?
10. **True or false:** The singing of the soul can compensate for the paltriness of old age.
11. **Class Discussion:** According to the poet, there is only one 'singing school', only one way through which the soul can sing louder and better. As a class, describe this in your own words.
12. All magnificent and enduring artworks are products of the soul. Which phrase indicates this?

13. **Group Discussion:** What is it about Byzantium that so attracted the poet? Bear in mind your answers to the other questions about this stanza.

Stanza 3

14. The poet is contemplating a Byzantine mosaic.
    - Who is depicted in this mosaic?
    - What is happening to them?
    - What does he want the sages to do?
    - What role would they play in his life?
    - What kind of things could they teach his soul?
15. The 'heart' is the aspect of the self associated with love and longing.
    - Does the poet's 'heart', even in old age, still experience desire?
    - Is he capable of fulfilling these desires? Why is this the case?
    - What impact does this state of affairs have on the poet's 'heart'?
16. **Class Discussion:** What does the poet want the sages to do with his 'heart'?

Stanza 4

17. Yeats imagines taking the form of a Byzantine piece of art, specifically a decorative metal bird.
    - Who manufactured this bird?
    - From what material was it fashioned?
    - Which phrase indicates that the bird was capable of producing musical tones?
    - Yeats imagines the decorative bird being placed by the Emperor's throne. What purpose would it serve?
    - **True or false:** Yeats imagines the bird resting upon an artifical tree branch.
18. How do you think the 'lords and ladies of Byzantium' would have reacted to this elaborate contraption? Give a reason for your answer.

Exam Prep

1. **Personal Response:** Yeats imagines being gathered up by the sages and led 'out of nature'. Take a moment to consider these odd but striking images. Do you find these notions pleasant or unpleasant?
2. **Theme Talk:** 'In this poem Yeats rejects nature and the body in favour of art and the mind'. Write a short essay in response to this statement.
3. **Exam Prep:** 'Yeats's poetry is driven by a tension between the real world in which he lives and an ideal world that he imagines'. Write a short essay in response to this statement, making reference to 'Sailing to Byzantium' and three other poems on the course.

Language Lab

1. What does the phrase 'dying generations' suggest about the brevity of life?
2. What does the phrase 'dying animal' suggest about the poet's attitude towards his ageing body?
3. Yeats refers to sexuality as 'that sensual music'.
   - What kind of music do you imagine when you hear this phrase?
   - Which phrase indicates that this 'music' bewitches people?
   - Does this 'music' bewitch young and old alike?
   - What, according to Yeats, does this bewitchment cause people to forget?

The Stare's Nest by My Window

The bees build in the crevices
Of loosening masonry, and there
The mother birds bring grubs and flies.
My wall is loosening; honey-bees,
Come build in the empty house of the stare.   [5]

We are closed in, and the key is turned
On our uncertainty; somewhere
A man is killed, or a house burned.
Yet no clear fact to be discerned:
Come build in the empty house of the stare.   [10]

A barricade of stone or of wood;
Some fourteen days of civil war:
Last night they trundled down the road
That dead young soldier in his blood:
Come build in the empty house of the stare.   [15]

We had fed the heart on fantasies,
The heart's grown brutal from the fare,
More substance in our enmities
Than in our love; O honey-bees,
Come build in the empty house of the stare.   [20]

Annotations

Stare: starling

Civil War: the Irish Civil War (1922-23), a bitter conflict fought between former comrades. On
one side were those who accepted the Anglo-Irish Treaty (1921). On the other side were
those who rejected this treaty.

[1] ***crevices:*** narrow openings or fissures in a wall

[2] ***masonry:*** stonework

[3] ***grubs:*** the larva or immature form of an insect

[9] ***discerned:*** recognised, perceived

[11] ***barricade:*** an improvised barrier

[17] ***fare:*** food, sustenance

[18] ***enmities:*** hostilities, rivalries

Tease It Out

1. Watch Video 35 and answer the following questions:
   - Why was Thoor Ballylee so important to Yeats?
   - In what year did he move from this tower?
   - What happened to the tower after he left it?
   - What happened to the tower in 2015?
2. The masonry that binds the stones of the tower together is 'loosening'. What use do the bees make of the gaps that this creates?
3. Birds also make use of these gaps. What do they use them for?
4. What do the 'mother birds' bring back to these 'crevices'?
5. One of the gaps in the wall is empty. What did this gap once house, and why might its previous occupants have moved on?
6. What does the poet want to happen in this gap?
7. **Class Discussion:** Consider the phrase, 'My wall is loosening', and answer the following questions:
   - The poet uses the word 'loosening' twice in this stanza. What is the effect of this repetition?
   - Is the poet bothered by the deterioration of his tower's walls, or does he view it as a positive development?
   - Can we read the 'crumbling' of the poet's walls on a symbolic or metaphorical level, perhaps as a description of something that's happening to the poet's life or psyche?
8. For how long has the Civil War been raging?
9. What has happened to the roads around the poet's home?
10. Which phrase indicates that the poet and his neighbours feel like prisoners in their own homes?
11. Describe in your own words what happened to the dead young soldier's body. Do you think the poet personally witnessed this occurrence or merely heard about it? Give a reason for your answer.
12. Name two other terrible events that have occurred.
13. Which phrase indicates that the poet is unable to learn the exact details of these terrible events? Suggest why this might be the case.
14. Suggest three different notions or ideals that had obsessed the Irish populace in the years after the 1916 rebellion.
15. Would you agree that the poet considers these 'fantasies' to be dangerous ones? Give a reason for your answer.
16. What impact has the obsession with these notions had on the psyches of the Irish people?
17. Which phrase indicates that the twisted minds of the Irish people now thrive on and are motivated by hatred rather than love?

Exam Prep

1. **Personal Response:** Working in pairs, list everything the creatures of the natural world do in this poem. List everything that human beings do. Together compose a paragraph contrasting these two sets of activities.
2. **Class Discussion:** 'This poem powerfully describes how an obsession with abstract ideals can twist the mind not only of an individual but of an entire population, leading to terrible consequences'. Write two paragraphs in response to this statement.
3. **Theme Talk:** 'This poem captures not only the violence of war but also the terrible 'uncertainty' it inflicts on a population, especially in a time before modern technology and communications'. Compare this poem's treatment of war and violence with those found in 'September 1913' and Easter 1916'.
4. **Exam Prep:** 'Yeats uses evocative language to create poetry that includes both personal reflection and public commentary'. Write a short essay in response to this statement, referring to 'The Stare's Nest' and at least two other poems on the course.

Language Lab

1. Again and again, Yeats returns to the refrain 'Come build in the empty house of the stare'. How do you imagine his tone as he repeats this phrase? Do you think the poet is pleading or demanding? Why do you think he contrasts the activity of the bees with the destruction that rages in the countryside around him?
2. Do you think it's possible that the people of Ireland, locked in a 'brutal' conflict, could somehow learn from or be inspired by the activity of the bees? Support your answer with reference to the text.
3. **Class Discussion:** Consider the metaphor of feeding the heart. Would you agree it's an effective way of describing our obsessions, fixations and fascinations? Can you think of any other metaphors for the same process?
4. '[T]he key is turned/ On our uncertainty'. What is responsible for 'locking' the poet and his neighbours in this state of uncertainty? Do you think this metaphor of imprisonment is an effective one? Give a reason for your answer.

In Memory of Eva Gore-Booth and Con Markievicz

The light of evening, Lissadell,
Great windows open to the south,
Two girls in silk kimonos, both
Beautiful, one a gazelle.
But a raving autumn shears   [5]
Blossom from the summer's wreath;
The older is condemned to death,
Pardoned, drags out lonely years
Conspiring among the ignorant.
I know not what the younger dreams –   [10]
Some vague Utopia – and she seems,
When withered old and skeleton-gaunt,
An image of such politics.
Many a time I think to seek
One or the other out and speak   [15]
Of that old Georgian mansion, mix
pictures of the mind, recall
That table and the talk of youth,
Two girls in silk kimonos, both
Beautiful, one a gazelle.   [20]

Dear shadows, now you know it all,
All the folly of a fight
With a common wrong or right.
The innocent and the beautiful
Have no enemy but time;   [25]
Arise and bid me strike a match
And strike another till time catch;
Should the conflagration climb,
Run till all the sages know.
We the great gazebo built,   [30]
They convicted us of guilt;
Bid me strike a match and blow.

October 1927

Annotations

Eva Gore-Booth: (1870–1926), a writer who campaigned for women's suffrage and workers' rights

Con Markievicz: Countess Constance Markiewicz, née Gore-Booth (1867–1927), a leading figure in the 1916 Rising

[1] *Lissadell:* A mansion in County Sligo where the Gore-Booth family lived.

[3] *silk kimonos:* a traditional Japanese dress

[4] *gazelle:* a small antelope known for its grace and elegance; Yeats is referring here to Eva

[7] *The older:* Constance

[7-8] *condemned to death, / Pardoned:* Constance was sentenced to death for her part in the 1916 Rising. Her sentence was later commuted, and she was released in 1917.

[8] *lonely years:* Constance's Polish husband returned to his homeland, and she was separated from her children.

[9] *Conspiring among the ignorant:* Yeats is critical of Constance's political activities in the years following the Rising.

[11] *Utopia:* a place or state considered to be perfect or ideal

[16] *Georgian:* a neoclassical style of architecture popular during the reigns of the British Kings George I-IV (1714-1830)

[21] *shadows:* ghosts, spirits

[22] *folly:* foolishness, error

[28] *conflagration:* large, destructive fire

[29] *sages:* men revered for their profound wisdom

[30] *gazebo:* small, roofed structure used for outdoor entertaining

[31] *They ... guilt:* In the newly independent Ireland, the Catholic majority often highlighted what they saw as the historical crimes committed by the Protestant Ascendancy, a class to which both Yeats and and the Gore-Booths belonged.

Tease It Out

1. Watch Video 36, which depicts Lissadell House in Co. Sligo, and answer the following questions:
   - What recent projects have been undertaken with regard to the house and its gardens?
   - What features of the house and its gardens strike you as appealing? Are there any features of the property that strike you as unappealing?
   - Is it a place where you would like to live or spend part of every year? Give a reason for your answer.
2. Where is the poet? Who is with him? What are these 'Two girls' wearing?
3. What time of day is it? What hints do we get that the weather is fine?
4. What does the adjective 'Great' suggest about Lissadell's windows? Could it suggest more than one thing?
5. The poet describes one of the girls as a 'gazelle'. What are gazelles known for? What does this comparison suggest about her appearance, especially about how she moves and carries herself?
6. What does the term 'raving' usually mean? What does it suggest about autumn's demeanour and appearance?
7. What impact does autumn have on the wreath of summer? What implement does autumn use to accomplish this?
8. With whom do you think Constance was conspiring later in her life? What was she hoping to achieve?
9. **Class Discussion:** The poet describes how Eva, the younger sister, dreamed of a 'Utopia'. What is a utopia and what does this phrase suggest about Eva's political beliefs?
10. The aged Eva is presented as an 'image' of the political views she served throughout her life. What does this suggest about the poet's view of Eva's political work?
11. The poet often felt like seeking out the two sisters. Do you think he ever actually did this?
12. Consider the phrase 'mix/ pictures of the mind'. What activity does this wonderful metaphor describe?
13. **Class Discussion:** Lines 19 and 20 repeat lines 3 and 4. Would you agree that the lines have a different tone or significance this time around?
14. Why does the poet refer to the sisters as 'shadows' in line 21?
15. Describe in your own words what the sisters now 'know'.
16. The sisters, according to the poet, fought battles that were 'common'. What does the word 'common' mean in this context? Could it mean more than one thing?
17. Does the poet feel that the sisters were wise to engage in such struggles? Give a reason for your answer.
18. What, according to lines 24 and 25, is the only enemy of those who are beautiful and innocent?
19. In lines 26 to 27, the poet imagines himself lighting a series of matches. What would he like to set fire to?
20. If he's successful in this endeavour, what would he like the sisters to do? Where do you imagine this occurring?

Exam Prep

1. **Personal Response:** 'In this poem Yeats vividly and passionately recreates a perfect memory'. Write a paragraph in response to this statement. Then write a short text in which you describe a perfect memory of your own.
2. **Class Discussion:** 'The innocent and the beautiful/ Have no enemy but time'.
   - What does Yeats mean by innocence in this context?
   - What impact does time have on innocence and beauty?
   - What other 'enemies' might innocence and beauty have?
3. **Theme Talk:** 'This is a very sexist poem, arguing that women, especially women from affluent and cultured backgrounds, have no business getting involved in political campaigns. Instead, they should focus on preserving their innocence and good looks'. Write a paragraph in response to this statement.
4. **Exam Prep:** 'Yeats emphasises the power of art to overcome old age, death and even time itself'. Write a response to this statement, making reference to 'In Memory' and at least two other poems on the course.

Language Lab

1. Can you identify two examples each of euphony and cacophony in this poem? How do they contribute to the poem's atmosphere?
2. **Class Discussion:** What literary device does the poet use to describe the autumn?
3. 'This is a poem that makes great use of seasonal imagery, moving from summer to autumn to winter'. Write a few lines in response to this statement.

Swift's Epitaph

Swift has sailed into his rest;
Savage indignation there
Cannot lacerate his breast.
Imitate him if you dare,
World-besotted traveller; he   [5]
Served human liberty.

Annotations

Jonathan Swift: (1667–1745) was Dean of St Patrick's Cathedral, Dublin. He wrote poems, essays and political pamphlets that criticised human greed and stupidity in all its forms. His works include *Gulliver's Travels, A Modest Proposal* and *The Drapier's Letters.* Yeats's poem is a translation, with some alterations, of the Latin epitaph on Swift's gravestone in St Patrick's Cathedral.

Epitaph: the inscription on a grave or tombstone

[2] *Savage:* fierce, violent

[2] *indignation:* anger aroused by injustice or unfairness

[3] *lacerate:* to tear, to wound, to cause emotional distress

[5] *World-besotted:* obsessed or infatuated with this world

Exam Prep

1. **Personal Response:** Google the term 'satire'; then watch Video 37. Who or what is being satirised in this extract? How is the satire being carried out? Is it easy to see why creators of satire, like Swift, might require moral courage?

2. **Class Discussion:** According to the poet, Swift served 'human liberty'. Suggest how Swift, as a writer, might be able to serve such a cause.

3. **Theme Talk:** 'Swift's emotions were 'Savage' but so were his writings'. Suggest one way in which a piece of writing might be said to exhibit a certain savagery.

4. **Exam Prep:** "Swift's Epitaph', like 'An Irish Airman Foresees his Death' and 'September 1913', features someone whose powerful, uncompromising principles causes him to jeopardise his own well-being'. Write two paragraphs comparing and contrasting these three poems.

Tease It Out

1. Have you ever read the novel Gulliver's Travels or heard the story it tells? Write down everything you can remember about this tale. Then Google its author, Jonathan Swift, and write down five facts about his life, including the title of one other work that he wrote.

2. What is an epitaph, and where do we generally find them written?

3. **Class Discussion:** According to the poet, Swift has 'sailed' out of this life. What does this suggest about the manner of his passing?

4. To be indignant is to feel anger at something that seems unjust or unfair. What does Swift's tendency towards indignation suggest about his personality?

5. Which word suggests that Swift's 'indignation' was especially intense and pronounced?

6. Based on your research into his life, suggest what might have provoked such strong emotions on Swift's part.

7. Which phrase suggests that these extreme feelings had a deeply negative impact on his state of mind?

8. Why will Swift no longer be troubled by such emotions?

9. Suggest two different ways in which people of today might 'Imitate' Jonathan Swift.

10. '[I]f you dare'. The poet suggests that there might be negative consequences for those who choose to imitate Swift. What might these consequences be and how might they arise?

11. Is the 'traveller' referred to in line 5 a specific person? Or is the poet addressing every reader of his poem? Give a reason for your answer.

12. Would you agree that every one of us, in one way or another, is 'besotted' with this world? Write a few sentences in response to this question.

An Acre of Grass

Picture and book remain,
An acre of green grass
For air and exercise,
Now strength of body goes;
Midnight, an old house   [5]
Where nothing stirs but a mouse.

My temptation is quiet.
Here at life's end
Neither loose imagination,
Nor the mill of the mind   [10]
Consuming its rag and bone,
Can make the truth known.

Grant me an old man's frenzy,
Myself must I remake
Till I am Timon and Lear   [15]
Or that William Blake
Who beat upon the wall
Till Truth obeyed his call;

A mind Michael Angelo knew
That can pierce the clouds,   [20]
Or inspired by frenzy
Shake the dead in their shrouds;
Forgotten else by mankind,
An old man's eagle mind.Somebody loves us all.

Annotations

[1-5] *an old house:* refers to Riversdale, a farmhouse in Rathfarnham, County Dublin, which Yeats leased in 1932 for thirteen years

[10] *mill:* a machine or device for grinding or crushing

[11] *rag and bone:* unwanted items, odds and ends, bric-a-brac

[13] *frenzy:* mental agitation, wild excitement, mania

[15] *Timon:* Timon of Athens. In Shakespeare's play of the same name, Timon becomes disillusioned with human society. He leaves the city of Athens and goes to live alone in a cave.

[15] *Lear:* King Lear. In Shakespeare's play of the same name, Lear exhibits great foolishness and arrogance. As a result he suffers greatly and goes insane.

[16] *William Blake:* (1757–1827) poet and artist. Yeats views Blake as a visionary who accesses truths beyond those associated with science, logic and reason.

[19] *Michael Angelo:* Michaelangelo Buonarroti (1475–1564) Renaissance artist best remembered for painting the ceiling of the Sistine Chapel and for his statue of David

[22] *shrouds:* garments in which the dead were wrapped for burial

Tease It Out

1. Which phrases suggest that the poet must focus on artistic and intellectual pursuits?
2. Will the poet be neglecting his body entirely? Give a reason for your answer.
3. Only these few activities, we're told, 'remain' to the poet. Suggest other activities the poet might have once enjoyed. Why might these activities no longer be available to him?
4. Which phrases indicate that the poet doesn't have much a social life anymore?
5. Consider the phrase 'Temptation is quiet'. Is the poet referring to a) sexual temptation, b) fun activities that might lure him away from the work of writing or c) something else entirely?
6. **Class Discussion:** Consider the term 'frenzy'.
   - Can you think of two or three examples of frenzied behaviour from fiction or real life?
   - **True or false:** The poet is terrified of experiencing such a frenzied state of mind.
   - 'The phrase 'old man's frenzy' is surprising and contradictory'. Discuss this statement as a class. Do you agree?
   - Why does Yeats admire Shakespeare's characters King Lear and Timon of Athens?
7. Which phrase indicates that William Blake achieved a great understanding of the universe?
8. The poet describes how Blake 'beat upon the wall'. What do you visualise when you read this line?
9. Which of Blake's activities does this beating represent?
10. **True or false:** Society, according to Yeats, has little interest in old men.
11. What image suggests that the mind of an old man can be powerful, perhaps even more powerful than that of a young man?
12. **True or false:** The great artist Michael Angelo had such a powerful mind when he was an old man.
13. What metaphor, in Stanza 4, is used for the discovery of a great new truth?

Exam Prep

1. **Personal Response:** The poet mentions the possibility of remaking himself: 'Myself must I remake'. What do you think such remaking might involve? Can you think of anyone you know (or know of) who remade him or herself? What did this process involve?
2. **Class Discussion:** 'Art for Yeats is about more than entertainment or even beauty. It's about a search for fundamental truth'. Discuss this statement as a class. In what sense can films, music and novels reveal certain truths about our human existence? Do Yeats's poems, in the opinion of the class, touch on any such truths?
3. **Theme Talk:** 'Yeats is a poet who refuses to surrender to old age'. Discuss this statement in relation to 'An Acre of Grass', 'Politics' and 'Sailing to Byzantium'.
4. **Exam Prep:** 'The poetry of Yeats is both intellectually challenging and emotionally rewarding'. Write an essay in response to this statement.

Language Lab

1. The poet describes how he might shake the dead in their burial shrouds. What does he mean by this? Rank the following in order of plausibility:
   - He can bring the dead back to life.
   - The souls of the dead in the afterlife will be jealous of his achievements.
   - He will discovery new truths that disprove the conclusions of previous writers and thinkers.
2. **Class Discussion:** The poet considers the different ways in which poets and writers might arrive at such 'truth'.
   - What image is used to describe regular, repetitive mental labour?
   - How might such labour differ from 'loose imagination'?
   - Can either process, according to the poet, lead him to the truth?
   - Do you think the poet found it easier to arrive at the truth when he was a younger man?

from **Under Ben Bulben**

V

Irish poets learn your trade,
Sing whatever is well made,
Scorn the sort now growing up
All out of shape from toe to top,
Their unremembering hearts and heads   [5]
Base-born products of base beds.
Sing the peasantry, and then
Hard-riding country gentlemen,
The holiness of monks, and after
Porter-drinkers' randy laughter;   [10]
Sing the lords and ladies gay
That were beaten into the clay
Through seven heroic centuries;
Cast your mind on other days
That we in coming days may be   [15]
Still the indomitable Irishry.

VI

Under bare Ben Bulben's head
In Drumcliff churchyard Yeats is laid,
An ancestor was rector there
Long years ago; a church stands near,   [20]
By the road an ancient Cross.
No marble, no conventional phrase;
On limestone quarried near the spot
By his command these words are cut:

Cast a cold eye   [25]
On life, on death.
Horseman, pass by!

Annotations

Ben Bulben: mountain composed of layers of limestone that overlooks the town of Sligo

[3] ***Scorn:*** treat with contempt or disdain

[6] ***Base-born products of base beds:*** The current generation are lacking in moral worth and incapable of appreciating or understanding great art. They have been begotten by parents who are themselves 'base' and lacking in a similar manner.

[7] ***peasantry:*** poor farmers that worked the land belonging to wealthy landowners

[8] ***country gentlemen:*** members of the landowning class

[11] ***lords and ladies:*** members of the aristocracy

[12] ***That were beaten ... centuries:*** These lords and ladies often commanded armies in the fight against English rule from the 12th to the 20th century. Again and again, they were crushed or defeated.

[16] ***indomitable:*** impossible to defeat or overcome

[19] ***ancestor:*** Yeats's great-grandfather, the Reverend John Yeats (1774–1848)

[22] ***marble:*** material typically used for creating gravestones

[22] ***conventional:*** following the usual or widely accepted way of doing things

Tease It Out

1. Yeats describes poetry as a trade:
   - Can you think of two or three well-known trades?
   - What does the writing of poetry have in common with these? In what ways is it different?
   - Do you find Yeats's description of poetry as a trade surprising? Give a reason for your answer.
2. Can you think of one or two ways in which poets might go about learning the 'trade' of poetry?
3. Poets, according to Yeats, should sing or write about 'whatever is well made'. Think about the idea of the 'well made' object. What are the first three examples that come to mind?
4. **True or false:** Yeats thinks poets should find inspiration in the younger generations of Irish people who are growing up around the country.
5. These younger generations, according to Yeats, are 'all out of shape'. What do you think he means by this? Rank the following in order of plausibility:
   - They have put on weight and need to spend more time at the gym.
   - They were born with poor character.
   - They are physically unattractive.
   - They are suffering from psychological stress or trauma.

6. **Class Discussion:** These younger generations, according to Yeats, are 'unremembering'. Working as a class, can you suggest a number of different things they might have forgotten?
7. The term 'base' has several different meanings. Which do you think is most relevant to line 6? Give a reason for your answer.
8. What two very different groups of people are mentioned in lines 7 to 8?
9. Another two groups are mentioned in lines 9 to 10? What does Yeats admire about each of these?
10. **True or false:** Yeats insists that Irish poets must be up with the times, must focus on contemporary society with all its changes and challenges.
11. Yeats refers to the 'indomitable' nature of the Irish people:
    - Is being indomitable the same as being victorious?
    - How, in the past, did the Irish people show their indomitable nature?
    - What, according to Yeats, will help them be indomitable in the future?
12. Where does the poet plan to be buried? What family connections does he have with this area?
13. What material is to be used for the headstone? Do you think this is a deliberate choice on the poet's part?

Exam Prep

1. Personal Response: 'This poem shows Yeats as a snob and an insufferable elitist. He looks down his nose at the ordinary people of contemporary Ireland, viewing them as base and unworthy'. Do you agree with this assessment? Write two or three paragraphs explaining your response.
2. **Class Discussion**: Working as a class, discuss the poet's mysterious epitaph:
   - What does it mean means to view something with a 'cold eye'? Consider the following definitions of cold and say which you think is most appropriate here: Objective; Unsympathetic; Disdainful; Unemotional.
   - Why does it mean to cast a 'cold eye' on life and death? What view of human existence is suggested by this phrase?
   - Who is the 'Horseman' in the poem's final line? Is Yeats addressing a specific person, the reader, a personification of death itself or something else?
3. **Exam Prep:** 'Yeats uses unforgettable language to explore the character of the Irish people'. Write an essay responding to this statement in which you refer to this poem and to 'September 1913', 'Easter 1916' and 'The Stare's Nest By My Window'

Language Lab

1. Consider Yeats's view of poetry as put forward in 'Under Ben Bulben':
   - Writing about something, according to Yeats, is the same as singing about it. What does this suggest about his view of poetry?
   - **True or false:** True poetry comes from craft and hard work as well as inspiration.
   - **True or false:** Poets can write about any subject they wish and still create great work.
   - List the various types of people that Yeats considers worthy subjects for poetry. What is it about each one that he finds worthy of celebration?
2. For generations, according to Yeats, Ireland's 'lords and ladies' lead men into battle:
   - For how long did they fight? What was the object of their struggle?
   - What phrase indicates that they frequently met with defeat?
   - What attitude did they exhibit as they fought? Is this surprising?
   - Can you think of any historical figure who might be considered one of these lords or ladies?

Politics

'In our time the destiny of man presents its meanings in political terms.'
Thomas Mann

How can I, that girl standing there,
My attention fix
On Roman or on Russian
Or on Spanish politics?
Yet here's a travelled man that knows   [5]
What he talks about,
And there's a politician
That has read and thought,
And maybe what they say is true
Of war and war's alarms,   [10]
But O that I were young again
And held her in my arms.

Annotations

Thomas Mann: (1875–1955) a great German novelist and writer

[3-4] ***On Roman … Spanish politics:*** The poem was written in 1938, a period of great political
unrest in Europe. The Spanish, Russian and Italian ('Roman') political systems all witnessed upheaval at this time.

[10] ***war and war's alarms:*** In 1938, Hitler invaded Austria and Czechoslovakia, causing great alarm
internationally and bringing a threat of war.

Tease It Out

1. Watch Video 38, which contains newsreel footage from 1938, the year in which the poem was written. What significant political events were happening in Europe? Having watched this footage, how would you characterise the mood and atmosphere of the time?

2. The poet is having a conversation with two other men. How does he describe them?

3. **True or false:** The poet expects that these men are knowledgeable about the problems facing Europe.

4. What prevents the poet from listening attentively to these two men?

5. **True or false:** The poet wishes he could focus more attentively on what his two male companions are saying. Give a reason for your answer.

6. What do you imagine the poet's relationship with the girl to be? Do you think they know one another, or do you think that this is the first time that he has seen her?

7. What is it that the poet wishes for in the last two lines of the poem? Why does he wish for this?

Exam Prep

1. **Personal Response:** This poem highlights how lust, even in old age, remains at the forefront of the male mind.
   - Would you agree that this is an accurate assessment of the poem?
   - How do you think the 'girl' feels about being the subject of the poet's attention?
   - Is it fair to describe 'Politics' as something of a sexist poem?

2. **Class Discussion:** 'Youth and age is one of Yeats' recurring themes'. Discuss this statement in relation to this poem, 'An Acre of Grass' and 'The Wild Swans at Coole'. In which poem is Yeats most accepting of the ageing process? In which poem is he least accepting?

3. **Theme Talk:** Does the poet believe it is his duty to deal with important political events? Or does he feel entitled to focus on private affairs of the heart? Explain your answer.

4. **Exam Prep:** Compare and contrast the ways in which 'The Second Coming' and 'Politics', respectively, deal with the prospect of social and political upheaval.

Language Lab

1. Do you think 'Politics' is a good title for this poem? Give a reason for your answer. What would you choose if you were asked to select an alternative title?

2. 'Why do you think that the poet uses the term 'Roman' instead of 'Italian'?

3. Yeats placed 'Politics' at the very end of his *Selected Poems*. Can you suggest why he decided to round off his poetic career with this fairly short and simple poem? What does this choice suggest about his priorities as a poet and as a person?

4. Consider the syntax of the sentence that forms the first four lines of the poem. Why do you think the poet chose to structure it in this manner? How does Yeats's syntax enhance his introduction and description of the poem's topic?

Emily Dickinson

Themes

Nature

In poem after poem, Dickinson celebrates the beauty of the natural world. In 'A Bird, came down the Walk', for instance, the poet lovingly highlights the bird's bead-like eyes, the softness of the feathers on its 'Velvet Head', its unfurling wings and the exceptional grace and elegance with which it moves through the air.

'I could bring You Jewels', meanwhile, celebrates the beauty of a little flower the poet has noticed growing in a nearby meadow, the poet detailing the intensity of its 'Topaz' petals and bright green stem. 'I taste a liquor never brewed' finds the poet revelling in summer days when the meadows are fragrant with life and growth, when birds, bees and butterflies flutter about in the pleasant summer heat.

'A narrow Fellow in the Grass', too, reflects the poet's love of the natural world. Its farm-boy speaker clearly loves nature and spends much of his time outside. He proclaims his affection for the various creatures of the earth, referring to them as 'Nature's People'. This implies that he has a give-and-take friendship with many of the birds and animals in his locality: 'I know, and they know me'.

Dickinson, it must be noted, is often playful in her depiction of the natural world. 'A Bird, came down the Walk', for instance, is cute and almost comedic in its depiction of the little traffic jam that occurs on the garden path, the bird darting aside to let the beetle pass him by: 'And then hopped sidewise to the Wall/ To let a Beetle pass'. 'I taste a liquor never brewed' is similarly light-hearted, especially in its depiction of the humming-bird becoming so drunk on nectar, air and dew that it reels from flower to flower the way a drunk person might reel from bar to bar.

'I could bring You Jewels', too, is mischievous in its approach to nature, specifically in the poet's exaggeration of the flower's charms. This little bloom, she declares, would make a more fitting gift than even the most spectacular piece of jewellery, blazing as it does with the intensity of emerald and topaz.

Dickinson is a poet who persistently identifies the extraordinary in the everyday. 'A Bird, came down the Walk', 'I could bring You Jewels' and 'I taste a liquor never brewed' aren't inspired by conventionally magnificent spectacles. Instead, they suggest that even the most mundane sight, such as a bird walking down an ordinary garden path, devouring a worm and taking flight, can appear extraordinary.

'I taste a liquor never brewed', for instance, reminds us of the intoxicating beauty that can be found in an ordinary field in summertime. 'I could bring You Jewels' goes even further in its praise of the everyday, the poet claiming that a wildflower growing near her house is more special and exotic than berries from the Bahamas or the colours of Vera Cruz. Dickinson's poetry, then, reminds us again and again that beauty and mystery can be found in the ordinary world around us, if only we take the time to stop and look.

In her poetry, Dickinson comes across as someone intensely sensitive toward the natural world. This is especially evident in 'I taste a liquor never brewed'. We sense that the poet, like the hummingbird, was capable of getting 'high' on nature, that the sights, sounds and smells of the natural world induced in her a sense of ecstasy and intoxication.

A similarly manic enjoyment of nature is depicted in 'The Soul has Bandaged moments', where the poet portrays herself dancing 'like a Bomb' in a 'delirious' response to nature's beauty. Many readers feel that perhaps there is something a little unhealthy about this 'hyper' response to the natural world, as if it were the 'manic' flip side to the numb 'depression' that Dickinson describes in many of her poems.

'I could bring You Jewels' and 'A Bird, came down the Walk', also highlight this sensitivity. The conclusion of 'A Bird, came down the Walk', with its strange, dense web of imagery, captures the sense of awe experienced by the poet as she watches the bird take wing. In 'I could bring You Jewels', meanwhile, the poet is clearly deeply affected by her observation of the little flower, declaring that there's no better gift she could find for her beloved: 'Better—Could I bring?'

'There's a certain Slant of light' is one poem where Dickinson focuses on nature's bleaker and more depressing aspects. The poem highlights the fact that the natural world can sometimes have a negative impact on our state of mind, altering our psyches as it brings us the worst kind of 'internal difference'.

Both 'A Bird, came down the Walk' and 'A narrow Fellow in the Grass', emphasise the brutality and danger that exist in the natural world. In 'A Bird, came down the Walk', the bird savagely devours a worm and is itself in a fearful state, being permanently on the look-out for potential predators. The speaker in 'A narrow Fellow in the Grass', despite his love of animals, is not naive about the dangers of the natural world. He knows that certain species of grass-snake are dangerous and not to be trusted, as evidenced by the fear he experiences when he encounters one coiled up or sliding through the meadow.

The Workings of the Mind

Dickinson's great subject, according to several critics, is the human mind itself. We see this in 'I heard a Fly buzz', which movingly depicts a mind disintegrating at the point of death. There is something powerful about the repetition of 'and then' in these lines, as the speaker mechanically lists the stages of her mental collapse. The phrase is repeated three times, suggesting a relentless and unstoppable process of shutting down, one that, once it commences, cannot be stopped or delayed. As we read, we can almost feel the speaker's consciousness dwindling away.

Dickinson is a poet especially gifted when it comes to the portrayal of mental anguish. 'There's a certain Slant of light', for instance, depicts a mind 'oppressed' by a formidable mental burden, one that brings with it great inner 'Hurt' or psychological damage. This is a state of mind that involves being altered on the inside, in the depths of our psyche, 'where the meanings' reside.

'After great pain, a formal feeling comes', meanwhile, details the disturbingly numb mental state that occurs in the wake of great trauma. Although the 'Pain' of the poem's title has ended, its departure brings no relief or joy. Instead, there is almost a total lack of feeling and emotion. The speaker's body behaves as if it is living – but there is something stiff and mechanical about its actions and movements, as if it is just going through the motions without any thought or care: 'The Feet, mechanical, go round'.

The poem finishes on a rather disturbing note, suggesting that the speaker might not survive this post-traumatic period. There is a danger that the mind might never again spark with life, that the body will not be re-ignited with energy and vitality. There is a risk that the speaker will just descend further into 'stupor', that the numbness will utterly paralyse her body and her mind.

'The Soul has Bandaged moments' presents us with someone who experiences great highs and lows, who seems to swing, rapidly enough, from utter dejection to ecstatic joy. It suggests someone who is bi-polar, someone whose mood alternates between extreme euphoria and deep depression. The poem vividly captures such wild mood swings. Such mood swings are vividly brought to life by the images that Dickinson uses to portray the soul, first, as a prisoner confined in a terrifying dungeon, and then as someone dancing 'like a Bomb, abroad'.

It is surely in 'I felt a Funeral, in my Brain', however, that we find Dickinson's most unforgettable portrayal of mental suffering. Here the speaker finds herself confronting what can only be described as a nervous breakdown, imagining that a funeral is taking place inside her brain: 'I felt a Funeral in my brain'. The speaker, it seems, can't actually see the funeral. Instead, she feels and hears this terrible event, experiencing it through the sounds made by the mourners and through the vibrations that accompany each noise. It's as if she can hear, but not see, what's going on inside her own head.

Unlike 'After great pain' and "There's a certain Slant of light', "Hope' is the thing with feathers' has an uplifting message, describing as it does an inner resource of some kind that we can all draw on to help us get through such difficult times. Even at our lowest, the poem suggests, a sense of hope prevails, encouraging us to persevere.

Death

'I heard a Fly buzz', as we've seen, movingly portrays the process of death, showing how the speaker's sense of vision, and her sense of logic, blur as consciousness ebbs away. The poem is bleakly witty in its depiction of the indignity that surrounds the speaker's passing. The speaker has prepared for death, she has made her will and gathered her family around her. The moment of her demise is intended to be the solemn climax of a life well lived.

The last thing she hears, however, is not the soothing words of her family but the buzzing of a fly. The last thing she sees is not the faces of her loved ones but a fly floating in front of her. The speaker's last experience in this world is of a miserable and insignificant insect 'stumbling' as it buzzes around the room. Many readers feel that the fly's interruption makes the moment of the speaker's death seem a little ridiculous, robbing it of its intended grace and dignity.

'I heard a Fly buzz' doesn't specifically deny the existence of the afterlife. And yet, when the speaker's vision fades to black at the end of the poem, we are left with the distinct impression that the speaker now feels that this black oblivion is all there is, that no afterlife awaits her. The last thing the speaker 'witnesses' is not the glorious arrival of the 'King' but the uncertain buzzing of a stumbling fly.

'I taste a liquor never brewed' is much more positive in its depiction of life after death, as the bird is welcomed into Heaven by saints and angels. Heaven is memorably depicted as a joyful and carefree city of rest. The bird finds itself in the presence of the 'Sun', which, as we have seen, is generally taken to be Christ himself.

Heaven is depicted as a very real place, as a town whose inhabitants live in houses with windows, wear hats, and celebrate the arrival of each new soul. This positive and light-hearted depiction of the afterlife contrasts sharply with many of the other poems in which Dickinson addresses the themes of death and dying.

'Hope' is the thing with feathers –

LINE BY LINE

Hope is the feeling that events will turn out for the best, that no matter how difficult or dire our circumstances, all will be good in the end. We often encourage those who are going through trying times not to lose hope. In this poem, Dickinson attempts to define what she understands hope to be and reflects on the role it plays in our lives.

Stanzas 2 and 3

The poet imagines life in terms of a voyage or a journey that we must each undertake. As we journey, we inevitably encounter challenges and hardships. The poet likens such hardships and trying times to adverse weather conditions, to strong winds and storms. Sometimes the hardships that we must endure are extreme. The poet uses remote and inhospitable landscapes to represent such times in life. She imagines being in the coldest place possible, some kind of freezing Arctic landscape: 'the chillest land'. She imagines being adrift on a sea that is as far from home as possible: 'on the strangest Sea'.

However, we are never alone as we journey through life. Every step of the way we are accompanied by a sense of hope. The poet imagines hope to be a bird that accompanies us through the good times and the bad. The bird is constantly singing to us, keeping our spirits up and up and encouraging us to go on. Its tune is most appreciated when times are especially tough: 'And sweetest – in the Gale – is heard'. It

is then that we most need to hear its uplifting music, to feel encouraged to journey on.

Hope is a strong and resilient presence in our lives. It is capable of surviving and withstanding gales and storms. There is a sense in which hope is an indestructible force. No matter what the world throws at it, it survives. This little creature never stops singing 'at all'.

Yet, Dickinson does hint at the possibility of hope being damaged, saying that it would have to be a 'sore' storm to 'abash' this little bird. The term 'sore' suggests violence and severity, but it also suggests malice. It is as if such a storm would be intent on harming the bird, that it is 'sore' or smarting from something that causes it to act in this cruel and vengeful manner. To 'abash' is to destroy the self-confidence, poise, or self-possession of someone or something. So, the effect of such a storm on this bird would be to make it meek and silent.

Yet the phrase 'And sore must be the storm' suggests that no such storm can exist. It is much like the expression, 'It's an ill wind that blows no good', which we might take to mean that there is no situation so bad that somebody does not benefit from it.

In the poem's final lines, Dickinson describes hope as a selfless creature, something that gives us so much but asks for nothing in return. All the while that she was journeying, this 'little Bird' never asked her for a single thing. Even when things were at their worst, 'in Extremity', the bird did not look for 'a crumb' from the poet.

Stanza 1

The first four lines of the poem raise a number of interesting questions about hope and the poet's understanding of it. Why does the poet place the word 'Hope' in quote marks at the start of the poem? Hope is an abstract concept. It is not something we can easily identify or define. The poet, therefore, places the term 'Hope' in quote marks to convey the fact that it is not something of which we have a sure or ready grasp.

Why does the poet say initially that it is the 'thing with feathers', rather than simply a bird? Again, this stems from the fact that the poet is attempting to define a complex, abstract concept. She begins by thinking of the term in the broadest manner possible – It is a 'thing' – before getting more specific.

It is interesting that the first image the poet attaches to or associates with hope is 'feathers': ''Hope' is the thing with feathers'. We instantly, of course, think of a bird – What else has feathers? But the poet does not wish to simply say that hope is a bird. Rather, she wants tease out the manner in which hope operates and features in our lives.

The word 'feathers' introduces the notion of flight, of something that can take to the air and, conversely, descend from above. It also suggests that hope is not a part of who we essentially are; it is a separate entity.

Why does the poet say that hope 'perches in the soul'? As we have just suggested, the poet presents hope as something independent of us. It is a feathered 'thing' that somehow inhabits us. The manner in which it does this is interesting. The poet says that hope 'perches' within us. To perch is to alight or roost on an object, typically a branch or horizontal bar. This implies that hope is somehow separate from us but has come to rest or reside within us.

Dickinson's description of hope as a bird perching in the soul is also interesting because it connects or associates something physical with something that is non-physical or abstract. Our soul is the non-physical aspect of our selves; yet somehow this 'thing with feathers' comes to settle within it.

Why does hope sing a 'tune without the words'? Hope does not convey or deliver a specific message to us. It moves us, inspires or generates a feeling within us, much as music without any lyrics does. Hope does not, for example, tell us to get up and keep going; rather, it lifts our spirits, gives us a sense that things will work out for the best, without articulating how or why.

Why does the poet say that hope 'never stops' singing? This suggests that hope is a permanent force or presence in the world. It also suggests that, while hope resides within us, its message is constant. We may not always hear it it can, perhaps, be drowned out by fear and doubt – but it is always singing to us. Dickinson emphasises hope's permanence by telling us never stops 'at all'. This suggests that there is no imaginable force or circumstance in the world capable of overwhelming or silencing hope. No matter how bad things get, hope will continue to sing; we just need to attune ourselves to its song.

FOCUS ON STYLE

The poem consists of three four line stanzas with an ABAB rhyme scheme.

The poem is centred on the extended metaphor of life as a journey that we must each undertake. It is a journey that will take us to strange, uncomfortable and terrifying places. The freezing landscapes and unfamiliar seascapes represent such times and places in our lives. We also encounter many hardships and setbacks along the way. These are represented in the poem by storms and violent winds.

The journey that each of us must take through life is essentially a solitary one. But Dickinson says that we are never entirely alone in life. We each have a special form of companion with us on our difficult journey – our sense of hope. The poet imagines hope to be a bird that is housed within our souls, constantly singing to us and keeping our spirits up, even in the most trying times.

THEMES

THE WORKINGS OF THE MIND

The 'chillest land' and the 'strangest Sea'. Both settings suggest periods of great psychological anguish. We might imagine that dwelling in or journeying through the 'chillest land' represents moments when we are almost numb or frozen with horror, or perhaps just psychologically exhausted. This idea of being frozen or numb with the cold is also present in 'After great pain', where the poet likens the sort of stupor or mental numbness that follows periods of intense anguish and suffering to the experience of someone freezing in the snow.

The 'strangest Sea' might represent times in our life when we feel utterly isolated and alone, cut off from the rest of the world. We are reminded here, perhaps, of the description in 'I Felt a Funeral' of being 'Wrecked' and 'solitary' in some strange and alien environment. However, unlike 'After great Pain' and 'I Felt a Funeral', ''Hope' is the thing with feathers' has an uplifting message, describing as it does some inner resource that we can all draw on to help us get through such difficult times. Even at our lowest, the poem suggests, a sense of hope prevails, encouraging us to persevere.

There's a certain Slant of light

LINE BY LINE

In this poem, Dickinson focuses on a particular variety of sunlight: 'There's a certain Slant of light'. Such light is typically evident on 'Winter Afternoons'. It has a cold, hard quality and is depressing rather than cheerful. The poet describes a 'Slant of light', and we can imagine this harsh glow angling out of the sky, breaking through the cloud cover in slanted shafts.

Damage

The light, we're told, 'oppresses' all those who witness it. Dickinson's use of the verb 'oppress' suggests that the light brings us misery and hardship. All those exposed to its glow find themselves suffering.

The damage caused by the light is psychological, rather than physical. It it brings a 'Hurt' that leaves no bodily wounds or injuries: 'We can find no scar'. Instead the light causes

'internal difference', changing us in a sinister fashion on the inside. It alters our very minds and souls, the place 'Where the Meanings are'.

Using a memorable turn of phrase, Dickinson refers to the light as the 'Seal Despair', suggesting how it robs us of all hope. All those exposed to its cruel glow find themselves sealed in their own anguish, trapped in utter hopelessness. They're unable to escape from, or even express, the negative emotions the light brings with it.

Oppressive

Dickinson's use of the verb 'oppress' also brings with it the idea of control and subjection, suggesting that the light dominates us in the same way that a tyrannical king might dominate his subjects. The light is presented as a cruel tyrant, from whose dominance no one can escape.

The winter light is, in many respects, worse than any human oppressor, like a corrupt president or abusive overlord. For such a human oppressor might be shown the error of their ways, might be taught to be a kinder and more compassionate ruler. The winter light, however, cannot be reasoned with in such a fashion. No one can 'teach' it anything: 'None may teach it- Any'. It is a merciless and implacable force of nature.

Dickinson uses an unexpected simile to capture the light's oppressive quality, comparing it to the hymns sung in a cathedral. Such 'Cathedral Tunes', she suggests, possess a great 'Heft' or weight, which suggests the sombre nature of their melodies. We imagine not uplifting gospel music, but gloomy and monotonous Latin psalms echoing through a cold cathedral. According to the poet, the winter light is similar to this liturgical music in that it 'oppresses' all exposed to it, dominating their minds and leading them into depression.

Affliction

The winter light is presented as if it were some airborne plague or a form of lethal radiation. The poet describes it as an 'affliction/ Sent us of the Air', as though it were an illness or disease, floating down through the winter air to torment us. The 'Hurt' that it brings to us, therefore, can be described as 'Heavenly' because it originates in the sky over our heads, often referred to as the heavens.

In the presence of this affliction, the landscape becomes incredibly still and silent. Yet, this is more an eerie stillness than a moment of soothing tranquillity. For the poet says that the landscape seems to 'listen', and even the shadows seem to 'hold their breath'. The entire countryside seems filled with fear and trepidation, as if nature itself were cowering before the 'Hurt' that the light brings with it.

The poem concludes with a note of relief, as the speaker describes the departure of the light. We greet the disappearance of the light with an extraordinary sense of relief. We are as glad, the poet suggests, as someone who has survived a brush with death: 'When it goes, 'tis like the Distance/ On the look of Death'

FOCUS ON STYLE

Form

'There's a certain Slant of light', like most of Dickinson's poems, uses four-line stanzas with an ABCB rhyme scheme. The poem is marked by the concision common to Dickinson's poetry, in which words and phrases are regularly omitted. Such compression is especially evident in line 9: 'None may teach it – Any –'.

We sense that Dickinson is punning on the word 'certain' in the poem's ope ning line. In one sense, of course, certain means specific or particular. The poet is referring to one specific type of light. But 'certain' also means definite and determined, suggesting the light's relentless and merciless quality.

It's possible, as we've seen, to read this line as suggesting that light cannot be taught anything, cannot be reasoned with or be diverted away from its purpose.

The same line also suggests, however, that the effect of the light cannot be explained to anyone who has not experienced it. The light's misery cannot be explained to someone who has never experienced its glow. You have to see it for yourself.

Riddling and Paradoxical Language

'There's a certain Slant of light', like many of Dickinson's poems, is distinguished by riddling and paradoxical language. There are several instances where the poem subverts or unsettles our expectations.

Light, usually associated with hope and growth, is depicted here as a grim and oppressive force. Music – by definition airy and weightless – is presented as having 'Heft' or weight. The 'Cathedral Tunes', and by extension the winter light, is depicted as something solid and tactile; pressing down upon the speaker like a burden she is forced to carry.

The concept of 'Heavenly Hurt' is another startling reversal of our expectations. Heaven, which we usually think of as a place of bliss and calm, is presented as a source of misery and suffering. The phrase is an example of an oxymoron, an expression where the adjective appears to contradict the noun it describes. In this case, 'Heaven' is not a concept that we usually associate with 'Hurt'.

Metaphor, Simile, Figures of Speech

In this final stanza, Dickinson uses 'personification' to describe the atmosphere of nervous tension that fills the landscape when the light shines down. (Personification occurs when the poet gives human qualities to inanimate objects.) In this instance, the landscape 'listens' and the shadows 'hold their breath,' just as a human being would in the presence of a force as oppressive and menacing as the winter light.

It could be argued that in this stanza death itself is personified. Death seems to be represented as a person who approaches us when we are close to dying. As our life slips away, death's 'look' – or face – comes close to us. If we recover, however, his face recedes into the 'distance'.

Atmosphere

This is a poem that skilfully conjures an atmosphere of dread and trepidation, especially in the final stanza with its depiction of nature itself fearfully waiting for the oppressive light to vanish. We are presented with a dark and shadowy landscape, that holds its breath beneath the dreary and oppressive winter light. The presence of the 'Shadows' indicates how gloomy and dreary the landscape appears beneath the pallid sun.

THEMES

THE WORKINGS OF THE MIND

This poem powerfully depicts a state of mental anguish. The poet describes a state of mind that involves being 'oppressed' by a great mental burden, being affected by inner 'Hurt' or psychological damage and being sealed within 'Despair' and bereft of hope.

It's a state of mind that involves being altered on the inside, in the depths of our psyche, 'Where the Meanings' reside. The term meaning is being used in two different senses here. On one level, it refers to understanding, to our ability to make sense of the words, concepts and actions that surround us. The light, then, interferes with this capacity, making it difficult for us to make sense of our environments. But the idea of meaning as purpose or significance is also involved here, suggesting that those exposed to the light's harsh glow lose all sense of purpose; for them, life becomes a pointless and monotonous chore.

Is it realistic for Dickinson to declare that such a negative state of mind is caused by the malevolent sunlight pouring from the sky? Many of us, no doubt, find the watery winter sunlight a bit of a downer. But must it induce such crippling despair?

Perhaps Dickinson is describing, with surprising accuracy, what we would today call clinical depression, with its sense of oppressive hopelessness. Those who suffer from such a disorder are often highly sensitive to atmospheric conditions and find their condition worsening in winter, with its pale, weak sunlight.

RELIGION

It's tempting to view this poem as presenting an unusually bleak view of religion. There's a sense in which the winter light is presented as a punishment sent from God himself:

- The phrase 'Heavenly Hurt', on this reading, suggests that the light has been sent down from Heaven to do us harm: 'Heavenly Hurt, it gives us'.

- The description of the light as an 'affliction', meanwhile, reminds us of the plagues sent to punish the unfaithful in the Old Testament of the Bible.
- The description of the light as 'imperial' suggests that it originates with God himself, who might be regarded as the 'emperor' of the entire universe.
- The Book of Revelation describes how the opening of four sealed parchments releases four different forms of suffering - war, famine, plague and death - into the world. Now, it seems, another seal has been opened, unleashing the winter light and the 'Despair' that comes with it.
- It is perhaps not surprising, therefore, that the poet associates this grim winter light with hymns sung in a cathedral.

God, then, is presented as merciless and vindictive, rather than gentle and forgiving. He sends the winter light into the world, presumably as a punishment for humanity's failings. But this is a collective and indiscriminate retribution. The light oppresses all who are exposed to it, irrespective of whether or not they have tried to live a good life. Both the sinner and the good person will experience the 'Heavenly Hurt'. The God of this poem, then, is a cold and judgemental overlord rather than a loving father who cherishes each of his children individually.

NATURE

Many of Dickinson's poems depict nature as a source of joy and inspiration. 'There's a certain Slant of light', however, focuses on nature's bleaker and more depressing aspects. As we've seen, the poem suggests that the natural world can have a negative impact on our states of mind, altering our psyches as it brings us the worst kind of 'internal difference'. Once again we find Dickinson focusing on nature in its everyday aspects, finding terror not in an earthquake or tsunami but in a simple slant of light. The poem reinforces our sense of the poet as someone especially sensitive to the natural world, someone whose entire mood and mind-set can be altered by the quality of light outside her window.

- Dickinson compares the air to a kind of ocean.
- The act of flying is compared to that of moving through water.
- The bird, for instance, is depicted as 'rowing' into the sky, his unfurled feathers functioning like oars that propel him upwards: 'And he unrolled his feathers/ And rowed him softer Home'.
- Butterflies, meanwhile, are depicted as 'swimming' through the air.
- When a flying creature takes wing it can disturb the air through which it moves. This is compared to the 'plashes' or splashes produced when we enter the water.

The poet imagines butterflies launching themselves from 'Banks of Noon', from ridges of plants and flowers on a sunny summer's day. They leap into the air, however, with extraordinary gentleness, causing no disturbances or splashes. As the speaker puts it, they swim 'plashlessly' through the air: 'Butterflies, off Banks of Noon/ Leap, plashless as they swim'.

Yet the bird's motion is even 'softer' than that of these imagined butterflies. According to the poet, it takes flight with more grace and elegance that any butterfly could muster: 'And rowed him softer home –/ Than … Butterflies'. She can only watch in awe as the bird propels itself upward, into the sky which is its 'Home' or natural element:

The poet imagines a boat rowing across an ocean of silver-coloured water. Think of the greatest silver mine in the world, with the richest 'seam' of silver. Well, not even the product of such a seam could match the colour of this imagined ocean, so glittering and lustrous is its surface as the boat rows across it. She imagines that the boat's oars dip delicately in and out of the ocean as it travels. With each stroke they 'divide' its silver waters into two halves or sections, one on the boat's port side and one on its starboard side: 'Oars divide the Ocean'.

The bird's unfurled wings, as it takes flight, are compared to the oars of this smoothly-travelling rowboat. Just as the boat's oars propel it across the ocean, so the bird's wings propel it upwards. Yet the motion of the bird's feathers is smoother and more gentle ('softer') than that of any oars could be.

FOCUS ON STYLE

Tone

This poem features several shifts in tone. The tone of the first two stanzas is casual, playful and innocent. The worm, for instance, is described not as a slimy wriggling thing but as a 'fellow', suggesting that it's some kind of gentleman. Even the grass is described as 'convenient'.

The movement of the verse here is simple, almost reminiscent of a nursery rhyme, with its full rhymes between monosyllabic words: 'saw' and 'raw' in stanza 1, and 'Grass' and 'pass' in stanza 2. This simplicity is heightened by the fact that each line consists of one phrase, and that there are no run-on lines.

The atmosphere darkens in stanzas 3 and 4, as the bird becomes agitated and ultimately flies away. The verse's 'nursery rhyme' quality is abandoned, and the language used becomes more sophisticated. Full rhymes are replaced by the half-rhyme between 'Crumb' and 'home' in stanza 4, and with no rhyme at all in stanza 3 ('around' and 'Head).

The absence of the expected rhyme comes as a jolting surprise to the reader, suggesting how the bird is jerked into alertness by its awareness of a sudden potential threat. Furthermore, the run-on line between stanzas 3 and 4 can confuse our initial reading of the poem, perhaps suggesting the bird's confusion and agitation as it searches for potential threats: 'He stirred his Velvet Head// Like one in danger'.

In the final stanzas, the tone shifts to one of joyous exultation as the poet celebrates the majesty of the bird taking flight. The poem's syntax becomes much more intricate, with a single complex sentence stretching across ten lines and taking in several different and complex metaphors.

VERBAL MUSIC

In this poem, Dickinson makes liberal use of assonance and alliteration. In line 12, for instance, assonance occurs between 'Velvet' and 'Head', with their repeated 'e' sounds. We also see it in the phrase 'rowed him softer home', with its repeated 'o' sound. Alliteration occurs in lines 17, 18 and 19, with their repeated 'o', 's' and 'b' sounds: 'Oars divide the Ocean', 'Too silver for a seam', 'Butterflies, off Banks of noon'. This use of assonance and alliteration creates a pleasant or euphonious musical effect, reflecting the majesty and beauty of the bird, especially when it takes wing.

Vivid Imagery

The poem's opening stanzas, as we've seen, present us with images that are playful and almost cartoon-like with their depiction of the bird hopping to one side in order to let the beetle pass by. Similarly light-hearted is the depiction of the butterflies leaping from banks of vegetation in order to flit and hover through the air.

'A Bird, came down the Walk' also presents us with the hauntingly beautiful image of a single row boat making its way across a vast and glittering ocean. Even more majestic, however, is the image of the bird powering itself homeward on its unfurled wings.

Metaphor, Simile, Figures of Speech

As we've seen, 'A Bird, came down the Walk' features a conceit or extended metaphor that compares the air to an ocean, butterflies to swimmers and the bird's wings to oars. Dickinson uses an excellent simile to capture the fear apparent in the bird's eyes, comparing them to 'frightened Beads'.

THEMES

NATURE

Like many of Dickinson's poems, 'A Bird Came Down the Walk' celebrates the beauty of the natural world, specifically that of the bird encountered on the garden path. The poet lovingly highlights the bird's bead-like eyes, the softness of the feathers on its 'Velvet Head', its unfurling wings and the exceptional grace and elegance with which it manoeuvres itself skyward.

The poem, like many works by Dickinson, is playful in its depiction of nature, the opening stanzas presenting us with images that are cute and almost comedic. We see this homeliness in the depiction of the little traffic jam that occurs on the walk, where the bird hops aside to let the beetle pass him by: 'And then hopped sidewise to the Wall/ To let a Beetle pass'. Yet the poem also emphasises the brutality and fear that exist in the natural world. The bird savagely devours a worm and is itself in a fearful state, being on the look-out for potential predators.

Dickinson is a poet who persistently identifies the extraordinary in the everyday. 'A Bird Came down the Walk' isn't inspired by a conventionally magnificent scene. It doesn't describe swans gliding on a lake in winter, or cormorants soaring from a geological wonder like the Cliffs of Moher. Instead it suggests that even the most mundane sight, such as a bird walking down an ordinary garden path, devouring a worm and taking flight, can appear extraordinary. Like 'I could bring You Jewels' and 'I taste a liquor never brewed', this poem reminds us that beauty and mystery can be found all around us if only we take the time to stop and look.

Several critics have suggested that it's possible to read 'A Bird, came down the Walk' as an allegory of a failed romantic relationship, with the male bird representing Dickinson's lost lover. We are reminded, perhaps, of the several intensely passionate correspondences that Dickinson conducted with various gentlemen over the course of her life, with Judge Otis Lord, for example, or the mysterious individual she referred to only as 'the Master'.

The poem, we imagine, is set in the garden of Homestead, the house where Dickinson lived and wrote from the age of 25. She speaks of 'the Wall' and 'the Walk', a very specific environment that she would have encountered every day of her adult life. It highlights, then, how to Dickinson this tiny farmstead served as an inexhaustible source of inspiration.

The poem also highlights Dickinson's intense sensitivity toward the natural world. The poet, we sense, is clearly someone deeply affected by her observations of nature, even in its most ordinary manifestations. The strange and dense web of imagery in the poem's final stanzas vividly conveys the awe felt by the speaker as she watches the bird take wing.

I heard a Fly buzz – when I died –

LINE BY LINE

In this poem the speaker addresses us from beyond the grave, telling us about the circumstances of her death. She describes lying on her deathbed, surrounded by various members of her family. We can imagine the speaker's mental and physical exhaustion, her body wracked, perhaps, by a combination of illness and old age. We can imagine that her family too are mentally and physically exhausted, having suffered the ordeal of watching a loved one drift towards death. We can imagine an atmosphere of great tension as they wait for the moment when the speaker will finally pass away.

A moment of calm

The speaker describes one oddly quiet moment that occurred as she lay upon her deathbed. The room had been noisy while the speaker was suffering on her deathbed. It would be noisy again as she experienced her final death throes. For a few moments, though, it was filled with quietness. The speaker compares this lull to the eerie stillness that can sometimes be experienced at the very centre of a storm system. 'The Stillness in the Room/ Was like the Stillness in the Air –/ Between the Heaves of Storm –'.

The loved ones

The speaker's loved ones had cried until they could cry no more: 'The Eyes around – had wrung them dry –'. We imagine an air of stress and expectancy, as the speaker's loved ones wait for the moment of death. We can imagine the unbearable tension they

experienced as they waited for the 'last Onset' or attack of the speaker's illness, when she would finally pass away. According to the speaker, her loved ones were so tense that they found themselves almost unable to exhale. The air they breathed in remained held or gathered firmly in their lungs: 'And Breaths were gathering firm'.

The speaker describes how her loved ones expect that at the moment of death a 'King' will be present. No doubt, the 'King' they have in mind is Jesus, the Lord of Heaven, who will descend in order to ferry his loyal and faithful subject into Paradise. Perhaps the speaker shares her loved ones' religious beliefs, or perhaps she is more sceptical about religion and life after death.

Will and testament

Because the speaker knows that the end is near, she has prepared her last will and testament, 'assigning', or passing on, her various valuables to her loved ones. The items that she allocates to her loved ones are described as 'Keepsakes', suggesting personal effects, little tokens that will remind loved ones of her after she is gone.

The fact that the speaker wills only such keepsakes, rather than stocks and property, reinforces our sense that she is a woman: In Dickinson's time, women were seldom permitted to own and administer such assets.

There is one aspect, or 'portion', of the speaker that is not 'assignable', however, one that she cannot simply give to whoever she wants. This is her immortal soul, the ultimate destiny of which she cannot control.

The fly

During this final moment of quiet, as the speaker prepares for her illness's final onset, a fly has been buzzing in the room. The fly, we are told, is moving in an 'uncertain' and 'stumbling' fashion. This suggests the jerky, erratic motions of an insect that has been trapped too long in a room and is desperate to escape.

The speaker starts to lose consciousness. She describes how at this moment a fly 'interposed' or positioned itself between her and the available light: 'There interposed a Fly... Between the light- and me'. This image of a fly blocking out the light is a puzzling one. How could such a tiny creature place itself between the speaker and the available light source? This cryptic statement lends itself to several possible interpretations:

Perhaps the image of the fly blocking out the light represents the ebbing of consciousness, the diminishment of the speaker's vision as her system begins to finally shut down.

Perhaps, as the speaker passes away, her sight begins to fail and her vision narrows to a little tunnel. A fly floats into this reduced field of vision, making itself the last thing the speaker sees before she dies and darkness engulfs her completely. The image of the light-obstructing fly might also refer to the afterlife. Perhaps, as she lingers between life and death, the speaker imagines for a moment that she can see the light of Heaven, the glow of paradise into which she's being summoned.

But at the very second her brain shuts down, she realises that this glow is only a hallucination. It is replaced by onrushing blackness and the buzzing, stumbling fly. The speaker realises that oblivion, rather than eternal life, lies in wait for her.

The fly can also be read as an embodiment of Satan himself, arriving at the speaker's deathbed in order to claim her very soul. It is not surprising that the devil would appear in the form of a fly, because he is sometimes referred to as the 'Lord of the Flies'. Or perhaps the speaker just sees the Devil as a giant fly, mixing him up with the fly that she hears buzzing in the room.

The Devil, then, in this unsettling insect form, blocks out not only the light of this world, from which the speaker's spirit is being wrenched, but also the light of paradise, which she will never reach, because the speaker's soul, on this reading, is instead bound for eternal damnation!

The gathered loved ones, presumably, don't think that Jesus will be physically visible at the loved one's deathbed. They probably think they'll 'witness' his presence by feeling his grace within their souls. Or maybe Jesus' presence will be evidenced by the serene and painless nature of the speaker's passing.

FOCUS ON STYLE

Form

'I heard a Fly buzz- when I died' uses a form common to most of Dickinson's poetry. It has four-line stanzas and an ABAB rhyme scheme. The poem has a regular rhythmic lilt, with four stresses in the first and third lines of each stanza, and three stresses in the second and fourth lines. The rhythm becomes jerky and irregular in the final stanza, suggesting the breakdown of the speaker's mental faculties at the moment of death.

Metaphor, Simile, Figures of Speech

Dickinson uses a fine simile to describe the momentary quietness in the room when the speaker is granted a brief respite from her suffering. The quietness, she says, is like that at the 'eye of a hurricane', the very centre of a storm. On either side of the storm's uneasily tranquil eye are great 'Heaves', a term that here refers not only to gusts or breaths, but also to the storm's force as it pushes and shoves against the landscape.

A similarly vivid metaphor is used to describe how the speaker's loved ones had exhausted their capacity for crying: 'The Eyes around – had wrung them dry –' Here, eye-balls are presented as being made from a spongy substance, a material that is squeezed in the act of crying so that moisture is forced out. According to the speaker, her loved ones' eyes had been 'wrung' in such a fashion until they had no moisture left to give, until they resembled a towel squeezed completely dry.

Tone and Atmosphere

'I heard a Fly buzz – when I died' wonderfully evokes an atmosphere of tension and expectation, as the speaker and her gathered loved ones prepare for the final onslaught of her illness. It joins other Dickinson poems in depicting a calm but uneasy interlude between bouts of suffering. In this regard, it is similar not only to 'The Soul has Bandaged moments', but also to 'After great pain, a formal feeling comes'.

THE WORKINGS OF THE MIND

Dickinson's great subject, according to several critics, is the processes and performances of the human mind itself. In this light, 'I heard a Fly buzz' can be regarded as a triumph. For it provides, especially in its last six lines, a moving depiction of how a mind disintegrates or dissolves as life leaves it.

There is something powerful about the repetition of 'and then' in these lines, as the speaker mechanically lists the stages of her mental collapse. The phrase is repeated three times, suggesting a relentless and unstoppable process of shutting down, one that cannot be stopped or delayed, once it commences.

As we noted, the speaker's vision fails as she passes away. It is arguable that her sense of logic fails as well, and that she confuses the fly buzzing in the corner of the room with the blackness that floods her vision. We sense that in the speaker's befuddled mind these two events become mixed up, and she hallucinates that a giant fly is blocking out the light

A similar confusion is evident in the speaker's declaration that 'the Windows failed'. As the speaker died the room seemed to fill with darkness. To her it seemed that the windows 'failed' – that they were suddenly incapable of performing their function. They could no longer let light into the room.

This mental befuddlement also lies behind the speaker's description of the fly's behaviour. The speaker is aware of three different aspects of the fly's appearance and demeanour:

- The buzzing sound it produces as it flies.
- The 'stumbling' and 'uncertain' nature of its movements around the bedroom.
- The blue colour of its wings.

In her confused mental state, the speaker experiences a moment of synaesthesia. This occurs when we experience something associated with one sense in terms of something associated with another sense. In this instance, the speaker experiences the fly's buzzing not only in terms of sound but also in terms of colour and movement: 'With Blue – uncertain stumbling Buzz-'. We sense that this occurs because her failing brain can no longer adequately process or organise the sensory input it receives from the speaker's eyes and ears.

There's a sense, too, in which the speaker's consciousness resembles the fly buzzing haplessly against the window, as her mind stumbles from one thought or sensation to the next. The poem's final line, with its repetition of the verb 'see' reinforces our sense of her diminishing capacity.

The first instance of this verb refers to the ability to perceive, while the second refers to the ability to focus. The speaker, therefore, first finds herself unable to focus on the buzzing fly in the corner of the room and subsequently becomes incapable of perceiving anything. As we read, we can almost feel her consciousness dwindling away.

DEATH

The presence of the fly introduces an element of indignity into the speaker's passing. The speaker has prepared for death; she has made her will and gathered her family around her. The moment of her demise is intended to be the solemn climax of a life well lived.

The last thing she hears, however, is not the soothing words of her family but the buzzing of a fly. The last thing she sees is not the faces of her loved ones but a fly floating in front of her. The speaker's last experience in this world is of a miserable and insignificant insect 'stumbling' as it buzzes around the room.

Many readers feel that the fly's interruption makes the moment of the speaker's death seem a little ridiculous, robbing it of its intended grace and dignity. It's a bit like a bride falling over as she makes her way up the aisle to be married.

We like to think that we can control our lives, that we can live with a certain poise and grandeur. But the poem reminds us that circumstances often intervene, upsetting our plans in ways both big and small. This is especially true when it comes to dying, the manner of our deaths being all-too-often unexpected and outside of our control.

RELIGION

The speaker and her gathered loved ones strike us as religious people. The speaker, as we've seen, believes that one portion of her is 'unassignable', her immortal soul. Her loved ones, meanwhile, wait anxiously for 'the King' to be 'witnessed' in the room. They seem to believe that as the speaker dies, Jesus, the King of Heaven, will appear and carry his loyal subject's soul to paradise.

These expectations are not borne out, however. The poem doesn't explicitly state that there is no heaven. And yet, when the speaker's vision fades to black at the end of the poem, we are left with the distinct impression that the speaker realises that this black oblivion is all there is, that no afterlife awaits her.

This poem, then, presents a rather ironic and sceptical view of religion. There's a sense in which it pokes fun at the gathered family's religious expectations by means of a crushing anticlimax. The last thing the speaker 'witnesses' is not the glorious arrival of the 'King' but the uncertain buzzing of a stumbling fly.

The Soul has Bandaged moments

LINE BY LINE

The poem's speaker is madly in love with someone. There are times when she is sure of her beloved's intentions, confident that he is faithful to her and loves her deeply. During these times, the speaker is deliriously happy. But there are occasions when the speaker is not sure of her beloved, when she becomes suspicious of his faithfulness to her. During these periods, the speaker is tortured and overwhelmed by jealous thoughts and suspicions.

The poem begins by describing an occasion where the speaker has been hurt by her lover's behaviour and is at the mercy of her suspicions and doubts. We don't know what – if anything – has triggered these suspicions. Perhaps her beloved has been behaving in a manner that is out of character. Perhaps the speaker has been made aware of her beloved's relationship with another. Someone may have told her this, or she might have seen him with someone else. Perhaps, however, the beloved has not done or said anything hurtful. Maybe it has been a while since she has heard from him, and she is assuming the worst.

Whatever has happened, some form of mental hurt has been inflicted upon the speaker. She has done her best to tend to this psychic hurt or wound. Her soul has been 'Bandaged'. The term 'Bandaged' suggests, perhaps, that the hurtful moment has passed, but the soul is still feeling weak and vulnerable. Perhaps the pain has not passed, however, and the bandages are merely disguising or concealing wounds that still smart.

In the wake of this trauma, the speaker is left feeling very weak and low. Her soul or psyche is so horrified by what it has experienced that it cannot move or 'stir'. It is as if the soul has been frozen with fear. The Soul's hair is described as 'freezing', which suggests that the Soul is both numb from the experience and unable now to react or respond to events.

In this weakened state, the soul is very vulnerable to jealous or suspicious thoughts. The poet personifies this jealousy, comparing it to a 'Goblin' that toys with the speaker's soul. The manner in which the Goblin behaves and interacts with the soul illustrates how suspicious or jealous thoughts take hold of the vulnerable mind, torturing and corrupting it.

The Goblin behaves in a seductive manner. He begins by greeting the soul rather formally, saluting her with 'long fingers', before tenderly rubbing or caressing the soul's hair. Finally the Goblin kisses the appalled soul. These actions suggest the manner in which suspicious thoughts can weasel their way into our minds, seducing us into believing them.

The Goblin's behaviour also hints at the forceful way in which suspicious thoughts take hold of us. There is something slightly violent or abusive about the manner in which the Goblin treats the soul. The verbs in stanza two progress rapidly from 'Salute' to 'Accost'. The Goblin lulls the soul with its formal salutation and the caressing of her hair, only to then 'Accost' or aggressively impose its will. All the while, the soul is frozen with fear, a passive victim to the Goblin's advances.

Such suspicious or jealous thoughts are contrasted with thoughts of love, which are personified by the 'Lover'. Whereas suspicious thoughts are rather brutal in their manner, boldly making their advances, thoughts of love are gentle and sweet. The 'Lover' does not even touch the soul, instead respectfully hovering over its lips.

> The poet uses an interesting term to describe the manner in which the Goblin kisses the soul. It is said to 'Sip' from the soul's lips. To 'sip' is to take in or absorb, to drink from something constantly, a little at a time. The Goblin feeds off the vulnerable soul, seeming to gain or benefit from its vulnerability. The image of the Goblin sipping from the soul's lips also seems to anticipate the description of the bee in stanza 4.

Love is described as something 'fair' – something associated with honesty, beauty and truth. But suspicious thoughts are ultimately damaging to this positive emotion. Such thoughts, the speaker says, attack or 'Accost' the fair 'Theme' of love.

Moments of escape

There are occasions when the speaker is free of all such doubts and suspicions, when she is sure of her beloved's devotion. During such periods, the speaker's soul is filled with ecstatic joy and soars free. The speaker describes these occasions as 'moments of escape'. The soul is no longer confined by crippling doubt and suspicion. Free of doubt, the soul experiences a sense of liberation and freedom. Nothing can contain it or hold it back. It is energised and capable of 'bursting all the doors'.

The speaker compares the soul to a bee that has been confined to its hive all winter. The bee has a favourite flower, a 'Rose', that it visits during the summer. Over the long winter months the bee is unable to leave the hive and visit the flower that it loves; it is 'Long Dungeoned' from this rose. Suddenly summer rolls around, and the bee is free to leave the hive. It flies in an ecstatic manner to the rose. In fact, such is its joy at the prospect of once again seeing the rose that it seems to not even need its wings to stay aloft ; it is 'delirious borne'.

When the bee eventually reaches the rose, it seems to become intoxicated with joy. It is as if the flower's nectar is an alcoholic beverage that the bee imbibes. (We are reminded here of the description of the bird in 'I taste a liquor'). The

> The American Civil War was fought in the United States from 1861 to 1865. The years of the Civil War corresponded with Dickinson's most intense period of productivity as a poet, during which she is thought to have written roughly half of her total number of poems. Although Dickinson never wrote specifically about the Civil War, some of the imagery she uses - such as 'She dances like a Bomb' - seems to reflect the bloody turmoil that raged across the country during these years.

bee reaches a state of ecstasy where all negative thoughts and feelings are forgotten. Having sipped from the flower, the bee knows nothing but 'Noon, and Paradise'. To the bee, at this moment, it seems that it will always be noon on a summer's day and that the world will forever be a paradise for it to enjoy. The cold, isolated days spent in the hive are now a distant memory.

We can imagine the speaker feeling the same as the bee, when she is again convinced that her beloved loves her. Her soul, which had been feeling wounded and weak, is suddenly lifted and re-energised. Whereas once the soul had been 'too appalled to stir', now it 'dances'. Whereas once the soul had felt bound in and confined, now it experiences great freedom and can travel far and wide or 'abroad'.

On these occasions, however, the soul seems incapable of measured joy and happiness. It loses all self-control and behaves in a reckless manner. It doesn't just quietly leave the space where it had been feeling weak and vulnerable, where it was trapped by fear, as a prisoner who has been released might walk slowly out of the prison. Instead, the soul bursts through the doors. Also, the manner in which it dances seems reckless and dangerous. Dickinson compares the soul's dancing to a 'Bomb', suggesting that the soul could explode at any moment, causing harm not only to itself but also to others. The behaviour is suggestive of a manic state of mind, of someone who goes from one emotional extreme to the other.

The soul is also said to swing 'opon the Hours'. We might think of the 'Hours' as representing the clock and the routine of the day. The soul, in its state of delirious happiness, pays no heed to this clock; it is as unconstrained by time just as it is by space. In fact, the soul seems to have fun with the whole notion of routine, swinging upon the 'Hours'.

Retaken moments

But it seems that these moments of ecstatic joy, times when the soul is entirely free of doubt and suspicion, are relatively short-lived. It doesn't take long - and it doesn't take much - for the soul to once again be overwhelmed by doubt. When such doubts and suspicions return, it is as if the soul has again been apprehended and incarcerated. It is as if the authorities have finally caught up with the escaped soul and are leading it back to its cell or dungeon. The soul is like a criminal or 'Felon' who escaped from jail only to be re-captured or 'retaken'.

The manner in which the soul is retaken is rough and brutal. Metal bands connected by a chain are placed around the soul's feet. Dickinson describes the soul's feet as 'plumed', suggesting that they have feathered wings that enable the soul to soar and fly. However, the shackles make it impossible for the soul to now take flight.

The apprehended soul is also prevented from singing. In a particularly disturbing image, the poet describes how 'staples' have been driven into the 'song' to silence the soul. The poet presents the 'song', the soul's expression of joy, as something corporeal rather than abstract. It is as if the 'song' is the soul's companion, someone that accompanies it during its moments of delirious happiness. However, when these moments come to an end, the 'song' is swiftly silenced. It is as if those who have shackled the soul have also brutally dealt with the 'song'. We can imagine how the metal staples have been used to bind its lips.

It is as if the soul has had some piece of twisted metal attached to its mouth that prevents it from expressing itself. When the apprehended soul eventually arrives at its prison cell, the Goblin or 'Horror' is there to welcome her once 'again'. Such moments, the poet says, are not spoken of. These are private humiliations, to be suffered and endured alone. Dickinson says that these moments are 'not brayed of Tongue'. To bray is cry or shout in a loud and harsh manner, like a donkey. Perhaps the soul, when it is feeling ecstatic, is able to shout in such a manner. However, when the soul has been wounded and tortured by suspicion, it suffers alone and in silence.

FOCUS ON STYLE

Conceits and Extended Metaphors

The poem uses the notion of prison and the soul as prisoner to describe the feelings of dejection and ecstasy that the speaker experiences. Whenever the speaker feels uncertain about her beloved's faithfulness to her, it is as if her soul has been incarcerated in some terrible dungeon where a horrible Goblin awaits her. Whenever these doubts are allayed or disappear, and the speaker is reassured of her beloved's love for her, it is as if her soul has been set free.

Vivid Imagery

The poem features a lot of what we might term 'gothic' imagery. There is the gloomy setting of the dungeon where the soul is confined during its periods of doubt and suspicion. There is the grotesque appearance of the Goblin, a hideous creature that toys with the soul, torturing and humiliating it. There is also the terribly violent images of the apprehended soul, with shackles upon its feet and, perhaps most brutally, the 'staples' in the 'song'.

Atmosphere

The atmosphere at the beginning and the end of the poem is dark and unsettling, full of menace and fear. This gloomy, nightmarish atmosphere lifts and changes in the middle of the poem, where for a brief spell the soul is free of doubt and experiences an ecstatic joy and sense of freedom.

THEMES

LOVE

The poem presents the idea of love as something beautiful and good; it is a 'Theme – so – fair'. Love is associated with such virtues as gentleness and respect, presented as something pure. The 'Lover', who personifies this notion of love in the poem, is so gentle and considerate when it comes to the soul that he merely hovers above its lips rather than boldly kissing them.

However, love can be undermined or threatened by suspicions and doubts. Such suspicions make us question whether the love we believed existed was ever so pure and true. The Goblin represents such suspicions in the poem. He takes advantage of the soul's vulnerable state to disabuse it of the notion that such pure love exists.

The poem illustrates how being in love can make us ecstatically happy. The speaker's soul seems to soar and fly when she is sure of her beloved's fidelity. It is said to dance and to

feel no bounds or restrictions. Being in love fills us with positive thoughts and feelings. However, being in love can also cause us to feel absolutely miserable. The poem begins and ends with descriptions of the speaker overwhelmed and horrified by thought that her beloved is not faithful to her. Such doubts torture the soul, leaving us feeling trapped, weak and alone.

THE WORKINGS OF THE MIND

The poem presents us with someone who experiences great highs and lows, who seems to swing, rapidly enough, from utter dejection to ecstatic joy. It suggests someone who is bi-polar, someone whose mood alternates between extreme euphoria and deep depression. The poem vividly captures what it feels like to feel so low and so high, using memorable images of the soul being confined in a terrifying dungeon, on the one hand, or dancing 'like a Bomb, abroad' and swinging upon 'the Hours', on the other. Such images bring the inner workings of the mind vividly to life.

I could bring You Jewels –
had I a mind to

LINE BY LINE

The speaker wants to give her beloved a gift. She considers several different possibilities. If she wished, she says, she could present her lover with a selection of precious stones: 'I could bring You Jewels – had I a mind to'. We imagine a fistful of glittering gems: diamonds, pearls and rubies.

Alternatively, she could present her lover with a selection of aromas or 'Odors'. These would come from the city of Santo Domingo, the capitol of the Dominican Republic and one of the most beuatiful cities in the Caribbean: 'I could bring You Odors from St. Domingo-'. We might imagine here not only the scent of the surf but also of the myriad exotic fruits and meats to be found in the city's bustling quayside markets.

She could also present her lover with a selection of 'Colors'. These would come from the city of Vera Cruz, a great port on the Gulf of Mexico: 'I could bring You … Colors –from Vera Cruz'. We imagine here the whitenss of the unspoilt beaches, the vivid green of the palm trees, the sparkling blueness of the Caribbean sea.

Finally, the speaker could give her beloved berries that come all the way from the Bahamas, a chain of islands in the Caribbean Sea: 'Berries of the Bahamas—have I—'. We imagine here succulent figs and cherries, and other still more exotic types of fruit that would have been all but unknown in Amherst where Dickinson was born and raised.

The flower

The speaker, however, rejects each of these possible gifts, instead deciding to offer her beloved a flower that she has seen growing nearby. Such a modest token of affection strikes her as more suitable or appropriate than the expensive items mentioned above: 'Suits Me- more than those'.

Dickinson uses a wonderful metaphor to describe this flower's brightness, comparing it to a tiny flame. It is, she says, a 'little Blaze' that can be seen 'Flickering … in the Meadow'. We can imagine it resembling a tiny camp-fire burning brightly in the meadow next to Homestead, the house in which Dickinson spent practically her entire adult life.

Dickinson provides a detailed description of this flower. Its petals are Topaz in colour, suggesting a vivid, iridescent blue. No human artist or decorator, she says, has ever managed to equal the intensity of this naturally-occurring shade: 'Never a Fellow matched this Topaz'. The flower's 'Swing' or stem, meanwhile, is described as 'Emerald', suggesting a lustrous green.

The flower is not merely the same colour as certain precious stones, such as topaz or emerald; like them, it is also an incredibly precious item. Indeed this little bloom, in the poet's view, is more valuable than any gem.

A 'dower' or dowry was the sum of money a woman's family gave to her husband when he married her. If a potential husband was unimpressed by the dowry on offer, a marriage had little chance of going ahead.

In the 16th Century, Francisco Bobadilo was the governor of the West Indies and was widely considered to be one of the richest men who had ever lived. This wealthiest of individuals, therefore, would expect any potential wife to be accompanied by an enormous dowry. The poet, however, says that this little flower, all by itself, would make a worthy dowry for such an incredibly wealthy gentleman: 'Dower itself- For Bobadilo'. The poet, then, presents this little flower as an item of incredible value.

Perhaps Dickinson was thinking of her own mother, Emily Norcross, whose dowry had to be transported for three days by horse-drawn carriage when she married Edward Dickinson in 1828, road and rail links being still very primitive in the Massachusetts of that time.

FOCUS ON STYLE

Form

Like the vast majority of Dickinson's poems, 'I could bring You Jewels' deploys an ABCB rhyme scheme. There are several instances of half rhyme, for example between 'those' and 'Cruz' in the first stanza and between 'Blaze' and 'those' in the second stanza. The poem is marked by the concision common to Dickinson's poetry, where words and phrases are regularly omitted. Such compression is especially evident in the poem's final line. Instead of 'What better gift could I bring you? ' we get the much more concise phrase: 'Better—Could I bring?'

Verbal Music

Like many of Dickinson's poems, 'I could bring You Jewels' is rich in assonance and alliteration. Assonance occurs in line 4, with its repeated 'c' sound ('Colors' and 'Cruz') and in line 5, with its repeated 'b' sound ('Berries' and 'Bahamas'). Assonance also occurs in line 3, with its repeated 'o' sound, in line 9, with its repeated 'e' sound ('Never' and 'Fellow'), and in line 11, which also has a repeated 'o' sound ('Dower' and 'Bobadilo').

This combination of assonance and alliteration lends the poem a pleasant musical quality, reflecting both the exotic splendours of the Caribbean and the more homely beauty of the flower in the meadow.

Vivid Imagery

In this poem, Dickinson uses several Caribbean or exotic images, referring to berries from the Bahamas, smells from Santo Domingo and colours from Vera Cruz. Dickinson, though she never travelled, was prone to using imagery from such exotic locales, journeying in her imagination where she never ventured in real life.

Metaphor, Simile, Figures of Speech

The speaker uses a wonderful metaphor to describe the little flower, comparing it to a tiny flicker of flame: a 'little Blaze/ Flickering to itself – in the Meadow'. The presentation of the flower as a 'Blaze/ Flickering' captures the brightness and warmth of its colours. In a further metaphorical flourish, the stem is described as the flower's 'Swing', and we can imagine the 'head' of the flower swinging back and forth as the stem bends in the breeze.

Tone

'I could bring You Jewels' is generally considered to be playful and light-hearted in tone. This owes something to Dickinson's use of hyperbole, or poetic exaggeration. No one, the speaker declares, has ever found a sapphire that could match the 'Topaz' of the flower's petals. Furthermore, she maintains that the 'Emerald' of its stem would be a sufficient dowry for Bobadilo. She puts forward these deliberately outrageous exaggerations in order to stress the beauty of the humble flower.

It has also been suggested that the poem's tone is one of confidence and swagger. The speaker advertises her poetic gifts and her literary skills. She could, if she desired, conjure up the jewels for us, or the colours of Vera Cruz, through her descriptive powers. The poem, then, can be read as a celebration of poetry's power to bring colours, sounds and smells – anything the poet might imagine – floating into our minds.

The poem's lighthearted tone also owes something to its 'riddle-like' qualities. We are never actually told that the 'little Blaze/ Flickering' with its 'Emerald Swing' is a flower. The reader has to work it out him or herself from the clues provided in the poem. In this respect, it is similar to 'I taste a liquor never brewed'.

THEMES

NATURE

Like many of Dickinson's poems, "I could bring You Jewels" celebrates the beauty of the natural world, specifically that of the little flower the poet has noticed growing in a nearby meadow. The poet lovingly describes the flower's blossom and stem, highlighting the intensity of its blue and green.

The poem, like many works by Dickinson, is playful in its depiction of nature, specifically in the poet's exaggeration of the flower's charms. She considers jewels as a potential gift but ultimately opts for the flower instead, declaring that this little bloom, in it's own way, is a spectacular piece of jewellery, blazing as it does with the intensity of emerald and topaz.

Dickinson is a poet who persistently identifies the extraordinary in the everyday. 'I could bring You Jewels' isn't inspired by what we'd ordinarily consider an example of nature's majesty, like a sunset or a mountain vista. Instead, the poem focuses on something most of us would regard as commonplace and unremarkable: a flower growing in a field.

The speaker claims that this little plant is more special and exotic than berries from the Bahamas or the colours of Vera Cruz. The poem, then, reminds us that beauty and mystery can be found all around us if only we take the time to stop and look. If we do so, we might find that things in our own backyards are as special as the exotic sights and smells of Caribbean islands or other exotic locations.

The poem also highlights Dickinson's intense sensitivity to the natural world. The poet, we sense, is someone who responds deeply to nature, even in its most ordinary aspects. She is clearly deeply affected by her observation of the little flower. There is a moving simplicity and sincerity about the poem's final line, in which the poet declares that there's nothing better she could give her lover: 'Better—Could I bring?'

LOVE

This little poem occupies a place within an ancient poetic tradition: the idea of the poem as a gift. It is easy to imagine Dickinson enclosing this poem with a letter to one of her close correspondents – a practice, in fact, that she often engaged in. 'I could bring You Jewels', therefore, functions as a token of the poet's esteem and admiration for someone she holds dear.

But who is the poem addressed to? Most readers are inclined to view it as a love poem, and are left with the impression that Dickinson is addressing a potential lover rather than a close friend.

Perhaps Dickinson is thinking of Judge Otis Philip Lord, a friend of her father's, with whom she enjoyed an intense and passionate correspondence. Or perhaps she's thinking of the gentleman she refers to as 'Master' in three extraordinarily passionate letters of 1858-61. The precise identity of this gentleman has never been established.

A CELEBRATION OF POETRY

It's unlikely that the speaker has a selection of precious stones lying around that she can simply hand over to her lover. And it's equally implausible that she owns a package of berries shipped thousands of miles from the Bahamas. And how could she present her lover with abstract, intangible things like colours and odours?

In a sense, though, the poet can 'give' her friend these extraordinary gifts by describing them in her poetry. She can present her lover with jewels and berries, with colours and odours, by writing a poem that summons up these things in the lover's imagination.

Perhaps above all else, then, this poem celebrates the power of poetry and the imagination. It can be read as a confident statement of the speaker's descriptive abilities. It asserts that poetry and literature have the ability to bring entire worlds to life in our imaginations.

THE WORKINGS OF THE MIND

There's an amusing moment of personification in line 6, where the flower is presented as if it were a person, capable of independent actions, choices and decisions. The flower, we're told, chooses to flicker 'to itself'. It enjoys its beauty for its own sake. It doesn't show off or care what anyone else thinks of it. This suggests that the flower's beauty is of the humble and everyday kind, rather than the spectacular and remarkable kind.

The speaker chooses the flower to be her gift, then, because it serves as a metaphor for her own psyche. She sees herself, like the flower, as modest rather than showy, as confident and independent rather than a follower of the crowd.

In this sense, the flower 'suits' her better than any other potential gift. In offering the flower, then, she presents her lover with something that is not only beautiful but also representative of her own personality.

A narrow Fellow in the Grass

LINE BY LINE

The first thing to note about this poem is that it's spoken by a man. This becomes clear in line 11 when the speaker refers to his boyhood: 'But when a Boy'. The speaker might be a farmer or farm labourer, someone who grew up in the countryside and is familiar with the meadows and wildlife of 19th-century New England, where snakes were fairly common. Perhaps Dickinson is imagining herself as her brother Austin, or as one of the farmhands who worked on the family farm.

Lines 1 to 4

The speaker describes a grass snake he's seen in the locality where he lives and works. He describes it in a fairly friendly and amiable manner: 'A narrow Fellow'. He notes that this creature can be glimpsed 'Occasionally' as it crawls through the grassy pastures. It's not an everyday sight, but it's common enough that one must remain alert for its presence.

The speaker describes the snake's movement as graceful and light, saying that it 'rides' or skims along the grass. He also describes how the snake moves quickly in and out of visibility, as suggested in line 3: 'You may have met Him – did you not'. The speaker highlights the suddenness with which the snake can appear at your feet: 'His notice sudden is'.

Lines 5 to 10

In stanza 2, the speaker further describes the unique movement of the snake. As the snake propels itself forward, it disturbs the grass through which it crawls. The speaker uses a simile to describe the snake parting the grass in much the same way as a comb parts hair: 'The Grass divides as with a Comb'. Here, you can visualise walking through the meadow when all at once you feel the grass parting under you and catch the briefest glimpse of the snake's crawling body: 'A spotted Shaft is seen'. But before you even have a chance to react, the grass 'closes' or returns to normal. You might then notice how the grass 'opens further on', parting a few metres away, as the snake continues its journey through the field.

The speaker tells us that the snake has a preference for cool, moist surroundings. He notes how it likes 'a Boggy Acre', poor land that is unsuitable for growing crops: 'A Floor too cool for Corn'.

Lines 10 to 16

The speaker then recalls the younger days he spent running 'Barefoot' through the meadows. He can remember coming across a snake 'more than once' during his childhood. Initially, he would mistake it for a discarded whip, unravelling on the ground: 'Have passed, I thought, a Whip lash,/ Unbraiding in the Sun'. The word 'Unbraiding' conveys a wonderful sense of the snake's sinuous movements.

When the boy bent down to retrieve the 'Whip', however, he quickly realised it was in a fact a snake. The whip 'wrinkled', or twitched, and disappeared: 'It wrinkled And was gone'.

Lines 17 to 24

The speaker then shifts into describing his love of nature, how close he feels to the natural world from working outside all day. He claims to be on friendly terms with many forms of wildlife: 'Several of Nature's People/ I know, and they know me'. He has a strong feeling of affection for and even friendship towards the animals, birds and insects he sees around him: 'I feel for them a transport/ Of Cordiality'.

The snake, however, is another story. While the speaker has attempted to portray the snake in as friendly a manner as possible throughout the poem, referring to it as 'Him' and a 'Fellow', there is no hiding the fact that the speaker fears the snake. It makes no difference whether he encounters the snake 'alone' or when 'Attended' by a companion: he still fears it.

In the poem's closing lines, the speaker gives us a vivid description of the physiological reactions that fear brings with it. Seeing the snake causes shortness of breath and a bone-chilling sensation: 'Without a tighter Breathing/ And Zero at the Bone'. Ultimately, the speaker cannot fully accept the snake as one of 'Nature's People'.

FOCUS ON STYLE

Tone and Atmosphere

The tone changes drastically over the course of the poem. It begins in a conversational manner, with the speaker appearing to ask the reader questions: 'You may have met Him? – did you not'. There is also something genial and playful about how the speaker refers to the snake as a 'narrow Fellow' who 'Occasionally rides', as if the snake is a gentleman whom the speaker sometimes encounters in the street.

By the end of the poem, however, the tone has changed drastically, as the speaker recounts his bone-chilling feelings of fear upon seeing the snake: 'a tighter Breathing/ And Zero at the Bone'. This brilliantly describes how our nerves prickle when we feel scared. Although he wants to be genial towards the snake and accept it as one of 'Nature's People', the speaker can't quite shake off that spine-tingling feeling.

Vivid Imagery

Interestingly, Dickinson never uses the word 'snake' in the poem. However, the way she describes the creature's movement leaves us in no doubt as to what it is. One effective thread of imagery throughout the poem is the association of the snake with hair. We see this in stanza 2, when she describes the snake combing the grass: 'The Grass divides as with a Comb'. In stanza 4, she again likens the snake to hair when she describes it as 'Unbraiding' or unravelling on the ground. These associations of the snake with hair give us a sense of its long, winding, smooth movement.

The speaker personifies the snake, as well as other creatures, throughout the poem. We see this in the way he refers to the snake as 'Him' and 'Fellow', and refers to the animal kingdom as 'Nature's People'. This demonstrates how close he feels to nature. Furthermore, in line 4, he compares the snake to a guest who does not give much notice before coming for a visit: 'His notice sudden is'. In stanza 3, he describes the snake as a discerning person with likes and dislikes: 'He likes a Boggy Acre'. We get the sense that the speaker is trying to overcome his fear of the snake by relating to it as if it were a person.

THEMES

NATURE

The speaker of the poem clearly loves nature and spends much of his time outside. He is knowledgeable about the snake's appearance, movements, and preferred habitat: 'He likes a Boggy Acre,/ A Floor too cool for Corn'. He has encountered the snake often enough to be able to describe its behaviour in detail: 'His notice sudden is'.

He proclaims his affection for wildlife, referring to the creatures as 'Nature's People'. This implies that he has a give-and-take friendship with many of the creatures in his locality: 'I know, and they know me'. Despite his love of animals, however, the speaker is not naive about nature. He knows that the snake is dangerous and not to be trusted, as evidenced by his feelings of fear: 'a tighter Breathing/ And Zero at the Bone'.

DEATH

The speaker is keenly aware of the danger and the possibility of death when he sees the snake. Though many snakes of New England are harmless, there are two venomous varieties: rattlesnakes and copperheads. Even when the speaker sees a harmless snake, he must wonder for an instant if it's one of the poisonous types. In the closing lines, the poet brilliantly describes the fight-or-flight response, the physical sensations we feel when we perceive danger: 'a tighter Breathing/ And Zero at the Bone'.

RELIGION

There are Biblical overtones to the poet's description of the snake. In the Book of Genesis, the serpent tricks Eve into eating fruit from the forbidden Tree of Knowledge, an act which results in Adam and Eve being thrown out of Paradise. The snake in the poem is also described as something of a trickster, one that appears in a 'sudden' manner, passing by your feet before you even have time to react. It is also portrayed as a deceitful creature that fools the boy into believing it's a 'Whip lash'.

I taste a liquor never brewed –

LINE BY LINE

'I taste a liquor never brewed' is one of Dickinson's happiest and most playful nature poems. The poem makes most sense if we imagine it being spoken from the point of view of a bird that goes 'reeling' through the meadows on a summer's day, sipping nectar from various flowers. The hummingbird was a creature that had a special significance for Dickinson, so much so that she referred to herself as 'the hummingbird' in several of her letters.

Stanzas 1 and 2

The bird describes how it travels through the fields on 'endless summer days'. We imagine here the long and lazy days in June and July, days so bright and sunny it seems they will never end.

As the bird journeys across the meadows, it becomes extremely drunk. Three different substances contribute to the bird's sense of intoxication: the nectar it sips from various wild flowers, the dew it drinks from grasses and the fresh summer air itself.

Line 2 mentions tankards that have been 'scooped' or shaped out of pearl. It's possible that this refers to white 'pearly' clouds, suggesting how intoxicating dew spills from the clouds the way beer might pour from a tankard.
It's more likely, however, that this line refers to white flowers. Just as 'Tankards' contain beer, so the flowers contain nectar. They are portrayed as being made from 'pearl' in order to reflect their intense, virginal whiteness.

The bird describes itself as a 'Debauchee', a person given to excessive indulgence. The bird, however, over-indulges in dew rather than in alcohol. It also describes itself as an 'Inebriate' or drunkard. But it gets drunk on the fresh summer air rather than on any alcoholic beverage.

The bird thinks of these summer substances as alcoholic beverages. But they are a liquor that was 'never brewed'; they are the product of no industrial process or human intervention, instead occurring naturally in the fields and meadows.

The bird compares theses summer substances to the beer from the Rhineland, an area in Germany famous for the quality of its brewing. The 'Vats' of the Rhineland's many breweries are filled with a bewildering variety of beers and ales. According to the bird, however, none can match the potency of the nectar it sips from the flowers of the meadow. No product of the Rhineland could be as intoxicating as the dew and the fresh summer air: 'Not all the Vats upon the Rhine/ Yield such an Alcohol!'

These substances leave the bird so intoxicated that it goes spinning and whirling through the meadows: 'Reeling- thro endless summer days'. The verb 'to reel' suggests movement that is wild, erratic and out of control, the type of motion one might associate with an extremely drunk person.

The bird, then, goes 'Reeling' between the blue flowers of the meadow, travelling from one to the other in search of nectar. Using a witty metaphor, the bird compares these flowers to pubs or 'inns'. Each flower is filled with intoxicating nectar, just as inns are filled with alcoholic beverages.

Stanza 3

The bird focuses on a purple 'Foxglove' plant, which, like the blue flowers mentioned above, is compared to a pub or inn: A bee enters the foxglove and nestles within its petals, just as a patron might enter a public house and make himself comfortable at the bar. The bee becomes 'drunken' on the foxglove's nectar, just as a pub's patron might become drunk on beer and spirits. Eventually, closing time will arrive and the pub's owner will ask the customer to leave. Similarly, the foxglove's petals will eventually tighten and close up, ejecting the bee from its comfortable drinking place: 'When 'Landlords' turn the drunken Bee/ Out of the Foxglove's door'.

The bird also describes how butterflies will 'renounce' or give up nectar the way an alcoholic might swear off alcohol. They are said to have vowed to never again consume a 'dram' or measure of this intoxicating substance. The bird, however, is determined to never stop drinking nectar. Unlike the bee, it will never permit itself to be ejected from the source of this substance it loves so much. Unlike the butterfly, it will never take a vow of abstinence. Indeed, the bird vows to consume even more nectar in the future: 'I shall but drink the more!' It's as if the bird will take advantage of the fact that the bee and the butterfly have stopped drinking, savouring the nectar they would otherwise have consumed.

Stanza 4

Unlike the ejected bee or the abstaining butterfly, then, the bird will continue with its drunken ways until the day it dies. On its death it will be welcomed into heaven by saints and angels. Heaven is depicted as a town or city where the saints run to the windows of their houses to see a bird entering paradise. The angels ('Seraphs') will 'swing their snowy Hats', throwing them into the air to celebrate the arrival of this 'little Tippler'. (The 'little Tippler' is the intoxicated bird, 'tippler' being a slang word for drinker).

Dickinson uses a final, memorable metaphor to describe the bird's arrival in heaven. The bird, she says, will be 'Leaning against the – Sun –'. The image of the bird being in physical contact with the sun suggests the intense, perhaps almost unbearable, brightness of Christ's presence, a presence that the bird will experience in paradise. The fact that the bird is 'leaning' suggests that it is tired after its busy life and welcomes the rest the afterlife will provide. It 'leans' in a way that recalls how a farmer might lean against a fence after a long day's work.

Many critics believe that this poem was influenced by the philosopher Ralph Waldo Emerson, who Dickinson greatly admired. Poets, Emerson believed, should be so attuned to nature that the sight, sound and taste of water alone are enough to intoxicate them. As Emerson himself puts it: 'The poet's habit of living should be set on a key so low that the common influences should delight him. His cheerfulness should be the gift of the sunlight, the air should suffice for his inspiration, and he should be tipsy with water.'

FOCUS ON STYLE

Form

'A Bird, came down the Walk' uses a form common to most of Dickinson's poetry. It has four-line stanzas and an ABAB rhyme scheme. It is written in 'ballad metre', which means there are four stresses in the first and third lines of each stanza, and three stresses in the second and fourth lines. Fittingly, for a poem that celebrates intoxicated states, the verse is fast-paced, 'reeling' from one line to the next.

Verbal Music

Like many of Dickinson's poems, 'I taste a liquor never brewed' makes wide use of assonance and alliteration. Assonance, in particular, is responsible for creating a pleasant, euphonious musical effect suited to a poem of celebration. The repeated 'e' sound in 'endless summer', and the repeated 'o' sounds in 'Out of the Foxgloves Door', for instance, generate a soothing music.

Metaphor, Simile, Figures of Speech

Much of the poem is structured around a 'conceit' or extended metaphor, one that compares the enjoyment of nature (especially nectar) to the enjoyment of alcohol. The bird, as we've seen, gets high on nature the way a drinker might get high on alcohol. This is why the bird describes itself as a 'Tippler' and 'Inebriate' and a 'Debauchee'. In stanza 1, as we have seen, white flowers are described as 'Tankards', or drinking glasses. In stanza 2, blue flowers are compared to 'inns', or pubs. This comparison is reinforced in stanza 3, where the speaker depicts a bee, drunk on nectar, being ejected from a Foxglove, just as a drinker might be ejected from a bar by its owner.

Vivid Imagery

The poem is distinguished by several playful and exaggerated images. A prime example is the image of heaven as a city, as a place where the saints run to the windows of their houses and where angels go 'swinging' their hats in what we can only take to be celebration. The image of a drunken bee being given his marching orders is also quite amusing.

Riddling and Paradoxical Language

The poem's riddling qualities also contribute to its playful and light-hearted tone. For instance, we are not actually told that the phrases 'Tankards scooped in Pearl' and 'inns of molten Blue' refer to flowers. Readers must figure these things out for themselves. The title phrase, 'I taste a liquor never brewed' has a similar riddling quality. We pause as we consider what the poet might be talking about. After all, what kind of liquor was never 'brewed' by human hand?

THEMES

NATURE

This poem, as is so often the case with Dickinson, celebrates the splendours of the natural world, specifically the pleasures of long, hot summer days. It depicts meadows fragrant with life and growth, flowers of such an intense blueness that they seem 'molten' or on fire; birds, bees and butterflies flitting hither and thither.

Like 'A Bird, came down the Walk', this poem is playful in its depiction of the natural world. There is something cute and almost comedic about the image of the bird becoming so drunk on nectar, air and dew that it reels from flower to flower, just as a drunk person might reel from bar to bar. Similarly playful are the depictions of the butterflies swearing abstinence and of the bee entering, and subsequently being ejected from, the foxglove's 'inn'.

The poem also reminds us of Dickinson's intense sensitivity to the natural world. We sense that the poet, like the hummingbird, is capable of getting 'high' on nature, that the sights, sounds and smells of the natural world induce in her a sense of ecstasy and intoxication.

The poem can also be read as a celebration of the everyday, suggesting the extraordinary beauty that can be found within an ordinary sight like that of a field in summer. Maybe Dickinson thinks that, like the hummingbird, we should be left blissful and ecstatic by the nature that surrounds us. We should be so open to the beauty of the natural world that it intoxicates us in the same way that liquor does.

This poem portrays an enjoyment of nature that is wild, manic and intoxicated. This is suggested in particular by the image of the bird reeling through the meadow. A similarly manic enjoyment of nature is depicted in 'The Soul has Bandaged moments', where the poet depicts herself dancing 'like a Bomb' in a 'delirious' response to nature's beauty. Many readers feel that perhaps there is something a little unhealthy about this 'hyper-sensitive' response to the natural world, as if it was the 'manic', flip side to the numb 'depression' that Dickinson describes in many of her poems.

DEATH

The poem's conclusion provides a memorable depiction of the afterlife, as the bird is welcomed into Heaven by saints and angels. Heaven is depicted as a joyful and carefree city of rest. The bird finds itself in the presence of the 'Sun', which, as we have seen, is generally taken to be Christ himself.

Heaven is depicted as a very real place, as a town whose inhabitants live in houses with windows, wear hats and who celebrate the arrival of each new soul. This positive and light-hearted depiction of the afterlife contrasts sharply with many of Dickinson's other poems that deal the themes of death and dying.

RELIGION

'I taste a liquor never brewed', then, presents a positive view of religion, suggesting that God will reward his faithful subjects, keeping a place for them in heaven's sunlit city.

This contrasts sharply with the view of religion expressed in 'There's a certain Slant of light', which depicts God tormenting us by sending down from Heaven a strange light that does us psychological harm. It also contrasts with the view of religion expressed in 'I heard a Fly buzz – when I died', which seems to mock religious hope.

We sense that God welcomes those who tirelessly appreciated nature during their lives, who relished the earth He created. The bird, then, is welcomed into heaven because of the drunkenness, gluttony, and excess it exhibited during its life. This is deeply ironic, of course, because such excessive behaviour is typically condemned by religion!

After great pain, a formal feeling comes –

LINE BY LINE

The speaker has recently experienced a bout of 'great pain', of extraordinary mental anguish. The pain has passed, but it has left a strange numbness and lethargy in its wake. The poet describes this state of mind as a 'formal feeling'. Several different meanings of the term 'formal' can be applied here:

- The feeling is marked by formality or ceremony. There is nothing spontaneous about it. It adheres to strict convention and ritual.
- It has the form or appearance of feeling but lacks any spirit.
- It is perfunctory, something that occurs in a mundane way, without care or thought.

Nerves

The speaker describes how different aspects of her body and her psyche are feeling and behaving in the wake of the pain she has recently endured. She first describes the condition of her 'Nerves'. As it is used here, the term 'Nerves' can refer to the body's nervous system, to the physical fibres that transmit signals around the body. Each nerve is also an aspect of the speaker's mental state, however. For instance, we might say of someone suffering from anxiety that his or her nerves are bad.

The speaker's nerves were recently in a highly elevated state. She experienced a state of anxiety and extreme tension, one that manifested itself both physically and mentally. But now this state of tension has passed. Where once her nerves were agitated, they now 'sit' still.

The speaker uses two literary devices to convey the state of her nerves and to describe the eerie calm that has come over her:

- First, she uses personification, depicting the nerves as people attending a ceremony. Perhaps we might imagine a crowd seated silently in a church, possibly attending a funeral service.
- She then uses a simile, comparing the nerves to 'Tombs'.

The images of people seated in a formal or ceremonious manner and of 'Tombs' convey a sense of rigidity and vitality and of a lack of emotion and spontaneity.

Heart

The speaker then describes how her inner self or psyche is holding up in the the aftermath of the pain that she has recently experienced. She uses the term 'Heart' to refer to this inner self. The 'Heart', we're told, has recently been forced to bear or carry a great weight: 'The stiff Heart ... that bore'. This suggests the intense strain to which her psyche was subjected during her recent bout of mental anguish. The 'Heart', we are told, is 'stiff', which suggests that, in the wake of this assault, her psyche is numb and unfeeling.

The speaker says that the 'Heart' cannot remember much, if anything, of the burden it was forced to carry. Did it carry this weight recently, or in the distant past? Did such an ordeal actually happen to it at all? Indeed, the 'Heart' is not itself sure how long it has existed for. Has it been around for centuries, or just for a normal human life-span?

The poem's reference to the heart's questioning conveys the intense disorientation that has gripped the speaker's psyche. In this moment of eerie calm, she finds herself confused and befuddled. She can't quite make sense of who or where she is. The terrible mental anguish that she has just experienced seems distant and unreal.

Feet

In this state of eerie calm and numbness, the speaker finds herself walking aimlessly in circles. There is something 'mechanical' and 'Wooden' about the manner in which she goes round and round, suggesting the unthinking or unconscious nature of her movement. In a sense, the speaker might be said to resemble a robot, mindlessly executing a pre-programmed set of instructions. She is no longer operating in a conscious manner; it is as if she has been hypnotised and is no longer controlling her own feet.

The speaker feels obsessively compelled to walk in this pattern. She simply must repeat this action over and over again. In this condition, she would walk through 'Ought' or anything placed along the path before her. If snakes or scorching hot coals were present on the path, the speaker would walk through or over them. If the path before her melted away, leaving only 'Air', she would continue walking anyway, presumably falling over the freshly created precipice.

The speaker, then, describes how her feet have grown 'Regardless', suggesting that they have become indifferent and uncaring. They are compelled to keep walking, irrespective of the surface on which they are walking.

Perhaps surprisingly, the speaker describes this state as one of 'contentment', suggesting that she experiences a measure of ease and satisfaction as she circles robotically. She compares what she feels to 'Quartz' or 'stone', suggesting an utterly rigid and unfeeling mental state. This contentment, then, is one of numbness and emptiness; after all, if you don't feel anything, you can't feel bad.

The speaker describes this period as the 'Hour of Lead'. Lead is an element with several vivid associations:

- It is a heavy metal and is proverbially associated with slowness and lethargy. For example, an unfit footballer might be said to have lead in his boots.
- Lead is also a poison, and prolonged exposure to it can cause serious illness or death.
- Lead is also characterised as a base metal, a crude or ugly substance for which people have little value.

The 'Hour of Lead' therefore suggests an especially grim mental interval, one characterised not only by lethargy and inertia but by feelings of worthlessness. Perhaps the speaker also feels

that her mind is slowly becoming toxic and poison-filled, as this period of eerie calm continues.

The speaker imagines how she will look back on this period of eerie calm, if she manages to outlive or survive this experience. She will recall this ordeal, as someone rescued from an Arctic snow-drift might recall the experience of nearly freezing to death: 'As Freezing persons, recollect the Snow'.

She mentions three stages that an Arctic survivor might experience. The first stage is the 'Chill' that sets in as cold overcomes the body. 'Stupor' follows as the mind's processes begin to shut down. Finally, a sense of 'letting go' leads to an acceptance of one's fate. The speaker, in her state of eerie calm, feels that she is undergoing a similar process. Unlike the Arctic survivor, though, who, presumably, was rescued at the last minute, it is unclear whether she will survive her ordeal.

FOCUS ON STYLE

Metaphor, Simile, Figures of Speech

The poet personifies the 'Nerves', describing them being seated in a 'ceremonious' fashion. The poet also personifies the inner self or 'Heart', presenting it as someone who has been traumatised and left feeling confused and discombobulated.

In the poem's final stanza, the poet compares this period she must now endure to what those trapped in snow might experience. If she does survive this period in her life, she might remember it with the same intensity as someone trapped in Arctic conditions and rescued at the last minute might remember the freezing conditions: 'As Freezing persons, recollect the Snow'.

Vivid Imagery

The 'Hour of Lead' is an especially powerful image. We can imagine someone being exposed to this poisonous substance in some horrific manner, perhaps being forced to inhale a cloud of lead-filled fumes, or having this metal injected into his or her system. Of course, the speaker in the poem has not experienced such torture, but such images convey her poisoned and lethargic state of mind.

Verbal music

Dickinson's use of repeated 'o' sounds in the poem serves to create a sense of weariness and exhaustion. The long 'o' sounds in 'grown', 'stone', 'bore' and 'before' create a sombre music that compliments the grim experience that the poet is describing.

THE WORKINGS OF THE MIND

Dickinson is a great poet of the inner self. Her poems are finely attuned to the workings of the human mind and to the vast range of human emotions and feelings. In 'The Soul has Bandaged moments', for example, the poet vividly captures the emotional swings that sometimes accompany being in love, describing how we can go from delirious highs to debilitating lows in no time at all. In 'I taste a liquor', she wonderfully describes what it is like to be full of joy and free of care. In contrast, 'There is a certain Slant of light' masterfully captures feelings of great despair and depression.

In 'After great pain', Dickinson describes the rather strange and disturbing psychological state that someone might experience after enduring some great mental trauma. Although the pain has ended, it is not followed by any sense of relief or joy. Instead, there is an almost complete absence of feeling and emotion. It is as if the speaker of the poem has been utterly drained of vitality and spontaneity.

Dickinson suggests this lack of spontaneity by describing the speaker's feeling as 'formal'. The body behaves as if it is living, but there is something stiff and mechanical about its actions and movements, as if it were just going through the motions, without any thought or care: 'The Feet, mechanical, go round'. The poet describes this lack of feeling as a form of 'contentment'. But this state of mind is brings no satisfaction; it is a stone's contentment, devoid of any feelings whatsoever.

The poem finishes on a rather disturbing note, by suggesting that the speaker might not survive this post-traumatic period. There is a danger that the mind might never again spark with life, that the body will not be re-ignited with energy and vitality. There is a risk that the speaker will just descend further into 'stupor', that the numbness will eventually paralyse the body and that all conscious thought will cease. At this point, the will to live will be lost and the speaker will let go, just as one who is trapped in snow might eventually lose their fight to survive.

John Donne Themes

Sex and Seduction

Donne's early poems, written while he was as a law student at Lincoln's Inn in London and a well-known 'visitor of ladies', present a cynical – we might say misogynistic – view of sex and seduction. 'Song: Go and catch a falling star', for instance, suggests that women can never be 'true' when it comes to matters of love and sexuality. According to Donne, women who are in relationships will always cheat. And women who are single will always sleep around in an inappropriate manner. This is especially true, the poet suggests, of 'fair' or beautiful women. In fact, finding a woman who is both 'true' and 'fair' is no more possible than catching a falling star or working out why the Devil has cleft feet.

The poet even imagines undertaking a 'pilgrimage' to see such a woman, as if she were one of the wonders of the world. But such a pilgrimage, he concludes, would be futile. For even the truest of beautiful women will not remain true for very long and will have slept with two or three men before his pilgrimage is concluded.

The poem, then, can be read as an extremely cynical piece of relationship advice from the poet to his male readers: avoid getting emotionally involved with women, he seems to suggest, because they cannot be trusted and will only hurt and betray you. Women, presumably, should instead be viewed only as objects of physical attraction.

Both 'The Flea' and 'The Dream' present a similarly cynical view of sex and seduction. In both poems, the poet's focus is entirely on the achievement of sexual satisfaction. In 'The Flea', for instance, we sense the poet's desperation to sleep with the object of his affection. He is willing to use any argument, no matter how outlandish, in order to overcome the lady's objections and lure her to his bedchamber. In 'The Dream', too, the poet is willing to deploy any argument he can to convince his beloved to sleep with him. As such, his characterisation of love as being something 'pure' and above the concerns of society is merely a cynical ploy, one designed to lure the object of his affections into bed.

Honour and Reputation

Both 'The Flea' and 'The Dream' are concerned with the theme of sexual virtue, with the idea that women become dishonourable or immoral if they engage in sex outside marriage. In 'The Flea', for instance, the lady is determined not to yield to the poet's advances, and she is conscious of how her honour will 'waste' away if she does so. To sleep with this man outside of wedlock would be a great 'sin' and 'shame'. In 'The Dream', too, the object of the poet's affections is concerned about her 'honour' and is fearful of the damage that sleeping with the poet might have on her reputation.

In both poems, the poet attempts to overcome the lady's objections. In 'The Flea', for instance, the poet asks the lady to 'mark', or consider, how a flea has sucked blood from the poet himself and is now sucking blood from the lady: 'It sucked me first and now sucks thee'. Their blood has, therefore, been mixed together inside the flea's body, their bodily fluids being 'mingled' just as they would be in sexual intercourse. And yet no shameful act or sin has been committed: 'Thou knows't this cannot be said/ A sin, nor shame, nor loss of maidenhead'.

In 'The Dream', meanwhile, Donne argues that love can only be 'pure' if it is untarnished by doubts and fears. To love in a 'pure' manner, he says, is to be 'brave', for it means not caring what others might think. But if people allow thoughts of shame and honour to enter their minds, it weakens and spoils this love: 'That love is weak where fear's as strong as he'.

In both poems, it should also be noted, the poet displays scant regard for the woman's honour, and for the lasting damage their night of pleasure would cause to the lady's reputation. There is an ironic contrast, therefore, between 'The Flea' and 'The Dream', on the one hand, and 'Song: Go and Catch a Falling Star' on the other. In 'Song: Go and Catch a Falling Star', the poet laments that there are no women who possess both beauty and sexual virtue. In 'The Flea', meanwhile, he has finally encountered such a woman. And he responds by doing everything in his power to seduce her, thereby compromising her sexual virtue forever.

Love and Marriage

In an early poem like 'The Flea', Donne exhibits what might be called a casual disregard for marriage and commitment, envying the flea's ability to enjoy itself 'before it woo' and comparing its bloated body to a marriage bed. 'The Flea' can be contrasted, therefore, with Donne's later poetry, which presents a more spiritual or romantic view of love and marriage.

In 'The Sun Rising', for instance, Donne emphasises that his relationship with his wife is the only thing of value, the only thing that matters to him. His beloved, he declares, is 'everything'. Being with her makes him feel like a king, like the wealthiest man in the world. The room in which they lie together is the only place that matters, the only place that really exists.

'The Anniversary', written on the first anniversary of Donne's meeting with his future wife, also highlights the centrality of love and marriage to the poet's life. He and his beloved are so important to each other that they 'rule' each other's lives. The poet is his lover's 'king' because he rules her, but he is also her 'subject' because she rules him.

'A Valediction: Forbidden Mourning' is also a testament to the depth of the poet's feelings for his wife. The poem, like many by Donne, approaches the subject of love in a rather intellectual and argumentative manner. But there are also moments of genuine emotion, especially related to the image of the mathematical compass at the poem's conclusion. The poem highlights how lovers remain in one another's minds even when they are physically distanced. The poet stresses that his wife will remain at the centre of his thoughts while he travels. Thoughts of her will ensure that he behaves appropriately while abroad and that he returns home to England when his journey is concluded.

The Mystical Nature of Love

Several poems by Donne present love as something spiritual and transcendent. Both 'The Sun Rising' and 'The Anniversary', for instance, suggest that love is immune to the passage of time. True love, according to the 'The Sun Rising', is 'all alike', is utterly unchanging. It doesn't 'know' or care about the seasons that come and go. It is unaffected by the passing 'hours, days, months'. 'The Anniversary' also depicts love as somehow magically outside the normal course of time. The poet imagines that the relationship between himself and his beloved is the only thing in the world not subject to ageing and decay (by the end of the poem, however, he has adopted a humbler and more realistic vision of love, accepting that love must triumph over time, not by being timeless and unchanging, but evolving as the years go by).

Both 'Song: Sweetest Love, I do not go' and 'A Valediction: Forbidding Mourning' suggest that the poet and his wife are joined by an almost mystical bond. In 'Sweetest Love', for instance, the poet suggests that his wife's sighs and tears 'waste' not only her own life but the poet's life, too. Each is like the 'life force' of the other. Therefore, on a spiritual or psychological level they can never be apart.

'A Valediction: Forbidden Mourning' makes a similar point, arguing that the poet and his wife are 'Inter-assured of the mind', enjoying an intense mental connection that they don't fully understand themselves. Their souls, he maintains, 'are one', and can never be breached or separated. He even suggests that their relationship has secret, sacred aspects and is associated with the celestial spheres rather than with this earthly domain.

Sin and Redemption

A recurring feature of Donne's 'Holy Sonnets' is the manner in which they emphasises Donne's extraordinary sinfulness. In 'Thou hast made me', for instance, Donne describes his heart as having turned to 'iron', wonderfully capturing how sin has corrupted his life and his mind. He claims to be such a terrible sinner that he cannot 'sustain' himself for even an hour without giving into the Devil's temptations.

'Batter my heart' makes a similar point. The poet is so corrupted by sin that he compares himself to a defective pot or vase, one that the sculptor has no choice but to cast aside. Sin has taken over his life, the way a usurper might seize a town not rightfully his. He even compares himself to sin's fiancé, emphasising the intense and intimate nature of his relationship with sin. In 'At the round earth's imagined corners', Donne goes even further, implying that he's more sinful than anyone else who has ever lived or died. His sins would, therefore, require an 'abundance' of forgiveness on God's part.

But the Holy Sonnets also highlight Donne's eagerness for redemption. In 'Thou hast made me' he is desperate to be cleansed of sin, for God to 'repair' his corrupt soul. In 'Batter my heart', meanwhile, he calls on God to forcibly 'untie' or 'break' his relationship with sin. He wants God to 'Batter [his] heart', to enter his life in a forceful, almost violent manner. He wants to be broken by God's love so that he can be made anew. 'At the round earth's imagined corners', too, highlights Donne's eagerness to atone for his sins and make himself right with God.

A striking feature of the Holy Sonnets is Donne's demand for what might be described as 'special treatment' from God. In 'Batter my heart', for instance, the poet is convinced that he is beyond any ordinary means of redemption. He is so sinful that he must be utterly demolished and remade. God, he insists, must 'bend' or apply all of His extraordinary 'force' in order to make this happen.

We also see this in 'Thou hast made me', when the poet calls on God to 'repair [him] now'. The poet doesn't want to bother with the usual business of redemption, with prayer, the sacraments and good deeds. Instead, he wants God to take immediate and decisive action, cleansing him instantly of sin. 'At the round earth's imagined corners' is similarly demanding. The poet insists that he, unlike ordinary Christians, cannot be guided to redemption by prayer and the sacraments. Instead, he needs Christ to enter his life directly in some special manner so he can be taught how to repent.

Song: Go and catch a falling star

LINE BY LINE

'Go and catch a falling star' was likely written in the 1590s, when Donne was a law student at Lincoln's Inn in London. Like other poems written during Donne's student days, it was not published in any book or periodical. Instead, it was copied out and circulated around London's literary scene. Donne's audience consisted of fellow students and literary gentlemen, many who would have been known to him personally. His goal, therefore, was to impress this almost exclusively male readership.

Stanza 1

The poem's opening stanza presents the reader with seven tasks or challenges. Donne first instructs his reader to 'Go and catch a falling star'. He is referring to the streaks of light that can be seen in the night sky and that resemble stars 'falling' or dropping from the skies. One could imagine, from a distance, that it might be possible to hold out a hand and catch one of these falling objects. But doing so, of course, is impossible. These streaks of light in the night sky are actually caused by meteoroids falling into the Earth's atmosphere and burning up.

Donne then instructs his reader to impregnate or 'Get with child' a 'mandrake root'. The mandrake is a Mediterranean plant whose roots can have an uncannily human appearance. Women who wanted to become pregnant would sleep with mandrake roots beneath their pillows, believing that it aided conception. But there is no magic ritual, of course, that might allow us to make a mandrake root pregnant.

Donne asks his reader to figure out the nature of time itself: 'Tell me where all past years are'. We could imagine a scholar in Donne's time asking such a question. Is time actually a substance of some kind? And what happens to time that is 'used up' after we have experienced it? But such a question, of course, is impossible to answer.

Donne then asks his reader to solve an arguably even more difficult riddle, wanting to know 'who cleft the devil's foot'. The Devil is traditionally depicted as having hoof-like feet that are 'cleft' or split into two toes. Donne wants his reader to figure out who is responsible for this aspect of the Devil's appearance. Did God grant him these goat-like feet? Or did the Devil himself choose such an appearance? Or did the Devil lose a bet with some quick-witted human being and end up with 'cleft' feet forever'?

Donne asks his reader to teach him how to hear the singing of mermaids, who were known for their enchanting voices. The reader, presumably, would have to locate a colony of mermaids somewhere off the English coast. He would also have to determine the time of the day when the mermaids are most likely to burst into song. He would then have to 'teach' this information to the poet. This task, of course, is just as impossible as those mentioned above.

Donne also wants to be taught how to avoid the emotion of envy. Donne brilliantly refers to 'envy's stinging', capturing how we experience envy as an almost physical pricking. Donne's reader would have to develop a series of techniques that 'keep off' or fend off this toxic emotion. He would then have to teach these tricks to the poet himself. But coming up with such techniques, given what we know of human nature, would be all but impossible.

Finally, Donne asks his reader to find the circumstance that would allow an honest person to get ahead in life. He uses a nautical metaphor to convey this. A person with an 'honest mind' is compared to a ship. Advantageous circumstances, meanwhile, are compared to a wind that will fill the ship's sails, allowing it to 'advance'. But such a wind, Donne implies, is impossible to locate. The poem, then, puts forward a very cynical view of human existence, suggesting that dishonest people prosper while honest people fall behind.

Stanza 2

Donne is convinced that women can be true or fair but not both. Indeed, Donne is convinced that his reader could travel around the world and never find a woman who possesses both of these qualities:

- His reader could travel for 'ten thousand days and nights', which equates to about 27 years.
- His reader could travel until he was an old man: 'Till age snow white hairs on thee'.
- His reader could even have supernatural abilities, such as the gift of second sight, and be capable of perceiving things that are invisible to ordinary men: 'If thou be'st born to strange sights,/ Things invisible to see'.
- His reader would return with tales of the 'strange wonders' he experienced while on his travels. Donne imagines sitting down with his returning reader to hear tales of strange people and faraway lands: 'Thou, when thou return'st, wilt tell me,/ All strange wonders that befell thee'.

But his reader will 'swear' that nowhere, even during such an epic journey, did he encounter a woman who is both true and fair.

Stanza 3

Donne concedes that it just might be possible for his reader to encounter such a woman in the course of such an epic journey. If his reader were to encounter such a woman, he must write to Donne immediately, telling him where she can be found: 'If thou find'st one, let me know'. Donne says that he would happily travel a great distance to see such a woman: 'Such a pilgrimage were sweet'.

But Donne quickly changes his mind and declares that he would not undertake a 'pilgrimage' in order to meet a woman his reader had deemed both true and fair. In fact, he wouldn't go to meet her even if she lived next door: 'I would not go,/ Though at next door we might meet'.

This is because no beautiful woman can remain true for very long:

- Donne's reader might come across a beautiful woman who is true at the time of their meeting: 'Though she were true, when you met her'.
- She might even remain true while the reader writes to Donne informing him of this discovery: 'And last, till you write your letter'.
- But before Donne arrives ('ere I come') she will have slept with two or three other men: 'she/ Will be/ false…to two, or three'.

Science and Superstition

Donne was living during a time of great scientific learning and discovery. But it was still also a very superstitious time, with people believing a great number of things that we might find strange or surprising today:

People believed that the sight of a shooting' or 'falling' star brought good luck or served as a portent or signal that good fortune was on its way.

Mandrake plants were believed to have magical powers and were much in demand throughout Europe at the time. Men would sometimes carry the plant in their pocket, believing that it would help them attract their desired lover. It was also believed that these plants emitted a terrifying scream when they were uprooted!

The first stanza also hints at the idea of witches, which people of Donne's time believed to be very real. The mentioning of the mandrake root calls to mind the strange plants and herbs that witches would use to make their magic potions. Witches were also commonly believed to be responsible for the envious thoughts that troubled people's minds.

DONNE'S METAPHYSICAL STYLE

Outrageous Claims and Demands

'Go, and catch a falling star', like many of Donne's poems, features outrageous claims and demands. The opening stanza, as we've seen, sets the reader a series of bizarre and impossible tasks. The second stanza makes the outrageous – not to say misogynistic – claim that nowhere on earth can there be found a woman who is both true and fair.

The poem's most extreme claim, however, comes in the third stanza, where the poet imagines hearing that a 'true' and 'fair' woman is living next door to him. The poet declares that by the time he had put on his coat and made his way next door, she would no longer be true. In fact, she would have slept with two or three other men! Here, of course, Donne is using hyperbole, or deliberate poetic exaggeration, in order to emphasise the falseness of the 'fairer sex'.

Inventive Metaphors and Similes

Stanza two features an inventive simile, comparing white hairs to snow. Donne personifies 'age', presenting it as someone who sprinkles white hair on us, whitening the surface of our heads just as snow whitens the surface of the earth when it falls.

Paradox and Contradiction

Donne is well known as a poet of paradox and contradiction. We see this in stanza 3. Pilgrimages are usually thought of as difficult and arduous journeys . But Donne's pilgrimage in this instance would be 'sweet'. The poet would take joy in this long journey, despite its difficulties, delighted at the prospect of the 'true' and 'fair' woman to whom he is travelling.

Form

The fact that the poem is titled 'Song' tells us that this lyric was intended to be chanted or sung, possibly with musical accompanied. The poem's short lines and regular rhyme scheme lend it to such a performance.

THEMES

SEX AND SEDUCTION

This poem presents a cynical – we might even say misogynistic – view of women. Women, the poet suggests, can never be 'true' when it comes to matters of love and sexuality. Women who are in relationships will always cheat. Women who are single will always sleep around in an inappropriate manner.

This is especially true, the poet suggests, of 'fair' or beautiful women. In fact, finding a woman who is both 'true' and 'fair' is no more possible than catching a falling star or working out why the Devil has cleft feet.

The poem's second stanza is wittily misogynistic. We can imagine Donne's male audience chuckling at his depiction of his reader travelling the whole world, encountering all kinds of 'strange wonders' but meeting no woman who is both true and fair.

This misogynistic attitude is most evident in the poem's final stanza. The poet, as we've seen, imagines undertaking a 'pilgrimage' to see such a woman, as if she were one of the wonders of the world. But such a pilgrimage, he concludes, would be futile, for even the truest of beautiful women will not remain true for very long and will have slept with two or three men before his pilgrimage is concluded.

The poem, then, can be read as an extremely cynical piece of relationship advice from the poet to his male readers: he seems to suggest that they should avoid becoming emotionally involved with women because they cannot be trusted and will only hurt and betray you. Women, presumably, should instead be viewed only as objects of physical attraction.

This poem takes an extremely bitter and cynical view of love. Women, the poet argues, are by their very nature inclined to be unfaithful. In fact, women are so untrustworthy in matters of the heart that it's impossible to find a woman who is both beautiful and faithful. And even if you do find such a woman, it's only a matter of time until her true treacherous nature is revealed: 'Though she were true, when you meet her … Yet she/ Will be/ False'.

The Flea

FIRST ENCOUNTER

In 'The Flea', the poet addresses a lady who he is trying to get into bed. The lady, however, is reluctant, feeling that her honour will be lost if she surrenders to his advances. This is especially true because she still retains her 'maidenhead' or virginity.

Donne, we must remember, was writing at a time when women were all too often branded dishonourable or immoral if they slept with a man outside marriage. The lady, then, resists the poet's advances in order to preserve her honour, denying him the pleasures of a sexual encounter. The poet tries to overcome her reluctance through a series of witty, outlandish arguments, all of which are based around the idea of the flea.

Their blood is already 'mingled'

The poet attempts to convince her how harmless or unimportant ('How little') sleeping together would be. He does so by asking her to 'mark', or consider, a flea hopping around the room:

- The flea has sucked blood from the poet himself. Now it's sucking blood from the woman: 'It sucked me first and now sucks thee'.
- Their blood has, therefore, been mixed together inside the flea's body: 'And in this flea our two bloods mingled be'. The flea is now filled with 'one blood made of two'.

- Their bodily fluids have been 'mingled' just as they would be in sexual intercourse.
- And yet no shameful act or sin has been committed. The woman's honour is still intact: 'Thou knows't this cannot be said/ A sin, nor shame, nor loss of maidenhead'.

The woman, therefore, has no reason to resist the poet's advances. Sleeping with the poet will prove no more sinful than being bitten by the flea. Indeed, because their blood has been combined, it's as if they've already slept together anyway.

The flea delights in its own physicality, pampering itself by feasting on blood until it's bloated and swollen: 'And pampered swells with one blood made of two'. It indulges in physical pleasure without 'wooing' or seeking any long-term commitment like that of marriage: 'Yet this enjoys before it woo'. The poet wishes that he and this woman could be more like the flea, that they too could enjoy the pleasures of the flesh before they are married: 'And this, alas, is more than we would do'.

A special kind of 'marriage'

The poet claims that the mingling of their bloods in the flea's body is a special kind of marriage, one 'more' meaningful and profound than any consensual union: 'Where we almost, nay more than married are'.

- He inisists, then, they have been 'met' or been joined together in wedlock despite the disapproval of their parents, and even the objections of the lady herself: 'Though parents grudge, and you, we are met'.
- The flea's body is presented as the temple where their marriage has been celebrated: 'this/ Our … marriage temple is.' It has become, therefore, a holy place.
- The flea also serves as their 'marriage bed'. Again Donne is referring to the mingling of their blood inside the insect's body. Their essences, he claims, have combined there just as a married couple's essences combine on the first night of marriage.

The poet argues, therefore, that because they are already 'married', she can have no objection to sleeping with him!

Killing the flea would be sinful

The lady, it seems, is so unimpressed by the poet's argumnets that she threatens to kill the flea. The poet, however, asks her to 'stay' or restrain herself, saying that if she does so she will spare three lives: 'three lives in one flea spare'. For by swatting the insect she will kill not only the flea itself but also a part of the poet and a part of herself. The flea, having sucked their blood, contains a little piece of each of them: 'This flea is you and I'.

The poet argues that by killing the flea the woman will commit three sins. She will murder the poet, or at least that part of him that is inside the flea. She will commit the sin of suicide or 'self-murder' because part of her is also inside the flea: 'Let not to this, self-murder added be'. She will commit the sin of sacrilege, the destruction of a sacred place. This is because, as we have seen, the flea has become the holy temple of their marriage.

The lady triumphs?

The lady ignores the poet's plea for mercy and acts in a 'Cruel and sudden' manner. She kills this innocent flea whose only crime was taking a single drop of her blood: 'In what could this flea guilty be,/ Except in that drop which it sucked from thee?' She swats the creature and her nail is 'Purpled' with its blood.

The lady laughs in triumph. She has disproved the poet's argument in favour of sparing the flea's life. She has killed the flea and yet no harm has come to herself or to the poet. Contrary to his warning, she has been guilty of neither murder nor suicide: 'Yet thou triumph'st and says't that thou/ Find'st not thyself, nor me the weaker now'. The poet, however, attempts to turn her triumph against her. ''Tis true', he agrees, that in killing the flea she has not damaged herself. But this merely proves that her fears about sleeping with him are false: 'then learn how false fears be'. Killing the flea caused little or nothing of her life force to waste away. Similarly, yielding to his advances will cause little or nothing of her 'honour' to waste away: 'Just so much honour, when thou yields't to me/ Will waste, as this flea's death took life from thee'.

DONNE'S METAPHYSICAL STYLE

Weird and Wonderful Arguments

This is another poem where Donne's Metaphysical style is in evidence, in particular his tendency to deploy zany and fantastical arguments:

- He argues that two people being bitten by the same flea amounts to a kind of sexual intercourse.
- He argues that two people being bitten by the same flea amounts to a kind of marriage.
- He argues that in killing the flea the lady will take 'three lives' and commit three very different sins.
- 'He argues that she will lose no more honour in yielding to him than she lost life force in killing the flea.

Donne offers an argument in favour of each of these outrageous and outlandish points. Yet he does not aim to convince us that they are actually true. He sets out rather to impress us with the inventiveness and ingenuity of his debating style.

Outrageous Claims and Demands

Another aspect of Donne's Metaphysical style is his tendency to make outrageous claims. We see this when he declares that the lady is literally killing him by denying him the pleasures of her body: 'Though use make you apt to kill me'. Indeed, he suggests that through 'use', or practice, the lady has become 'apt', or skilled, at killing him.

Inventive Metaphors and Similes

Another aspect of Donne's Metaphysical style is his tendency to use metaphors that compare two seemingly very different things. We see this in stanza 2, where the flea is compared to a temple in which the poet and the lady have been married. The flea, he declares, is a church with 'living' and 'jet' black walls where he and his lady have been 'cloistered' or sheltered (Donne's use of the word 'cloistered' reinforces the impression that the flea's body has become a holy place. To cloister someone is to confine him or her to the holy and peaceful seclusion of a monastery).

SEX AND SEDUCTION

'The Flea' was written in the 1590s, when Donne was a law student at Lincoln's Inn in London. The poem would have been copied out and circulated among London's literary set.

In Donne's time, believe it or not, there was a tradition of love poems that mentioned fleas. Donne's goal is to push this concept further than any of his rivals or contemporaries. He wants to come up with arguments and metaphors that impress his exclusively male audience with his wit and ingenuity.

'The Flea', then, is more a display of dazzling argumentative skill than it is a genuine attempt at seduction. After all, we may wonder whether such a bizarre discussion about a flea would be sufficient to seduce any reasonable woman!

In this famous poem of seduction, we sense the poet's desperation to sleep with the object of his affection. He seems happy to resort to almost any tactic to lure this lady to his bedchamber. He is willing to use any argument, no matter how outlandish, to overcome her objections.

'The Flea' is a highly playful poem. There is something teasing, almost flirtatious, about the way the poet and the lady clash wits. The poet's arguments and comparisons are meant to dazzle and amuse rather than be taken seriously.

LOVE AND MARRIAGE

'The Flea', it might be argued, presents a cynical view of love and marriage, the poet's focus being entirely on the achievement of sexual satisfaction. The poet, in fact, seems to have a casual disregard for marriage and commitment, envying the flea's ability to enjoy itself 'before it woo' and comparing its body to a marriage bed.

HONOUR AND REPUTATION

'The Flea', as we have seen, is concerned with the theme of sexual virtue, with the idea that women become dishonourable or immoral if they engage in sex outside marriage. We see this in how the woman is determined not to yield to the poet's advances and she is conscious of how her honour will 'waste' away if she does so. To sleep with this man outside of wedlock would be a great 'sin' and 'shame'.

There is an ironic contrast between 'The Flea' and 'Song: Go and Catch a Falling Star'. In 'Song: Go and Catch a Falling Star', the poet laments that there are no women who possess both beauty and sexual virtue. In 'The Flea', meanwhile, he has finally encountered such a lady. And he responds by doing everything in his power to seduce her, thereby compromising her sexual virtue forever.

The poem, therefore, highlights a double standard that prevailed in Donne's time and that to lesser extent still exists today. It's okay, the poem suggests, for a young man like Donne to be a 'visitor of ladies'. But women, on the other hand, are harshly judged if they sleep around. The poet, it should also be noted, displays scant regard for the woman's honour, and for the lasting damage their night of pleasure would cause to the lady's reputation.

The Dream

LINE BY LINE

Stanza 1

The poet is obsessed with a particular lady. However, he has been unable to lure her into bed. While sleeping in his chamber, he dreams that he and the lady are making love. His dream is interrupted when that very lady comes into his room and wakes him up.

We might ask how the lady managed to enter the poet's chamber. It's likely that both the poet and the lady are 'at court' and are resident in some great palace or manor where they would have had easy access to one another's accomodation.

Ordinarily, the poet would have been annoyed to have such a 'happy dream' broken, to be awakened from such an erotic reverie. But because it's the lady herself who woke him, he can't be too irritated:

- He addresses the lady with soft, endearing words, calling her 'Dear love'.
- It was wise, he declares, for the lady to wake him. The subject or 'theme' of his dream, the poet's idea of making love to this woman, is so powerful and 'strong' that it needs to be acted upon. It is a 'theme' more suited to the 'reason' or rationality of the waking world, than to the 'phantasy' of dreams.
- Anyway, his dream, in a sense, wasn't broken at all. He was dreaming about the lady and now the lady is really here. So his dream has been continued: 'My dream thou brok'st not, but continued'st it'.
- His dream of lovemaking was interrupted before it could reach its conclusion. But maybe he and the lady could 'act' or complete this lovemaking in the real world: 'let's act the rest'.

The poet, therefore, urges the lady to 'Enter [his] arms' and succumb, finally, to his advances.

Stanza 2

Donne flatters the lady, declaring that her eyes are brilliantly bright and radiant. It was the brightness of her eyes, he claims, rather than any noise she made, that roused him from his slumbers. Her eyes, he declares, are so bright that they woke him like a torch shining in his face.

The lady, he declares, is so beautiful that she has an angelic appearance. Indeed, when he first woke up he thought it was an angel rather than a human being standing in his room: 'Yet I thought thee … an angel, at first sight'.

Donne also claims that the lady is capable of seeing into his heart and reading his mind, of knowing his deepest thoughts and desires. When she entered the room and he was sleeping, she knew exactly what he was dreaming: 'thou knew'st what I dreamt'. Not only this, but she knew that he was close to reaching the climax of his dream: 'thou knew'st when/ Excess of joy would wake me'.

But angels, the poet knows, are not capable of reading the thoughts of humans. It is 'beyond an angel's art' to do so. And so, the poet declares, the lady must be some kind of a goddess or divine being if she can read his mind and know his deepest thoughts and desires. To consider her a mere angel would, therefore, be disrespectful, irreverent or 'profane': 'it could not choose but be/ Profane, to think thee any thing but thee'.

The Lady is 'so true'

Throughout the poem Donne makes references to 'truth' and to what is 'true'. In the opening stanza, he tells the lady that she is 'so true', that simply thinking about her is sufficient to make dreams reality and fantastical tales or imaginings real lived experiences that are recorded in the annals of history: 'Thou art so true that thoughts of thee suffice/ To make dreams truths, and fables histories'.

The term 'true' has a number of relevant meanings here:

- Donne is suggesting that the woman is very real and authentic, as opposed to some figment of his imagination.
- But he is also implying that the lady is sincere and honest. There is nothing, he suggests, disingenuous or duplicitous about her behaviour.
- She is also 'true' in the sense of being loyal and faithful to him. Her entering his room, he suggests, is a clear sign that she is committed to him and wishes to make love to him.

Making love would, therefore, not only make his fantasy a reality but it would somehow demonstrate the sincerity of her love and feelings for the poet.

Stanza 3

We can imagine the lady has been sitting on the poet's bed, listening to his flattering words. Perhaps he has been holding her hand and gazing into her eyes as he speaks. But his words fail to convince her to get into bed with him, and eventually she stands up and starts to leave the room.

As the lady makes her way towards the door, the poet expresses his disappointment and frustration. He tells her that when she entered the room, and all the while she remained there, she was acting in accordance with her true impulses and desires.

She entered his room, he suggests, because she wanted to demonstrate how 'true' her feelings are for him. As such, her presence in the room revealed her true feelings and character, not only to the poet but to herself: 'Coming and staying show'd thee, thee'.

But when she gets up and leaves the room, the poet doubts that she is acting in accordance with her true desires and impulses. She is allowing fears of how society will judge her to determine her behaviour. As such, she is no longer being true to herself: 'now/ Thou art not thou'.

The poet associates love that is uneffected by earthly concerns with the 'spirit'. Such love, he says, is 'pure', untarnished by doubt and fear. To love in such a manner is to be 'brave', for it means not caring what others might think about the manner in which we behave and act. But if people allow thoughts of shame and honour to enter their minds, it weakens and spoils this love: 'That love is weak where fear's as strong as he'.

Donne tells the lady that she is being guided by her fears, by thoughts of shame and the need to preserve her 'honour', rather than her natural desires. As such, her love for the poet is not 'all spirit, pure and brave'. It is mixed up with thoughts of 'fear, shame' and 'honour'.

One last hope

As the lady leaves his room, the poet holds out one last hope. He imagines that she came to rouse his passions and is now leaving with the intention of returning to excite even greater passion.

In this regard, the poet says, she is treating him like a candle. New candles can sometimes be difficult to light because their wicks are soft. However, a candle that has been lit and extinguished is much easier to reignite. As such, it was customary to light and extinguish new candles in order to prepare the wicks and ensure that they would light quickly when required.

Donne suggests that when the woman entered the room she roused his passion. Her leaving the room now dampens or extinguishes this passion. However, just like the new candle that has been lit and extinguished, the poet's passion can be quickly reignited or aroused: 'Perchance as torches, which must ready be,/ Men light and put out, so thou deal'st with me'.

The poet says he will hold this happy thought and 'dream' or imagine that the lady will soon return to his room: 'then I/ Will dream that hope again'. Without such hope, he would rather 'die'. The final line can be read as a dramatic threat, a last effort to make the woman return. The poet will literally die if she does not make love to him and restore his faith in their relationship. However, the word 'die' also has sexual connotations and can mean to orgasm. Donne, of course, intends such a pun. If the woman does not return to satisfy him, he will have to take matters into his own hands.

THEMES

THE MYSTICAL NATURE OF LOVE

Like 'Sweetest Love' and 'A Valediction: Forbidding Mourning', this poem presents love as something spiritual and transcendent. Donne talks of love being 'all spirit' and 'pure', suggesting that when people are truly in love their relationship transcends the physical and the earthly.

Donne argues that true love ought to be unaffected by any earthly concerns. Lovers, he suggests, should not care what others in society think about their actions and behaviour. Thoughts of 'shame' or 'honour' only weaken love's bond. If someone is truly in love, the poet claims, he or she should be true to their feelings and not allow fear to dictate or determine what they do. Love that is devoid of fear and doubt is 'pure', something spiritual that transcends all earthly fears and concerns.

HONOUR AND REPUTATION

However, unlike 'Sweetest Love' and 'A Valediction', this poem is not addressed to the poet's wife, but to an unmarried lady that the poet is looking to seduce. The fears that the poet alludes to are, for the lady in question, very real. Women who engaged in sex outside marriage were judged harshly by society and were classed as being dishonourable and immoral for their behaviour.

Donne, of course, is very conscious of this. He, therefore, uses the idea of 'pure' love to convince the lady to overcome her fears of society's opinions and values. If she is afraid and ashamed to make love to him, then her love is not pure: 'That love is weak where fear's as strong as he;/ 'Tis not all spirit, pure and brave'. Rather than being considered strong for resisting the poet's seductive efforts and protecting her character and reputation, the lady is presented as 'weak' and cowardly for allowing such concerns to guide her judgement and determine her actions.

In this regard, 'The Dream' can be compared to 'The Flea', another poem where the poet displays scant regard for the woman's honour, and for the lasting damage their moment of pleasure would cause to the lady's reputation.

SEX AND SEDUCTION

Ultimately, of course, 'The Dream' is a clever poem of seduction. Donne is willing to deploy any argument he can to convince his beloved to sleep with him. As such, his characterisation of love as being something 'pure' and above the concerns of society is merely a cynical ploy, something constructed to help him achieve his desired objective. It is he, and not the lady, who is ultimately being false and disingenuous.

DONNE'S METAPHYSICAL STYLE

Outrageous Claims and Demands

This is another poem where Donne's Metaphysical style is in evidence, in particular his tendency to make outrageous claims:

- He claims that it was the power and intensity of the lady's eyes that woke him from his slumbers, that they shine as brilliantly as a torch or a flash of lightning.
- He claims that the lady is so 'true' that just thinking about her is enough to make dreams reality: 'Thou art so true that thoughts of thee suffice/ To make dreams truths'.
- He claims that the lady is capable of reading his mind and knowing his deepest desires, dreams and thoughts: 'thou sawest my heart,/ And knew'st my thoughts'.

Inventive Metaphors and Similes

Another aspect of Donne's Metaphysical style is his tendency to use metaphors that compare two seemingly very different things. In the final stanza, he compares the sexual arousal of men to the lighting and extinguishing of candles, suggesting that just as candles which have been recently lit and extinguished can easily be lit again, so can men be easily re-aroused: 'Perchance as torches, which must ready be,/ Men light and put out'.

Weird and Wonderful Arguments

This is another poem where Donne deploys highly imaginative and fantastical arguments to achieve a desired goal or objective. Here he argues that his beloved woke him from his slumbers because she knew he was dreaming that he was making love to her. He claims that such erotic dreams are 'too strong' for fantasy and that they need to be acted out in reality. His beloved, he argues, should agree with him on this, because she is a lover of truth and, therefore, should wish to 'make dreams truths'.

Tone

The tone of the first two stanzas is bright and positive as the poet seeks to charm the lady who has entered his room. He is, at times, complimentary ('thou wak'd'st me wisely', 'Thou art so true', 'I thought thee … an angel') and seductive ('Enter these arms, for since thou thought'st it best,/ Not to dream all my dream, let's act the rest'). However, the tone of the last stanza is different. Here the poet comes across as wounded, cynical and rather bitter, accusing the lady in question of not being 'brave' and 'true'.

The Sun Rising

LINE BY LINE

The sun is an interfering 'old fool'

The poet has spent the night in bed with his beloved. The morning has arrived and the sun's rays come pouring in through the window. The poet is anything but happy with this. The sun's bright beams are a clear reminder that the day has begun and it is now time to get back to their day-to-day lives. They must now leave the chamber – and each other – and go about the business of the day.

The poet personifies the sun, imagining that it has arrived at their particular house and is now peering in through the curtains, calling upon them to get out of bed and go about their duties.

- The sun, he declares is an 'old fool'. It is like an elderly person whose mental faculties are beginning to decline.
- The sun, as a result, has become 'unruly', has started to behave in a disorderly or disruptive manner.
- It has also become 'saucy', suggesting that it's given to rude and inappropriate behaviour.
- The sun, however, is still as 'pedantic' as it ever was, meaning that it is finicky and overly fussy. It is especially pedantic, of course, when it comes to timekeeping.
- The sun is also described as 'busy' or meddlesome. It goes around interfering in the affairs of others, reminding them that their hours of play or rest are at an end.

The sun, then, is personified in an extremely unflattering fashion. It is both an interfering busybody and a rather confused elderly person, capable of all kinds of rude and rowdy behaviour.

The poet is irritated and asks the sun why it is bothering him: 'Why dost thou thus?' He asks the sun to leave him and his lover alone, to go away and bother other people instead:

- The sun, he suggests, should 'chide' or scold schoolboys who have slept in and are late for their lessons.
- It should also chide apprentices who are 'sour' or unhappy at having to spend yet another day at work. These apprentices, we imagine, are lingering in bed, rather than rushing to the workshops of their masters.
- It should wake the king's 'court-huntsmen' who need to rise and ready themselves for a day in the saddle: 'Go tell court huntsmen that the king will ride'
- It should 'call' peasants, the poor agricultural labourers, to the duties or 'offices' of the harvest: 'Call country ants to harvest offices'.

Time, Donne suggests, is 'run' or regulated by the sun because we use the sun's 'motions', its journey around the sky, to determine hours and days, months and years. Donne, in the poem's opening stanza, uses the term 'season' in the older sense to mean an appropriate period of time. For lovers, then, we might say there is a 'season' or appropriate time for lovemaking, a 'season' or appropriate time for taking a long walk on the beach, and a 'season' or appropriate time for enjoying a romantic meal together.

Donne wishes that these seasons weren't regulated by the sun's motions: 'Must to thy motions lovers' seasons run?' He wishes that the seasons of lovers behaved differently to ordinary time, that a walk on the beach could last months, or a night of passion for a hundred years.

The sun is weak, the lovers powerful

The sun's beams are usually considered to be extremely 'strong'. They are also 'reverend', or worthy of great respect. Many religions and religious practices, after all, are based around the sun and its light.

The poet, however, disputes this view of the sun's intrusive light. The sun, he suggests, has no reason to believe that its beams are 'so reverend and strong'. The poet, after all, can simply 'eclipse' or block them out by closing his eyes: 'I could eclipse and cloud them with a wink'. But the poet says that he will not 'eclipse' or 'cloud' the sun in this manner, because it would mean losing sight of his beloved: 'But that I would not lose her sight so long'.

The poet compares the sun's beams to the eyes of his beloved. His lover's eyes, he suggests, are far brighter and more radiant. They are so dazzling that the sun itself could be blinded by looking into them: 'If her eyes have not blinded thine'.

The wealthiest king

The poet makes the extraordinary declaration that he's ruler of the entire Earth. His lover, he declares, is 'all states', is every country and kingdom in the world. And he, as the man in his beloved's life, is the 'prince' or ruler of all these lands: 'She's all states, and all princes, I'.

The sun, he declares, as it embarks on its daily journey around the world, will notice that things have changed. It will notice that the kings it saw yesterday are no longer in their palaces. They might now be employed as huntsmen or as lowly peasants in the fields. If the sun asks about these fallen kings it will be told that their powers and titles have been transferred to the poet himself: 'thou shalt hear,/ All here in one bed lay'. The poet and his beloved, then, are the only true princes in the world. Any other princes the sun might encounter, as it journeys around the world, are merely players or actors. These false princes play at being the poet and his beloved: 'Princes do but play us'. They pretend to exercise power that really belongs to the poet himself.

The poet declares that all the world's honours – all noble titles, all stately offices – belong to him now. Any other honours the sun might witness, as it journeys around the world, are only 'mimic'. They are mere imitations of the true honours that have been awarded to the poet.

The poet also declares that the all the world's wealth now belongs to him. Any other apparent wealth the sun might witness, as it journeys around the world, is merely 'alchemy'. It is counterfeit and ultimately worthless, as all genuine riches are rightfully the poet's now.

The poet urges the sun to look for the islands of the East Indies, famous for their spices, and the islands of the West Indies, famous for their gold mines. These islands, according to the poet, will not be where the sun 'left' them or last saw them. Instead, they will 'lie' with the poet in his bedroom.

These lines are famously open to interpretation. Perhaps the poet is suggesting that the ownership of these islands has been transferred to him, and that the deeds and relevant paperwork are with him in his bedroom. Or perhaps he's making the rather surreal suggestion that the islands have magically been shrunk down and transported to his bedroom, where he studies them as if they were a unique and extraordinary ornament.

Contracting

The poet then pushes things even further, declaring that beyond their bedroom nothing really exists: 'Nothing else is'. Everything in the world has been 'contracted' or compressed into these four walls.

The sun, he suggests, should be happy that the world had been 'contracted' in such a fashion. The sun's duty, he reminds it, is to 'warm the world'. But the sun is old now – having been around for billions of years – and like an old pensioner needs to slow down and take it easy: 'Thine age asks ease'. Thankfully, the sun now only needs to 'warm' a single chamber, the poet's bedroom, for these four walls contain everything that exists: 'Shine here to us, and thou art everywhere'.

Each day it need only circle their bed to perform its duty. The bed is the centre around which it will revolve and the walls of the bedroom will define its circular orbit: 'This bed thy centre is, these walls thy sphere'.

Science and Superstition

John Donne lived through an exciting period of scientific discovery and many of his poems exhibit a keen interest in this new learning. However, at the time of this poem's composition, it was still widely believed that the sun revolved around the Earth. Although Copernicus had detailed his theory of the Earth and the other planets rotating around the sun in 1543, it took more than a century for this to become widely accepted. As such, 'The Sun Rising' describes a geocentric understanding of the universe, in which the sun revolves around the Earth.

The mentioning of 'alchemy' in the third stanza reminds us that, despite the great advances in science in the 17th century, ancient beliefs and superstitions still prevailed. Alchemists believed it was possible to turn base metals like iron and lead into gold. They based their theories on the assumption that the world and everything in it are composed of four basic elements (air, earth, fire and water). It was thought that by changing the proportions of these constituent elements, base metals could be transformed into gold.

DONNE'S METAPHYSICAL STYLE

Outrageous Claims and Demands

Donne, like the other Metaphysical poets of his generation, was fond of making outlandish claims and statements that were designed to provoke the reader. This is nowhere more apparent than in 'The Sun Rising':

- He declares that his beloved's eyes are so radiant that they are capable of blinding the sun itself.
- He declares that he's the ruler of the world, the wealthiest man in the world and the true holder of all the world's honours.
- He even declares that the entire world has been 'contracted' into his bedchamber, that nothing else exists.

Inventive Metaphors and Similes

The poet uses a metaphor to describe the workers in the fields, calling them 'country ants'. The comparison suggests both their great number and their industriousness. An equally vivid metaphor is used to describe the passage of time. The future is compared to a roll of fabric or material. As time progresses, pieces of cloth are torn from this roll, used and then discarded. The past, therefore, is compared to a pile of rags, all the 'hours, days and months' that have been used up by time's relentless progress.

The poem, as we've seen, is very playful in its personification of the sun, presenting it as an elderly and raucous busybody. Donne playfully depicts the sun looking down on the Earth's surface as it makes its daily journey around the world, noticing various kings, continents and islands. The sun, Donne suggests, has a rather high opinion of itself, regarding its beams as both powerful and worthy of respect. The final stanza, as we've seen, emphasises the sun's great age, depicting it as an elderly worker who needs to start thinking about retirement.

Form

'The Sun Rising' is a lyric poem consisting of three ten-line stanzas following a ABBACDCDEE rhyme scheme. The poem is a variation on the 'aubade' form, a morning love song usually about lovers separating at dawn. Donne, as usual, comes up with his own inventive twist. Instead of pleading with his lover to linger a little longer, he berates the sun for waking them and for signalling that their night together is at an end.

'The Sun Rising' is also a famous example of apostrophe, which occurs when a poet addresses an inanimate object. Donne, in this light-hearted poem, addresses the sun in a variety of tones, conveying everything from irritation, to triumph to sympathy.

THEMES

LOVE AND MARRIAGE

The poem was likely written around 1604, not long after Donne and Anne were married. They were living in Surrey, not far from London, in a small house belonging to a cousin of Anne's. Donne was 32 at the time and had just been released from prison, having served a short sentence for marrying Anne without her father's approval. Despite these difficult circumstances, it seems that this was a happy time in the poet's life, as 'The Sun Rising' seems to illustrate.

The poet emphasises the strength of his feelings for his beloved. He longs to spend more time with her and is irritated that the sun has risen, signalling that their night together is at an end.

The poet praises his beloved's beauty, declaring that he is unwilling to close his eyes in order to shut out the sun's intrusive light. He doesn't want to lose sight of her beauty for even a second. He uses hyperbole to emphasise the radiance of her eyes, declaring that they are capable of blinding the sun itself.

In the second half of the poem, Donne emphasises that the love they share is the only thing of value, the only thing that matters to him. His beloved, he declares, is 'everything'. Being with her makes him feel like a king, like the wealthiest man in the world. The room in which they lie together is the only place that matters, the only place that really exists.

These sentiments, of course, are common in love poems and love songs from the middle ages to the present day. But Donne, typically, puts his own twist on these common sentiments and pushes them to an extreme. We are not, of course, meant to take these statements literally. They are deliberately hyperbolic or exaggerated in order to emphasise the intensity of the poet's feelings for his beloved and the extraordinary richness she brings to his life.

THE MYSTICAL NATURE OF LOVE

This poem, like 'The Anniversary', emphasises the mystical nature of love. 'True love', Donne suggests, is 'all alike'. These feelings never change, remaining constant as the years go by. The passage of time, therefore, is irrelevant to true love. True love doesn't 'know' or care about the seasons that come and go, each with its particular 'clime' or set of weather conditions. The passing 'hours, days, months' change much about the world. But they have no effect on true love.

The Anniversary

LINE BY LINE

In the poem, Donne celebrates the love he felt for Anne More, the woman who was to become his wife. Donne first met Anne around 1597, when he started working for her uncle, Sir Thomas Egerton, and they quickly fell in love. This poem was written on the anniversary of their first meeting.

Powerful and admirable things

The poet mentions a number of prestigious people, concepts and entities:

- He mentions 'kings' and their 'favourites'. These 'favourites' were courtiers who enjoyed an especially close relationship with the king. They frequently gained power and prestige as a result.

- He mentions 'beauties' and 'wits'. The term 'beauties' refers to those known throughout the land for their extraordinary good looks. The 'wits', on the other hand, are famous for their intelligence, for their original and inquiring minds.

- Donne also mentions the 'glory of honours'. This refers to noble titles and grants of land that might be bestowed by the crown on its loyal servants. It also refers to powerful and lucrative positions within the government, some of which were held for life (Donne's boss, Sir Thomas Egerton, for instance, was made 'Lord Keeper of the Great Seal').

- Finally, Donne refers to 'the sun itself', which 'makes' or regulates time. For we count hours, months and years according to the Earth's annual journey around the Sun.

Each of these, the poet notes, is subject to ageing and decay. Each is 'elder by a year, now' than it was on the day he first saw his beloved. Each draws closer to its destruction with every passing year: 'All other things to their destruction draw'.

The kings and favourites will age and pass away. Mental prowess and physical beauty, too, will be destroyed by the passage of time. Political power and prestige, too, will inevitably prove fleeting; the 'glory of honours', after all, can be lost as well as won. Even the 'sun itself', which exhibits a fire and fury beyond human comprehension will eventually fizzle out and expire.

The poet's relationship with Anne

Only the poet's relationship with Anne is immune to such ageing and destruction because the love they feel for one another will never decay, will never diminish in intensity: 'Only our love hath no decay'. Their love, unlike the kings and courtiers, unlike the sun itself, will exist forever.

Their love, then, is presented as being outside the ordinary course of time. The whole idea of 'yesterday' or 'tomorrow' doesn't apply to the love that they share. Instead, their emotions exist in an unchanging and eternal present: 'But truly keeps his first, last, everlasting day'.

A love continued in heaven

Yet the poet quickly realises there is a problem with this argument. His and Anne's love may be ageless, but their bodies are not. Death, then, will come for them just as it will come for the nobles or princes mentioned in Stanza 1. Eventually their physical bodies will be no more: 'Alas, as well as other Princes, we … Must leave at last in death, these eyes, and ears'. The poet and his beloved, like everybody else, will be laid in the grave: 'Two graves must hide thine and my corse'.

Two separate graves

The poem, as we have seen, was written on the anniversary of Donne's first meeting with Anne Moore, the niece of his employer Sir Thomas Egerton. Donne's relationship with Anne was largely conducted in secret, as the couple knew that Anne's family would be bitterly opposed to any relationship between them.

The couple realise, therefore, that it will be extremely difficult for them to marry. And because they are not married, they will be buried separately, each with his or her own family. The poet laments that they must be separated at death in this manner: 'If one might, death were no divorce'.

The couple's relationship, therefore, has a bittersweet quality, represented by the 'sweet salt tears'. It is sweet because it is characterised by the passion and excitement of new love. But it is bitter because they realise that it will be extremely difficult for them to marry or openly be together.

Yet their souls will continue to exist. Their souls will 'remove' themselves from their buried bodies and journey to heaven, existing forever 'above' this earthly world: 'When bodies to their graves, souls from their graves remove'.

Their souls, therefore, will be able to 'prove' or sustain their relationship after death: 'But souls … then shall prove/ This'. It's possible, perhaps, that their love will even increase in the heavenly afterlife: 'or a love increased there above'.

The poet, however, isn't entirely satisfied with the idea of continuing the relationship in Heaven. Here on Earth they enjoy a unique and private relationship. The poet fears that such an exclusive, unique relationship won't be possible in the afterlife. In paradise, the poet and his beloved might 'be thoroughly blessed', but they'll be no different from the rest of God's faithful souls: 'But we no more, than all the rest'.

The poet chooses life

The poem concludes, therefore, with the poet focusing on this life rather than on the next. He and his beloved must 'live' and love each other 'nobly', in a true and honest fashion. They must make the most of the years together as they pass: 'Let us … live, and add again,/ years and years unto years'.

They must 'refrain' or control the 'true and false fears' that affect every relationship. 'False' fears relate to things that will never happen; for example, he and his lover hurting or betraying each other. 'True' fears, on the other hand, are directed towards difficulties that inevitably arise in life, things like sickness and old age.

The poet seems confident he and his beloved will attain the milestone of having been together for sixty or 'threescore' years. He declares that they will 'write' something on each anniversary of their first meeting, perhaps imagining an exchange of cards or letters.

But their relationship will remain fresh, passionate and exciting. Each anniversary will be like their first anniversary, each new year will stretch before them as if it were only the second year of their relationship: 'till we attain/ To write threescore, this is the second of our reign'.

DONNE'S METAPHYSICAL STYLE

Weird and Wonderful Arguments

This is another poem where Donne's Metaphysical style is in evidence. We see his tendency to deploy outlandish and fantastical arguments. In Stanza 1, for instance, he argues that the affection between him and his beloved is the only unchanging thing in the world. In Stanza 2, meanwhile, he argues that relationships between human beings can be continued and even improved on in heaven.

Inventive Metaphors and Similes

Donne, like the other Metaphysical poets of his generation, was especially fond of using conceits or extended metaphors in his work. This poem is structured around a conceit or extended metaphor that compares lovers to kings:

- This notion is introduced at the very beginning with the phrase 'All Kings'.

- In lines 23 to 24, the poet describes how he is both his lover's king and subject.
- A similar point is made in lines 13 to 14, where he declares that they are princes of each other: 'as well as other Princes, we/ (who prince enough in one another be)'.
- At the poem's conclusion, therefore, their relationship is described as a 'reign', or a period of rule.

Another aspect of Donne's Metaphysical style is his tendency to use metaphors that compare two seemingly very different things. We see this in line 18, where thoughts are described as 'inmates' or prisoners of the soul. According to the poet, love is the soul's only natural and constant emotion: 'souls where nothing dwells but love'. All 'other thoughts' (for example those associated with hatred, fear and jealousy) are merely the soul's 'inmates'. They are imprisoned in the soul during this life but they are released from it at the moment of death and do not travel with it to heaven.

THE MYSTICAL NATURE OF LOVE

'The Anniversary' is another poem where Donne presents love as an almost mystical bond. The first stanza depicts love as somehow magically outside the normal course of time. The poet imagines that the relationship between himself and his beloved is the only thing in the world not subject to ageing and decay.

By the end of the poem, however, he has adopted a humbler and more realistic vision of love. The poet, in stanza 3, no longer craves a changeless, timeless relationship. He concludes by suggesting that the only way love can triumph over time is not by being timeless and unchanging, but by altering and adapting with the lovers as the years go by.

LOVE AND MARRIAGE

The poet is highly conscious that every relationship has its lows as well as highs. The poet's relationship is characterised by 'true oaths' exchanged between him and his beloved, promises that they will always love one another and will always remain faithful.

But it is also characterised by worry, difficulty and conflict. They experience 'false fears', moments when one lover worries about being betrayed by the other. They also experience 'true fears' when they worry about the conflicts and difficulties that inevitably arise in any relationship.

The poem concludes, then, with the poet stressing that he and his beloved must 'love nobly', in a true and faithful fashion. They must overcome the worries, difficulties and conflicts that affect every relationship. By working together, they can ensure that their relationship retains its freshness and excitement for sixty years or even more.

He and his lover are so important to each other that they 'rule' each other's lives. The speaker is his lover's 'king' because he rules her, but he is also her 'subject' because she rules him.

All kings are scared of treason, of being betrayed by one of their subjects. Yet the poet and his lover are 'safer' than other kings because they each have only one subject, a subject extremely unlikely to betray them: 'Who is safe as we? where none can do/ Treason to us, except one us two?'

DEATH

Donne is a poet keenly aware of the passage of time and its effects. This awareness is evident in 'The Anniversary', as he notes how every person and object in the universe, no matter how powerful or prestigious, is inevitably drawn towards its destruction. The bodies of the poet and his beloved, too, will age, die and be laid in the grave.

The poem, like several others by Donne, touches on the idea of the afterlife. The poet seems confident that the souls of both he and his beloved will make it to heaven, where they will continue their relationship. Indeed, so assured is he of his place in paradise that he almost complains about it, lamenting the fact that 'there above' their love affair will lack some of the uniqueness it enjoys here on Earth.

This poem, then, contrasts forcefully with the three Holy Sonnets on the course, especially with 'Thou hast made me'. In these sonnets, Donne expresses a deep and profound concern with sin, with the possibility that only hell awaits him after death. In this poem, however, he seems convinced that heaven is his ultimate destination.

Ordinary lovers

The poet describes ordinary lovers, whose love is purely earthly or 'sublunary'. These lovers share a connection that is grounded or 'elemented' in the physical. They are connected only through the ordinary physical senses of sight, sound and touch: 'whose soul is sense'. Their relationships, because they are based on such a physical connection, cannot 'admit' or cope with separation.

Donne and his wife, in contrast, experience a form of love that is somehow mystical or unearthly. Indeed, their bond is so mysterious that they don't fully understand it themselves: 'That our selves know not what it is'. Donne describes how they are 'Inter-assured' of mind, enjoying a psychological and spiritual connection. The poet and his wife, therefore, are less bothered by physical separation, by being unable to hold hands, kiss or look into each other's eyes: '[We] Care less, eyes, lips, and hands to miss'.

Donne uses a metaphor from metallurgy, the study and manipulation of metals, to emphasise just how special his relationship is. Ordinary relationships are described as 'Dull', suggesting that are base, lumpen and valueless. Donne's relationship, on the other hand, is described as 'refined', suggesting metal that has all its impurities removed, leaving a perfect, priceless substance.

Donne draws a contrast between the earth, on the one hand, and the 'spheres' or heavens on the other (ancient thinkers, from Plato to Copernicus, believed that space was divided into perfect spheres rather than being an endless empty expanse). Donne associates ordinary relationships with the earth. His own relationship, meanwhile, is associated with the heavens.

- Disturbances of the earth – earthquakes, landslides and so forth – are keenly felt by the population at large.
- Disturbances in ordinary relationships, similarly, are noticed by the broader community. We notice the troubled couple arguing or giving one another the silent treatment.
- Disturbances of the heavenly spheres, however, are hardly noticed by the population at large.
- This disturbance in Donne's relationship, similarly, should go unnoticed by the broader community. He and his wife shouldn't cry or weep or moan. They should give no indication at all that anything is amiss.

A union of their souls

Donne declares their two souls are so intimately bound together that they are essentially 'one'. When he travels further and further away, their mingled soul will stretch, growing thinner and thinner. But it will never break or sever. Their mingled soul will experience an 'expansion' but never a 'breach'. Donne uses a wonderful simile to illustrate this, comparing their mingled soul to a gold bar that is beaten by a goldsmith. The gold, he imagines, will thin and expand as it is beaten until it's as thin as the air itself: 'Like gold to airy thinness beat'. But it will never break.

The compass metaphor

Donne uses a striking metaphor to illustrate the connection he shares with his wife, comparing their two souls to the 'feet' or legs of a mathematical compass. Their souls are bound together by love, just as the compass's legs are fastened by a hinge.

- When no circle is being drawn, the two feet of the compass are united. This represents the time Donne and Anne spend together at home.
- When a circle is being drawn the two feet are separated. This represents the period of Donne's travels, when he and Anne must be apart.
- Donne compares Anne to the 'fixed foot' of the compass, to the foot that remains stationary while the compass is in use. This represents how she must remain at home while the poet travels.
- Donne, himself, meanwhile is compared to the 'other' foot of the compass, to the foot that holds the pencil and traces the circle's rounded or oblique shape. This represents how Donne must soon depart on his travels: '[I] must,/ Like th' other foot, obliquely run'.
- The 'other foot' travels around the 'fixed foot'. Donne, metaphorically, will travel around Anne. She will remain at the centre of his thoughts no matter where he goes.
- The fixed foot ensures that the other foot traces a 'just' or proper circle. The thought of Anne, similarly, will ensure that Donne behaves in a 'just' fashion as he travels. The thought of his wife will ensure that he doesn't sleep with any other women or behave otherwise inappropriately.

The fixed foot ensures that the other foot's tracing of a circle begins and ends at the same point. This represents how thoughts of Anne will ensure that the poet returns home. He won't remain on the continent, abandoning his wife and starting a new life in Florence or Madrid. Anne, he insists, will make his journey end at home, right where it begun.

Science and Superstition

Donne was writing during a period that saw not only the beginnings of modern science but also the persistence of ancient superstition. He describes how people at the time would 'reckon' or consider earthquakes, attempting to understand what they 'did' in a rational fashion. But they also looked for meaning in such phenomena, regarding them as mystical omens or signs of God's displeasure.

The notion that outer space can be neatly divided into perfect spheres that rotate around one another also contains elements of science and superstition. It was believed, for instance, that the interaction of the spheres produced beautiful music. But sometimes the spheres clashed, producing a 'trepidation' or disturbance that echoed throughout the universe, being 'greater far' than that produced by any earthquake. The concept of celestial spheres, of course, strikes us as ridiculous today. But it can be regarded as a stepping stone towards our modern understanding of the universe.

DONNE'S METAPHYSICAL STYLE

Outrageous Claims and Demands

This is another poem where Donne's Metaphysical style is in evidence. Throughout the poem, he makes a number of outrageous claims in an effort to comfort his wife and prevent her from mourning his departure:

- He claims that their love is something scared, something that only they can know and fathom, and that it would be a 'profanation' if the general public were to witness them grieving.
- He claims that their love is based on a spiritual bond and that, therefore, they will not miss being able to touch, hold and see each other when Donne is away: 'But we ... Care less eyes, lips, and hands to miss'.
- He claims that because their love transcends this earthly realm, their separation will not have any physical or emotional effects.

Perhaps the most outrageous claim that the poet makes is that he and his wife can never be truly separated because they share the one soul: 'Our two souls, therefore, which are one ... endure not yet/ A breach, but an expansion'.

Inventive Metaphors and Similes

Another aspect of Donne's Metaphysical style is his tendency to use metaphors that compare two seemingly very different things.

- We see this in the opening stanza when the poet compares their parting to a 'virtuous' man's death.
- He compares the impact that separation has on ordinary lovers' relationships to the effects of earthquakes. Turmoil in the relationship he shares with his wife, in contrast, is compared to disruptions amongst the heavenly spheres.
- The poet compares the manner in which their single soul will expand as he travels to the expansion of hammered gold.

Donne, like the other Metaphysical poets of his generation, was especially fond of using conceits or extended metaphors in his work. 'A Valediction', as we have seen, ends with Donne using the extended analogy of a mathematical compass to illustrate the manner in which his soul is connected to his wife's. The comparison also illustrates just how central Anne is to the relationship.

Paradox and Contradiction

The poem centres around a paradox or contradiction, which the poet makes every effort to overcome. On the one hand, Donne wishes to argue that he and his wife share a love that is deeper, richer and more profound than any other. On the other hand, he wishes to convince his wife that they should feel no grief or pain when they separate. In order to overcome this contradiction the poet ends up having to resort to a further paradox. Their separation, he claims, will actually be a form of an expansion of their shared 'soul'.

THEMES

LOVE AND MARRIAGE

'A Valediction: Forbidding Mourning' is a testament to the depth of the poet's feelings for his wife. The poem, like many poems by Donne, approaches the subject of love in a rather intellectual and argumentative manner. But there are also moments of genuine emotion, especially related to the compass metaphor at the poem's conclusion.

There is a sense, as in 'Sweetest Love, I do not go', that the poet is desperate to avoid a scene and any 'tear-floods' or 'sigh-tempests' that might accentuate his guilt at leaving Anne behind. But the poet, we sense, is also making a heartfelt effort to console his wife. And perhaps also console himself.

The poem highlights how lovers remain in one another's minds even when they are physically distanced. The poet, as we've seen, stresses that Anne will remain at the centre of his thoughts while he travels. Thoughts of Anne will ensure that he behaves appropriately while abroad and that he returns home to England when his journey is concluded.

THE MYSTICAL NATURE OF LOVE

The poet emphasises the mystical nature of his relationship.

- The relationship has certain secret and sacred aspects, something that must not be shared with ordinary people.
- Their relationship is associated with the celestial spheres rather than with this earthly domain.
- They are 'Inter-assured of the mind', enjoying an intense mental connection that they don't fully understand themselves.
- They also enjoy an extraordinary spiritual bond. Their mingled souls 'are one' and can never be breached or separated.

The poet's marriage, therefore, is presented as being far superior to ordinary relationships. Ordinary couples are associated with the profane rather than the scared and with the sublunary earth rather than the heavens. Ordinary couples are grounded in a purely physical connection, lacking the intense mental and spiritual bonds enjoyed by the poet and his wife. Ordinary couples cannot bear to be apart because they need to see and touch one another to maintain their relationship. For the poet and Anne, however, given their mystical union, such physical separation will be easy to endure.

Batter My Heart

LINE BY LINE

In 'Batter my heart', as in the other Holy Sonnets, Donne presents himself as an extraordinary sinner:

- God has attempted to redeem the poet from sin. God, as the poet puts it, has attempted to 'mend' him as if he were a defective object: 'you… seek to mend'.
- We might 'knock' or tap such a defective object, for instance, in an effort to remove its dents. Or we might attempt to cover up its imperfections by breathing on it and rubbing it to make it shine: 'breathe, shine'
- But the poet, like an object too defective to be repaired, is so sinful that he is beyond any conventional redemption.
- Such an utterly defective object, of course, needs to be scrapped and rebuilt from scratch. The poet, similarly, needs to be destroyed and then remade.

The poet, therefore, calls on God to 'Batter [his] heart', to forcefully strike his heart over and over again. The 'heart', of course, represents our most intimate thoughts and feelings. The poet, therefore, is calling on God to assault, and ultimately demolish, his mindset, his lifestyle, his very personality.

The poet, then, describes how he wants God to 'break, blow [and] burn' him. It's as if the poet wants his limbs to be snapped. It's as if he wants to be lashed by howling gales. It's as if he wants to be consumed by roaring flames. These powerful, violent metaphors wonderfully convey how the poet wants God to forcefully end his current sinful existence.

Once this process of destruction or demolition is complete, the poet wants God to 'make [him] new,' to reshape his lifestyle and personality. We might say that he wants to be born again, to begin an entirely new life that would be lived in service to God.

The poet, therefore, needs to be 'overthrown'. He needs to be utterly destroyed, reduced to nothing. He will then 'rise' and 'stand' once more, being rebuilt or reconstituted as a new, more virtuous version of himself. This process of destruction and recreation, the poet suggests, will require a great effort from God. God, he insists, must 'bend' or apply all of His extraordinary 'force'.

Lines 5 to 8

In these lines, the poet uses a famous conceit, comparing himself to a town that has been 'usurped' or taken over by a foreign power.

- The townsfolk know that their loyalty is 'due' to their rightful king, who is currently absent from the town, rather than to the usurper who currently occupies the town. The poet, similarly, knows that his true loyalty lies with God, who is absent from his life, rather than with sin, which currently occupies his life.
- The town's citizens 'labour' to cast out the usurper and 'admit' their rightful ruler back into the town. The poet, similarly, struggles to turn away from sin and let God back into his life.
- The citizens' efforts, however, are in vain or 'to no end'. They cannot expel the usurper from their town. The poet, similarly, finds it impossible to live a life that is not dominated by sin.

The rightful king has appointed a viceroy or govener to the town. God, similarly, has given the poet the gift of reason, the faculty of rationality and logic.

The viceroy's role is to govern the town properly while the rightful king is away. Reason's role, similarly, is to govern the poet's life, ensuring that he lives in dignity and decency.

The viceroy, however, has proved to be a 'weak' governor and has allowed the town to be taken over by the enemy. Reason, similarly, has turned out to be weak when it comes to governing the poet's life and has allowed him to be taken over by sin. Rationality and logic, after all, are all too often useless in the face of temptations such as lust, gluttony or anger.

The viceroy, we're told, has also turned out to be 'untrue' or untrustworthy, suggesting that he has actively collaborated with the enemy. Reason, similarly, has turned out to be untrustworthy. Reason, after all, can be seduced by all kinds of fancy arguments that seem to justify sinful behaviour, that lead us away from the path of righteousness.

The viceroy, then, has effectively allowed himself to be taken prisoner by the enemy. The poet's faculty of reason, similarly, has been 'captived' by sin. Only a direct and forceful intervention by God himself, one that reshapes his soul and personality, will be enough to cast sin out of his life.

Lines 9 to 14

The poet, in these lines, addresses God the way one might address a lover.

- He tells God how much he loves Him and how he would gladly ('fain') be loved in return: 'Yet dearly I love you and would be loved fain'.
- The poet, however, is trapped in an intense relationship with sin, which is God's eternal enemy. The poet emphasises the intensity of this relationship by memorably declaring that he and sin are engaged to be married. 'But [I] am Betrothed unto your enemy'. The poet calls on God to 'divorce' him from this degrading relationship. He wants God to forcibly 'untie' or 'break' the knots of his addiction to the pleasures of this world.
- Donne, memorably, declares that he wants to be imprisoned by God: 'Take me to you, imprison me'. He wants God to take full control of his life and personality. Otherwise, he will just drift back to a sinful existence.

The poem concludes with Donne calling on God to 'enthral' and 'ravish' him. The term 'enthral' has two different meanings. It can mean to enslave, reinforcing our sense that Donne wants to submit utterly to God's will. It can also mean to captivate, suggesting how Donne wants God to utterly occupy his attention. His mind must be filled with thoughts of God's goodness; otherwise, he will start to experience temptation again, and sinning will seem like an alluring prospect.

The term 'ravish', similarly, has two very different meanings. It can mean to delight, suggesting how Donne wants to be thrilled and overjoyed by God's presence in his life. It can also mean to sexually violate, suggesting how Donne wants God to forcefully enter his life and his mind.

The poem's final lines are based around two paradoxes or contradictory statements. The first paradox occurs when the poet says that he can only be free if he is enthralled or enslaved. He can only be released from the grip of sin if he allows God's love to completely take over his life.

The second paradox relates to the idea of ravishing. Normally, in Donne's time, sexual activity was considered to leave one less pure or 'chaste'. Donne, however, states that being ravished is actually the only route to purity and chastity. It's only through God forcefully entering his life and mind that he can become a pure and virtuous person.

DONNE'S METAPHYSICAL STYLE

Outrageous Claims and Demands

Donne is known for his tendency to make outrageous demands, and this is nowhere more evident than in 'Batter my heart'.

- He demands that God batter or assault his very psyche.
- He calls on God to break him and burn him.
- He wants God to imprison, enthral and even ravish him.

Indeed, many readers have been disturbed by the violence that characterises these demands, which strike us as far more extreme than the requests one might find in conventional prayers.

Inventive Metaphors and Similes

Donne, like the other Metaphysical poets of his generation, was especially fond of using conceits or extended metaphors in his work. And it's often been suggested that 'Batter my heart' is organised around three such comparisons:

- In lines 1 to 4, as we have seen, the poet compares himself to a defective object of some kind. Critics have suggested that Donne is referring to a vase or piece of pottery. We can see how some, though maybe not all, of the verbs in these lines might relate to the potter's craft.
- In lines 5 to 8, as we've seen, the poet compares himself to a captured or usurped town.
- In lines 9 to 14, meanwhile, the poet compares himself to a person trapped in a degrading relationship.

The scholar Raymond-Jean Fontain has argued that Donne derives these conceits from the Bible. In the Old Testament, when the people of Israel disobeyed God, the prophets compared them to an imperfect pot, a captured city or a woman betrothed to her true love's enemy. In 'Batter my heart', Donne adapts these biblical images to describe his own predicament as a sinner desperate for redemption.

Form

'Batter my heart', like the other Holy Sonnets on the course, is a variation on the Shakespearian sonnet, being divided into three quatrains and a final rhyming couplet. The poem is a kind of prayer to the Holy Trinity, or 'three-personed God', and the idea of the Trinity determines its structure. Just as the Christian God is divided into three distinct persons, so the poem is divided into three distinct parts: lines 1 to 4, lines 5 to 8 and lines 9 to 14. The poet also uses verbs in sets of three: 'knock, breathe, shine' and 'break, blow, burn'.

THEMES

SIN AND REDEMPTION

A recurring feature of Donne's poetry is the strange joy he takes in presenting himself as a terrible person. His sins, he seems to suggest, are far greater than those of the average man or woman. His whole life and personality, he suggests, have been taken over by sin:

- He is so corrupted by sin that he compares himself to a defective pot or vase, one that the sculptor has no choice but to cast aside.
- Sin has taken over his life, the way a usurper might seize a town not rightfully his.
- He even compares himself to sin's fiancé, emphasising the intense and intimate nature of his relationship with sin.

But the poem also highlights Donne's desperation for redemption. He wants God to forcibly 'untie' or 'break' his relationship with sin. He wants God to 'Batter [his] heart', to enter his life in a forceful, almost violent manner. He wants to be broken by God's love so that he can be made anew.

In 'Batter my heart', as in the other Holy Sonnets, Donne demands what might be described as 'special treatment' from God. God, we imagine, has reached out to the poet through prayer and the sacraments, offering him redemption from his sinful ways. The poet, however, is convinced that he is beyond such ordinary means of redemption. He is so sinful that he must be utterly demolished and remade.

A striking feature of 'Batter My Heart' is the demanding or challenging tone the poet takes with God. God has already taken action to cleanse the poet of sin. But the poet feels that God 'As yet' has not done enough. The poet, therefore, will require a greater effort from God from now on. God, he insists, must 'bend' or apply all of His extraordinary 'force'.

The poem's closing lines, however, are arguably more humble in tone. The poet accepts that he must surrender to God's love, and that he must allow God to enter his life and dominate his existence. It is only by doing so that he be can free from sin and live a 'chaste' or righteous life.

Thou hast made me

LINE BY LINE

This poem, like the other Holy Sonnets, was written sometime between 1611 and 1615. This was a difficult time in Donne's life. It was a time of financial difficulty. His once promising diplomatic career was a thing of the past, and he had spent a decade scraping a living doing bits and pieces of legal work. It was also a time of great responsibility, as he had a wife and ten children to support. He also had to contend with a series of illnesses that affected both himself and the other members of his family.

Donne feels that the end of his life is fast approaching: 'for now mine end doth haste'. He is not an old man, being only in his early forties. But he is so mentally and physically drained that death seems a real possibility. He uses a wonderful metaphor to describe what he views as his approaching demise: 'I run to death and death meets me as fast'. We can imagine death and the poet running to meet each other like lovers across a field in an old romantic movie.

Wasting away

The poet is highly conscious that he is a sinful person. Sin, he suggests, corrupts not only his immortal soul but his physical body. Sin resides within his body like some disease. It causes his body to 'decay' and his 'flesh' to shrivel up and 'waste' away: 'my feebled flesh doth waste/ By sin in it'.

Sin, the poet laments, has taken quite a toll on his body. He has grown 'feeble'. His eyesight has begun to fail to the point that all his perceptions are 'dim'. Donne, then, presents himself as having prematurely aged from years of hard work, childcare and financial worry.

The poet laments that for him life's pleasures are a thing of the past: 'And all my pleasures seem like yesterday'. Perhaps he is suggesting that he no longer has the time or money to engage in pleasurable activities. Perhaps he misses being part of the glittering social and cultural life of London. Or perhaps he's so depressed that he can no longer take joy in life's simple pleasures, like the sunset or the singing of a bird.

The poet wonders why God went to the trouble of creating him if He's only going to let him rot away: 'Thou hast made me, and shall thy work decay?' The poet wants God to 'Repair' him. He wants God to take away his sins. Doing so will not only cleanse his soul, it will also restore his body. Sin, as we've seen, is presented as the cause of the bodily decay that has affected the poet.

Spatial metaphor

The poem is structured around the conceit of the speaker being unable to look in various directions: 'I dare not move my dim eyes any way':

- He's afraid to look in front of him. This represents how he is terrified to contemplate the future, for he knows he only has a short while to live before death comes: 'death before doth cast/ Such terror'.
- He's reluctant to look behind him. This represents his unwillingness to contemplate the past. Doing so fills him with 'Despair', reminding him of all the pleasures he can no longer enjoy.
- He is terrified to cast his eyes downward. This represents his terror of hell. He feels that sin weighs him down, threatening to drag him downwards into eternal damnation: 'to towards hell doth weigh.'

There are times, however, when the speaker can look 'upwards', when he can pray to or commune with God: 'Only thou art above'. At such moments the poet feels himself 'rise again'. He feels the burden of sin lessen and senses himself growing closer to God. Perhaps, too, he experiences relief from the feelings of terror and despair that have so gripped him. The poet accepts, however, it is only with God's 'leave' or permission that such moments can occur: 'and when towards thee/ By thy leave I can look'.

God and the Devil

The poem's final lines focus on the Devil, who is presented as the common foe to both God and man. The Devil is very 'old', having been around in one form or another since the creation of the universe, and has mastered the 'art' of temptation. He can be extremely 'subtle' in his temptations, preying on each individual's weaknesses and insecurities. He can make sinful acts appear harmless or even justified.

Donne, therefore, finds it almost impossible to resist the Devil's wiles and stratagems. He is incapable of passing even sixty minutes without a sinful deed or thought: 'That not one hour I can myself sustain.' No matter how hard he tries, he cannot maintain or sustain a righteous way of life.

The poet knows it's only with God's help that he can resist temptation. He must rely on God's 'grace', on His favour and assistance. It only through such grace that the poet will be able to 'prevent' or overcome the Devil's 'art'. Donne uses a vivid metaphor to depict this. God's grace is comaped to a winged bird that will carry him along, safely above the traps and snares placed by the Devil.

Donne also uses the metaphor of the magnet to describe his relationship with God. He imagines God functioning 'like adamant' or a magnet, pulling his 'heart' upwards: 'thou like adamant draw mine iron heart'. This wonderfully suggests how God will help the poet to focus on what might be described as higher things, on faith, hope and charity rather than on sinful thoughts and ideas.

DONNE'S METAPHYSICAL STYLE

Outrageous Claims and Demands

'Thou hast made me' like many of Donne's poems features outrageous claims and demands. We see this when he demands that God immediately 'repair' his sin-damaged soul. An outrageous claim, meanwhile, features in line 12 where the poet suggests that he can't go a single hour without sinning.

The poem opens with a commanding or challenging tone. The poet wonders why God went to the trouble of creating him only to let his body and soul be corrupted by sin: 'Thou hast made me, and shall thy work decay?' The poet seems almost irritated with God's inaction. It's as if he believes he can convince God to do things his way, to take action where and when Donne requires: 'Repair me now'.

The poem's closing lines, however, are much more humble in tone. He accepts that it is only with God's 'leave', or permission, that he can pray or contemplate goodness: 'and when towards thee/ By thy leave I can look'. The poet emphasises that he is powerless in the face of sin and temptation. It is only with God's help that he has any chance of turning away from sin and focusing on higher things.

Inventive Metaphors and Similes

Donne's Metaphysical style is once again in evidence in this poem, in particular his tendency to use metaphors that compare two seemingly very different things. We see this in line 14, where God is compared to a magnet that will draw the poet's 'iron heart' upwards towards contemplation of the divine. God has been compared to many things over the centuries, but a magnet is surely one of the more unusual. Lines 5 to 10, meanwhile, as we have seen, are structured around the conceit of the speaker being terrified to look in various directions: 'I dare not move my dim eyes any way'.

Form

Like 'Batter my heart', and 'At the round earth's imagined corners', this is one of Donne's Holy Sonnets. It is a 'Shakespearean' sonnet, divided into three quatrains and a couplet, each with a different focus.

The first quatrain focuses on the terrible reality of growing older, the second on the poet's inability to look in any direction, and the third on the Devil's subtle 'art'. The closing couplet, meanwhile, attempts to resolve the various questions raised throughout the poem.

THEMES

SIN AND REDEMPTION

In 'Thou hast made me', like the other Holy Sonnets, Donne emphasises his own extraordinary sinfulness. He describes his heart as having turned to 'iron', wonderfully capturing how sin has corrupted his life and his mind. He claims to be such a terrible sinner that he cannot 'sustain' himself for even an hour without giving into the Devil's temptations.

But the poem also highlights Donne's eagerness for redemption. He is desperate to be cleansed of sin, for God to 'repair' his corrupt soul. In 'Thou hast made me', as in the other Holy Sonnets, Donne demands what might be described as 'special treatment' from God. We see this when he calls on God to 'repair [him] now'. The poet doesn't want to bother with the usual business of redemption, with prayer, the sacraments and good deeds. Instead, he wants God to take immediate and decisive action, cleansing him instantly of sin.

For the poet, it's important to note, hell is no metaphor or abstraction – it's something very real and very scary. He is keenly aware that his sins will condemn him to damnation. He thinks of them as a dead weight dragging him downwards into eternal torment. This is especially the case because the poet is getting older and feels that he could die at any minute.

This poem is unusual in that it suggests sin causes not only the soul but also the body to decay. As the poet puts it, 'my feeble flesh doth waste/ By sin in it'. The poet, then, seems to suggest that sin is responsible for the weakness of his flesh and the dimness of his eyes. In healing his soul, therefore, God will also restore his body.

The poem opens with a commanding or challenging tone. The poet wonders why God went to the trouble of creating him, only to let his body and soul be corrupted by sin: 'Thou hast made me, and shall thy work decay?' The poet seems almost irritated with God's inaction. It's as if he believes he can convince God to do things his way, to take action where and when Donne requires: 'Repair me now'.

The poem's closing lines, however, are much more humble in tone. He accepts that it is only with God's 'leave', or permission, that he can pray or contemplate goodness: 'and when towards thee/ By thy leave I can look'. The poet emphasises that he is powerless in the face of sin and temptation. It is only with God's help that he has any chance of turning away from sin and focusing on higher things.

DEATH

'Thou hast made me', lke other poems by Donne, emphasises the poet's keen awareness of death. Death, he stresses, is not only inevitable, but could also happen at any time. This comes across in the striking personification of death as a kind of lover the poet rushes to embrace. There is a real urgency, therefore, to Donne's appeal for redemption.

Donne is a poet keenly aware of transience, of how everything fades with the passage of time. This poem, in particular, focuses on how the passage of time affects the body. It powerfully captures the frailty and indignity of ageing, which each of us must endure as death approaches. The poet presents his final years as a time of physical suffering, of 'dim eyes' and 'feeble flesh', a time when all life's pleasures are in the past.

The afterlife is another theme that recurs throughout Donne's poetry. In this poem, as we've seen, the poet regards death as a terrifying prospect and senses the real possibility that hell rather than heaven awaits him after death. It is only through God's help and intervention that he will be able to enter the heavenly kingdom.

This poem, then, can be contrasted with 'The Anniversary'. In 'The Anniversary', the poet regards death as essentially no big deal and seems certain that he and his beloved will be free to continue their relationship in paradise.

At the round earth's imagined corners

LINE BY LINE

The poem's opening lines refer to the Book of Revelation, chapters 8 to 11. These chapters describe how the end of the world will be signalled by the sound of seven trumpet blasts blown by angels. Donne longs for the end of the world to come. He longs to hear these trumpets ringing out: 'At the round earth's imagin'd corners, blow/ Your trumpets, angels'.

Donne imagines what the end of the world would be like:
- The souls of every single person who has lived and died will 'arise' from death
- This would be an extraordinary number of souls: 'numberless infinities'
- Each soul would reunite with its body.
- These remains, of course, are 'scattered' all over the world, some buried in graveyards, others lost at sea.

Donne lists some of the different ways in which people have died since the world began. He first mentions the victims of

'the flood', which is associated with the story of Noah and his Ark: 'All whom the flood did … o'erthrow'. He then mentions those who will be consumed by flames as the end of the world approaches. The Book of Revelation describes how the end of the world will be preceded by infernos, asteroid strikes and other catastrophic events.

The poet also mentions other more mundane causes of death:
- Those who died because of 'war'.
- Those who died due to a 'dearth' or scarcity of food.
- Those who died naturally of 'age'.
- Those who died from disease or 'ague'.
- Those who were the victims of 'tyrannies', of wicked rulers or regimes.
- Those who took their own lives out of 'Despair'.
- Those who were put to death in accordance with the 'law'.
- Those who were killed by 'accident' or chance.

There are also, of course, those who will still be living when the end of the world arrives. These people will have suffered through the various crises and catastrophes that precede the end of the world. They will hear the angels' trumpets sounded at the earth's four 'corners'. Then they will see or 'behold' God Himself as He enters His creation. These survivors will have made it to the end of the world without dying, and now they will never 'taste death's woe'. They will never endure the terror and uncertainty of death. Their souls will never depart from their bodies and their bodies will never rot in the ground. Instead, they will ascend, body and soul, into heaven.

This, of course, is why Donne is so eager for the end of the world to occur during his lifetime. He wants to be one of the few who never has to die, who avoids 'death's woe' and makes it directly to paradise.

A change of heart

But the poet suddenly has a change of heart, deciding that he is no longer so eager for the world to end. He addresses Christ, asking Him to let the souls of the dead 'sleep' a little longer.

Donne believes himself to be a very sinful man. In fact, he fears that he might be the most sinful man to have ever lived: 'above all these my sins abound'. The poet, therefore, needs to ask for Christ's 'grace', for His favour or forgiveness. Because he is such a terrible sinner, he would require an 'abundance' of this 'grace', an extraordinary level of forgiveness. It would be too late, he feels, to ask for such forgiveness when the end of the world has come: "Tis late … When we are there'. The poet, therefore, wants the end of the world to be delayed. This will allow him the time he needs to get himself right with God. He wishes to remain on the earth's 'lowly ground' and atone for his sins.

The poet is desperate to 'repent'. He wants to not only express remorse for the things he has done, but to also renounce sin and lead a better life. But he feels that he is incapable of doing so. He is too prone to sinning, too susceptible to temptation. He needs Christ to come directly into his life and teach him how to be a better human being.

Science and Superstition

John Donne lived through an exciting period of scientific discovery and many of his poems exhibit a keen interest in this new learning. He uses the term 'imagined' to describe the Earth's corners because he knew very well that the planet is round. The 'corners' that he has in mind are the corners of a map of the world (English maps from the Renaissance often featured illustrations of angels blowing trumpets in the four directions: North, South, East and West). Donne, therefore, calls on the angels to take up position at four equivalent points around the world.

DONNE'S METAPHYSICAL STYLE

Outrageous Claims and Demands

Like the other Metaphysical poets of his day, Donne enjoyed making outrageous claims, statements and comparisons. In this instance he demands no less than the end of the world itself. Equally outrageous is his claim that he is the most sinful person who has ever lived or died.

Inventive Metaphors and Similes

The poet, as we have seen, wants Christ to enter his life and teach him how to repent. Receiving Christ into his life is compared to receiving a letter of 'pardon'. Envelopes containing official documents were sealed with wax to ensure privacy. Donne, however, imagines an envelope that has been sealed, not with wax but Christ's own 'blood'. A pardon sealed in blood seems more serious than one sealed with wax. The mention of blood, of course, also brings to mind Christ's crucifixion, where he suffered for the sins of all mankind.

Paradox and Contradiction

There is something paradoxical about the poem's opening line, which describes how the earth is round but also has corners. The 'four corners of the earth' is an everyday phrase, and one that also occurs in the seventh chapter of the Book of Revelation: 'I saw four angels standing on the four corners of the earth'.

Form

'At the round earth's imagined corners' is a Petrarchan, or Italian sonnet. In the octet, or the first eight lines, the poet calls on God to end the world immediately. In the sestet, or the last six lines, meanwhile, he calls on God to delay. The poem's 'volta' or turn occurs with the word 'But' in line 9, where the poet changes his mind about wanting the world to end.

Tone

The poem opens with a commanding tone, with the poet adopting an almost God-like role, calling on the world to end and issuing instructions to the angels and the souls of the dead. The poem's closing lines, however, are much more humble in tone, with Donne presenting himself as a human being upon the earth's 'lowly ground', someone deeply flawed and desperately in need of God's mercy and grace.

Detail from the cover of the 1632 edition of *Death's Duel*, the last sermon preached by Donne. The image is an engraving of Donne, posing in his burial shroud before his death.

SIN AND REDEMPTION

Throughout his poetry, Donne seems to get a perverse pleasure in presenting himself as a terrible person. His sins, he seems to suggest, are far greater than those of ordinary people. In this poem, he even implies that he's more sinful than anyone else who has ever lived or died. His sins would, therefore, require an 'abundance' of forgiveness on God's part.

The poem also highlights Donne's eagerness for repentance and redemption. He is desperate to atone for his sins and make himself right with God. Donne, however, feels that his redemption can only be achieved with special treatment. He cannot, like other Christians, be guided to redemption by prayer and the sacraments. Instead, he needs Christ to enter his life directly in some special manner so he can be taught how to repent.

The fear of hell and damnation is another recurring feature of Donne's poetry. To Donne, we remind ourselves, the prospect of hell was something very real and something to be greatly feared. We see this when he decides that he does not want the world to end. The ending of the world, Donne knows, will bring with it the final judgement, when God assesses the souls of all who have lived. The poet fears that, due to his sinful nature, he will fail this judgement, and will be cast into damnation rather than ascending directly into heaven.

DEATH

This sonnet is a powerful meditation on mortality. The first eight lines (the octet) forcibly remind us that death lies in store for each of us. The poet describes the 'numberless infinities' of people who have lived and died throughout the ages. They may have met their ends through a myriad of different ways, but they all have the grave in common.

The poem, too, highlights Donne's own terror of dying. Indeed, he calls on God to end the world so he won't have to face dying. He would prefer to still be alive when the world ends so he can be transported directly to heaven without ever having to die. It is only concern about his soul's sinful state that causes him to think better of the world ending immediately.

Seamus Heaney Themes

Art, Craft and Creativity

Celebration of Craft

'The Forge' is one of Heaney's most passionate and vivid celebrations of craft. The poet admires the effort and exhaustion that goes into the labour, which is evident in the way the blacksmith 'expends himself'. The poet is also attracted by the physicality of the work – by the beating of metal; the sudden, almost dangerous 'fantail of sparks'; and the settling of roasting hot metal in water: 'hiss when a new shoe toughens in water'.

But the blacksmith's work is not only practical and everyday; it is also artistic and creative. Working in 'shape and music', the blacksmith seems to combine the sound and rhythm of a musician with the transformative, sculpting ability of a fine artist. Heaney compares the anvil to an 'altar', bolstering the idea of the forge as a special, almost sacred place. All the poet knows of it is 'a door into the dark'. We get the sense that the forge is reserved for blacksmiths only; that laypeople have no business crossing the threshold of this sacred space.

'The Harvest Bow' is a similar celebration of craft and manual labour. The poet praises the skill with which his father wove the bows, tightening the strands of straw 'twist by twist' until the 'love-knot' came together. He describes the 'fine intent' or intense concentration his father brought to this task and how eventually his fingers seemed to move automatically, as though he no longer needed to think about what he was doing: 'Until your fingers moved somnambulant'.

The father's inherent craftsmanship also features in 'A Call'. The father exhibits great care and precision, combing carefully through the leeks and ensuring that he's careful, too, to remove each weed at the root so that they won't grow back. But he also possesses the gentleness and sensitivity necessary to nurture a garden, removing the weeds 'gently', so as not to upset the soil bed.

'Sunlight' and 'The Pitchfork' also celebrate different aspects of craft. 'Sunlight' celebrates the everyday precision of the aunt as she goes about her baking, following her through the process of preparing and baking the scones as she wrestles dough into shape, places it in the oven, cleans off the bakeboard and waits for the scones to rise. 'The Pitchfork' meanwhile celebrates how the titular instrument has been carefully shaped and sculpted until it has become smooth and balanced. The farmer appreciates just how well-suited it is to the task at hand, admiring the 'springiness, the clip and dart of it'.

The Nature of Art

'The Forge' is a potent allegory for the poetic process. The poet, like the blacksmith, must expend himself in his efforts. He must work really hard to produce 'shape' (form, stanzas etc.) and 'music' (sound effects and verbal music). Poetry must be at centre of the poet's life, just as the anvil is 'somewhere at the centre' of the forge. Poetry must be an immovable priority in the poet's life, just as the anvil is 'Set there immovable' in the forge.

Poetry and art originate from a mysterious and unknowable place in the psyche. Like the forge, this part of the mind remains hidden and mysterious. We can experience only glimpses into its workings, just as the poet knows only the door of the forge and the darkness of its interior.

'Bogland' too focuses on the poetic process. Heaney was keenly aware that memory was important to him as a poet: 'memory was the faculty that supplied me with the first quickening of my own poetry'. It is memory, perhaps above all, that sustains Heaney as a poet, nourishing his talent and arousing his inspiration. There is a sense in which he feels that a poet must excavate the layers of his remembrance, much as the turf cutters and archaeologists dig into the layers of bog, in an attempt to extract the material for poetry from his personal store recollection.

In 'The Harvest Bow', the poet comes to see the bow not merely as a humble piece of craftsmanship but as a genuine piece of art. He thinks of it as a 'device', as a tool or implement that allows his father to communicate things that otherwise would have remained unsaid. But the term 'device' in its older usage also means an emblem, and the bow works as a powerful symbol for the poet, representing not only the father's personality but also the harvest and the traditions associated with it in the parish where he grew up.

'The Skunk' and 'The Pitchfork' also focus on aspects of poetic creativity. 'The Skunk' celebrates the fascination of words themselves, especially ancient, fundamental words like 'wife'. Such words, especially when we haven't used them for a while, possess the power to intrigue and captivate us. In the right circumstances, the poet suggests, language can be more potent and intoxicating than a freshly broached cask of wine. 'The Pitchfork', meanwhile, acknowledges that no poem can achieve the perfection imagined at the beginning of its composition. Each work, at best, can only come 'near' such perfection.

The Anxiety of the Artist

In 'The Forge', we sense that the poet cannot help but compare the hands-on usefulness of the blacksmith's craft with the more abstract utility of poetry. There is a thread of this concern through Heaney's work: an anxiety about the legitimacy of writing poetry, about whether it is a 'proper' job for a man. This is more understandable if we consider Heaney's traditional rural upbringing, where men did practical physical labour and poetry was possibly considered pretentious or grandiose.

Though the poet admires the blacksmith, there is a sense in which he also feels inadequate by comparison, working with a pen and paper rather than 'the bellows'. The blacksmith does real work involving 'real iron'. The material that Heaney works with, on the other hand, is only imagined in his readers' heads.

This anxiety about the uselessness of poetry is also present in 'The Skunk'. We see this in lines 13 to 14: 'The beautiful, useless/ Tang of eucalyptus'. The smell of the eucalyptus tree may be beautiful but it serves no practical value. Similarly, the lines themselves may be beautiful but they also serve no practical value. Like all poetry, they are 'useless' in any practical sense.

Such anxiety also features in 'The Harvest Bow', heightened no doubt by the fact that Heaney's father was a no-nonsense, pragmatic man. However, on this occasion the poet detects a similarity between them. For harvest bows, like poems, are beautiful but serve little practical value. Making the harvest bow, then, shows the father's hidden artistic side, with the poet remarking on how his father's hands 'Harked to their gift and worked with fine intent'. The father weaves the bow with the same skill and intensity with which the poet puts together a poem.

Perhaps the father's weaving grants the poet a sense of permission – if it's okay for his father to produce the beautiful but useless bows, it is okay for him to compose his poems. The similarity between the poet and his father only goes so far, however. Heaney responds to the harvest bow with the intense spirituality of a poet, feeling that he is able to glean 'the unsaid' from its loops. To his father, however, it is more 'throwaway': part of a tradition and nothing more.

Crediting the Marvellous

'Lightenings VIII' powerfully makes the point that the marvellous is very much a matter of perspective. What is ordinary and mundane to one person is extraordinary to another. To the monks, the flying ship is an extraordinary sight – it is like nothing they have ever seen before or will ever see again and they will remember it for the rest of their lives. To the crewman, however, the flying ship is just his place of work. But the opposite is also true. To the monks the oratory is just a place where they eat, work and pray. But to the crewman, it is truly extraordinary. It is as wonderfully alien to him as the bed of a deep-sea trench would be to us. The poem suggests then that the ordinary world around us can be a source of awe, mystery and inspiration, if we look at it in the right way. If we are open to experience and view our lives with fresh eyes, as the crewman views the oratory, the world might suddenly appear as the truly marvellous place it actually is.

'The Forge' and 'the Pitchfork' show the poet finding the marvellous in the most unlikely workday scenarios. In 'The Forge', he sees the humble workshop as a space of truly marvellous creation. 'The Pitchfork', meanwhile, presents the simple, everyday instrument, comprising of 'Riveted steel' and 'turned timber' as being almost perfect. 'Bogland' features a similar sense of mystery and wonder. The poet seems awestruck as he contemplates the different objects that have been preserved by the bog: the butter dug out after a hundred years, the preserved trees, the 'astounding' Great Irish Elk. He also seems awestruck at the thought of how endlessly deep the bog is, how layer after layer can be stripped away to reveal yet more bogland underneath.

'The Skunk' is yet another poem where Heaney finds the marvellous in the everyday. The skunk is a familiar sight in California – as common as a fox or a squirrel would be in Ireland. However, he knows that to native Californians, the skunk is a nuisance, barely a step above vermin. Yet the poet finds great mystery in this everyday creature. To him it is the 'Ordinary, mysterious skunk'. He realises that it's a common rodent, but he also, as we've noted, sees it as something special, as a creature of poise and elegance.

'Postscript' too is a poem that stresses the importance of being present in the moment, and of keeping oneself open to life and its sensations. The opening line emphasises the importance of making the time for such experiences 'And some time make the time to drive out west'. Doing so, the poem suggests, is by no means a frivolous activity; it's necessary for a sense of perspective, for our mental and emotional wellbeing.

The Process of Memory

In 'Bogland', the bog is like a museum preserving the history of the Irish race. It holds the evidence of the past, the flora and fauna that once existed on the island and the remains of past civilisations, all the layers that have been 'camped on before' by Ireland's previous occupants.

Yet the bog also serves as a metaphor for the mind or consciousness of the Irish race. As Heaney puts it: 'I had a tentative unrealised need to make a congruence between memory and bogland and, for the want of a better word, our national consciousnesses. Within our national consciousness we remember all that has happened to us as a race, handing it down to the next generation in history, song and story.

'Sunlight' and 'A Constable Calls' are in their very different ways wonderful poems of childhood memory. In 'A Constable Calls', the poet vividly reconstructs and imaginatively re-enters an incident from his childhood, wonderfully capturing a child's perspective on events. We see this in the way he describes the speaker's boyish fascination with the officer's gun. He is captivated by the details of the constable's weapon: 'its buttoned flap, the braid cord/ looped into the revolver butt'.

'Sunlight' illustrates how we often remember distant times and places in a positive light, how our minds filter out the negative details and enable us to imagine that things were better than they actually were. When the poet thinks back on the summers he spent at Mossbawn, it seems that the rain never fell and there were no disturbances or interferences from the outside world. His memory seems to combine the best elements of these summers and fuse them into a single perfect afternoon.

'The Skunk', 'The Harvest Bow' and 'Tate's Avenue' all provide fascinating insights into the strange and surprising ways that memory functions. The poet's memory, the skunk and his wife are inextricably linked in 'The Skunk'. When the poet was lonely in California, the skunk's appearance triggered memories of his wife. In turn, when he is back in Dublin with his wife, Heaney can't help but be reminded of the skunk: 'It all came back to me last night'. Heaney, then, describes the powerful, irresistible manner in which smells, tastes, sights, sounds and even words trigger memory.

In 'The Harvest Bow', as the poet examines the 'golden loops' of the bow pinned up on his dresser, he finds himself vividly remembering an occasion from his childhood. With astonishing clarity, the poet recalls an evening walk with his father to a local fishing spot. Heaney uses a typically brilliant metaphor for this process of memory, in how the bow stimulates such intense recollection. The loops of the bow, he suggests, are a kind of screen on which footage of long-ago events is replayed for him to savour and relive.

'Tate's Avenue', meanwhile, describes the process of memory as an almost inner Instagram. We find the poet flicking through different mental images, as if he were swiping through an internal photo stream. The poem, we might imagine, is set during a moment of ease or relaxation, one in which the poet finds his mind idling or drifting through memories of the past. Maybe he is on a train or a plane, in a space where it is possible to tune out from what is going on around you and become lost in your own thoughts.

Love and Relationships

The Skunk' and 'Tate's Avenue' are both powerful celebrations of married love, showing how the love between two people can grow and remain intense even after years of marriage. When the poet was in California he had been with his wife for 'eleven years'. Yet his feelings towards her were still passionate, and he missed her deeply during this spell abroad. He wrote her love letters and was reminded of her by the sensual delights of California: by the sweet smell of eucalyptus trees or by a sip of Californian wine.

'Tate's Avenue' similarly celebrates the resilience and longevity of a long-term relationship, not the just the excitement and passion of the young love in its earliest stages. The poet fondly recalls how he and his wife explored the world together as the years went by and their relationship continued to flourish and deepen. He relishes how their horizons expanded over time, from the claustrophobic walled yard, to the Northern Irish seashore, to the exotic Guadalquivir river in Spain, and then, no doubt, even further afield.

'The Underground' presents an arguably more complicated picture of marriage. The poem's first nine lines capture the joy and excitement of early married life. The second half of the poem is dark and unrealistic, perhaps even a little bizarre, as the poet presents himself in a similar situation to Orpheus: forced to lead his wife on a journey through the darkness but doomed to lose her if he looks behind. The nightmarish scenario suggests the poet's feelings of anguish and confusion as he takes up his role as husband. He has been thrust into a new set of responsibilities that will eventually require him to function as father, breadwinner and protector.

'The Harvest Bow' is poem that explores the complicated relationship between the poet and this rough, tough no-nonsense man. Specifically, it focuses on the difficulties they experienced in communicating. The poet suggests that his father could express his inner self, the mellowed silence that existed within him, through making the harvest bows. Making harvest bows allowed the father to convey or communicate something of his personality.

'A Call' also focuses on such difficulties in communication. The poet is a highly articulate man who loves to express his thoughts and feelings in words. Why then does he struggle to express his feelings for his father when they speak on the phone? Perhaps it has to do with the difficulty that many men seem to have when it comes to expressing their feelings – it is not something that comes naturally to them. Perhaps it is a generational thing – the poet would have grown up in a time when fathers and sons would rarely articulate their feelings for one another. Perhaps the poet knows that if he speaks these words he will make his father uncomfortable, and he does not want to do this.

LINE BY LINE

The poet is fascinated by the forge, and by the blacksmith who works there. It seems he's drawn to this little workshop and likes to hang around outside. We sense that he's spent hours staring at the pieces of scrap metal in the forge's yard. He's studied 'old axles' the blacksmith would have removed from carts before replacing them with new ones. He sees wheels that the blacksmith decided were beyond repair and that now sit 'rusting' outside the forge.

When the poet lingers outside the forge, he can hear the noises of the blacksmith's trade. For instance, he hears the sound of the blacksmith's hammer colliding with his anvil. Each tap of the hammer produces a 'short-pitched ring', a chime that seems to be both high-pitched and short in its duration. The blacksmith, then, produces a kind of tinkling sound, as he shapes and thins out a piece of metal with continuous well-aimed tapping.

Sometimes the poet hears a sharp hissing sound emanating from the forge. He imagines that the blacksmith is thrusting a freshly beaten, red-hot horseshoe into a bucket of water to cool. This cooling process solidifies and toughens the iron, fixing it in shape: 'hiss when a new shoe toughens in water'.
The poet, however, has never actually been inside the forge itself. The blacksmith, it seems, has never offered to show him around the building's interior. And he's probably too intimidated by the blacksmith to request such an invitation. This particular tradesman, as we shall see, comes across as a rather gruff and unapproachable individual.

From time to time, the poet has looked through the building's open door, peering into the gloom of its interior. It's too dark inside, however, for him to see much. All the poet 'knows' of the forge, therefore, is its doorway and the darkness to which it leads: 'All I know is a door into the dark.' On occasion, however, as he peers in through the door, the poet has witnessed little eruptions of sparks, the result of heat and friction as metal grinds against metal within the forge. Such bursts occur suddenly, and at 'unpredictable' intervals, as the blacksmith goes about his work. The poet describes how these surges issue outward from the anvil, expanding in a 'fantail' shape.

Imagining the interior

The poet imagines what the interior of the forge might be like, focusing especially on the blacksmith's anvil. He imagines that this particular anvil follows the classic design, having one square end, known as the heel, and one horned end, known - unsurprisingly - as the horn: 'Horned as a unicorn, at one end and square' (The 'horn' of an anvil is used for hammering metal into curved shapes).

- He imagines the anvil as a solid rectangular block, resembling 'an altar' in a church.
- He imagines that it must be extremely heavy, an 'immoveable' object.
- He imagines that the anvil 'must be somewhere in the centre' of the forge.

This of course makes sense from a practical point of view, permitting the blacksmith to move around the anvil as he works, striking the metal on its surface from a variety of different angles. But it also seems appropriate that the anvil, the blacksmith's largest and most important piece of equipment, should be his workroom's focal point. The poet imagines the blacksmith at work within the forge. His labours are exhausting; as he drains or 'expends himself' in his efforts at the anvil. The blacksmith's work, of course, is practical in nature as he produces marketable products for everyday use, things like horseshoes, wheels and axles.

But the poet also presents the blacksmith as a kind of artist, as someone working in 'shape and music'. He's a kind of musician whose 'hammered anvil', as we've seen, produces music of a kind, a tinkling pitch and rhythm. But he's also a sculptor of sorts, shaping raw metal into useful and even beautiful objects. The poet often sees the blacksmith standing at the door of the forge, taking a break from his work. He leans against the door's side jamb, smoking a cigarette and watching the world go by: 'Sometimes, leather-aproned, hairs in his nose,/ He leans out on the jamb'.

Heaney provides us with a memorable portrait of the blacksmith. Given his hairy nose and the 'iron hoops rusting' outside his business, we get the impression that he isn't too bothered with superficial things like grooming and branding. He is a tough, country workman of the old school: a no-nonsense, slightly gruff character.

Watching the cars go by

As he smokes, the blacksmith watches cars passing by his forge. He can remember a time when most people travelled by horse and cart rather than by car, when roads were filled with the 'clatter/ Of hoofs' rather than with the zoom of car engines. The poet describes how the 'traffic is flashing in rows' as it passes the forge, a phrase that conveys several meanings at once. The word 'flashing' suggests the greatly increased pace of modern life. Once people travelled on horseback or on foot and had time to take in their surroundings. Nowadays we tend to whizz around in our cars, utterly unmindful of the environments we pass through (and even when we do find ourselves walking, we're in such a hurry, so preoccupied with the stresses and strains of modern living, that we pay little attention to what's going on around us).

'Flashing', no doubt, also suggests the blacksmith's opinion of the automobiles he watches from his doorway. These might be fancy or 'flash', as the expression goes, and they might have glossy, 'flashing' paint jobs. But they're also flimsy, mass-produced and ultimately disposable, especially compared to the carts the blacksmith would have worked on, each of which was unique and designed to last a lifetime.

The fact that the cars go flashing by in 'rows' suggests the conformity of modern living. We travel to and from school and work, in an orderly and regulated fashion, each of us sealed in our almost identical, mass-produced pods. We allow ourselves to be herded 'in rows' like obedient cattle. The blacksmith grunts at the sight of the passing traffic, almost as if he can't find the words to express his contempt for this flashily conformist procession and the new world it represents. He flicks his cigarette in its direction, a classically aggressive

gesture of contempt. Then he retreats back into the forge, slamming the door behind him as he does so: 'Then grunts and goes in, with a slam and flick'. These gestures reveal not only the blacksmith's scorn for the traffic and the modernity it represents but also his anger and frustration that his skills are no longer as valued as they once were. But surely there is also an element of defiance; we sense the blacksmith's determination to persevere with his craft even in the face of the world's indifference.

The poet imagines that, once the blacksmith's back in the forge, he gets down to business: 'To beat real iron out, to work the bellows.' The mass-produced vehicles passing outside are manufactured from cheap artificial alloys and various plasticky materials. The blacksmith, however, still works with genuine metal. It's only the blacksmith, and those few others that practise his dying art, who continue to use 'real iron'.

FOCUS ON STYLE

Form

'The Forge' is written in the form of a sonnet. It has fourteen lines. The octet is concerned with the forge itself whilst the sextet focuses on the blacksmith. It has an ABBACDDC.

Metaphor, Simile, Figures of Speech

The anvil is central to the poem and Heaney uses effective figures of speech to describe it. Using a simile, he describes it as being 'Horned as a unicorn'. This gives us a striking visual of the anvil's horn and also suggests that there is something mystical and magical about the anvil. Using a metaphor, Heaney also describes the anvil as 'an altar'. This emphasises how central the anvil is to the blacksmith's work, and how there is something mysterious and sacred about it.

Verbal Music

The poem is full of sounds. Heaney describes the 'short-pitched ring' of the anvil, the 'hiss' of the red-hot horseshoe as it is plunged in water, the 'clatter/ Of hoofs', and the 'grunts' of the blacksmith. These various sounds underscore the poet's assertion that there is a kind of 'music' in the work of the blacksmith.

Imagery

'The Forge' is filled with vivid imagery, from the rusty 'axles and iron hoops' outside the forge, to the beautiful plumes of sparks that randomly fly off the anvil: 'The unpredictable fantail of sparks'. Perhaps the most memorable image in the poem, however, is that of the blacksmith himself. He is a little scruffy in his work gear: 'leather-aproned, hairs in his nose'. He is a traditionalist with little patience for the modern world, who 'grunts' at the rows of traffic outside the forge. He is brusque in his manner, returning inside 'with a grunt and flick'. In just a few lines, Heaney portrays the blacksmith's appearance, his personality and the way he carries himself.

CELEBRATION OF CRAFT

'The Forge', perhaps more than anything else, is a celebration of the blacksmith's craft. The poet admires the effort and exhaustion that goes into the labour, evident in the way the blacksmith 'expends himself'. The poet is also attracted by the physicality of the work – by the beating of metal; the sudden, almost dangerous 'fantail of sparks'; and the settling of roasting hot metal in water: 'hiss when a new shoe toughens in water'.

But the blacksmith's work, as we noted above, is not only practical and everyday but also artistic and creative. Working in 'shape and music', the blacksmith seems to combine the sound and rhythm of a musician with the transformative, sculpting ability of a fine artist.

He also compares the anvil to an 'altar', bolstering the idea of the forge as a special, almost sacred place. All the poet knows of it is 'a door into the dark'. We get the sense that the forge is reserved for blacksmiths only; that laypeople have no business crossing the threshold of this sacred space.

The blacksmith, as we have seen, has a dismissive and defiant attitude to modernisation. We sense that the poet celebrates the blacksmith's individuality and authenticity: this is someone who does his own thing and follows his own calling, irrespective of the changes in the world at large. Perhaps the poet even shares a little of the blacksmith's hostile attitude towards our conformist, mass-produced society.

The poet associates the anvil with a unicorn, a mythical horse that has a single horn protruding from its forehead. The unicorn is a fantastic beast, a purely imaginary creature. This suggests that the blacksmith's work involves a degree of fantasy and imagination, as well as hard physical labour. Scottish mythology celebrated the unicorn as a beast that would die rather than be captured, suggesting the blacksmith's dogged refusal to change his ways in the face of modernity.

The unicorn also suggests the boundless imagination that poets and artists strive for. In spiritualism, for example, the unicorn is a symbol of change and transformation, while modern day investors use the term for new companies and ideas that can literally change the world: Skype or Google, for example.

THE NATURE OF ART

'The Forge' can be read as an allegory for writing poetry. Different aspects of the poem function as metaphors for creativity:

- Poetry and art originate from a mysterious and unknowable place in the psyche. Like the forge, this part of the mind remains hidden and mysterious. We can experience mere glimpses into its workings, just as the poet knows only the door of the forge and the darkness of its interior.

- Poetic inspiration is 'unpredictable', just as the appearance of the blacksmith's 'sparks' is random. When it occurs, however, it is wonderful.
- The poet, like the blacksmith, must expend himself in his efforts. He must work really hard to produce 'shape' (form, stanzas etc.) and 'music' (sound effects and verbal music).
- Poetry must be at the centre of the poet's life, just as the anvil is 'somewhere in the centre' of the forge.
- Poetry must be an immovable priority in the poet's life, just as the anvil is 'Set there immovable' in the forge.
- Poetry, like the anvil, has a 'square' part (representing form, hard work, drafting) and a part that is 'Horned as a unicorn' (representing fantasy, imagination, wonder and invention).
- Like smithing, poetry has somewhat fallen out of fashion. It is undervalued in the modern mass-produced world.

THE ANXIETY OF THE ARTIST

We sense that the poet cannot help but compare the hands-on usefulness of the blacksmith's craft with the more abstract utility of poetry. There is a thread of this concern through Heaney's work: an anxiety about the legitimacy of writing poetry, of whether it is a 'proper' job for a man. This is more understandable if we consider Heaney's traditional rural upbringing, where men did practical physical labour and poetry was possibly considered pretentious or grandiose.

Though the poet admires the blacksmith, there is a sense in which he also feels inadequate by comparison, working with a pen and paper rather than 'the bellows'. The blacksmith does real work involving 'real iron'. The material that Heaney works with, on the other hand, is only imagined in his readers' heads. In the title, Heaney is possibly playing on the dual meaning of the word 'forge'. Besides being the name for the blacksmith's workplace, 'to forge' means to fake or to imitate. Perhaps this pun expresses Heaney's anxiety that the work he does has no real-world application – at least, not in the way that the blacksmith's work does.

CREDITING THE MARVELLOUS

On the face of it, the forge is an unpromising location for a poem. It's not aesthetically pleasing, with the rusty 'old axles and iron hoops' piled up outside, and the unpolished grumpy blacksmith with 'hairs in his nose'.

However, the poet sees this humble workshop as a place of truly marvellous creation. The 'unpredictable fantail of sparks' that explodes as the blacksmith strikes the metal is beautiful and unexpected. The blacksmith creates 'music' as he works, causing the anvil to 'ring' with his hammer. The anvil itself is marvellous, described as being 'Horned as a unicorn' and standing like an 'altar', 'immovable' in the centre of the forge.

Bogland

'Seamus Heaney in Toner's Bog' by Liam O'Neill

LINE BY LINE

'Bogland' opens by comparing the landscape of Ireland to the prairies of North America. Prairies are vast grasslands reaching for hundreds of kilometres. The Irish landscape, in contrast, is relatively tiny; you can travel for only a few hours by car before reaching the sea. One might say it's cramped and claustrophobic in comparison to the prairies' endless plains. The prairies also exhibit an endless flatness, while the Irish landscape on the other hand is known for being rugged, mountainous and uneven.

The prairies are almost featureless, stretching out monotonously in every direction. The Irish landscape, on the other hand, is filled with geographical features, such as mountains, lakes and hills. In the prairies you can see for tens or even hundreds of kilometres. In the Irish landscape, however, you can only see as far as the next hill, lake or mountain. Then the eye must 'concede' or give way: 'Everywhere the eye concedes'. The rugged horizon seems to 'Encroach' or push up against the viewer.

In the prairies, because there are no distractions, one's gaze tends to drift all the way towards the horizon. In Ireland, however, some feature of the landscape will inevitably attract or distract the eye. Heaney, for instance, mentions how the eye is 'wooed' or seduced by the sight of a mountain lake: 'the eye … is wooed into the cyclops' eye/ Of a tarn'. This 'big sun' can be usefully compared to the description of a 'tarn', or mountain lake, in the Irish landscape. In a wonderful metaphor, Heaney likens this tarn to a 'cyclops' eye' (the cyclops was a mythical one-eyed giant). He emphasises how the eye is 'wooed' or seduced by the tarn, which gently draws the gaze into its depths.

Heaney, using a wonderful phrase, refers to the prairies as 'unfenced country'. This describes how the prairie ranges were kept open, without walls or barriers, so cattle could wander freely, grazing on their abundant grass lands. But it also suggests how, as we've noted, the prairies possess few natural impediments, such as hills and mountains. The prairies, therefore, permit one to travel for hundreds of miles without encountering the slightest obstacle. While the Irish landscape, of course, has no such wide-open spaces, it has its own 'unfenced country' in the form of its bogs: 'Our unfenced country/ Is bog'. Just as the prairies allow one to wander vast distances along the surface of the earth, so the bogs allow one to burrow vast distances into the earth, striking deeper and deeper into its depths.

The bog's depths

In the 19th century, the voyagers who traversed the great plains of America were known as pioneers. These men and women were fearless and intrepid explorers, who set out to explore environments and landscapes no European had ever before witnessed. The closest Irish equivalent to these pioneers are the turf cutters who dig into the bog, revealing its secrets. As Heaney puts it: 'Our pioneers keep striking/ Inwards and downwards'. The American pioneers witnessed extraordinary sights as they journeyed westwards across the

American plains. But our turf-cutting pioneers have made some incredible discoveries of their own:

- They found the perfectly preserved skeleton of a 'Great Irish Elk', which has been extinct for approximately 11,000 years. Heaney uses a wonderful metaphor to depict the elk's skeleton set up in a museum, describing it as 'an astounding crate full of air' (we can imagine the skeleton's bare bones resembling a kind of crate or box).
- They found butter that had been buried in the bog over 'a hundred years' ago. It was 'salty' after its decades amid the peat and had been leached of its original yellow colour but was nevertheless still perfectly edible.
- They have found the trunks of ancient trees, of 'great firs'. These trunks had been softened by the bog's swampy wetness until they were 'waterlogged' and reduced to a spongy or pulpy consistency. But their original shape was still preserved.

Each layer of bogland the turf cutters remove reveals evidence of earlier civilisations: 'Every layer they strip/ Seems camped on before'. Each level of the bog contains remnants of the people who were alive when that level formed the bog's surface. In this way, those who probe the bogs of Ireland are on an archaeological journey into the country's past. Heaney's description of how each layer of bog seems 'camped on' wonderfully captures the brevity of human life. Each generation of Irish people is only 'camping' on the island. We're here only temporarily before we must give way to the younger generations coming up behind us.

The phrase 'big sun' refers to an optical illusion whereby the sun seems bigger when it's close to the horizon. This effect is especially pronounced in locations, like the American prairies, where the horizon is often far off in the distance. As the sun sinks down over the edge these of these great plains 'at evening', it seems like it's being 'sliced' or cut in half by the horizon line.

The word 'camped' also underlines the impermanence of each civilisation – Celtic, Viking, Norman – that invaded and occupied the island over the preceding centuries and millennia. Each was only 'camped' here. Though they didn't realise it at the time, each civilisation was only passing though, simply occupying the island for a relatively brief period before being replaced by the next civilisation to come along. The word 'camp', of course, can also refer to a military force, especially one in medieval times, reminding us of how each civilisation had to forcibly remove the one that came before in order to settle here.

A description of bogland

The poem emphasises the strange splendour of Ireland's boglands, which Heaney once described as 'a very beautiful, benign place.' Heaney praises the oddly pleasant texture of the peat that comprises this boggy landscape, comparing it to 'black butter'. This memorably conjures the peat's pleasant softness and its yielding, almost creamy qualities.

Heaney seems especially fascinated by the bog's shifting, malleable nature:

- The buttery material of which the bog consists constantly changes shape. Merely to step on it is to alter its contours, for it is constantly 'melting and opening underfoot'.
- The bog's surface, too, is constantly altering. Its exterior cools and solidifies each night, 'between the sights of the sun', generating a crusty upper layer. However, this crust melts again each morning when the sun rises, bringing with it the relative heat of the day.
- Bogland exhibits no definition. There is nothing lasting, crisp or distinct about its shape. The shifting, melting substance of the bog is 'Missing its last definition/ By millions of years'. It's been millions of years since the bog was last 'defined', was last cast in an enduring definite shape, and millions of years until it will be again.
- It seems as if nothing solid could ever exist in such an environment: 'They'll never dig coal here'.

Heaney presents the bogland as a 'kind' landscape, an adjective that encompasses its haunting physically beautiful character, the softness of peat that makes it up and the almost miraculous preservative qualities it exhibits. Using another fine metaphor, Heaney compares a tarn or mountain lake to a 'cyclops' eye' (the cyclops was a one-eyed giant in Greek mythology). Such tarns, he suggests, seduce the eyes of all who see them, gently drawing our gazes into their depths: 'the eye… is wooed into the cyclops' eye/ Of a tarn'.

Heaney imagines that the bog reaches ever downwards in stratum after stratum, that each layer stripped away will only reveal another. He imagines that the turf cutters could keep delving through the bog until they encounter the island's very foundations. He suggests that the turf cutters might even encounter the Atlantic Ocean, which he imagines is constantly percolating through or under the bedrock of the island. He fancies that the 'bogholes' we witness on the bog's surface are filled with ocean water that has filtered up through the bog's countless layers, all the way from the Atlantic as it ripples through the foundations of the country: 'The bogholes might be Atlantic seepage'. The edges of the bog, where it blends into ordinary farmland, are relatively dry. But the centre is incredibly moist.

Heaney concludes by imagining that this central portion of the bog might in fact be 'bottomless'. If the turf cutters were to dig here, at the bog's 'wet centre', their 'inwards and downwards' voyage of discovery would never end. They would be able to strip away new layers of bogland for hundreds or even thousands of years, with each one revealing new historical treasures and evidence of ever earlier civilisations.

THEMES

THE PROCESS OF MEMORY

Heaney had this to say about 'Bogland' and memory: 'I began to get an idea of bog as the memory of the landscape, or as a landscape that remembered everything that happened in and to it. In fact, if you go round the National Museum in Dublin, you will realise that a great proportion of the most cherished material heritage of Ireland was 'found in a bog''. In a sense, then, the bog is like a museum preserving the history of the Irish race. It holds the evidence of past, the flora and fauna that once existed on the island and the remains of past civilisations, all the layers that have been 'camped on before' by Ireland's previous occupants.

Yet the bog also serves as a metaphor for the mind or consciousness of the Irish race. As Heaney puts it: 'I had a tentative unrealised need to make a congruence between memory and bogland and, for the want of a better word, our national consciousness'. Within our national consciousness, we remember all that has happened to us as a race, handing it down to the next generation in history, song and story. Similarly the bog records an impression of 'everything that happened in and to it', serving as a potent metaphor for our national consciousness:

*   Like the 'bottomless' bog, our national consciousness goes back thousands of years.
*   Like the bog, it contains different layers of memory, each one closer to the present.
*   Like the bog, our national consciousness is shapeless and fluid, rather than solidly defined. The story of Irish civilisation changes depending on who is recounting it, with different individuals regarding historical events in radically different lights.

The other sense of 'definition', that of meaning or significance, is also relevant here. Our national consciousnesses cannot be pinned down to any one such meaning, to any one coherent or definite narrative. Like the bog it is 'Missing its last definition/ By millions of years'. It's a story that shifts and alters like the peat itself. It is also possible that Heaney is suggesting the Irish race is overly introspective and excessively inward looking. Our pioneers, he says, keep striking 'inwards and downwards'. On one level this refers to those digging into the bog. Yet on a metaphorical level it refers to the Irish people generally. We constantly 'strike inwards', obsessing about our own present, and downwards, obsessing about our own past, in particular the injustices the country has suffered.

ART, CRAFT AND CREATIVITY

The poem can also be taken as a symbol for the poet's memory. Heaney was keenly aware that memory was important to him as a poet: 'memory was the faculty that supplied me with the first quickening of my own poetry'. It is memory, perhaps above all, that sustains Heaney as a poet, nourishing his talent and arousing his inspiration. There is a sense in which he feels that a poet must excavate the layers of his remembrance, much as the turf cutters and archaeologists dig into the layers of bog, in an attempt to extract the material for poetry from his personal store.

FOCUS ON STYLE

Metaphor, Simile, Figures of Speech

There are several memorable metaphors in this poem:

*   Heaney uses an excellent metaphor to describe the impressive American sunset, claiming that the prairies 'slice a big sun at evening'. We can imagine how the sun's disc might seem to be sliced or cut in half by the horizon as it sinks slowly downwards.
*   A tarn is described as the eye of a cyclops, a mythical one-eyed giant.
*   A similarly fine metaphor is used to depict the elk's skeleton set up in a museum. It is described as 'an astounding crate full of air' (we can imagine the skeleton's bare bones resembling a kind of crate or box).
*   Heaney memorably compares the bog's melting, shifting soil to 'black butter'.
*   He compares those who dig into the bog to the 'pioneers' of the American West.

The poem concludes with an instance of hyperbole, or deliberate poetic exaggeration: 'The wet centre is bottomless'. Of course Heaney doesn't believe that the bog is actually bottomless. He exaggerates for effect, to emphasise how incredibly deep the bogs actually are.

Imagery

'Bogland' is replete with imagery of softness and wetness, as Heaney masterfully conjures up the yielding nature of the bog. He describing its buttery soil 'Melting and opening underfoot'. He emphasises the moistness of this landscape, featuring a centre so wet you could sink down into it forever and holes that are filled with 'seepage' from the Atlantic itself. He describes a substance that can never be defined or cast into any kind of definite shape, where nothing hard like coal could ever be discovered. Only items that are waterlogged and pulpy can be salvaged from its depths.

II

Heaney associates these childhood summers at Mossbawn with security, calmness and love. He begins the poem by saying there was an 'absence' of something during these sunlit days.

- Perhaps the poet is describing how these long summer days were devoid of stress and hurry. There was a lazy, relaxed atmosphere about the farm and the poet was free to do what he wished with his time.
- Perhaps the poet is alluding to the innocence of childhood, to the absence of the fears and anxieties that we often experience as we get older.
- Perhaps the poet is referring to the absence of the violence and conflict that had engulfed the North when he was writing the poem. The Mossbawn of his childhood is presented as a refuge from such conflict.

The poet describes the absence as 'sunlit', suggesting that the sun perhaps facilitated this absence. Its bright rays allowed no room for anything unpleasant to lurk and hide. On these long summer afternoons, there was an 'absence' of darkness. The absence of stress and anxiety is also suggested when the poet later says, 'here is a space/ again'. It is as if these long afternoons afforded everyone a breathing space, an opportunity to relax and to take timeout from the hustle and bustle of the day-to-day life. When the aunt has put the scones in the oven, she sits down and relaxes, waiting for them to bake.

But the 'space' that the poet describes might also be an imagined space. Whenever he thinks about this place and this time in his life, he is reminded of the security and peace that he experienced back then. Now that the poet is older, he can revisit this place in his mind and experience some of its calm.

Heaney also refers to 'love' in the poem's closing lines, suggesting that above all else, it was this that he experienced most on those long summer afternoons. Perhaps it is the thought of his aunt going about her business in the kitchen that epitomises such love. The aunt is depicted as a nurturing and wholesome presence with her 'broad lap' and 'whitened nails'. We can imagine how her presence in the warm kitchen must have made the young poet feel safe and secure. But it is also likely that it is Mossbawn itself that epitomises this love, that within its grounds and its walls the poet felt perfectly happy and secure.

The poet compares the love that he experienced in Mossbawn to a scoop that has been sunk deep into a bin of flour: 'here is love/ like a tinsmith's scoop/ sunk past its gleam/ in the meal-bin'. A scoop is a utensil with a short hand and deep bowl used, for example, to take flour from a bag or a bin. In this case, the scoop has been crafted from tin by a tinsmith. The shiny metal surface of the scoop would reflect or 'gleam' in the sunlight. However, in this instance, the scoop is sunk deep into the flour in the bin, to the point where its surface is no longer exposed to the light: 'sunk past its gleam/ in the meal-bin'.

The image suggests perhaps the abundance of the love that the poet felt during these summer days in Mossbawn. The image suggests a sense of almost womb-like security. Like the tinsmith's scoop, which is sunk deep in the flour, the poet felt that the love he felt here was all-embracing, that it surrounded him and cushioned him from harm.

FOCUS ON STYLE

Verbal Music

There are several examples of alliteration in this poem. We see this with the repeated 'h' sound in 'helmeted pump in the yard/ heated its iron,/ water honeyed' and with the repeated 's' sound in 'measling shins:/ here is a space/ again, the scone rising'.

Assonance occurs throughout the poem, through the constant repetition of 'u' and 'o' sounds. We see this in lines 4 and 5 for example: 'water honeyed// in the slung bucket'. Assonance also occurs with the repeated 'ea' sound in 'meal' and 'gleam'. Assonance and alliteration produce a pleasant and euphonious musical effect, appropriate to the poem's atmosphere of peace and comfort. The repeated broad-vowel sounds slow the pace of the verse, lending it a relaxed easy quality appropriate to the peaceful and sunny afternoon it describes.

Metaphor, Simile, Figures of Speech

This is a poem that is all about atmosphere. The various images that the poet presents us with conjure up the atmosphere of his childhood home on these long summer days. There is a perfect stillness and calmness to the place. There is an almost entire absence of movement in the poem. In fact, the only movement described is that of the aunt's hands scuffling or scurrying over the bakeboard as she prepares the scones for the oven. There is also almost an entire absence of sound. The only sound the poet describes features in the poem's second last stanza, where he mentions the ticking of the 'two clocks' in the kitchen.

This atmosphere of stillness and silence seems to correspond with the process of memory that is happening here. The poet is recalling an idealised version of these childhood days, rather than a specific, actual event. As we observed above, such recollections of treasured times often preserve the positives and eliminate the negatives, until we are left with a memory that is ideal.

THEMES

THE PROCESS OF MEMORY

Just as he does in such poems as 'A Constable Calls' and 'The Forge', Heaney convincingly conveys to us a child's mentality. The poem captures the innocence of the child's mind. We get the sense that the poet at this time was barely conscious of the larger world beyond his family home, that he was utterly unaware of any happenings beyond this place.

The poem also illustrates how we often remember distant times and places in a positive light, how our minds filter out the negative details and enable us to imagine that things were better than they actually were. When the poet thinks back on the summers he spent at Mossbawn, it seems that the rain never fell and there were no disturbances or interferences from the outside world. His memory seems to combine the best elements of these summers and fuse them into a single perfect afternoon.

ART, CRAFT AND CREATIVITY

Heaney often uses traditional skills as a metaphor for his own poetic craft. This is especially evident in 'The Harvest Bow', which draws many analogies between the craft of weaving the bows and that of writing poetry. We also see this in 'The Forge' and in 'The Pitchfork'. This tendency is arguably also present in 'Sunlight'. This poem stresses the care and patience involved in baking bread, characteristics that are also important in the creation of poetry.

This is one of many poems where Heaney praises craft and manual labour. He celebrates his aunt's baking ability, following her through the process of preparing and baking the scones as she wrestles dough into shape, places it in the oven, cleans off the bakeboard and waits for the scone to rise.

IMAGINED SPACES AND LANDSCAPES

Although the place that the poem describes, the poet's childhood home, Mossbawn, is an actual place where the poet spent his childhood, there is a sense in which the description is very much imagined. Just as we all tend to recall the summers of our childhood as perhaps being graced with more sunshine than was actually the case, so the poet seems to imagine a rather idealised version of the place where he grew up. The place that he describes is soaked in sun and seems blissfully peaceful. The poet vividly remembers his aunt baking in the kitchen.

MASCULINITY AND FEMININITY

There has been much discussion about the poem's final comparison of love to a scoop sunk into a meal bin: 'like a tinsmith's scoop/ sunk past its gleam/ in the meal-bin'. Many critics interpret this image symbolically, as suggesting the perhaps old-fashioned view that men cause most of the conflict and violence in the world while women are associated with care and nurture.

The metal scoop made by a tinsmith is associated with masculinity, with forges and tools. The meal bin is associated with femininity, with cooking and domesticity. Perhaps the poem suggests that love and the absence of conflict become possible only when feminine values predominate over masculine ones, when the scoop is sunk into the meal bin's flour. Mossbawn, associated with the poet's 'broad-lapped' aunt is one place where such feminine values predominate and love is allowed to exist.

THE PROCESS OF MEMORY

Heaney wrote this poem around the same time he wrote 'A Constable Calls' and 'The Tollund Man', poems that deal with the bitter conflict in Northern Ireland. Yet in this poem, there is the sense of Mossbawn as a place of refuge from conflict. The poet's childhood home is presented as place of complete security and comfort:

- It is a place associated with nourishment and wholesomeness; with water in the bucket and bread in the oven. Depictions of the sun as a griddle and of the water as honey reinforce this association.
- The aunt is depicted as a nurturing and wholesome presence, with her 'broad lap' and 'whitened nails'.
- It is a place of warmth, both from the sun and from the oven. There is almost a sense in which the poet thinks of Mossbawn as a place of permanent good weather: the sun fills 'each long afternoon'.
- Heaney stresses that this is a place of love and kindness: 'and here is love'.
- The 'helmeted pump' seems to stand guard, so no trouble can enter.
- This is a place from which violence and conflict are completely absent. The sun pours down upon this welcome absence. The poem depicts a breathing space, a refuge where conflict cannot enter: 'here is a space/ again'.

A Constable Calls

LINE BY LINE

Seamus Heaney grew up on a farm in Co. Derry, Northern Ireland, during the 1940s. The Northern Ireland of the poet's youth was a divided place. On the one hand, there was the Protestant majority who dominated the state: controlling the parliament, the civil service and the police. On the other, was the Catholic minority, to which Heaney and his family belonged. This Catholic minority suffered discrimination and inequality at the hands of the Protestant-dominated state institutions.

This poem is based on a memory from the poet's childhood. A constable, or police officer, arrives on a routine visit to the farmhouse. He's come to note the 'tillage returns', to record the different varieties of crop growing on the farm and the area of land devoted to each one. This would enable the authorities to determine how much tax the poet's father had to pay and to bill him accordingly.

The Constable arrives

The constable arrives on a bicycle, which he leaves leaning 'at the window-sill' of the house. Heaney provides a typically vivid and detailed description of the bike's various features.

- He describes its 'mud-splasher', which was a piece of rubber fabric draped over the front wheel. Like the mud-guard, it protected the constable's uniform from getting dirty as he cycled around the countryside performing his duties.
- He describes the 'fat black' grips on its handlebars.
- He describes the bike's dynamo, a little electrical device that charged as the constable pedalled and powered the bike's front light. The dynamo, because of its stubby shape, reminds the childhood speaker of a 'spud' or potato.

We might think of bicycles as a simple and old-fashioned means of transport, but in the 1940s, when cars were still extremely rare in Ireland, a bike was an important piece of equipment. Without his bicycle, the constable would not have been able to travel around the district and carry out his duties.

The speaker presents the bike almost as a kind of weapon. Its dynamo is depicted as 'gleaming and cocked back', like a gun ready to fire. Similarly, its 'flat black handlegrips' resemble the handle of a gun. There's even something menacing about the speaker's depiction of the 'mud-splasher', which is presented as 'cowl' or hood that might be draped over a prisoner's head. Tellingly the constable keeps it 'gleaming', just as he keeps the holster of his revolver 'polished'. For the speaker, then, the constable's bicycle is a machine of menace and violence, one that facilitates an agent of a hostile regime.

Throughout the poem, the constable is associated with an oppressive weight. His boots are associated with heaviness and his pedals are described as being 'relieved' when he steps off them. Tellingly, the speaker associates these boots with the 'law', suggesting that like many Northern Irish Catholics he regards 'the law' as an oppressive force. His policeman's cap is also associated with heaviness and pressure, leaving a wedge-shaped indentation in his sweatdamp hair: 'The line of its pressure ran like a bevel'. Its weight is also hinted at when he uses both hands to replace it on his head: 'fitted his cap back with two hands'. The ledger in which he makes his returns too, is described as 'heavy'.

Arithmetic and fear

The constable enters the farmhouse and takes a seat. He removes his cap and places it beside his chair: 'His cap was upside down/ On the floor, next his chair'. His hair is described as 'slightly sweating', suggesting the exertions of his cycle to the farmhouse. The constable begins recording the tillage returns, taking down this information in his ledger or record book: 'He had unstrapped/ The heavy ledger'. The father lists the different crops growing on his farm, describing the amount of land devoted to each in terms of 'acres, roods and perches', which are measurements of area.

The poet describes this moment as one of 'Arithmetic and fear'. The 'arithmetic' relates to the calculations the constable makes in his ledger, adding up the volumes of the various crops that grow on the farm and working out the taxes due on each one. The 'fear', meanwhile, is experienced by the young speaker. Any small child might be frightened by the presence of an armed police officer in their kitchen. But in this instance the unease is even greater because the constable is a member of the RUC, the Protestant controlled police force; to the young speaker, he represents oppressive state power.

The young speaker's fear is evident in how he finds himself 'staring' at the constable's gun, taking in its every detail: 'the polished holster/ With its buttoned flap, the braid cord/ Looped into the revolver butt.' We sense that he is simultaneously horrified and fascinated by this weapon; though it terrifies him, he can't take his eyes off it.

A small deception

The speaker's father has 'a line/ Of turnips' growing on his land that he doesn't want the authorities to know about (presumably the father wants to avoid paying tax on the sale of these vegetables). The turnips have been planted far from prying eyes. They grow at the very end of the potato field, where the father ran out of potato seed when he was sowing the season before.

The constable has nearly completed the tillage returns. But he wants to be sure he's recorded absolutely everything, asking the father: 'Any other root crops?/ Mangolds? Marrowstems?

Anything like that?' The father, of course, says no, failing to mention the secret turnips. The young speaker, already uneasy in the constable's presence, is terrified by this little piece of fraud. He imagines that his father might be taken to the 'barracks' for lying to the constable. Perhaps the speaker himself might be jailed also for not speaking out against his father's deception.

The verb 'assume' in line 25 has two meanings. In one sense it means to understand or realise. The speaker, then, realises that his father isn't being totally honest with the constable and is practising a small deceit on the state. But it also means to take on responsibility. The speaker then 'assumed/ Small guilts' in the sense that he feels implicated in and responsible for the deception that is taking place.

Thankfully, the constable leaves without inspecting the fields and discovering the illicit turnips. He replaces his cap, adjusts his baton and closes his ledger. Then he gives the speaker a look as he takes his leave: 'And looked at me as he said goodbye'. We can imagine that the young speaker was terrified by the constable's gaze. Maybe he felt the constable was inspecting him for signs of guilt. Maybe he felt the constable somehow suspected the existence of the illicit crops.

The constable is briefly visible outside the window, securing the ledger to his bicycle's carrier: 'A shadow bobbed in the window./ He was snapping the carrier spring/ Over the ledger'. Then the only sign of him is the ticking sound his bike makes as he cycles down the lane away from the speaker's house: 'the bicycle ticked, ticked, ticked'.

There is an interesting reference to the 'domesday book' in line 30. The Domesday Book was a record of all the lands of England made in 1086 by King William I, twenty years after he had violently conquered the country. Heaney describes the constable's ledger as a kind of mini-Domesday Book. Instead of recording the wealth of an entire country, it records what's growing on the farms of a single district.

FOCUS ON STYLE

Imagery

Heaney is nothing if not a poet of description. We see this in his comprehensively detailed descriptions of the bicycle with its handlebars, dynamo and mud-splasher. It's also evident in his description of the constable's holstered weapon with its flap and cord. The constable's movements are also precisely described: how he unstraps, closes and secures his ledger, how he adjusts his 'baton-case', how he carefully replaces his cap. It is important to note, however, that the speaker never describes the constable's demeanour or facial expressions. He is presented only in relation to his uniform and equipment. It's as if for the young speaker the constable is completely identified with his job, with the role he plays as representative of an unloved and oppressive regime.

Metaphor, Simile, Figures of Speech

The metaphors in 'A Constable Calls' capture the aggressive, invasive nature of the constable's visit, at least as it would have been perceived by the young poet and his family. The bike's mud-splasher, as we've seen, is compared to a sinister rubber hood, one that might perhaps be used in the abduction of a prisoner. There's a sense of this, too, when the bike's 'cocked' dynamo is compared not only to a potato but also to a gun. Even the constable's hair is associated with pressure, as the line left by his cap is compared to a bevel drilled into a concrete surface.

CONFLICT AND VIOLENCE

In many respects, the poem describes a minor incident, a routine visit by a police officer to a farm. Yet the poem skilfully highlights the tensions that existed between Catholics and Protestants in the Northern Ireland of the poet's youth. The constable represents the institutions that oppress the speaker's family and other Catholics all across Northern Ireland. Nevertheless, the speaker's father has no alternative but to invite him in, to answer his questions and to account for himself to this representative of an alien authority. The constable's presence in the speaker's home, then, represents a kind of violation, perhaps even a humiliation.

It's unsurprising, therefore, that throughout the poem the constable is presented as a menacing or even terrifying figure, one who brings with him not only 'arithmetic' but also 'fear':

- As we've seen, he is associated with an oppressive heaviness, suggesting the repression to which Northern Ireland's Catholics were subjected.
- His bicycle, as we noted, is depicted not only as an innocent mode of transport, but also as a kind of weapon, as a machine associated with menace and violence.
- He is associated with weaponry, with his baton in its case and with his revolver in its 'polished holster'.
- He is also associated with enforcement and imprisonment, with 'the black hole in the barracks'.
- As we have seen, his ledger is described as a 'domesday book', associating it too with conquest and violence.
- Even the depiction of him, in the poem's closing stanza, as a 'shadow' adds to this sense of menace and unease.

Tellingly, the speaker records only one word his father uttered to the constable: 'No'. But this single syllable captures the father's anger and resentment at having to account for himself to this oppressive government, which refuses to recognise his rights. Perhaps this is part of his motivation for not being completely honest with his tillage returns. On the one hand, of course, he simply wants to avoid paying tax on the sale of 'a row of turnips'. But there's also a sense in which he wants to 'get one over' on what he regards as a hostile and oppressive state.

It's important to note, however, that the constable, as far as we can tell, doesn't behave badly during this brief visit. The speaker's father doesn't shout at him, abuse him or defy him in any way. All these tensions remain bubbling beneath the surface. Eventually, however, the tensions described in the poem would flare up into the terrible conflict known as the Troubles, which began several decades after the events described in this poem. The constable's bike, as we've noted, produced a ticking sound as he cycled.

Perhaps it's not too fanciful to hear in that ticking a timer counting down to the beginning of the Troubles, which at that time were still years in the future. It's a noise that also brings to mind the many bombs that exploded with such terrible loss of life in that devastating conflict.

THE PROCESS OF MEMORY

'A Constable Calls' is a wonderful poem of childhood memory, one in which we witness the poet vividly reconstructing and imaginatively re-entering an incident from his childhood. Heaney wonderfully captures a child's perspective on events. We see this in the way he describes the speaker's boyish fascination with the officer's gun. He is captivated by the details of the constable's weapon: 'its buttoned flap, the braid cord/ Looped into the revolver butt.'

Heaney also wonderfully evokes the 'small guilts' of childhood, the silly and naïve worries that can seem so great to us when we are children. The young speaker, as we've seen, 'assumes' or takes on the guilt of his father's little deception, worrying that by not alerting the constable to this fraud he's become implicated in a terrible crime.

The fact that he mentions how the constable looked at him as he departed further reinforces our sense of the fear that gripped him. The young speaker, we imagine, worries that the constable is scanning his face for signs of deception. He even worries that he and his father might be hauled off to the barracks for not being completely honest with the tillage returns. Here we see Heaney wonderfully capturing the fears that strike us as ridiculous when we're adults but seem very real and vivid when we're children.

LOVE AND RELATIONSHIPS

'A Constable Calls' provides a subtle but effective portrait of the poet's father. It's fair to say that in this poem the father comes across as the strong silent type:

- He's a farmer, a man well used to the physical demands of making a living off the land, as he sows and harvests various crops.
- He's a man of few words; as we noted above, the only thing he says to the constable is 'No'.
- He's not afraid to defy the authorities by growing turnips without reporting doing so.
- He's not afraid to face down the constable, another powerful masculine presence.
- He calmly lies about the hidden crops, giving no evidence of being frightened or intimidated by the constable's and his revolver, his composure contrasting starkly with the fear the young speaker experiences.

The father, then, comes across as a rough, tough no-nonsense farmer. However, poems like 'The Harvest Bow' and 'A Call' present a different and arguably softer side of the father's personality.

The Skunk

Heaney with his wife, Maria, and sons, Michael and Christopher, in 1969

LINE BY LINE

The poet remembers a period he spent working in California during the 1970s. He was obliged to spend a few months away from his wife and children, who remained behind in Ireland. The poet, naturally enough, felt very lonely for his family during this time of separation. In fact he missed his wife so much that many aspects of California's landscape and lifestyle reminded him of her. He thought of her, for instance, when he caught the scent of the eucalyptus trees that are ubiquitous in that part of the world: 'The beautiful, useless/ Tang of eucalyptus spelt your absence.'

Perhaps the poet longed to share this beautiful aroma with his wife. Or maybe it reminded him of her perfume. In any event, this wonderful phrase suggests that the trees were communicating with the poet, speaking to him through the medium of scent in order to emphasise just how far away his wife was. Californian wine, too, reminded the poet of the wife he'd left behind, particularly the 'aftermath' of every sip. This aftertaste or lingering finish reminded him of his wife's scent. He was reminded especially of how, when they lived together back in Dublin, he'd inhale her aroma from her cold pillow after she'd left the bedroom in the morning.

The writing desk

While in California, the poet would spend his evenings writing. His desk, it seems, was situated at a large French window, or glass door, that looked out on to the yard of the property where he was staying. Beyond this window was a 'verandah', or covered porch.

The light from his desk lamp would illuminate this verandah. But its glow would 'soften', or diminish in intensity, as it reached the verandah's edge and blended with the darkness of the yard beyond: 'My desk light softened beyond the verandah.' The poet recalls how on these evenings the house would be extremely quiet, its silence broken only by the humming of the refrigerator. He also recalls the orange tree that grew in the yard; specifically how its fruit seemed larger in the evening time: 'Small oranges loomed in the orange tree.' This effect was created, no doubt, because the fruit's bright rind seemed even brighter as the darkness gathered.

No doubt, the poet composed poetry during these evenings at his writing desk. But he also found himself writing love letters to his wife. This was something he hadn't done for a long time, not since the early days of their relationship eleven years ago: 'After eleven years I was composing/ Love-letters again'. Remember that this poem is set during the 1970s, a pre-internet era when there was no Skype, social media or even email to keep in touch. Furthermore, transatlantic phone calls were extremely expensive, making letters by far the most efficient and cost-effective means to communicate.

The skunk's nightly visits

Each evening, as the poet sat at his writing desk, a skunk would appear in the garden of the property. The poet was fascinated by this creature and was especially taken by its lustrous, glossy tail:

- He describes the tail as 'damasked', suggesting not only its luxuriance but also its distinctive black and white patterning.
- He compares the tail to a black and white chasuble, the vestment worn by a Catholic priest as he celebrates a funeral: 'damasked like the chasuble/ At a funeral mass'.

- The tail was so extravagant that it seemed to parade the skunk around the place: 'the skunk's tail/ Paraded the skunk.' It seemed to the poet that the tail was leading the animal, rather than the other way around.
- He describes how the tail was 'Up', as if the skunk, peacock-like, was keen to show off its most extravagant feature. The word 'Paraded', too, conveys the skunk's confident, self-assured demeanour, how it strutted around the yard like it owned the place.

The skunk would sniff the verandah on the other side of the French door, just 'five feet' from where the poet sat at his writing desk: 'Snuffing the boards five feet beyond me'. The word 'Snuffing' brilliantly conveys the skunk's action of rubbing its nose against the verandah, suggesting the sniffling, snorting sounds it produced as it checked the wooden boards for scents.

The poet watches the skunk

The poet found himself waiting each evening for the skunk to appear: 'Night after night/ I expected her like a visitor.' We can picture him at his writing desk, anticipating the skunk's arrival and wondering when it will show up. We can imagine his heart skipping a beat each time it finally appeared in the garden: 'And there she was'. We sense that he was surprised, perhaps even a little shocked, at how important its nightly visits became to him.

- It seems that the skunk, just like the taste of wine and the smell of eucalyptus, began to remind the poet of the wife he missed so much:
- The skunk, like the poet's wife, is female and exhibits a peculiarly feminine beauty.
- It's a 'glamorous' creature, showing off its glossy, patterned tail as if it were sporting the latest and most fashionable gown from Paris or Milan.
- As we've seen, the skunk swaggers around the yard with great self-confidence, with poise and assurance worthy of a runway model.
- Unlike a model, however, the skunk doesn't care who's looking.

The link between the skunk and the poet's wife, while it seems bizarre at first, actually makes a certain kind of sense. In the skunk, he sees a little of his wife, of her beauty, her demeanour and her attitude. In his loneliness, then, the poet nearly began to depend on the skunk's visits. It's as if, when the skunk was nearby, he no longer missed his wife quite so much.

Remembering the skunk

The poem's first five stanzas, as we've seen, are set some years ago, during the poet's stint in California. The final stanza, however, is set in the present day when the poet is back in Dublin with his wife and family. He describes how 'last night' he was 'stirred', or sexually aroused, by the sound of his wife undressing: 'stirred/ By the sootfall of your things at bedtime'.

His wife, having disrobed, reached into a bottom drawer for her nightdress: 'Your head-down, tail-up hunt in a bottom drawer/ For the black plunge-line nightdress'.

Suddenly, the poet finds himself reminded of the skunk. The position and motion of his wife searching for the nightdress remind him of the skunk 'snuffing' the boards of the verandah. The black nightdress on her white skin, no doubt, reminds him of the skunk's damask coat. Suddenly, he is transported back to his time in California all those years ago, when he would spend each night waiting for the skunk to make its appearance: 'It all came back to me last night'.

A voyeur is someone who gains pleasure from watching others. The poet, then, is a voyeur in the sense that he gets a thrill from watching the skunk go about its business each evening. The poet's observing of the skunk does have a slightly erotic component. For the poet, as we've seen, regards the skunk as an elegant, sensual creature and associates it with his wife's confident, expressive mannerisms.

Voyeurs are typically tense and nervous because their activities involve an invasion of privacy. The poet, as we watches the skunk, experiences something of this tension: 'I began to be tense as a voyeur.' Perhaps the poet feels that watching the skunk is an intrusive act. Perhaps he feels that at night the verandah and the yard belonged to the skunk more than to him, and that the creature should be left to do its thing unobserved. Or maybe this tension stems from his fear that the skunk won't make an appearance on this particular evening and that he'll be denied the thrill of watching it wander and snuffle about the yard.

FOCUS ON STYLE

Verbal Music

Heaney is well known for his ability to vividly capture different sounds. There are several instances of this in 'The Skunk'. In line 5 he compares the soft hum of the refrigerator to a horse whinnying. In line 22 he memorably compares the swishing sound of his wife removing her underwear to the soft noise of soot falling down a chimney. Taste and smell are evoked in stanza 4, which memorably describes the smell of the eucalyptus tree and the aftertaste of wine. The senses of smell and taste are intermingled in line 16. The wine's aftertaste reminds the poet of the aroma his wife's hair would leave on the pillow when they were back home in Ireland together.

Metaphor, Simile, Figures of Speech

There are several memorable similes in this poem. The poet compares the skunk's tail to a priest's 'chasuble', emphasising how mysterious and sacred the creature has become to him. Because the poet and his wife live together, he has not written her love letters for a long time. He is not used to writing the word 'wife' and the word seems strange and mysterious to him. He evokes this strangeness and mystery by comparing the word to an old and precious cask of wine. The cask has long been in storage, but now the poet is about to open it once more.

The word 'wife', in an unexpected but effective metaphor, is compared to a cask of wine. Because the poet hadn't written this word for a long time, it's compared to a cask that's been stored in a cellar, put aside until needed. We 'broach' a cask by inserting a syringe, known as a 'barrel thief', and drawing up a portion of the liquid, which allows us to taste and sample the vintage within. By writing the word 'wife' again, after many years, the poet felt as if he were sampling a rare and valuable vintage.

As he wrote the word 'wife', the slender 'i' vowel seemed to release from the word into the night air, just as the opening of a cask would release the scent of wine: 'as if its slender vowel/ Had mutated into the night earth and air// Of California'. The description of the vowel as 'mutated' suggests how the poet's relationship with his wife has changed and matured over the course of their relationship. The word 'wife' meant something different to the poet eleven years into their marriage than it had done at the beginning. This is similar to how the taste of wine will mature and deepen with time.

THEMES

LOVE AND RELATIONSHIPS

'The Skunk' is a powerful celebration of married love. It shows how the love between two people can grow and remain intense even after years of marriage. When the poet was in California, he had been with his wife for 'eleven years'. Yet his feelings towards her were still passionate, and he missed her deeply during this spell abroad. He wrote her love letters and was reminded of her by the sensual delights of California: by the sweet smell of eucalyptus trees or by a sip of Californian wine.

The poem also celebrates erotic and sexual love, showing how the desire between the poet and his wife is undiminished by over a decade of marriage. In the poet's mind, the skunk becomes associated with his wife. The poet looks forward to the nightly visits of the skunk, because its glamour, mystery and confidence remind him of his wife's sexuality. The eroticism of married life is also celebrated in the poem's concluding stanza, where the poet is 'stirred' or aroused by the sound of his wife undressing and by the sight of her 'tail-up hunt' for her nightdress.

It could also be argued that the poem illustrates how 'absence makes the heart grow fonder'. The time spent in California is the poet's first extended period of separation from his wife since the beginning of their marriage. This separation seems to have intensified his feelings towards her. The whole idea of marriage, of her being his 'wife', began to seem fresh and new once more. He found himself 'composing/ Love letters again', as he did when he was a love-struck young man at the beginning of their relationship.

THE PROCESS OF MEMORY

'This poem provides a fascinating insight into the strange and surprising ways in which memory functions. In the poet's memory, the skunk and his wife are inextricably linked. When the poet was lonely in California, the skunk's appearance triggered memories of his wife. In turn, when he is back in Dublin with his wife, he can't help but be reminded of the skunk: 'It all came back to me last night'.

The poem also explores the sensory aspects of memory. Heaney describes the powerful, irresistible manner in which smells, tastes, sights, sounds and even words trigger memory:

- The skunk's tail reminds the poet of a priest's robe at a funeral: 'damasked like the chasuble/ At a funeral mass'.
- The smell of the eucalyptus tree reminds him of his wife: 'The beautiful, useless/ Tang of eucalyptus spelt your absence.'
- The aftertaste of wine reminds him of his wife's scent: 'The aftermath of a mouthful of wine/ Was like inhaling you off a cold pillow.'

An interesting feature is how the poet remembers remembering. In present-day Dublin, his wife's hunt for the nightdress reminds him of how in California, all those years ago, wine and eucalyptus reminded him of her! The processes of memory, then, are complex and irregular, operating through all kinds of unpredictable layers and circuits.

CREDITING THE MARVELLOUS

'The Skunk' is another poem where Heaney finds the marvellous in the everyday. The skunk is a familiar sight in California – as common as a fox or a squirrel would be in Ireland. However, the poet knows that to native Californians, the skunk is a nuisance, barely a step above vermin. Yet the poet finds great mystery in this everyday creature. To him it is the 'Ordinary, mysterious skunk'. He realises that it's a common rodent but he also, as we've noted, sees it as something special, as a creature of poise and elegance.

The poet, then, simultaneously holds two contradictory views of the skunk. On the one hand he's 'mythologised' the animal, building it up into a symbol of his wife's sexuality: confident, mysterious and even glamorous. On the other hand, he constantly 'demythologises' the creature, reminding himself, even as he waits each night for its appearance in his garden, that it's only a skunk.

The Harvest Bow

LINE BY LINE

Where Heaney grew up, there was a tradition of weaving small bows from straw each autumn at harvest time. The poet now has one of these bows in his house, 'pinned up on [his] deal dresser'. He contemplates this bow, recalling how it was woven by his father several years before:

- It was made from several stalks of harvested wheat, which his father 'plaited' or intertwined.
- It was created 'twist by twist', the father wrapping one strand of wheat around another again and again. The strands would gradually be tightened into a very rigid plait or braid: it 'tightens twist by twist'.
- This length of braided straw would be knotted into an elaborate bow shape, which Heaney describes as a 'love-knot'.

Using a wonderful metaphor, Heaney compares the wheat in the bow to some kind of metal capturing its golden, metallic sheen. But this is a 'metal' that does not rust or decay because the process of plaiting the harvest bow dries out the straw, preventing it from rotting. We sense that the poet's father made a number of these bows each year, and quickly got back into the knack of weaving them each harvest time. The poet suggests that his father had a talent for this kind of work, a 'gift' to which his fingers 'Harked' or responded. He recalls how his father worked a 'fine intent', with intense concentration as he interlaced the straw.

The description of the bow as 'throwaway' suggests that it is fragile and disposable, a 'frail device' made out of straw. These objects were not intended to last a long time. They were usually worn for a brief time during the harvest, and then cast aside.

Eventually the father's fingers seemed to move automatically, as though he no longer needed to think about what he was doing. Heaney, in a typically inventive turn of phrase, describes how his father's fingers were sleepwalking, how they 'moved somnambulant'. This suggests the unconscious ease with which the father wove the bows, his fingers seeming to operate independently of his conscious mind. He no longer needed to concentrate or even look at his fingers as they interlaced the straw.

What type of person was the father?

The poet's father worked as a farmer and cattle dealer. The poet recalls how he carried a stick, an 'ashplant' or a 'cane stick', with him everywhere he went. Such implements would be used not only as a walking stick but also, no doubt, for driving livestock along the country roads. Heaney remembers his father working with roosters or 'game cocks' on their farm, recalling how he 'lapped the spurs' of these unruly birds, trimming back the sharp growths of bone that protruded from their claws. The poet recalls how his father had devoted his whole lifetime to practical tasks such as this on and around the family farm.

We sense that the poet is surprised – and perhaps even a little charmed – that his father took so readily to making the harvest bows. This is a man who was a stick-wielding cattle-dealer, a farmer used to working out in the elements, a man devoted to difficult, practical tasks around the farm. There is something incongruous about seeing such an individual engrossed in the intricate, almost dainty, craft of making the harvest bows.

The father's personality

All through his life, the poet's father remained a man of few words. In his younger days, his silences seemed tense and sullen, maybe even a little cranky. In his later days, however, his silences seemed tranquil and almost welcoming. This is because the father mellowed as he aged, becoming calmer and more at peace with himself. The poet artfully describes the transformation of his father's personality. The 'silence' contained within his psyche changed over time, just as wine in a barrel ages to become smoother and more soothing.

The poet, however, feels that his father can communicate with him through the harvest bow. The surface of the bow, in an unusual but effective comparison, is likened to a piece of braille text. When the poet touches the bow he can 'read' this text, just as a visually impaired person might read a passage of braille: 'I tell and finger it like braille'.

The poet, then, describes a form of communication that takes place through the medium of touch. Such messaging occurs through items that, like the harvest bow on the poet's dresser, are 'palpable', that can be felt and handled. Touching the bow allows to poet to 'glean' or understand aspects of his father's life and personality, aspects that the father had always left 'unsaid': 'Gleaning the unsaid off the palpable'.

The poet, it seems was given the harvest bow by his father and has treasured it ever since, having it pinned on the dresser before him as he writes. He describes it, therefore, as a 'love-knot', as if it were a token of affection from father to son. However, he's aware that this bow was a 'throwaway' love token, a most casual gift. Maybe the poet just happened to be visiting his father as he finished one of the many bows he would make during that particular harvest time. We can imagine the father casually tossing the completed bow to his son and thinking no more about it. And even if it was a more meaningful gift, we can imagine the poet's father playing it down and not wanting to make a big deal out of it.

Childhood memories

The poet remembers walking with his father through the countryside near their home. He recalls how he carried his fishing rod, indicating that his father was taking him to a nearby river or lake to do a spot of fishing: 'Me with the fishing rod'. He remembers how his father, as always, was carrying his walking stick, which he used to whack 'the tips off weeds and bushes'. We can imagine him doing this almost absentmindedly as they walked along, simply for the enjoyable sensation of whipping the heads off the plants. The way his father whacked

the hedgerows reminds the poet of shooters beating bushes to scare up birds that might be hiding in them. The father, however, manages to flush nothing from the undergrowth as they walk along. This is, no doubt, because he was striking the bushes idly or absent-mindedly.

The poet uses a wonderful turn of phrase to describe how, as the years passed, the father's hands 'aged around' these various sticks. This is wonderfully cinematic image – we visualise the hand ageing in time-lapse cinematography, as if we are fast-forwarding through a video.

But it's hard not to detect here a note of sorrow about the father's life, a suggestion that he never flushed out or revealed the opportunities that life had for him, that he never fulfilled his potential. The poet's father, as we have seen, was in his own way a contemplative, creative man. However, he was never afforded the opportunity to explore this creative potential. Instead, he spent a 'lifetime' herding cattle and tending to game cocks. Perhaps if he had being born in a different place or a different time, he could have been a diplomat or an investment banker, or even a writer like his son.

The poet describes how his father's stick 'Beats out of time', a phrase that suggests several different meanings. Perhaps the poet's suggesting that his father had little or no sense of rhythm, that the beating of his stick doesn't keep time with their steps as they walk along. Or perhaps the poet is suggesting that his father was 'out of time' in the sense that he was born at the wrong time, coming of age in an Ulster that had changed little since the 1700s, where the only profession and lifestyle open to him was that of a farmer or cattle dealer. Had he come of age, as his son did, in the rapidly modernising Ireland of the 1950s, he would have had far more opportunities in training and self-development.

In pagan times, people wore harvest bows to honour the spirit of fertility, a magical god-like presence that brought a bountiful harvest each autumn. People believed this 'spirit of the corn' somehow inhabited these bows at harvest time. Pinning such a bow to your lapel would gain the spirit's favour, coaxing it to keep you safe through harvest season and beyond.

The poet thinks of the 'townland' or parish in which he was raised as a 'tongue-tied' place. To be tongue-tied, of course, is to be lost for words, to be unable to explain or articulate oneself clearly. The poet suggests, therefore, that the people surrounding him as he grew up were a tongue-tied lot, that they never learned the vocabulary with which to express themselves in a deep and complex fashion. There is a sense, too, in which these people were suspicious of such fluency. Their natural language was silence.

FOCUS ON STYLE

Metaphor, Simile, Figures of Speech

There is an interesting simile in line 11 where the poet compares the feel of the harvest bow to a braille manuscript, as if he can read it by touch: 'I tell and finger it like braille'. Another simile occurs at the poem's conclusion when the bow's loops are compared to a snare or small trap: 'Like a drawn snare'. A metaphor occurs in line 5 where the bow is compared to a 'corona' or crown.

There is also a metaphorical expression in line 20, where the late summer evenings are described as having a 'big lift', suggesting the open and expansive evening sky. Heaney also uses a wonderful metaphor to describe the vividness of his childhood recollection, saying that when he looks into the bow's loops he can actually see the past. The bow is described almost as a magical object: 'And if I spy into its golden loops/ I see us walk between the railway slopes'.

The bow's looped design reminds the poet of a snare, which, in ancient times, would have been used to catch 'the spirit of the corn' rather than a wolf or deer. He thinks of a 'snare' that's been stepped in, that's been triggered or 'drawn' tight. The bow, therefore, managed to snag 'the spirit of the corn', which, for a moment at least, would have inhabited its loops. It also, as we've seen, managed to capture the father's personality.

It's a snare, however, that's been 'slipped', whose target has somehow managed to escape from its drawn or tightened loops. The 'spirit of the corn', it was believed, would inhabit such bows for a short time, around the harvest, before moving on. It's also been 'slipped' by the father's personality: for his character was best expressed during the process of the construction as he delicately wove it 'twist by twist'.

He thinks of a snare whose strands have been polished or 'burnished' by an animal's efforts to free itself, that is still warm from having closed around an animal's ankle. This wonderfully suggests how the spirit of the corn would leave a trace behind in the bow's loops, even when harvest time was over and it had departed this golden corona. Similarly, a trace of the father's personality, of the mellowed silence that existed within him, is expressed by the bow even now, sitting mutely as it does on the poet's deal dresser.

THEMES

LOVE AND RELATIONSHIPS

This is another poem that explores the complicated relationship between the poet and his father. Specifically, it focuses on the difficulties they experienced in communicating. Like many men of his background and generation, the poet's father wouldn't have been given to self-expression or to talking about his feelings. The poet, however, suggests that his father could express his inner self, the mellowed silence that existed within him, through making the harvest bows: 'As you plaited the harvest bow/ You implicated the mellowed silence in you'.

To 'implicate' means to convey or communicate. Making harvest bows, then, allows the father to convey or communicate something of his personality. He expresses himself through making these little bows, just as an artist might express himself by creating a sculpture or a painting. But the verb to 'implicate' can also mean to interweave or entwine, suggesting that the poet's father wove his inner self into the very harvest bows he created. It's as if the 'mellowed silence' that existed in him was infused into the bows themselves, as if his father's personality is somehow encoded in the straw: 'You implicated the mellowed silence in you/ In wheat'.

In making the bow, the poet's father tied the plaited straw into a complicated crown-like knot, which the poet describes as a corona. According to the poet, it is a 'knowable corona', because it allows him to know his father. As we noted, the bow functions almost like a braille text because when the poet touches it, he feels he can learn unsaid things about his father's life and personality.

However, this communication brings sorrow as well as happiness. The poet realises that his father never had the chance to realise his full potential. He realises that his father had hidden depths, gifts that were destined to remain unexplored. He realises that his father never managed to 'flush out' all the opportunities life might have had in store for him. But he realises too that his father was born 'out of time'. As we noted already, he grew up at a time before educational opportunities were widely available. He grew up in a place, a 'tongue-tied townland', where there was little scope for self-expression and self-development and where such concepts, if anything, were frowned upon.

Despite all this complication, however, the poem conveys the strong connection that existed between father and son. This is beautifully suggested in the portrait of them walking together through a late summer's evening, strolling through the railway slopes together in companiable silence. It's a moment that, even while it was happening, the poet realised he would always remember and return to again in his mind.

THE PROCESS OF MEMORY

As the poet examines the 'golden loops' of the bow pinned up on his dresser, he finds himself vividly remembering an occasion from his childhood. It all comes back to him with astonishing clarity. As we noted, he recalls an evening walk with his father to a local fishing spot. He remembers how they followed the route of a railway line, walking in between the banks that sloped upwards from either side of the tracks (the nearest town to where Heaney grew up, Castledawson, had a train station, and the railway line ran behind the back of the family home). He remembers how it was harvest season, late August or September, and how his father was wearing one of the bows he made every year at this time.

Heaney remembers how such evenings had a 'big lift', suggesting the optical effect by which the sky can seem higher and further away on those evenings when summer transitions into autumn. Heaney uses a typically brilliant metaphor for this process of memory, for how the bow stimulates such intense recollection. The loops of the bow, he suggests, are a kind of screen on which footage of long-ago events is replayed for him to savour and relive.

As he looks at the bow on his dresser, the poet recalls his tongue-tied townland with heartbreaking clarity. It's as if this long-ago parish has been woven into the bow's fabric. He recalls how, even as he walked along beside his father, he was 'already homesick' for those harvest evenings. This is a phrase that wonderfully captures the nostalgia we sometimes feel for a golden moment, even while that moment is still in the present. Our enjoyment of such special times can sometimes be tinged with a sorrow born from our knowledge that these moments can't last, that everything must change.

THE NATURE OF ART

The poet comes to see the bow not merely as a humble piece of craftsmanship but as a genuine piece of art. He thinks of it as a 'device', as a tool or implement that allows his father to communicate things that otherwise would have remained unsaid. But the term 'device' in its older usage also means an emblem, and the bow, as we have seen, works as a powerful symbol for the poet, representing not only the father's personality, but also the harvest and the traditions associated with it in the parish where he grew up.

The poet associates the bow with a saying by Coventry Patmore: 'The end of art is peace'. In what sense might the 'end' or objective of this artwork be described as 'peace'?

- Creating the bow allowed the father to express the peace or 'mellowed silence' that existed within him.

- Creating the bow allowed the father to express creativity that otherwise would have lain dormant within him forever, granting him a measure of peace or release.
- The bow generates an element of peace or reconciliation between the poet and his father, allowing him to understand his father in a new way.

The 'motto' that the poet associates with the bow is something of a paradox, with contradictory meanings. On the one hand, it suggests that the objective of art is to create peace. On the other, it suggests that peace will be the conclusion of art; that art can only be made out of conflict and turmoil. We sense here an anxiety experienced by many writers and artists – they long for a life of serenity and tranquillity but worry about what would fuel their art were serenity to ever be achieved.

THE ANXIETY OF THE ARTIST

Heaney, like many artists, experienced a sense of anxiety about his work as a poet. Although his poems necessitated a great amount of commitment, time and effort to produce, they had no practical value. His anxiety was heightened by the fact that his father was, in contrast, a no-nonsense, pragmatic man, someone whose whole lifetime was devoted to practical tasks.

However, on this occasion the poet detects a similarity between himself and his father. Harvest bows, like poems, are beautiful, but serve little practical value. Making the harvest bow, then, shows the father's hidden artistic side, with the poet remarking on how his father's hands 'Harked to their gift and worked with fine intent'. The father weaves the bow with the same skill and intensity with which the poet puts together a poem. Perhaps the father's weaving grants the poet a sense of permission – if it's okay for his father to produce the beautiful but useless bows, it is okay for him to compose his poems.

It's worth nothing, however, that the similarity between the poet and his father only goes so far. Heaney responds to the harvest bow with the intense spirituality of a poet, feeling that he is able to glean 'the unsaid' from its loops. To his father, however, it is more 'throwaway': part of a tradition and nothing more.

CELEBRATION OF CRAFT

This is one of many poems where Heaney celebrates craft and manual labour. He praises the skill with which his father wove the bows, tightening the strands of straw 'twist by twist' until the 'love-knot' came together. He describes the 'fine intent' or intense concentration his father brought to this task and how eventually his fingers seemed to move automatically, as though he no longer needed to think about what he was doing: 'Until your fingers moved somnambulant'.

LINE BY LINE

This poem describes an evening in London. The poet and his wife had just been married and had arrived in that great city for their honeymoon. The poet's wife was still wearing her 'going-away coat'. This was a fancy white coat worn by a bride when she left her wedding and set off on her honeymoon.

The couple, according to the poet, had been 'mooning around' London. They'd been wandering around the city in a relaxed and casual fashion, and taking in the sights, maybe stopping into a favourite pub for a drink or two.

On this evening they were due to attend one of 'the Proms', a series of concerts that takes place each year in London's famous Albert Hall venue. They travelled there by underground rail: London's famous Tube service. They got off the train in a 'vaulted tunnel', in one of the many older Tube stations with an ornate and arching roof.

However, all their 'mooning around' had left them late for the concert: 'mooning around, late for the Proms'. They exited the train and ran through the Underground station, rushing to reach the Albert Hall before the performance began: 'There we were in the vaulted tunnel running'. The poet recalls how his wife, was 'speeding ahead' as they ran through the station.

The poet's wife was still in front as they left the station and continued rushing through the streets towards the Albert Hall. The poet remembers how, as she ran, her going-away coat 'flapped wild' in the breeze. The coat was blown vigorously this way and that, causing its buttons to fall off. The poet describes how the fallen buttons lay in the street, leaving a kind of trail between the tube station and the Albert Hall.

Pan and Syrinx

In one of the Greek myths the goat-god Pan chased a nymph called Syrinx through the fields in an effort to have sex with her. As she ran, she called out to the other gods for help. The gods responded by transforming her into a reed, thereby rescuing her from Pan's attentions. Presumably, in the gods' opinion, life as a plant was preferable to the ravishes of Pan.

The poet thinks of his wife running through the London streets as Syrinx. He thinks of himself as Pan running behind her: 'me then like a fleet god gaining/ Upon you before you turned to a reed'. We must remember that the poem describes a newly married couple at a time when sex before marriage was extremely uncommon. The poet's comparison of himself to Pan captures the sexual anticipation and excitement he feels on his honeymoon. The comparison between his wife and Syrinx, meanwhile, suggests the unease and apprehension she might have felt regarding sex, especially in this era when information about sexuality was scarce and such issues were rarely openly discussed.

Dying echoes

Line 10 presents us with a sudden jump forward in time. Whereas lines 1 to 9 are set before the concert in the Albert Hall, lines 11 to 16 are set later that evening, as the poet struggles to make his way from the Albert Hall back to the Underground station (it's notable that in the poem's first nine lines the poet uses the past tense, whereas in the last six he uses the present tense).

The poet uses the image of echoes dying to symbolise the passage of time between these events: 'Our echoes die in that corridor'. This refers to the corridor that led from the station itself to the street above. We can imagine the couple laughing and exclaiming as they dashed down this corridor in an effort to get to the Proms in time. We can imagine how the echoes produced by their laughter bounce around the corridor's walls, diminishing in intensity until they 'die' or completely fade away.

The poet as Orpheus

The poem refers to the Greek myth of Orpheus and his wife Eurydice, who died after being bitten by a snake. Orpheus journeyed into the underworld, the land of the dead, determined to recover his wife and return with her to the land of the living. A gifted musician, he used his musical abilities to charm the lord of the underworld and was permitted to take Eurydice back with him.

However, there was a catch: he had to walk ahead of his wife and not look back until they had safely returned to earth. If he turned around before they'd made it out of the underworld, Eurydice would remain forever with the dead. Orpheus had nearly led Eurydice to the surface when he was startled by a noise behind him and tragically looked back, causing him to lose his wife forever.

As the poet makes the return journey from the Albert Hall, he compares himself to Orpheus:

- Just as Orpheus led Eurydice through the underworld, so the poet must lead his wife from the Albert Hall back to the Underground Station: 'retracing the path back'.

- His wife walks behind him on this journey, just as Eurydice was forced to walk behind Orpheus.
- Like Orpheus in the underworld, the poet leads his wife through an unnerving alien landscape. He passes through dark disorientating streets, the phrase 'moonlit stones' suggests that only the moon illuminates the cobblestones he walks upon. He passes through an eerily empty station, one that is dark, cold and draughty 'After the trains have gone', their service finished for the night.
- He listens intently for his wife's footsteps following behind, just as Orpheus must have listened for the footsteps of Eurydice as he guided her from the land of the dead: 'all attention/ For your step following'.
- The poet finds himself in an agitated state of mind, just as Orpheus must have been as he led Eurydice on their ill-fated journey from the underworld. He feels 'tensed', suggesting the worry and nervousness that fills him. He describes himself as 'bared', suggesting he feels exposed and vulnerable as he makes his way through the city and the station.
- Orpheus lost Eurydice by looking back. Similarly, if the poet looks back his wife will be 'damned' or lost forever: 'and damned if I look back.' The poet seems terrified that if he looks behind his wife will simply disappear for good.
- The poem's last line can also be read as a statement of determination, one that suggests the poet's stubborn refusal to look behind. The colloquial expression 'damned if I do something' conveys a great reluctance or refusal to do the thing in question. In this instance it conveys the poet's refusal to look back until he has led his wife to safety.

The poet, as we noted, feels lost and disorientated as he walks the city streets. But he is guided by the buttons that fell from his wife's coat earlier that evening. As he comes across each fallen button he picks it up: 'lifting the buttons'. Finding each one reassures him that he is on the right track, that he is indeed retracing his steps from the Albert Hall to the station.

The poet, therefore, compares himself to Hansel in the fairy story. Hansel led Gretel through the forest, using white pebbles as a guide. Similarly, the poet leads his wife through the streets of the city, using the fallen going-away coat's buttons to retrace his route.

FOCUS ON STYLE

Metaphor, Simile, Figures of Speech

'The Underground' is particularly rich in allusions. As we've seen, the references to Hansel and Gretel and Orpheus and Eurydice in the last two stanzas highlight the fears the poet feels as he begins married life.

The reference to the lustful god Pan chasing the nymph Syrinx, meanwhile, captures the poet's sexual excitement on his honeymoon. It also captures the trepidation he imagines his wife to be experiencing, one common to many newly-wed brides in earlier times.

The poet imagines his wife being transformed not only into a 'reed', as Syrinx did in the legend, but also into 'some new white flower'. Here we imagine this woman in her white going-away coat being transformed into some never-before-seen blossom. The fact that this flower would be 'japped' or stained with 'crimson' has two different meanings. It refers to how, while they were in a pub on the night in question, the poet's wife accidentally stained her coat with beetroot. But this image also evokes sexual relations between the couple and suggests the loss of virginity.

Verbal Music

The poem has an irregular rhyme scheme. Each line rhymes with another in the same stanza, but in an irregular pattern. Furthermore, many of these are half or even quarter rhymes. In the first stanza, for instance, 'running' rhymes with 'gaining' while 'ahead' rhymes with 'reed'. In the second stanza, meanwhile, 'crimson' rhymes with 'button' while 'trail' rhymes with 'hall'.

Tone and Atmosphere

This is a poem with two very different atmospheres. The opening section is realistic, joyous and full of life. The poet describes the excitement that he and his wife felt as they raced to the Albert Hall. In stark contrast, the atmosphere of the second section is unrealistic, eerie and haunting, with its stark streets and empty tube station.

THEMES

LOVE AND RELATIONSHIPS

The poem's first 9 lines capture the joy and excitement of early married life. We can imagine the feelings of freedom and exhilaration they experience as they begin their honeymoon in London, the wife still proudly wearing the 'going-away coat' from her wedding. They spend their time 'mooning around, enjoying what the city has to offer in a relaxed and casual fashion. We sense their excitement at going to a show in the famous Albert Hall, the two of them racing in order to get to the performance in time.

The second half of the poem is dark and unrealistic; perhaps even a little bizarre, as the poet presents himself in a similar situation to Orpheus: forced to lead his wife on a journey through the darkness but doomed to lose her if he looks behind. These closing lines brilliantly convey an atmosphere of dread and loneliness. They summon up not a bustling, brightly-lit city but an eerie unnerving landscape of empty streets and deserted stations, one lit only by the moon and the flickering lamps of the underground.

The poet's feelings of anxiety and vulnerability, of being 'bared and tensed' also contribute to this sinister atmosphere, as does his sense of being lost and disorientated, of having to navigate his way back to the station by means of the buttons that fell from his wife's coat earlier.

A reference to Hansel and Gretel further reinforces this menacing, lonesome atmosphere. We might think of 'Hansel and Gretel' as a harmless fairy story. But it's also, in its own way, a dark and frightening tale, one that depicts two children abandoned in the depths of an unfamiliar and terrifying forest.

This is a poem, then, that describes two very different sides to a new marriage or relationship. The opening 9 lines, as we've seen, capture the energy and exhilaration of beginning something new, of really getting to know this new person, of setting out on the journey that every marriage or relationship represents.

However, the poem also registers the poet's fears and anxieties as he sets out on married life. The nightmarish scenario depicted in lines 11 to 16 suggests the poet's feelings of anguish and confusion as he takes up his role as husband. He has been thrust into a new set of responsibilities that will eventually require him to function as father, breadwinner and protector.

The tensions experienced by the poet also stem from a larger unease, typical of the 1960s, about the nature of sexuality. The poet's fears find their greatest expression when he depicts himself as an Orpheus-like figure, terrified to look behind. Here we sense his fear that this new marriage, only just begun, might not last, that his new bride might eventually be lost to him.

The Pitchfork

LINE BY LINE

At the heart of this poem is the notion of perfection and the possibility of its existence in the world. When we say that something is perfect, we can mean a number of things:

• It is highly suitable for something or exactly right.
• It is precisely accurate or exact.
• It is as good as it is possible to be.
• It is flawless.

But nothing that actually exists is completely perfect or flawless. True perfection is something that we can only imagine. It is something that exists in the abstract, but not in reality.

Take circles, for example. Mathematically speaking, a circle is the set of points in a plane that are equidistant from a given point. For a circle to be perfect, you'd need all those points in the circle's circumference to match up exactly. And for all those points to match up exactly, you'd need this precision to remain constant no matter how closely you looked. But the closer you look at any drawn circle or any object that is circular, you will begin to see inconsistencies. Only in the abstract world of pure mathematics can we find our perfect circle – a world of points and infinitely-thin lines.

The same goes for any other object or thing that exists in the world. We might have an idea or an understanding about what constitutes a perfect chair or a perfect apple, but no actual chair or apple will be absolutely perfect. Each individual object that exists has its own flaws and quirks, no matter how small or insignificant, that render it less than perfect. Some objects will come closer than others to reaching a state of perfection, but each will ultimately fall short.

The farmer considers the pitchfork

The poem describes a farmer who has given some thought to this notion of perfection. The farmer reflects that perfection can only be imagined, although some objects come closer to it than others do. The farmer considers the different implements he uses in his work and thinks about which one comes closest to being perfect. We can imagine him looking at the various tools in his shed, at the shovels and forks and other implements. Having given the matter some thought, he decides that it is his pitchfork that comes 'near to an imagined perfection'.

The pitchfork is a simple object, comprising of a steel head that is riveted or fixed to a timber handle. The timber of the handle has been 'turned' or machine-carved to a rounded state. Yet the farmer considers it to be almost perfect. The pitchfork's perfectness can be assessed according to the criteria we gave above:

It is highly suitable for something or exactly right
The pitchfork is well 'balanced' and the ideal 'length'. The weight of the head in proportion to the weight of the handle allows it to be handled with ease. In fact, the farmer sometimes holds it aloft like a javelin, noting how 'accurate and light' it feels. The pitchfork has been 'sharpened', perhaps through use or with a sharpening tool. It has the right amount of 'give' or flexibility: 'The springiness'. It has been 'tested' and proven to work. When it comes to threshing wheat at harvest time, there is no better implement or tool. It can be used with speed, allowing the farmer to swiftly work through the wheat: 'the clip and dart of it'.

It is precisely accurate or exact
The pitchfork achieves an almost mathematical state of perfect. The farmer considers the abstract qualities 'Smoothness', 'straightness' and 'roundness', and how these are present in the pitchfork.

It is as good as it is possible to be
To the farmer, the pitchfork is not just a useful tool that is easy to handle and work with. He considers it to be an almost perfect object, independent of the use for which it is intended. To him, it is an object of great beauty. The details on the grain on the ash handle strike him as beautiful: 'He loved its grain of tapering, dark-flecked ash'. The polished handle is beautifully shiny or lustrous: 'sheen'.

The farmer thinks about how the pitchfork feels almost perfect. The timber handle has been 'Sweat-cured', polished through repeated use, lending the tool a wonderfully tactile feel. He seems to love to handle this implement, even when he is not working. In playful moments he imagines himself being a 'warrior' or an 'athlete', and that the pitchfork is his spear or javelin.

It is flawless
The farmer considers the pitchfork to be an all-but-perfect implement. It is ideal for the work for which it is used. The pitchfork feels great to work with and is aesthetically pleasing. But, of course, the pitchfork is not absolutely flawless. As we have already said, the farmer does not believe that this implement is perfect, only that it comes 'near to an imagined perfection'. Yet the farmer would probably be hard-pressed to say where the flaws lie in this tool.

The pitchfork as space probe
The farmer has an interest in space travel and exploration. He has learned about 'probes', robotic spacecraft that explore the outer reaches of space. His curiosity is sparked by them. He imagines how, when their mission is complete, they drift beyond their destination, ending up in the farthest reaches of the solar system: 'when he thought of probes that reached the farthest'. They no longer have engines propelling them along; they are merely drifting: 'Evenly, imperturbably through space'. There is something quite serene about this image of a space probe 'sailing' quietly through space, 'absolutely soundless'.

When the farmer thinks about this space probe, he imagines it as a long, cylindrical vessel with sharp metal 'prongs' at one end. In short, he sees it as being shaped like a pitchfork: 'He would see the shaft of a pitchfork sailing past'. This pitchfork-probe was launched with a certain destination in mind – given a 'simple lead' – and propelled in that direction. Once it reached its destination, however, it was switched off and left to drift. It continues to move with intent through space, rather than aimlessly drifting. It is as if, somewhere along the way, the probe has learned 'at last to follow that simple lead'. It surpasses its original trajectory, goes 'Past its own aim' and carries on through to the 'other side'.

Different visions of perfection
The farmer imagines the probe travelling far beyond the known parts of space, eventually reaching 'an other side' or dimension. Here too those who live in this dimension also have an idea or understanding of perfection. Like the farmer, they believe that perfection can only be imagined, that nothing perfect actually exists. Certain objects or things can approach or come near to this imagined perfection, but nothing that actually exists can be considered perfect.

However, here in this place far removed from our planet, they have a different understanding of what perfection entails. On earth, we imagine that achieving perfection is all about careful planning and plotting. Something can be considered perfect if it achieves its goal or hits its target. In the other dimension that the probe reaches, they do not place the same value on such control. Perfection is something that happens when things are out of our hands. This understanding of perfection entails spontaneity and surprise; it arises in the unexpected rather than the expected.

The poet uses the image of a javelin being held and aimed to represent how we think about perfection on earth: 'perfection... is imagined... in the aiming'. He uses the image of the 'opening hand', the moment that the javelin is thrown and released to represent the different vision or understanding of perfection that exists in this other dimension: 'perfection... is imagined' in the 'opening hand'.

FOCUS ON STYLE

Verbal Music

The poet uses rich verbal music to suggest the rich beauty of the pitchfork's handle. The poet uses repeated 'a' sounds in line 8 to convey the pleasing tone and colour of the timber that has been polished through use: 'its grain of tapering, dark-flecked ash'. Heaney also uses some wonderfully sonorous, lush language in lines 9 to 10, words such as 'burnish' and 'sheen' to convey the lustrous quality of the handle that has been achieved through repeated handling and rubbing.

Assonance is also used when the poet describes the probe journeying through space: 'its prongs starlit and absolutely soundless'. The long 'o' sounds seem to convey or correspond with the vast, silent space through which the probe travels. The poet uses short, one-syllable words, that trip off the end of the tongue to convey how the pitchfork can be deftly handled: 'the clip and dart of it'.

Imagery

The poet's description of the probe, shaped like a pitchfork and drifting silently through space, is wonderful. Heaney captures the manner in which the probe moves in a perfectly straight line, without any external interference: 'Evenly, imperturbably'. The probes 'prongs' reflect the light of the surrounding stars: 'its prongs starlit'. The probe also emits no sound as it travels. It is in a constant state of motion and has no need for engines or thrusts: 'absolutely soundless'. It is a beautifully serene and peaceful image.

To convey a certain understanding of perfection, Heaney also uses the image of the hand of a javelin thrower opening to release the javelin. As we discussed above, the image suggests that perfection can be understood very differently to the way we normally think about it. Rather than being achieved through careful planning and calculation, perfection arises in a more spontaneous fashion, when things are released from our control and allowed to behave as they need or want to behave.

Metaphor, Simile, Figures of Speech

The poem describes how the farmer thinks of the pitchfork as a 'javelin'. Both are 'light' to handle and the pronged and sharpened head of the pitchfork allows for 'accurate' work, just as a javelin's pointed head allows for precise aim.

THEMES

ART, CRAFT AND CREATIVITY

The idea of perfection presented in the poem is something that might apply to the poet and his work. We can imagine how each time the poet writes a poem he is aiming for perfection. But no single poem can ever be perfect; so each work can only come 'near to an imagined perfection'.

The different understandings or visions of perfection described in the poem's closing lines might also be relevant to the poet and the manner in which he approaches his work. On the one hand, we can think of the perfect poem as one that conforms to the established criteria of form and rhyme etc. The poet careful plans and structures his writing in order to come as close as possible to this notion of perfection. Perhaps, however, the perfect poem is not the one that achieves technical excellence and conforms to such traditional understandings of form and meter. Perhaps the perfect poem can be imagined in a different way, arising out of a more free-flowing, spontaneous effort, surprising the poet when it happens rather than being the product of careful planning.

Like a number of Heaney poems, 'The Pitchfork' is a great celebration of craftsmanship. The pitchfork has been carefully shaped and sculpted until it has become smooth and balanced. The farmer appreciates just how well-suited it is to the task at hand, admiring the 'springiness, the clip and dart of it'. We also get a sense of craftsmanship from the description of the probe that has been carefully designed to travel to the remotest parts of space. To the farmer, this vessel has very similar qualities to the pitchfork he works with – both have been shaped and streamlined to a state approaching perfection.

CREDITING THE MARVELLOUS

The poem reminds us how fascinating and marvellous the everyday world can be, if we are capable of looking at it in a certain way. Even the most mundane, everyday items can be a source of wonder and admiration. The farmer is fascinated by the pitchfork he works with. This simple, everyday instrument, comprising of 'Riveted steel' and 'turned timber' strikes him as being almost perfect. It is smooth and pleasant to handle. It is beautifully balanced and enables allows him to work with speed and ease: 'the clip and dart of it'. It is a thing of great beauty: 'He loved its grain of tapering, dark-flecked ash'.

The farmer is someone with an almost childlike sense of wonder and imagination. We see this in the description of him playing with the pitchfork, imagining it to be a 'javelin' or a 'spear': 'he played the warrior or the athlete'. He is fascinated by space travel, thinking about how the probes that travel through space are capable or journeying far beyond their intended destination. We also get the sense of how playful his imagination is when he associates the shape of such probes with the pitchfork: 'He would see the shaft of a pitchfork sailing past'.

Lightenings VIII

LINE BY LINE

The poem describes an incident from the 'annals' or historical records of Clonmacnoise, a monastery in County Offaly founded in 544 AD by Saint Ciarán. The opening lines describe an ordinary part of the monastery's routine.' There is a peaceful atmosphere as the monks gather to pray in their 'oratory' or chapel: 'when the monks of Clonmacnoise/ Were all at prayers inside the oratory'. The oratory was and still is open-roofed, so that as the monk prayed they were exposed to God's creation.

These lines suggest the silence, order and repetition of life at the monastery, where everything is regulated and scheduled. The monastery's large community is highly organised. Each monk has a role – some are blacksmiths, carpenters or farmers. Others are artists, who spend their days creating precious metal objects or illuminated manuscripts. The monks lead simple lives of prayer and routine, with up to eight prayer services a day. They are in the midst of one of these services at the beginning of the poem.

Suddenly, however, in this orderly and predictable setting, something utterly unexpected happens. Through the open-air

roof of the oratory, the monks see a ship floating in the sky: 'A ship appeared above them in the air.' This must have been an extraordinary sight for the monks, as shocking and unexpected as the sighting of an alien spacecraft might be to us today.

These people live in the earth's upper atmosphere just as we live on its surface. The earth's surface is to them what the seabed or ocean floor is to us. They travel through the clouds, their natural environment, dropping their anchor whenever they want to stop. We can imagine how the anchor might nestle or lodge in the crook of a tree, bringing the ship to a halt in the clouds above.

But now the anchor seems to have fallen off by accident – it trails along behind, connected by the anchor line. The anchor drags along the ground, while the ship proceeds through the sky, maybe a couple of hundred metres above it. Suddenly, however, the anchor gets stuck in the rails of the open-air oratory, causing the ship to shake violently in the air as its progress is halted: 'the big hull rocked to a standstill'.

Then the monks see a figure leave the deck of the airborne ship above. This 'crewman' begins to lower himself down the rope.

His legs or shins are crossed over the rope in an effort to secure himself. He grapples his way down the rope, hand after hand laboriously: 'shinned and grappled'.

When he reaches the bottom of the rope, he attempts to pull the anchor free with one hand, while clinging to the rope with the other. However, he struggles 'in vain' to release the huge, heavy anchor.

Though they lead lives of strict routine, peace and quiet, the monks at Clonmacnoise also occasionally endure Viking raids. They associate strange ships with danger. This time, however, the ship is not coming up the Shannon but is directly over their heads – a truly awesome sight.

It soon becomes apparent that the crewman cannot breathe the air on the surface of the earth, in the same way that humans can't breathe under water. He and his kind have their natural environment in the higher reaches of the earth's atmosphere. To him, the oratory floor might as well be the bottom of the ocean.

For a moment, the monks are frozen in shock, staring at the crewman as he struggles for breathe and attempts to free the anchor from the altar rail. For them, this must have been a moment of true shock and awe; not just to have witnessed this unidentified flying object in the sky, but to have it physically intrude into their world.

The abbot calls on his fellow monks to wake up and take action. He realises that this other-worldly crewman can't breathe on the earth's surface and that he's in danger of drowning: 'This man can't bear our life here and will drown … unless we help him.' At this, the other monks spring into action and help the crewman to free the anchor: 'So/ They did, the freed ship sailed'.

The crewman then scuttles back up the long anchor rope to the safety of his ship. We can picture him gasping as he breathes his own atmosphere again. We can imagine how he is stunned by his experience of the earth's surface, an environment like nothing he has ever seen before 'the man climbed back/ Out of the marvellous as he had known it.'

THEMES

CREDITING THE MARVELLOUS

The poem powerfully makes the point that the marvellous is very much a matter of perspective. What is ordinary and mundane to one person is extraordinary to another. To the monks, the flying ship is an extraordinary sight – it is like nothing they have ever seen before or will ever see again and they will remember it for the rest of their lives. To the crewman, however, the flying ship is just his place of work.

But the opposite is also true. To the monks the oratory is just a place where they eat, work and pray. But to the crewman it is truly extraordinary. It is as wonderfully alien to him as the bed of a deep-sea trench would be to us.

The poem suggests then that the ordinary world around us can be a source of awe, mystery and inspiration, if we look at it in the right way. If we are open to experience and view our lives with fresh eyes, the way the crewman views the oratory, the world might suddenly appear as the truly marvellous place it actually is.

FOCUS ON STYLE

Imagery

The poem centres on an extraordinary image, the sudden appearance of a ship above the open-aired oratory at Clonmacnoise. It is an incredible sight: 'A ship appeared above them in the air.' However, the language used to depict this fantastical occurrence is understated. Heaney focuses on the small, practical details, such as the 'big hull' coming 'to a standstill', and the efforts of the crewman to climb down and free the anchor: 'shinned and grappled'. By not sensationalising the wild, incredulous sights described, Heaney's language lends the events of the poem a quiet authority.

Tone and Atmosphere

The poet doesn't spend any time speculating about the origins of the airborne ship – whether it is ghostly, angelic or just a mass hallucination on the part of the monks. He merely describes what happens in a matter-of-fact way. This down-to-earth, almost deadpan reporting of the events provides a striking and effective contrast to the poem's fantastical imagery.

LINE BY LINE

The poet makes a phone call to his father. He calls the landline in his parent's house, which is located on a table in the hallway. His mother answers the phone and says that his father is busy in the garden: 'The weather here's so good he took the chance/ To do a bit of weeding.' She asks him to hold the line while she fetches his father from the garden: "Hold on', she says, 'I'll just go out and get him.'"

While he waits, the poet pictures his father gardening. The poet imagines his father kneeling beside a 'rig' or bed of leeks: 'So I saw him/ Down on his hands and knees beside the leek rig'. We sense that the father approaches this work with real care and finesse. The poet pictures him closely examining the leek plants as he searches for weeds growing between them: 'Touching, inspecting, separating one/ Stalk from the other'. He imagines that is father is careful to pluck each weed by the root so that it won't grow back. We sense that the father is not one for half measures and feels satisfaction in a job well done: 'Pleased to feel each little weed-root break'.

We sense that the father has a great love for the leeks that he takes such pains to grow, that he really appreciates these graceful, fragile plants. Strangely enough, it also seems that the father has a certain affection for the weeds that he plucks. He seems 'rueful' or regretful that he must end their lives in order that his leeks might thrive.

The poet continues to wait for his father to come to the phone. He can hear a loud ticking as he waits, reminding him that there are several clocks in his parent's hallway, their noise amplified by the emptiness of the hallway: 'The amplified grave ticking of hall clocks'.

He imagines how his parent's hallway must look in the sunlight. He pictures the phone lying 'unattended' on the hall table. He thinks of sunlight reflecting on the pendulums of the clocks. He finds the hallway to be a very calm and pleasant environment. The medieval story of Death and Everyman comes to the poet's mind. The poet imagines that if this story took place in modern times, Death would probably summon Everyman over the phone. The poem was written in the early nineties. If it were today, we might imagine Death summoning Everyman by Twitter or Instagram!

The medieval tale of Death and Everyman emphasises the inevitability of death. In the medieval story, Death appeared at the door of a character called Everyman in order to summon him into the next world.

The poet is just thinking about his father's death when the man himself comes to the phone. We can imagine that having just contemplated his death, the poet is relieved to hear the old man's voice. He wants to tell his father how much he loves him and cares for him, but he doesn't do it. The words are almost spoken, but the poet checks himself and holds them back: 'I nearly said I loved him'.

FOCUS ON STYLE

Imagery

The poem is rich with vivid, memorable imagery. The poet describes the leek rig that his father is attending to, imagining the stalks as 'tapered, frail and leafless'. The various objects described in the poem serve as effective metaphors for or symbols of the father's frailty and pending death. Like the leeks, the father is 'frail' and can be seized by death at any moment.

Particularly striking is the image of the father being summoned by Death, just as Everyman was in the medieval play. We imagine the father walking in from the garden to the beautifully sunlit hallway, with its 'sunstruck pendulums' to answer the phone. No sooner does he pick up the receiver though, than he disappears, vanishing into the afterlife, leaving the phone unattended on the hall table.

The father's imagined passing is oddly peaceful and beautiful. It is the departure of a man who lived a gentle, fulfilled life. But there is also an element of sorrow here, in the emptiness of the hallway he leaves behind, a hollowness that amplifies the 'grave ticking' of the hall clocks. Of course, 'grave' here has two separate meanings, suggesting both the sombre sound of the pendulums and the grave where the poet's father will eventually be buried.

Verbal Music

The assonance in line 7 with its broad vowels creates a pleasant, euphonious sound. Assonance also features in the phrase 'sunstruck pendulums' with its repeated 'u' sounds. Onomatopoeia occurs in line 12: 'The amplified grave ticking of hall clocks'.

Form

The poem is almost a sonnet. The poem has fifteen lines, one more than the traditional sonnet. The sonnet portion of the poem, the first fourteen lines, concludes with the father's imagined death. The fifteenth line, where the poet describes the father speaking, is set apart and stands on its own. It's very much an after-thought. The poet's imagining of his father's death has been so deep that he is so surprised to hear his father's voice. The father was quite old when the poet wrote this poem and we sense that the poet is preparing himself mentally for his eventual passing.

THEMES

LOVE AND RELATIONSHIPS

In 'The Harvest Bow', Heaney describes his father as a strong silent farmer with 'almost a contempt for speech'. In 'A Call' we get the impression that the father is perhaps most comfortable when he is out working in the garden. It is hard to imagine that he is very talkative on the phone. We can imagine him taking the call but saying relatively little, happy to get back to his work when the conversation ends.

The poet, however, is someone who is given to expression. He is a highly articulate poet who loves to express his thoughts and feelings in words. Why then does he struggle to express his feelings for his father when the old man comes to the phone? Perhaps it has to do with the difficulty that many men seem to have when it comes to expressing their feelings; it is not something that comes naturally to them, and they may have been taught to think of it as 'unmanly'. Perhaps it is a generational thing – the poet would have grown up in a time when fathers and sons would rarely articulate their feelings for one another. Perhaps the poet knows that if he speaks these words he will make his father uncomfortable and he does not want to do this. The result will just be silence at the other end of the phone.

Although the poet's father is not given to expressing his feelings in words, we get the impression that he is a gentle and sensitive man. The poet imagines his father ruefully removing the weeds from his leek bed, seeming to regret the need to kill these invading plants. We also get the impression that the poet's father is a man who takes pride in his work, deriving great pleasure from doing things properly.

ART, CRAFT AND CREATIVITY

We sense that the father is someone who takes great pride in his work. He exhibits great care and precision, combing carefully through the leeks and removing each weed at the root to ensure that they won't grow back. But he also possesses the gentleness and sensitivity necessary to nurture a garden, removing the weeds 'gently', so as not to upset the soil bed. 'A Call', then, is a poem that celebrates the craft of gardening, just as 'The Forge' celebrates the craft of the blacksmith.

IMAGINED SPACES AND LANDSCAPES

Many of Heaney's poems feature a speaker who imagines a location or environment. In this instance, the speaker imagines his parents' hallway and his father working in the garden. We have to remind ourselves that the speaker never actually sees the hallway's 'sunstruck pendulums' or his father kneeling beside the leek rig. He's on the other end of the phone the whole time. However, his description of this imagined space is so vivid that we feel we've witnessed it ourselves.

The Burren, Co. Clare, near the Flaggy Shore

LINE BY LINE

In *Stepping Stones*, a book of interviews, Heaney describes the joy he derives from driving: 'Often when I'm on my own in the car, driving in spring or early summer … I get this sudden joy from the sheer fact of the mountains to my right and the sea to my left, the flow of the farmland, the sweep of the road, the lift of the sky.' 'Postscript' captures something of this 'sudden joy', being a great hymn to the energy and locomotion of driving, to the pleasures of being behind the wheel.

The Flaggy Shore

The poet advises a visit to the Flaggy Shore, a stretch of coastline in County Clare, famous for its limestone rock formations and fossils. 'September or October', he suggests, is the perfect time to visit this rugged location. At this time of year the wind and light go 'working off each other', combining to create spectacular effects across this mile-long stretch of coast road.

The title captures the manner in which the poem was composed, quickly, fluently and with relatively little effort. Heaney commented on the writing of this piece: 'Now and again a poem comes like that, like a ball kicked in from

nowhere.' The poem, then, was written outside of or after the poet's usual writing process, which involves painstaking thought, effort and revision.

Postscripts are often more casual and relaxed in tone than the main body of the work. The poem has something of this carefree zest (the word 'postscript' comes from the Latin postscriptum, which means 'after writing'. A postscript can be a remark added to a letter after the letter has been signed. It can be a section added to a book, usually just before the book goes to print).

There's a wonderful element of personification in the opening lines. The wind and light caress the landscape like two sculptors shaping a single piece of clay. Sometimes they work in tandem, collaborating to generate particular visual effects, the breeze rippling a mountain lake so that it perfectly reflects the pale autumn sun. But sometimes, we sense, they compete or tussle with one another, each altering and revising the other's handiwork. Imagine looking out 'one side' of the car, towards the ocean, as we zip along the coast road. We'd see the interplay of these two elemental forces, the wind and the light, producing a magnificent effect: 'So that the ocean on the one side is wild/ With foam and glitter'. We can imagine the wind making the ocean tempestuous or 'wild', stoking its surface into mountainous, foaming waves. We can picture the autumn sunlight glittering as it reflects on this turbulent surface.

Now imagine looking out the other side of the car, so that your gaze turns 'inland'.

- You'd see a place of 'stones'. The landscape surrounding the Flaggy Shore is extremely stony and rugged, full of boulders, erratics and moraines.
- You'd see the lake known as Lough Muree, with 'a flock of swans' adrift on its waters. The swans, with their 'headstrong-looking heads', would come across as proud and assertive creatures.
- Some swans would have their heads '[t]ucked' in tight to their bodies. Others would have their heads 'cresting' on the lake's surface. Still others would have their heads plunged below the waterline, keeping 'busy underwater' as they search industriously for food.

Wind and light would once again contribute to the beauty of the scene. Their interplay would lend Lough Muree a 'slate-grey' appearance, so it almost blends it with the stony surrounding landscape. The swans' feathers would be 'roughed and ruffling', tousled, disarrayed and rearranged by the wind's gusts.

The feathers of particular swans might stand on end, revealing different layers and shades of white. The underside of some feathers would be spotlessly white, others a dusky grey: 'Their feathers roughed and ruffling, white on white'.

A lightning rod attracts a bolt of lightning and leads it down into the earth where its energy dissipates. Heaney imagines a bolt of lightning that remains on the earth's surface, a crackling and fizzing ball of electricity. This is the comparison used to describe the swans, wonderfully capturing their intense white plumage. Each swan, he says, is a bolt of earthed lightning, a creature of pure white light that illuminates the lake on which they glide.

Remember, we're driving. We have to keep at least one eye on the road, meaning we can manage only a few fleeting glances at the beauty that surrounds us. The poet, however, advises that there's no point in parking and getting out of the car, as doing so won't allow us to get more out of this experience: 'Useless to think you'll park and capture it/ More thoroughly.' We can 'capture' this landscape 'thoroughly', then, in a few brief glimpses, snatched and savoured from our station behind the wheel. Indeed, there's a sense that stopping would diminish the experience of this particular vista. The energy

and propulsion of driving, its endless forward momentum, contributes to the exhilaration we experience as we glance at the lake on one side of us, and at the ocean's 'foam and glitter' on the other.

Being present and absent

The poet wonderfully captures how driving makes one feel both present and absent, how it promotes a sense of being both in the landscapes through which we drive and also somehow at a remove from them: 'You are neither here nor there'. On one level, of course, as we motor along the coast we're a part of the Flaggy Shore's landscape. But on another we're sealed away from the world around us, ensconced within the bubble of the car.

The poet, in another unexpected turn of phrase, describes how we'd be a 'hurry' as we drive. We wouldn't be merely 'in a hurry'; we would actually be a hurry. This phrase wonderfully captures the exhilarating sense of speed we'd feel as we power along the coastline. We'd feel that our bodies, minds and very souls were filled with energy and propulsion.

The poem also shows how experienced drivers often enter a strangely meditative state while driving. While their attention, of course, remains focused on the road, another part of their mind drifts freely, experiencing unexpected images and associations as one thought leads on to another. As we traversed the coast road, the poet suggests, we'd enter just such a reflective state of mind, with 'known and strange things' passing through our minds. We'd find our minds drifting not only to known or familiar topics, but also to strange or unexpected ones.

The poem's final lines emphasise the importance of mindfulness, of being open to the world around us. The beauty of the Flaggy Shore will render our hearts off-guard, making us susceptible to such a state. Then finally, as we drive along between the ocean and the lake, we will find our hearts opening as we experiences a sense of oneness with the world around us.

Heaney uses a wonderful metaphor to describe this sense of mindfulness: As we drive along, winds from the sea would buffet or forcibly nudge the car in which we drive, impacting the side of the vehicle: 'big soft buffetings come at the car sideways'. The poet imagines these gusts of wind, affecting not the car's position on the road but our very hearts, blowing them open so we for once are truly present in the landscape that surrounds us.

Tone and Atmosphere

The tone of the poem is conversational and informal. The fact that it begins with the word 'And' gives the sense that we are being dropped into the poem in mid-conversation. It has a free-flowing and unconstrained feel, containing no full stops in its first ten lines.

Verbal Music

Also contributing to the poem's lively rhythm are its many examples of alliteration. Lines such as 'inland among stones/ The surface of slate-grey lake is lit', with its repeated 's' and 'l' sounds, contribute to the poem's rapid flow of imagery. Similarly, the description of the swans with 'Their feathers roughed and ruffling, white on white', with its repeated 'r' and 'w' sounds, lends the poem an urgent rhythm.

The poet imagines a car being struck reasonably forcibly by the wind as it drives along the coast. However, this impact is presented as benign, as an oddly soothing disturbance, rather than a violent and dangerous one. He describes how these gusts are not only big and imposing, but also soft and gentle. The word 'buffeting' itself contributes to this paradoxical effect. It describes a reasonably violent, forceful action but the word has a soft, almost soothing verbal music.

Metaphor, Simile, Figures of Speech

Perhaps the most striking metaphor in the poem is that of the swans as 'earthed lightning'. The long-necked, elegant swans are like forks of lightning tethered to the earth. With their 'white on white' colouring, they seem to light up the 'slate-grey lake'. Their 'ruffling' feathers, meanwhile, give them the flickering appearance of flames.

Imagery

'Postscript' is full of energetic, kinetic imagery. Everything seems to be busy and on the move, from the poet in his car to the wind and light 'working off each other'. Every surface seems to be dancing in the breeze, such as the surface of the ocean 'wild/ With foam and glitter' and the swans' feathers 'roughed and ruffling'.

THEMES

CREDITING THE MARVELLOUS

This is a poem that has the idea of mindfulness very much to the fore: it stresses the importance of being present in the moment, and of keeping oneself open to life and its sensations. The opening line emphasises the importance of making the time for such experiences 'And some time make the time to drive out west'.

On the one hand, the poet is reminding himself to take time out of his busy life 'to drive out west' to one of his favourite places. This opening line, however, can also be read as a general address to all of us to 'make the time', to make room in our busy lives for the places and experiences that really move us and replenish us. Doing so, the poem suggests, is by no means a frivolous activity – it is necessary for a sense of perspective, for our mental and emotional wellbeing.

We are often advised when we see something spectacular on our journey to stop, to pull over and take it all in. We can only be mindful, we are told, by slowing down. The poet, however, gives us the opposite advice. Our trip to the Flaggy Shore should suffer no such interruptions – we must keep driving. There is a certain kind of mindfulness, the poem suggests, that comes from movement, pace and rhythm. The heart can be open to experience, even when we are in the driver's seat.

IMAGINED SPACES AND LANDSCAPES

The poet advises us to go the Flaggy Shore at a particular time when conditions are just so, when the wind and light are interacting perfectly, when the weather conditions are in a particularly atmospheric state. In a sense, then, the poet presents us with an imagined space, an idealised version of this coastline: the wild, glittering ocean; the 'slate-grey lake'; the swans that look like balls of 'earthed lightning'.

Perhaps the poet has actually experienced the Flaggy Shore under such conditions. But it is more likely that the picture he paints for us fuses elements of different trips he has taken there over the years. Perhaps he's seen the Flaggy Shore on an exquisitely blustery afternoon, but surely he has never actually witnessed the splendour he advises us to seek out.

Tate's Avenue

Heaney with his wife, Maria, near the beginning of their relationship

LINE BY LINE

The car rug (circa 1963)

The poet finds himself thinking about various rugs that he has shared with his wife over the many years they have been together. The first rug he remembers is a 'car rug' from the early sixties. This was the 'first' rug he and his future wife owned as a couple. It likely came with the poet's first car, which he purchased in 1963, a time when many cars came with a rug intended for picnics or day trips.

He remembers how, when they drove in his new car to the seaside, this car rug was 'Spread on sand by the sea'. The rug itself, it should be pointed out, doesn't strike us as being especially attractive, Around its edges were old-fashioned woollen tassels or 'tails'. Its colour scheme was a mixture of various browns: brown and 'fawn', or greyish brown, for the main body of the rug, with sepia or reddish brown for the tassels. In a wonderful phrase, the poet describes how the rug was 'Breathing land-breaths' capturing its stale and musty odour from being stowed in the car.

But this rug, despite its unattractiveness, was their 'comfort zone'. In one sense of course, this simply means that it was a comfortable place to sit, that it spared them the discomfort of the seaside's sand and rocks. But the term 'comfort zone' as we shall see also serves as a powerful metaphor for their relationship. The poet in an interesting turn of phrase describes the car rug as 'vestal', meaning related to virginity. Perhaps this suggests that the rug is new and unsullied. It's a phrase that also tells us something about their relationship in its earliest stages, suggesting perhaps that it had yet to develop fully physically. We must remember that during the early 1960s, when this stanza is set, sex before marriage was still relatively uncommon.

The Spanish rug (circa 1969)

The poet finds himself thinking about a different rug, one they shared on their first trip to Spain in 1969. The poet has now achieved some success and is already a minor literary celebrity, having just published his second book of poems *Door into the Dark*. It is quite possible, therefore, that the poet and his wife have been invited to Spain to attend a literary gathering there.

The description of the rug certainly suggests that the poet and his wife had a great time. We get the impression that they ventured off by themselves, out into the Spanish heartlands, with a basket of local wine and food. The poet remembers sitting on a rug by the banks of the Guadalquivir river, which flows through Cordoba and Seville in Southern Spain, and enjoying their feast.

The rug that the poet remembers from this particular occasion was eventually strewn with scraps from the meal they enjoyed. Scattered all over its surface are 'crusts' from the baguettes, shells from the cooked eggs, bits of the local cheese, olive stones and 'rinds' from the salami scattered all over the rug. Heaney describes the rug as 'scraggy', with food scraps entangled in its fibres. These scraps made the rug uncomfortable to lie on.

The description of the rug gives us a sense of how relaxed and carefree the couple were on this occasion, 'drunk' from the local Spanish wine. We can imagine that this is one of their first trips abroad, and likely their first trip to Spain, and they are just lapping and soaking up the culture. We also get a sense of how at ease they are with each other, having been together for a number of years.

The Belfast rug (circa 1961)

Now the poet finds himself remembering another rug, one that he and his wife lay on briefly back in 1961. At this time, the poet and his future wife were both living in Belfast. But at this stage they were only acquaintances rather than lovers. It is likely, in fact, that they were both attached to other people at the time. The parks in Belfast were locked-up on Sundays because the civic authorities were heavily influenced by the Presbyterian community, who believed that Sundays should be preserved for worship and reflection. For this reason, until 1965, Sunday saw Belfast parks under lock and key.

One Sunday, they found themselves in the same back yard on Tate's Avenue in central Belfast. We imagine that this is some kind of social gathering and that they have both been invited around for lunch by a mutual friend, for example. The yard, in which they found themselves, seemed claustrophobic, with its 'walls' and 'high and silent' dustbins. The back yard that the poet remembers consisted of lumpy earth, suggesting that it was barren and uncared for rather than a well-attended garden. The portrait of the backyard suggests rented accommodation for students or graduates rather than a family home.

The poet remembers how his future wife was lying on a rug in the yard reading. He recalls how she twirled her hair distractedly, lost in her book. The poet was deeply attracted to this woman and felt that she was deeply attracted to him as well. He took the brave step of lying down beside her on the rug. The poet's future wife didn't respond positively to this advance, but she didn't push him away either. She just ignored him and went on reading. The poet uses the colloquial expression 'nothing gives' to describe this lack of response, meaning 'nothing doing' or 'nothing happening'. But the expression nothing gives' also refers to the ground on which they both lay, suggesting the unyielding nature of the surface.

The poet lay 'at [his] length', his body stretched out alongside his future wife. The lumpy earth made him deeply uncomfortable but he was determined not to move from the rug. He wanted to remain pressed against her for every second possible: 'But never shifted'. The poet describes how he was 'Keen-sensed' during these minutes he spent next to his future wife. His senses were heightened by his attraction to her, and he was keenly aware of her smell and her touch. But the poet also remained conscious of the discomfort of lying on this hard, lumpy earth.

Finally, they moved. Maybe they were called in for dinner by the mutual friend who has been hosting them. Maybe they were disturbed by one of the flies that populate the 'high and silent' dust bins. But now they know they have something. Though nothing has been said, they know they like each other. It is the first move in what will become a life-long attachment.

THEMES

THE PROCESS OF MEMORY

This poem describes the process of memory as an almost inner Instagram. We find the poet flicking through different mental images as if he were swiping through an internal photo stream. The poem, we might imagine, is set during a moment of ease or relaxation, one in which the poet finds his mind idling or drifting through memories of the past. Somehow the poet finds himself thinking about the rug that came with his first car. But this memory triggers a remembrance of another rug and then another, wonderfully illustrating the associative manner in which the memory works.

The poet, as we have seen, finds himself remembering the rug he and his wife would use when they visited the beach in the early stages of their relationship. He remembers a rug they sat on during an exquisitely sensual trip to Spain. These are two fine memories, but they are not the ones that he recalls most fondly. They are not the ones that he finds himself returning to again and again. Instead, he finds himself dwelling 'again' and again on a rug associated with an ordinary morning in an ugly back yard in Belfast in the early 60s. Maybe it's easy to see why this is the rug that he always returns to, for this was the beginning of his relationship with his wife, when everything seemed fresh and new and full of possibility.

LOVE AND RELATIONSHIPS

'Tate's Avenue' celebrates the resilience and longevity of a long-term relationship, not the just the excitement and passion of the young love in its earliest stages. The poet celebrates how he and his wife explored the world together as the years went by and their relationship continued to flourish and deepen. He relishes how their horizons expanded over time, from the claustrophobic walled yard, to the Northern Irish seashore, to the exotic Guadalquivir river in Spain, and then, no doubt, even further afield.

The rugs described in the poem serve as a symbol of their relationship over the years. Placing a rug on the ground creates a space apart from the surface in which it has been laid. Similarly, the bond the couple share can be thought of as a place apart, as being somehow separate from the surrounding network of human commitments and relationships. We think of it as a comfortable space – usually, it is more comfortable to sit on a rug rather than on sand or earth. Similarly, the poet views his relationship with his wife as a comfort zone, for it provides them both with calmness and reassurance, nourishing them as they journey through life.

Gerard Manley Hopkins Themes

The Beauty of Nature

Nature's beauty is a theme that Hopkins returns to again and again. 'As Kingfishers Catch Fire, Dragonflies Draw Flame', for instance, is one poem where he celebrates the immense beauty and variety of the natural world. It conjures up the fiery colourful beauty of kingfishers and dragonflies, as well as humbler aspects of the natural world like the noise of stones tumbling into a well.

In 'Spring', meanwhile, we get a sense of the poet being almost overwhelmed by the beauty of the springtime countryside, declaring that 'Nothing is so beautiful as Spring'. The sights and sounds of spring induce in Hopkins a kind of ecstasy, a kind of natural high. He is electrified by the sound of birdsong and is so overcome by the beauty of the sky that he feels its blueness washing all about him.

In 'The Windhover' Hopkins relishes the sight of a falcon, which is depicted as a fierce and dangerous hunter. The falcon, then, possesses a 'Brute beauty', beauty of a brutal and ferocious kind. It exhibits poise, confidence and control as it goes 'striding' through the sky, manipulating the air-thermals on which it cruises. To the poet, the falcon seems caught up in an 'ecstasy' as if it relishes its own strength, power and control.

'Inversnaid' continues this celebration of nature, lauding the beauty of a Scottish 'burn' or stream at each stage of its journey to the lake below. Hopkins captures the thundering energy and momentum of the burn's waters in their upper course. He describes the fertility of its banks during its middle course and he relishes how it meanders, 'combs' and 'flutes' during the last phase of its journey.

There are moments in Hopkins' poetry where he presents a very modern view of environmental stewardship. 'God's Grandeur', for instance, suggests that it is humanity's duty to manage our environment in a sustainable manner, so the beauties of nature can be passed on to the next generation. The poem is keenly aware of how humanity has failed in this duty, of how the Industrial Revolution has ravaged the landscape in England and beyond. For generations we have carelessly trampled God's creation, guided only by selfishness and greed.

This tendency is also evident in 'Inversnaid' where the poet points out what an unimaginably terrible place the world would be without such places of wild and unspoilt beauty. He concludes with a desperate plea that locations like 'Inversnaid' be spared by industry, building and development: 'Let them be left,/ O let them be left'. As we know today, however, such pleas all too often go ignored in the name of progress.

God's Presence in Nature

In 'Pied Beauty,' Hopkins, using a topical coinage, describes how God 'fathers-forth' everything we see around us. The phrase, tellingly, is in the present tense, suggesting God's work of creation is ceaseless and ongoing. God's creative abilities, Hopkins suggests, are a mystery no human being could ever understand: 'who knows how?' We can only shake our heads in awe at his remarkable accomplishments.

And God, Hopkins believes, is present in a very real way in every aspect of His creation. This theme is especially evident in 'God's Grandeur', for instance, in which he describes how God's presence throbs and pulses through the world. Hopkins compares it to a current of electricity that 'charges' every aspect of the natural world. God's presence, the poet suggests, exists 'deep down' in every single aspect of creation.

In 'As Kingfishers Catch Fire, Dragonflies Draw Flame', meanwhile, Hopkins describes how God has imbued everything in nature with its own unique and individual essence. Each creature and object expresses this essence through its actions and appearances. Each creature and object, therefore, makes God present in the world.

'God's Grandeur' stresses that God's presence in nature means that the natural world can never be 'spent', can never be exhausted or destroyed. Mankind in his greed and stupidity may pollute and ruin the natural world, but God's presence nourishes and sustains it. We see this when Hopkins describes the 'Holy Ghost' tending to the world just as a bird tends to an un-hatched egg. Despite man's destructive efforts, nature will always restore itself.

The Relationship Between God and Man

'As Kingfishers Catch Fire, Dragonflies Draw Flame' emphasises the distinction between humanity and the rest of God's creations. According to Hopkins, non-human creatures and objects come into this world with a simple purpose: to express through their actions and appearances the essence God has placed within them. Human beings, however, have a higher purpose: to make Christ present in the world by behaving as a 'just man'.

All too often, however, we fail in this purpose by lapsing into sinning. In 'God's Grandeur', for instance, Hopkins laments the fact that the human race no longer respects God's authority. According to Hopkins, we no longer 'reck', no longer respect or recognise, the 'rod' that symbolises God's divine power. We disrespect God's authority by murdering, lying and cheating. But we also do so through our environmental misdeeds, when our 'toil' stains the magnificent world He has gifted us and in which He is everywhere present.

In 'Spring', meanwhile, Hopkins presents the world as a kind of fallen place, one that inevitably corrupts every human being. Children, he believes, possess a special kind of innocence, but as they grow older, as they experience more of this corrupting world, that innocence will inevitably 'cloud' and 'sour'.

It is only through Christ, Hopkins believes, that the human race can be redeemed from its sinful ways. 'Spring', for instance, calls on Christ to 'Have' and 'get' the children of the world before they are exposed to sin and its corrupting ways. The poet wants Christ to be an active presence in children's lives as they grow up, shielding and counteracting the world's wicked influence, so they can retain some of their innocence.

'As Kingfishers Catch Fire, Dragonflies Draw Flame', meanwhile, calls on us to turn away from sin and live in a Christ-like fashion. By doing so we will make Christ present in our eyes, limbs and features. We will seem 'lovely' in the eyes of God as he recognises Christ's presence within us.

'The Windhover' highlights how Christ's sufferings on the cross offer every human being the possibility of salvation, from sin and hell, and the potential of eternal life. Christ's death on the cross, like the falcon's destruction by the wind, exhibited a kind of 'brute beauty'. It was beautiful in the sense that it offers each of us salvation. It was 'Brute' in the sense that it involved physical force and violence, as Christ's body was tortured and maimed.

The crucifixion, then, is not merely a historical event. We see this in Hopkins' choice of tense, when he writes 'the fire that breaks from thee then' rather than 'the fire that broke from thee then'. The crucifixion, therefore, is presented as an event that resonates through all of history, that still offers every human being the opportunity of salvation.

In 'Felix Randal', Christ is depicted working through the sacraments of the church. When Hopkins gives Felix the sacrament of communion his heart becomes 'heavenlier', suggesting that his soul becomes cleansed of sin and fit to enter heaven. Communion is describe as our 'sweet reprieve', which is the cancellation or postponement of a punishment. For it is through communion – and the other sacraments – that we are given the opportunity to escape the punishments of hell and gain heaven's eternal rest. Communion is also described as a 'ransom', bringing to mind, once again, Christ's sacrifice on the cross. Christ, Hopkins suggests, was paid as a kind of 'ransom' in order to free humanity from sin.

There are several moments in his poetry where Hopkins highlights the intensely personal nature of his feelings towards Christ. This is especially evident in 'The Windhover' where Hopkins refers to Christ as 'my chevalier' and 'my dear', suggesting the intense bond he feels with his Lord. We sense the poet's deep personal gratitude that Christ suffered for his sins in order that he might reach the kingdom of heaven.

Physical and Mental Suffering

Throughout his life, Hopkins suffered from poor physical health. He also suffered from bouts of depression, which overshadowed in particular his final years in Dublin. The poet's suffering is most starkly captured in a series of sonnets he wrote towards the end of his life, which have become known as his 'Terrible Sonnets'.

'Inversnaid' was written at a time when Hopkins was on the verge of the depression and despair that would characterise this last period of his life. There is a darkness at the heart of the poem, something disturbing in its central image is that of 'the pool so pitchblack' – the little whirlpool in the brook's path that fills Hopkins with such horrified fascination. It's as if staring into its murky 'fell-frowning' depths gives him some premonition of the personal abyss into which he soon will fall, the despair in which he will soon find himself drowning.

'Felix Randal' too focuses on physical and metal suffering. There is something almost unbearably moving about this 'powerful' tradesman being broken by sickness until he ended up weeping in the arms of a visiting priest. Felix suffered mentally, too. At the beginning of his illness he was so overcome with such despair and anger that he cursed God. Finally, as his illness neared its end, his mind started to give way and his 'reason rambled' as he slipped into some form of dementia.

'No worst, there is none', one of the 'Terrible Sonnets' mentioned above, could be described as a howl of mental torment. The poet has been 'Pitched past pitch of grief'. He is experiencing a mental state that is far beyond ordinary grief or sorrow. Hopkins' mental torment is more or less unrelenting, with only the briefest of pauses between one bout of suffering and the next. His torment also keeps getting worse. To Hopkins, it seems that his sufferings will keep increasing in intensity forever, that there is 'no worst', no rock-bottom for him to hit. It is hardly surprising, therefore, that the poet thinks of himself as a pitiful 'wretch', crying out in agony over and over again. His only 'comfort' is the oblivion offered by sleep or death.

'I wake and feel the fell of dark', another of Hopkins' 'Terrible Sonnets, also provides an extraordinary account of mental suffering. The poet suffers from insomnia and lies awake for hour after hour imagining that day will never come. He experiences such dread that he imagines darkness as a foul creature that holds him in his grip. He experiences 'black hours' of mental anguish.

But the poet also endures physical suffering. He experiences the physical ailments of gall and heartburn. He feels like his whole body is unbalanced and off-kilter. He even resents having a body at all, viewing it as a 'curse'. Hopkins, then, experiences his mind and body as having an almost unbearably 'bitter' quality. Indeed, he is in such a miserable state that he compares himself to the 'lost' souls who suffer in hell.

'Thou art indeed just, Lord' is perhaps the least intense of the three 'Terrible Sonnets' on the course. Here, Hopkins presents his suffering in a more rational, restrained and subtle fashion. He contrasts his situation with that of the countryside in springtime, in order to emphasise how he feels creatively, spiritually and professionally barren. He contrasts himself with the birds of springtime, who are busy building nests for the mating season to come: 'birds build'. Hopkins, on the other hand, can't seem to 'build' anything at all: 'but not I build; no'. He describes how he 'strain[s]', making extraordinary efforts to lead a productive life. But his efforts are all in vain.

Doubting God's Goodness

'Felix Randal' is one of the earliest poems by Hopkins to tackle the theme of religious doubt. We see this when Felix becomes 'impatient' with God's will and curses God for allowing him to become sick. Felix's doubts are overcome when Hopkins administers the sacraments and he 'mends' his relationship with God. However, in a later sonnet like 'Thou art indeed Just, Lord', however, there is no easy answer to such doubts.

'No worst, there is none' powerfully deals with Hopkins' sense of abandonment by God. In the throes of mental torment, Hopkins calls out to God and the Virgin Mary for comfort and relief. God, however, is unable or unwilling to help him. Hopkins, who was a loyal and devoted priest, feels abandoned by the God he has served so faithfully.

A similar sense of abandonment is also evident in 'I wake and feel the fell of dark'. The poem describes how Hopkins 'cries' out to Christ again and again, looking for comfort, answers and relief. But he is dismayed to find that his cries, like 'dead letters' ,go unanswered or unheard. Hopkins suspects that God actually wants him to suffer. It's as if God commanded or decreed that his body and his mind would have a 'most bitter' quality. Hopkins even seems to resent the fact that God gave him a body, rather than letting him exist forever as a purely spiritual being.

'Thou art indeed just, Lord' is another powerful poem of religious doubt. In it, Hopkins asks an age-old question: if God is good why does He let wicked men triumph and sinners get ahead in life? Furthermore, why does He let His faithful servants suffer? Hopkins has sacrificed so much for God yet nothing in his life succeeds. Meanwhile, sinners who have sacrificed nothing – who are the slaves or 'thralls' of lust – get ahead in life. Hopkins, like many other people throughout history, wonders why God allows this to happen.

There is a strong sense of frustration, perhaps even anger, in this poem. Everything Hopkins tries to do ends in disappointment and failure. He cannot understand why God allows this to happen, especially when Hopkins has served Him so faithfully. Hopkins almost suspects that God has turned against him and is actually his enemy rather than his friend.

In many of his poems, Hopkins draws a moral message from the natural world. The beauty of nature leads him to contemplate God's goodness. In this poem, however, the beauty of nature seems to tie in with Hopkins' angry questioning of God's justice. Each spring the riverbanks grow thick with leaves while God lets Hopkins' life remain barren and empty. Hopkins' only hope is that God will make his life fertile and fulfilling, just as He sends rain to water the plants on the riverbank. Hopkins, therefore, calls out desperately for God to 'send my roots rain'.

LINE BY LINE

I

God, according to Hopkins, is a being of extraordinary grandeur, of splendour and magnificence.

- And this grandeur, according to Hopkins, is present not only in God himself but also in the world He has created.
- Hopkins describes how the world is 'charged' with this grandeur, suggesting that it pulses through every aspect of creation like an unstoppable electrical current: 'The world is charged with the grandeur of God'.
- We will experience God's grandeur, then, when we contemplate the world around us. We might experience it when we stop to admire a sunset, for instance. Or when we watch birds flitting about the trees in summertime.
- At such moments, according to Hopkins, God's grandeur emanates from the world and reaches our senses.
- God's grandeur, according to Hopkins, 'flame[s]' from the world, just as rays of light or 'shining' emanate from silvery foil when it's shaken in the sunlight: 'It will flame out, like shining from shook foil'.

God's grandeur, then, is present in countless individual aspects of creation. But His grandeur, we're told, also 'gathers to a greatness'. This suggests how everything in nature is interrelated, how every plant, animal and insect combines or 'gathers' to form a single ecological system that covers the entire world. And this extraordinary global system, of course, is the ultimate illustration of God's magnificence.

II

Hopkins imagines God holding a great staff or 'rod' that symbolises his universal authority. Nowadays, however, human beings are increasingly reluctant to 'reck' or recognise this 'rod'. We are more and more unwilling to turn away from our sinful ways, and instead to acknowledge God's authority and follow his commandments.

Hopkins' use of a rhetorical question suggests his amazement at humanity's behaviour. God, after all, has given us this magnificent world that is 'charged' with His very own grandeur. Hopkins wonders 'why then (therefore)' we don't show God thanks by repenting our sins and acknowledging his authority: 'Why do men then now not reck his rod?' To Hopkins, our sinful ways and our disregard for God's authority smacks of extraordinary ingratitude.

III

Hopkins focuses especially on one aspect of mankind's selfish and sinful behaviour: our mismanagement of the natural world. Such mismanagement, Hopkins declares, has become much worse over recent decades. For several 'generations' now, humanity has been treating the natural world with utter carelessness and contempt. Hopkins, we remember, was writing about a century after the Industrial Revolution had begun. Vast polluted cities had sprung up in England and around the world. Huge factories endlessly belched out gouts of acrid smoke. Pollution was rife and nature seemed everywhere in retreat.

Hopkins, then, addresses the ideas of 'toil' and 'trade'. But he doesn't mean all forms of work or commercial activity. Instead he's referring to this modern industrial production that has such terrible environmental consequences:

- 'Trade', according to Hopkins, has left everything 'seared' or burned: 'all is seared with trade'. This suggests how industry tends consume and burn up natural resources, such as timber, coal, oil and various minerals.
- 'Toil' has left everything 'bleared' or blurred. This describes how industry causes air pollution, how clouds of fine smoke and other pollutants emerge from factory chimneys, making the entire cityscape seem blurred and hazy.
- 'Toil' has left everything smeared or 'dirty': 'all is…smeared with toil'. This wonderfully describes how industrial waste travels far from the factories that produce it – floating on the winds, carried by rivers and streams, seeping through the very soil – until the entire environment bears a faint trace of pollution.
- Human beings, since the Industrial Revolution, have become associated with 'smudge' and 'smell', with pollutants and soot and toxic waste. We spread such filth over the natural world, until everything 'wears' a 'smudge' associated with our cities and industrial complexes.
- Hopkins laments that 'the soil/ Is bare now'. Bare soil describes soil that has been stripped of its topsoil, its upper productive layer, leaving only bare rocks and clay. The phrase describes the impact of pollution and over-farming on our natural environment.

Hopkins laments that human beings are 'shod', that we wear shoes and as a result no longer feel the soil against our feet: 'nor can foot feel, being shod'. Hopkins, of course, doesn't want everyone to start going around in bare feet. Instead he's using footwear to symbolise how we are no longer at one with the natural world that surrounds us. Our feet's lack of contact with the earth represents our lack of sympathy with and understanding of nature.

IV

Mankind, then, has inflicted extraordinary damage on the natural world. Yet despite all this destruction and pollution ('for all this'), there is still hope. For nature's resources, Hopkins insists, can never truly be exhausted or consumed: 'And for all this, nature is never spent'. The natural world, despite mankind's destructive activities, will always find a way to restore itself. This endless renewal is possible because God's presence flows through the entire world. God's presence, Hopkins stresses, exists 'deep down' in every aspect of His creation. Hopkins refers to God's presence as a 'freshness' because it ensures that nature will always be refreshed or rejuvenated. It is the 'dearest' or most precious thing that Hopkins can imagine, ensuring as it does that nature will always be reborn.

Each evening the sun sets in the blackness of the western sky and the 'last lights' of the day slowly disappear: 'And though the last lights of the black West went'. In the morning, however, the sun 'springs' once more from the 'brink' or edge of the eastern sky and light returns: 'Oh, morning, at the brown brink eastwards, springs' (Hopkins memorably describes how the sky before sunrise can have a brownish tint, as night slowly gives way to morning).

Here, Hopkins is using the sunrise to illustrate nature's infinite capacity for renewal. The sun's disappearance represents how forests, fields and other aspects of the natural world retreat due to man's depredations. The sun's reappearance, meanwhile, represents how forests and fields will always, eventually, return. Such a return may take decades or even centuries. But sometime, maybe long after humanity itself has disappeared, growth will return to barren meadows and polluted cityscapes.

Hopkins uses an inventive metaphor to describe how God presides over the world. The Earth, rather wittily, is compared to an egg. And we can see how the planet's oval shape might lend itself to such a comparison. The Holy Spirit meanwhile is compared to a mother bird with a 'warm breast' and bright wings. A mother bird might 'brood over' an un-hatched egg, sitting on it and using her feathers to keep it warm and protected. The Holy Spirit, we're told, 'broods over' the Earth in a similar fashion. We're invited to imagine the Holy Spirit as a powerful but invisible presence that folds itself around the world, that transmits waves of spiritual energy into each creature on the planet's surface, that helps to preserve all life on earth.

FOCUS ON STYLE

Syntax

Hopkins is known for using unusual syntax or word order in order to create rhythmic effects. We see this at the poem's conclusion when he writes 'the Holy Ghost over the bent/ World broods' rather than, as we might expect, 'The Holy Ghost broods over the bent world'.

We also see this tendency when Hopkins writes 'the ooze of oil/ Crushed', rather than what we might expect, 'The ooze of crushed oil'. The unusual word order has the effect of energising the verse and leaving the key word 'Crushed' highlighted in a prominent position.

The word 'Crushed' completes the statement begun in line 3 but stands alone by itself at the beginning of line 4, its isolation highlighting its significance. It signals a change in the poem's focus, introducing the theme of environmental damage, the crushing of nature's beauty by man. The word 'Crushed' might also suggests the disappointment that the poet feels when he looks at the beauty of nature and the damage that man does.

Compression

Hopkins is a poet who is perfectly happy to leave out words, and even entire phrases, in order to create a specific rhythmic effect. This tendency towards compression is evident in the line 'There lives the dearest freshness deep down things'. Ordinarily, of course, we would say something like 'the dearest freshness lives deep down *in* things'.

Words With Many Meanings

Hopkins often uses words that have more than one meaning. The word 'charged' in the poem's opening line, as we've seen, is used in the sense of electricity. However, we also detect here a shade of the word's other meanings. To be 'charged' is to be accused of a crime, in this instance bringing to mind mankind's crime of failing to respect God's creation. To be 'charged' is also to be given a task, in this instance bringing to mind how humanity is charged with the great duty of protecting God's creation.

The description of the world as 'bent' can also be understood to mean different things. Perhaps it is a reference to the curved nature of the globe. However, the world 'bent' can also mean corrupt or morally crooked and so might be describing the activities of man.

Instress and Inscape

Hopkins uses 'inscape', a profusion of assonance and alliteration, to capture the essence of an object or sensation. In the phrase 'ooze of oil' for example, with its onomatopoeic quality, we can almost hear the oil slicking and flowing. The phrase 'shining from shook foil', meanwhile, features alliteration with its repeated 'sh' sounds and assonance with its repeated 'o' and 'i' sounds. This lends the phrase a pleasant, sprightly music, in keeping with its description of silver foil glittering in sunlight.

The poem's concluding lines are rich in alliteration, generated by its repeated 'b' sound in 'bent', 'brood', 'breast' and 'bright', and the 'w' sound in 'world', 'warm' and 'wings'. This creates a euphonious musical effect that suggests the gentle, redemptive quality of the Holy Spirit.

THEMES

GOD'S PRESENCE IN NATURE

The poem describes how God's presence throbs and pulses through the world. Hopkins compares it to a current of electricity that 'charges' every aspect of the natural world. God's presence, the poet suggests, exists 'deep down' in every single aspect of creation. A similar point is made in 'As Kingfishers Catch Fire, Dragonflies Draw Flame', where Hopkins describes how God has imbued everything in nature with its own unique and individual essence.

Hopkins also illustrates God's presence in nature when he describes the 'Holy Ghost' tending to the world just as a bird tends to an unhatched egg. Because God is present in nature, it can never be 'spent', destroyed or exhausted. Mankind in his greed and stupidity may pollute and ruin the natural world, but God's presence nourishes and sustains it. Despite man's destructive efforts. therefore, nature will always restore itself.

THE BEAUTY OF NATURE

'God's Grandeur', like many of Hopkins' poems, deals with the beauty of nature. It wonderfully captures how beauty seems to 'flame out' from the natural world, how nature, if we look at it in the right manner, will strike us as being ablaze with beauty.

The poem contains less direct descriptions of nature than, say, 'Spring' or 'Pied Beauty'. However, Hopkins does provide a memorable portrait of the sunrise, depicting how the light has a brownish tint before the sun springs from the eastern 'brink' of the world. Hopkins, as we've seen, views nature's beauty as a gift God has given to mankind. But we don't have to be religious to share Hopkins' view of the natural world as a gift of sorts. It is a privilege, after all, to watch the sun rise or listen to birdsong.

And it is a privilege that none of us has earned, as it has been gifted to us by the natural world itself.

'God's Grandeur' presents a very modern view of stewardship. It is humanity's duty, the poem suggests, to manage our environment in a sustainable manner, so the beauties of nature can be passed on to the next generation. He is keenly aware of how humanity has failed in this duty, of how the Industrial Revolution has ravaged the landscape in England and beyond. For generations we have carelessly trampled God's creation, guided only by selfishness and greed. Equally modern is Hopkins' depiction of how the entire natural world 'gathers' together to create a single greatness. Here he seems to pre-empt modern theories of how everything from dung beetles, to bees, to elephants are inter-related, how even seemingly minor changes to the environment can have devastating consequences.

SIN AND REDEMPTION

God's authority, as we've seen, is represented by His 'rod'. We might visualise this as the sceptre he wields on His heavenly throne or as a shepard's crook that He uses to steer us away from sin and spiritual harm.

In the past, Hopkins suggests, mankind was relatively good at respecting God's authority. Over the course of recent generations, however, we have come to disregard His authority more and more. A similar point is made in 'Spring', which also suggests that humanity in the distant past was more respectful of God's laws. We disrespect God's authority by murdering, lying and cheating. But we also do so through our environmental misdeeds, when our 'toil' stains the magnificent world He has gifted us and in which He is everywhere present.

As Kingfishers Catch Fire, Dragonflies Draw Flame

LINE BY LINE

When Hopkins was in training to become a Jesuit priest at Stonyhust College in Lancashire, England, he was struggling with a personal moral dilemma. He had a great love for the beauty of the natural world but he felt, as Robert Bernard Martin has put it, 'that to put too much love into the perception of one flower ... was to neglect man's primary duty of love of God'.

But his reading of the medieval theolgian, Joannes Duns Scotus, helped Hopkins to resolve this dilemma. Duns Scotus postulated that the material world was a symbol of God, not divorced from him, a view to which Hopkins wholeheartedly subscribed emotionally. 'As kingfishers catch fire' is, as Martin puts it, an 'explicit statement of the liberation [Hopkins] felt to love the phenomenal world because of its ultimate identity as part of God'.

Lines 1 to 8

Hopkins believes that God has given everything in the world a unique spiritual essence. This essence 'dwells' or lives 'indoors', meaning that it exists deep within each creature and object: 'that being indoors each one dwells'.

Every single creature and object was created with a single purpose in mind: 'Each mortal thing does one thing and the same'. They all 'came' into the world to express the unique spiritual essence God has placed within them.

Each creature and object expresses its essence through its actions and appearances:

- The birds known as kingfishers, for instance, express their essence through their colourful appearance. Hopkins describes how their feathers seem to blaze or 'catch fire' when struck by sunlight.
- Dragonflies, too, use colour to express their essences. They too seem to flare up when the sunlight hits them. Their multi-coloured wings seem to 'draw' or attract 'flame'.
- Even humble, ordinary stones have a unique essence that dwells within them. They, too, express their essence through their actions and appearances. A stone, for instance, might express its essence through the sound it makes when thrown or 'tumbled' into the round mouth of a well: 'As tumbled over rim in roundy wells/ Stones ring'. Hopkins seems to have in mind a stone that bounces against the sides of the well shaft as it falls, producing a chiming or ringing sound with each collision.
- Even a man-made object like a guitar string has a unique spiritual essence. It 'tells' or expresses this essences through the note it makes when plucked by a musician: 'each tucked string tells' ('Tucked' is an old word for plucked).
- A bell, Hopkins suggests, expresses its essence when it rings. Hopkins then refers to bells that might be 'hung' in the tower of a church or cathedral. The bell's 'bow' or curved outer shell is 'swung', causing it to strike the clapper and produce a ringing sound that can be heard in a 'broad' area around the bell tower.

The behaviour of each object and creature, therefore, expresses its truest and deepest nature: 'What I do is me'. Each thing's actions and appearances are likened to a shout or cry, one through which it joyfully declares its unique spiritual essence: 'Crying What I do is me: for that I came'.

Lines 9 to 14

In the poem's final six lines, Hopkins focuses on 'the just man':

- The 'just man' is someone who 'justices' on a regular basis, who makes a constant, ongoing effort to be a good person: 'I say more: the just man justices' (here we see Hopkins playing with language as he transforms the noun 'justice' into the verb 'to justice'. You 'justice', of course, when you behave in a just and righteous manner).
- The just man is someone who 'keeps gráce', who lives in accordance with God's law and stays free of sin.
- The just man ensures that all his 'goings', all his doings and activities, are 'graces'. Everything he does, therefore, is a 'grace', an act of decency and good will.
- The just man is aware that he is being observed by God the father. He endeavours, therefore, to act in a Christ-like manner, to exhibit the values of compassion, forgiveness and humility. He 'Acts in God's eye [like] Christ'.

But Hopkins pushes this last point a little bit further, declaring that when we act in a Christ-like manner, Christ is actually present within us.

- When we act in a Christ-like manner, Christ inhabits our 'limbs', our eyes and the 'features of [our] faces'.
- When we look into the eyes of the just man, we look into the eyes of Christ himself. Christ, according to Hopkins, is present 'in eyes [that are] not his [own]'. He is present in the eyes of everyone at any given moment who is behaving in a Christ-like fashion.
- Christ, then, can be present in 'ten thousand places' at once, existing everywhere someone is behaving in a Christ-like manner.
- The presence of Christ within us, Hopkins declares, is a 'lovely' one. Here Hopkins is using the term 'lovely' to mean not only pleasant and attractive, but also admirable and worthy of respect.

Hopkins imagines God the father looking from heaven. God the father, Hopkins imagines, sees that His son, Christ, is present all over the world. Christ is visible 'to the father' not only 'in [the] eyes' but also 'through the features' of every just man and woman. And to God the father, that is a 'lovely' sight.

THEMES

THE BEAUTY OF NATURE

In many of his poems, Hopkins focuses on the uniqueness, or 'inscape', of each creature and object, devising complex and original poetic lines to capture that uniqueness. 'Kingfishers' is arguably Hopkins' greatest celebration of this individuality. Every aspect of nature, the poem suggests, acts in a way that expresses or spells out the unique essence that exists within it.

The poem, then, celebrates the immense beauty and variety of the natural world. It conjures up the fiery colourful beauty of kingfishers and dragonflies, as well as humbler aspects of the natural world like the noise of stones tumbling into a well.

Hopkins also celebrates the beautiful sounds made by certain manufactured objects: strings on musical instruments and church bells. While these man-made objects are not technically part of the natural world, they blend with it in the poem's celebration of life's rich tapestry.

SIN AND REDEMPTION

This poem emphasises the distinction between humanity and the rest of God's creations. Non-human creatures and objects come into this world with a simple purpose: to express through their actions and appearances the essence God has placed within them. Human beings, however, have a higher purpose: to make Christ present in the world by behaving as a 'just man'. Non-human creatures fulfil God's plan for them automatically, simply by existing. They have no choice in the matter. Human beings, on the other hand, have been given free will. We can choose to go against the purpose God has in mind for us by living in a sinful rather than a just manner.

The poem, therefore, calls on us to turn away from sin. We must live the lifestyle of the 'just man' as outlined above. We must behave in a Christ-like fashion and make Christ present in our eyes, limbs and features. By doing so we will fulfil God's plan for us. We will seem 'lovely' in the eyes of God as he recognises Christ's presence within us.

GOD'S PRESENCE IN NATURE

'Kingfishers' also refers to another of Hopkins' central themes: the presence of God in nature.

- God, the poem emphasises, has placed a unique essence inside each creature and object.
- Each creature and object expresses this essence through its actions and appearances.
- Each creature and object, therefore, makes God present in the world.

God's presence, therefore, pulses and vibrates through the entire natural world, like unstoppable waves of electricity.

FOCUS ON STYLE

Form

'As Kingfishers Catch Fire' is a perfectly formed Petrarchan sonnet. It has the typical Petrarchan rhyme scheme: ABBAABBA CDCDCD. It is divided into an octet (eight lines) and a sestet (six lines). There is a shift in focus between the octet and the sestet. In the octet, Hopkins discusses how every creature and object expresses its inner essence through its actions and appearances. The sestet, on the other hand, deals with issues of morality.

Playing with Vocabulary

In this poem, as always, we find Hopkins playing with vocabulary. In line 9, as we've seen, the noun 'justice' is transformed into the verb 'to justice', meaning to live in a just and righteous fashion according to God's law.

In line 7, meanwhile, the noun 'self' is transformed into the verb 'to self'. Everything in nature, according to Hopkins, 'selves', meaning it expresses its own inner qualities. Everything 'goes itself', acting in accordance with its own nature. Everthing 'speaks and spells' itself, expressing its inner essence that God gave it.

Hopkins sometimes uses a long phrase as if it were a single adjective. We see this in lines 2 to 3. Instead of saying 'heavy' stones or 'polished' stones, Hopkins refers to 'tumbled over rim in roundy wells' stones!

Words with Many Meanings

Hopkins is well known for deploying words that have multiple meanings. The phrase 'catch fire' in the poem's opening line, as we've seen, describes how the kingfishers seem to blaze when the sunlight hits them. But it might also describe the fish these birds pluck from the water, suggesting that they catch fish whose skins gleam and glimmer. The verb 'draw', too, has multiple meanings. It can describe, as we've see, how the dragonflies seem to attract flame. But it might also describe how their flickering wings 'draw' or paint patterns of blazing colour in the air.

Another example of this unusual arrangement of words occurs in the poem's last two lines: 'Lovely in limbs, and lovely in eyes not his/ To the Father through the features of men's faces'. We could translate this into ordinary speech, as follows: 'Christ's loveliness is visible to the Father in the features of men's faces, in men's limbs and in eyes that are not Christ's own eyes'.

Inscape and Instress

In 'As Kingfishers Catch Fire', as in many of his poems, Hopkins sets out to capture the 'instress' or unique essence of various objects. He does so through 'inscape', a profusion of assonance, alliteration and other musical effects:

- In line 1, Hopkins uses assonance and alliteration to create a pleasant verbal music, reflecting the colourful splendour of kingfishers and dragonflies. Assonance is present through the repeated broad 'a' sound in 'dragonflies draw fame'. Alliteration, meanwhile, features through the repeated 'f ' sound in 'fire', 'flies' and 'flame'.
- It could be argued that there is an 'onomatopoeic' quality to lines 2 and 3. The large number of broad vowel sounds and the alliteration of 'rim into roundy', with its repeated 'r', create a hollow, echoing music that mimics the sound of a stone falling down a well.
- Onomatopoeia also occurs in lines 3 to 4. The repeated 'b' sound in 'bell' and 'bow', and the rhyme between 'swung' and 'tongue' gives these lines a loud, booming quality, suggestive of the ringing bell they describe.

Metaphor, Simile, Figures of Speech

Hopkins uses a metaphor to describe the effect of sunlight striking the dragonflies' and kingfishers' bodies. It appears, he says, that these beautiful creatures have caught fire. Hopkins also uses a wonderful metaphor to describe the sound of the bell ringing, declaring that the bell is shouting out its name. The bell, he suggests, 'flings' its name throughout the surrounding countryside: 'each hung bell's/ Bow swung finds tongue to fling out broad its name'.

Sprung Rhythm

Hopkins was known for his unique 'sprung rhythm'. He would combine syllables to create bouncing, irregular rhythmic effects. These were quite unlike the rhythms of ordinary speech and the regular rhythms of traditional verse. An example can be heard in lines 3 to 4 ('each hung bell's/ Bow swung finds tongue to fling out broad its name') which, if read aloud, have a procussive rhythmic quality that mimics the chiming of the bell the lines describe.

Syntax

Unusual syntax or word order is another signature feature of Hopkins's poetry. We this, for instance, in lines 2 to 3, 'As tumbled over rim in roundy wells/ Stones ring'. We would ordinarily put it like this: 'Stones make a ringing sound when they are thrown over the rims or edges of roundy wells'.

.

LINE BY LINE

Hopkins came to St Beuno's College to begin his study of theology in 1874. St. Beuno's is located in rural North Wales and commands spectacular views of the Vale of Clwyd and Snowdonia. Hopkins immediately fell in love with Wales, its language and its countryside. 'Spring' was one of a number of poems that he wrote during this happy time in Wales, and it wonderfully reflects his appreciation of the natural beauty of the Vale of Clwyd.

The delights of springtime

The poem's first eight lines focus on the delights of springtime, celebrating various features of the season. Hopkins first celebrates 'weeds', by which he means daisies, dandelions and other wildflowers. To Hopkins, these 'weeds' are not a pestilence or an irritation. They are 'long and lovely and lush', having a beauty of their own that deserves to be praised.

Hopkins uses an interesting metaphor to describe these 'weeds' in line 2, referring to them as 'wheels'. It is possible to imagine the central portion of the wildflower as the wheel's 'hub' and its petals as the 'spokes'. Hopkins then turns to the beauty of a thrushs' eggs. He uses another wonderful metaphor here, comparing the eggs to little patches of sky that have somehow fallen to earth. The eggs are a delicate blue in colour, like the sky above. But the eggs, of course, are lower or closer to the ground than the sky. Hopkins, therefore, describes them as 'little low heavens'. The poet also celebrates the thrush's song, which floats through the forest, echoing from the trees' wooden boughs. It moves, as Hopkins puts it, 'through the echoing timber'. Anyone who hears this song, according to Hopkins, will find it a thrilling, almost electrifying experience. He uses an unusual simile to capture this effect, comparing the notes of the thrush's song to bolts of lightning: 'it strikes like lightnings to hear him sing'.

Hopkins next focuses on a pear tree, which is starting to put out leaves and blossoms: 'The glassy peartree leaves and blooms'. The tree is described as 'glassy' because its leaves are brand new and are shiny and glossy in appearance.

Hopkins then focuses on the sky itself. The sky, he declares, possesses a 'richness', suggesting that it is a blue of unusual depth and intensity. The sky is so blue that it seems tangible to Hopkins, more like a liquid than a collection of gases. The sky, he declares, is 'in a rush', which suggests it washes over the earth below. Its blue seems to be 'descending' or cascading downwards like a waterfall. The peartree's branches seem to 'brush' this rushing torrent of colour: 'they brush/ The descending blue'.

Spring, of course, is the birthing time for lambs. And Hopkins, as he wades through the countryside, is happy to see these loveable newborn creatures 'racing' about the place. The lambs, he declares, are having a 'fling'. This suggests the colloquial sense of 'fling', as in 'having a good time'. But it also suggests the energetic nature of the lambs' movement, how they run, jump and 'fling' themselves around the meadows in which they play.

The meaning of spring

Hopkins compares the springtime countryside to the Garden of Eden.

- The Garden of Eden existed in a state of 'sweet being', a state of utter beauty and perfection. The countryside in springtime, according to Hopkins, exhibits a faint trace or echo of this 'sweet being'.
- The Garden of Eden existed at the very 'beginning' of the world. The springtime countryside, too, is a place of 'beginning', when all of nature seems fresh and new.

These thoughts of Eden lead Hopkins to consider his usual concepts of sin and redemption. Hopkins claims that 'Innocent mind' and 'Mayday' exist in every 'girl and boy'. To Hopkins, 'Mayday' is associated with purity and innocence, perhaps due to the fact that May is traditionally regarded as the month of the Virgin Mary. As they experience the world, however, children inevitably become corrupted by sin. Each 'Innocent mind', Hopkins declares, will 'cloy', 'cloud' and 'sour with sinning'. Each child's innocence, therefore, is presented as a pure and perfect liquid that slowly becomes polluted over time. First, it cloys, becoming disgustingly sweet. Then it turns cloudy and sour.

The poet calls on Christ to somehow prevent this process of corruption. He requests Christ to 'Have' and 'get' each boy and girl, to take them to Him before their innocence is clouded and soured: 'Have, get … Christ, lord … Innocent mind and Mayday in girl and boy'. Hopkins, therefore, makes a passionate plea to Christ, who he addresses as the 'maid's child' because he was born of a maid or virgin. According to the poet, the majority of these children are 'worthy the winning'. They are worth the effort it would take for Christ to 'win' them, to take them to Him and preserve their sinless nature: 'Most, O maid's child, thy choice and worthy the winning'.

THEMES

SIN AND REDEMPTION

'Spring', like many of Hopkins' poems, is greatly concerned with the idea of sin. Hopkins presents the world as a pernicious place, one that inevitably corrupts every human being. Children, he believes, possess a special kind of innocence, but as they grow older, as they experience more of this corrupting world, that innocence will inevitably 'cloud' and 'sour'.

Only Christ, Hopkins believes, can prevent this process of corruption. Christ must 'Have' and 'get' these children before they are exposed to the world and its corrupting ways. He wants Christ to be an active presence in their lives as they grow up, shielding and counteracting the world's wicked influence, so they can retain some of their innocence.

'Spring' presents the world as a kind of fallen place. In the beginning, Hopkins suggests, the world knew a kind of perfection, hosting the Garden of Eden, which was a kind of paradise on Earth. But those days are long since gone.

The countryside in springtime, according to Hopkins, is reminiscent of the 'Eden garden', giving us a brief and partial glimpse of this utopian world. But the perfection of those early days can never come again.

Perhaps Hopkins is taking the biblical tale of Eden seriously here and thinking back to a time before Adam disobeyed God and sin entered the world. Or perhaps he is suggesting that humanity has grown ever more sinful and selfish over the centuries, since the beginning of our time on earth. Or perhaps, as in 'God's Grandeur', he is thinking ecologically and referring to the fact that human beings, with each passing year, make the world a more and more imperfect place.

THE BEAUTY OF NATURE

'Spring' highlight's Hopkins' intense love of the natural world. We sense that he is almost overwhelmed by the beauty of the springtime countryside, declaring that 'Nothing is so beautiful as spring'. The sights and sounds of spring induce in him a kind of ecstasy, a kind of natural high. He is electrified by the sound of birdsong and is so overcome by the beauty of the sky that he feels its blueness washing all about him.

There is something sensual, almost sexual, in Hopkins' description of spring as a time of 'juice and joy'. The 'joy' suggests the simple pleasures of springtime – the gambolling lambs, the blue skies and the pleasant sound of birdsong. The term 'juice', meanwhile, suggests rebirth and renewal. The leaves, blooms and flowers are rich with sap and moisture, as they emerge after the barrenness of winter. The thrush's eggs, too, are filled with liquids that will in time give rise to new life.

FOCUS ON STYLE

Form

Like many of Hopkins' poems, this is a Petrarchan sonnet. It has the typical Petrarchan rhyme scheme: ABBAABBA CDCDCD. It is divided into an octet (eight lines) and a sestet (six lines). There is a shift in focus between the octet and the sestet. In the octet, Hopkins discusses the beauty and joy of springtime. The sestet, on the other hand, deals with issues of innocence and sin. These defining features of the Petrarchan sonnet are also evident in 'God's Grandeur'.

Syntax

Hopkins is known for using unusual syntax or word order. We see this in lines 11 to 14, for instance, where the words are ordered in a very different way from everyday speech. Were we to express this in normal speech, we might say something along the lines of 'Take hold of the innocent minds of all girls and boys before they are clouded, cloyed and soured with sinning'.

Compression

Hopkins is well known as a poet of compression, one who frequently leaves out words and even entire phrases in order to create particular musical effects. Such compression is evident in the poem's third line where the poet omits the word 'like'. This makes us read faster, maintaining the pace of the verse and suggesting the buzzing energy of springtime: 'Thrush's eggs look little low heavens ...'

Words With Many Meanings

Hopkins is well known for deploying words that have multiple meanings. The word 'strain' in line 10, for instance, can be read in a number of ways. It might mean a snatch of melody or song, suggesting that springtime is a 'faint echo' of the way the world was in its early Eden-like state. But 'strain' can also mean trace or streak, suggesting that the Garden of Eden has left an impression on this world, one that is still visible in springtime.

We also see this with the word 'fair' in line 8. It suggests the 'fair' weather of springtime. It suggests the 'fairness', the beauty and attractiveness, of springtime. It also brings to mind the colloquial or dialect sense of fair, meaning 'to a high degree', suggesting that limbs are having a remarkable 'fling' for themselves as they race around the countryside.

Inscape and Instress

Hopkins uses 'inscape', a profusion of assonance and alliteration, to capture the essence of an object or sensation. We see this in the description of the weeds, for instance, where the alliteration created by the repeated 'l' sounds captures the weeds' beauty and abundance. We also see this in the description of the thrush's song, where a profusion of assonance captures the bird's sweet and energetic tune. We see this with the repeated 'e' and 'i' sounds in 'echoing timber' and the repeated 'i' sounds in the phrases 'rinse and wring' and 'strikes like lightnings'.

Metaphor, Simile, Figures of Speech

The poem, as we've seen, is rich in metaphor and simile. Wildflowers are compared to 'wheels', while the thrush's eggs are compared to patches of sky and its melodies to bolts of lightning. Hopkins also uses the metaphor of laundry to describe the effect of the thrush's singing. The thrush's song, he says, cleanses the ears of those who hear it, just as one might clean a garment or a towel. First, it 'rinses' our ears, washing away the noise and babble we have to put up with on a daily basis. Then it 'wrings' them, squeezing out any unpleasantness that might remain.

Sprung Rhythm

Hopkins was known for his unique 'sprung rhythm'. He would combine syllables to create bouncing, irregular rhythmic effects. These were quite unlike the rhythms of ordinary speech and the regular rhythms of traditional verse. An example can be heard in lines 10 and 11 ('A strain of the earth's sweet being in the beginning/ In Eden garden'), which, if read aloud, have a rather jerky but rather pleasant musical quality.

Playing with Vocabulary

Hopkins is a poet who loves to play with vocabulary. We see this in line 6, where he uses the noun 'leaves' as a verb, by which he means to grow or put out leaves: 'The peartree leaves'.

We also see this tendency in line 2, where the weeds 'shoot' out of the ground. Hopkins brings to mind not only 'shoot' as a verb, meaning to move suddenly and rapidly, but also a noun, meaning a plant's roots or tendrils.

Pied Beauty

'skies of couple-colour as a brinded cow'

LINE BY LINE

Hopkins loves aspects of nature that have a 'pied' or patchwork appearance. He also loves aspects of the natural world that have a 'dappled' appearance, which means marked with spots or rounded patches. These irregular surfaces, to Hopkins, are far more attractive and engaging than regular ones.

Hopkins reminds us that sometimes the sky itself can have a 'pied' appearance. The sky, at such times, is 'couple-colour[ed]', being formed from two very different shades. We can imagine a sky streaked with blue and white, or blue and pink, or even two contrasting shades of grey.

Fallen chestnuts, too, might be said to exhibit a 'pied' appearance. Hopkins describes chestnuts that are 'Fresh... falls', suggesting that they have just tumbled from the branches on which they grew. Their shells have cracked open, revealing their red and yellow interiors. Their overall, appearance, therefore might be described as a patchwork of blacks, browns, yellows and reds.

The landscape itself exhibits a 'pied' or patchwork appearance. The landscape, as Hopkins puts it using a typical coinage, has been 'plotted' or divided into various plots and fields. Some fields are associated with the 'plough', suggesting that they're being used to grow crops. Some are described as a 'fold', which suggests that animals are grazing on them. Some are described as 'fallow', which means they've been left idle so that their nutrients and fertility might be restored. When viewed from above, therefore, the landscape seems to have been 'pieced' together like a patchwork quilt from all these different-looking plots of land. Trout, meanwhile, might be said to have a dappled appearance. Their skin, as Hopkins points out, is covered in 'rose-moles', in rounded markings that are a reddish brown in colour. This proliferation of markings lends them a 'stippled' effect when we watch them swimming in a clear summer stream. Their skin, rather than a continuous surface, seems to be composed of innumerable little dots.

Finches, too, might be described as dappled. Anyone who has studied these birds will have noted how their wings are marked with countless rounded dots, an assemblage of blacks, browns greys and yellows. Hopkins then turns to the various workers that might be seen throughout the countryside. He has in mind, no doubt, 'trádes' or occupations like that of ploughman, harvester or shepherd. He focuses on the clothing worn by these workers, on their 'gear and tackle and trim'. Their clothing, he suggests, has a pied appearance. And we can imagine how a farmer's work jacket might have patches stitched over various areas of wear and tear. Indeed, we can imagine that 'gear' might be a patchwork to begin with, having been assembled from bits and pieces of older worn-out garments.

Hopkins then turns his atention to God, who 'fathers-forth' everything special and beautiful we see around us. God, he maintains, creates everthing that is 'counter', that exhibits a shifting, changing nature. God, he suggests, is also responsible for everyting that is 'original' and unique or 'spare'. And God, of course, is responsible for everything that is 'strange', every aspect of the natural world that fills us with wonder and fascination.

GOD'S PRESENCE IN NATURE

Hopkins, using a tpical coinage, describes how God 'fathers-forth' everything we see around us. This suggests a number of things:

- The phrase, tellingly, is in the present tense, suggesting God's work of creation is ceaseless and ongoing.
- It presents God as a father and the natural world as His child. But God, of course, is a father who doesn't need a mother to bring life into existence. He can simply bring it 'forth' himself.
- It presents God as a benign, paternal figure, who presides over and tends to His creation.

Hopkins emphasises God's beautiful and unchanging nature. God not only creates the beautiful world that surrounds us, but is also Himself a beautiful being. The beauty of the world constantly alters, as individual aspects of nature appear, evolve and pass away. God's own beauty, however, is 'past change'. It exists in a state of unimaginable perfection, utterly constant and unchanging as the millennia go by.

Hopkins, we sense, is mystified by God's creative abilities, especially by His ability to create things that are 'fickle' or 'freckled'. God's creative abilities, Hopkins suggests, are a mystery no human being could ever understand: 'who knows how?' We can only shake our heads in awe at his remarkable accomplishments.

The poem, then, concludes with a call for human beings to praise God. We must laud God the way we would a great athlete or artist. We must give 'Glory' to God, thanking Him for surrounding us with beautiful things, especially things that are 'Pied' or 'dappled'.

FOCUS ON STYLE

Form

'Pied Beauty' is written in a form Hopkins invented, termed the 'curtal' or shortened sonnet. It consists of two sections: the first six lines in length and the second five lines in length. 'Pied Beauty', like most sonnets, has a shift or 'volta' between its two sections. The section lists a number of 'Pied' or 'dappled' things, while the second focuses on God's creative efforts.

Playing with Vocabulary

The poem features a number of neologisms or newly coined words or phrases:

- He invents a new adjective 'couple-colour', for instance, to describe an object that has two contrasting shades.
- He invents a brand new noun 'rose-moles' to describe the spots or circular markings on a trout's skin.
- In line 9, meanwhile, he coins the adjective 'adazzle', meaning bright.

Hopkins' playfulness is most pronounced in lines 8 to 9, where he focuses on aspects of nature that are 'fickle' or 'freckled'. Fickle things shift and change from one moment to the next. Something 'fickle', like a cat, for instance, might be 'swift' one moment and 'slow' the next.

'Freckled' things, meanwile, exhibit two contrasting features at the same time. Hopkins describes aspects of nature that are 'freckled ... With swift [and] slow', that are 'freckled ... With ... sweet [and] sour' and 'freckled ... With ... adazzle [and] dim'. A mountain stream, for instance, might be described as 'freckled' because it can be both 'swift' and 'slow' at the same time.

Metaphor, Simile, Figures of Speech

Hopkins, using a wonderful metaphor, compares each fallen chestnut to a 'fire-coal', to a smouldering lump of coal that's been taken from a hearth. He also uses a most unusual simile to describe a partly cloudy sky, comparing it to a cow that is 'brinded', which means streaky or patchy in appearance.

Inscape and Instress

Hopkins uses 'inscape', a profusion of musical effects, to emphasise the beauty of various aspects of the natural world. Assonance, for instance, features in 'finches-wings', where the repeated 'i' sounds create a pleasant musical effect. Alliteration, meanshile, features in line 5, where the repeated 'p', 'f' and 'l' sounds also create a pleasant verbal music appropriate to the countryside's patchwork of fields. Line 2 employs both assonance and alliteration. Its repeated 'c' sound and broad vowel sounds create a euphonious effect that mirrors the beauty of an English summer sky.

Syntax

Hopkins is known for using unusual syntax or word order to create powerful rhythmic effects. This is especially evident in lines 7 to 10. Using more conventional syntax, we might write the lines as follows: 'He whose beauty is past change fathers-forth everything that is contradictory, original, unique and strange, everything that is fickle or freckled ...' Hopkins' departure from ordinary syntax can leave the reader temporarily mystified, just as he himself is mystified by the sheer extent of God's creative abilities.

The Windhover

LINE BY LINE

This sonnet was written in May 1877. Hopkins, at the time, was studying in the Jesuit house of theological studies, St Beuno's College, near St Asaph in North Wales. This was a particularly happy period in the poet's life. Hopkins enjoyed taking regular morning walks through the the Vale of Clwyd and the rest of the countryside around St. Beuno's, relishing the open expanses and the play of light upon the landscape. 'The Windhover', inspired by the sighting of a falcon on one such morning walk, was written a few months before Hopkins' ordination and was described by the poet himself as 'the best thing [he] ever wrote'. 'The Windhover', like many of Hopkins' poems, is a Petrarchan sonnet. The octet, or first eight lines, describes the falcon's flight. The sestet, or final six lines, meditates on the significance of the falcon's flight.

The poet describes how he 'caught' or caught sight of a falcon. Hopkins' uses one of his favourite techniques to describe the bird, mashing several adjectives together to create a single compound phrase: 'dapple-dawn-drawn'. This suggests how the falcon's feathers are 'dappled', marked with a pattern of circular spots. Hopkins, as 'Pied Beauty' suggests, had a great weakness for such dappled patterning in nature. The term 'dawn-drawn', meanwhile, suggests how the falcon has been 'drawn' or attracted by the dawn's light to set out on its day's hunting.

The kingdom of daylight

Hopkins uses an interesting extended metaphor in these opening lines:

- Daylight is compared to a kingdom, to a bright and glittering realm.
- The morning, meanwhile, is personified as the kingdom's ruler (personification, we remember, occurs when an abstract concept is presented as if it were a person).
- The falcon in turn is presented as the kingdom's crown prince or 'dauphin'.
- Just as a prince loyally serves his king, so the falcon is depicted as the loyal 'minion' or servant of the morning.

The falcon, then, is presented as a creature of light and brightness. It is also presented as a noble or regal being, as a courtly 'minion' or a princely 'dauphin'.

The falcon rides upon the air

Hopkins refers to the falcon's 'riding/ Of the ... air', describing how the bird glides upon currents of air as it travels across the sky. He declares that the bird was 'striding/ High there', suggesting that the bird, as it glided upon these thermals, exhibited confidence grace and power. Hopkins deploys another of his favourite techniques to describe these thermals, using a long phrase as a single adjective. Instead of saying the 'warm' air or the 'rippling' air he says the 'rolling level underneath him steady' air. These air-currents were sometimes rolling and sometimes level as the falcon passed over them. But his flight path remained steady, suggesting how he almost effortlessly adjusted to compensate for the shifts or changes in the air 'underneath him'.

The falcon spirals and swerves

The poet watched as the falcon folded or wimpled one of its wings. Then it 'wrung' or rotated the rest of its body around this 'wimpling wing', so that it moved in tight, highly controlled circles. Hopkins describes how the bird seemed to exhibit 'ecstasy' as it spiralled in this fashion, as if it delighted in its own skill and agility.

Hopkins uses a typically inventive metaphor to describe the falcon's folded wing, comparing it to a rein: 'the rein of a wimpling wing'. Reins, of course, are the straps to guide and steer horses. It's a metaphor that presents the falcon as a horseman, and the air itself as the horse on which he rides. It suggests that the falcon uses its folded wing to expertly manipulate the currents of air it passes through as it spirals around the sky.

Hopkins compares the falcon to a skater who expertly steers around a 'bow bend', a long curve in the frozen path on which he's skating. Hopkins seems to imagine the skater taking this bend at pace, angling his body and balancing on the heel of a single skate. He imagines the skater's heel 'sweeps clean', that he moves in a smooth and continuous arc, expertly tracking the curve in the path. It's a vivid metaphor, one that conveys the grace and elegance of the falcon's 'swing' across the sky.

The falcon encounters the 'big wind'

The falcon, it seems, had been enjoying perfect conditions for flying. But then the weather changed suddenly and a 'big wind' started blowing. This seems to have been quite a gale, one severe enough to damage any bird that flew directly into it. And yet the falcon, seemingly with little regard for its own safety, flew right into the teeth of the gale.

The falcon's flight into the wind is depicted in military terms, as an assault on a hostile power. Hopkins imagines the falcon and the wind as two opposing warriors parleying before a battle, discussing terms on which combat might still be avoided. The 'big wind' gave the falcon the opportunity to call off hostilities. If the falcon turned back and ceased its attack, the wind would leave it unharmed. The falcon, however, 'rebuffed' or rejected these terms of surrender. Instead, it continued its attack, flying directly into the teeth of the gale.

The falcon, it is important to note, has nothing practical to gain from flying into the gale. It seems to view this 'big wind' as an irresistible challenge, the way a mountain climber might

feel compelled to climb Mount Everest. Perhaps the falcon wants to test its strength against the wind's overwhelming force. Perhaps it wants to demonstrate its 'mastery' of the skies, to show that no other creature or force will ever dominate it.

Meditating on the falcon

The sonnet's last six lines (or sestet) shift from the past to the present tense. We imagine that Hopkins is back at St Beuno's sitting at his desk meditating on what he saw 'this morning', especially on the falcon's flight into the 'big wind'.

The falcon, Hopkins suggests, exhibited 'beauty' during this flight. The adjective 'Brute', however, suggests this was a forceful, almost violent, beauty as the falcon flew onward despite the damage inflicted on its body by the wind. The adjective 'Brute' also means unpleasant but necessary, suggesting that the falcon, on one level, had no choice but to confront the wind in this manner. By doing so, it was responding to its deepest instincts as a hunter.

To Hopkins, the falcon's flight into the wind was an 'act'. By this he means no ordinary action, but a feat, a deed that requires great strength, skill and bravery. Hopkins thinks of the 'air' into which the falcon flew so stubbornly and the 'pride' it seemed to exhibit as it did so. The term 'plume' picks up on this notion of pride. On one level, it refers to the bird's plummage, its covering of feathers. But on another level, to 'plume' means to engage in an extravagant of self-conscious display, suggesting the falcon, as it flies into the wind, is perfectly aware of the prowess it is exhibiting.

The falcon, finally, was defeated by the sheer ferocity of the wind into which it flew. Hopkins recalls how the bird seemed to 'Buckle', suggesting how its body bent and crumpled in the face of the wind's onslaught. The bird, then, was in a state of utter collapse. We can imagine it falling from the sky, lifeless and exhausted. The phrase 'here/ Buckle' suggests the vividness with which Hopkins can recall the events of the morning. It is as if the falcon's body is crumpling again before his mind's eye as he sits in his study in St. Beuno's.

Line 9, it should be noted, is a list of individual terms rather than what might be considered a proper sentence. This breakdown in sentence structure, it has been suggested, reflects the breakdown of the bird's body as it is crushed by the wind's overwhelming force. But it also suggests Hopkins' inability to fully process what he saw that morning. When he thinks about the falcon's flight, he is so overcome with emotion that he can't quite organise his thoughts into a coherent sentence. All he can do, as suggested by the vocative 'oh', is gasp inwardly in amazement. Line 9 is also remarkable for its wonderfully jerky rhythm, which reflects the falcon's flight into the wind, capturing how the bird pressed forward and was blown back, pressed forward and was again blown back.

FOCUS ON STYLE

Sprung Rhythm

Hopkins was known for his unique 'sprung rhythm', the combining of syllables to create bouncing, irregular rhythmic effects. This is especially evident in line 6 ('As a skate's heel sweeps smooth on a bow-bend'), which creates a smooth, yet propulsive, rhythmic effect, one that reflects the elegance of a skater gliding around a curve or the falcon gliding across the sky.

Metaphor, Simile, Figures of Speech

Hopkins often uses the metaphor of fire to describe the beauty of the world around us. Beauty, he suggests, emanates from beautiful objects like flames from a burning coal (we see this in 'God's Grandeur', for instance, where he describes how beauty will 'flame' out from objects in the natural world). We see this when he describes how 'fire' seemed to 'break' from Christ's suffering body during the crucifixion. The term 'break' suggests a sudden eruption or explosion of flame. Hopkins isn't suggesting, of course, that Christ spontaneously combusted. The flames are metaphorical, representing the unparalleled meaning and beauty of this moment.

Compression

The phrase 'a billion/ Times told lovelier' is an example of Hopkins' use of compression. We might unpack the phrase by re-writing it as follows: 'The fire that breaks from you, Christ, will be told of a billion times and is a billion times lovelier'. This captures how the 'fire' of the crucifixion, the beauty and majesty of that extraordinary event, will be retold countless times as the story spreads around the world and is passed on from generation to generation.

This phrase also captures the unsurpassed beauty of the crucifixion. Many events, like that of the falcon crumpling in the wind, are beautiful. And the beauty they exhibit is compared to 'fire' that emanates from their bodies. But the crucifixion is the most beautiful event of all. And the 'fire' that emanates from Christ's suffering body is a 'billion times ... lovelier' than that emanating from the falcon's body or any other sight.

Inscape and Instress

Hopkins uses 'inscape', a profusion of assonance and alliteration, to capture the essence of an object or sensation. We see this in the first four lines, which are exceptionally rich in assonance and alliteration. Alliteration, for instance, features in the first line, with its succession of 'm' sounds, and in the second line, which features a series of 'd' sounds. 'R's and 'w's, meanwhile, feature in the fourth line.

Assonance is equally prominent. We see this in the repeated 'o' and 'i' sounds in the opening line and the repeated 'a' sounds in the second line. A combination of 'i' and 'e' sounds, meanwhile, features in lines 2 and 3.

This combination of alliteration and assonance creates an extraordinary euphonious, ringing verbal music, that reflects the majesty of the falcon as it swerves and spirals in the sky above.

Words With Many Meanings

Hopkins has a tendency to deploy key words that can be interpreted in several different ways. The word 'Buckle' in line 10 is a perfect example of this tendency.

- The term 'Buckle', as we've seen, can mean to collapse under a great weight or force. It brings to mind, therefore, how the falcon's body bent and crumpled as it flew into the 'big wind'. It also brings to mind how Christ's body was broken on the cross.
- But the term can also mean to join or fasten together. It suggests how the poet's recollection of the falcon's flight into the wind combine or fuse at this point in the poem ('here') with the idea of Christ subjecting himself to the ordeal of the crucifixion.
- Finally, the term suggests a knight buckling his helmet or breast-plate as he prepares for battle. The term, on this reading, reinforces our sense of Christ as a 'chevalier' who takes on sin and death on behalf of all humanity.

Imagery

Hopkins, as we've seen, believes that many things are at their most beautiful when broken. He provides two examples of this phenomenon: a freshly ploughed field and embers from a fireplace. We can imaging Hopkins in St. Beuon's gazing out his window at fields in the surrounding countryside or contemplating the fireplace in his study.

Fields, he suggests, are at their most beautiful when their topsoil has been broken and upturned by ploughing. Hopkins describes how a ploughman's 'shéer plód', his utterly monotonous and plodding labour, will produce a field of 'sillion'. 'Sillion' is a brand new term coined by Hopkins himself to describe freshly ploughed soil that is so rich and glossy it seems to glitter or 'Shine' in the sun.

The poet suggests that 'embers', too, are at their most beautiful when broken. Embers, in this instance, refers to small pieces of coal in a dying fire. Such embers, nearly extinguished, exhibit only a faint blue glow. But when they 'Fall' through the grate and strike the base of the fireplace, they break and burst into flame again, blazing with brief but exquisite light.

THE BEAUTY OF NATURE

Like many of Hopkins' poems, 'The Windhover' reveals the poet's love of the natural world. The poet relishes the sight of the falcon, which is depicted as a fierce and dangerous hunter. The falcon, then, possesses a 'Brute beauty', beauty of a brutal and ferocious kind. This contrasts with the gentler aspects of nature celebrated in 'Spring' and 'Pied Beauty'.

The falcon is presented as a regal being, reminiscent of a knight or prince. It exhibits poise, confidence and control as it goes 'striding' through the sky, manipulating the air-thermals on which it cruises. It is also an elegant creature, gliding smoothly and crisply through the air. To the poet, the falcon seems caught up in an 'ecstasy' as if it relished its own strength, power and control. Perhaps most notable of all is the bird's 'valour' or bravery, which we see in its willingness to test itself against the 'big wind'.

The poet declares that his heart has been in 'hiding'. This reminds us that the poem was written during the last year of study for the priesthood. He has been suppressing his artistic vocation in favour of his priestly one. He had been focusing, not on the beauty of the natural world, but, instead, on spiritual matters. Certain important aspects of his personality, then, had been hidden away. But seeing the falcon 'stirred' his heart. He was no longer capable of suppressing his love of nature or his poetic creativity. He feels compelled to let these aspects of his personality come to the fore again and to give them free expression.

The poet associates the falcon with achievement and mastery: 'the achieve of, the mastery of the thing'. This may refer to the falcon's own achievement and mastery, to the strength and skill it displays as it powers through the sky. However, it might also refer to God, who displayed great achievement and mastery by creating the falcon in the first place.

THE RELATIONSHIP BETWEEN GOD AND MAN

Hopkins, no doubt, has a crucifix on the wall of his room in St. Beuno's. We can imagine how Hopkins, as he writes about the falcon, glances up every now and again at this image of Christ's suffering. It suddenly dawns on him that the falcon and Christ are similar in many respects.

This brings Hopkins back to one of his central themes – the relationship between man and God. For Hopkins, this relationship centres on the crucifixion. Christ's sufferings on the cross offer every human being the possibility of salvation, from sin and hell, and the potential of eternal life.

Hopkins stresses the physicality of the crucifixion, emphasising that it was a brutal and arduous ordeal. Like the falcon, then, Christ exhibited great 'valour' as he subjected himself to unimaginable physical pain. Christ's acceptance of the cross, like the falcon's assault on the wind, was an 'act', a feat of remarkable bravery and conviction.

Christ's death on the cross, like the falcon's destruction by the wind, exhibited a kind of 'beauty'. The 'beauty' of the crucifixion, of course, stems from the fact that it offers each of us salvation. The 'beauty' of the crucifixion, like that of the falcon's demise, is a 'Brute beauty'. It was 'Brute' in the sense that it involved physical force and violence, as Christ's body was tortured and maimed. But it was also 'Brute' in the sense that it was a horrific but necessary event, being the only way that humanity would be worthy of salvation.

It's 'No wonder', the poet declares, that Christ exhibited his greatest beauty and magnificence when he was broken on the cross. As is often the case, many things are at their most magnificent when they break. He provides two other examples of such things, which are described in 'Imagery' below.

The crucifixion, of course, is a historical event, one that took place over 2,000 years ago. But it is also one that is still very real today, offering each Christian the opportunity of salvation. We see this in Hopkins' choice of tense, when he writes 'the fire that breaks from thee then' rather than 'the fire that *broke* from thee then'. The crucifixion, therefore, is presented as an event that resonates through all of history, that still offers every human being the opportunity of salvation.

The poet likens Christ to a 'chevalier' or knight. Just as a chevalier exhibits great bravery on the battlefield, so Christ exhibited great bravery on the cross. This concept of Christ as a kind of knight in shining armour is set up earlier in the poem when Hopkins compares the falcon to a horseman. Many stories about knights highlight how they fight on behalf of someone else, risking their lives so their lord or lady doesn't have to. Christ, Hopkins suggests, acted in such a fashion during the crucifixion, sacrificing his own life on behalf of all mankind.

The poem also highlights the intensely personal nature of the poet's feelings towards Christ. We see this in line 10, where the capitalised 'AND' signals a sudden shift in the poem, as Hopkins starts addressing Christ directly. The vocative 'O' indicates a gasp of emotion and we can imagine Hopkins being overcome with awe and admiration as he contemplates the crucifix above his desk. The fact that Hopkins refers to Christ as 'my chevalier' and 'my dear' suggests the intense bond he feels with his Lord. We sense the poet's deep personal gratitude that Christ suffered for his sins in order that he might reach the kingdom of heaven.

Inversnaid

One of several mountain streams in Inversnaid, near Loch Lomond. This is claimed to be the particular stream that inspired Hopkins' poem

LINE BY LINE

This poem was inspired by a trip Hopkins made to the Scottish Highlands, where he was very taken with the wild beauty of this landscape. In this poem, he celebrates the movement of a stream, or 'burn', as it flows down the hillside to the lake below.

Hopkins first focuses on the burn's upper course, when it is more a waterfall than a stream per se. Its course is described as a 'highroad', suggesting the great height from which it gushes. The burn, we're told in line 2, goes 'roaring down', suggesting its power and force. The burn, at this early stage of its course, doesn't have proper banks or a definite course. Instead, it travels in a 'rollrock' fashion, bouncing and deflecting from the various obstacles in its path.

The colour of the burn's surface is a dark or 'darksome' shade of brown, one that Hopkins compares to a horse's coat. This comparison reinforces our sense of the burn's strength and power by comparing it to a galloping horse. Its surface bucks, rocks and tosses like the muscled back of a racehorse galloping at full pelt.

The burn's waters encounter a rocky outcrop that causes them to slow and deepen, forming a kind of mini whirlpool. The water in this pool is so dark that Hopkins describes it as 'pitchblack'. It seems unpleasantly thick and soupy, as if it were a broth or stew: 'the broth/ Of a pool so pitchblack'. This black little whirlpool is described as 'féll-frówning'. The fact that it is 'frówning' suggests its depressing, gloomy appearance. The fact that it is 'féll', meanwhile, suggests that its gloomy pitch-black waters are sinister, evil and threatening.

On the surface of this pool Hopkins sees a rather unpleasant layer of foam or froth. This froth is a brownish 'fawn' in colour. It 'rounds and rounds', circling on the surface of the whirlpool

in a spiral pattern: 'Turns and twindles'. Finally, it is sucked into the pool's pitch-black depths.

Hopkins switches focus from the burn's upper course to its middle course. Its waters leave the whirlpool and continue on their journey. Now the burn is a proper 'brook' or stream, with proper 'braes' or banks. It easily treads or steps its way through the various 'groins' it encounters.

Hopkins notices that the burn's banks are covered in dew on this Highland morning. The banks, he declares, are sprinkled or 'degged' with dew. He also describes them as being 'dappled' with dew. To be 'dappled', we remember, is to be marked with spots or rounded patches. This suggests that the banks are covered with innumerable little blots of moisture: 'Degged with dew, dappled with dew/ Are the groins of the braes'.

Hopkins describes the plant life that grows upon these banks. There are packs or clusters of wiry heather ('heathpacks'). There are 'flitches' or thin strands of fern. There is an ash tree that 'sits over' the burn's waters. The tree is covered with berries that give it a beautiful or 'bonny' appearance.

Hopkins finally focuses on what might be described as the mature phase of the burn's course towards the lake. It meanders through 'coops', a word Hopkins coined to describe enclosed hollows. It forms 'combs', which he defined as uneven and rippling stretches of water.

We're told that the foaming water 'Flutes' as it nears the lake that is its 'home' or final destination: 'Flutes and low to the lake falls home'. The word 'flute' may refer to the musical instrument, suggesting that the water 'Flutes' or makes a pleasant musical sound as it meets the lake. Or it may refer to flutes as in champagne glasses, suggesting that the foam breaks into fizzy flute-shaped rivulets as it finally falls towards the lake.

The poet's plea

The poet is well aware that places like Inversnaid are under threat in our industrial age. 'What would the world be, once bereft/ Of wet and of wildness?', he asks, wondering what this earth will resemble once it's 'bereft' or deprived of such beautiful wilderness locations. The answer, of course, is that the world would be a terrible place without 'wet and wildness', without unspoilt countryside and unpolluted rivers. 'Let them be left,/ O let them be left', he says, pleading for such areas of unspoiled countryside to be left alone by industry and development. The poem's last line, therefore, is a defiant cry for the wilderness to survive long into the future: 'Long live the weeds and the wilderness yet'.

FOCUS ON STYLE

Inscape and Instress

Hopkins uses 'inscape', a profusion of assonance and alliteration, to capture the essence of an object or sensation. Alliteration predominates in the first stanza. We see this with the repeated 'r' sounds in line 2: 'rollrock highroad roaring down'. Line 3, also, is rich in alliteration with the repeated 'c' sound in 'coop and in comb', and the 'f' sound in 'fleece of his foam'. This alliteration lends the stanza a powerful rhythmic pulse, capturing the freshness and energy of the brook as it rushes down the slope.

A similar vibrancy is evident in stanza 3. Once again, alliteration is used extensively. We see it in the repeated 'd' sound in 'Degged with dew, dappled with dew', the 'br' sound in 'braes of that brook', and the 'f' sound in 'flitches of fern'.

Playing with Vocabulary

Hopkins is famous for playing with language. He often invented or coined new words to convey his desired meaning. In the second stanza, for instance, he comes up with a new verb 'twindles' to capture the water's unique movement. 'Twindles' is a verb that Hopkins made up himself, meaning to 'twist' and 'dwindle' at the same time.

The poet is also renowned for the way he combines existing words to create new compound words. For example, he uses the word 'rollrock' in line 2 to convey the rolling of the water over the rocks and the word 'pitchblack' to describe the darkness of the pool. In line 5, he combines the words 'fawn' and 'froth' to capture the colour of the foam that the churning water creates. Two other such combinations, 'heathpacks' and 'beadbonny', are used to describe the plantlife on the burn's banks.

In the third stanza meanwhile, Hopkins uses a number of words from the Scottish dialect, including 'braes', 'degged', 'bonny' and 'burn', which reinforce our sense of the poem's Highland setting.

THE BEAUTY OF NATURE

Hopkins, as we've seen, celebrates he beauty of the burn at each stage of its journey to the lake below. He captures the thundering energy and momentum of the burn's waters in their upper course. He describes the fertility of its banks during its middle course and he relishes how it meanders, 'combs' and 'flutes' during the last phase of its journey.

Hopkins comes across once again as someone highly sensitive to the natural world, someone who responds to nature in a profoundly emotional fashion. In a poem like 'Spring', this response was a positive one. In 'Inversnaid', however, his response also has a negative dimension. To Hopkins, the 'pitchblack' whirlpool, with its thick, broth-like waters, is a bleak and terrible sight. Contemplating it causes him to be overcome by sorrow. His mind is left 'drowning' in 'Despair' just as a little woodland creature might become trapped in the whirlpool before drowning in its black waters.

Though Hopkins wrote a long time ago, he often exhibits an environmentalism fitting to our own age. We see this in the poem's final stanza where he points out what an unimaginably terrible place the world would be without such places of wild and unspoilt beauty. He concludes with a desperate plea that locations like 'Inversnaid' be spared by industry, building and development: 'Let them be left,/ O let them be left'. As we know today, however, such pleas all too often go ignored in the name of progress.

PHYSICAL AND MENTAL SUFFERING

There is a darkness at the centre of the poem, something disturbing in its depiction of the natural world that was absent in earlier poems such as 'Pied Beauty'. The poem's central image is that of 'the pool so pitchblack' – the little whirlpool in the brook's path that fills Hopkins with such horrified fascination. It's as if staring into its murky 'fell-frowning' depths gives him some premonition of the personal abyss into which he soon will fall, the despair in which he will soon find himself drowning.

'Inversnaid' was written at a time when Hopkins was on the verge of the depression and despair that would characterise the last period of his life. He had sacrificed an incredible amount for God and had served His Church faithfully only to be rewarded with mental anguish and physical illness.

There is an implied contrast between Hopkins himself and the landscape he admires. The burn's banks are a riot of fertility, of heather and ferns and trees. Hopkins, on the other hand, considered his own life to be barren and infertile. The poem, then, looks forward to Hopkins' 'terrible sonnets' such as 'No worst, there is none' and 'I wake and feel the fell of dark' in which he explores personal feelings of incredible despair and devastation.

331

Felix Randal

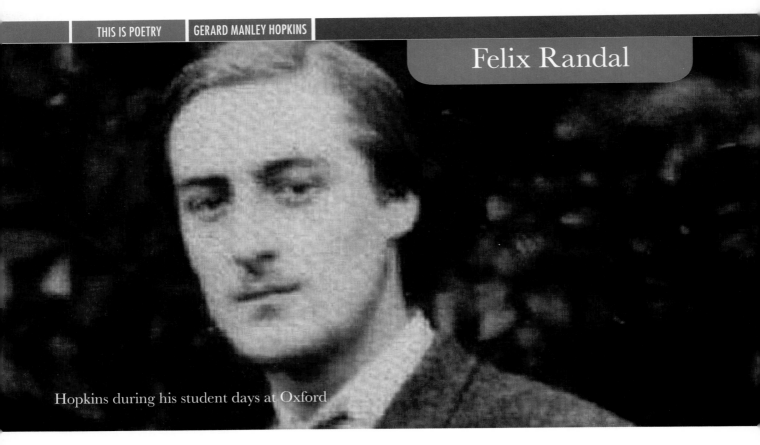

Hopkins during his student days at Oxford

LINE BY LINE

This poem was written in the early 1880s when Hopkins was working as a priest in various parishes between Liverpool and Manchester. Hopkins was horrified by the circumstances of the poor in those industrial cities, which were polluted, dirty and ridden with disease. This poem was inspired by the death of one of his parishioners, a thirty-one-year-old blacksmith (the real-life blacksmith was called Felix Spencer. It is unclear why Hopkins felt compelled to use a different name in his poem).

Lines 1 to 4

One of Hopkins' priestly duties was tending to the sick. He would visit people who were seriously ill, praying with them, offering them spiritual comfort and helping them come to terms with their illness. One man he tended to was Felix Randal, a 'farrier' or blacksmith. Hopkins, at the opening of the poem, has just heard the news of Felix's death: 'Felix Randal the farrier, O he is dead then?' He realises that his duty of care towards Felix is now at an end: 'my duty all ended'.

Hopkins describes Felix's physical appearance before the blacksmith became ill. Felix was 'big-boned', suggesting that he had a large and imposing frame. He was 'hardy', suggesting that he was vigorous, fit and strong. Hopkins, using a typical compound or hyphenated term, claims that Felix was 'hardy-handsome', suggesting that he had rugged good looks bound up with his strength and physicality.

Felix's illness, however, caused him start 'pining, pining', to waste away both mentally and physically (here, The repetition of 'pining' wonderfully captures the slow and relentless progress of Felix's illness). Hopkins, during his visits to Felix, has 'watched' this process of decline. It was an experience, we sense, that Hopkins found painful and depressing.

Hopkins memorably compares Felix's body to a 'mould', describing it as his 'mould of man'. Felix's soul, meanwhile, might be thought of as a liquid metal that is poured into the mould. Hopkins describes how Felix's reason – his faculty of sense and understanding – began to 'ramble' around his mould or body: 'reason rambled in it'. This image of reason rambling, of moving in an unpredictable or erratic fashion, powerfully suggests how Felix's mind, towards the end of his illness, began to breakdown , allowing a form of dementia to set in.

Felix's initial illness weakened his body's defences, allowing other diseases to infect him. By the end, it seems, he suffered from four distinct conditions. Hopkins, using a wonderful turn of phrase, describes how these 'four disorders' were 'fleshed' within him, suggesting that they had taken over the very organs and tissues of his body.

Hopkins describes how these different diseases 'contended' or competed. Perhaps he's describing how each illness fought against Felix's failing immune system. Or perhaps he's suggesting that the diseases 'contended' with one another, each of them attempting to drive out the others so it could have Felix's body all to itself. Eventually, then, this strong and big-boned blacksmith was 'broken' by sickness, was left defeated and destroyed by the various diseases that affected him: 'Sickness broke him'.

Lines 5 to 8

When Felix first became ill, he was 'impatient', which in this instance means angry and rebellious. Indeed, Felix became so angry and rebellious that he cursed God for allowing him to become sick: 'Impatient, he cursed at first'. Some months before Felix's death, however, his 'heart' became 'heavenlier' or holier. He made his peace with God and began to focus on the next life rather than this one: 'a heavenlier heart began some/ Months earlier'. This change of heart, according to Hopkins, was brought about by the sacrament of Holy Communion.

Shortly before Felix's death, Hopkins anointed him with oil as he administered the Last Rites, the sacrament of the sick. According to Hopkins, this sacrament 'mended' Felix, soothing and repairing him on a spiritual level. It allowed him to find an inner serenity during his last days and perhaps accept his imminent demise.

And now Felix has passed away. The phrase 'Ah well!' suggests a tone of resignation. It's as if Hopkins realises that Felix is gone now. There is nothing more that can be done for him. Life simply has to go on.

Lines 9 to 11

Hopkins thinks about the bond that forms between priests and the sick people they visit. This process 'endears' sick individuals to the priests who tend to them. They come to like or even love their priestly visitors: 'This seeing the sick endears them to us'. But this process also 'endears' the priests to the people in their care, suggesting that they devlelop a fondness for the sick people they visit: 'us too it endears'.

Hopkins' visits, it seems, had a great affect on Felix. His 'tongue', the words he spoke and the prayers he prayed, 'taught [Felix] comfort', comforting the blacksmith spiritually and psychologically. Hopkins would 'touch' Felix when the blacksmith wept due to mental as well as physical distress. And such a 'touch', such a hug or friendly arm around the shoulder, would cause Felix's tear to quench or subside.

But Hopkins, too, was affected by these visits. The sight of the blacksmith crying filled Hopkins with sorrow and pity, touching him in a deep and meaningful way: 'Thy tears that touched my heart'. His great sympathy for the suffering blacksmith comes across in the simple but moving repetition of Felix's name: 'Felix, poor Felix Randal'.

Lines 12 to 14

Hopkins imagines Felix back in the days before he became ill. These, according to Hopkins, were Felix's 'more boisterous years'. The term 'boisterous' suggests that Felix was energetic, noisy and cheerful in both his demeanour and behaviour. Before his illness, according to Hopkins, Felix was 'powerful amidst peers', suggesting that he was stronger than any other blacksmith who worked in the forge or in the surrounding area. Hopkins imagines a young and healthy Felix hard at work

'fettling' in the forge. 'Fettle' is an old northern English term meaning to shape or make, suggesting how Felix would have forged brand new horseshoes from molten metal. 'Sandal', on this reading, is a playful metaphor for horseshoe. But 'fettle' also means to shave or scrape, suggesting how Felix, as part of his trade as farrier, would have shaved excess growth of bone from horses' feet. 'Sandal', on this reading, refers to the horse's hoof.

Felix, during those 'boisterous years', never predicted or 'forethought' that he would end up broken by sickness. He never imagined that all too soon he would start 'pining, pining' away to nothing. All such thoughts were 'far' from the mind of this fit, healthy and physically imposing blacksmith.

Hopkins emphasises the imposing nature of the animals with which Felix worked. He pictures Felix making horseshoes for a 'great' or powerful 'drayhorse', which was a type of horse used for pulling carts and other vehicles. Such a drayhorse, he suggests, would have a 'battering' sandal, suggesting the sheer force with which its hooves strike the ground. This description of the drayhorse reinforces our sense of Felix's own strength and power. For he must have had a commanding physical presence, given that he managed, tamed and worked with such fierce and 'battering' animals.

FOCUS ON STYLE

Compression

Hopkins was very much a poet of compression, one who was happy to leave out what he regarded as inessential words in order to add to his rhythmical effects. We see this in line 3, for instance, with the phrase 'till time when reason rambled in it'. Using more ordinary language we might write 'till [the] time [came] when reason rambled in it'. Compression is also evident in line 8 when the poet asks God to grant Felix his rest in the next life: 'God rest him all road ever he offended!' Let's unpack this phrase:

- 'God rest him' is a common phrase, meaning 'May God grant him rest' or 'May God grant him the peace of heaven'.
- 'all road' is a Lancashire phrase, meaning 'in any event' or 'anyway'.
- 'ever he offended', meanwhile, is a classic example of Hopkins's tendency towards compression. We might rewrite as 'whoever he might have offended or sinned against'.

The entire phrase, then, might be rewritten as 'May God grant him rest, anyway, whoever he might have sinned against during his life'.

Playing with Vocabulary

Hopkins was a great lover of language and delighted in using unusual words in his poetry. We see this tendency, for instance, when he uses the word 'random' to describe Felix's forge. Here Hopkins is using the word 'random' in an older sense, which refers to walls made from uncut, irregular stones.

Hopkins' delight in playing with vocabulary also comes across in his tendency to coin new words and phrases. He comes up with the term 'Heavenlier', for instance, meaning holier or more heavenly and the compound-term 'hardy-handsome', which describes Felix's rugged good looks.

Sprung Rhythm

Hopkins unique sprung rhythm can be heard in the poem's final line, which creates a percussive, and swinging rhythmic effect, one reminiscent perhaps of the blacksmith's hammer clashing against an anvil.

Words with Many Meanings

Hopkins is well-known for using words that suggest several meanings at once. We see this with 'child' in line 11. This refers to the fact that Felix was in Hopkins' spiritual care. Felix was Hopkins' responsibility, just as a child might be his or her father's. But it also suggests how illness had reduced Felix to the status of a child, had left him uncertain, vulnerable and helpless.

We also see this when Hopkins describes how he 'Tendered' the sacrament of communion to Felix. On one level this simply means that he gave or administered the sacrament. But on another level it brings to mind the tenderness – the extraordinary gentleness and kindness – of Christ himself.

THEMES

SIN AND REDEMPTION

An important theme in Hopkins' poetry is that of the relationship between man and God. This poem has a particular focus on the sacraments of the church, emphasising how they bring us closer to God and allow us to enter heaven after we die:

- When Hopkins gives Felix the sacrament of communion his heart becomes 'heavenlier'. This phrase, as we've seen, suggests that Felix's thoughts turn from things of this world to things of the next. But it also suggests that his soul becomes cleansed of sin and fit to enter heaven.
- Communion is described as our 'sweet reprieve', which is the cancelation or postponement of a punishment. For it is through communion – and the other sacraments – that we are given the opportunity to escape the punishments of hell and gain heaven's eternal rest.
- Communion is also described as a 'ransom'. It brings to mind the last supper and the crucifixion, recalling how God sacrificed his only son. Christ, Hopkins suggests, was paid as a kind of 'ransom' in order to free humanity from sin.
- The sacrament of the sick, as we've seen, is said to have 'mended' Felix. As we've seen, It mended him psychologically, helping him find peace as he faced death. But it also 'mended' his soul, cleansing it of sin.

The poem also touches on the theme of religious doubt. We see this when Felix becomes 'impatient' with God's will and curses God for allowing him to become sick. The poem, then, raises an age-old question about God's fundamental goodness: If God is so good, Hopkins wonders, then why does he allow his faithful servants to suffer? Felix's doubts are overcome when Hopkins administers the sacraments and he 'mends' his relationship with God. However, in a later sonnet like 'Thou art indeed Just, Lord', however, there is no easy answer to such doubts.

PHYSICAL AND MENTAL SUFFERING

There is something terrible about how this 'big-boned' and 'boisterous' man started 'pining' away to nothing. There is something horrific about the description of four terrible diseases taking root in his flesh and 'contending' with each other to dominate his ailing body. There is something almost unbearably moving about this 'powerful' tradesman being broken by sickness until he ended up weeping in the arms of a visiting priest.

Felix suffered mentally, too. At the beginning of his illness he was so overcome with such despair and anger that he cursed God. Finally, as his illness neared it send, his mind starts to give way and his 'reason rambled' as he slipped into some form of dementia. Felix, it seems, was plagued with mental anguish as his illness progressed. The poem, then, looks forward to the intense mental anguish Hopkins himself suffers in the 'terrible sonnets', such as 'I wake and feel the fell of dark' and 'No worst, there is none'. Hopkins, as we've seen, used words and touch in an attempt to comfort Felix. For Hopkins himself, however, there will be no one to produce such comfort.

The poem also makes the valid point that when we are young and strong, like Felix during his 'more boisterous years', we seldom think about illness. We give no 'forethought' to the difficulties that may await us. Perhaps the poem's abiding message, then, is that we shouldn't take health for granted and should make the most of it while it is ours to enjoy.

No worst, there is none

LINE BY LINE

The poem was probably written in 1885 towards the end of the poet's life when he was working in University College Dublin. At the time, Hopkins was in poor mental and physical health. He found his duties exhausting and unrewarding. Furthermore, he was lonely and miserable in Ireland, a country where he found it difficult to fit in and had few friends. As he put it in a letter, these and the other 'terrible sonnets' were the product of a 'continually jaded and harassed mind'.

Endless torment

Hopkins declares that he has been 'Pitched past pitch of grief'. His torment occupies a place on the scale of suffering that is beyond ordinary 'grief'. He is close to complete despair and possibly even to madness. Furthermore, his mental torment keeps getting worse. He personifies his 'pangs' or pains, depicting them as willing students. Each new pain, he suggests, has learned from earlier pains how best to make him suffer. He describes each new 'pang', therefore, as having been 'schooled' by the pangs that went before ('forepangs').

Each new pain 'wrings' his mind in a way that is 'wilder' and more violent than the last. We visualise the poet's mind, therefore, being tugged and twisted like a damp dishcloth. It is an image that vividly conveys the extreme nature of his suffering. Hopkins, therefore, feels that there is no limit to his torment. There is no such thing as rock bottom, no 'worst' possible situation for him to be in. No matter how badly he's suffering, new and more vicious pains will come along.

Calling for comfort

In the face of such torment, Hopkins calls out to Christ for help. He describes Christ as his 'Comforter', suggesting that in the past thoughts of Jesus have soothed his troubled mind. Hopkins also calls out to the Virgin Mary, who he describes as 'mother of us'. This of course suggests how Mary, in the Catholic Church, is depicted as the universal mother of all mankind.

On this occasion, however, the poet's pleas for help seem to fall upon deaf ears. Christ offers him no comfort and Mary provides no relief. The poet seems to have been abandoned, therefore, by the God he has served so faithfully.

The heaving cries

The poet cries out again and again in torment and distress. His cries, we're told, 'heave' from him, and we can imagine his chest heaving as he moans and groans in despair. Hopkins uses a typical compound adjective to describe these cries, declaring that they are 'herds-long'. This suggests that each cry is a 'long' and drawn-out sob of misery. It also suggests that there are a great many ('herds') of such desperate cries (other compound adjectives include 'world-sorrow' and 'no-man-fathomed').

This image of 'herds of cries' is peculiar and surreal. The poet's cries are presented almost as living things, as poor bewildered beasts that 'huddle' together like cattle on a freezing winter evening. The comparison of the cries to living animals may seem weird and outlandish, but it successfully conveys the poet's distress, suggesting that he finds himself in a debased and animalistic state. His self-respect and dignity have been stripped away.

The poet's torment is caused not only by his own miserable circumstances but also by some universal problem, some great sorrow that affects the entire world: 'a chief/ Woe, world-sorrow'. Hopkins doesn't describe the precise nature of this 'world-sorrow'. Some critics feel that Hopkins is referring to the tragedy of sin, that the great 'sorrow' he has in mind is mankind's failure to obey God's law. However, Hopkins could also be referring to the apparent distance between God and man. On this reading, the 'world-sorrow' is God's apparent unwillingness to answer our prayers and his apparent willingness to let evil men triumph.

Age-old anvil

There is some disagreement about what is beaten on the 'age-old anvil' in line 6. Grammatically, it is the poet's 'cries' that 'wince and sing' on the anvil: 'My cries heave … huddle … wince and sing'. But this seems to make little sense. How, after all, can 'cries' be beaten on an anvil? As the critic Norman White suggests, it makes more sense to read this as the poet's soul or mind being hammered on an 'age-old anvil', suffering mental torment as thousands have before throughout the ages, mental torment that makes the poet 'wince' in pain and 'sing' out in agony.

A brief lull

There seems to be a brief interval or 'lull' in the poet's torment when his sufferings pause or 'leave off': 'Then lull, then leave off'. However, this reprieve is extremely short-lived. No sooner has one bout of suffering ended than the next one begins. There will be no real let-up in the poet's mental agony.

The poet personifies his mental torment as one of the Furies – the terrifying demons from Greek mythology who relentlessly pursued and tortured their victims. He imagines this 'Fury' shrieking out, calling for his torment to commence once again, insisting that there be 'No lingering'. The 'Fury', he imagines, wants to express its 'fell' or evil personality, by getting immediately back to its malevolent work: 'Let me be fell'.

The 'Fury', the poet imagines, declares that it has to be 'brief': 'force I must be brief' (here, the term 'force', or 'perforce', means 'of necessity'). The Fury's very nature, then, means that it has to be very 'brief' or quick. Perhaps this means it can only allow the briefest of lulls in the poet's torment. Or perhaps it means it is eager to complete its mission of torturing the poet until he finally goes insane.

Despair's abyss

Hopkins compares the human mind to a vast landscape that features many different terrains. One of those terrains is a place of vast, forbidding 'mountains', of 'sheer' cliffs and terrifying drops that seem to have no bottom. This terrain, of course, represents the darker aspects of the mind, those associated with extreme mental anguish (it is likely that Hopkins' descriptions of these mountains and cliffs was inspired by his sighting of the Alps during a trip he took to Switzerland in 1868, just before he commenced his novitiate to become a Jesuit).

Hopkins depicts himself as a frequent visitor to this bleak terrain, suggesting that he is no stranger to the mind's darker aspects. He suggests that he is 'hung' from one of these 'sheer' cliffs, with the unfathomable abyss yawning below.

The poet seems aware that most people simply won't get what he is describing. Only those who have also 'hung there' above despair's abyss will appreciate his words. The rest of us who have never (ne'er) dangled above this chasm will 'hold [his words] cheap'. We will not understand his complaints or take them seriously: 'Hold them cheap/ May who ne'er hung there'.

A crumb of comfort

The poet maintains that human beings are simply not cut out for the kind of mental torment he's going through. The human mind, he claims, is a weak and fragile thing with limited powers of endurance ('small/ Durance'). It cannot deal with the 'steep' cliffs and 'deep' abyss that form the landscape of despair: 'Nor does long our small/ Durance deal with that steep or deep'. We cannot cope with this kind of extreme suffering for very long without simply falling apart.

Yet there is some comfort for the beleaguered poet, some shelter from the storm that has engulfed his mind: 'Here! creep,/ Wretch, under a comfort serves in a whirlwind'. Though his existence is miserable, he can take comfort from the fact that his life will one day be over: 'all/ Life death does end'. Death will bring a final halt to his trials and sufferings. Furthermore, there is the comfort of sleep. When the poet is sleeping, it seems, his sufferings disappear or are at least diminished. The poem's conclusion, then, is a shocking indication of the extent of the poet's misery: his only relief comes from death or unconsciousness.

PHYSICAL AND MENTAL SUFFERING

This poem could be described as a howl of mental torment. The poet has been 'pitched past pitch of grief'. He is experiencing a mental state that is far beyond ordinary grief or sorrow. Hopkins uses a number of very powerful images to describe the extraordinary torment he suffers:

- He feels that his mind is being violently 'wrung' like a piece of cloth.
- He feels that his mind is being beaten on an anvil.
- He personifies his suffering as willing school children, each pang learning from the 'pangs' that have come before.
- He also personifies his suffering as a Fury, a malevolent demon from Greek mythology.
- He describes his mental suffering in terms of a bleak, mountainous landscape.
- He compares his mental torment to a violent 'whirlwind'.

Hopkins' mental torment is more or less unrelenting, with only the briefest of pauses between one bout of suffering and the next. His torment also keeps getting worse. To Hopkins, it seems that his sufferings will keep increasing in intensity forever, that there is 'no worst', no rock-bottom for him to hit. It is hardly surprising, therefore, that the poet thinks of himself as a pitiful 'wretch', crying out in agony over and over again. His only 'comfort' is the oblivion offered by sleep or death.

DOUBTING GOD'S GOODNESS

This poem powerfully deals with what is arguably Hopkins' darkest theme: his sense of abandonment by God. In the throes of mental torment, Hopkins calls out to God and the Virgin Mary for comfort and relief. God, however, is unable or unwilling to help him. Hopkins, who was a loyal and devoted priest, feels abandoned by the God he has served so faithfully.

A similar sense of abandonment is evident in 'I wake and feel the fell of dark', where Hopkins describes his prayers to God as 'dead letters' that will never reach their destination. We also see it in 'Thou art indeed just, Lord', where Hopkins accuses God of 'thwarting' him and treating him like an enemy while allowing sinners to get ahead in life. This theme is arguably also present in 'Felix Randal', where the dying Felix curses God for making him ill.

FOCUS ON STYLE

Compression

There are several examples in this poem of what we might describe as Hopkins' 'shorthand' style. We see this in the following phrase: 'Hold them cheap/ May who ne'er hung there'. A more conventional writer might express a similar sentiment like this: 'Those who have never hung from those terrible cliffs may well hold my words cheap and not take them seriously'. Entire words are left out as Hopkins compresses this sentence into a short, powerful poetic phrase. We see a similar effect in line 13, where Hopkins writes 'a comfort serves in a whirlwind' rather then, what me might expect, 'a comfort *that* serves in a whirlwind'.

Inscape and Instress

Hopkins, as he so often does, uses intense musical effects to capture a specific sensation – in this case, the sensation of despair. The opening lines, in particular, are marked by a jarring cacophony. This cacophonous effect is largely down to Hopkins' use of repetition. The repetition of the word 'pitch' in line 1, and the close proximity of 'pangs' and 'forepangs' in line 2, lend the opening a jerky, grating quality.

This is also reinforced by the alliteration in the first line, where the repeated 'p' sound in 'Pitched past pitch' creates a harsh musical effect. The assonance and alliteration in 'wilder wring' with its repeated 'w' and 'i' sounds is also far from easy on the ear. A similarly unpleasant effect is created by the repeated 'h' sound in line 5: 'My cries heave, herds-long; huddle in a main'. This repetition is almost onomatopoeic, suggesting the poet's gasps and cries as he laments his suffering.

Words with Many Meanings

Hopkins's enjoyment of using words that have multiple meanings is evident in his use of the word 'pitched' in the opening line: 'Pitched past pitch of grief'. This phrase can be interpreted in at least three different ways:

- To 'pitch' is to throw or hit an object. Hopkins' mind has been thrown beyond grief into some new and even more terrible emotional state.
- The word 'pitch' also suggests the notes on a musical scale. On this reading, Hopkins is suggesting that there is a 'scale' of suffering just as there is a scale of musical notes.
- To 'pitch' something can also mean to blacken it, to roll it round in wet tar. Hopkins' mind has been blackened by suffering. It is now more 'pitch' black than the blackness we associate with grief and mourning. It has entered a new kind of darkness.

I wake and feel the fell of dark

LINE BY LINE

'I wake and feel the fell of dark' was written during the summer of 1884. Hopkins was living in Dublin at the time, teaching at the Royal University of Ireland. This was a deeply unhappy period in Hopkins' life. He was disillusioned with the work at the University, writing to his mother that 'I believe most of it is [useless] and that I bear a burden which crushes me and does little to help any good end'.

Hopkins despised Dublin, describing it in a letter to a friend as a 'joyless place'. He also felt very alienated and alone, living far away from his family and friends and lacking the kind of psychological support he desperately needed. A year after his arrival in Dublin, he wrote to his friend Bridges, 'I must absolutely have encouragement as much as crops have rain'. Hopkins also mentioned to his friend how he had recently written a number of sonnets, stating that 'if ever anything was written in blood one of these was'. This was the first mention of the group of sonnets usually known as the Terrible Sonnets, or, more exactly, the Sonnets of Desolation.

Insomnia and dread

The poem opens with a powerful portrayal of insomnia and dread. The poet wakes in the middle of the night and can't get back to sleep. We sense his disorientation when he wakes to find it is 'not day' but still the hours of darkness. To Hopkins, it feels like morning will never come. He feels that he's been lying there in the dark for an incredibly long time. He personifies the light of morning, depicting it as a friendly presence. But the light, he declares, has been delaying its arrival. And it will delay 'yet longer', further prolonging this seemingly endless night.

Hopkins, as he lies there, is filled with an extraordinary sense of dread. We see this when he compares the dark to the 'fell' or hide of an animal: 'I wake and feel the fell of dark'. He is so distressed that the darkness that surrounds him seems almost tangible. He can almost 'feel' it brushing against him and breathing on him like some foul beast.

Mental anguish

The poet then experiences 'black hours'. The word 'black', of course, suggests not only the literal blackness of the night-time but also the mental anguish the poet experiences as he lies awake through the night.

Line 3 features apostrophe, which occurs when a poet addresses an inanimate object. Hopkins, in this instance, addresses his own 'heart', by which he means his psyche or inner self. He says that his 'heart', over the course of this one night, has travelled down terrifying 'ways' or roads and has witnessed 'sights' so horrific they defy description: 'What sights you, heart, saw; ways you went!'

This metaphor of the heart's journey through some nightmarish landscape powerfully captures the poet's tortured mental state. However, the heart's journey isn't over. It 'must' experience 'more' of these 'sights' and 'ways', must continue to suffer until the morning finally arrives. The poet is keen to point out that he speaks with 'witness', from deep and intense personal experience: 'With witness I speak this'. This kind of mental anguish isn't just something he's imagining or has heard about second hand.

Hopkins suddenly corrects himself, declaring that where he said 'hours', he meant 'years' or 'life'. He's asking us to go back and re-read line 2 in the following ways:
- 'What [years], O what black [years] we have spent'
- 'What [life], O what black [life] we have spent'.

Perhaps Hopkins is once again emphasising the extraordinary length of this one night, at least as it seems to him, stressing that every hour is like a year or even an entire lifetime. Or perhaps he is emphasising how his entire life has been a difficult one, how he has suffered not just over the course of this extraordinary night, but over his entire lifetime.

Where is God's comfort?
Hopkins, as he lies there in the dark, engages in a 'lament'. This can be understood as a passionate expression of his grief. But it can also be understood to mean a complaint, as if he were reaching out to God to complain about his plight and to ask for it to be improved. His 'lament', he declares, consists of 'countless' individual 'cries', suggesting that he calls out again and again in desperation.

Hopkins describes Christ as his 'dearest' friend. But Christ, unfortunately lives 'away' from him, existing in heaven while the poet himself exists on Earth. The poet's 'cries', his efforts to communicate with Christ, are compared to letters sent in the post. But his 'cries', it seems, go unheard. He compares his 'cries', therefore, to 'dead letters', which are letters that cannot be delivered to their intended recipient.

Physical anguish
Hopkins, as he lies there in the dark, experiences not only mental anguish but also physical discomfort. He declares that he is suffering from 'heartburn', a type of reflux where acid from the stomach rises upwards causing intense physical discomfort. The poet also experiences the reflux of 'gall' or bile, a substance secreted by the liver that aids in the digestive process. Gall, it seems, rises all the way through the poet's digestive system, leaving a 'bitter' taste in his mouth (Hopkins, it is worth noting, doesn't say that he *has* gall and heartburn - he says he *is* gall and heartburn. He experiences his whole system as being sickly, unbalanced and out-of-sorts).

This memorable phrase also suggests the psycho-somatic nature of Hopkins' various ailments, as described in Robert Martins' biography of the poet. After all, digestive problems, like those experienced by Hopkins, are often brought on by stress. Perhaps Hopkins realises on some level that he lets himself get too worked up and too stressed out, that he himself is the cause of the gall and heartburn that afflicts him.

Let's focus on lines 9 to 10: 'God's most deep decree/ Bitter would have me taste'. This is an instance of Hopkins playing with syntax or word order to produce a percussive rhythmic effect. We might re-write it as follows: I taste bitter to myself and others because God decreed or commanded that I have such a taste.

Hopkins experiences himself as something 'bitter', a sensation emphasised by the short, powerful phrase 'my taste was me'. But what does it mean for someone to experience themselves as bitter? Hopkins, on one level, is referring to the bitter 'taste' in his mouth caused by gall and excessive stomach acid. But he is also referring to physical discomfort more generally, to how his whole body feels as if it has been flooded with poison or some other bitter substances. Finally, he is also using the idea of tasting bitter to oneself in a metaphorical sense to refer to his mental anguish. He experiences all his thoughts, emotions and ideas as being 'bitter' – they bring him only disappointment and regret rather than happiness and satisfaction.

It was God's will, Hopkins believes, that he must experience himself in this bitter fashion. God, he suggests, descreed or commanded that this must be the case. And this decree was not lightly issued. Instead, it was a 'most deep' or solemn one, suggesting that God is absolutely determined that Hopkins' mind and body must be filled with bitterness.

The body as burden
Hopkins imagines that his soul existed long before his body did. But then he was transformed from a spiritual being drifting through God's heaven into a creature of flesh and blood that must exist here on Earth:
- First, a structure of bone was 'built' inside his spritual form.
- Then his spiritual form was 'filled' out with 'flesh'.
- Finally, his spiritual form was filled to the brim with blood.

Hopkins, we sense, resents ever having been incarnated or embodied. He wishes he could have existed forever in a purely spiritual form. To him, his body is a 'curse'. It is a 'curse' in the sense that it is a torment. But is is also a 'curse' in the sense that it is a malediction, a prophecy, threat or promise of further suffering.

The poet and the 'lost'
The poet suddenly realises that he is like the 'lost' or damned souls that suffer in hell: 'I see/ The lost are like this'.
- The 'lost', like him, experience a 'scourge'. The 'scourge' endured by the 'lost' is that of hell's various torments. The 'scourge' endured by the poet is that of the mental and physical anguish he experiences on this seemingly endless night.
- The 'lost', like him, are described as 'sweating'. The 'lost', of course, sweat due to the fires of hell. The poet, on the other hand, sweats due to a fever brought on by mental and physical anguish.

The situation of the 'lost' is, however, 'worse' than that of the poet. The 'lost' have no hope whatsoever, as they have been amned to an eternity in hell. The poet, on the other hand, still has a slight hope that his situation here on earth might improve and that he might find peace in heaven when his life is over.

FOCUS ON STYLE

Syntax

Hopkins is known for using unusual syntax or word order. For example, in the second line he says 'what sights you, heart, saw' where we might normally say 'What sights you saw, heart'. Unusual syntax is also a feature of line 12 where the poet says 'Selfyeast of spirit a dull dough sours'. Converted into 'normal' language, the line might go something like this: 'A dull dough sours the selfyeast of the spirit'.

Compression

Hopkins is well known as a poet of compression, one who frequently leaves out words and even entire phrases in order to create particular musical effects. Such compression is evident in the poem's fourth line: 'And more must, in yet longer light's delay'. If we fill in the gaps, we end up with a line such as 'And you must endure more sights such as this, as the light's arrival is set to be delayed even longer'.

Words With Many Meanings

Hopkins has a tendancy to deploy key words that can be interpreted in several different ways. The word 'fell' is an example of this tendency. 'Fell' as we mentioned above, can mean the hide of an animal. But it can also mean evil or wickedness, suggesting that Hopkins experiences the darkness as something sinister or menacing. Finally, 'fell' is a dialect word for vale or valley. The 'fell of dark' on this reading is a valley of darkness. Hopkins' night of mental and physical suffering, therefore, is compared to a journey through a bleak and mountainous terrain that the sun's light never reaches.

Inscape and Instress

Hopkins uses 'inscape', a profusion of assonance and alliteration, to capture the essence of an object or sensation. In 'I wake and feel the fell of dark', the poet uses repeated long vowel sounds to lend the verse a slow, melancholy air, reflecting his mental anguish. We see this in the poem's opening line, for instance, which features long 'a' and 'e' sounds. Cacophany, too, features in this regard. Line 11, for instance, features clashing, repeated 'b' and 'f' sounds, creating a jarring verbal music that captures the poet's unsettled state of mind.

The poem's second line is a masterpiece of emphasis. The poet uses the declarative structure 'What hours', suggesting that these hours can't be easily described or explained. We might use the expression 'What a goal!' or 'What a song!', for instance, when referring to a goal or song that resists easy description. The line's use of repetition further emphasises the length and horror of these 'hours', reinforcing our sense that the poet is experiencing a true dark night of the soul.

Metaphor, Simile, Figures of Speech

The poet compares his soul to yeast that might be used in baking. Hopkins, using a typical coinage, refers to 'Selfyeast', suggesting yeast that is compared to his soul or his very self. The poet's soul longs to rise upwards, to return to its heavenly home, just as yeast rises during the baking process. The poet's soul, however, is trapped in his body and this earthly realm. He compares it, therefore, to yeast that has been spoiled and cannot rise.

THEMES

PHYSICAL AND MENTAL SUFFERING

This poem provides an extraordinary account of physical and mental suffering.

- The poet suffers from insomnia and lies awake for hour after hour imagining that day will never come.
- He experiences such dread that he imagines the darkness is a foul creature that holds him in his grip.
- He experiences 'black hours' of mental anguish.
- He endures the physical ailments of gall and heartburn.
- He feels like his whole body is unbalanced and off-kilter.
- He even resents having a body at all, viewing it as a 'curse'.

Hopkins, then, experiences his mind and body as having an almost unbearably 'bitter' quality. Indeed, he is in such a miserable state that he compares himself to the 'lost' souls who suffer in hell.

DOUBTING GOD'S GOODNESS

'I wake and feel the fell of dark' is the poem where Hopkins most doubts God's fundamental goodness:

- Hopkins 'cries' out to Christ again and again, looking for comfort, answers and relief. But he is dismayed to find that his cries, like 'dead letters', go unanswered or unheard.
- Hopkins suspects that God actually wants him to suffer. It's as if God commanded or decreed that his body and his mind would have a 'most bitter' quality.
- Hopkins even seems to resent the fact that God gave him a body, rather than letting him exist forever as a purely spiritual being.

The attitude towards God in this poem, then, is very different from that expressed in 'God's Grandeur' or 'Pied Beauty', where God is depicted as a benevolent Father, worthy of praise.

Thou art indeed just, Lord ...

LINE BY LINE

This poem was written in 1889, when Hopkins was living in Dublin. In January of that year, Hopkins made his annual retreat. Religious retreats involve a brief withdrawal from society to a quiet place for prayer, study, to reflect or to meditate. They usually cover a period of a few days and are held at a religious house. On this particular occasion, Hopkins went to St Stanislaus's College in Tullamore.

The poet's notes from this retreat capture the struggles and doubts he was wrestling with at the time. He describes feeling that his time in Ireland has been fruitless and wasted: 'What is my wretched life? Five wasted years almost have passed in Ireland. I am ashamed of the little I have done, of my waste of time … All my undertakings miscarry: I am like a straining eunuch. I wish for death: yet if I died now I should die imperfect, no master of myself, and that is the worst failure of all. O my God, look down on me …'.

What caused the poet perhaps the greatest strife was the idea that God did not care about him, that He was doing nothing to help him in his endeavours. Hopkins seems to have believed that if only he had some assistance from God, he would be capable of doing some good: 'I do not feel that outwardly I do much good, much that I care to do or can much wish to prosper; and this is a mournful life to lead … Yet it seems to me that I could lead this life well enough if I had bodily energy and cheerful spirits. However, these God will not give me'. Two months after the retreat Hopkins wrote 'Thou art indeed just', in which he captures these feelings of failure and questions God's fairness and justice.

The poet's conflict

In this poem, Hopkins sets out to 'contend' or take issue with God. The world, to Hopkins, seems a very unjust place. When the poet looks at the world around him, he sees many examples of people who do not lead good or virtuous lives. But these people do not suffer for their behaviour or actions. In fact, many of them, the poet believes, are prospering and thriving, despite their immoral ways. The poet asks God why this is the case: 'Why do sinners' ways prosper?'

The poet, in contrast, is a loyal and dutiful priest, one of God's faithful servants. He has devoted his entire life to God. Yet everything he attempts to do in life ends in failure and disappointment. The poet asks God why this is the case: 'why must/ Disappointment all I endeavour end?'

The poet, then, finds himself wrestling with two conflicting or contradictory beliefs. On the one hand, as a Christian and a priest, he must believe that God is 'just', and is careful to begin his plea by stating: 'Thou art indeed just, Lord'. But he also believes, as we've seen, that the world is an unjust place. How can God, if He is 'just', preside over such unfairness?

Hopkins 'pleads' his case carefully like a lawyer in a courtroom. He addresses God in a respectful manner, the way a lawyer would a judge, calling Him 'sir'. Yet he feels that what he has to say about the state of affairs in the world is also reasonable and right: 'but, sir, so what I plead is just'.

Contrasting Lives

What baffles and hurts the poet most is the fact that God seems to be actively preventing or thwarting him from succeeding and prospering in life. Hopkins is God's friend yet God seems to treat him very badly. In fact, Hopkins thinks, if God were his enemy, He couldn't treat him any worse: 'How wouldst thou worse, I wonder, than thou dost/ Defeat, thwart me?'

Hopkins compares himself to the 'sots and thralls of lust'. The term 'thralls' suggests people who are enslaved by lust. The term 'sots' suggests people who are intoxicated by lust, who are so overcome with lustful thoughts they can no longer think straight.

- These 'sots and thralls' give into lust on a regualar basis – they sleep with prostitues, consume pornography or have extramarital affairs. Hopkins, as a celibate, never gives in to such lustful temptations.
- These 'sots and thralls' have 'spare hours' – hours when they are not engaged in lustful pursuits – which they devote to various projects in the realms of business, politics and art. Hopkins, on the other hand, has no 'spare hours'. Every minute of every day is spent in prayer or in servitude to the Church: 'I that spend/ Sir, life upon thy cause'.
- These 'sots and thralls' seem to 'thrive' more than Hopkins. Their projects, hopes and ambitions meet with success, while his never do.

The term 'spends life', of course, describes how Hopkins passes his time. But it also suggests a suggests an expenditure of his energy and resources in the service of God's cause. We get a sense, too, of how Hopkins, with his vow of celibacy, sacrifices his own ability to bring new life into the world.

The barrenness of Hopkins' life

Hopkins directs God's attention to riverbanks and 'brakes' or woodland thickets. He asks God to consider these aspects of the natural world, as if he were introducing evidence to a courtroom hearing: 'See, banks and brakes/ Now'.

Hopkins is writing, it seems, in springtime, when such 'banks and brakes' are returning to life. These river banks and woodland areas grow 'thick' with leaves. Their surfaces become covered with herbs like 'chervil', that form a heavy, lace-like layer (chervil is a form of parsley, whose leaves, as Hopkins puts it, form a 'fretty' or delicate pattern).

Hopkins compares himself to these 'banks and brakes'. He sees how they endure the barenness of winter but experience new life 'again' each spring: 'leavèd how thick! lacèd they are again'. Hopkins' life, in contrast, seems destined to remain barren forever.

Hopkins, no doubt, experiences himself as being creatively barren, feeling that he is not writing any poems of lasting value. He also experiences himself as being spiritually barren, feeling that he is incapable or forging a proper connection with God. He also considers himself to be professionally barren, feeling that his priestly duties are utterly futile and make no difference to his parisheners.

In the poem's final line, Hopkins compares himself to a tree that has been deprived of water. He wants God to change his circumstances, to help him lead a more productive life. Doing so, he suggests, would be like exposing such a tree to a welcome rainfall: 'O thou lord of life, send my roots rain'.

FOCUS ON STYLE

Form

Like so many of Hopkins' poems, 'Thou art indeed just' is a Petrarchan sonnet. It has a typical Petrarchan rhyme scheme: ABBAABBA CDCDCD. It is divided into an octet (eight lines) where Hopkins outlines his complaints against God and a sestet (six lines) where he compares himself to nature and hopes for a solution to his troubles.

Syntax

The poem's opening is relatively simple in terms of syntax. We are presented with more or less straightforward sentences in which it is reasonably easy to work out what's going on. As the poem goes on, however, the syntax becomes more cluttered, difficult and convoluted. This is evident in lines 5 to 9, where most readers require several readings of the text in order to properly follow the poet's meaning. This contorted word order reflects his confused and angry state of mind. At the beginning of the poem, he speaks rationally and his intense emotions are

kept in check. As the poem goes on, however, his confusion, bitterness and frustration come bubbling to the surface and are reflected in the increasingly difficult and tortured syntax.

Inscape and Instress

The poem's closing lines are typical of Hopkins in that he uses intense and musical language in order to describe the natural world in an effort to capture the uniqueness, or 'inscape', of each natural thing he depicts. We see alliteration, for instance, with the repeated 'b' sounds ('banks' and 'brakes', 'birds' and 'build'), in the repeated 'l' sound ('leaves' and 'lace') and in the repeated 'fr' sound ('fretty' and 'fresh'). Assonance also occurs in these lines in the repeated broad-vowel sounds. The phase 'fretty chervil', in particular, creates a pleasing euphonious effect.

DOUBTING GOD'S GOODNESS

This is a powerful poem of religious doubt. In it, Hopkins asks an age-old question: if God is good why does He let wicked men triumph and sinners get ahead in life? Furthermore, why does He let His faithful servants suffer? Hopkins has sacrificed so much for God, yet nothing in his life succeeds. Meanwhile, sinners who have sacrificed nothing – who are the slaves or 'thralls' of lust – get ahead in life. Hopkins, like many other people throughout history, wonders why God allows this to happen.

There is a strong sense of frustration, perhaps even anger, in this poem. Everything Hopkins tries to do ends in disappointment and failure. He cannot understand why God allows this to happen, especially when Hopkins has served Him so faithfully. Hopkins almost suspects that God has turned against him and is actually his enemy rather than his friend.

It has also been suggested that in this poem Hopkins expresses doubts about his religious vocation, especially his vow of celibacy. Hopkins sacrificed the sexual side of his nature for God. He also gave up his ability to 'breed', to father children. But in this poem, he suggests that God has given him little or nothing in return. There's a sense in which he regrets these huge sacrifices, referring to himself in a demeaning fashion as 'Time's eunuch'. Is it possible that Hopkins envies those sinners who are 'thralls of lust', who are slaves to sexual passion?

In many of his poems, Hopkins draws a moral message from the natural world. The beauty of nature leads him to contemplate God's goodness. In this poem, however, the beauty of nature seems to tie in with Hopkins' angry questioning of God's justice. Each spring the riverbanks grow thick with leaves while God lets Hopkins' life remain barren and empty. Hopkins' only hope is that God will make his life fertile and fulfilling, just as He sends rain to water the plants on the riverbank. Hopkins, therefore, calls out desperately for God to 'send my roots rain'.

MENTAL AND PHYSICAL SUFFERING

This poem is one of Hopkins' 'terrible' sonnets – poems in which Hopkins describes his great mental anguish. Other poems in this group include 'No worst, there is none' and 'I wake and feel the fell of Dark'. 'Thou art indeed just, Lord' is perhaps the least intense of the three. Here, Hopkins presents his suffering in a more rational, restrained and subtle fashion.

Hopkins. as we've seen, contrasts his situation with that of the countryside in springtime, in order to emphasise how he feels creatively, spiritually and professionally barren. He contrasts himself with the birds of springtime, who are busy building nests for the mating season to come: 'birds build'. Hopkins, on the other hand, can't seem to 'build' anything at all: 'but not I build; no'. He descibes how he 'strain[s]', making extraordinary efforts to lead a productive life. But his efforts are all in vain.

Hopkins also frames this lack of productivity in terms of sexual reproduction. He compares himself to a 'eunuch', a man who has been castrated. Just as such a eunuch can 'breed' no children, so Hopkins can produce no works.

Sometimes it seems that Hopkins manages to produce a 'work' or two. But these works don't 'wake'. They have no life in them, they produce no impact and they have no lasting value. Perhaps Hopkins is writing poems that fail to have any merit or lasting impact on the reader. Or perhaps he is referring to sermons he has been giving as a priest that fail to inspire his congregation. He might even be referring to initiatives that he started within his parish that failed to take off.

The poet's mental anguish, then, resonates throughout the poem. It powerfully conveys Hopkins' desperate and 'straining' attempts to make something of his life, and his sense of failure and disappointment when these attempts come to nothing.

Paula Meehan Themes

The Strength and Power of Women

Many of Meehan's poems feature strong female characters, women who, though their lives are hard, find the strength to persevere and endure. Her poems offer us a vivid insight into what life was like for many women living in Dublin's inner city in the 50s and 60s.

The poet's own mother had to work hard all her life to maintain the household and look after the family. Meehan describes her mother's life in 'The Pattern'. Nearly all the poet's memories of her mother involve work of some kind. Meehan describes how on one occasion her mother 'must have stayed up half the night' to finish mending a dress for her to wear to school the next day. Even her leisure activity, knitting, is work of a kind: we can imagine her knitting hats, gloves and other useful items. In 'Hearth Lessons', the mother is presented as quite a formidable woman. Each week she must manage the little money that the father earns and ensure that the family survives.

The women in the poet's childhood neighbourhood were often the primary breadwinners in their respective households, bringing home a wage that kept utter poverty and despair at bay. Their jobs often involved doing difficult, repetitive work. In 'The Exact Moment I Became a Poet', Meehan describes a local sewing factory where many of her classmates' mothers, aunts and sisters worked. She recalls how one of her primary school teachers warned the class to behave themselves or they might 'end up' working in such a sewing factory.

The young poet was deeply upset by how her teacher presented the sewing factory as a worthless and undesirable place of employment. Meehan appreciated the drudgery of such work, but even at a young age she recognised that the women working in the sewing factory retained a certain dignity and pride despite their circumstances. She realised that the women of the factory took great pride in what they did, in producing garments that were well made and hard-wearing. Miss Shannon's words, she realised, 'robbed' the women of this 'dignity', making their 'labour' seem utterly menial and pointless.

This ability to take pride in the work that had to be done was also evident in the poet's mother. In 'The Pattern', Meehan describes how her mother would polish the floor of the family flat in a methodical manner, ensuring that it gleamed and shone when she was done. In 'Buying Winkles', meanwhile, we see how the lady selling the winkles takes great pride in what she is selling, telling the young poet to tell her mother that she 'picked them fresh this morning'. She also remains good-humoured, patiently telling the young poet how to remove the winkle from the shell, despite the fact that she would have told the young girl how to do this on numerous other occasions. This woman, we must remember, would have been up early in the morning to collect the winkles that she now sells on the streets in the cold of the evening.

'Cora, Auntie' is another poem that offers us a portrait of a woman who possessed great strength and spirit. The poet's aunt Cora is presented as a flamboyant and fearless individual, someone who lived life on her own terms. The opening lines of the poem present us a with memorable image of the aunt facing death down like a gunslinger in a Western movie. But instead of being armed with pistols, the aunt faces death with 'a bottle of morphine in one hand/ and a bottle of Jameson in the other'. The startling addition of the red sequins to the wedding dress tells us something about the aunt's personality. We get a sense of someone who liked to do things differently, to bring her own unique style to situations and occasions. The fact that the poet kept these sequins over the years tells us just how powerful a presence this glamorous woman was in her life.

Poverty and Hardship

Meehan's poems give us an insight into the poverty and hardship that were common in Ireland when the poet was a child. 'Buying Winkles' suggests that money was very tight in the poet's family. The mother would 'spare' the poet sixpence, suggesting that each week they were just getting by, living hand to mouth. The condition of the tenement block in which the young poet lived also hints at this hardship. We get the impression that the building was not well maintained and that the bulb on the stairs had been blown for a considerable amount of time. The description of the men 'heading out for the night' suggests, perhaps, how many of the men in the locality would regularly go and drink in bars as a means of escape from the hardship that they had to endure.

'The Pattern' highlights the fact that there were few options available to people to improve their lot in life. This was especially true when it came to women. The poet's mother was born into the Ireland of the 1930s. The country was extremely poor. It was also a narrow and closed-minded place. There were extremely limited opportunities for education and advancement. This was especially so for the working class into which the mother was born.

'Hearth Lesson', meanwhile, highlights the toxic effects that poverty can have on a relationship. For the poet, even as a child, understood that poverty caused the constant strife between her parents: 'Even then I can tell it was money/ the lack of it day after day,/ at the root of the bitter words'. The constant lack of money made both of her parents tense, irritable and frustrated. It led to unceasing tensions between them, to blazing rows and 'brooding' periods of silence. The father's wages, it is made clear, were never quite enough to cover the family's expenses. The mother, we sense, had to scrimp and save as she managed the household budget. There was always the pressure of unpaid bills, of upcoming expenses that needed to be covered from the household's meagre resources.

Family

'The Pattern' is a moving exploration of the relationships between mothers and their eldest daughters. Such relationships, Meehan suggests, all too often turn sour: 'Some say that's the fate of the eldest daughter'. We get the impression that much of the tension between Meehan and her mother arose because of the great differences between them. The poet, we sense, is someone given to introspection, to reflecting on her own life, to contemplating her own thoughts and emotions. She is prone to looking into the mirror, searching for a 'glimmer of her true self'. The mother, on the other hand, is not given to such introspection. She spent little time, the poet imagines, contemplating her own face when she saw it reflected in the floor's polished surface. She simply shrugged and moved on with her work.

'My Father Perceived as a Vision of St. Francis', meanwhile, emphasises how even close family members can sometimes be a mystery to us. Sometimes, family members keep things hidden from one another. We see this when the poet declares that the box room contained 'secrets'. There were items hidden about the room, she sensed, that her brother didn't want her to discover. Sometimes, family members simply stay quiet about aspects of their lives. The poet's father, for instance, had never told her that he feeds the birds each morning. Sometimes, we don't notice certain things about family members, even ones that we see regularly. The poet, for instance, had never noticed how age was catching up with her father: 'He was older than I had reckoned'. It was only on this particular morning that she noticed 'for the first time' how his shoulder was stooped and that his leg was stiff.

And yet, 'The Pattern' suggests, we are often more alike our parents than we might like to admit or acknowledge. In this poem, we can detect some of the mother's meticulousness in how the young poet explores the city, getting to know it section by section. The mother, meanwhile, exhibits something of the daughter's introspection when she's photographed in the Phoenix Park. The poet wishes that she had a chance to explore these similarities. She wishes her mother had lived on until the poet herself had matured: 'I wish now she'd

lasted until after/ I'd grown up'. They would have been two independent women, neither reliant on the other. They would have been unburdened of family commitments: 'without tags like mother, wife,/ sister, daughter'. They could have got to know each other afresh, first as acquaintances and then, perhaps, as friends: 'We might have made a new start'. The poem's great tragedy, then, is that the mother passed away before such a new start could be made.

'Prayer for the Children of Longing' highlights the suffering and agony that families endure when they lose a child. The poet mentions the terrible moment when the police come to knock on the door to inform the parents that their child has died. Such loss is felt most acutely at Christmas time. The description of the spirits of the dead children singing reminds us of the innocence of the child and how at this time of year the young should be singing carols and enjoying the magic of Christmas.

Meehan's poetry also captures the joy, love and support that families provide. In 'Cora, Auntie', for example, the poet remembers the women that played important roles in her childhood – her mother, grandmother and aunts. Meehan compares these women to 'stars' whose light is only now reaching her. It is as if only now as an adult she can fully appreciate their strength and character: 'Cora, Marie, Jacinta, my aunties,/ Helena, my mother, Mary, my grandmother-/ the light of those stars// only reaching me now'. The poem also highlights how powerful the love between family members can be. Meehan describes how it was 'love unconditional' that kept her aunt Cora alive towards the end.

Nature and Spirituality

In Meehan's poetry, the natural world is presented almost as a single organism, as if all its animal and plant life combine to form a unitary life-force or intelligence. Meehan developed this understanding of the natural world when she lived in California during the 1960s. She was influenced by Buddhism and Eastern philosophy, by the hippie movement and by American poets such as Gary Snyder who combined mysticism and environmentalism.

There are moments when Meehan suggests that the natural world is worthy of veneration, that we might pray to nature just as religious people pray to God. In 'Prayer for the Children of Longing', Meehan appeals directly to the great fir tree that has been erected in the middle of Dublin city. She imagines the landscape of the tree's native land. The poet associates this natural landscape with 'clarity', tranquillity and 'silence'. She prays that the tree might somehow bring these conditions to bear on these urban streets, to grant the people of Dublin's north inner city a chance to heal.

In 'The Statue of the Virgin', the statue adopts a very spiritual view of nature, regarding the earth as a divine being. The earth, however, is very different from the God of the Catholic faith. First, it is female rather than male. Second, it wants people to express rather than repress their sexual desire. The earth, according to the statue, calls on human beings to be fertile too, to engage in 'coupling' or sexual activity: 'when the earth herself calls out for coupling'.

The sun, too, is presented as a kind of goddess, one that the statue venerates or worships. The sun is described as our 'centre', reflecting the fact that our whole lives, in a sense, are spent orbiting the sun. The earth, meanwhile, is compared to a dancer that traces a circle, over and over again, around the sun's central point. The sun is described as our 'molten mother'. The term 'molten', of course, reinforces our sense of the sun's incomprehensible heat, causing us to envision a sphere of churning lava. The description of the sun as our 'mother' also reminds us that we depend on the sun's heat and light for our very survival.

There are also moments, Meehan suggests, when it is possible for human beings to commune with nature, to attain an almost mystical oneness with the natural world. Such communion in Meehan's poetry is presented as a source of healing and renewal. In 'Death of a Field', the poet laments the fact that a local field is set to be destroyed in order that a housing estate can be built. The poet highlights the great loss of flora and wildlife that will result. She suggests that we undervalue and under-appreciate the importance of the field and the rich life it contains. At the poem's conclusion, she imagines walking out into the field at night in order to connect with the field. The poet describes how she longs to establish an intimate, spiritual connection with the field, imagining how it might wrap or coat her in its silky dew.

This is how he appeared to her for a single sunlit moment in an ordinary 'Finglas garden'. This vision, no doubt, was partly caused by the fact the poet had just woken up and had been jerked out of a dream by the sound of the horse next door. But Meehan's visionary spiritual experience, in this instance, is prompted, not by conventional religion but by nature itself. The poet, we sense, was overwhelmed by the beauty of the scene in the yard before her, by the sight of the father suddenly struck by sunlight as he was surrounded by a 'pandemonium' of birds. The poem, then, is typical of Meehan's work, in that spirituality and nature are closely linked.

Social Justice

Meehan is a poet with an acute sense of social justice. Even as a primary school student, she was keenly aware of social inequality. In 'The Exact Moment I Became a Poet', she describes how she realised early on that people in her part of inner city Dublin were denied the opportunities granted to those from more privileged parts of the city. And this lack of opportunity, of course, was passed down from one generation to the next. In this poem, society is compared to a nightmarish factory where generation after generation of 'mothers, aunts and neighbours' from inner city Dublin are processed. The image of these women being 'trussed up' suggests how they were constrained by lack of opportunity. The image of them being mutilated by a giant sewing machine suggests how their underprivileged lives left them mentally and physically damaged.

'Prayer for the Children of Longing', meanwhile, outlines what any healthy, functioning society should offer and provide to its young. It should provide security, sheltering them from drugs and violence. It should provide them with a secure and healthy space in which to grow and develop. It should inspire them and nurture and develop their dreams and aspirations. Society should be blowing the young people's minds with exciting possibilities. The streets of Dublin's north inner city should have been able to promise them all these things and then deliver on these promises. But society has failed these children.

'The Statue of the Virgin' is yet another poem that highlights Meehan's acute sense of social justice. We see her once again giving voice to the voiceless. In this instance, she invites, or we might say forces, the reader to remember the story of Ann Lovett in all its grim sorrow. The poem draws a stark contrast between and Ann and the society of which she was a part. The rest of the town was 'tucked up' safe and warm, while Ann, alone in the cold of a January night, suffered the agony of childbirth. The image of the towns being 'tucked up' in scandals, bargains, prayers and promises is a powerful one. It suggests that such concerns envelop their minds just as sheets and blankets envelop their bodies when they go to bed at night.

These lines remind us that the people of the town failed Ann as her pregnancy wore on. No one noticed that things weren't quite right with her. There was no one Ann felt she could turn to, no older member of society with whom she could share her 'secret'. The people of the town were too wrapped up in their own affairs – in 'bargains' and business dealings, in their hopes and 'prayers', 'promises' they had to keep or get out of.

In 'Them Ducks Died for Ireland', Meehan urges us to 'salute' not only the great heroes but also those in the background of history's great events. She reminds us that those ordinary workers also made great sacrifices and displayed great courage. Such a 'salute', of course, could take many forms. It could be an exhibition or a school project, or a poem of remembrance like this one.

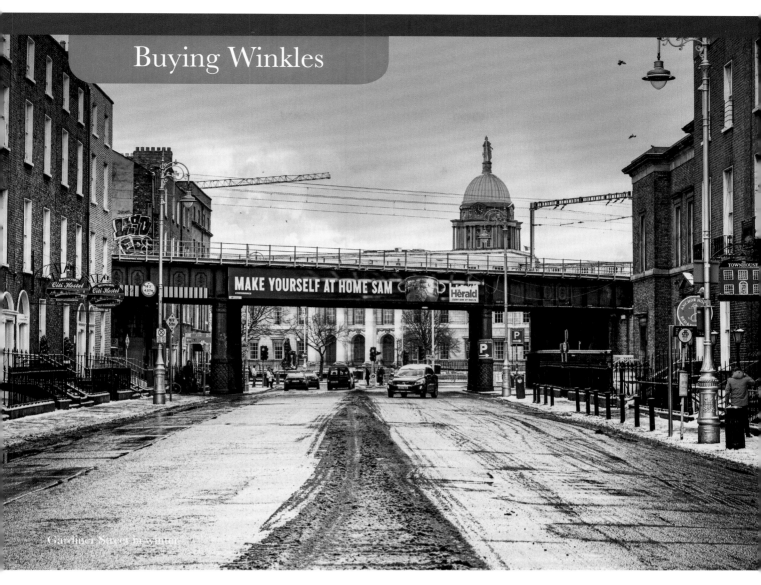

Buying Winkles

Gardiner Street in winter

LINE BY LINE

This poem relates to a period when the young poet and her family lived in a flat on Gardiner Street in Dublin city centre. On certain, special occasions the poet's mother would give her a 'tanner' or sixpence coin to go and buy a bag of winkles. The poet says that her mother would 'spare' her this sum of money, suggesting that it was something she could barely afford to give. The young poet would then dash excitedly out of the flat. As she would leave, her mother would warn her to be careful and not to talk to any strange men along the way.

The poet would descend the stairs of the apartment complex. She recalls how the light bulb in the stairwell had 'blown' and never been fixed. The young poet found this dark space scary, and would imagine that it was haunted. She would descend the stairs as quickly as she could to avoid the ghosts she imagined lurking here: 'I'd dash from the ghosts/ on the stairs where the bulb had blown'. When she finally emerged from the dark stairwell onto Gardiner Street, she would feel great 'relief' to be out in the open.

Winkles, also known as periwinkles, are small, edible shellfish. They are common to Irish shores and can often be found attached to rocks at low tide. They are easy to gather by hand and were commonly sold in paper bags or in newspaper wrapping.

The young poet would be happy if it was a clear evening. On such occasions she would be able to gaze up at the 'strip of sky' visible between the rows of 'tall houses' that lined the street. When the sky was clear she might be able to see some stars. On some rare occasions the moon would be visible in this strip of the sky. When this happened it made the occasion all the more special: 'A bonus if the moon was in the strip of sky'.

But even if the weather was not good and it was raining, the poet was still 'happy'. She loved the way the winkles would look when they were wet from rain. The shells would take on a rich, dark blue colour and 'glisten'. To the poet these shells were 'like little/ night skies themselves'.

The Winkle Seller

The young poet would buy the winkles from a woman outside the Rosebowl bar. This woman would have gone out early in the morning to gather winkles from rocks at low tide along the shores of Dublin Bay. She would then bring the winkles into the city and set herself up in this familiar spot where locals and passersby could purchase these delicious delicacies.

- The poet vividly recalls the manner in which this woman would be set up:
- She would be sitting on an 'orange crate', a timber box used for transporting fruit.
- She would have buckets or 'pails' full of winkles that she had picked from the rocks that morning.
- These pails were kept inside a pram, which was a convenient way to transport and hold the heavy load.
- She would use newspaper to wrap the winkles. She would twist the paper at the end to create a cone shape that would securely hold a large quantity of winkles.

As the young poet waited to buy the winkles she would glimpse into the Rosebowl Bar every time the door swung open. She seems to have been intrigued by the place:

- She recalls the way the light was reflected in the 'golden mirrors' that adorned the walls.
- She recalls the distinctive odours that would emanate from the bar, wafting out to where she stood on the street. The poet recalls the particular musk of the men gathered inside mixed with the odour of alcohol.
- Meehan also recalls the warmth of the place. We can imagine how snug and cosy this place seemed on a cold winter's evening.

The poet describes how she 'envied each soul in the hot interior'. We can imagine how the activity and the atmosphere might have appealed to the young poet. Here was a space where people could relax and be at ease, enjoying jokes and banter. Perhaps, considering the tensions that sometimes existed at home, this place struck the poet as an ideal escape from strife that sometimes defined family life.

As she was purchasing the winkles, the young poet would ask the woman to demonstrate the exact way to extract the winkle from its shell. The woman would happily go through the steps with the young girl:

- She would take a long pin which was used to fasten her shawl.
- She would then use this pin to remove the small disc covering the entrance to the shell, which protected the winkle inside. This disc is compared to an 'eyelid', something the winkle can close to seal itself off from the world outside.
- When this barrier was removed, the woman would gently press the pin into the winkle, causing it to tighten and 'grip' the pin.
- This would enable the woman to 'slither' or extract the winkle from the shell.

The young poet would request this demonstration each time she purchased winkles. We get the impression that she knew very well how to do this, but she would ask the woman to show her again because she knew that if she did, she would get to eat the extracted winkle. And it was this 'extra winkle', the poet says, that always tasted the 'sweetest'. Tasting the winkle was like tasting or experiencing the sea: 'The sweetest extra winkle/ that brought the sea to me'.

Heading back home

When the demonstration was finished, the woman would wrap the winkles in sheets of newspaper. She would place a quantity of winkles onto a sheet of paper and then twist the paper at both ends, creating a secure pouch or package that the customer could carry home. When these packages were ready, the young poet would race home proudly.

The poet uses a memorable metaphor to describe the bulging packages of winkles she would carry home, comparing them to 'torches'. We can imagine how the newspaper was twisted in such a way that when it was filled or loaded with winkles, it took on the appearance of a torch. The glistening winkles would be like the flame that would burn at the head of the torch.

The comparison conveys how, to the young poet, these winkles possessed some special, magical quality. It was like as if the packages of winkles were torches that would aid the young girl on her journey back home through the dark and perilous streets. The comparison also suggests the immense pride that the young poet experienced as she made her way home bearing these very special packages.

Metaphor, Simile and Figures of Speech

The poet uses a wonderful simile to describe the manner in which the winkles' dark shells would take on a deep blue colour when wet, comparing them to 'little/ night skies'. She also uses a memorable simile to describe the appearance of the packages of winkles that she would carry home, comparing them to 'torches'.

Playful Language

'Buying Winkles' wonderfully captures the young poet's excitement at being given this very special task. Meehan captures the thrill that she felt as she raced out of the flat, down the dark stairs and out on to the street where she weaved a 'glad path' through the men heading out to the pub that evening.

Vivid Imagery

The poem offers us a wonderful snapshot of life in inner city Dublin in the 1950s. The poet mentions specific places such as Gardiner Street, where her flat was located, and the Rosebowl Bar. We get a sense of life in this part of the city during the evening, with the women in the poet's neighbourhood relaxing at the doors to their buildings and leaning out of upstairs windows.

The men would be heading out to the local bars. The image of the woman selling the winkles is especially memorable. We can picture the cart upon which she sat and the pram that was used to transport and hold the buckets of winkles. Meehan also captures something of the dialogue of inner city Dublin, remembering how the woman would give her a message for her mother: 'Tell yer Ma I picked them fresh this morning'.

THEMES

THE STRENGTH AND POWER OF WOMEN

In many of Meehan's poems we encounter strong female characters, women who, though their lives are hard, find the strength to persevere and endure. The woman selling the winkles on the streets of Dublin is someone who has been up early in the morning gathering the winkles along the shore. It is now evening – and a cold evening at that – and she sits on the footpath in the city, selling the winkles she has gathered.

Although her life is very difficult, she takes pride in what she is selling, telling the young poet to tell her mother that she 'picked them fresh this morning'. She also remains good-humoured, patiently telling the young poet how to remove the winkle from the shell, despite the fact that she would have told the young girl how to do this on numerous other occasions.

The poem also gives us the impression that there is strong community of women in the area that support each other and look out for one another. As the young poet passes along the streets on her way to buy the winkles she waves 'up to women at sills or those/ lingering in doorways'.

CHILDHOOD

The poem wonderfully captures the simple pleasures of childhood. We get a sense of how magical something as simple as a bag of winkles can be to a young child. Such simple pleasures are also evident in the delight the young poet takes in seeing the moon or stars visible between the rows of houses.

The poem also illustrates just how exciting the world can appear to children. The young poet races down the stairs of her tenement building, imagining that ghosts dwell in the dark stairwell. She seems to relish being out at this late hour,

waving to the women standing in doorways or leaning out the windows of their flats. As the young poet makes her way down the street, she jumps 'every crack in the pavement', superstitiously believing that threading on these cracks will bring her bad luck. The young poet's return journey home is particularly magical. She proudly carries the packages of winkles home as if they contained the most wonderful riches.

POVERTY AND HARDSHIP

The poem gives us an insight into the lives of hardship and poverty that were common in Ireland when the poet was a child. The poem's opening line suggests that money was very tight in the poet's family. The mother would 'spare' the poet sixpence, suggesting that each week they were just getting by, living hand to mouth.

The condition of the tenement block in which the young poet lived also hints at this hardship. We get the impression that the building was not well maintained and that the bulb on the stairs had been blown for a considerable amount of time. The fact that the poet mentions how she would envy 'each soul in the hot interior' of the bar also suggests that she was not dressed well for the cold and, perhaps, also that her own flat might not have been that warm.

The description of the men 'heading out for the night' suggests, perhaps, how many of the men in the locality would regularly go and drink in bars as a means of escape from the hardship that they had to endure. As we mentioned above, the young poet seems to have been intrigued by the glimpses of these men drinking in the bar, envying the cosy scene she witnessed.

The Pattern

LINE BY LINE

This poem describes the poet's complicated relationship with her mother, Helena, who was born in Dublin in 1933. In 1968, the Meehan family moved to Finglas from Dublin's inner city. There Meehan attended St Michael's Girls' Secondary School. During these years Meehan's relationship with her mother became very difficult. Though they lived in the same house, they grew 'bitter and apart'. They seldom spoke to one another. When they did speak, their conversations turned into rows so explosive the poet describes them as 'wars'.

The poet remembers one shocking incident when her mother struck her across the face. This clearly affected the poet deeply – she can still recall the stinging sensation she experienced: 'the sting of her hand/ across my face in one of our wars'. We are not told what caused the mother to lash out in this way. Perhaps this incident occurred when the poet was expelled from St. Michael's Holy Faith Convent for organising a student protest. Or perhaps the mother didn't approve of the hippy-influenced music scene the poet was drawn to when she was about fifteen years old.

The two grew even further apart when the poet went to study English, History and Classical Civilisation at Trinity College. By the time the mother died at the tragically young age of forty-two, they had grown utterly estranged. The poet's complicated feelings towards her mother continued even after the mother's death. Many years have passed, but the poet has never gone back to visit her grave.

Polishing the floor

The poet thinks back to her childhood, when she would have been seven or eight years old. At that time her family lived in a flat on Séan MacDermott Street in Dublin city centre. The poet remembers how her mother would scrub and polish the floor of the flat's living-room.

- We get a sense that the mother was methodical in her work. She would start 'at the door', covering an area within an 'armreach' of where she kneeled. Only when that area was completed would she move on to the next.
- The mother was also clearly disciplined in her work. She would scrub and polish until 'her knees grew sore', only then stopping for a cup of tea.
- She was also someone who took pride in her work and was determined to do a good job. We see this in how she buffed the wax polish until it exhibited 'a high shine'

The poet, along with her brothers and sisters, were instructed to remain in the bedroom while their mother scrubbed and polished. The poet describes how the lavender scent of the polish would filter or 'percolate' through the air of the apartment: 'The smell/ would percolate back through the flat to us'. Finally, when the mother was finished, she would call the children into the living-room so they could amuse themselves by skating in their socks on the freshly polished floor.

Altering the dress

The poet now focuses on a different memory, recalling an evening in late summer when was twelve or thirteen years old. The following day would see the young poet start secondary school and her mother was altering a 'crimson' dress for her to wear.

The young poet stayed up quite late, long after her younger siblings had gone to bed, keeping her mother company while she worked at these alterations. The young poet and her mother, we sense, enjoyed a moment of friendly intimacy as they sat together by the fire. We can imagine the two of them chatting while the mother cut and sewed.

The mother, while they sat by the fireside, recounted a story from her own teenage years. The dress being altered once belonged to the mother herself and she wore it during her own teenage years. Once she was wearing it when her father caught her out on a date with a boy. Her father responded by flying into a terrible rage.

- He insulted the mother's boyfriend, using terms such as 'lout' and 'cornerboy'.
- He insulted the mother, it is implied, by using terms such as 'slut' and 'prostitute'. We can imagine the shock and shame the mother must have felt being addressed in this manner by her own father. Even years later she still can't bring herself to repeat these slurs: 'I needn't tell you/ what he called me'.
- We can imagine the mother's humiliation as she was dragged 'in by the hair ... in front of the whole street'.
- He brutally removed the makeup she had been wearing for her date in what can only be described as a form of assault. There is a real violence to how he holds her head 'under the kitchen tap'. We can imagine the mother's agony as he went at her with the scrubbing brush and carbolic soap that were usually used for scrubbing clothes.

This was clearly a traumatic incident for the mother, one that has lingered vividly in her memory.

Eventually, the teenage poet had to go to bed herself. She woke up the next morning to find the alteration complete and the dress ready for her first day at her new school. Her mother had also provided her with 'three new copybooks' and a new tip or 'nib' for her fountain pen. Also waiting for her was a St Christopher medal, a small silver pendant 'strung on a silver wire' so it can be worn around the neck. These were traditionally worn by travellers as charms to keep them safe on 'perilous' journeys through 'unchartered realms'.

The poet, however, was put off by the fact the dress was second-hand. To her this previously owned item was a 'stigma', a mark of disgrace. It 'spelt poverty', showing clearly to her friends and neighbours that her family was struggling to get by. Wearing the dress made her feel embarrassed and ashamed.

The poet, then, exhibited little 'grace' or gratitude for the mother's efforts in altering the dress. We can imagine her grumbling as she puts it on and leaving it crumpled on the ground when she takes it off. We can even imagine her wearing it in a deliberately ungraceful fashion, failing to adjust it so it fits her figure properly. She was relieved when she grew too big to wear the dress and did not have to wear it anymore: I grew enough to pass// it on by Christmas to the next in line'.

The poet recalls how in her early teenage years she developed a new sense of curiosity and independence. Each day after school she would wander the streets of Dublin, roaming further and further from the family home on Séan MacDermott Street: 'I was sizing/ up the world beyond our flat'.

There was something deliberate and meticulous about the way the poet explored the city:

- The phrase 'sizing up' suggests that she was carefully considering and forming opinions about the world at large.
- She would explore the city 'patch by patch', getting to know one area before moving on to the next.
- Gradually she developed a sense of the city's geography, of how its streets, squares and diamonds fitted together.
- She was especially fascinated by the river, and would stand there for hours watching it pulse by.
- She would also watch ships 'coming and going' in Dublin Port.

The young poet was certain that one day she would board such a ship and let the river carry her out beyond the harbour to the open sea. She would make her way to some exotic, far-off destination, such as Zanzibar, off the coast of East Africa, or the great Indian city of Bombay, or the ancient civilisation of Ethiopia.

The mother in the Phoenix Park

The poet now focuses on a photo of her mother which was taken many years ago in the Phoenix Park. The mother was heavily pregnant at the time. There is something graceful or regal about the mother's bearing. She looks like she could be a member of an aristocratic family, those who are 'born to' or inherit great estates with their 'formal gardens'. She looks like she could be the owner of the rose garden in which she sits, rather than a woman from a flat on Séan MacDermott Street who is visiting a public park.

But the poet also gets the impression that her mother was experiencing great sorrow. The mother seems utterly wrapped up in these sorrowful thoughts. She is so distracted that she only half realises she is being photographed: 'She stares out as if unaware/ that any human hand held the camera'. She seems utterly disconnected from what's going on around her: 'wrapped/ entirely in her own shadow'.

Knitting and skeins

The poem concludes with another two memories related to the mother's knitting. First, the poet recalls her mother knitting by the fire. She remembers how her mother would be silent, lost in concentration and focusing on her knitting pattern. She would give a 'sporadic' or occasional 'mutter' when she came to 'a hard place in the pattern'. Like many people she would attempt to make sense of the instructions by reading them aloud.

Second, she would remember helping her mother create neat balls of wool. She would have to kneel before her mother holding a 'skein', a large, knotted clump of wool. She was required to hold the skein stretched taut between her hands. This would allow her mother to draw out a continuous thread of wool, which she would roll into neat balls.

The poet would frequently become distracted and loosen her grip upon the skein. She'd find herself fascinated by the shadows the fire cast on the ceiling. She would imagine that the shadows were clouds and that she herself was a kite swimming among them: 'If I swam like a kite too high/ amongst the shadows on the ceiling'. She would be equally fascinated by the light the fire cast on the floor. She would imagine that these were flickering pools and she was a fish travelling through their depths: 'or flew like a fish in the pools/ of pulsing light'.

The mother, it seems, would be frustrated by her daughter's lapses in concentration. She would snap the daughter out of her daydreams by yanking on the skein. This would remind the daughter to focus on the skein and hold it at the appropriate tightness. The poet uses a wonderful metaphor to describe this, declaring that her mother was reeling her back to reality like a fish being reeled onto land: 'she'd reel me firmly/ home, she'd land me at her knees'.

The mother, it seems, has been teaching the daughter how to knit. She has urged the daughter to properly follow the various knitting patterns they have been using. But the daughter, it seems, is unwilling or unable to do so: 'One of these days I must/ teach you to follow a pattern'. We can imagine how the daughter might let her imagination run away with her, departing from the pattern's plan, as she knits rows and stitches of her own devising.

THEMES

FAMILY

This poem is a moving exploration of the relationships between mothers and their eldest daughters. Such relationships, Meehan suggests, all too often turn sour: 'Some say that's the fate of the eldest daughter'. We get the impression that much of the tension between Meehan and her mother arose because of the great differences between them.

The poet, then, views herself as very different to the mother. The phrase 'Little has come down to me of hers' refers to physical heirlooms the poet has inherited from her mother. But it also reflects the poet's belief that she has inherited few of her mother's traits and characteristics.

The poet, we sense, is someone given to introspection, to reflecting on her own life, to contemplating her own thoughts and emotions. She is prone to looking into the mirror, searching for a 'glimmer of her true self'. The mother, on the other hand, is not given to such introspection. She spent little time, the poet imagines, contemplating her own face when she saw it reflected in the floor's polished surface. She simply shrugged and moved on with her work.

The poet, as we highlight below, comes across as highly imaginative. The mother's relative lack of imagination comes across in her 'sensible' colour choices when she knits. The poet is rather dreamy and prone to lapses in concentration. We see this when she repeatedly loses focus and and lets the skein of wool go slack. The mother, on the other hand, values focus and concentration in all she does, whether it is knitting, sewing, polishing the floor or unravelling a skein of wool. The mother – focused but unimaginative – always follows the 'pattern' when she knits. The daughter, prone to letting her imagination run away with her, never does.

Perhaps, however, the poet and her mother are not so different after all. There is something about the mother's meticulousness, for instance, in how the daughter explores the city, getting to know it section by section. The mother, meanwhile, exhibits something of the daughter's introspection when she's photographed in the Phoenix Park. As we've seen, she seems so distracted, so lost in her own thoughts that she is unaware of what's going on around her.

The poet wishes that she had a chance to explore these similarities. She wishes her mother had lived on until the poet herself had matured: 'I wish now she'd lasted until after/ I'd grown up'. They would have been two independent women, neither reliant on the other. They would have been unburdened of family commitments: 'without tags like mother, wife,/ sister, daughter'. They could have got to know each other afresh, first as acquaintances and then, perhaps, as friends: 'We might have made a new start'. The poem's great tragedy, then, is that the mother passed away before such a new start could be made.

BECOMING A POET

'The Pattern' shows us how, even as a child, Meehan was a highly imaginative person. She can spend hours watching the river flowing by lost in fantasies of faraway lands or studying the fireplace's patterns of light and shadow. An interesting feature of this passage is how the poet imagines kites swimming and fish flying. This suggests pure imaginative freedom. The poet conjures a world where the rules of physics don't apply and in which anything can happen. In the poet's imagination, the ocean can be composed of air, while the sky can behave like water.

The poet's burgeoning imagination is evidenced when she imagines a robe that has been dyed in a colour of extraordinary purity, a shade so intense it couldn't possibly exist in the real world. The robe, in the poet's imagination, morphs and twists, transforming into a 'word' or a piece of text. Here we sense not only the poet's active imagination, but also her growing fascination with the written word. She is beginning to realise that through writing she can capture these visions and convey them to other people.

POVERTY AND HARDSHIP

The mother was born into the Ireland of the 1930s. The country was extremely poor. It was also a narrow and closed-minded place. There were extremely limited opportunities for education and advancement. This was especially so for the working class into which the mother was born.

The mother had a very limited and constrained life. She had little education and no career outside the home. The poem suggests that she married the first man she ever dated and had her first child the following year. From a relatively young age, therefore, she was expected to devote herself to a life of housework and childcare.

If the mother had been born in a different time, during a different phase of Irish history, she could have flourished like her daughter and achieved a fulfilling life. History, then, has brought the mother 'to her knees', robbing her of such fulfilment. The photograph taken in the Phoenix Park shows her wrapped/ entirely in her own shadow', lost in melancholy thoughts of what her life might have been.

Perhaps the mother, like the poet, once dreamed of faraway places like Zanzibar. But she realises now that she will never make such journeys. Her life is confined to her flat and a few square miles of Dublin city: 'the world beyond her/ already a dream, already lost'.

THE STRENGTH AND POWER OF WOMEN

The mother, however, didn't succumb to these difficulties – instead, she stayed strong for the sake of her family.
- The mother is presented as extremely hard-working. Nearly all the poet's memories of her, in fact, involve work of some kind. Even her leisure activity, knitting, is work of a kind: we can imagine her knitting hats, gloves and other useful items.
- We get the sense that the mother had to be extremely resourceful and resilient in order to steer the family through a lifetime of hardship and poverty. We see this when she re-purposes a dress declaring that there is 'Plenty of wear in it yet'.
- The mother is highly protective of her 'brood' and will do anything, we sense, to protect her six children: 'It'll be over my dead body anyone harms a hair of your head'.
- But the mother is also capable of great tenderness towards her daughter. We see this when she 'must have stayed up half the night/ to finish the dress', determined that her daughter will look good on her first day back. Tenderness is also suggested when she gives her daughter the copy books, the nib and the St. Christopher's medal.

The poem, then, highlights the central role that mothers play in the lives of their children. We see this when the poet describes how she and her siblings would skate around their mother on the freshly polished floor. She uses a beautiful simile to describe this, declaring that the children orbited the mother just as planets orbit the sun.

Meehan, at the poem's conclusion, sees 'Tongues of flame' in her mother's eyes. Perhaps this is simply an optical effect, the mother's dark eyes reflecting the glow of the fireplace. Or perhaps the young poet is thinking of the tongues of flame that in the Bible descended on the apostles, granting them extraordinary powers and abilities. Perhaps the poet senses that her mother, too, is capable of extraordinary things. But the mother, alas, was never granted the opportunity to fulfil this potential.

Continuity

This poem is very much about the patterns of inheritance, how traits or characteristics repeat across the generations, like stitches in a knitted garment.

The grandfather's ferocious temper, evident when he drags the mother 'in by the hair', is passed down to the mother, and comes across when she strikes her daughter in the face.
The grandfather's meticulousness is evident when he scrubs 'every spick of lipstick and mascara' from the mother's face. The mother is similarly meticulous when she polishes the floor of the apartment. The poet herself, in turn, is meticulous in her explorations of Dublin town.

Sometimes, of course, we don't like the idea of inheriting our parents' characteristics. The mother, for instance, describes the grandfather as a 'tyrant', perhaps not realising that she has inherited some of his tyrannical ways. The poet makes a similar point, declaring that 'Little has come down' to her from her mother. But the poem, as we've seen, suggests that they have more in common than she might think.

The Statue of the Virgin at Granard Speaks

LINE BY LINE

This poem is centred on the poetic device known as personification. Personification, we remember, occurs when an inanimate object is depicted as if it had human characteristics. Meehan, in this instance, personifies a statue of the Virgin Mary. The statue in question can be seen in a grotto on the outskirts of the town of Granard, County Longford. The statue is presented as being capable of speech. It is presented as being capable of experiencing physical sensations like cold and discomfort. It is presented as being capable of emotional states like puzzlement and sexual desire.

The grotto in which the statue stands came to national attention due to the tragic death of Ann Lovett, a 15-year-old schoolgirl from the town. Ann had become pregnant but had managed to keep the pregnancy secret from her family and friends. On 31 January 1984, knowing her baby was coming, she went to the grotto alone to give birth. By the time Ann was discovered, her baby was already dead. Ann herself passed away some hours later. The story became a national scandal and greatly influenced the debate on women, sexuality and pregnancy in Irish life.

1

It is All Souls' Night, the Night of 2 November. It is extremely cold: 'It can be bitter here at times like this'. It is extremely windy, with a gale 'sweeping' through Northern Ireland, 'across the border' and down into County Longford. The wind, according to the statue, carries 'seeds' or pellets of ice that are capable of cutting 'to the quick', which suggests that they can penetrate the skin to damage vital and sensitive organs.

The people of Granard, unsurprisingly, are all 'tucked up safe' in bed. Indeed, not even 'wild things', such as badgers and foxes, are forced to endure these icy conditions. These creatures are normally active during the nighttime. But this particular night is so bitter that they have 'gone to earth', finding shelter in burrows, hedges and the hollows of trees.

The statue complains, therefore, that she alone is exposed to the elements on this brutal All Souls' Night. The statue, of course, is utterly immobile and must remain in its grotto, despite the terrible weather: 'and I/ stuck up here in this grotto'. It must continue with its 'vigil' all night long (A vigil, we remember, is a period of watching and waking that takes place during the hours usually devoted to sleep).

The statue, therefore, must endure the utter darkness of this overcast November night. There isn't a single star or planet glinting in the sky that might cheer it up as it maintains its vigil. It must also endure the wind's cacophony: 'The howling won't let up'. The sound of the wind, it seems, resembles a series of long mournful cries that just go on and on. The statue must also endure the wind's unpleasant odour. The statue describes how it can 'taste' this unpleasant mixture of turf-smoke and stagnant water, suggesting that the wind is blowing directly into its mouth.

The statue refers to the Northern Ireland Troubles, which were on going when the poem was written. The statue imagines the sinister activities that are taking place in 'garrison towns' such as Newry, or 'walled cities' such as Derry, or in the 'ghetto lanes' of East and West Belfast.

'Garrison towns' were towns in which the British Army were permanently stationed. Such towns tended to grow and prosper because of the British presence. The term 'ghetto' meanwhile refers to a city district reserved for people of a particular faith. Parts of Belfast were sometimes referred to as ghettos because they were predominantly inhabited by either Catholics or Protestants.

Men, in these towns, cities and ghettos, engage in 'death tactics'. They plan and carry out assassinations, bombings and shootings. They 'hunt each other' and engage in 'night manoeuvres', heading out each night to murder and maim under cover of darkness.

There's an element of fantasy or 'poetic licence' as the statue suggests that the wind informs it about these grisly nighttime killings. It's as if the wind, as it sweeps through Northern Ireland, picks up and carries the whispering of the conspirators as the plan their 'night manoeuvres', the sound of the gunshots, the screams of the dying.

2

The statue describes how the people of the locality come to the grotto. They address the statue as if it were Mary, the mother of Jesus: 'They call me Mary'. They speak to it as if it were a divine being, referring to it as 'Blessed' or 'Holy'. They even 'kneel before' the statue and pray to it.

Visitors to the grotto also associate the statue with the concept of the virgin birth, which states that Mary was 'mated' or had sex with 'no mortal man'. Instead, she was still a virgin when she gave birth to Jesus, who was conceived through a miraculous intervention on the part of the Holy Spirit.

The statue, however, seems surprised that the local people address it in this way: 'They call me Mary'. It seems perturbed that people come and kneel before it offering up their prayers. The statue, then, seems clear in its mind that it is not actually the Virgin Mary. It is no divine or semi-divine being. It didn't experience any miraculous virgin birth and didn't witness the crucifixion in Palestine two thousand years ago. It's just a sculpted piece of marble that has spent decades perched within its grotto.

The statue, using a wonderful simile, compares the prayers of the local people to sparks that drift upward from a bonfire then 'wink out'. The statue views their prayers, like such sparks, as being beautiful but fleeting. The prayers express noble sentiments and feature beautiful turns of phrase. But they serve no lasting purpose. The statue can't imagine that they are heard or answered by any spiritual being. It seems puzzled by all this praying, by what it regards as an utterly futile activity.

3

The statue emphasises that the weather isn't always terrible in Granard: 'It can be lovely here at times'. Each season, according to the statue, bangs its own particular beauty to the fields beside the grotto.

The statue thinks of spring and early summer when boys and girls who have made their first communion come to the grotto. At that time of year wildflowers such as 'cow parsley' and 'haw blossom' bloom in the surrounding area. The statue describes how these wildflowers are a 'riot' in the hedgerows, suggesting their abundant unstoppable growth. They exhibit a pristine whiteness, one far more striking than that of the 'frocks' worn by the communion girls.

In midsummer, meanwhile, the grotto is frequently visited by newly-married couples: 'Or the grace of a midsummer wedding'. Midsummer, of course, is a time of extraordinary fertility. We can imagine lavish, luscious growth in the surrounding area, as plants, trees and flower all flourish.

At such moments the statue is filled with sexual desire:
- It longs to be 'incarnate' or made flesh. It longs to exchange its immobile plaster form for one made of flesh of blood, so it can touch and be touched.
- The statue uses a wonderful metaphor to describe this impulse, declaring that it wants to 'break loose of [its] stony robes'.
- The statue, then, wants to lie with a human man. It wants to be 'tousled' or caressed in a bed that is 'honeyed' or sweetened with physical 'intimacy'.

Tellingly, the statue tends to experience these moments of desire when a newly-married couple has come to visit it. It's as if the statue envies the couple's passion and affection. These moments of desire also occur in summertime, reflecting the widespread assumption that sexual desire and activity are more prevalent during the summer months.

The statue associates the season of autumn with 'burial[s]' and we can imagine how funeral parties might stop at the grotto as they make their way from church to cemetery. In autumn, according to the statue, the landscape engages in 'pageantry', in an elaborate beautiful display. The wind is sweetened with the scent of fallen pears as it causes clouds to 'scud' or career eastward across the sky. Berries grow so abundantly in the surrounding area that they are a heavy 'burden' to the hedgerows on which they flourish. 'Windfalls', fallen apples and pears, lied hidden in the 'orchard grasses'.

4

On this November night, however, the weather is absolutely terrible. The fierce winds sound like 'keening', which suggests human beings wailing over the body of a deceased loved one. The gale blows relentlessly and the statue must endure its howling night long, without a single break or 'respite': 'But on this All Souls' Night there is/ no respite from the keening of the wind'.

The sound of the wind, the statue suggests, is so loud that it could wake the corpses in the nearby graveyard: 'I would not be amazed if every corpse came risen/ from the graveyard' (This of course is an instance of hyperbole or deliberate poetic exaggeration).

In what sense are the dead the 'conscience of the town'? When the people of the town make moral judgments they invoke the dead. The say things like 'My grandfather would be so ashamed of me if he saw me doing this' or 'What would your Aunt Josephine say if she could see you in such a state?' The dead are imagined to be morally flawless and provide an impossible standard against which the living must measure their behaviour.

The statue imagines that the awakened corpses would howl in 'exaltation' or delight as they wandered around the cemetery. They would be elated, she imagines, to be active and animate again after years or centuries in the grave. They would produce an unpleasant or cacophonous sound, 'a cacophony of bone', that mingles with the roaring of the gale.

- When the dead were still alive, their lives were governed by the town's Catholic morality.
- But even in death they are still involved in this morality. For they remain, according to the statue, the 'conscience of the town'.
- The dead's only 'release' from this moral system can come through the destruction of the town itself.

355

- It imagines their revived corpses shouting at the sky, begging or 'imploring' God to trigger the day of 'judgment' and the end of the world.

For this would mean the end of the town and their 'release', finally, from its system of morality.

5

On stormy nights such as this one, the statue finds itself thinking of Ann Lovett and her tragic passing: 'On a night like this I remember the child'.

- She recalls how Ann was only fifteen years old on that terrible day: 'She...who came with fifteen summers to her name'.
- She recalls how Ann took refuge in the grotto: 'and she lay down alone at my feet'.
- She recalls how Ann, in the throes of childbirth, was utterly alone, lacking any moral or medical support: 'without midwife or doctor or friend to hold her hand'.
- The statue recalls how Ann, as she gave birth alone, was 'in extremis', was in an extreme state of mental and physical distress.

Ann, like many people, responded to a terrible situation by praying for help from God. To Ann, the statue represented the Blessed Virgin. Ann wanted the statue to 'intercede with heaven', to act as an advocate or intermediary. Ann hoped that the statue would reach out to God on her behalf, that the statue would ask God to alleviate her plight.

The statue, however, did nothing practical to help Ann: 'I did not move,/ I didn't lift a finger to help her'. Nor did the statue respond to Ann's request to 'intercede with heaven'. It didn't reach out to God on Ann's behalf. It didn't 'whisper the charmed word' that might have moved God to act and help Ann in her hour of greatest need.

THEMES

NATURE AND SPIRITUALITY

The statue adopts a very spiritual view of nature, regarding the earth as divine beings of a kind. The earth, however, is very different from the God of the Catholic faith. First, it is female rather than male. Second, it wants people to express rather than repress their sexual desire. In summer time, as we've seen, the earth is maximally fertile. And the earth, according to the statue, calls on human beings to be fertile too, to engage in 'coupling' or sexual activity: 'when the earth herself calls out for coupling'.

The sun, too, is presented as a kind of goddess, one that the statue venerates or worships. The statue longs for the winter solstice, which falls on 21 December each year. That date represents a 'turn back to the light'. The days slowly start to get longer and the sun's presence is felt more in the world.

The statue, at the end of the poem, prays to the sun directly: 'O sun'. The statue's prayer, like many prayers, involves a list or 'litany' of names for the deity being prayed to:

- The sun is described as our 'centre', reflecting the fact that our whole lives, in a sense, are spent orbiting the sun. The earth, meanwhile, is compared to a dancer that traces a circle, over and over again, around the sun's central point.
- The sun is described as a 'burning heart', suggesting the extraordinary potency of its flames.
- The sun is described as our 'molten mother'. The term 'molten', of course, reinforces our sense of the sun's incomprehensible heat, causing us to envision a sphere of churning lava. The description of the sun as our 'mother', meanwhile, reminds us that we depend on the sun's heat and light for our very survival.

The statue calls on the sun to 'have pity' on us poor human beings. It's as if the statue wants the sun to intervene in human affairs and somehow make the world a better place. We sense, however, that the statue's prayers, like those of Ann on the day she died, are likely to remain unanswered. The earth's dance, we fear, is destined to remain a 'foolish' one, as we human beings will almost certainly remain thoughtless, selfish and judgemental. We will continue to produce societies where innocent people like Ann are victimised and destroyed.

SOCIAL JUSTICE

The poem draws a stark contrast between and Ann and the society of which she was a part. The rest of the town was 'tucked up' safe and warm, while Ann, alone in the cold of a January night, suffered the agony of childbirth. The image of the towns being 'tucked up' in scandals, bargains, prayers and promises is a powerful one. It suggests that such concerns envelop their minds just as sheets and blankets envelop their bodies when they go to bed at night.

These lines remind us that the people of the town failed Ann as her pregnancy wore on. No one noticed that things weren't quite right with her. There was no one Ann felt she could turn to, no older member of society with whom she could share her 'secret'. The people of the town were too wrapped up in their own affairs – in 'bargains' and business dealings, in their hopes and 'prayers', 'promises' they had to keep or get out of.

These lines also suggest that that the town was characterised by the judgemental sexual morality associated with the church. 'Prayers', of course, were central to life. We get the impression that the townsfolk were quick to judge those involved in 'little scandals' that occurred around the parish. But some townsfolk, of course, despite their prayers and judgement, were likely to behave in scandalous behaviour themselves.

RELIGION

Sectarianism

The poem, it must be said, presents a very negative view of Christianity. The mention of the Northern Ireland Troubles, for instance, reminds us that Christianity, over the centuries, has given rise to a wide variety of violent conflicts. These conflicts tend to be sectarian in nature, involving a clash between different sects or branches of the Christian faith.

The Troubles, we remember, were in part such a sectarian conflict, a struggle between a Catholic community on one side, and a Protestant community on the other. The statue refers to the 'various names of God', suggesting how both sides in the conflict have a different understanding of God and use different prayers and phrases to address the divine. But each side believes that God is with them. They believe that by killing they are doing God's will and 'invoke' or seek his blessing as they engage in their 'death tactics'.

A Faith of Misery and Suffering

The poem focuses on the Catholic version of Christianity in particular, presenting it as a faith obsessed with misery and suffering. We see this when the local people refer to the statue as 'Mother of all this grief'. There is an element of metonymy here, which occurs when we refer to something by the names of something with which it is closely associated. Jesus, in this instance, in referred to as 'all this grief' because he is so closely associated with suffering and sorrow.

But the term 'Mother of all this grief' also brings to the mind the Catholic religion as a whole. Mary, after all, is frequently referred to as the mother of the church. The phrase suggests that the Catholic faith is centred on grief and suffering, that it celebrates and elevates misery and suffering. This is evident in the way visitors to the grotto dwell on the crucifixion and associate the statue with that grisly event: 'They fit me to a myth of a man crucified'. The statue, in their minds, is linked to the various tortures Jesus suffered: being whipped or scourged, falling several times as he carried the cross through Jerusalem, having a 'thorny crown' placed mockingly on his head, enduring the 'hammer blow of iron' as his wrists and ankles were nailed to the cross.

The statue's own hardships arguably reinforce our sense of Catholicism as a religion of suffering. The statue, as we have seen, must maintain its vigil all night long no matter what the weather, enduring 'seeds of ice' and the incessant howling of the wind. This calls to mind the tendency in Catholicism to make the body suffer in order that it be cleansed of sin.

Sexuality

The poem also reminds us of how the Catholic faith represses and mistrusts sexuality. This is suggested by the fact that a virgin, a woman 'mated to no mortal man', plays such a central role in the religion. The faithful utter phrases like 'Blessed, Holy, Virgin', suggesting that for them Mary's holiness is wrapped up in her asexual nature.

In the Catholic faith, then, sexual activity is regarded, metaphorically speaking, as a stain or tarnish. Mary, being a virgin, is regarded as 'immaculate' or unstained. The statue, on the other hand, longs to be 'maculate' or stained. It longs to take on a human form and engage in sexual activity. The mention of a 'midsummer wedding', meanwhile, brings to mind the Church's disapproval of sexual relations outside of marriage. Midsummer is a time of maximum fertility, when, as the statue puts it, 'the earth herself calls out for coupling'. But good Catholics must refrain from such 'coupling' unless they've been married in the eyes of God.

The statue's description of how it's trapped in 'stony robes' serves as a powerful metaphor for this sexual repression. The statue, in these lines, presents itself as a sensual human being held prisoner within a hard outer casing that prevents it from expressing its sexuality. The people of Catholic Ireland, similarly, are held prisoner within the church's rules and regulations, strictures that prevent them from expressing their sexuality.

Guilt and Shame

This repressive morality, unsurprisingly, gives rise to great deal of shame and guilt when it comes to sexual matters. This is heartbreakingly evident in the case of Ann Lovett, who, as we have seen, felt obliged to keep her pregnancy a secret. This is emphasised by a famous instance of metonymy: 'and she pushed her secret out into the night'. Metonymy, as we noted above, occurs when we refer to something by the name of something with which it is closely associated. Ann's baby, in this instance, in referred to as 'her secret' because he was so closely associated with secrecy and shame.

The Failure of Catholicism

It was this shame, of course, that caused Ann to give birth alone 'without midwife or doctor or friend to hold her hand'. It was this shame that led to her tragic and all too avoidable death. There is a bitter irony, then, in the fact that Ann sought refuge in the grotto and called out to the Virgin Mary for help, as it was the faith represented by the grotto and its Virgin that had led to her predicament in the first place.

The statue, as we've seen, describes how it 'didn't lift a finger to help' Ann in her hour of need. In one sense, of course, this shouldn't surprise us. For the statue, as we pointed out above, is only an immobile piece of plaster. It is no divine or semi-divine being. It could neither help Ann in any practical way nor intercede on her behalf with God.

But the statue's failure to act can also be read on a symbolic level. The statue can be seen as a symbol for the church. The statue's inability to help, meanwhile, can be seen as a symbol of the Church's failure. The church failed not only Ann but entire generations of Irish people by offering them judgement rather than kindness, by making them ashamed of their sexuality and their very selves.

Cora, Auntie

LINE BY LINE

The poem is a tribute to the poet's aunt, Cora. Cora was the poet's mother's sister. She lived in Dublin until 1961, when she emigrated to England. Meehan was six at the time. Cora remained in London for the rest of her life.

Cora's last year

The poet recalls how Cora looked shortly before she died. She was sick with cancer and had been receiving chemotherapy. The treatment and the long illness left her aunt frail and weak. Her body had 'withered'. Her skin looked 'Old' and she very frail and thin. Meehan describes her emaciated body looked like a 'bag of bones'.

Meehan describes how close to death her aunt was at this point. She personifies 'Death', imagining it as some sinister figure that was always lurking close to Cora at this time. But Cora remained unperturbed by death, treating it with defiance and good humour.

- Meehan recalls how her aunt would fearlessly confront the fact that she was going to die. She describes Cora as a gunslinger and 'Death' as a foe or enemy she had to face. The strong pain medication the aunt was taking and the whiskey that she would drink are compared to pistols that Cora would use in a face-off with Death.
- She recalls how her aunt would never treat her pending death in a sombre or serious manner. Instead, Cora is described as 'laughing at Death', as though he were some ridiculous, comical figure.
- Cora would use humour to ward off any negative thoughts of death, making light of the fact that she was going to die. Meehan compares her aunt to a medieval knight taking part in a jousting contest. Humour is compared to the 'lance' that her aunt carries. As she charges towards her adversary, Death, she tilts or lowers this lance in order to knock her opponent from his horse: 'humour a lance// she tilted at Death'.

Although the aunt was in a lot of pain, she did not behave like someone defeated or tortured by her condition. The poet recalls her aunt tolerating or 'bearing the pain'. Nor did she speak like someone who felt persecuted. There was, Meehan says, no 'crucifixion' in her voice. Instead, when Cora spoke, the poet heard tones of exaltation, great happiness and 'glory' in her voice.

Rather than become morose and withdrawn, it seems Cora became even more of a force in her final year. We get the impression that Cora was always flamboyant and exuberant and that she remained this way until the very end. The poem,

after all, opens with the memorable image of her holding a bottle of morphine in one hand and a bottle of whiskey in the other.

This aspect of Cora's character further reinforces Meehan's description of what it was like to head out onto the London streets with Cora. At this stage, due to her weakened condition, Cora had to use a 'motorised invalid scooter' to get around. Meehan recalls how her aunt would career recklessly down the street out in front of the trams. She was, as Meehan says, the bane of the tram drivers operating in the area: 'Scourge of Croydon tram drivers'. If she was not on the street she would be driving recklessly along the footpaths, forcing anyone who was walking at a leisurely pace to jump out of her way. Meehan characterises such pedestrians as 'High Street dossers', a term we can imagine her aunt might have used for anyone who got in her way. A dosser is a slang term for someone who is idle or lazy.

Despite the fact that her illness and treatment had left her looking old and haggard, Cora remained in many ways youthful. The aunt's hair, which had fallen out when she was receiving chemotherapy, 'grew back'. The poet recalls how the hair was 'thick and curly as when she was a girl'. And her eyes, though they grew 'darker and stranger' as her conditioned worsened, always held a youthful twinkle: 'always a girl in her glance'.

The aunt's name, the poet points out, has associations with youth. Cora comes from the Greek Kore, which means 'the girl' or 'the maiden'. In Greek mythology, Kore was another name for Persephone, the goddess of fertility and vegetation who was associated with the blossoming of the flowers and plants in spring and summer: 'promising blossom, summer, the scent of thyme'.

The wedding dress

The poet switches to a different memory of her aunt. She recalls a time when her aunt was a young woman preparing for her wedding. It was nineteen sixty-one and Cora was 'nearly twenty-one'. The poet vividly remembers her aunt standing up on the kitchen table in her 'white satin dress'. Around the table stood the poet's mother, her other aunts and her maternal grandmother. They are sewing red sequins to the bottom of the dress. As the women standing around the table attach the sequins, Cora 'moves slowly round and round'.

Meehan was a young child at the time. She recalls how she was barely tall enough to 'see over' the table. As the women attended to Cora's dress, she walked around them, orbiting the table. She also remembers being under the table 'singing'. But it is the sequins that were being sewn to the hem of the dress that the poet remembers most vividly. They were of the most intense red colour: 'red as berries'.

Cora was set to emigrate to England shortly after the wedding. Meehan tells us that she was 'weeks from taking the boat to England', which is euphemism for the fact that her aunt had to leave Ireland in order that she and her husband could find stable employment and survive. Meehan recalls how the cards that the aunt received before she departed remained standing on the mantelpiece for weeks after Cora left. These were cards from her family and friends, wishing her luck as she embarked on newly married life abroad. The poet remembers how the cards had the traditional images or 'emblems of luck' that often feature on wedding cards.

Meehan also remembers how the cards had images of large keys, which the poet describes as 'emblems ... of access'. These keys were meant to symbolise how her marriage was unlocking a whole new life for her. But the term 'access' suggests that in moving to England, Cora was accessing opportunities that were just not available to her in Ireland at the time.

Finding the sequins

The bright red sequins that Cora had sewn into the hem of her wedding dress really captured the young poet's imagination. After her aunt left for England, she spent a year searching the house for sequins that had fallen from the dress and got scattered around the house. Meehan remembers how she would find them everywhere, 'in the pillowcase,/ under the stairs,/ in a hole in the lino'. These small items would be discovered in the most unlikely of spots, 'in cracks and crannies' all over the house.

In her search for the sequins, the young poet discovered a variety of other items, bits of jewellery that had broken, fallen and got lost: 'odd beads and single earrings,/ a broken charm bracelet, a glittering pin'. The young poet treasured each item she found, gathering them all 'into a tin box'.

The poet has kept this tin and she opens it now 'in memory' of her aunt. The items inside the tin are described as 'coinage', suggesting the sequins and other bits of jewellery are like valuable old coins. But the term coinage can also refer to anything made, invented or fabricated. As such, the word calls to mind the aunt's creative spirit, her ability to turn situations, no matter how difficult or grim, into occasions of fun and excitement.

Opening the tin reveals once again the aunt's 'glamour', her singular enchanting style. Meehan describes her aunt as an 'emigrant soul', calling to mind the fact that the aunt had to leave Ireland and move to England. But the term also conveys the fact that the aunt is now dead and her soul has moved on to another realm.

THEMES

THE STRENGTH AND POWER OF WOMEN

The poem offers us a wonderful portrait of someone with great character and spirit. Cora is presented as a flamboyant and fearless individual, someone who lived life on her own terms. The opening lines of the poem present us with a memorable image of the aunt facing death down like a gunslinger in a Western movie. But instead of being armed with pistols, the aunt faces death with 'a bottle of morphine in one hand/ and a bottle of Jameson in the other'.

The startling addition of the red sequins to the wedding dress tells us something about the aunt's personality. We get a sense of someone who liked to do things differently, to bring her own unique style to situations and occasions. The fact that the poet kept these sequins over the years tells us just how powerful a presence this glamorous woman was in her life.

FAMILY

The poet also remembers the other women that played important roles in her childhood. Meehan compares them to 'stars' whose light is only now reaching her. It is as if only now as an adult she can fully appreciate their strength and character: 'Cora, Marie, Jacinta, my aunties,/ Helena, my mother, Mary, my grandmother-/ the light of those stars// only reaching me now'. The poem also highlights how powerful the love between family members can be. Meehan describes how it was 'love unconditional' that kept the aunt alive towards the end.

BECOMING A POET

We get the sense that Cora offered the young girl a different way of seeing things, opening her eyes to the possibility of transcending the circumstances of her life. Cora represented 'glamour' and individuality. She showed the young poet the possibility of striking out on your own, of being true to yourself. Meehan seems to have been quite taken with the aunt from an early age, imagining her to be like one of the charatecrs in the books she read as a young child. She compares the vivid redness of the sequins to the colour of maidens' lips and the red of the 'blood on the snow' in 'Child's old ballads'.

We get the impression that Cora might have been something of an influence on Meehan becoming a poet. Meehan compares the red of the sequins to the pen she uses to compose the poem, saying the sequins are 'as red as this pen/ on this white paper'. The description of the poet snatching a moment out of the 'chaos' of her life to write these lines at her own kitchen table might also be a reflection of the wonderful mayhem of Cora's life.

The Exact Moment I Became a Poet

LINE BY LINE

This poem is set in 1963 when Meehan was 8-year-old pupil in Central Model Girls' School, Gardiner Street. The poet remembers an occasion when she and the rest of her classmates had become distracted from their lessons and were chatting and laughing. She recalls how Miss Shannon, her teacher at the time, attempted to silence the classroom.

Miss Shannon, in an effort to gain the class's attention, rapped her duster against the easel that was holding up her blackboard. A 'cloud' of chalk dust flew upward from the duster, leaving her 'half obscured' for a moment. She urged her pupils to be quiet, issuing them a stark warning. If they didn't 'Attend' or pay attention at school they would never find a good job later in life. They will only be able to secure employment in the local 'sewing factory': 'or mark my words you'll end up/ in the sewing factory'

The poet is upset

The young poet was deeply upset by Miss Shannon's words, by how her teacher presented the sewing factory as a worthless and undesirable place of employment. After all, some of her classmates had mothers who worked there. These classmates, no doubt, would be embarrassed to hear their mothers' workplace referred to in such a fashion. Indeed, the young poet herself also experienced such embarrassment; her own aunt worked in that very factory, as did a number of her neighbours.

The young poet was particularly upset by Miss Shannon's use of the phrase 'end up'. This phrase, she realised, suggested a negative or undesirable outcome. It implied that those who worked in the sewing factory had failed in life. It implied that they were stuck in lowly, meaningless jobs no one would ever willingly sign up for.

The young poet felt that the 'labour' in the sewing factory had its own particular 'dignity'. She must have realised that this work, while not fancy or highly-paid, was important in its own way. She must have realised, too, that the women of the factory took great pride in what they did, in producing garments that were well made and hard-wearing. Miss Shannon's words, she realised, 'robbed' the women of this 'dignity', making their 'labour' seem utterly menial and pointless.

The poet acknowledges that she's engaging in 'back construction', that she's altering or reconstructing a memory. We see this when she depicts her eight-year-old self using terms like 'dignity' and 'labour'. The poet accepts that she didn't actually know these terms when she was eight years old. However, she did have some grasp of the feelings and concepts to which these terms relate: 'Not that I knew it then, / not in those words'.

A vision formed by words

Miss Shannon's words triggered the young poet's imagination, leading to a strange and disturbing flight of fancy:

- She found herself imagining the sewing factory with its crew of 'mothers, aunts and neighbours'.
- She imagined that these women had been 'trussed', which suggests that their legs and arms were tied together, and placed on a 'conveyor belt'.
- She imagined that the women were being 'sewn up' like chickens being readied for the oven: 'the way my granny/ sewed the sage and onion stuffing/ in the birds'.

We imagine a procession of women, tied-up and helpless, being shunted along the conveyor belt until one by one they come to some monstrous sewing machine that mutilates their bodies.

THE EXACT MOMENT I BECAME A POET

FOCUS ON STYLE

Metaphor, Simile and Figures of Speech

The poem concludes with a most memorable metaphor:

- Human beings are compared to chickens.
- Our self-esteem is compared to the 'lovely shiny feathers' that cover a chicken's body.
- Hurtful words are compared to hands that pluck the chicken's figures.

Plucking hands will leave a chicken 'naked', utterly stripped of its feathers. Hurtful words, similarly, can leave a human being emotionally naked, stripped of our dignity and self-esteem. Meehan, then, captures the power of hurtful words, such as those spoken by Miss Shannon in that long-ago classroom, to leave us diminished, belittled and humiliated.

Verbal Music

'The Exact Moment I Became a Poet', like many of Meehan's poems, is rich in imagery. The poet wonderfully captures an everyday classroom scene (the teacher banging her duster amid a loud of chalk dust) as well as the surreal and nightmarish image of the 'trussed' women on the conveyor belt.

BECOMING A POET

Meehan, in this poem, describes a crucial moment in her childhood, one when she first realised the power of words. She suddenly understood that words could have a powerful effect on the imagination. Her teacher's comments triggered a flight of fancy image that was not only distressing but also exceptionally vivid: 'I saw them'. For a moment, in her mind's eye, she could see the 'trussed' women on the conveyor belt with a strange and disturbing clarity.

She suddenly understood, too, that words could powerfully affect the emotions. Miss Shannon's remarks about the factory, she realised, had the power to hurt not only the factory workers themselves, but also hurt the workers' daughters nieces and neighbours who sat beside her in the classroom, so that they felt weak, vulnerable and exposed: 'words could pluck you,/ leave you naked'.

The eight-year-old Meehan, then, at that precise moment 'became a poet'. She didn't, of course, immediately start writing poems and getting them published. But she knew that she would spend her life devoted to language. She would begin to learn, starting right now, how to make language work for her. She would harness the power of words to shape images in people's minds. She would use language, just like Miss Shannon had done in the classroom, to affect the emotions of those who heard and read her.

Miss Shannon, on this occasion, used language in a negative fashion. Her words, as we've seen, were wounding and diminishing. The eight-year-old Meehan, we sense, is determined to use language in a much more positive fashion. She will interrogate the powerful in society while providing a voice for the voiceless, weak and vulnerable.

SOCIAL JUSTICE

We sense that the poet, even as a primary school student, was keenly aware of social inequality. She realised that people in her part of inner city Dublin were denied the opportunities granted to those from more privileged parts of the city. And this lack of opportunity, of course, was passed down from one generation to the next.

The poet's daydream vividly conveys this social inequality. Society is compared to a nightmarish factory where generation after generation of 'mothers, aunts and neighbours' from inner city Dublin are processed. The image of these women being 'trussed up' suggests how they were constrained by lack of opportunity. The image of them being mutilated by a giant sewing machine suggests how their underprivileged lives left them mentally and physically damaged.

CHILDHOOD

'The Exact Moment I Became a Poet' wonderfully captures the mentality of childhood. The poem Meehan reminds us that eight-year-old children can understand ideas such as 'labour' and 'dignity', even if they lack the words to express such concepts. It also reminds us that children tend to have exceptionally vivid imaginations that sometimes lead them to strange and disturbing flights of fancy.

THE STRENGTH AND POWER OF WOMEN

The poem also touches on the strength and power of women, another of Meehan's recurring themes. She reminds us that in the inner city Dublin of the 50s and 60s it was working women like these – often doing difficult, repetitive work – who were the primary breadwinners in their respective households, bringing home a wage that kept utter poverty and despair at bay.

The poet, looking back, realises that Miss Shannon, in one way, was correct in her assessment of the sewing factory: 'allowing also/ the teacher was right'. Meehan's own experiences of life have taught her that such factories are exhausting and dehumanising places in which to make a living: 'and no one knows it like I do myself'. Meehan herself, then, wouldn't want to spend her life working in such a place of employment. But Meehan, even as she accepts the truth of Miss Shannon's comments, insists that the 'mothers, aunts and neighbours' who worked there retained a certain 'dignity'. She insists that their labour, while far from glamorous, had value and meaning.

My Father Perceived as a Vision of St. Francis

LINE BY LINE

This poem is set in the house in Finglas where Meehan spent her teenage years. She had returned to stay in the house for a few days. She was visiting her father who still lived there, her mother having passed away some years before.

The poet recalls how she was woken by a 'piebald horse' that was kept in the garden next door. The horse whinnied loudly, causing her to wake 'out of a dream' with a start. It was still dawn when the poet was so rudely awakened. Everyone else in the house was still asleep: 'The rest of the house slept'.

The poet lay in bed and listened to the sounds of the early morning. She heard the clinking sound of glass bottles as the milkman left his delivery 'on the doorstep'. She heard 'the first bus' of the day pull up at the bus stop on the road outside. Then the poet heard her father start moving about downstairs. She heard him 'rake' the previous night's ashes from the fireplace. She heard him 'plug in the kettle' as he prepared to make a cup of tea. Finally, she heard him as he 'unlocked' the back door and 'stepped out' into the garden.

The poet went to the window. It was so early that the sun had not yet fully risen; the eastern half of the sky was bright, while the western half was still dark and speckled with stars. She notes how autumn is transitioning into winter: 'Autumn was nearly done'. It is a cold morning, the first on which frost is visible on the roof slates of the housing estate.

The poet watches her father in the garden below. She suddenly realises that her father is becoming an old man: 'He was older

than I had reckoned'. She notices for the first time that he is showing the effects of age: his hair is silver, his shoulder is stooped and his leg is stiff. She wonders what he is doing in the garden at this early hour: 'What's he at? / So early'.

Suddenly, an enormous flock of birds descended upon the garden: 'They came then: birds'. The flock, it seems, consists of hundreds of birds and a wide variety of species are represented: 'birds / of every size, shape, colour'.

Birds must have come from all over the housing estate: from the 'hedges and shrubs' of neighbouring gardens, from the eaves of houses, from the roofs of garden sheds. They must have come from further afield as well, from the nearby industrial estate and from 'outlying fields'. The poet even imagines that birds have come from Dubber Cross, a green area several miles away, and from the ditches of the North Road, which leads from Finglas to Dublin Airport.

We realise that the father, unbeknownst to the poet, had been feeding the birds on a daily basis. The birds of the surrounding area had got used to receiving a dawn snack from him. They would gather expectantly in his garden every morning. Suddenly, the father 'threw his hands up' and cast 'fistfuls' of breadcrumbs into the air. The garden, at that moment, became a 'pandemonium', a scene of extraordinary disorder. We can imagine the chaos that ensued as with birds flapping and squawking as they scrambled for the crumbs.

Until that point, the chimney of a nearby house had prevented the sun's rays from directly reaching the garden. But then the sun climbed a little higher in the sky, clearing this obstruction: 'The sun // cleared O'Reilly's chimney'. Direct sunlight suddenly struck the garden and the poet's father was illuminated.

The poet, for a moment or two, saw her father very differently:
- The father seemed 'radiant', which suggests that bright light was being emitted from his body.
- The father seemed 'whole' as if his various physical infirmities had miraculously been healed.
- The father seemed 'young again', as if the aging process had been miraculously reversed.
- The father seemed transfigured into Saint Francis of Assisi.

The poet emphasises that he was a 'perfect vision' of Francis as he stood there surrounded by birds. It's as if the great saint's mighty spirit had descended upon the father, transforming him utterly.

The transfiguration described by the poet, then, is a truly remarkable one. She sees an ordinary Dubliner transformed into a saint and miracle worker, one of Europe's greatest cultural and spiritual figures.

Birdlife, of course, are the connection between these two seemingly very different men. Saint Francis is known for his kindness towards birds of all kinds. The poet, as sunlight hits the garden, realises that her father has in his own way been displaying such kindness, as he feeds the birds of the locality each morning.

FOCUS ON STYLE

Vivid Imagery

Especially memorable is the depiction of the father surrounded by birds while the sun 'cleared O'Reilly's chimney'. There is something cinematic, meanwhile, about the poet's description of how birds have come from all over the surrounding area. We are taken from the garden of the housing estate to the outlying fields of Finglas, the poet's descriptions functioning like a camera that pans slowly across a landscape.

Equally vivid is the depiction of the frost that had 'whitened' the roof slates of the housing estate. This indicates that 'Autumn was nearly done', that winter was coming. It brilliantly reflects how the father was entering what might be described as the winter of his life as old age takes hold.

THEMES

NATURE AND SPIRITUALITY

A vision occurs when someone sees something that isn't really there, or that no one else can see. Visions are usually considered different to hallucinations. People who are hallucinating think that false perceptions are reality. Someone experiencing a vision, on the other hand, doesn't think their perceptions are real in any ordinary sense. They realise that they are seeing an alternative or mystical version of reality.

The key word in the poem's title, then, is 'perceived'. The poet doesn't believe that her father has been de-aged, healed and transformed into a 13th century Italian saint. Rather, this is how she 'perceived' him. This is how he appeared to her for a single sunlit moment in an ordinary 'Finglas garden'.

This vision, no doubt, was partly caused by the fact the poet had just woken up, had been jerked out of a dream by the sound of the horse next door. Human beings, of course, are more susceptible to such visionary moments when we're not quite fully awake. The vision might also have been caused in part by the poet's heightened emotional state. She must have experienced a sense of shock as she suddenly noticed how old age was beginning to affect her father, coupled, no doubt, with the sorrowful realisation that he wouldn't be around forever. She must have experienced feelings of tenderness towards her father as she learned for the first time about his daily kindness towards the birds of the locality.

Visions are thought of as spiritual experiences prompted by religion. But Meehan's visionary spiritual experience, in this instance, is prompted, not by conventional religion but by nature itself. The poet, we sense, was overwhelmed by the beauty of the scene in the yard before her, by the sight of the father suddenly struck by sunlight as he was surrounded by a 'pandemonium' of birds. The poem, then, is typical of Meehan's work, in that spirituality and nature are closely linked.

FAMILY

The poem emphasises how even close family members can sometimes be a mystery to us. Sometimes, family members keep things hidden from one another. We see this when the poet declares that the box room contained 'secrets'. There were items hidden about the room, she sensed, that her brother didn't want her to discover. Often family members simply stay quiet about aspects of their lives. The poet's father, for instance, had never told her that he feeds the birds each morning. Sometimes, we don't notice certain things about family members, even ones that we see regularly. The poet, for instance, had never noticed how age was catching up with her father: 'He was older than I had reckoned'. It was only on this particular morning that she noticed 'for the first time' how his shoulder was stooped and that his leg was stiff.

Hearth Lesson

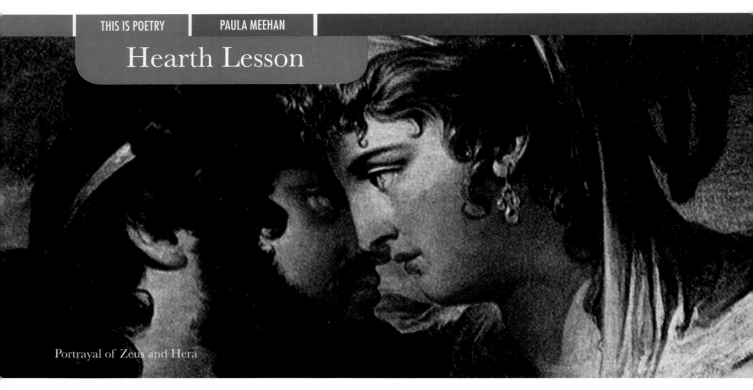

Portrayal of Zeus and Hera

LINE BY LINE

In this poem, Meehan remembers her childhood, specifically the years when she and her family lived on Séan MacDermott Street in Dublin city centre. During this period the relationship between her parents was quite turbulent. They would regularly fight and argue. The poet remembers how she would crouch 'by the fire' while these arguments raged around her.

The poet wittily compares her parents to Zeus and Hera, who in Greek mythology were king and queen of the gods. Zeus and Hera, according to legend, were husband and wife but endured a famously fractious marriage. The poet compares her father's insults to the thunderbolts Zeus would hurl at his enemies. Her mother, meanwhile, looked at the father with such contempt that she is reminded of Hera's 'killing glance' (Hera, according to legend, could cause those who displeased her to drop dead merely by looking at them).

Seeing and raising

The poet mentions some of the accusations that were traded between the parents during these rows. The father, for instance, would accuse the mother of having a 'fancyman', of being too friendly and flirtatious with another man. He would also accuse her of putting on 'airs and graces', of pretending that she is posher and more important than she really is. He would even accuse 'every last one' of her siblings of being mentally unwell.

The mother, meanwhile, would accuse the father of spending too much time at the local snooker club. She would also accuse him of being too obsessed with horse-racing, suggesting that

he spends all his time thinking about jockeys and horses, ignoring his wife completely. She would wittily suggest that the only way for her to get his attention would be to 'neigh' like a horse herself.

The poet compares her parents to two poker players gambling on which has the better hand of cards. The first player opens the betting by placing a certain value of chips in the centre of the table. The second player 'sees' or matches this amount and 'raises' the stakes by adding more chips of his own. Then the first player 'sees' or matches this greater amount, before raising the stakes even further.

Her parents, according to the poet, behaved in a similar fashion. Her father would open their brutal game with a particular criticism of her mother. Her mother would 'see' or match this, by saying something just as critical about the father. She would then 'raise' or escalate the row by saying something even more negative. Her father would not only 'see' or match this insult, but also escalate the row even further, saying things that are even more hurtful.

Umpire, net and court

The poet compares her parents' rows and arguments to the sport of tennis. In a rally, tennis players trade shots. Her parents, similarly, trade insults and accusations. The poet compares herself to the net in these peculiar tennis matches. Tennis players, of course, attempt to hit the ball over the net. Her parents, similarly, attempted to speak over the young poet's head. This suggests that they didn't want her know the precise nature of their disagreements and phrased their arguments in words she was unlikely to understand.

The poet also compares herself to the matches' umpires or referees. This suggests that at times she was called upon to adjudicate in her parent's arguments. We can imagine, for instance, the father urging the young poet to agree with him that the mother's siblings are crazy, or the mother asking for her opinion on the father's obsession with horse-racing.

Finally, the poet compares herself to the court on which these matches were contested. This suggests that some of the insults and accusations involved her. Maybe we can imagine the mother accusing the father of ignoring her or the father accusing the mother of not providing her with a proper diet.

The last, astonishing word

The poet views her parents' various rows and arguments as a single on-going competition, the objective of which was to have the 'last word'. Both parents, she suggests, were attempting to come up with an argument or insult to which there could be no reply, which stunned the other into silence. This cruel game, we sense, dragged on for months or even years, with neither participant able to silence the other in such a definitive fashion.

Suddenly, however, their grim competition came to an end. And it did so in a manner no one in the household was 'prepared' for or expected:

- The poet's father at the time worked as a bookmaker's clerk. Every payday he 'handed up his wages' to the mother. She would then use the money to manage the household, purchase the groceries and pay various bills.
- The poet remembers one particular 'teatime' when the father handed over his wages as usual. The mother 'straightened' the notes he'd given her, as if she were preparing to count them and start budgeting for the week to come.
- 'Suddenly', according to the poet, the mother exhibited a great weariness. We can imagine her shoulders slumping and an exhausted expression flashing across her face.
- Then, without warning, she cast the entire week's wages into the fire.
- The mother accompanied this extraordinary gesture with a single, simple phrase: "It's not enough', she stated simply'.

But this simple phrase, accompanied by the gesture of burning the banknotes, is 'the last, the astonishing word' in their long-running competition. The father, we imagine, stood there in a shocked and astonished silence while the money burned. For once, he had no comeback, insult or argument of his own with which to respond. The mother had finally and definitively won.

Meehan describes how the flames, as they consumed the banknotes, emitted a multi-coloured glow: 'blue and pink and green'. The poet also describes how the flames 'sheered' or swerved from the cinders at the bottom of the fireplace to the chimney breast at its top, causing shadows to jump and flicker across the room.

There was something 'alchemical', almost mystical, she says, about this colour. Alchemy, we remember, was a forerunner to chemistry that involved using fire, metal and other materials in a variety of processes that were both magical and scientific

We might wonder, of course, if the burning money really caused the flames to jump in such a fashion and exhibit such a weird 'alchemical' glow. Perhaps this 'marvellous sight' is a trick of memory. Perhaps the poet, as she looks back on this long ago experience, recalls the flames as being more dramatic than they really were.

THE STRENGTH AND POWER OF WOMEN

'Hearth Lesson' is also typical of Meehan's poetry in that it highlights the strength and power of women. The poet's mother comes across as quite a formidable woman.
- She ensured that her husband 'handed up his wages' each week.
- She steers her family as best she can through a period of poverty and hardship.
- She is more than able to stand up to her husband during their many rows, matching his arguments and insults.
- It is the mother, as we have seen, who has the 'last word' in the long-running competition with her husband.

We get a sense that the mother was a woman of extraordinary potential, someone who could have achieved great things in life. This potential, however, remained unfulfilled due to the poverty and hardship in which she found herself. The phrase 'It isn't enough', then, may refer not only to the father's wages, but also to the mother's circumstances. She wanted more from life and was desperate for opportunities and possibilities that never could be hers.

We might question however, if the mother hasn't gone too far in this regard. We sense that the father, like many men, was largely defined by his work, by his ability to provide for his wife and family. For a long time, however, his wages were inadequate to do so. Everyone in the household knew this: 'And we all knew it wasn't [enough]'. But it has never, we sense, been spoken aloud.

The mother not only gives voice to this unpleasant truth, but she also casually burns the wages he worked hard to bring home. By doing so, she undermines her husband's very identity, highlighting his inadequacy as a breadwinner. The father, we imagine, must have been left feeling worthless and humiliated by his wife's 'astonishing word'.

FOCUS ON STYLE

Metaphor, Simile and Figures of Speech

The poet uses a number of imaginative comparisons to describe the arguments between her parents. She compares her parents to the gods Zeus and Hera, to poker players and to tennis players. She uses an equally simile to capture the flames' brightness and vibrancy, comparing them to 'trapped exotic birds'.

Vivid Imagery

Meehan's gift for vivid imagery is on display when she describes the behaviour of the flames as they consumed the banknotes, capturing how they emitted a bizarre multi-coloured glow and skittered in the fireplace.

Playful Language

'Hearth Lesson', though it is a serious poem, provides us with a hint of Meehan's trademark playfulness. We see this when she compares her parents, two ordinary working-class Dubliners, to the Greek gods Zeus and Hera. Such light-heartedness is also evident in her depiction of the parents' insults; in the father's accusation that the mother's family are all crazy, for instance, or in the mother's claim that only by neighing like a horse could she get her husband's attention.

THEMES

POVERTY AND HARDSHIP

The poem highlights the toxic effects that poverty can have on a relationship. The poet, even as a child, understood that poverty caused the constant strife between her parents: 'Even then I can tell it was money/ the lack of it day after day,/ at the root of the bitter words'. The constant lack of money made both of her parents tense, irritable and frustrated. It led to unceasing tensions between them, blazing rows and 'brooding' periods of silence.

The father's wages, it is made clear, were never quite enough to cover the family's expenses. The mother, we sense, had to scrimp and save as she managed the household budget. There was always the pressure of unpaid bills and of upcoming expenses that needed to be covered from the household's meagre resources.

This hardship, the poet emphasises, dragged on 'day after day', year after year, leaving the mother psychologically worn down. We see this when the poet describes how the mother was overcome by an extraordinary weariness as she contemplated the 'rumpled' notes.

The burning of the wages, while astonishing and theatrical, is also self-destructive and wasteful. There is the obvious question of how the family are going to manage for the rest of the week. There are several ways of looking at this gesture:

- We can view it as a gesture of exhaustion. Perhaps the mother simply couldn't take another week struggling to make ends meet. Burning the notes, in a strange sense, simplified her situation. Having no money meant there was no need for careful budgeting.
- We can view it as a gesture of defeat and resignation. The mother wants her family to enjoy a reasonably high standard of living. But she realises that her husband's wages are 'not enough' to achieve this and never will be.
- We can also view it, of course, as an attempt to win the long-running and bitter competition with her husband.

CHILDHOOD

'Hearth Lesson' provides a brutal and unflinching portrayal of childhood. The young poet's crouched position by the fireplace suggests the trauma she endured as she listened to her parents 'battle it out'. It also suggests her desire not to be drawn into these disagreements, to somehow escape this toxic environment. We can picture her staring into the fire, making herself as small as possible, wishing she was somewhere else.

There is something witty about the poet's comparison of her parents to Zeus and Hera. But it also suggests the trauma she endured. To the young poet, the arguments of these fully grown adults were epic and explosive, like the clash of two vengeful gods. Her parents, as we have seen, attempted to shield her from the content of their argument, using language that she as a young girl is unlikely to understand. But not all of the balls 'are lobbed over her head'. She still understands enough. Even more traumatic for the poet were those times when her parents gave one another the silent treatment. There were lengthy periods, it seems, when the mother and father would refuse to speak to one another. And if they absolutely had to communicate, they would use the young poet as a go-between rather than address one another directly.

Their silence, according to the poet, was accompanied by a great deal of 'brooding' or moodiness. We can imagine the young poet walking on eggshells amid a tense and toxic atmosphere. Small wonder, then, that she describes these periods as a 'particular hell'. Indeed, she actually preferred her parents' arguments to these days of unbearable, silent tension: 'Even then I can judge it's better/ than brooding and silence'. This trauma, we sense, has remained with the poet into adulthood. Simply hearing the expression 'money to burn' or 'burning a hole in his pocket' causes her to relive this ordeal. The poet's use of the present tense highlights the immediacy of these recollections: 'I am crouched...I'm net, umpire...Even then I can tell'. It's as if she's back on Séan MacDermott Street, enduring the anguish of her parents' disagreements.

LINE BY LINE

This poem was commissioned by the community of Dublin's north inner city to remember their children who died from drug use. Meehan read the poem on the occasion of the lighting of the Christmas tree on Buckingham Street. Gathered around the tree on this occasion were the families of those who had lost children to drug use.

Where has the tree come from?

It is coming up to Christmas. The lights on a large Christmas tree in Buckingham Street in the heart of the north inner city are being turned on. This magnificent or 'Great' tree has come from a forest in the 'far northern' hemisphere. We might imagine a forest in Norway, perhaps, where many large fir trees are grown. The tree has only recently been cut down and transported to Dublin. The poet observes how it is still coated with sap, the watery fluid that circulates through plants and trees: 'Still rich with the sap of the forest'.

The poet imagines how this 'far northern forest' must look at this time of year. She pictures a place of ice and snow. We can imagine the landscape covered in a blanket of snow, its rivers and lakes frozen. Snow covers the trees and shards of glittering ice hang from the branches.

The poet imagines the 'silence' and the stillness of this northern winter landscape. We can imagine a still winter's day, the sky clear and blue overhead. We can imagine the snow that covers the landscape adds to the silence, blanketing the forest floor and branches of the trees, silencing any rustling sounds: 'The snow's breathless silence'.

The streets of Dublin's north inner city

Dublin witnessed epidemic levels of heroin addiction in the 1980s. This epidemic was concentrated in small pockets of Dublin's inner city, particularly in areas with a history of poverty and disadvantage. A report commissioned at the time found that in north central Dublin, for example, 10% of 15 to 24 year-olds had used heroin in the previous year.

Meehan focuses on the manner in which drug use has devastated the north inner city, blighting and destroying the lives of the young. She personifies the 'streets' in order to convey the manner in which this area has affected the lives of the young people who must live and socialise here. These streets should represent a safe place, a space where the young can grow, develop and mature. However, the streets in this area are hostile and dangerous, blighted by drugs and violence.

Meehan thinks about the manner in which these streets have destroyed many young lives. She thinks of how some children have been seduced or coaxed into taking drugs. We can imagine how dealers might encourage the young to accompany them to some secluded place where they offer them a chance to try something that will '[blow] their minds'.

The poet refers to the young people who have tragically lost their lives to drugs as the 'children of longing'. The phrase suggests how these children's lives remained unfulfilled. They were 'longing' for something better than they got, for a way out of the cycle of poverty and drug addiction that characterised the lives of so many people living in Dublin's north inner city in the 80s and 90s.

It is possible that Meehan's choice of this phrase was influenced by the book Children of Longing, which was published in 1970. This book was contains accounts of the firsthand experiences and aspirations of black teens and young adults. It was edited by Rosa Guy, an American writer who drew on her own experiences to create fiction for young adults that usually concerned individual choice, family conflicts, poverty, and the realities of life in urban America and the West Indies.

The poet describes how those who take drugs are immediately bewitched or 'spellbound' by them. It is as if they have been placed under an evil spell from which they can never escape. And once they are hooked on drugs, they are caught in a vicious cycle of addiction that will ultimate destroy them. Meehan describes how the 'streets' have 'defeated' so many young people. She describes the burden and the toll that living with addiction brings, crippling lives that were once full of hope and potential. The poet describes how many of the young have been 'brought them to their knees', left felling powerless and without hope.

She describes how the streets have stolen the young away from the care and protection of their families: 'out of reach of our saving'. She describes how the streets have claimed the lives of some of the young people. The poet imagines the 'scream'

of the victim, the sound of the police or ambulance siren and the 'knock on the door' when the police come to inform the parents of what has happened.

What does the poet wish for?

The poet appeals to the tree, asking it to grant this area of Dublin a moment of stillness and silence, a brief respite from the pain and suffering which the heroin epidemic has wrought. The poet longs for the freezing temperatures of the forest where the tree grew to somehow 'freeze' the streets of Dublin's north inner city. For a brief spell, Meehan imagines, the city streets would stand frozen, as still and silent as a northern winter forest.

For this brief moment, all the pain, violence and suffering of the streets would be suspended:

- The poet imagines a young person using a needle to inject drugs into their veins. She imagines the needle being frozen 'in its tracks', not reaching the arm of the user (The term 'track' might also refer to the scar created by continuously injecting a needle into the same point in the body over and over again. The needle, therefore, has punctured the track mark but it is frozen before the drug is injected).
- The poet imagines someone raising a knife to stab another person in the back. She imagines the knife being frozen just before it reaches its victim.
- The poet imagines that freezing conditions will for a moment stop the killing on the streets. It will freeze the 'scream' of the victim, the 'siren' of the police or ambulance, and the 'knock on the door' when the police call to the victim's house to inform his or her parents of the tragedy.

But this moment wouldn't just freeze the activities in the streets. It would also allow those who have gathered around the tree a moment of respite from their mental anguish and pain.

In this frozen moment there would be a suspension of all human emotion. The poet imagines a state of mind which she associates with the frozen northern landscape:

- For this brief moment their minds will not be burdened or preoccupied with any painful thoughts or memories. They will become as clear as 'ice'.
- For a brief moment they will not feel any anguish, pain or regret. There would be an absence of feeling, a numbness, which the poet associates with the 'comfort of snow'.
- For this brief moment they will forget the tragic events that have scarred their lives. Meehan associates this with the 'cool memory of trees'.

There is something cold and inhuman about the state of mind that the poet describes, but she knows it will offer those who are suffering a moment of relief from their anguish and pain. For a brief moment they will feel nothing at all. The poet imagines that in this frozen moment the spirits of these lost children will return. She imagines that in the absolute silence and stillness it will be possible to hear the 'breath of the children'. Meehan also imagines that these children are singing. In the frozen silence it will be possible to hear the 'song of the children'.

As those gathered around the tree speak the names of those loved ones they have lost to drugs, Meehan prays that their spoken names might somehow merge with the wind that blows 'through the branches' of the tree and that they become one with the soothing sounds of the river that flows through the city: 'Let their names be the song of the river'. These lines conjure up powerful images of freedom and release. The poet's final wish that 'their names be the holiest prayers' captures her wish that these children should never be forgotten.

FOCUS ON STYLE

Metaphor, Simile and Figures of Speech

The poet uses personification throughout the poem. She appeals to the tree that has been placed on Buckingham Street, calling on it to somehow act in a manner that might bring peace and solace to an area in Dublin that had been blighted by drugs and violence. The poet also personifies the 'streets'. It is as if the 'streets' have behaved in a sinister manner, seducing the children and wrecking their lives. It is the 'streets' that promise the children a bright future, only to betray them and stab them in the back. The 'streets', of course, represent the greater society.

Vivid Imagery

Meehan wonderfully captures the beauty and atmosphere of the 'far northern forest' where the tree grew. She describes the pristine snow that coats the landscape and the utter stillness that is to be found in such places.

THEMES

SOCIAL JUSTICE

The poem outlines what any healthy, functioning society should offer and provide to its young. It should provide security, sheltering them from drugs and violence. It should provide them with a secure and healthy space in which to grow and develop. It should inspire them and nurture and develop their dreams and visions. Society should be blowing the young people's minds with exciting possibilities.

The streets of Dublin's north inner city should have been able to promise them all these things and then deliver on these promises. But society failed these children. It has, Meehan suggests, betrayed them. The phrase 'knife in the back' might be read as a description of such a betrayal. Rather than raise them to the heights to which they aspired, the streets 'brought them to their knees', broke their dreams and crippled them with addiction.

NATURE AND SPIRITUALITY

In Meehan's poetry, the natural world is presented almost as a single organism, as if all its animal and plant life combine to form a unitary life-force or intelligence. Meehan developed this understanding of the natural world when she lived in California during the 1960s. She was influenced by Buddhism and Eastern philosophy, by the hippie movement and by American poets such as Gary Snyder who combined mysticism and environmentalism.

There are moments when Meehan suggests that the natural world is worthy of veneration, that we might pray to nature just as religious people pray to God. There are also moments, Meehan suggests, when it is possible for human beings to commune with nature, to attain an almost mystical oneness with the natural world. Such communion in Meehan's poetry is presented as a source of healing and renewal.

In this poem, Meehan appeals directly to the great fir tree that has been erected in the middle of Dublin city. She imagines the landscape of the tree's native land. The poet associates this natural landscape with 'clarity', tranquillity and 'silence'. She prays that the tree might somehow bring these conditions to bear on these urban streets, to grant the people of Dublin's north inner city a chance to heal.

FAMILY

The poem highlights the suffering and agony that families endure when they lose a child. The poet mentions the terrible moment when the police come to knock on the door to inform the parents that their child has died. Such loss is felt most acutely at Christmas time. The description of the spirits of the dead children singing reminds us of the innocence of the child and how at this time of year the young should be singing carols and enjoying the magic of Christmas.

Death of a Field

LINE BY LINE

Planning permission has been granted for the construction of forty-four houses in a field close to where the poet is living. A site notice or 'Notice' has been placed at the entrance to the field. Such notices give a description of the nature and extent of the development and state to which planning authority the planning application is being made. Such a notice must be placed on site for five weeks from the date of receipt of the planning application.

In this case, the planning authority is Fingal County Council and planning permission is being sought for the construction of forty-four houses. Although no construction has yet taken place, the field, according to the poet, is 'lost' at this very moment. It is as if the site notice is a form of death warrant, an irreversible sentence that canot be overturned. The houses will be built and the field site will eventually be destroyed.

The poet thinks of the field as an intricate organism. She imagines that all the plant life in the field combines to form a unitary intelligence. The field's 'flora' or plant life – its grasses, flowers and herbs – function like some form of collective memory. These flowers and plants have been growing here for many years. It is as if they carry within them a shared memory or understanding of the field.

There is a sense in which the field's mix of different flowers, grasses and herbs is its identity. The moment these plants are lost, the field ceases to have an identity. It is as if its mind has been cleansed of all memories: 'the memory of the field disappears with its flora'.

The poet describes the impact that the field's loss will have on the wildlife in the area. Much of the hedging around the field will be destroyed, leaving many birds without a place to build their nest. The birds that do remain – 'the woodpigeons in the willow' and the 'finches in what's left of the hawthorn hedge' – will struggle to find the food they need to survive. These birds would have lived off the worms and grubs in the field's soil. Meehan imagines how these birds will continue to sing in the summer, but that their song will now be a 'hungry' one.

The field's plant life will also suffer. Meehan personifies some of the plants and flowers that grow in the field. She mentions 'yarrow', a wildflower with feathery leaves and heads of small white or pale pink aromatic flowers, which has long been used in herbal medicine. She describes how this plant will be left 'yearning' and will be left with an intense longing for the field in which it has long blossomed. She describes the scarlet pimpernel's 'plight' or predicament. It is as if this flower is going to be left destitute, without a home.

The poet thinks of how the field served as a discreet space for the young people in the area to get up to mischief. The field, with its long grass and hedges, would have provided the ideal place for the local kids and teenagers to smoke their first cigarette or take their 'first tokes' or inhalations of marijuana. The field was also where many teenagers would experience their earliest, and somewhat awkward, sexual experiences: 'first gropes'.

The houses

When the field has been destroyed, the construction of the houses in the estate will commence: 'The end of the field as we know it is the start of the estate'. Meehan imagines how these houses will eventually become family homes. The poet thinks of the many joyful moments and events that will take place in these homes. Each house, she says, will become a 'cargo of joy'. It is as if each house is a form of container that will eventually be filled with times of happiness and cheer. The house functions, she suggests, as a form of vessel that holds and contains these happy moments, its 'cargo of joy', carrying them through the years.

But these houses will also be places of 'sorrow'. Meehan thinks of the troubles that many families experience – the tragedies, setbacks and disappointments, the arguments, the bitter words and the brooding silences. For some, these houses will become places where negative feelings foster and flourish. They will be, for some, a 'nest of sorrow'.

The poet also thinks of the myriad cleaning products that these houses will contain. Each house, she says, will be a 'nest of chemical'. Detergents, surface cleaners, dishwashing tablets and air fresheners will quickly fill the cupboards and shelves. Meehan mentions a number of common 'chemical' cleaning products, such as 'Pledge', which is used when dusting, and 'Brasso', which is used to polish metal.

Meehan laments the fact that so many natural herbs will be destoyed in order that the houses be built.

- She mentions dock leaves which are used to soothe nettle stings. The cooling properties of their leaves are also used to soothe insect bites and stings, as well as scalds, blisters and sprains.
- The teasel herb is used to make certain medicines. People traditionally take teasel to treat skin conditions such as psoriasis. It is also put on the skin to treat arthritis.
- She mentions 'herb robert', which has traditionally been used to improve the functioning of the liver and gallbladder.

The fact that she juxtaposes herbs with a variety of 'chemical' products suggests that nature's potent and powerful remedies are being sacrificed and replaced with commercial products that are, in many cases, bad for the environment.

A walk at night

Soon the field will be gone. And the only record of its existence will be a map of the area as it was prior to the estate's construction. Meehan imagines this map file saved on 'some architect's screen'. In time, she says, the field will become 'solely map memory'.

The poet decides to take a last walk out into the field at night. This will enable her to experience the field alone, without the disturbing presence of architects, engineers and construction workers. In the stillness and silence of the night, she will be able to experience the field in an intimate way, sensitive to its every sound and movement.

Meehan describes how she will be 'Barefoot' so that she can 'know the field/ Through the soles of [her] feet'. She will be able to feel the texture of the grass and the dew that will be forming its blades in the cool of the night. In the silence of the night, she imagines how she will be able to hear the the gentle rustling of the trees' many leaves. She thinks how each green leaf is like an individual being, each producing its own distinctive sound, which she likens to song: 'hear/ The myriad leaf lives green and singing'.

The poet wishes that she could somehow come to 'possess' the field, that she could somehow seize or take control all the beauty, vitality and life that it contains. The poet longs to preserve this rich natrual treasure. The poet also imagines the field somehow coming to 'possess' her. She imagines being coated in the field's dew. She imagines how this 'slick' and shiny substance would coat or cover her like a 'caul' or membrane. She would be held within this silky covering, which would be rendered white in the moon's pale light: 'it possess me/ Through its night dew, its moon white caul/ Its slick and shine and its profligacy'.

THEMES

NATURE AND SPIRITUALITY

In Meehan's poetry, the natural world is presented almost as a single organism, as if all its animal and plant life combine to form a unitary life-force or intelligence. Meehan developed this understanding of the natural world when she lived in California during the 1960s. She was influenced by Buddhism and Eastern philosophy, by the hippie movement and by American poets such as Gary Snyder who combined mysticism and environmentalism.

In 'Death of a Field', the poet presents the field as a living organism. It has its own distinct 'memory', which is held within the flowers and herbs that grow there. Each element in the field, every blade of grass and every leaf that grows upon the branches of the trees is considered a living being that possesses its own distinctive identity.

The field, the poet suggests, comprises of a mind-boggling variety of life – and, also extraordinary potential for future life. She mentions the 'seeding head' of the plants, the dry cluster of seeds that sit atop the different plants in the field. Each seed is capable of becoming a new plant. There is the potential for so much future life in these clusters of seeds that the poet says it would be impossible to calculate the loss when the field is gone: 'Who amongst us is able ... To number the losses of each seeding head?'

Meehan also mentions the vast number of insects that can be discovered in the field. Some of these insects are responsible for spreading the seeds that gather at the tops of the flowers and for carrying pollen from plant to plant: 'The million million cycles of being in a wing'. There is a sense here of life

constantly renewing itself, of endless fertility. Meehan describes the 'profligacy' of the natural world, the abundance of life that is evident in 'every beat of time'. She suggests that we have no idea of the magnitude of loss that occurs when a field like this is destroyed: 'Who amongst us is able to number the end of grasses/ To number the losses of each seeding head?'

Meehan also believes that it is possible for human beings to commune with nature, to attain an almost mystical oneness with the natural world. Such communion in Meehan's poetry is often presented as a source of healing and renewal. We see this in the poem's final lines, where Meehan describes walking out into the field at night in her bare feet. She is sensitive to its every sound and movement and describes a longing to 'possess' the field or to have the field 'possess' her.

FAMILY

The description of the houses as 'Nest[s] of sorrow' and 'cargo[es] of joy' suggests that in an estate of forty-four houses there are inevitably going to be families that enjoy a relatively happy and peaceful life and those who are going to be afflicted with troubles and difficulties. Meehan, of course, knew all too well, as many of her poems testify, that family life is not always easy.

SOCIAL JUSTICE

Many of Meehan's poems highlight the plight of individuals that society has neglected, forgotten or ignored. Here she highlights the 'plight' of a field that is going to be destroyed in order that a housing estate can be built. The poem suggests that when it comes to such trade-offs, we do not appreciate what is being sacrificed and lost.

FOCUS ON STYLE

Playful language

Meehan uses wonderfully playful language to capture the manner in which the field has served as a location for the town's teenagers to escape and hide. She describes the corners of the field and the secluded spots in the long grass and amongst the trees as 'hidey holes'. Here, she says, teenagers have traditionally experienced their 'first smokes, first tokes' and 'first gropes'.

Metaphor, Simile and Figures of Speech

Meehan describes how the magpies in the field sound 'like flying castanets'. Castanets are small wooden rattles, made in the shape of two bowls or cups, fitted together, tied by a string and then fastened to the thumbs. The comparison captures the rhythmic clicking sound that the magpies make.

Meehan compares the houses to nests, suggesting how these are places of sanctuary where children can be born and raised. But, as we mentioned above, the poet highlights how these structures might protect the inhabitants from external threats and dangers, but it does not safeguard against the sorrows that can afflict families within their homes.

In the poem's final lines, Meehan compares the coating of night dew to a membrane or 'caul'. The comparison brings to mind a kind of cocoon, the silky case spun by the larvae of many insects for protection. The poet imagines being coated and wrapped in this dewy substance. Perhaps she hopes that this 'caul' will preserve, insulate or protect her from the hardships that she is experiencing.

Them Ducks Died for Ireland

Statue of Countess Markieviecz

LINE BY LINE

'Them Ducks Died for Ireland' comes from a sequence titled 'Six Sycamores', which explores the beauty of Georgian Dublin whilst also exploring its complicated history. As Meehan put it: 'Because I grew up in a Georgian house, albeit a tenement slum, I know how they work ... I love those buildings; the intricacies of the craftwork, and the imagination ... and yet what they stand for ... I have real problems with that'. The sequence was commissioned by the Office of Public Works, whose headquarters are on St Stephen's Green in Dublin.

Light in the OPW

The poet is in the OPW building on St Stephen's Green working on her commission. This Georgian mansion has floorsboards made of oak and old-style 'sash' windows. Meehan is thinking about history, about time and the passage of time. In an extraordinary metaphor, she compares time to the evening light that is pouring through the sash window and spilling onto the 'oaken boards'. She presents time as a tangible presence in the room, a liquid substance that flows down the window panes and gathers in puddles on the floor.

The Green as lung

The Green, in a memorable metaphor, is compared to a 'great lung'. This reminds us of how plants, through the process known as photosynthesis, take in carbon dioxide and emit oxygen.

The poet thinks of nature's 24-hour cycles. Each evening the sun sets, the moon rises and the stars appear. Each morning the opposite happens: the moon sets, the sun rises and the stars disappear once more.

She also thinks of nature's yearly cycles, the constant 'seasons turn' from spring to winter and back again. These natural rhythms, she suggests, constantly alter the Green's plants, trees and grasses, shifting the nature of the gasses they 'exhale'.
The poet is standing close to the 'sash window' of the OPW, looking out at the Green below. Her breath, as she exhales, forms a mist on the 'pane' of the window before her. In a vivid simile, the oxygen emitted by the Green is compared to the breath exhaled by the poet: 'The Green...exhaling like breath on the pane'.

Memories of 1916

Meehan remembers that St Stephen's Green was seized by rebel forces during the 1916 Rising. The rebels dug trenches around the Green and erected barricades. They were attacked by British artillery and many buildings around the Green went up in flames.

The poet wonderfully compares the pond at the centre of the Green to a 'mirror'. She imagines that it must have reflected the flames that consumed the buildings around the Green. She also imagines that it must have reflected the dark palls of 'smoke' that drifted overhead.

The poet remembers the Irish patriot Countess Markievicz, who along with Michael Malin, commanded the rebel forces on the Green. The poet imagines the Countess striding confidently across the green. We can picture her dressed in full military uniform, issuing orders and encouraging her men to resist the British bombardment.

The rebels had declared a republic free of British rule. And, as Markievicz walked across the Green, the destiny of that fledging republic walked with her. Her actions and decisions as a commander would help determine if the Republic survived or was quickly extinguished: 'a Republic's destiny in a Countess' stride'.

Patriots like Markievicz were utterly dedicated to their cause and were willing to pay 'the bloodprice' for Irish freedom. They were prepared to kill British soldiers. They were also prepared to kill Irish people they felt were collaborating with the British state and to give their own lives for the cause they served. The Countess's colleague, Michael Malin, for instance, was among the 16 leaders executed after the surrender of the rebels. Markievicz, too, was condemned to death, only to have her sentence commuted because the British authorities were reluctant to execute a woman.

The sight of this 'bloodprice', of the rebels killing and being killed, had a complicated effect on the Irish people. For some, it was a 'summons' to national 'pride'. They wanted to fight on, to follow the rebels' example and finally end British rule in Ireland. But for others, it was a cure or 'antidote' to national pride. They were horrified by the bloodshed and destruction of the Rising and became wary of nationalism in all its forms, realising the violence it could lead to.

Those who pick up the pieces

Meehan, however, wants to focus on the ordinary people who are forgotten by history. She doesn't want to write about famous commanders like the Countess. She doesn't even want to write about the rank and file soldiers who fought and died around the Green. Instead, she wants to write about those who worked in the background of the conflict.

- She mentions 'stretcher bearer[s]' who carry wounded soldiers to safety. Meehan no doubt remembers that St Stephen's Green served as a field hospital during the Rising. But such stretcher bearers can be seen in many conflicts around the globe.
- She mentions 'nurse[s] in white' who tend to the wounded and the dying. Meehan, of course, has in mind not only the nurses who attended the wounded in 1916 but also those nurses who have served in countless other conflicts before and since.
- She mentions the ones who 'pick up the pieces'. This brings to mind the workers who cleared away the rubble in the wake of the Rising, who set about repairing

Dublin's damaged streets and buildings. But such repair work, of course, is necessary after every conflict.

Commanders like Countess Markievicz are at the centre of historical events. The nurses, stretcher bearers and construction workers, on the other hand, 'live at the edge' of these events. They can be glimpsed working away at the periphery of the action, or they appear once the action is concluded in order to 'pick up the pieces'.

Meehan points out how these ordinary workers all too often die while working 'at the edge' of these great historical moments. A construction worker might be killed by falling rubble, for instance, or a nurse might be struck by a stray bullet.

Meehan emphasises what these ordinary workers 'endure'. This suggests their physical and mental strength and their ability to keep going, even in adverse circumstances. It also suggests the courage they exhibit as they undertake tasks that are often dangerous or even life-threatening. These are people who are determined to get the job done no matter what. Meehan, therefore, stresses the importance of remembering and honouring these ordinary workers. We must 'salute' these unknown heroes just as we salute the major personalities like Countess Markievicz.

Each conflict leaves behind psychological wounds, a legacy of bitterness and division. Eventually these wounds are healed. The bitterness and division prompted by the conflict is resolved or, at least, forgotten. Remembering these ordinary workers, Meehan suggests, is much easier once such healing has occurred: 'When we've licked the wounds of history, wounds of war// we'll salute the stretcher bearer'. A nation, the poet suggests, must come to terms with the big issues of a conflict before it can 'salute' those who lived and died at the conflict's 'edge'.

These ordinary heroes are never the subjects of biographies or documentaries. They hardly feature in the history books. They do, sometimes, leave a vague trace in the historical record. Their names might be mentioned in passing in a newspaper report. We might glimpse them in the corner of a photograph. Or their actions might be recorded in reports that have been filed, archived and forgotten.

Meehan has come across one such report while conducting research for her 'Six Sycamores' sequence. The report in question was written by the Park Superintendent of Stephen's Green in 1916. The report describes the damage caused to the Green by the events of the Rising, recounting how birds were shot, 'garden seats broken' and 'shrubs destroyed'.

Meehan sits by the sash windows in the OPW and reads this 'archival footnote' in the 'fading light' of evening. She realises that this Park Superintendent was one of the ordinary heroes mentioned above. It was his job to pick up the pieces once the great events of the Rising had concluded. He had to repair the park benches, replant the shrubberies and replace the birds that had been shot.

We erect statues to our great heroes, making the 'gesture/ of commemorating them ... in bronze and stone'. But we erect no statues to the ordinary workers like the Park Superintendent. We make no 'gesture' of commemoration towards them. They survive only as an 'archival footnote'.

The poet exhales as she stands before the window of the OPW and her breath forms a mist upon the glass. This 'breathmark', she realises, will exist only for a moment before vanishing.

Both the statues and the archival footnotes, the poet realises, are as 'fragile' as this 'breathmark'. They too will exist only briefly before vanishing. The statues may exist for hundreds of years before they weather away. The archival footnote too may last for a long time before it is disposed of or disintegrates. But the lifespan of these objects in the grand scheme of human existence covers only the briefest of moments.

THEMES

SOCIAL JUSTICE

In 'Them Ducks Died for Ireland', as in many of her poems, Meehan sets out to speak on behalf of those who have been forgotten. She urges us, as we have seen, to 'salute' not only the great heroes but also those in the background of history's great events. She reminds us that those ordinary workers also made great sacrifices and displayed great courage. Such a 'salute', of course, could take many forms. It could be an exhibition or a school project, or a poem of remembrance like this one.

The poet also makes the point that no form of commemoration will last forever. She is highly conscious of time's passage, presenting it as an almost palpable, liquid presence in the drawing room of the OPW. And time, she emphasises, will erode all forms of memory, from archival records to statues made of bronze or stone.

FOCUS ON STYLE

Form

The poem, somewhat unusually for Meehan, has a regular form. It is a Petrarchan sonnet, rhyming ABBA BCCB DEFDEF.

Playful use of language

In the 'Six Sycamores' sequence, Meehan combined two very different tones. She used sonnets written in hightened poetic language. She also included snatches of ordinary Dublin speech.

We see this in 'Them Ducks Died for Ireland', which combines a sonnet written in such complex, metaphorical verse with a title that is a snippet of Dublin street talk. We can imagine an ordinary Dubliner hearing about the wildfowl that were shot in St Stephen's Green and remarking that 'Them ducks

died for Ireland', wittily comparing these unfortunate birds to those who martyred themselves for Irish freedom.

The sonnet form represents, for Meehan, the beauty of the Georgian mansions she was writing about, while the snippets of everyday speech reflect the ordinary lives that are lived in and around these beautiful buildings. As Meehan put it in an interview:

I wanted to put them together, to say this is a sonnet, but this is an actual human voice, unornamented in plain speech with its own vignette out of life. Just as the ordinary life goes on in these beautiful structures, these edifices. So I wanted to get a conversation between the casual throw-away vernacular of the little pieces and the more tightly wrapped language and ritualised energy of the sonnets.

THIS IS POETRY   EILÉAN NÍ CHUILLEANÁIN

Eiléan Ní Chuilleanáin Themes

Death and Grief

Death is a constant presence in Ní Chuilleanáin's poetry. 'The Bend in the Road', for instance, suggests that our dead loved ones are never truly gone. Instead they exist all around us, 'in the tree, in the air'. Perhaps she means this literally, reflecting the spiritual belief that when we die, our spirits, our very essences, merge somehow with the natural world, becoming one with the soil, with plant-life, with the very air itself. It's more likely, however, that this 'presence' is merely a metaphor for memory. Perhaps it describes how the poet's memories of our loved ones, even after they have passed away, remain vividly in our minds. Perhaps it describes how their faces, as the poet so memorably puts it, are 'never long absent' from our thoughts.

'Deaths and Engines' offers a darker approach to death and dying. The poem presents death not only as inevitable but also as predetermined. The moment of each person's death has been scheduled with such certainty that it could be represented on a mathematical graph or predicted by a skilled palm reader. We will recognise this moment when it comes. We will know – with the certainty of passengers in a car accelerating down a blind alley – that our end has finally come.

The poet emphasises how our deaths will bring extraordinary grief and suffering to those who love us. The poem, however, ends with an acceptance of death. The poet says that death is ultimately something extremely 'light'. We spend much of our lives greatly fearing this moment, only to find that when it arrives it is less terrible than we imagined. Transitioning from life to death is actually pretty easy. There is even a sense that dying might actually be something of a relief, as we cast off the burdens and obligations of being alive.

Several of Ní Chuilleanáin's poems can be viewed as elegies, as poems of mourning for those who have passed away. 'Fireman's Lift', for instance, is a lament for the poet's mother. The dates below the poem memorialise their relationship: in 1963 the poet and her mother visited Parma cathedral together while in 1994 the mother passed away. We can view the depiction of the angels is intended as a tribute to her mother, suggesting how she strove to help others throughout her life. And maybe the image of the Virgin ascending to Heaven represents Ní Chuilleanáin's hope that her mother, too, will enter Paradise after her death.

In 'Kilcash', meanwhile, Ní Chuilleanáin translates a famous lament for Lady Iveagh, a great woman whose passing left the people of Kilcash feeling lost and devastated. There's a sense in which even nature itself mourns her passing: the estate of Kilcash becomes a nightmarish place of impenetrable mists and daytime darkness. It's a place where streams run dry, where the songbirds refuse to sing, where the sky turns dark even in daytime.

In 'Following', the poet looks back at the death of her own beloved father who passed away in 1970. The young woman in the poem discovers that the dead father is somehow still alive. She even gets to share a whiskey with him in the comfort of his library. We can imagine how this represents how Ní Chuilleanáin's own father, in a metaphorical sense, is also still alive. He lives on in the memories and the behaviour of those who loved him and were influenced by him. The poem concludes with a startling image of growth and renewal as the crushed flowers come to life again. This represents how Ní Chuilleanáin's father, even in death, will remain very much part of her inner life. The fact that the flower grows from the pages of the book suggests that her long-dead father will continue to influence and inspire her literary pursuits.

Mental Suffering

Mental suffering, in its various forms, is another of Ní Chuilleanáin's central themes. 'Lucina Schynning in Silence of the Nicht', for instance, details the poet's response to her father's final illness. It describes how the poet found this situation so horrific that she was overcome by a sudden and powerful urge to flee, to leave the hospital and, indeed, the city far behind.

The poem highlights the darkness that consumed the poet's mind when she found herself sleeping overnight in a ruined castle in the countryside. Negative thoughts came crashing over her like 'waves of darkness'. She found herself dwelling on images of plague and disease. She imagined whole towns and villages being overrun with mice and beetles. She found herself thinking of bacterial plagues such as the Black Death, which killed millions in medieval Europe. Such sickness would first turn their victims pale. Then the victims' flesh would assume a clay-like complexion, as the life slowly left their bodies.

'The Second Voyage' is another powerful study of mental suffering, describing how Odysseus has been tormented and frustrated by the seemingly endless nature of his journey home. He has been travelling across the ocean for so long that the very sight of its waves fills him with disgust and horror. He is absolutely desperate to find his way back to Ithaca. He weeps in despair at his plight, his tears tasting 'Like his own sweat or the insults of the sea'.

376

'The Second Voyage' also conveys the effects that a long and difficult period of isolation can have on the human psyche. He speaks to his oar as if it were a person. We see this in phrases like 'Our shipwreck', and 'I'll take you with me' and 'I'll plant you'. He thinks of the waves as if they were individual human-like entities, rather than random accumulations of water. He has developed an irrational aversion to water and is horrified by the thought that water is everywhere, from kettles to canals, and that no matter how far he goes he cannot escape it. Such ideas might strike us as bizarre and disturbing, as the fevered imaginings of the mentally unwell. Yet such abnormal trains of thoughts are typical of the survival strategies or 'coping mechanisms' used by people who are forced to endure long periods of isolation.

'Deaths and Engines' presents a more mundane form of mental discomfort, capturing the stresses we sometimes experience when we travel by plane. It is common, after all, for people to feel nervous and anxious when awaiting take-off. But the sight of the crashed plane on the ground introduces a whole new level of anxiety into the mix for the poet. As she sits aboard the return flight, her mind almost inevitably fills with panicked thoughts of crashing and dying.

Spirituality

'Lucina Schynning in Silence of the Nicht' offers a mystical and spiritual understanding of the natural world, hinting at its restorative powers. By exposing herself to the elements, by sleeping rough and washing in the stream's 'cold water', the poet undergoes a form of spiritual or mental renewal. Her recovery is aided by her connection with the wildlife in the area, particularly the insects and animals that she encounters. There is a sense in which the natural world is looking out for her, offering her much needed protection and solace.

We sense that the poet at the end of the poem is ready to return to the hospital where her father lies dying. She left a horrific situation in the hospital and it will be no less horrific when she returns. But her sojourn in the natural world has left her grounded and serene. She is ready now to face the traumatic reality of her father's final illness and be by his side during his final days.

In 'On Lacking the Killer Instinct', another poem that touches on her father's final illness, Ní Chuilleanáin also presents a spiritual view of the natural world. The poet is deeply affected by the sight of the hare 'absorbed, sitting still' on the middle of the country track. She realises she was wrong to leave her dying father behind and that she is in fact capable of dealing with the trauma of his suffering.

When she returns to the city she thinks about the hare on the hillside path. We sense that this is a memory the poet will draw strength from as she stays by her dying father's bedside.

She will find inspiration in the hare's stillness, calmness and composure: 'And I thought of the hare in its hour of ease'. She will try to exhibit at least some of that 'ease' as she grapples with her father's final illness, not only for her own sake but also for that of her father and her family at large.

'The Bend in the Road' also finds a kind of spirituality in nature. The poem's first and last lines both begin with the phrase 'This is the place', emphasising the importance of this seemingly banal location, this ordinary bend in the road, to the poet. This is because the bend in the road is an especially still and tranquil place, one that encourages mindfulness and reflection. Stopping here, then, leaves the poet's faculty of memory highly stimulated. As a result, she experiences intensely vivid recollections of her departed loved ones. These memories are so vivid that they prompt what might be described as a spiritual experience. The poet, for a moment, can sense the 'presence' of her loved ones all around her.

'Fireman's Lift', meanwhile, finds spirituality in art rather than in nature. The poem reminds us how great works of art can sometimes produce an almost spiritual response in those who view them. The poet and her mother, we sense, experienced such a response as they 'stepped// Back' so they could see 'the work entire' and were overcome by sheer wonder at Correggio's achievement in conceiving and executing such a monumental work. They experienced a moment of heightened emotion as they contemplated the angels, realising that that they were witnessing a true portrayal of love: 'This is what love sees'. They also, we sense, experienced a moment of calm or psychological healing as they stood there in the extraordinary 'fall-out of brightness' that emanated from the centre of the fresco.

'Translation' depicts a bleak and oppressive form of spirituality, looking back to a time when the Catholic Church was very much the dominant force in Irish life. Sexuality was treated with suspicion. Female sexuality, in particular, was regarded as dangerous and unpredictable. The Church and its various religious orders were willing to take extreme, even cruel, measures in order to police and control sexual morality.

The bleakness of this form of spirituality comes across in the phrase 'The high relief of a glance'. Here Ní Chuilleanáin is referring to a holy picture – maybe of Jesus, or of the Virgin Mary – that was placed 'high' on the laundry wall. The picture was meant to provide the inmates with 'relief' as it gazes down on them while they work. Its 'glance' was meant to offer them with the hope and consolation of religious faith. But the picture's colours had been 'bleached' away by the 'White light' pouring through the laundry window, its eyes erased or 'blinded' by the steam and chemicals rising from the laundry floor.

The image of the 'blinded' picture powerfully captures the failure of religion in 20th century Ireland. It captures how the Catholic faith had become obsessed with a narrow sexual morality, growing blind to all other aspects of spirituality. It also captures how the Church and its religious orders had grown blind to the great harms they were inflicting on the laundry's inmates.

Family

The importance of family is another of Ní Chuilleanáin's central themes. 'Lucina Schynning in Silence of the Nicht', for instance, highlights the deep love and respect the poet had for her father, Cormac Ó Cuilleanáin, who was a professor of Irish at University College Cork (UCC) and helped foster her imagination, creativity and love of the written word. The poet's intense love for her father is evident in the 'waves of darkness' that washed over her as she witnessed his final illness. As we've seen, she was unable to bear the sight of his suffering and fled to the countryside.

The father's life and death inspired two other poems on the course, 'Following' and 'On Lacking the Killer Instinct', a fact that emphasises his central importance to Ní Chuilleanáin's imagination. 'Following' describes not only how the young woman in the poem went 'Following' her father across the bog, but also suggests how Ní Chuilleanáin has been following in her father's footsteps her whole life as she continues his devotion to literature and the written word. 'On Lacking the Killer Instinct', meanwhile, celebrates the vigour and cunning the father exhibited in his younger days, as he dramatically evaded British troops in 1921. The poet praises not only the physical dexterity he showed as he was cornered 'in the narrow road', but also his speed of thought; how he was 'clever' and exhibited 'bright running' to evade his pursuers.

The poet's deep love for her father is evident in how she behaved while he 'was dying in a hospital'. She loved him so much and was so distraught at his condition that she fled up into the hills to avoid the stress of his suffering and imminent demise. Yet she clearly felt guilty about this decision and eventually returned to the city: 'And I should not/ Have run away'.

In 'To Niall Woods and Xenya Ostrovskaia, married in Dublin on 9 September 2009' the poet turns from her father to her son. This poem is a wonderful example of an 'epithalamium', a poem written to celebrate a wedding day. The poet suggests that her son Niall Woods and his Russian bride Xenya Ostrovskaia are destined to be together. She suggests that Niall and Xenya must 'Leave behind the places that [they] knew'. Perhaps the most moving line in the poem is the poet's simple declaration that 'You will have to trust me'. Here we sense the poet, as a mother, attempting to reassure her son and her new daughter-in-law as they embark on their new life together.

'The Bend in the Road' wittily highlights how families develop their own internal mythology. The titular bend is a perfectly ordinary place. But it's a place that the poet and her family frequently speak about and recall. It has been transformed, through the telling and retelling of a simple story, into a location of significance for the family: 'Over twelve years it has become the place/ Where you were sick on the way to the lake'.

In 'Translation', meanwhile, the centrality of family is highlighted by the bizarre but brilliant depiction of the inmates' remains filtering through the soil of Glasnevin cemetery, as they attempt to connect with the buried bodies of their relatives. It's an image that highlights how, in life, the laundry's inmates were forcibly disconnected from their families (many long-term inmates were encouraged to become 'lay nuns', a process that involved taking a new name). But it also highlights how, in death, if we research and retell their stories, the inmates might be connected to their families once more.

Love

'Street' highlights how we can become infatuated with people we see regularly in our neighbourhood. The young man, in this instance, develops a powerful fascination with the butcher's daughter who passes regularly along the street. The infatuation in this case is rather one-sided. It is likely that the butcher's daughter is unaware of the young man's feelings. She might not even know he exists. The poem ultimately presents a most mysterious portrait of love, or at least of infatuation. We can choose to view the man who falls in love with the butcher's daughter as a death-obsessed oddball who has stalker-ish tendencies or as a spontaneous romantic who is overcome with awe and admiration for strong-willed women.

'Fireman's Lift' is concerned not with romantic love but with what might be termed 'brotherly love' or community spirit. We exhibit such love when we act like the angels in the painting, when we strive to help others reach their goals or destinations. For the poet, such behaviour is the very definition of love.

'All for You', too, can be regarded as a love poem of sorts, one that highlights the speaker's devotion to her young companion and her desire for him to receive what is rightfully his. Ní Chuilleanáin has described how the inspiration for this mysterious poem began in advertising of all places: 'I absolutely hate the use of the word 'you' in advertising, and I hate phrases like 'We have all your favourites' or 'We know what you want', because they are lies. And I started with the idea that I would write a poem based on that – but then it became clear that this was far too negative a sentiment to build a poem on and so I began to think what is the opposite of that – and the opposite way of saying 'you' with real reference to the person you are talking to is the 'you' of love.

LINE BY LINE

This poem describes an incident that took place in 1970 when the poet was 28 years old and was still living in Cork city with her family. At the time, her beloved father was terminally ill and lay dying in one of the city's hospitals. Understandably, the young poet was deeply traumatised by this situation.

The young poet found herself leaving the hospital and the city. The decision to leave, we sense, was a spontaneous one. We sense that the poet, overcome with the horror of her father's lingering death, felt a sudden, overwhelming desire to escape. The young poet found herself journeying into the countryside. Eventually she found herself in the ruins of an ancient castle and she ended up spending the night alone here.

The poet settled down for the night in one of the castle's rooms. We are not told what equipment or supplies she had brought with her, if she had a tent or a sleeping bag, for example. But we know that she had a book by the Scottish poet William Dunbar and a candle that enabled her to read: 'I was reading my book in a ruin/ By a sour candle'.

The poet found herself imagining the feasts that might have been held in the castle in centuries gone by. She thinks of how lords and ladies of the castle would have feasted on roast meat and 'Strong drink' while enjoying the music of the castle's minstrels.

The poet, however, had no such comforts and was essentially sleeping rough. This ruined building offered no 'shield from the air', no protection from the elements. There was a time when the castle's windows had shutters and panes of glass. But these features were long since gone. The windows were open to the elements now and the wind came 'Blowing in' around the poet, where she sat with her book and candle. The roof of the castle had also long since fallen in. When the poet looked up, she could see the moon above her in a cloudless sky: 'I felt/ Moonlight on my head, clear after three days' rain.'

Eventually, the poet fell asleep. She woke several times during the night and heard bats squeaking above her as they flitted between the towers of the castle. When she woke in the morning, she found that several sheep had wandered into the roofless room while she was sleeping. She describes how the sheep 'stared' at her, suggesting that these animals were surprised at the arrival of this stranger.

The poem's title 'Lucina Schynning in Silence of the Nicht' is taken from 'The Birth of Antichrist', which was published in the early sixteenth century by the Scottish poet William Dunbar. The poem's opening line translates this phrase from the Scottish dialect into modern English. This is the book it seems that the young poet was reading by candlelight when she stayed overnight at the castle.

The poet describes how she 'slept safely', suggesting that she felt safe and secure in this environment, despite the fact that it was open to the elements and to bats, sheep and other creatures. The poet spent the morning exploring the castle and the surrounding area. She 'washed' in a stream that ran beside the castle. The water in the stream was 'orange' in colour, having drained or 'channelled' into the stream from surrounding bogland. The stream's banks were covered in 'cresses', which are green leafy plants. Perhaps the poet simply washed her hands and face in these orange waters. Or maybe she stripped off and immersed herself, eager to cleanse her entire body.

Near the castle was a 'desert', upon which stood a little church or chapel. 'Desert', derived from the Irish word díseart, means a place of retreat and hermitage. The poet entered the chapel, noting the hole in its roof and the mosaic on the floor. Mosaics are images that are made by combining hundreds of little pieces of coloured stone. This particular mosaic, according to the poet, depicted 'beasts', suggesting that it featured sheep, cows and other biblical animals.

The poet found the 'desert' an extremely pleasant place to be. She found herself relaxing, as the stress and tension associated with her father's illness temporarily left her mind and body: 'In the desert I relaxed'. She found herself feeling 'amazed', suggesting that she was overcome by a sense of joy, wonder and optimism.

The poet continued to wander in the area surrounding the castle.

- She had a pleasant encounter with some 'Sheepdogs' who 'embraced' her. We can imagine the poet petting these animals, only for them to rise up on their hind legs as they paw and lick her in an affectionate manner.
- She noted that birds, bees and other insects that are highly active in the area: 'the grasshopper/ Returned with lark and bee.' The use of the word 'Returned' here suggests that the poem is set in springtime, that the natural world is coming to life again after the stillness of winter.
- She noticed a hare 'sitting still' on one particular track. The hare struck her as being 'absorbed', utterly lost in concentration and indifferent to what was going on around it.
- She returned to the stream where she had bathed earlier and relished the chirping sound of its quickly flowing waters.

FOCUS ON STYLE

Imagery

Many of Ní Chuilleanáin's poems feature startling and unusual images that remain with the reader long after they have read the poem. 'Lucina Schynning in Silence of the Nicht' is no different in this regard. The poem is comprised of a series of memorable images relating to this particular moment in the poet's life. There is the image of the poet sitting alone in a ruined castle, reading a book by candlelight. There are the dark and terrifying images of 'plague' and 'disease', of swarms of insects emerging from the spines of books.

The poem refers to the historical events of 1649, when the English statesman Oliver Cromwell invaded Ireland with a large expeditionary force. Cromwell spent Christmas of that year in Cork city and his vast army found whatever lodgings they could find in the surrounding area. The poet imagines that a squadron of his men were billeted in the castle. Before moving on, she imagines, these soldiers would have smashed the windows in the nearby 'desert' chapel. They were motivated to do so because of their hatred of the Catholic religion.

The poem features a wonderful description of the mosaic on the chapel floor that depicts certain animals or 'beasts'. This act of vandalism would have exposed the chapel's mosaic to the elements. The poet playfully personifies the animals depicted in the mosaic, presenting them as if they were living, breathing creatures. She imagines that they would have gazed out through the freshly broken windows, 'amazed' at the sight of the sky beyond the chapel walls.

Many of Ní Chuilleanáin's poems feature references to strange or mysterious buildings to which the speaker is granted access. In 'Lucina Schynning', the poet has come to a deserted castle. Though this place is in a state of utter disrepair – the roofs have fallen in and the windows broken – the poet feels at home here. She sleeps peacefully during the night and experiences the peace and serenity of the chapel, with its beautiful mosaic floor.

Quests and Journeys

The poet's coming to this location can be seen as a form of pilgrimage, a journey or search of spiritual significance. The poet's behaviour at this location also calls to mind the certain traditional religious practices. Her lack of creature comforts, the fact she had to sleep rough and bathe in cold water, can be seen as rituals of self-mortification, which the saints of old would have subjected themselves to in order to cleanse their bodies of sin. The act of washing the body in cold water is a traditional part of many religions, seen as a source of purification.

DEATH AND GRIEF

This poem highlights the trauma caused by the final illness of a loved one. Ní Chuilleanáin's father, after all, was a major figure in her life. We sense that the poet was deeply traumatised by watching him waste away in a hospital bed. The poet found this situation so horrific that she was overcome by a sudden and powerful urge to flee, to leave the hospital and, indeed, the city far behind.

MENTAL SUFFERING

The toll that this difficult period took on the poet's mental health is evident throughout the poem. The opening lines, for instance, hint at her agitated, depressed state of mind. The description of the candle as 'sour' suggests, perhaps, the anger and bitterness that the poet felt at the time. It might also suggest the poet's loss of interest in or enthusiasm for life, that this had soured as a consequence of her father's illness. The fact that she is reading William Dunbar's 'The Birth of Antichrist' also suggests that she is in a dark psychological place and that this apocalyptic text is the one that appeals to her or resonates with her at this moment in time.

The poem's first 16 lines also suggest that the poet has been driven to an extreme emotional state, one that borders on mental illness or insanity. The term 'crazed, which she uses to describe the condition of the window in the room where she sleeps, can also be used to describe someone who is insane or has lost all emotional control. The description of the 'Moonlight' on her head also suggests mental instability. For centuries, people believed that certain phases of the moon prompted mental illness and irrational behaviour. The poet makes reference to this concept of 'lunacy' in line 16, where she describes the 'disease of the moon gone astray'.

Lines 12 to 16, meanwhile, hint at the dark thoughts that consumed the poet's mind. Negative thoughts came crashing through her mind like 'waves of darkness'. She found herself dwelling on images of plague and disease. She imagined whole towns and villages being overrun with mice and beetles. The poet, in a masterful metaphor, describes how the mice and beetles came crawling out of the 'spines of books', suggesting that these dark thoughts were inspired by various novels and history books she had read over the years. She found herself thinking of bacterial plagues such as the Black Death, which killed millions in medieval Europe. Such sickness would first turn their victims pale. Then the victims' flesh would assume a clay-like complexion, as the life slowly left their bodies.

SPIRITUALITY

The poet, however, declares that these 'waves of darkness' are now behind her, that she has recovered, to some extent, from the trauma that had afflicted her. There is a sense in which the castle and 'desert' have provided her with the support and comfort she needed at this difficult moment in her life. Perhaps the poet, on a conscious level, did not know what she was doing when she left the hospital and wandered into the hills. But she realised, on an unconscious level, that she needed to get back to nature, that the proximity of the natural world would help her overcome the anguish and the agitation that had gripped her.

The poem, therefore, offers us a mystical and spiritual understanding of the natural world, hinting at its restorative powers. By exposing herself to the elements, by sleeping rough and washing in the stream's 'cold water', the poet undergoes a form of spiritual or mental renewal. Her recovery is aided by her connection with the wildlife in the area, particularly the insects and animals that she encounters. There is a sense in which the natural world is looking out for her, offering her much needed protection and solace. Rather than disturbing or frightening her, for example, the bats that fly through the room when the poet sleeps offer her a sense of security: 'The bats flew through my room where I slept safely.' The sheepdogs that she encounters greet her with great love and affection: 'Sheepdogs embraced me'.

We sense that the poet at the end of the poem is ready to return to the city and the hospital. She left a horrific situation in the hospital and it will be no less horrific when she returns. But her sojourn in the castle has left her grounded and serene. She is ready now to face the traumatic reality of her father's final illness and be by his side during his final days.

FAMILY

This poem, like many by Ní Chuilleanáin, emphasises the importance of family. It highlights the deep love and respect the poet had for her father, Cormac Ó Cuilleanáin, who was a professor of Irish at UCC and helped foster her imagination, creativity and love of the written word. The poet's intense love for her father is evident in the 'waves of darkness' that washed over her as she witnessed his final illness. As we've seen, she was unable to bear the sight of his suffering and fled to the countryside. The father's life and death inspired two other poems on the course, 'Following' and 'On Lacking the Killer Instinct', a fact that emphasises his central importance to Ní Chuilleanáin's imagination.

The Second Voyage

LINE BY LINE

Odysseus, King of Ithaca, is one of the great heroes from Greek mythology. He led an army from his island nation to participate in the legendary Trojan War. Odysseus, along with his fellow Greek kings, laid siege to the great city of Troy. However, the city's walls held firm and the siege dragged on for ten bitter years.

Odysseus was known not only for his skill and bravery but also for his intelligence and quick wittedness. It was Odysseus, according to legend, who conceived the 'Trojan Horse', the ruse that allowed the Greeks to finally capture Troy. After Troy's fall, Odysseus headed back to Ithaca. However, his journey home, as recounted in Homer's epic poem *The Odyssey*, was frustrated by shipwrecks and misfortune. For nearly ten years he wandered the Mediterranean, visiting various islands and experiencing many adventures, before finally finding his way back home.

Odysseus' present situation

We join Odysseus at some point during his wanderings. We don't know, precisely, how long it has been since he left Troy and started on his journey back to Ithaca. We sense, however, that he has been travelling for several years at least. Odysseus set out from Troy with a ship full of Ithacan companions. By the time we join him, however, his men are gone. They have perished, we imagine, in various shipwrecks and adventures, leaving him utterly alone upon the ocean's surface.

Odysseus seems to be aboard a tiny craft. It doesn't have a sail, meaning he has to row his way across the ocean. Line 13 suggests that Odysseus has recently been shipwrecked.

Perhaps, therefore, we find him piloting a little barge or boat he has used to escape the wreck of a greater vessel. He might even be using a piece of wreckage as a makeshift lifeboat.

Odysseus takes a break from rowing, rests 'on his oar', and studies the ocean. Its surface is described as 'simmering', suggesting that the water is not only choppy and turbulent but also extremely hot. Its depths are described as 'Uncertain', suggesting that Odysseus cannot tell how deep it really is. He makes out shoals of 'slim fishes' swimming by beneath his vessel. Odysseus describes how they pass in a 'fatal' or deadly 'formation', as if he can imagine them nibbling on his drowned corpse were he to fall overboard.

Odysseus, we sense, is utterly weary of the ocean. After voyaging so long, the very sight of its waters fills him with disgust. He is sick of contemplating water that stretches in every direction, an utterly monotonous vista, uninterrupted by land or any distinguishing features.

Odysseus and the waves

Odysseus thinks of the waves that surround him as if they were human beings. The surf on top of each wave is presented as 'ruffled' or curly locks of hair that sits upon its forehead. Inserting his oar into the water, meanwhile, is like driving it between a particular wave's jaws.

The waves, Odysseus declares, move past his vessel in a manner that is both 'mincing' and 'crocodiling'. The fact that they 'mince' suggests that they move in what strikes him as a prim or dainty fashion. The fact that they are said to 'crocodile' suggests they are deceptive, dangerous and could strike at any moment with deadly force.

Odysseus doesn't think of the waves as a brief and random accumulation of water molecules. Instead, he thinks that each wave, like a human being, has a fixed and definite body. Each wave, according to Odysseus, has taken a 'battering' as it travelled over the ocean's surface. He expects, therefore, that each wave should have distinguishing features, that it should be 'ridged / Pocked or dented' in a distinctive manner.

But the waves, according to Odysseus, choose to conceal their distinguishing features and all adopt a similar appearance. They do so, he maintains, because they are cruel and callous, lacking even 'a single/ Streak of decency'. They don't want to make the ocean less monotonous and therefore more bearable for wanderers like him. The waves, then, suppress their individuality and exhibit 'less character than sheep'. They pass by in a monotonous flock of sheep, each moving at the same pace in the same direction.

Odysseus dearly wishes that the waves would express their individuality. Then he would be able to recognise particular waves as they passed by, making the ocean's surface far more interesting. He could greet a 'notorious' or deadly wave with the 'admiration' of one warrior saluting another. He could assign names to individual waves; just as Adam, in the Bible, was said to name the various creatures that inhabited the Garden of Eden: 'we could name them as Adam named the beasts'. He might encounter a wave that gloated and 'rejoice[d]' at his miserable, shipwrecked condition. Odysseus, we sense, would prefer such gloating to the current endless monotony he surveys.

The prophecy
It has been prophesised that Odysseus could never go home until he first found a 'land that knows nothing of the sea'. When he discovers such a kingdom he must make a sacrifice to the gods. Only then will he finally be permitted to return to Ithaca.

Adrift on his tiny vessel, Odysseus fantasises about discovering such a land. He imagines mooring his boat on its coastline: 'I know what I'll do he said;/ I'll park my ship in the crook of a long pier'. He imagines turning his back on the ocean and walking up a hillside: 'I'll face the rising ground and walk away'. He imagines waking on an on, travelling 'up riverbeds' and 'Over gaps in the hills'. He would leave the 'tidal waters' of the ocean and of rivers mouths far behind.

Odysseus imagines carrying his oar with him on this hike: 'And I'll take you with me he said to the oar'. Eventually he would come to 'warm/ Silent valleys' so far inland that their inhabitants are utterly unfamiliar with the ocean and its ways. He imagines meeting a farmer so ignorant of the sea that he mistakes the oar for a 'winnowing fan', an implement used by grain famers. Odysseus would finally have fulfilled the prophecy. He would finally have discovered a 'land that knows nothing of the sea' and would be permitted by the Gods to return to Ithaca. He imagines pausing for a while on this very spot: 'There I will stand still'. He imagines driving the oar into the ground where it would serve as a 'a gatepost or a hitching-post'. Then he would walk back to where his ship was 'park[ed]' and set sail, at last, for his native land.

Odysseus, it seems, is worried that all is not well back in Ithaca, that the kingdom might have a taken a turn for the worse during the years he's been away. He is eager, therefore, to 'go back and organise [his] house'. We can imagine that he's keen to restore his relationship with his wife, Queen Penelope, and with his children. No doubt he also wants to ensure that his house or palace – as well the kingdom as a whole – is being administered correctly. Perhaps he will have to eliminate sinister and self-serving elements that have gained influence while he's been away.

Odysseus despairs
In reality, however, Odysseus is still aboard his little craft, drifting on the ocean's surface: 'But the profound/ Unfenced valleys of the ocean still held him'. The water all around him is still turbulent and unpleasantly hot: 'The sea was still frying under the ship's side'. He has only his oar to keep himself safe and out of the water's clutches: 'He had only the oar to make them keep their distance'.

Odysseus, it seems, has been travelling for so long that he has grown to hate not only the ocean but also water in general. But he finds himself thinking of how water is inescapable, of how it exists everywhere in a multitude of forms:

- He thinks of various waterways: a 'black canal' on which 'pale swans' float and 'flat lakes' that 'bisect' or divide a countryside overgrown with rushes.
- He thinks about fountains he's seen in various city squares. Using a fine simile, Ní Chuilleanáin compares such a fountain to a willow tree. We can imagine how the wide, downward curves of water issuing from the fountain might resemble the willow's bent over branches.
- He even thinks of water being poured into a kettle, making a 'clattering' sound as it does so.
- He also remembers smaller or less significant instances of water flowing: a fountain in a city square, horse troughs, a kettle being filled.
- He remembers troughs where horses go to drink.
- He even remembers muddy trickles of water by a roadside, next to which frogs and spiders made their homes.

Odysseus, at the poem's conclusion, becomes filled with despair at his present shipwrecked state, at his endless journey home, at the inescapable presence of the water he's come to despise so much. He begins to weep in misery and frustration: 'His face grew damp with tears that tasted/ Like his own sweat or the insults of the sea', the fact that his tears taste like the 'insults of the sea' suggests his rage and frustration at his inability to find his way back to Ithaca. He seems to feel like the ocean's plaything, toyed with by the waves as they send him hither and thither and laugh at his misery. We leave him there, sobbing as his little craft drifts onwards at the water's mercy.

FOCUS ON STYLE

Quests and Journeys

Many of Ní Chuilleanáin's poems depict a person who goes on a journey and is changed in some fundamental way by what they experience. This theme is certainly present in 'The Second Voyage'. Odysseus has been utterly altered by his seemingly unending journey back from the war. Once he was a minor king who led men into battle, but now he's all alone, a rag-clad vagrant on a makeshift craft, having conversations with his oar. He once led men into battle and was the quick-thinking commander who master-minded the fall of Troy itself. But now he weeps in impotence and frustration before the 'insults of the sea'.

The Poem's Title

If the 'first voyage' was the relatively uneventful cruise from Ithaca to Troy with the rest of the Greek fleet, then this 'second voyage' is the return journey, the decade-long, shipwreck-bedevilled, extraordinary journey back, one that will leave Odysseus changed forever.

Spirituality, Myth and Folklore

'The Second Voyage' is typical of Ní Chuilleanáin's poetry in that it makes fresh and imaginative use of existing material. In this case, she draws on Homer's epic poem the *Odyssey*, the most famous and original account of Odysseus's travels. Yet Ní Chuilleanáin makes Odysseus very much her own, and she presents his story as a distinctly modern take on his voyage and the terrible hardships it entailed. Line 11 features a Biblical reference, recalling how in the Bible, Adam, as the first man, was given the task of coming up with names for every other creature God had created.

Metaphor and Simile

'The Second Voyage' is a poem distinguished by Ní Chuilleanáin's typically inventive use of metaphor. Ní Chuilleanáin uses several brilliant metaphors to describe the ocean. She mentions its 'profound' or deep 'Unfenced valleys' and we can imagine how the ocean's wave-tossed surface might be said to resemble a landscape of peaks and valleys. Its turbulence, meanwhile, is captured when Ní Chuilleanáin compares it to cooking oil, describing how it is 'sizzling' and 'frying' under Odysseus's ship. The twisted strands of seaweed floating in its waters are imaginatively compared to 'scribbles'.

Personification, meanwhile, features in the poem's last line, where the poet refers to the 'insults of the sea'. This line suggests the sea is deliberately frustrating Odysseus's homeward journey, and mocking or insulting him as it does so.

THEMES

MENTAL SUFFERING

'The Second Voyage' is a powerful study of mental suffering. Odysseus has been tormented and frustrated by the seemingly endless nature of his journey home. He has been travelling across the ocean for so long that the very sight of its waves fills him with disgust and horror. He is absolutely desperate to find his way back to Ithaca. He weeps in despair at his plight, his tears tasting 'Like his own sweat or the insults of the sea.'

Odysseus, as we've seen, fantasises about finding a land that knows nothing of the sea. But his fantasy is disturbed by the notion that the ocean might rise and flood even the most inland-lying of valleys. We see this when he imagines leaving the oar as a 'tidemark', a device used along the shoreline to measure the level reached of the tide. Odysseus, then, has been travelling so long that he cannot imagine being fully free of the ocean.

'The Second Voyage' also conveys the effects that a long and difficult period of isolation can have on the human psyche. We see this in the rather strange thoughts that drift through Odysseus' mind:

- He speaks to his oar as if it were a person. We see this in phrases like 'Our shipwreck', and 'I'll take you with me' and 'I'll plant you'. There is a sense, perhaps, in which the oar has taken the place of his lost companions.
- As we've seen, he thinks of the waves as if they were individual human-like entities, rather than random accumulations of water.
- He has developed an irrational aversion to water and is horrified by the thought that water is everywhere, from kettles to canals, and that no matter how far he goes he cannot escape it.
- He even thinks that the waves are deliberately persecuting him by concealing their individuality.

Such ideas might strike us as bizarre and disturbing, as the fevered imaginings of the mentally unwell. Yet, such abnormal trains of thoughts are typical of the survival strategies or 'coping mechanisms' used by people who are forced to endure long periods of isolation.

Deaths and Engines

LINE BY LINE

Landing in Paris Airport

The poet recalls a time she was onboard a flight to Paris. She remembers how the plane turned down sharply towards the runway, as it descended on its final approach into Charles de Gaulle airport. As the plane tilted and turned in a 'stiff curve' above the outskirts of Paris, the poet could see the suburban houses below. 'We came down above the houses'. It was winter and a layer of snowfall covered the city.

At the periphery or 'edge' of the airport, where the runway commences, the poet saw the remains of a crashed plane. The front half of the plane had been completely destroyed in the crash, leaving only the 'back half'. The poet could see into the severed fuselage, the central portion of the aircraft's body. The inside of the fuselage had been consumed by fire. All that remained was a hollow 'burnt-out' tube, which the poet compares to a long, dark 'tunnel'. These charred remains stood out starkly against the snow that covered the runway.

It seems that the wreckage had been there for a while. The poet observed how the wreckage was 'frozen' or encrusted in ice, suggesting that it had been there for days, weeks or even months. Perhaps the plane had crashed elsewhere in France and had been brought to Paris for study.

Sitting on board the return flight

The poet recalls sitting on board the return flight to Ireland a number of days later. It was an evening flight and the poet observed how the runway, illuminated by the lights at either side, was still white with snow. The plane had taxied out to the top of the runway and the pilot was awaiting confirmation from the control tower that he was clear for take-off.

As she sat in her seat waiting for the plane to begin accelerating down the runway, the poet began to feel anxious and uncertain. She found herself thinking about the wreckage she had seen on her arrival. We can imagine how her mind would have been busy with thoughts of plane crashes, with worry that something might go wrong on her return journey.

The poet waited for the pilot to speak over the plane's 'loudspeakers', but no communication was forthcoming. Perhaps she was hoping that the pilot would update the passengers about the weather conditions and reassure everyone that everything was fine. But 'No sound came over/ The loudspeakers'.

In her anxious state, sitting in an environment that makes her feel very uncomfortable, the world around the poet began to feel strange and unfamiliar. She thought of the pilot in the cockpit, imagining him being 'lonely', isolated and remote from everybody else on board. She imagined that he was sighing and that these sighs were audible over the loudspeakers in the cabin. Such thoughts and imaginings about the pilot stem, of course, from the poet's own feelings of anxiety and panic.

The mood among the poet's fellow passengers seems to have been rather somber. We can imagine that many of the other passengers were sitting silently, static in their seats in preparation for take-off. There is something about waiting for a plane to take-off, the poet suggests, that induces feelings of tension and anxiety.

Imagining a crash

The poet, as she waits for take-off, is filled with a dreadful certainty that the plane will crash during its journey back to Ireland. The plane, she is convinced, will depart from its flightpath and 'curve' downwards until it 'Meets the straight skyline' or horizon, crashing into the earth. The poet is convinced, therefore, that she is doomed. Only having some super, miraculous power of flight will allow her to escape the coming disaster: 'Soon you will need wings of your own'.

The poet describes the metal wings as 'cold', implying that there is something lifeless and soulless about such metal structures. The poet imagines that if the plane crashes her body too will turn 'cold', as her life and spirit ebb away. It is as if the coldness of the wings will somehow be transmitted to her, that it is 'contagious'.

The inevitability of death

As the engines roar into life, the poet feels convinced that each human life has an inevitable and pre-determined end, one that we can do nothing to avoid. She suggests that each human existence can be presented as a mathematical graph. One line on the graph represents a person's life. Another line represents time. The point where these lines cross represents the moment of this person's death. When that moment comes, each person is utterly 'Cornered' and helpless to alter the situation. There is nothing we can do to escape death and prolong our existence.

The poet, we imagine, is nervously fidgeting with the knife and fork that have been provided for her in-flight meal. She crosses them on the tray in front of her, reminding her of how the lines of life and time might cross on her imaginary graph.

The moment of our deaths, the poet suggests, might be foretold by the lifeline in our palms. Perhaps a skilled palm reader could, in theory, determine the moment of our demise by noting where the lifeline breaks on its course across the palm.

There are moments when people seem to cheat death, when they survive accidents and hazardous situations. The poet associates such survival with 'images of relief', with lucky escapes and hospital care. But such survival changes nothing because the moment of our death is still set in stone and waits for us in the future. The time will inevitably come when these 'images of relief' can no longer help us: 'These [images] will fail you sometime.'

The moments of our death

The poet imagines a car that is accelerating towards the wall at the end of a blind alley. The wall is only metres away, meaning that it is 'too late to stop', even if the driver slams on the brakes. At the moment of our deaths, the poet suggests, we will feel like the passengers in such a car. We will realise that nothing can be done to prolong our existence. We will accept that the inevitable, pre-determined moment of our death has finally arrived.

FOCUS ON STYLE

Gapped and Mysterious Narratives

'Deaths and Engines' like many of Ní Chuilleanáin's poems, features a gapped and mysterious narrative. The poem can be divided into three quite distinct segments: the poet's arrival in Paris, covered in the first stanza, the poet's wait for take-off, which is covered in stanzas two and three, and a meditation on the inevitability of death, which is covered in stanzas four and five.

The transitions between these segments are sudden and abrupt. We move from the poet's arrival directly to her departure while learning nothing about her time in France. Equally jarring is the transition from segment two to segment three, where we are jolted from images of a plane crashing to images of an injured man in hospital.

Imagery

Ní Chuilleanáin's poems are known for their startling imagery, and 'Deaths and Engines' is no different in this regard. Especially vivid is the bleak image of the crashed plane, black and frozen on the snow-covered outskirts of the Paris airport. Equally memorable are the 'images of relief' mentioned in the fourth stanza, where the poet depicts a survivor of some horrific accident. She describes a man with 'cut lips' and a bloodied face, relieved but no doubt traumatised, who is chatting with visitors who stand around his hospital bed.

DEATH AND GRIEF

Much of the time we are so busy with our lives that we give little or no thought to death. But there are moments when our minds become sharply focused on death's inevitability. For many people, being on an airplane gives rise to such anxious thoughts. The poet, prompted by the sight of the crashed aircraft, experiences one such moment as she sits aboard the return flight on the runway.

The poem presents death not only as inevitable but also as pre-determined. The moment of each person's death has been scheduled with such certainty that it could be represented on a mathematical graph or predicted by a skilled palm reader. We will recognise this moment when it comes. We will know – with the certainty of passengers in a car accelerating down a blind alley – that our end has finally come.

The poem, however, ends with an acceptance of death. The poet says that death is ultimately something extremely 'light'. We spend much of our lives greatly fearing this moment, only to find that when it arrives it is less terrible than we imagined. Transitioning from life to death is actually pretty easy. There is even a sense that dying might actually be something of a relief, as we cast off the burdens and obligations of being alive.

The poet emphasises how our deaths will bring extraordinary grief and suffering to those who love us. She uses a remarkable metaphor to convey this, declaring that when we die, our bodies will explode into little pieces that fly off in every direction: 'You will be scattered like wreckage'. These body parts, she declares, will 'spin' through the air, finally coming to rest 'in the hearts' of our loved ones: 'Will spin and lodge in the hearts/ Of all who love you.' This is a rather strange and unsettling imagine, but one that powerfully conveys the reality of bereavement.

Each person we love will be affected differently – each will have their own particular memories and relationship with us. We are, after all, different things to different people. The poet says that each piece of the 'wreckage' that is created when we die will be 'a different shape'.

MENTAL SUFFERING

The poem captures just how stressful and uncomfortable travelling by plane can sometimes be. It is common, after all, for people to feel nervous and anxious when awaiting take-off. But the sight of the crashed plane on the ground introduces a whole new level of anxiety into the mix for the poet. As she sits aboard the return flight, her mind almost inevitably fills with panicked thoughts of crashing and dying.

The poem illustrates how at such moments of intense anxiety and stress the world can start to seem strange and unfamiliar. The poet begins to have strange thoughts of the pilot being isolated and lonely in the cockpit, sighing to himself. She even imagines that she can hear these sighs over the plane's loudspeaker. In reality, of course, the pilot was probably chatting happily with his co-pilot as he prepares to get the flight underway.

Street

LINE BY LINE

I

The poem focuses on a young man's response to seeing the local butcher's daughter as she passes along the street where he lives or works.

On this particular occasion, the girl is striding down the street in her butcher's attire. A bloodied knife hangs from her belt. The fact that the girl's knife is dripping with blood suggests that she has just come from her work in the 'shambles' or slaughterhouse, where she slaughters animals, dismembers their corpses and cuts them up into joints and pieces of meat. All of this, of course, is bloody business, and the girl's knife will be dripping with blood at the end.

Perhaps on this occasion the daughter is on an errand. Perhaps she is delivering some meat to a local customer. But she hasn't changed out of her blood-stained work attire. She hasn't even removed her dripping knife from its ring on her belt.

The young man is so struck by this sight that he immediately '[falls] in love' with her. What grabs is attention, in particular, is the blood that drips from her knife as she strolls along the pavement. When she has passed by he stands staring at the 'dark shining drops on the paving-stones'.

II

The butcher's daughter, we sense, regularly passes along the street as she runs errands. And the young man, no doubt, is always excited and delighted to see her pass by. We can imagine him keeping an eye out for her, hoping that she will pass by.

Finally, 'One day' the young man decides to follow the girl as she returns from whatever errand she has been on. He follows her along the street and down a lane that leads to the family home. The lane is described as being at the back of the shambles, suggesting that the butcher's family lives adjacent to their place of work.

When the young man arrives at the entrance, the door is 'half-open'. He walks up to the door and peers inside. Inside the door are a set of stairs that lead up to the family living quarters. The stairs are kept very neat and orderly. We are told that they are 'brushed and clean'. The girl has removed her shoes and placed them neatly on 'the bottom step'.

However, the girl has managed to get blood on the soles of her bare feet. Perhaps blood from her knife dripped onto the floor when she was removing her shoes and she stepped in this before climbing the stairs. The blood on her heels leaves a 'red crescent' mark each time she presses her foot down on one of the steps. Each step she takes diminishes the amount of blood on her foot and so the marks begin to fade as she climbs: 'Each tread marked with the red crescent/ Her bare heels left, fading to faintest at the top'.

LOVE

This poem highlights how we can become infatuated with people we see regularly in our neighbourhood. The young man, in this instance, develops a powerful fascination with the butcher's daughter who passes regularly along the street. The infatuation in this case is rather one-sided. It is likely that the butcher's daughter is unaware of the young man's feelings. She might not even know he exists.

Many readers are taken aback by the young man's fascination with the blood that drips from the knife. Perhaps this suggests something abnormal about his psychology, an obsession with death and violence. But we can also read this fascination in a more positive light. Perhaps the young man views the blood as a symbol of the daughter's strength and independence of mind. For this is a young woman, after all, who does what might be considered traditional masculine work: the slaughtering of animals. And she makes no attempt to prettify herself when she leaves the shambles to run an errand. Instead, she walks boldly along the street with her dripping cleaver, indifferent to what others might think of her.

What are we to make of the young man's decision to follow the butcher's daughter? Perhaps this is a spontaneous, harmless gesture, born of his fascination with this proud and strong-willed woman. Or perhaps there is something inappropriate, maybe even stalkerish, about how he follows her down the lane and peers inside the doorway to her home.

The poem, then, presents a most mysterious portrait of love, or at least of infatuation. We can choose to view the man who falls in love with the butcher's daughter in two very different ways. We can view him as a death-obsessed oddball who has stalker-ish tendencies. Or we can view him as a spontaneous romantic who is overcome with awe and admiration for this strong-willed woman.

FOCUS ON STYLE

Imagery

There is something very cinematic about this poem. Each section seems like a scene from a movie. We can imagine how the first four lines might work on the big screen.

We have an establishing shot of the street, followed by a medium range shot of the butcher's daughter walking down the street.

- The camera zooms in on the knife that dangles from the ring on her belt and drops of blood that fall to the pavement.
- We then cut to the young man who is, perhaps, standing inside the window of the newsagents or pharmacy where he works.
- The girl catches his eye and he is immediately infatuated.
- He walks out onto street as she passes and sees the blood dripping from the knife. He walks over to where the drops have landed and stares silently at the 'dark shining drops on the paving-stones'.

We can imagine how the second part of the poem could be one continuous shot, as we follow the girl down the street, turning down the passageway alongside the shop, walking by the shambles at the back before reaching the entrance to the house. The door is pushed open and we see the shoes neatly arranged on the bottom step. As the camera moves in on the stairs, we see the 'red crescent' blood marks on each of the steps, fading as we reach the top.

Gapped and Mysterious Narratives

'Street' plunges us into a narrative with little or nothing in the way of background information. We have no idea who the 'He' mentioned in the opening line is. Is this the first time he has seen the butcher's daughter, or does he see her regularly?

Rather than providing us with a coherent story that enables us to make easy sense of the characters and events described, the poet gives us two segments of the narrative, leaving us to fill in the gaps ourselves. We transition abruptly from an account of the unidentified young man observing the butcher's daughter walking down the street to an occasion where he decides to follow her home.

The poem also ends in an abrupt manner, with little or no sense of resolution or conclusion. The reader is left wondering where the narrative will go and what will happen next. Will the young man continue to follow the girl up the stairs, and, if so, what are his intentions at this moment? Or will he simply turn back and leave the property, returning to his place of work or to his own home?

Many of Ní Chuilleanáin's poems feature references to strange or mysterious buildings to which someone is granted access. In 'Street', the young man who follows the butcher's daughter comes to a door that has been left 'half-open'. We might wonder why the girl did not close the door after her. Has she been expecting the young man? Has the door been deliberately left open so that he may enter? Like with so many of Ní Chuilleanáin's poems, the reader is left guessing as to what the significance of certain details are and what comes next.

Fireman's Lift

A detail from Correggio's fresco 'The Assumption of the Virgin'

LINE BY LINE

This poem is set in the great cathedral of Parma, Italy, which is famous for its 'cupola' or dome. The interior of the dome features a massive fresco by the great Italian painter Correggio, which was created between 1526 and 1530. This powerful painting depicts the miracle of the Assumption: how the Virgin Mary was raised body and soul into heaven without actually having to die beforehand. Correggio painted a vast spiral of clouds, circling upwards towards a clear patch of golden light, which represents heaven itself. The Virgin is poised in this circle of brightness on the verge of entering Paradise. Seated on the spiralling clouds around her are choirs of angels.

The light in the painting

In 1963, when she was twenty one years old, Ní Chuilleanáin visited the cathedral with her mother. She remembers the two of them standing there, gazing up at the dome's interior: 'I was standing beside you looking up'.

The poet and her mother took a step back to get a better view of this massive painting: 'We saw the work entire'. They imagined how Correggio himself must have 'longed' to take such a step back all those years ago, as he stood there painting

on scaffolds high above the ground. He must have longed, the poet feels, to somehow see himself in action, to somehow watch himself bringing a masterpiece into existence.

We get a sense of the power and physicality Correggio must have exhibited as he worked, as his arm 'swept' across the dome's surface in 'large' and decisive strokes. He is presented as an heroic figure, working tirelessly for six years to make his great vision a reality.

The poet and her mother, it seems, were especially struck by Correggio's depiction of light. The light in the painting is described as a 'fall-out of brightness', suggesting the intense and shimmering waves of illumination that seem to drift downwards and outwards from its centre. Ní Chuilleanáin uses a wonderful metaphor to describe this exquisitely-painted glow. It's as if, she says, the ceiling of the dome 'splits wide open', exposing the cathedral to the light of heaven itself: 'Where the church splits wide open to admit…the fall-out of brightness.' The light is so realistic it's as if she's looking 'through' the dome at some flawless summer sky: 'looking up/ Through… the cupola'.

The light in the painting, while intense, is also soft and peaceful. It has a wonderfully liquid quality that 'Melted and faded' the bodies of the angels it shines down on. Their forms were soft and blurred rather than crisp and distinct, with the bodies of individual angels blending into one another and into the painting's background.

The poet describes how it seemed that 'Loose' body parts 'Floated' in the painting's surface: 'feet and elbows and staring eyes'. According to the poet, these seemed to drift and shimmer like strands of almost transparent seaweed in a rock pool: 'Clear and free as weeds.'

The Virgin travels upwards

The poet imagines that the Virgin has passed through the spiral of clouds in the painting, travelling towards the glory of heaven at the painting's centre: 'The Virgin was spiralling to heaven'. The Virgin has moved upwards 'Past mist and shining', passing misty billows of cloud illuminated by the light pouring down from Paradise.

The poet imagines that the angels seated on the spiral of clouds have assisted the Virgin on her journey heavenward: 'we saw them Lifting her'. She imagines that the Virgin is 'Hauled up in stages', as the 'Celestial choirs' of angels pass her from one level of the cloud-spiral to the next.

The poet imagines that the angels have been working in 'Teams', their arms 'heaving' the Virgin upwards. Each team of angels crowds around the Virgin, supporting her weight and lifting her: 'Teams of angelic arms were heaving,/ Supporting, crowding her'.

The angels' effort

The poet is moved taken by the intense physical effort the angels seem to be making as they heave the Virgin upwards, as 'she passed through their hands'. Their jaws are clenched in exertion so that their features become more defined: 'a jaw defining itself'. The poet describes this process by using a number of images associated with building and construction:

- Their shoulders of certain angels are 'yoked' or intertwined as they work together to heave the Virgin upwards.
- Certain angels are bent double, so that their backs resemble a 'roof' or fat surface: 'The back making itself a roof'. We can imagine the Virgin stepping on their backs and using them to pass from one level of the cloud-spiral to the next.
- Their legs of certain angels are compared to bridges because they span the gaps between different levels of the cloud spiral, allowing the Virgin to continue on her journey.
- The hands of certain angels are compared to 'cradles', others to 'cranes', and their arms are said to resemble 'pillars'. This is because of how they lift and support the Virgin on her journey.

The poet imagines the angels making one final collective effort as the Virgin nears the end of the cloud-spiral: 'as she came to the edge of the cloud.' As they do so their muscles bunch together, straining and shifting with the effort involved: 'the muscles clung and shifted'. They will push the Virgin on the final stage of her journey, heaving her off the end of the cloud spiral and into heaven itself.

Ní Chuilleanáin uses the term 'purchase' here, which refers to a team of angels gripping or finding 'purchase' on the Virgin's body as they prepare to heave her upwards one last time: 'a final purchase together/ Under her weight'. But 'to purchase', of course, also means to pay for something, reminding us that the price of the Virgin's ascent is the angels' strenuous and painstaking efforts.

LOVE

'Fireman's Lift' is concerned not with romantic love but with what might be termed 'brotherly love' or community spirit. We exhibit such love when we act like the angels in the painting, when we strive to help others reach their goals or destinations. For the poet, such behaviour is the very definition of love: 'This is what love sees'. What love 'sees', the act of love, is one of helping others, of straining every sinew to assist those in need.

This idea of love as a kind of assistance is reflected in the poem's title. The fireman's lift is a technique used to carry an injured or incapacitated person. The injured person is placed across the shoulders of the carrier, allowing him or her to be carried quickly out of harm's way.

Such love is often shown by nurses, doctors and other medical personnel, especially in their efforts to make dying people as comfortable as possible. Ní Chuilleanáin wrote this poem around the time of her mother's death in 1994. In an interview, she described how impressed and moved she was by the nurses who tended to her mother in her final illness.

We can show love, then, by assisting others physically, like the angels in the painting like the nurses who tended the poet's mother, or a first responder using the fireman's lift to carry someone to safety. But we can also lift those in a less obvious fashion, giving them a metaphorical 'lift' with regard to their studies, their working life, or their personal or financial problems.

SPIRITUALITY

'Fireman's Lift' reminds us how great works of art can sometimes produce an almost spiritual response in those who view them. The poet and her mother, we sense, experienced such a response as they 'stepped// Back' so they could see 'the work entire'. They experienced a moment of heightened emotion as they contemplated the angels, realising that they were witnessing a true portrayal of love: 'This is what love sees'. They also, we sense, experienced a moment of calm or psychological healing as they stood there in the extraordinary 'fall-out of brightness' that emanated from the centre of the fresco.

The poet and her mother, of course, might have been responding to the artwork's religious message. They might have been inspired by the painting to contemplate the mystery of heaven, the infinite kindness of the Virgin, the miracle of the Assumption. But their spiritual response was also triggered, no doubt, by artistic pleasure, by sheer wonder at Correggio's achievement in conceiving and executing such a monumental work of art.

DEATH AND GRIEF

'Fireman's Lift' can also be considered an elegy or poem of lament for the passing of the poet's mother. The dates below the poem memorialise the poet's relationship with her mother. In 1963 the poet and her mother visited Parma cathedral together while in 1994 the mother passed away. The poet doesn't directly describe her mother in this piece. But we can perhaps interpret the depiction of the angels as being intended as a tribute to her mother, suggesting how she strove to help others throughout her life. And maybe the image of the Virgin ascending to Heaven represents Ní Chuilleanáin's hope that her mother, too, will enter Paradise after her death.

FOCUS ON STYLE

Imagery

'Fireman's Lift' is a an 'ekphrastic' poem, a poem inspired by a painting or artwork. Ní Chuilleanáin, through her rich poetic imagery, manages to capture in words some of this massive work's majesty, vividly depicting its soft light that issues from heaven in a 'fall-out of brightness', the spiral of clouds full of 'mist and shining', and the vast 'teams' of angels that are 'Supporting' and 'crowding' her as she journeys upwards.

Several telling details make her depiction live in the imagination: the fact that the angels' heads are bowed in worship and respect as the angels pass by, the way their muscles are said to have 'clung and shifted' with their final effort, the description of the Virgin herself as angelic: 'her/ Fair face and hair so like their own'.

Ní Chuilleanáin's imagination takes her in a surprising direction as she imagines that the angels have helped the Virgin to her present position, heaving and pushing her up the cloud-spiral. There is something moving about the angels' efforts. But it is also a zany and peculiar notion: teams of angels crowding around the Virgin in a concerted effort to lift her onwards.

Metaphor, Simile, Figures of Speech

'Fireman's Lift' is especially rich in metaphor. Ní Chuilleanáin, as we've seen, uses a range of metaphors associated with building and architecture to describe the efforts of the angels as they heave the Virgin upwards. Their backs are compared to roofs, their legs to bridges, their hands to cranes and cradles, their arms to pillars. This series of construction-based metaphors is appropriate for a poem inspired by a great building.

Ní Chuilleanáin also touches on the natural world, using a pair of tree metaphors. She describes the dome as a 'big tree'. Initially, this might seem like an outlandish comparison, but we quickly see just how inventive and original it is. Many trees, after all, have branches that curve downwards, lending them a dome-like apppearance.

In lines 16 to 18, meanwhile, Ní Chuilleanáin imagines the branch of a tree weighed down by the fruit it bears. For her, this is the perfect metaphor for love. The branch is 'loaded with fruit', just as we might be 'loaded' with the weight of a person we're helping.

- The weight of the fruit has caused the branch to bend down at an 'angle'. Similarly, we might bend under the strain of helping a fellow human being. This strain might be physical; but it could also be psychological, emotional or financial.
- The weight of the fruit has given the branch a 'crick', caused it to be twisted in a painful or damaging way. Similarly, we might suffer from the strain of helping others.
- The branch's suffering brings something beautiful into existence; fruit that can be enjoyed by the world at large. Similarly, our suffering when we help others brings something beautiful into existence.

In doing so, we demonstrate what can only be described as love in its truest sense: 'This is what love sees, that angle:/ That crick in the branch loaded with fruit'.

LINE BY LINE

'All for You' opens with the speaker and her companion approaching a large manor house in the countryside. They are riding, it appears, on a single donkey.

The property they are approaching seems very grand. The main house is surrounded by various grounds and outbuildings. They pass through one of the property's outer gates and into the 'stableyard'.

They dismount and their donkey 'walks on' by itself towards one of the stables. It walks 'straight in' through the stable's 'wide door', suggesting that it moves without hesitation. Once inside the stable, it begins eating straw from a trough.

The speaker and her young companion, meanwhile, enter the manor house itself. Its entry hall is dominated by a staircase that's described as 'great' and 'Sprawling', suggesting its grandeur and impressive width. This massive and ornate feature 'slouches back', sloping gently upwards towards the building's upper floors. On either side of this imposing staircase stretch the 'warm wings', or welcomingly well-heated sections, of this remarkable building.

The speaker and her companion enter the manor's cellars. The speaker describes how steps 'wind and warp', or turn and twist, through these underground 'vaults'. Using a wonderful metaphor, she refers to the foundations' arched supports as 'thick ribs'. We can imagine these rows of curving struts might resemble a rib cage, curving to support the building up above. Different staircases and passageways meander through the gaps between these buttresses: 'As the steps wind and warp/ Among the vaults, their thick ribs part'.

The vaults contain many different rooms: a storeroom, a chapel and even a barracks or guardroom. This reinforces our sense that we are in a truly great manor, one worthy, perhaps, of being called a castle. The vaults also contain what seems to be a large kitchen. The heat that emanates from this underground cookery is wittily compared to the breathing of its ovens: 'the breath of ovens/ Flows out'. The ovens are fuelled by 'brushwood', wood gathered from shrubs, undergrowth and small trees. The roots of the brushwood, which have been torn from the soil and cut up or 'butchered' for the ovens, burns with a great 'rage' or intensity.

The speaker and her companion enter a well-stocked larder. There are chests full of tea and shelves stacked with 'shining' tins of food. There are enormous 'ten-pound jars' of preserves, which are made by sealing fruit and sugar in a can or jar. Over time, the fruit becomes not only 'shrivelled' but also incredibly sweet. The speaker describes the jars as 'rich', suggesting how succulent and tantalising their contents must appear. The larder is clearly organised and carefully maintained, with its 'labelled' shelves and its tins arranged in 'ranks' or neat rows.

Ní Chuilleanáin described her inspiration for the manor house which features in this poem: 'It's a house that I remember or partly remember and have partly made up. The house I grew up in was rather odd because it was an official house. My father was the warden of Honan Hostel [in UCC]. So we had this house which was much much bigger than anything we were used to and it had rooms with all kinds of strange functions. There was a room full of onions and there was a room that contained the vestments of the chapel at the bottom of the garden. And that feeling of a house that has all kinds of parts to it just came to me.'

The speaker, somewhat unexpectedly, suggests that her companion sleep right there in the storeroom: 'Where better to lie down/ And sleep, along the labelled shelves'. Initially, this seems like a bizarre suggestion. Why does the poet suggest that her companion sleep on a shelf in the basement rather than in one of the manor's bedrooms? But maybe this larder would actually be a pleasant place to rest. There is an atmosphere of comfort and cosiness in this basement hideaway, warmed by the heat that emanates from the nearby kitchens. Furthermore, it's a place of richness and plenty, its air scented with tea and its shelves well-stocked with nourishing and wholesome produce.

FOCUS ON STYLE

Gapped and Mysterious Narratives

'All For You' is an example of Ní Chuilleanáin at her most mysterious. The poem plunges us straight into a narrative with little or nothing in the way of background information.

It's difficult, for instance, to say for certain in which century these events take place. Certain features of the poem – the fact that the speaker and her companion travel by donkey, the wood-burning oven – suggest a medieval setting. But the mention of tinned food suggests a modern one.

The image of the speaker and her companion riding on a single donkey adds to the sense of mystery. It suggests that they are extremely poor. A donkey, traditionally, is the humblest of mounts, and would be ridden only by those unable to afford even the lowest quality horse or pony. Furthermore, it's almost impossible for a donkey to carry two fully grown adults, suggesting that the poet's companion is either a child or a very young teenager.

Equally mysterious is the precise nature of the relationship between the speaker and her companion, as we are given no information, however, about the relationship between these two people. Is the speaker the companion's mother? Is she an older sister? Is she a teacher or some kind of guardian?

Another mysterious aspect of the poem is the fact that the speaker and her companion seem expected in the manor. They are permitted to enter and move about freely. The fires have been left lighting and the larders are fully stocked. But no one is present. Ní Chuilleanáin has described how she borrowed this aspect of the poem from fairy tales: 'There's a motif in fairy tales where somebody comes to a house and it's a completely strange house but still they seem to be expected. There is a stable for the horse, there's a meal, there's a bed'.

'All For You', like many of Ní Chuilleanáin's poems, features a strange and mysterious building to which the speaker is granted access. It also, like many of her poems, features a key, which in this instance remains in the pocket of the speaker's companion. The companion, it seems, didn't seem to need to use the key to access the manor, so we are left wondering what mysterious door or chest the key will eventually unlock.

The poem also ends in an abrupt manner, with the speaker and her companion resting in the fully-stocker larder. There is little sense of resolution or conclusion. The reader is left wondering what will happen next as the speaker and her companion continue to explore the house.

Imagery

Like many of Ní Chuilleanáin's best poems 'All for You' works as a flowing succession of images, each one dissolving into the next. There's something cinematic about how we're carried from the stableyard into the entrance hall, then down into passageways that 'wind and warp' their way through the vaults, until we reach the larder with its jars of shrivelled fruit. We might compare it to a single long and artfully-composed tracking-shot by a gifted Hollywood director.

Metaphor, Simile, Figures of Speech

This poem contains several skilfully-realised metaphors. The mansion's arched foundations, visible in its vaults, are memorably compared to ribs. The heat that fills the kitchen is described as the ovens' roasting 'breath'. It is also described as the 'rage' of the wood that burns there. There's something of a hidden metaphor in line 13 where the tins of food, we're told, are arranged in 'ranks'. This suggests a comparison between the tins' neatly arranged rows and the precise line-up of soldiers on parade. There's an element of synasthesia in the phrase 'dry fragrance of tea-chests'. Here dryness, something we associate with the sense of touch, is used to describe a smell, wonderfully capturing the rich but mild aroma in question.

FAMILY

But through this fog of mystery we discern a classic story of lost inheritance regained. Twice the poet's young companion is told that the manor and its estate are 'for you', are rightfully his.

But some years ago a series of events occurred that denied the young companion this inheritance. The poem, as we've seen, doesn't specify exactly what occurred. But it's difficult to imagine such a disinheritance occurring without conflict, without some kind of war, or coup, or violent dispossession. Perhaps the speaker is conscious of this violent past when she thinks of the brushwood being 'torn out and butchered' or when she thinks of the tins arranged in 'ranks' as if they were soldiers.

The companion, then, has been raised far from the grandeur of the mansion's richness and plenty. So far, he hasn't been allowed to savour the luxurious lifestyle that should have been rightfully his. Instead he's lived a life of terrible poverty, as indicated by the fact that he and the speaker are forced to ride on a single donkey. All this time, however, he has kept a key to the manor, a powerful symbol of all that was wrongfully snatched away from him.

But now circumstances have changed somehow, allowing the companion to reclaim his inheritance. He sets out with the key in his pocket, accompanied only by the speaker and their donkey. Eventually the companion reaches the manor and enters its stableyard, returning to a place that has grown 'strange' to him, that he no longer recognises.

We sense that this young man can't quite believe that the mansion and its estate is really his, that he can't quite come to grips with this sudden transition from rags to riches, from being a disinherited pauper to being, quite literally, lord of the manor. Perhaps the speaker repeats the phrase 'It is for you' in an effort to reassure the speaker that this miraculous transition is actually happening. She also reminds him that he 'still' holds the key in his pocket, reinforcing his belief that rightful ownership of the place has always and always will be his. Maybe the speaker's suggestion that the companion sleep down in the basement is an effort to manage this transition; the companion will get used to these new surrounds before properly taking up residence and cementing his new status as owner.

This sense of ownership is reinforced by the way the speaker and her companion enter the property and find no-one waiting for them in its halls and vaults. It's as if the manor's previous occupants have abandoned it, aware that its rightful owner is returning. But they have done so with good grace, leaving the larder stocked and the ovens burning.

The manor, as we've seen, is 'strange' to the speaker's companion. But is it also strange to the donkey? The donkey seems to know where it's going: it walks across the stableyard by itself, heading straight for the stable, which it enters without hesitation. Perhaps the donkey has been with the companion's family for a long time and remembers the manor from before they were disinherited and evicted.

LOVE

Ní Chuilleanáin has described how the inspiration for this mysterious poem began in advertising of all places: 'I absolutely hate the use of the word 'you' in advertising, and I hate phrases like 'We have all your favourites' or 'We know what you want', because they are lies. And I started with the idea that I would write a poem based on that – but then it became clear that this was far too negative a sentiment to build a poem on and so I began to think what is the opposite of that – and the opposite way of saying 'you' with real reference to the person you are talking to is the 'you' of love'.

The poem, then, can be regarded as a love poem of sorts, one that highlights the speaker's devotion to her young companion and her desire for him to receive what is rightfully his.

Following

LINE BY LINE

I

The poem describes a young woman whose father has recently passed away. Her father, it seems, was a highly cultured individual. He was a well-read man who had amassed a large library. He had a taste for good whiskey and fine tailoring.

The young woman finds herself visiting a fair that is taking place in the main square of an Irish town. Such fair days were important social occasions and brought people together from all over the surrounding area. Certain farmers, we imagine, have come into town to sell vegetables, herbs and other produce. Others have come to sell cows and horses. Also present are 'dealing men', who travel from farm to farm and fair to fair buying and selling animals. The people of the town itself, no doubt, are also out in force, bringing a real sense of hustle and bustle to the square.

The young woman is in the middle of this hustle and bustle when she suddenly sees her dead father. Her father, when she glimpses him, is walking briskly through the crowd. He is still extremely well-dressed and is wearing a familiar overcoat.

The young woman immediately starts to follow her father through the fair, 'Shouldering' her way through the crowd in order to keep up with him. She pushes her way through a pack of 'beasts', of cows or horses. She navigates a group of 'dealing men', who, lost in conversation, don't even notice her and fail to move out of the way: 'the dealing men nearly as slow to give way'.

Her view of her father is obscured by all the people and animals milling about. They criss-cross in front of her so that she can't see him properly. But she focuses on his distinctive coat, tracking its 'trail' through the crowded fair.

The young woman follows her father to the edge of the square where the crowd is thinner and she can see him more clearly. She catches 'a glimpse' of his hard-brimmed hat, of his 'shirt-cuff', of the handkerchief folded stylishly in the pocket of his suit jacket.

II

The young woman follows the well-dressed man out of the town and into the surrounding countryside. She follows him for hour after hour, all day and into the night. Eventually, she finds herself 'tracing his light footsteps' across some vast bog. The sun has long since set and she has only 'starlight' by which to navigate the treacherous boggy ground.

This remote bog is an unnerving environment to navigate alone, especially in the middle of the dark, when the flickering starlight gives even everyday objects a distorted and threatening appearance. Its unsurprising, therefore, that the young woman's imagination runs away with her:

- She thinks that a reanimated corpse is 'Gliding before her' along the boggy ground. This corpse, she imagines, has 'risen' somehow from the house in which it was being waked and is wearing a white gown or 'habit' in which the deceased would traditionally be buried.
- The boggy 'ground', she imagines, is covered with human 'trunks' or torsos. At least some of these trunks still have arms attached to them and they seem to gesture towards the poet as she passes across the bog.
- The ground, she imagines, is also littered with female hands that sway as if they were busily sewing, as if they were 'dragging needles' through a piece of fabric.
- The young woman passes holes, created by turf cutters, that are filled with water. She imagines that human heads are 'Half-choked' or partially submerged in these bog holes. These severed heads, she imagines, are still alive in some nightmarish sense and have 'Mouths that roar' at her as she passes by.

III

The young woman continues to follow her father across the countryside. Eventually she follows him into what seems to be a large house with a room that serves as a dedicated library. The young woman finds her father 'Seated' in this library. He has poured two glasses of whiskey, suggesting that he is waiting for her to join him.

Lines 19 to 20 emphasise, once more, that the father is a meticulous dresser. His clothes, we're told, have all been 'finely laundered'. Both the 'facings' and the 'linings' of his suit have been 'Ironed'. A 'facing' is a piece of fabric stitched onto the edge of a garment. Facings act as interesting visual details while also providing the garment with structure and support.

The poem's conclusion mentions three items that can be found within the library:

- There is a 'foxed leaf', a sheet of paper that has grown discoloured with age, turning a yellowish shade of brown. The leaf, however, is described as 'smooth' rather than crumpled, suggesting that it has been carefully looked after.
- There is a luxurious handkerchief, a 'square of white linen', on which three drops of the young woman's blood have been spilled. The drops are described as heart's blood, suggesting they came from an artery rather than from a vein.
- There are 'crushed flowers' that have been dried out and preserved.

All three items have been carefully placed in a single book. The 'foxed leaf', we're told, has been 'hidden' in its pages. The handkerchief has been 'shelved' between the book's 'gatherings' (gatherings or signatures are sections of a book that are folded, stitched and bound in order to produce a finished volume). The crushed flowers have been placed 'among its pages'.

These items, no doubt, are mementos of the young woman's youth. The 'foxed leaf', we imagine, might feature one of her earliest drawings or pieces of writing. The handkerchief might have been bloodied when her father tended to her after she cut herself during some youthful game. The 'flowers' might have been picked by her in some garden of her childhood, only for her father to preserve them by crushing them in the pages of one of his books. The fact that the father kept these items so carefully for so long indicates the intense affection and admiration he holds for the young woman.

The poem concludes with a startling image as the dried and crumpled flowers come to life once more. Their stalks and leaves blossom and expand. As they do so, they damage the book in which they have been stored, cracking its spine and undoing the glue and threads that hold it together: 'The crushed flowers among the pages crack/ The spine open, push the bindings apart'.

THEMES

DEATH AND GRIEF

In this poem, published in 1994, the poet looks back at the death of her own beloved father who passed away in 1970. We can imagine how Ní Chuilleanáin, in the months following her father's death, might have glimpsed him at some fair or other such gathering. But for Ní Chuilleanáin, of course, this glimpse was only imaginery, a trick of the light or the mind, something that many bereaved people experience.

The young woman's horrific journey across the bog represents the misery and despair Ní Chuilleanáin must have experienced in the months after her father's passing. The young woman in the poem discovers that the father she thought was dead is somehow still alive. She even gets to share a whiskey with him in the comfort of his library. We can imagine the way in which this represents how Ní Chuilleanáin's own father, in a metaphorical sense, is also still alive. He lives on in the memories and the behaviour of those who loved him and were influenced by him.

The poem concludes with a startling image of growth and renewal as the crushed flowers come to life again. This represents how Ní Chuilleanáin's father, even in death, will remain very much part of her inner life. The fact that the flower grows from the pages of the book suggests that her long-dead father will continue to influence and inspire her literary pursuits.

FAMILY

We can draw certain parallels between Ní Chuilleanáin and the young woman in the poem.

- The young woman's father is a man of culture, learning and refinement. Ní Chuilleanáin, no doubt, thinks of her own father in the same way.
- The reference to the library suggests that the young woman relates to her father through books. The same was true for Ní Chuilleanáin whose father helped inspire her creativity and love of the written word.
- The young woman in the poem is aware that her father has kept certain objects that reveal his deep love for her. This suggests that Ní Chuilleanáin also felt secure in her father's love.

The poem, then, highlights the poet's intense love and respect for her father, Cormac Ó Chuilleanáin, who was a professor of Irish at UCC and a major influence in her life. The poem's title suggests not only how the young woman in the poem went 'Following' her father across the bog. It also suggests how Ní Chuilleanáin has been following in her father's footsteps her whole life as she continues his devotion to literature and the written word.

FOCUS ON STYLE

Gapped and Mysterious Narratives

'Following', like many of Ní Chuilleanáin's poems, features a gapped and mysterious narrative. We are plunged into the narrative with little in the way of back ground information. In fact, the first word of the poem is 'So...'. It is as if the speaker has already begun her tale and we, her readers, join her only half-way through.

The poem has what Ní Chuilleanáin has described as a 'segmented narrative'. We move from segment to segment – from the fair to the bog and from the bog to the library – in an abrupt and jarring fashion. The poem's conclusion is equally abrupt. There is little sense of resolution or conclusion. The reader is left wondering what will happen next between the young woman and her father.

Ní Chuilleanáin has described how many of her poems feature 'somebody [who] comes to a house and it's a completely strange house but still they seem to be expected'. We see this in 'Following' when the young woman arrives at the library to find a glass of whiskey poured and waiting for her. Ní Chuilleanáin has described how she borrowed this motif from fairy tales.

'Following' is imbued with a surreal and dream-like quality.

- We see this when the young woman spies her seemingly dead father at the fair.
- We see this in the nightmarish phenomena she encounters as she crosses the bog.
- There is something dreamlike too about the young woman's inability to catch up to her father as she follows him across the bog.
- Especially surreal is the startling image of the crushed flowers returning to life at the poem's conclusion.

Imagery

The poem presents us with a sharp contrast between the young woman's father and the dealing men:

- The dealing men are associated with manual labour, with a 'block' and a 'plumber's bend'. The father, on the other hand, is associated with books and the life of the mind.
- The dealing men are heavy and 'slow', while the father goes 'skimming along' with light footsteps.
- The dealing men are associated with the noisy and chaotic fair. The father, on the other hand, is associated with the 'clean' light of the library, which is a place of stillness and order.

'Her company laments her/ That she fed with silver and gold'

Kilcash

LINE BY LINE

In 'Kilcash', Ní Chuilleanáin translates a Gaelic poem from the early nineteenth century. The poem mourns the passing of Margaret Butler, also known as Lady Iveagh, who owned a great wooded estate around Kilcash Castle in South Tipperary.

The poet depicts Lady Iveagh as a fundamentally decent person, who did the right thing by the people of her estate. She was also a formidable figure who commanded the respect of everyone she encountered. She was a lady, he says, who 'lived with such honour'. No other woman, the poet declares, was held in such high esteem: 'No woman so heaped with praise'. She was of such standing that even noblemen travelled from abroad to pay her their respects: 'Earls came across oceans to see her'.

This was the time of the Penal Laws, when the Catholic religion was all but banned in Ireland. Lady Iveagh, however, assisted in keeping the Catholic religion alive in Kilcash and its surrounding areas. She organised semi-secret masses so that those living in the area 'could hear the sweet words of mass'. Because Lady Iveagh was such a prominent and influential person, the British authorities were reluctant to intervene.

After Lady Iveagh's death, Kilcash passed into the ownership of the English government. Its woods were cut down and its grounds declined. Its great house was left empty and fell quickly into ruin. Once tales of this great estate (and of its illustrious owners) travelled not only around Ireland but also around Europe. But those days are gone: 'No word of Kilcash nor its household'.

The destruction of the forests

The poet laments the loss of Kilcash's woodlands. After Lady Iveagh's death, its great forest parks were sold to the English government and chopped down. All the estate's trees have been felled and shipped off to England, leaving the locals with no source of timber or firewood: 'What will we do now for timber/ With the last of the woods laid low'.

It was the policy of the English government at the time to cut down Ireland's woods and forests. Timber, of course, was a valuable resource. Yet this policy also stemmed from the fact that Irish rebels used the country's dense woodlands as a refuge. To this day, Ireland remains one of the most deforested countries in Europe.

The decay of Kilcash's grounds

The poet laments how, since Lady Iveagh's death, her estate has fallen into ruin:

- Its 'neat gates' have been 'knocked down'. Its great avenue has been neglected and is now completely overgrown with weeds.
- Once there were pleasantly shaded pathways that led all through the estate. But the destruction of its forests has left these 'long walks' exposed to the elements: 'The long walks affording no shade now'.
- Once the estate had the 'smooth wide lawn' we might associate with such a grand property. But the removal of the trees left it exposed so that it's been 'all broken' by the elements: 'No shelter from wind and rain'.
- Once Lady Iveagh's horses would graze on the estate's paddock. But following her death those 'fine creatures' are gone. Only cows graze there now: 'The paddock has turned to a dairy'.

The poet returns to this theme in stanza five, lamenting how the estate's 'forest park' is now a 'leafless' and treeless waste-ground. Where once there was lush woodland there is now only 'Bare naked rocks and cold'. In Kilcash there is now 'No hazel, no holly, no berry' to be found.

The poet turns his attention to the house at the centre of the estate, where Lady Iveagh once resided. This, he says, was a 'fine house', one 'that was famed in its day'. The house, we imagine, was well known for its splendour as well as for its famous resident. With Lady Iveagh's death, however, its 'day' has passed. Like the rest of the estate, it has fallen into ruin. We're told that it no longer keeps 'out the weather', suggesting that its windows have been broken and that its roof has fallen in.

The silence of Kilcash

Kilcash has become a place of eerie silence. Once geese and ducks were kept there. But with the estate's decline these birds have disappeared and their 'commotion' is no more. The 'shout' or great cry of eagles is also no longer to be heard, presumably because there are no longer any high trees for them to rest on. The birds that nest in the few remaining trees are silent. The cuckoos are 'dumb' and the other musical birds are 'stilled'.

Lady Iveagh's staff kept beehives, which supplied wax and honey. But now, following her death, the hives are no longer maintained. These 'stores' of wax and honey have been 'Deserted' by the insects that once lived in them. The great 'roar' of the bees' buzzing is no longer to be heard: 'The roar of the bees gone silent'.

The poet describes how the 'bell' of Lady Iveagh and her family is 'silenced now' This probably refers to the bell that would signal the semi-secret Sunday Masses Lady Iveagh would organise for the people of Kilcash. But now following her death those services have been discontinued and the bell is heard no more.

In stanza 5, the poet describes how weird, unnatural conditions hold sway in Kilcash now. The estate's streams have all 'run dry'. A strange mist fills the estate that 'no sunlight' can burn off or 'sweep aside'. It becomes dark all of a sudden in the middle of the day: 'Darkness falls among daylight'. In these lines there is a powerful sense of the supernatural, as if Kilcash were a cursed or haunted landscape. We are presented with a nightmarish scene fit for any tale of horror, one in which nature itself seems to be lamenting Lady Iveagh's death.

The poet's despair

The poet is greatly affected by the death of Lady Iveagh and by the decline of her once great estate. This is the 'cause' of his 'long affliction', of his great and unending despair. His sorrow is shared by the people of Kilcash, who have also been left 'depressed' by the estate's decline.

The people of Kilcash no longer have Lady Iveagh's protection from the worst excesses of English rule. Indeed, it seems that without her influence they have been 'tamed' by their English overlords. When Lady Iveagh was alive, the people of Kilcash could practice their religion semi-openly because her influence shielded them from government interference. But now with Lady Iveagh out of the picture the Catholic faith has once again gone underground.

According to the poet, then, the people of Kilcash are now in a pitiful state. The hunters who 'follow' the paths of the surrounding mountains look down on the estate and pity its inhabitants. Their lives, it seems, are worse than those of animals. Indeed, even deer roaming the surrounding hills feel sorry for them: 'Even the deer...Look down upon us with pity'.

The loss of Irish Freedom itself

Yet the decline of Kilcash is 'not the worst' of the poet's ills. For he is even more troubled by the loss of Irish freedom in general. 'Kilcash', like many poems and ballads, personifies Irish freedom as a beautiful young woman. In this instance the concept of Irish liberty is depicted as a 'gentle maiden', a kind of royal princess who once ruled over the 'company' of Irish men and women.

The poet believes that an independent Ireland was a prosperous Ireland. He depicts, therefore, how this maiden gave her subjects great riches, how 'she fed [them] with silver and gold'. He also believes that independence meant Ireland and its people were safe from persecution. He also notes how the maiden never terrorised or 'preyed on' the people she ruled over. Indeed, she protected the weaker subjects, acting as a 'friend' to the 'poor souls' among them.

Now, however, Ireland has been conquered and subjected to English domination. The poet depicts this by describing how the maiden of Irish liberty has been exiled overseas, 'Summoned to France and to Spain'. She has travelled to the Continent with the 'prince of the Gaels', which refers to the many Gaelic chieftains who fled to the continent after their defeat by the English crown.

The poet prays that Ireland may one day be an independent nation again. He depicts this by describing how the maiden may return to her 'company' and rule over it once more: 'My prayer to Mary and Jesus/ She may come safe home to us here'.

The return of Irish freedom would naturally be greeted with great 'rejoicing', with music, dance and celebratory bonfires: 'To dancing and rejoicing/ To fiddling and bonfire'. The poet also prays that the house of Kilcash might somehow be restored to its former glory: 'Kilcash built up anew'. He prays that it will never decline again, that the house will stand until 'the end of the story', until the end of time itself. The poet's hopes were only partly realised. For while the castle of Kilcash still stands, it has never been restored to its former glorious state.

FOCUS ON STYLE

Form

One of this poem's standout features is the fact that it's translated from 18th century Irish. The original Irish language version of this poem was famously set to music. There is a reasonable chance you will hear the song – or at least its melody – at some moment in your life. Ní Chuilleanáin's version has many features we associate with songs and ballads:

- It is written in regular stanzas of eight lines.
- It features a regular, rolling iambic rhythm.
- It contains several lists, a common feature of ballads from Ireland and indeed from elsewhere.
- It features a regular rhyme scheme of ABCBDEFE.

It is worth noting that Ní Chuilleanáin makes extensive use of half rhyme: for example 'praise' and 'Mass' in stanza one, 'down' and 'overgrown' in stanza two, 'Gaels' and 'Spain' in stanza six, 'here' and 'bonfire' in stanza seven.

Metaphor, Simile, Figures of Speech

'Kilcash', for the most part, uses plain rather than figurative language. However, there's an arresting metaphor in line 24, where the cuckoo's song is compared to a lullaby. It's easy to imagine the cuckoo's sweet music as an effort to lull the world asleep as evening comes.

Personification occurs towards the end of the poem, where the concept of Irish freedom is presented as a 'gentle maiden' who's been forced overseas. There's also an example of symbolism here. The poet refers to 'the prince of the Gaels', this one noble warrior symbolising all the defeated Irish chieftains who emigrated to the continent over the centuries.

THEMES

DEATH AND GRIEF

The poem is a powerful lament for this great woman. Her death has left the people of Kilcash feeling lost and devastated. As we noted, there's a sense in which even nature itself mourns her passing: the estate of Kilcash becomes a nightmarish place of impenetrable mists and daytime darkness. It's a place where streams run dry, where the songbirds refuse to sing, where the sky turns dark even in daytime.

'Kilcash', like many of Ní Chuilleanáin's poems, emphasises the importance of memorialising the dead. The people of Kilcash will not forget Lady Iveagh. They will remember her in their prayers, praying for her along with the rest of those who died while remaining faithful to the Catholic religion: 'And their names with the faithful departed'. And the poem itself is a fine memorial to this departed woman, one that has survived for centuries right down to the present day.

THE SORROWS OF HISTORY

'Kilcash' is a powerful study of historical suffering, detailing the oppression endured by the Irish people in the eighteenth century. The poet, as we've seen, laments the loss of Irish freedom, which he personifies as a 'gentle maiden' that's vanished to foreign lands. According to the poet, when Ireland was a free country its people were prosperous and safe from oppression. But now Ireland has been subjected to English rule and its people suffer greatly.

The poem reminds us of how Ireland, like many colonies, was stripped of its natural resources by its colonisers, its precious woodlands being chopped down and shipped off to England. As the poet regretfully asks: 'What will we do now for timber'. The poem reminds us of how for two centuries the Irish were prevented from practising their own religion, with the Catholic faith being effectively banned throughout the country. It was only in secret, or in some cases under the protection of influential patrons like Lady Iveagh, that the Mass and the other Catholic sacraments could be conducted.

The poem also illustrates how the country was robbed of its leadership. Some Irish leaders, of course, were executed or killed on the field of battle. But many others were forced into exile. These are referred to collectively as 'the prince of the Gaels', as if they were a single lost leader, a single great chieftain forced overseas to find service in the Catholic nations of France and Spain. Other prominent and influential figures, like Lady Iveagh herself, had their power-bases dismantled when they died, ensuring their heirs could not continue in their spirit of defiance.

Translation

A still from the film *The Magdalene Sisters (2002)* directed by Peter Mullan

LINE BY LINE

The Magdalene Laundries were a series of asylums that existed in Ireland throughout the 19th and 20th centuries. These institutions, administered by religious orders such as the Sisters of Mercy and the Sisters of Charity, initially focused on helping prostitutes or 'fallen women'.

These asylums focused on penance rather than rehabilitation. Living conditions were harsh, sometimes prison-like. The inmates worked long hours for no pay, usually in laundries attached to the institutions.

But the scope of these institutions quickly expanded beyond former sex workers. Some inmates were unmarried mothers. Others were young women who had been 'caught' engaging in sexual activity. Even young women viewed as overly flirtatious could find themselves committed.

Poor orphans with no one to provide for them could end up in the laundries as could mentally challenged girls who couldn't easily be looked after at home. Some inmates had been victims of rape or sexual abuse and were packed off to the laundries in order to hush up any resulting scandal. Others were simply deemed troublesome by their parents or guardians and were no longer wanted around the family home.

Most inmates were committed to the laundries by their own families without any trial or legal proceeding. And leaving these institutions was not easy. Many women remained in the laundries for years, decades or even for their entire lives.

This poem relates to a particular incident that took place in 1993. An order of Dublin nuns sold a portion of their land to a developer, who intended to build apartments on the site. His workmen found the remains of 155 women, all former Magdalene inmates, buried in unmarked graves on the convent grounds. The women's remains were eventually cremated and reburied in Glasnevin cemetery. Ní Chuilleanáin read this poem at the reburial ceremony. The last Magdalene Laundry closed in 1996.

Reburial in Glasnevin

The poet describes Glasnevin cemetery on the day of the reburial. The gravediggers have been busy:
* A shallow grave has been cut or scored into earth.
* The inmates' cremated remains have been placed in this score, which has then been filled with soil.
* The soil has been 'frayed' and 'sifted'. It has been loosened and sieved by the gravediggers' tools so that it resembles a fine dust.
* The gravediggers 'even the score', tamping down the soil to make the new grave level with the surrounding grass.

The identities of the reburied inmates are unknown. Yet the poet assumes that among their number are women from every county in Ireland. After all, women from every corner of the land served in the laundry at one time or another.

The phrase 'evens the score', of course, also has another meaning. The work of the gravediggers somehow represents a small element of compensation for the poor inmates. Their honourable reburial today makes up – to some extent – for the indignity of their bodies being stashed away and forgotten in an unmarked grave.

The inmates at work

The poet thinks of the inmates' years of confinement, imagining them at work in their laundry room:

- She imagines the 'stone drains' around the edges of the room into which dirty water would disappear.
- She imagines the steam that must have emanated from the laundry's sinks and irons, picturing little clouds of steam moving and shimmering through the room.
- Lines 5 to 6 wonderfully personify the steam that fills the laundry. The hissing it makes when released from the irons is compared to a giggling sound, while its fluid, unpredictable movement around the laundry is described as a kind of dance.

The poet focuses on the working conditions that must have pertained in the laundry. She imagines water draining down plug-holes, leaving behind worn and dirty bars of soap that resemble 'rotten teeth'. She imagines how 'every grasp seemed melted', how the inmates must have felt that their hands were melting from being immersed all day in boiling hot water. She imagines the laundry's never-ending racket; the shuffling of inmates moving slowly and steadily around, the humming of equipment.

Return to the soil

A layer of grass and topsoil has been placed over the inmates freshly dug resting place. But this covering isn't exactly level. For the buried remains leave this 'veil' of earth ridged, bumpy and uneven.

Ní Chuilleanáin, in a typically vivid and unexpected image, describes the inmates' cremated remains spreading through the earth of the cemetery. She describes the remains of each individual woman 'shifting' through the soil as they go 'searching for their parents'. We imagine each set of remains moving like a worm of dust and ashes through Glasnevin, seeking to make contact with the remains of family members that might also be buried there.

If they could link up with buried relatives in this way, their resting place would no longer be completely anonymous. They would find their 'names', and they would lie beneath headstones that were at least inscribed with the appropriate surname.

Assisting the inmates now

The poet calls on her listeners and readers to somehow help the reburied inmates, to 'Assist them now'. She wants us to remember their plight, their confinement and the terrible treatment they received, and to retell their story as best we can. By doing so we will give a voice to these voiceless victims.

It will be 'As if' one protesting inmate had spoken out in the laundry during her confinement there: 'As if…one voice/ Had begun'. The poet imagines this woman suddenly protesting in the middle of a working day, her voice loud enough to be heard over the laundry's ever-present background noise: 'one voice/ Had begun, rising above the shuffle and hum'.

This inmate, once her protest has 'begun', will not be silenced 'Until' she feels her point has been made. We can imagine her repeating again and again that she is not 'evil' or 'fallen', but an ordinary woman deserving of respect. Her protest is compared to a musical 'note' that's repeated insistently, becoming more intense with each repetition.

But this repeated 'note', this insistent chant of protest, fills not only the laundry room but also the inmate's own mind. It reaches every corner of her mind, what the poet memorably describes as 'every pocket in her skull'. It blares in every aspect of her consciousness, drowning out all other thoughts and concerns. She can think of nothing but these words of protest she keeps repeating, nothing but this objection to the great injustice she has suffered: 'Until every pocket in her skull blared with the note'.

Hearing the inmate now

Ní Chuilleanáin wants 'us', not only those gathered in the cemetery but also the Irish people as a whole, to hear the inmate's protest and complaint: 'Allow us now to hear it'. We can do so, the poem suggests, by telling and retelling the stories of this particular woman and the thousands of women like her. We must seek justice and compensation for former inmates who are still alive. And we must seek to restore the good names of those who have already passed on.

If we take such action the inmate's protest will become 'sharp as an infant's cry'. It will be almost impossible for the world to ignore the terrible injustice that she suffered, just as it's almost impossible for a human being to ignore the crying of an infant.

The poem concludes with a wonderfully strange and surreal image as the inmates spirits rise in the form of steam from their new grave. The steam billows into the air, even as the 'grass takes root' on that freshly dug resting place: 'While the grass takes root, while the steam rises'.

What would the inmate say?

The poem's final six lines switch to what might be described as a first-person narrative. It is as if that one protesting inmate was speaking to us directly, her voice reaching out to us somehow from beyond the grave. She describes how her remains now lie in 'earth sifted to dust', in soil rendered fine and grainy by the gravediggers' efforts.

She tells us about the 'idiom', the set of words and phrases that were used to hurt her throughout her life. The inmate here is probably referring to words like 'fallen woman', 'whore' and 'Magdalene' itself, words that branded her as something unworthy and less than human. Such terms, she says, covered her like a 'baked crust', of dirt or grime. These terms of abuse were like a 'parasite that grew' inside her. They affected her life like an enchantment or evil 'spell'.

Now however, she has been, 'washed clean' of the 'idiom' that clung to her like a layer of encrusted filth. The parasite that tormented her has been eliminated. The dark 'spell' of demeaning insults has been 'lifted'.

The poem concludes by returning to the extraordinary image of steam rising from the inmates' freshly dug grave. The protesting inmate describes how she can finally 'rise and forget'. As her spirit rises into the air in the form of steam, she can finally let go of the guilt, anger and shame that defined her existence. It's as if the ceremonial reburial brings a measure of peace to her soul and to the souls of her fellow inmates.

The inmates, then, will be permitted to 'forget' the injustices they suffered at the hands of the Irish state. But the people of Ireland never will. The protesting inmate describes how her spirit rises like a 'cloud' over the graveyard and her 'time'. This cloud of shadowing steam serves as a powerful symbol of Ireland's great shame with regard to the Magdalene affair, and indeed with regard to that entire period in the nation's history.

THEMES

SPIRITUALITY

This poem depicts a bleak and oppressive form of spirituality, looking back to a time when the Catholic Church was very much the dominant force in Irish life. Sexuality was treated with suspicion. Female sexuality, in particular, was regarded as dangerous and unpredictable. The Church and its various religious orders were willing to take extreme, even cruel, measures in order to police and control sexual morality.

The bleakness of this form of spirituality comes across in the phrase 'The high relief of a glance'. Here Ní Chuilleanáin is referring to a holy picture – maybe of Jesus, or of the Virgin Mary – that was placed 'high' on the laundry wall. The picture was meant to provide the inmates with 'relief' as it gazes down on them while they work. Its 'glance' was meant to offer them the hope and consolation of religious faith. But the picture's colours had been 'bleached' away by the 'White light' pouring through the laundry window, its eyes erased or 'blinded' by the steam and chemicals rising from the laundry floor.

The image of the 'blinded' picture powerfully captures the failure of religion in 20th century Ireland. It captures how the Catholic faith had become obsessed with a narrow sexual morality, growing blind to all other aspects of spirituality. It also captures how the Church and its religious orders had grown blind to the great harms they were inflicting on the laundry's inmates.

FAMILY

The importance of family is a prominent and recurring feature in Ní Chuilleanáin's work. In this poem, the centrality of family is highlighted by the bizarre but brilliant depiction of the inmates' remains filtering through the soil of Glasnevin cemetery, as they attempt to connect with the buried bodies of their relatives.

Many long-term inmates were encouraged to become 'lay nuns', a process that involved taking a new name. But now the inmate describes how she has been washed clean of her 'temporary name'. Researching and retelling the inmates' story, then, involves remembering these victims by their real names: the names given to them by their parents at birth, rather than the names given to them by the nuns in the laundry.

FOCUS ON STYLE

In 'Translation', Ní Chuilleanáin cleverly uses several metaphors associated with clothing and laundries. The plot dug up for the reburial is presented as if it were a 'frayed' garment. Each aspect of the protesting inmate's mind or consciousness is compared to a different 'pocket' of her skull. The protesting inmate compares insults and derogatory language to a 'crust of grime' that can only be 'washed clean' if we tell her story. The poet hauntingly depicts the inmates rising from the grave in the form of the steam that would have surrounded them all those days they spent labouring in the laundry.

In the laundry, the inmate carried a set of keys for the different utility rooms, store rooms and so on. She remembers gripping them so tightly that all the individual keys 'bunched' together, as if her fist were clenched in bitterness, shame and anger. Now, however, at this moment of reburial and letting go, she imagines relaxing her grip, as if the feelings of rage and humiliation that grip her are disappearing. The keys 'slacken' or loosen in her hand, then 'fall' altogether.

The poem's title has several meanings. 'Translation' is the technical term for transferring human remains from one grave to another. But the title also, of course, refers to a change of language, reminding us that the 'idiom' used to describe the inmates must change from one of insult to one of respect.

The Bend in the Road

Ní Chuilleanáin pictured with two of her grandchildren on her appointment as Ireland Professor of Poetry

LINE BY LINE

One afternoon, about 12 years ago, the poet, her husband and her young son Niall were driving to a lake. We get the impression that the weather was hot and humid, making conditions in their car were muggy and uncomfortable.

Suddenly, Niall began to feel carsick: 'the child/ Felt sick in the car'. So the family 'pulled over/ and waited' by the side of the road. They 'opened the windows' of the car, letting in the fresh air and allowing all three of them to breathe more 'Easily'. After a short while, Niall began to feel 'better' and they continued with their journey.

There was nothing very remarkable about the spot where the poet and her family pulled over. It was a perfectly ordinary 'bend in the road'. There was a house that cast a 'shadow' over their parked car, offering them relief from the heat of the sun. There was a 'tall tree' that resembled a cat's tail.

The poet describes how 'nothing moved' while they waited in the car, emphasising that the bend in the road was especially still on that particular afternoon. The poet's personification of the tree adds to this tranquil atmosphere. Personification, we remember, occurs when a non-human object is presented as if it had human qualities and the tree, in line 4, is presented as if it were capable of waiting: the tree 'waited too'. We get a sense that the tree stood perfectly unmoving on the roadside, unruffled by even the slightest breeze.

From time to time, as the years went by, the family would drive past this particular bend in the road. And every time they did so, the poet and her husband would recall that afternoon, mentioning to Niall that 'this is the place/ Where you were sick one day'. Now, in the present day, the poet has parked her car by the bend in the road and has got out for a look around. She has driven past this location many times since that day, twelve years ago, when she and her family were forced to stop on their way to the lake. But this is the first time, since that long ago afternoon, that she has actually stopped here.

The poet stands alone on the roadside, reflecting on the changes that have occurred over the previous twelve years:

- Her son has grown from a boy into a young man. In fact he has grown taller than either of his parents: 'You are taller than us now'.
- The tail-shaped tree, too, has grown: 'the tree is taller'.
- The house that offered them shade is still there. But its walls have become covered by creeping plants such as ivy: 'the house is quite covered in/ With green creeper'.

The poet is no longer the same person she was twelve years ago. She has changed in all kinds of ways, both psychological and physical. And the same is true for her husband and her son. Perhaps this is why the poet, when she describes the incident twelve years ago, refers to herself and her own family as if they were strangers. She uses 'they' rather than 'we', for instance, and 'the child' rather than 'our child'. It's as if the poet, when she looks back, finds her own family unrecognisable compared to the people they are today.

The poet, as she pauses by the roadside, thinks about 'all that went on' since she first stopped here twelve years ago. She thinks especially about loved ones who have passed away over the previous twelve years. Their passing has left great 'absences' in the life of the poet. But they are by no means forgotten because the poet finds herself frequently thinking about their faces: 'Their faces never long absent from thought'.

The poet, standing at the bend in the road, remembers visiting her loved ones during their last weeks and months.

- Their bodies were 'alive then'. But they were barely so.
- They had grown so thin and frail that the space their bodies took up was 'airy'. Their bodies seemed barely solid or substantial, as if they were composed of air rather than of solid matter.
- She recalls how they were extremely ill, were 'wrapped and sealed' by sickness.
- The poet recalls how her loved ones, near the end of their lives, were utterly exhausted, utterly worn out by sickness and old age.
- The poet remembers 'Guessing' that her loved ones would not be able to carry this burden 'for long'. Soon they would give in to exhaustion and slip away into the eternal sleep of death.

The poet, as she stands at the bend in the road, can feel these departed loved ones all round her: 'This is the place of their presence'. She can sense them in the tail-shaped tree, in the clouds, and even in the air itself. These loved ones may have departed physically but, at this moment on the roadside, they are present for the poet in a profound and meaningful way.

FOCUS ON STYLE

Imagery

Ní Chuilleanáin's startling use of imagery is evident when she describes how at certain moments those we've lost are still present all round us. Their souls or essences are depicted as an almost physical substance, a strange invisible material that can be 'piled' or 'wrapped' or 'packed'. Their essences float above us like a 'cumulus cloud', which is an aggregate of water vapour, or like the air itself, which is a mixture of gases. This image is one that is difficult to visualise precisely. However, it powerfully conveys how the dead remain present in the minds and lives of the living.

Metaphor, Simile, Figures of Speech

'The Bend in the Road', like many of Ní Chuilleanáin's poems, is rich in metaphor and simile. The 'tall tree', for instance, is compared to a 'cat's tail', which wonderfully suggests its long thin shape. It also suggests, perhaps, that its branches have a springy, tensile quality.

An equally vivid metaphor is used to describe the exhaustion experienced by the poet's loved ones towards the end of their lives. Their exhaustion, their overwhelming need to sleep, is compared to an incredible burden they were forced to carry, a 'piled weight' that dragged them down.

Ní Chuilleanáin uses another metaphor to describe the illness that afflicted her loved ones as they approached death. Her loved ones, she declares, were 'wrapped and sealed by sickness', a metaphor that compares illness to a kind of physical substance, a layer of paper and wax that covers the afflicted person's body.

The poem's opening stanzas feature simple, everyday phrases like 'They opened the window' and 'you are taller now than us'. The final stanza, however, creates a more complex musical effect. The entire stanza consists of a single nine-line sentence, which rushes constantly onwards from one phrase to the next. The stanza also features a great deal of repetition, with words like 'air', 'piled', 'wrapped' and 'absent' repeated – or nearly repeated – over its nine lines. These techniques combine to create a heightened verbal music reminiscent of a spell or prayer or incantation. It's a tone that wonderfully reflects the poet's intense emotions as she experiences vivid memories of her departed loved ones.

FAMILY

The bend in the road, as we've seen, is a perfectly ordinary place. But it's a place that the poet and her family frequently speak about and recall. It has been transformed, through the telling and retelling of a simple story, into a location of significance for the family: 'Over twelve years it has become the place/ Where you were sick on the way to the lake'.

Many families, of course, have such locations. A nondescript stretch of woods might become the place where little Ciara got lost. A street corner might become the place where Dan happened to meet his favourite rugby player. These stories may be simple, perhaps even boring, but they are told again and again until the places associated with them become a part of family lore.

SPIRITUALITY

The poem's first and last lines both begin with the phrase 'This is the place', emphasising the importance of this seemingly ordinary location to the poet.

This is becasue the bend, as we've seen, is an especially still and tranquil place, one that encourages mindfulness and reflection. But it's also because the bend triggers the poet's memory. She finds herself thinking of the first time she stopped here, which leads to her thinking of all the occasions she and her husband mentioned that incident, which leads to her thinking of all that has changed over the intervening twelve years.

Stopping here, then, leaves the poet's faculty of memory highly stimulated. As a result, she experiences intensely vivid recollections of her departed loved ones. These memories are so vivid that they prompt what might be described as a spiritual experience. The poet, for a moment, can sense the 'presence' of her loved ones all around her.

GRIEF AND DEATH

The poet maintains that our dead loved ones are never truly gone. Instead, they exist all around us, 'in the tree, in the air'. Perhaps she means this literally, reflecting the spiritual belief that when we die our spirits, our very essences, merge somehow with the natural world, becoming one with the soil, with plant-life, with the very air itself.

Or perhaps this 'presence' is merely a metaphor for memory. Perhaps it describes how the poet's memories of our loved ones, even after they have passed away, remain vividly in our minds. Perhaps it describes how their faces, as the poet so memorably puts it, are 'never long absent' from our thoughts.

On Lacking the Killer Instinct

LINE BY LINE

A prize-winning photograph

The poet is reading her morning paper when she is struck by a prize-winning photograph; a dramatic image of a hare escaping from two greyhounds. It seems to be a most dynamic action shot, one that captures the hare's great speed as she 'shoots off to the left', evading her pursuers' clutches.

The hare leaves the two greyhounds 'tumbling over'. We imagine the hounds falling over one another in a tangle of limbs while the hare bolts away for cover. The poet describes the dogs as 'absurdly gross', ridiculously oversized and bulky, emphasising how clumsy they seem in contrast to the compact and nimble hare.

The poet studies the hare, discerning various emotions in its eyes and facial expression.

- The look in the hare's eye is one of 'fear', betraying the terror of a hunted animal.
- But its expression is also one of 'speed', of focus, alertness and quick-thinking. It seems to be deploying every ounce of concentration in its effort to stay alive.
- The poet also detects a sense of 'power' in the hare's face. It seems that the hare has a sense of its own power, of its strength and dexterity as it triumphs at least temporarily over the hounds. This expression is one of 'glad power', suggesting how the poet discerns an element of joy in the hare's eye.
- Tellingly, the hare's eye is described as 'bright', suggesting how it shines with the pleasure and excitement of the chase.

This last point is crucial, reminding us of the thrill we often feel at moments of great crisis, when the adrenaline starts pumping through our bodies, maybe even when we're running or fighting for our lives. It captures how 'in the moment' of such danger, a human (or an animal) can often feel exhilarated and alive.

The photograph prompts a memory, reminding the poet of an incidence that took place during her youth. This was about thirty years ago, at a time when her father was 'dying in a hospital'. The poet remembered how she 'fled up in to the hills' in order to escape the trauma of her father's slow and painful death. The verb 'fled' suggests a sudden and unplanned retreat. We get the impression that the poet left the hospital and the city impulsively, finding herself incapable of handling her father's final illness.

As she wandered through the countryside, she saw a hare 'Right in the grassy middle of the track'. The hare, she remembers, was 'sitting still'. To the young poet, the hare seemed 'absorbed', as if it was meditating or lost in thought, utterly indifferent to the world around it.

The poet felt guilty, it seems, for fleeing into the countryside, for attempting to avoid the trauma of her father's final illness: 'And I should not/ Have ran away'. The next morning she returned to her dying father's bedside: 'I went back to the city/ Next morning'.

The father in 1921

The photograph prompts another memory, bringing to mind a story her father told her about the Irish War of Independence. This incident took place in 1921. Her father, who was only nineteen at the time, found himself running between the 'high hedges' of a narrow country road, a lorry-load of British soldiers in hot pursuit.

The father faced terrible consequences if the soldiers apprehended him; he might have been beaten up, arrested or even shot dead on the spot. Yet he described how he felt happiness and delight as he ran dextrously around the road's sharp corners, with his pursuers closing in behind him: 'Such gladness, he said, cornering in the narrow road'.

The father heard the lorry growling behind him as the soldiers bore closer. But he managed to sneak into a farmhouse, unseen by the chasing soldiers: he 'risked an open kitchen door.' This was a risk, of course, because the house's occupants might well have handed him over to his pursuers.

- The father found himself in a 'country kitchen'. He grabbed a towel and pretended to dry his face in a desperate effort to disguise himself.

- The soldiers quickly arrived and entered the kitchen, questioning the father along with the five other people who were present: 'The soldiers/ Found six people in a country kitchen'.
- Thankfully, for the father, the people living in the house had no interest in cooperating with the British authorities.
- They lied to the soldiers, pretending that the poet's father was a family member who'd been present the whole time.
- The soldiers believed them, decided not to pursue the matter, and departed: 'The lorry left'.

The house's kindly occupants let the father stay overnight and he walked out next morning into a 'blissful dawn'. The word 'blissful' probably refers not only to the beauty of the morning, but also to the father's state of mind, to the mixture of relief and exhilaration he experienced having survived the previous night's terrifying encounter. On this particular morning, he is glad simply to be alive, and he is in no mood to take the dawn's beauty and freshness for granted.

THEMES

FAMILY

This poem, like many by Ní Chuilleanáin, emphasises the importance of family. It highlights the deep love and respect the poet had for her father, Cormac Ó Cuilleanáin, who was a professor of Irish at UCC and helped foster her imagination, creativity and love of the written word.

The poem celebrates the vigour and cunning the father exhibited in his younger days, as he dramatically evaded the British troops in 1921. She praises not only the physical dexterity he showed as he cornered 'in the narrow road', but also his speed of thought; how he was 'clever' and exhibited 'bright running' to evade his pursuers.

The poet's deep love for her father is evident in how she behaved while he 'was dying in a hospital'. She loved him so much, was so distraught at his condition, that she fled up into the hills to avoid the stress of his suffering and imminent demise. Yet she clearly felt guilty about this decision and eventually returned to the city: 'And I should not/ Have run away'.

SPIRITUALITY

Many of Ní Chuilleanáin's poems present what we might describe as a spiritual view of nature. The poet's sojourn in the countryside changes her. She is deeply affected by the sight of the hare 'absorbed, sitting still' on the middle of the country track. She makes what seems like the bizarre decision to bathe in a bog pool. But it's as if doing so cleanses her psyche washes away her doubts and feelings of inadequacy. She realises she was wrong to leave to her dying father behind and that she is in fact capable of dealing with the trauma of his suffering.

When she returns to the city she thinks about the hare on the hillside path. We sense that this is a memory the poet will draw strength from as she stays by her dying father's bedside. She will find inspiration in the hare's stillness, calmness and composure: 'And I thought of the hare, in her hour of ease'. She will try to exhibit at least some of that 'ease' as she grapples with her father's final illness, not only for her own sake but also for that of her father and her family at large.

FOCUS ON STYLE

Imagery

Like many of Ní Chuilleanáin's poems 'On Lacking the Killer Instinct' proceeds by means of image rather than argument. The poem wonderfully depicts the process of memory, enacting how in our minds one thought leads on the next, one remembered image calling forth another.

The prize-winning photograph in the newspaper summons up two distinct images in the poet's memory, both related to the her father. She remembers the story of his pursuit by British soldiers during the War of Independence.

She also remembers a hare she saw around the time of her father's death. Her mind is carried or 'borne' back into the past, and she experiences an extremely vivid memory of that day in the countryside. It's as if she can somehow 'see' that long-ago hare again: 'I see her suddenly again'.

In lines 15 to 21 the poet returns to contemplating the photograph. But this causes her to think once more about the incident in 1921, which in turn triggers further memories of the time of her father's death. The poem, then, does a wonderful job of depicting how memory actually works, how we jump from one remembered image to the next in an unpredictable fashion and how we are often 'borne back' in a runaway train of thought.

The poet identifies certain parallels between her father's and the hare in the photograph. Both the hare and the poet's father are described as 'clever' because of the mental sharpness and physical agility they exhibit in evading their pursuers. The hare's dexterity as she 'shoots off to the left' reflects that of the father 'cornering in the narrow road'. In the hare's 'bright' eye there is the intelligence to leave the hounds frustrated. Similarly the poet praises the 'bright' or quick-thinking running that led her father to seek refuge in the farmhouse and thereby escape the soldiers.

Both the hare and the father experience a sense of exhileration in the face of death. Both experience a powerful sense of 'gladness', a sense of power, energy and joy, in the act of running for their lives.

Metaphor, Simile, Figures of Speech

There are also several instances of assonance that contribute a pleasant musical effect. We see this in the repeated 'a' sound in 'grassy middle of the track' the repeated 'u' sound in 'summer dusk', and the repeated 'o' sound in 'lorry growling'. The repeated broad vowel sounds in phrases like 'cornering in the narrow road', 'blissful dawn' and 'hare in her hour of need' also contribute to this effect.

'On Lacking the Killer Instinct' is written in plain almost prosaic language, making it unusual among Ní Chuilleanáin's poems. But it does feature one memorable metaphor; the sound of the lorry is compared to the 'growling' of a wild animal. This not only captures the engine's angry rasping sound, but also deftly links the soldiers pursuing the poet's father with the hounds chasing the hare in the prize-winning photograph.

The Poem's Title

The poet considers the terrible risk her father took when he ran into the open farmhouse: 'Should he have chanced that door?' Things could have worked out very differently. The soldiers might not have given up so easily. They might have responded to the householders' lack of cooperation by burning down the 'sheltering house'. His escape attempt, therefore, risked bringing doom not only to himself but also to the innocent household that had 'harboured' him: 'what good/ Could all his bright running have done/ For those that harboured him?'

But the father exhibits the 'killer instinct', which is defined as 'an aggressive and ruthless determination to win or attain a goal'. He quickly assesses the situation and does what he deems necessary for his own survival.

The hare in the prize-winning photograph might also be said to exhibit the 'killer instinct'. It exhibits quickness of thought and movement, doing whatever it takes to escape the pursuing hounds.

There is a sense, however, that the poet lacked the ruthlessness and focus associated with the 'killer instinct' around the time of her father's death. She found herself unable to see things through, to remain by his bedside until he had passed away, and instead she fled into the hills.

To Niall Woods and Xenya Ostrovskaia, married in Dublin on 9 September 2009

LINE BY LINE

I

This poem is set in a fantastical, magical version of Europe, one that resembles a land of fairytale. The poem describes a couple who live on opposite sides of the continent: a boy who lives in Ireland and a girl who lives in Russia. Both, it seems, live in rural environments, in villages surrounded by fields.

The boy and girl have never met. But each has heard, somehow, about the other. And they know that it's their destiny to be together. Perhaps they were both visited by a magical bird, who informed each about the other's existence. Or perhaps they experienced some strange shared dream.

In any event, both the boy and the girl have heard the same prophecy and have received the same set of mystical instructions. They must wait until they see a particular star in the night sky. Then they must set out to find one another: 'That is the time to set out on your journey'. The boy will depart from Ireland and the girl will depart from Russia. They will meet somewhere in the middle of Europe and start a new life together.

The mothers of the boy and girl will experience mixed feelings when this moment of departure comes. They will be sad, of course, to see their children leave and start a new life in a foreign land. But they will understand, too, that their children must find happiness and fulfil their destiny. Their mothers, then, will offer the boy and girl support and encouragement, giving them their 'blessing' as they set out on their extraordinary journey.

The boy and girl, like many fairytale figures, come from extremely humble origins. They receive no gold coins, no jewellery or fine clothes as they set out on their respective journeys. Their mothers, alas, can offer them nothing but a 'blessing'. Indeed, they are both so poor that they set out with only the most meagre of provisions, each carrying 'half a loaf' of bread.

But the bread also serves a symbolic function. They both set out with half a loaf, symbolising how they are both half of a greater unity, one that will only be complete when they finally come together in the middle of the European continent.

II

In order to be together, the boy and girl must 'leave behind the places that [they] knew'. They must leave behind the only homes they've ever known – the characters and landscapes they've been familiar with all their lives – and set up home in some foreign land. They will both, therefore, experience a great deal of homesickness as they embark on their new life together.

But stories, she suggests, will allow the boy and girl to rediscover the lives they'll have left behind: 'All that you leave behind you will find once more,/ You will find it in the stories':
* When the boy and girl were children, they 'saw' Sleeping Beauty. Their parents would have read them this ancient tale, the words and illustrations bringing the princess vividly to life in their imaginations.
* The boy and the girl, as they start their new life together, will once again 'see' Sleeping Beauty: 'you will see her again'. They will re-read this old tale together, no doubt in some old story book, and the words and illustrations will once again bring the princess vividly to life.

411

• Re-reading Sleeping Beauty, and other fairy stories they first heard when they were children, will allow them to reconnect with their childhoods and the homelands they have left behind.

III

The boy and girl, according to the poet, will find themselves captivated by one illustration in particular: a picture of Sleeping Beauty asleep in her 'high tower' with her companion – a magical talking cat – curled up sleeping 'beside her feet'.

Then, according to the poet, the boy and girl will experience something extraordinary. They will see the illustration of the talking cat magically come to life. The cat will 'wake up' and leap from the pages of the story book into their lives.

This strange being will live with the girl and boy. It will 'speak in Russian and Irish', their native languages (though this magical creature, we sense, will be fluent in every human language). It will tell them a 'different tale' every evening. Some of these tales will come from Russia, such as 'Tsarevitch Ivan and the Fire Bird'. Others will be Irish in origin, such as 'the King of Ireland's Son and the Enchanter's Daughter'.

The cat's stories, then, will allow the boy and girl to foster a connection with their native lands. These stories will allow them – in an imaginative or metaphorical sense – to revisit the countries in which they were born and spent their childhoods.

IV

We get the impression that the magical cat, will be like a living encyclopaedia of stories, that it will know folk tales from every country in the world. In fact the only story 'the cat does not know' is that of Ruth, which appears in the Old Testament of the Bible.

Ruth was from the land of Moab. When her husband died, she made the following promise to her mother-in-law Naomi: 'Wherever you go, I will go; wherever you lodge, I will lodge; your people shall be my people, and your God my God'. Naomi decided to return to her native land of Israel. Ruth 'stood by her word' and went with her.

Ruth and Naomi settled near Bethlehem, where Ruth found work helping with the 'barley harvest'. At first Ruth found Israel to be a strange and alienating environment. But gradually she 'trusted to strangers', coming to understand and appreciate the people of her new home.

The poet describes how Ruth 'went out at night' to visit the home of a man called Boaz, with the hope that he might marry her. Ruth, perhaps understandably, was 'afraid' as she made her way to Boaz's house, uncertain of how things would turn out. But eventually, after several complications, she and Boaz were married and lived happily together.

The poet would like to share the story of Ruth with the boy and girl. But she finds herself unable to do so: 'I have not time to tell you how she fared'. All she can do is mention the key aspects of the story. Ruth, the poet emphasises 'stood by her word' when she followed Naomi. And she 'trusted to strangers' when she found herself in a strange kingdom where she knew no-one.

FOCUS ON STYLE

Gapped and Mysterious Narratives

The poem features a primary narrative: the story of the boy and girl. It also features a secondary narrative, or story-within-a-story: the story of Sleeping Beauty, which is read by the boy and girl.

The poet playfully blurs the line between these primary and secondary narratives, having the talking cat step out of the storybook and into the lives of the boy and girl.

The poet also takes the unusual step of addressing her characters directly. She tells them a few details from the Book of Ruth but declares that she doesn't have time to relate Ruth's story in full.

This poem, like many by Ní Chuilleanáin, leaves much unexplained. Why must the boy and girl wait until a particular star appears before setting out on their respective journeys? Why is the cat, who seemingly knows every story ever told, unwilling or unable to learn the story of Ruth? Why doesn't the poet have enough time to tell her characters Ruth's story in full? But these unanswered questions, rather than leaving the reader frustrated, add to the poem's sense of mystery and atmosphere.

Imagery

This poem is also notable for its startling imagery. Especially memorable, of course, is her depiction of the illustration that comes to life, of the talking cat stepping out of the story book and coming to live with the boy and girl in their new home.

Also notable is her depiction of the star that will be witnessed by the boy and girl in their respective homelands. The poet, using an unexpected metaphor, compares this star to a tent: 'the same star/ Pitching its tent on the point of the steeple'. But we can imagine how such a star, when glimpsed above the rooftops of a village, might seem triangular in shape, how it might resemble a glittering tent that has been pitched on the steeple of the local church.

Myth and Folklore

'To Naill Woods' is typical of Ní Chuilleanáin's work in that it delves deeply into the realm of myth and folklore. The poet, with the story of the boy and girl, creates her very own fairytale, one that contains several features common to such narratives: a couple that are destined to be together, a long journey undertaken with little in the way of provisions, an inanimate object (in this case, an illustration of a cat) that comes to life.

The poet also refers to several pre-existing folk tales:

- 'The King of Ireland's Son and the Enchanter's Daughter', for instance, describes a prince who must overcome several fantastical challenges in order the win the hand in marriage of a magician's daughter.
- 'Tsarevitch Ivan and the Fire Bird' meanwhile, is a Russian folktale about a magical bird that each night steals a golden apple from the 'emperor's garden'. The emperor's son, Ivan, sets out on a quest to catch the bird. Along the way he meets and falls in love with a beautiful princess.
- The poet, of course, also refers to 'Sleeping Beauty', a fairytale that exists in many versions around the world.

By referencing these tales, the poet reinforces her message to her son and her new daughter-in-law. Niall and Xenya, like the characters in these folktales, will face challenges trials and setbacks. But Niall and Xenya, like these fictional princes and princesses, will overcome the challenges they face and live 'happily ever after'.

FAMILY

This poem is a wonderful example of an 'epithalamium', which is poem written to celebrate a wedding day. The poet, in this instance, is celebrating the marriage of her son Niall Woods to his Russian bride Xenya Ostrovskaia. We can imagine how the poem might have been presented to the bride and groom on the day of their wedding, or perhaps even recited at the reception or the ceremony.

The poet, then, draws several parallels between Niall and Xenya's situation and that of the boy and girl:

- She suggests that Niall and Xenya, like the boy and girl, are destined to be together.
- She suggests that Niall and Xenya, like the boy and girl in the story, must 'Leave behind the places that [they] knew'. Niall and Xenya, once married, would neither be setting up home in Russia nor in Ireland, but in a third country unfamiliar to both of them.
- She suggests that Niall and Xenya, like the boy and girl, can use stories to reconnect with their respective homelands.

She suggests that Niall and Xenya, like the boy and girl, should look to the story of Ruth for guidance and inspiration. They, like Ruth, must keep their word, remaining faithful and true to one another. They, like Ruth, must learn to trust in strangers as they make their new home in a foreign land. If they can manage to do so then they – like Ruth – will live 'happily ever after'.

LOVE

This poem offers a moving portrayal of love, capturing both the excitement at the beginning of a relationship as well as the ups and downs that come with long-term commitment.

Perhaps the most moving line in the poem is the poet's simple declaration that 'You will have to trust me'. Here we sense the poet, as a mother, attempting to reassure her son and her new daughter-in-law as they embark on their new life together. The poet herself has lived and loved. She knows the challenges that Niall and Xenya will face as they navigate the ups and downs of married life together. She also knows that her son and daughter-in-law have what it takes to overcome those challenges. But, of course, she cannot prove to them that they will be all right. They will simply have to take her word for it.

Sylvia Plath Themes

Order and Chaos

In many of her poems, Plath describes longing for order and a fear of being overwhelmed by chaos. In 'The Arrival of the Bee Box', for instance, the bees are a chaotic force, swarming hectically and frenziedly within their box. They are like a wild and disorderly mob. Only the box imposes order on them, containing their fury. Tellingly, the poem's opening lines associate the box with order: 'I ordered this, this clean wood box'. However, once the box is opened, order will be removed. The chaos represented by the bees will be free to make its way into the world.

In 'Finisterre', meanhile, chaos is represented by the 'formlessness' of the sea. The sea is presented as a vast, shapeless void churning chaotically. The poem shows chaos slowly encroaching on order as the sea reduces the coastline to nothing. It breaks down the mighty cliffs of Finisterre until they are worn, rheumatic fingers, then little rocks, then nothing at all.

In both poems, Plath seems to regard chaos with what can only be described as fear and horror. In 'The Arrival of the Bee Box', the poet finds releasing the bees an unpleasant and perhaps even frightening prospect: 'How can I let them out?' In 'Finisterre', meanwhile, the poet seems horrified by the violence and menace of the raging sea's assault upon the land. Yet there is also a sense in both poems in which the poet finds the prospect of chaos an attractive and intoxicating one. In 'Finisterre', after all, its formlessness is described as a 'beautiful' formlessness. In 'The Arrival of the Bee Box' meanwhile the poet 'can't keep away' from the bees' frenzy, and she decides at the end of the poem to release this 'box of maniacs' into the world. To Plath, then, chaos is simultaneously both horrific and irresistible.

'Black Rook in Rainy Weather' is another poem that presents the world as a random and chaotic place. The leaves fall haphazardly, not according to some 'ceremony' or hidden pattern. The weather is described as 'desultory', which means without plan or purpose. Even inspiration occurs in a manner that is entirely haphazard and unpredictable.

The poet, we sense, longs to discern order amid this chaos (we get a sense of this, perhaps, when she refers to the rook 'Ordering its black feathers'). She is forced to conclude, however, that things seem to happen chaotically rather than according to some divine plan or higher purpose. Studying the leaves reveals no 'portent' – no sign of deeper meaning. There's no use looking for any purpose or 'design' in the weather or the natural world.

'The Times Are Tidy', on the other hand, describes a perfectly ordered environment, a space where the same things happen over and over again in a perfectly regular and predictable fashion. Anything that might disrupt this regularity has been carefully eliminated. The prevalence of machines – like the mayor's automated rotisserie – reinforce our sense of a mechanised and totally rational world. But it's one where there's little room for heroism, creativity or craft. There's no scope for individualism in this 'province of the stuck record'. In these tidy times no disruptive influences will be tolerated; each human being must conform and function as one of society's obedient cogs.

Poetic Inspiration

'Black Rook in Rainy Weather' presents an almost spiritual view of inspiration, associating it with miracles, with mystical fire and with communication or 'backtalk' from the heavens above. Inspiration is even personified as an angel that might 'Suddenly' descend from heaven and 'flare' beside the poet, appearing without warning in a burst of heavenly light.

But the angel's appearances are described as 'random' as well as 'rare', reminding us that inspiration strikes in a haphazard and unpredictable way. We can't know in advance when it will strike. The poet must remain alert and hope she's lucky enough to be in the right place at the right time to be inspired.

However, the poet is aware that good writing requires perspiration as well as inspiration. Hard work will be required, then, if she is turn a moment of inspiration into a finished poem. The poem, she declares, will have to be 'patched together', suggesting a process that involves false starts and redrafting. She will have to arrange and rearrange words like the rook adjusting its feathers.

To write poetry, Plath believed, it was necessary to explore the darkest recesses of the mind, to explore the deepest reaches of the soul. Plath felt probing the unconscious mind was a risky business, for it risked disturbing all kinds of inner demons. In 'Finisterre', the ocean is often taken as a metaphor for the unconscious mind. It is presented as a place of great danger, furious and treacherous, with 'no bottom, or anything on the other side of it'. 'Mirror', too, explores this theme; The woman looking into the mirror's depths can be taken as a metaphor for such self-exploration.

'The Arrival of the Bee Box' is another poem that touches on this theme of poetry and the unconscious. The bee box, according to many readers, represents the hidden aspect of the mind, the dark and mysterious parts the true poet must explore. Like the bee box, our unconscious mind is almost completely sealed: we cannot know what it contains until we begin to explore it. Just as the poet is terrified and disgusted by the bee box, so Plath was nervous about exploring her unconscious mind, and horrified by the demons that might lurk there. By opening up her unconscious, she will unleash her inner demons, just as she will release the bees. Yet just as she can't stay away from the bee box, so Plath was drawn back again and again to probe around the edges of her unconscious, for she felt that only by exploring this hidden aspect of herself could she create great poetry.

Femininity and Motherhood

'Morning Song' is a brutally honest poem, one that addresses both the positive and negative emotions associated with becoming a mother for the first time. The poet is clearly fascinated by her child and delights in her new baby's innocence. She describes her child's 'clean' mouth and the 'clear' sounds that rise from the crib, suggesting a pristine and newborn being that has yet to sullied and corrupted by this all-too ugly world.

Perhaps the most striking feature of 'Morning Song' is the emotional distance experienced by the poet, now that her child has left her and body and has become just one more 'element' of the world. The poet, during these first few days, can't quite believe that she's actually her child's mother, that she created and is responsible for this tiny newborn being: 'I'm no more your mother'. Our sense of this distance is reinforced when the poet describes her child in non-human terms, as a moth, a cat, a statue and a watch. The poet, then, wonderfully captures the difficulties that can be involved with the adjustment to motherhood, how it can take days or even weeks for a new mother to settle into this most challenging role.

The poem, however, concludes on an optimistic note, with an image of the newborn baby cooing happily in its crib. There is a wonderful sense of freshness and experimentation in these lines, as the poet describes how her child seems to 'try' out different sounds. It's as if, even now, during these earliest days of life, her child was playing with language and taking the first tentative first steps towards speech. The poem's title captures this optimistic tone, suggesting not only an actual morning, but also the morning of the child's life, when the world is new and there is so much to be learned, explored and experienced for the very first time.

'Child', like 'Morning Song', documents the pressures of motherhood. But, unlike 'Child', it offers no ray of hope or optimism. Every mother wants their child to experience only the beautiful and delightful aspects of the world and to shield them from all the horrors and ugliness that exist in this world. In 'Child', however, we sense that Plath feels that she is utterly failing, that she has nothing positive and good to offer her child.

This theme of motherhood is aso present in 'Finisterre' through the depiction of Our Lady of the Shipwrecked. Our Lady, after all, is often thought of as the 'mother' of the human race. Yet in this poem she is depicted as having failed her children. Despite her serene and beautiful smile, 'her lips sweet with divinity', she is cold, distant and uncaring. She no longer hears the pleas of those who pray to her, either of the despairing sailor or of the peasant woman. She is unmoved by the plight of the lost souls that drift like mist aroud the cliffside.

Mental Anguish

Plath's poetry is notable for its unparalled depiction of mental suffering. Her work takes on a journey from faint hints of unease in 'Black Rook in Rainy Weather' to the total despair of 'Child'. 'Black Rook in Rainy Weather' describes how the poet has been going through an uninspired period. And Plath, we must remember, was someone for whom artistic creativity was bound up in mental well-being. She is terrified, therefore, that if this lack of inspiration goes on too long it will plunge her into a state of 'total neutrality': into a depressive limbo-like existence drained of passion and emotion. A moment of inspiration, however, would offer her 'respite' or relief from this fear.

Both 'Mirror' and 'Finisterre' are potent explorations of mental anguish. In 'Finisterre', the sea's violent fury is often taken to represent Plath's tumultuous mental state. The ocean is presented as a terrifyingly vast 'exploding' force that 'cannons' into the coastline, making an endless and oppressive roaring sound; a 'doom-noise'. 'Mirror', meanwhile, features a woman gripped by a fit of loneliness or despair, examining herself in the looking glass as she cries and wrings her hands: 'She rewards me with tears and an agitation of hands'. We get a sense that much of the woman's turmoil stems from the fact that she has lost her way in life, has lost her sense of her own identity. She gazes into the mirror in an attempt to locate and reconnect with her true self: 'Now I am a lake. A woman bends over me,/ Searching my reaches'.

'Poppies in July' and 'Elm' document Plath's response to the breakdown of her marriage in the sumer of 1962. 'Poppies in July' is a masterful depiction of an agitated, anguished state of mind. To most people, the sight of a field of poppies in summer would be a thing of great joy, a scene of beauty and inspiration. But to the poet, the flowers conjure up highly disturbing images of hellish fire and of mouths that have been beaten and bloodied.

The poet even expresses a masochistic longing to experience pain, to be beaten and to 'bleed'. Perhaps she feels that pain, like some form of shock therapy, might jolt her out of her anguised state of mind (Plath would have been familiar with such treatments, having undergone electroconvulsive therapy in 1953). Or perhaps she feels that physical pain would be a welcome distraction from the mental pain she is currently experiencing.

'Elm', meanwhile, is a masterpiece of personification, one where Plath uses the figure of the elm tree to express her own mental anguish. The elm suffers various torments: being lashed by poisonous rain, burned by the sun, whipped by the wind, and then 'dragged' and 'scathed' by the moon. These torments serve as powerful metaphors for Plath's own mental ordeals, reflecting the tortured state of mind she experienced around the time of the poem's composition. 'Elm', it must be said, also offers a very beak depiction of romantic love. Love is presented as something transitory and insubstantial, like a shadow or a cloud. We are most foolish, the poem suggests, to 'agitate' our hearts for this illusion. But, of course, we can't stop ourselves from doing so.

Plath's poetry often expresses feelings of inadequacy and worthlessness. We see this in 'Mirror' where the speaker looks at her reflection with 'tears and an agitation of hands'. She turns away to the soft glow of candles and the moon, as if she does not like what she sees in the mirror. Perhaps she feels inadequate about her appearance, her personality or the way she is living her life.

In 'Elm', meanwhile, the creature that plagues and tortures the tree is associated with 'faults', which suggests cracks or fault lines. These faults or cracks are described as 'isolate', suggesting that to begin with they are quite far apart from one another. They are also described as 'slow', suggesting that they only gradually expand. Eventually, however, the cracks spread and combine, causing the object to fall apart. These faults and cracks, of course, serve as a powerful metaphor for the poet's feelings of inadequacy, of the flaws and faults that she perceives in herself.

The phrase it 'is something … to be visited at all' in 'Pheasant' also hints at Plath's feelings of inadequacy. It suggests the loneliness and isolation she might have experienced while living in the countryside, far from friends and acquaintances in London. It also hints, perhaps, at a sense of low self-esteem. Maybe the poet feels so down and lacking in confidence that she is surprised that anyone or anything would ever want to come and visit her. 'Child', too, provides us with an insight into the poet's feelings of inadequacy. She feels that she is failing her child, that she is not capable of offering it the things it needs to thrive and be happy.

'The Arrival of the Bee Box' is another poem that vividly depicts mental turmoil. Plath reacts to the bee box with horrified fascination. This is partly due to her finding the sights and sounds of the bees disgusting and unsettling. But it is also because the bee box represents her own anguished mental state. The bees buzz and vibrate inside the box just as anguished thoughts churn and agitate inside her troubled mind. Plath imagines releasing the bees into her garden. This seems to represent her belief that she might be able to free her mind from such negative and destructive thoughts. If she can overcome this seemingly irrational fear of the bee box, perhaps she can also overcome the deeper mental turmoil that affects her.

There are several instances where Plath's poetry seems to prefigure her tragic death by suicide, where the poet expresses what might be described as self-destructive thoughts or desires. Such desires are arguably expressed in 'Finisterre' when the poet describes herself walking into the sea mist. She describes how this mist 'erases' the rocks and yet she enters it. It's as if on some level she herself desires to be erased from existence.

Such desires also surface in 'The Arrival of the Bee Box', when the poet imagines herself wearing the protective garments of a beekeeper; she describes the face covering as a 'funeral veil'. There is a sense here that she is anticipating her own demise, or on some level even desiring it. This tendency is perhaps also evident when she imagines herself being transformed into a tree: 'I wonder if they would just forget me/ If I just undid the locks and stood back and turned into a tree'. There is a sense in which the poet seems to desire this transformation, to leave behind the human condition, with all its trials and tribulations. A similar tendency is evident in 'Poppies in July' where the poet expresses her desire to sleep, to ingest some sedative that would plunge her into a deep slumber that would allow her to escape her anguished state of mind.

'Child' provides us with an insight into the almost unbearbale mental anguish that Plath was experiencing at the very end of her life. Her description of the 'dark/ Ceiling without a star' at the end of the poem captures her despair and lack of hope. The 'dark/ Ceiling' might be understood metaphorically as a description of the poet's psychological state or condition. To her the world seems bleak and without hope. She feels utterly trapped and alone. When she contemplates the future, it seems an endless vista of blackness, without a ray or shard of hope.

An advert from 1950s America that reflects the atmosphere of blissful confidence described in the poem

LINE BY LINE

This poem can read as a fairytale of sorts, one that paints a vivid portrait of an imaginary little town and its community. The town is presented as a rich and comfortable place, its great wealth indicated by its cows producing milk that's incredibly thick with cream: 'The cow milks cream an inch thick.' Cream and fat, we note, are often used as symbols for richness, plenty and prosperity.

It's a place where technological innovation has made life easier. For instance, the town's mayor has a fancy new automated rotisserie that 'turns/ Round of its own accord' (a rotisserie is a spit or skewer that rotates over a fire to ensure that meat is evenly cooked). In these lines we can almost visualise the mayor throwing a gala banquet for the townsfolk to show off this new toy.

The town is also a very safe place. Once it would have been threatened occasionally by fearsome dragons. But that was long ago and these terrible beasts have 'withered' and shrunk over the centuries, evolving from huge and fiery serpents into tiny 'leaf-size' lizards.

Witches once posed a different type of threat to the community. We are presented with the traditional fairy-tale witch, an old woman or 'crone' accompanied by a demonic familiar in the form of a 'talking cat'. According to the speaker, such witches wreaked havoc upon the townsfolk. They used their magic to ruin crops, for instance, or used herbs to make love potions that controlled people's minds.

Thankfully, however, such witchcraft is a thing of the past, its last practitioner having been burnt alive over eighty years ago along with her cat and the 'love-hot herb' she used in her concoctions. The town's children, we're told, are safer now that witchcraft has been eliminated. Black magic no longer interferes with agriculture, allowing cows to produce their extraordinary milk.

The town, then, is a place of great prosperity and safety. But such comfort comes at the price of terrible boredom. The poet describes a place where nothing ever changes, wittily referring to it as the 'province of the stuck record'. A stuck record, of course, endlessly repeats the same few seconds of music. Similarly, it seems that in this town the exact same day occurs over and over again. It's a place where life is unexciting, predictable and dull.

There is no room for heroism in this safe but monotonous community. Once upon a time heroes were called on to don their suits of armour and ride off to defeat the dragons that menaced the town's welfare. But as we've seen, the passage of time has eliminated such hazards and threats: 'History's beaten the hazard.'

Now there's 'no career' for a hero in this town and nothing for him to fight against: 'There's no career in the venture/ Of riding against the lizard'. Heroes born here are 'unlucky' because they'll find no opportunity to express their heroism. They're simply born too late to show off their strength, selflessness and courage.

And heroes aren't the only ones surplus to requirements. Skilled craftspeople, too, are increasingly no longer needed, as machines now handle tasks once done by hand. The town's best cooks would once have found employment at the mayor's banquet. But now they remain 'jobless' as the new automated rotisserie turns around on its own.

THEMES

A BITING CRITIQUE OF 1950s AMERICA

This poem was written during the 1950s, which was a time of great success and confidence in American life. This was a period when the United States loomed over the world as its one true superpower.

Nazi Germany and its allies had been defeated in the Second World War while the Soviet Union had yet to emerge as a serious rival to American might. It seemed certain that even outer space itself would soon fall to American conquest. It was also a time of great economic prosperity in America; here it seemed everyone could find respectable and well-paying employment. Advances in medicine made diseases that had tormented earlier generations a thing of the past. Consumer goods like cars, central heating, fridges and televisions became freely and cheaply available, bringing a level of everyday comfort that would have been unimaginable a decade previously.

The little fairy-tale town Plath sketches so memorably serves as a powerful allegory for the U.S. during this 1950s period of confidence and dominance. The post-war wealth is symbolised by the inch-thick cream issuing from the cows, technological advancement by the mayor's new spinning gadget. America's enemies like Germany and Japan have gone the way of the witches and dragons that once menaced the town. They've been burned up or have been shrunk down to insignificance.

But Plath, like many writers and artists, had mixed feelings about this shiny new America, regarding it as a place of great dullness, conformity and conservatism. Like the town in her little story, 1950s America is a 'province of the stuck record', a place of boredom where nothing ever really changes. She sees little scope for heroism in this monotonous country. Furthermore, she was keenly aware that technology had downsides as well as benefits. As the 'jobless' cooks symbolise, in a world increasingly run by machines, many old skills and talents would fall by the wayside.

HEROISM AND THE YOUNG

'But the children are better for it' might be regarded as the poem's most important line. Plath was twenty-five when she wrote this poem and she seems deeply concerned with what this new America meant for young people. In previous generations, young Americans had been ravaged by diseases like polio, had slaved in farms and factories, had bled to death on the battle fields of France. Now they only worried about who to invite to the prom as they drove brand new cars to drive-in movie theatres. A new word – 'teenager' – was coined in order to sell products to these affluent youngsters.

But does Plath really believe that children are better off in this brave new world? She hardly wants a return to poverty and disease. Nor does she want to send young Americans marching off to war. However there's a sense in which she feels her younger countrymen are too pampered and over-indulged. They lack the opportunity for heroism in these 'latter-days' to which they've been born, in this repetitive and monotonous country where 'History' has already run its course. The potential heroes among them are simply 'unlucky', having been born at a time when all the great battles have been fought and all challenges overcome.

ORDER AND CHAOS

In 'The Times Are Tidy', Plath powerfully describes a perfectly ordered environment. She depicts a place where the same things happen over and over again in a perfectly regular and predictable fashion. Anything that might disrupt this regularity has been carefully eliminated. The prevalence of machines – like the mayor's automated rotisserie – reinforce our sense of a mechanised and totally rational world. But it's one where there's little room for heroism, creativity or craft. There's no scope for individualism in this 'province of the stuck record'. In these tidy times, no disruptive influences will be tolerated; each human being must conform and funcntion as one of society's obedient cogs.

POETIC INSPIRATION

We sense too that Plath views this ordered, tidy world as somehow deeply uncreative. This mechanical realm is no place for individualists and dreamers, for artists and craftsmen who follow their own course of self-expression. Indeed many artists, writers and musicians found the conformist America of the 1950s a deeply uninspiring place, one in which they struggled to find acceptance.

Black Rook in Rainy Weather

LINE BY LINE

The poem was written in the winter of 1958 when Plath was living in Massachusetts. A journal entry from February captures Plath's mood and her struggles to forge her identity as an artist: '[E]ach night, now, I must capture one taste, one touch, one vision from the ruck of the day's garbage. How all this life would vanish, evaporate, if I didn't clutch at it, cling to it, while I still remember some twinge or glory. Books & lessons surround me: hours of work. Who am I?'

The weather, as the poem's title informs us, is rather rainy. Winter, it seems, has lent the landscape a bleak and desolate appearance. The poet, as she trudges through this dreary scene, observes a rook perched on a branch: 'On the stiff twig up there/ Hunches a wet black rook'. The rook sits 'hunched' upon its perch, almost as if it's trying to protect itself from the miserable weather.

This poem discusses moments of inspiration, moments when the poet gets the ideas for her poetry, when she is filled with energy, positivity and creativity.

- At such moments she sees the world in an intense and heightened way. The ordinary sights around her seem to blaze with light. These moments 'set the sight on fire/ In [her] eye'.
- Such moments, she declares are 'a miracle', suggesting that for her they are a holy or sacred phenomenon.
- But such moments are also an 'accident', suggesting that they occur in a random and unpredictable manner.

When inspiration strikes, common household objects seem consumed by heavenly or 'celestial' fire: 'light may still/ Lean incandescent// Out of kitchen table or chair'. Inspiration can 'hallow' or make sacred a moment that would otherwise be completely unimportant: 'hallowing an interval/ Otherwise inconsequent'. We sense, however, that the poet has been going through a barren period in terms of her creative life. It has been a while, it seems, since she experienced such a moment of inspiration.

At first the poet does not expect such a moment of inspiration to occur today, as she wanders through the wintry New England landscape: 'I do not expect a miracle/ Or an accident'. She doesn't expect to be struck by ideas, energy and creativity. She doesn't expect the sights that surround her – such as the 'wet black rook' on its twig – to take on the fiery glow of inspiration.

But then she allows herself a moment of hope. Inspiration could strike her, even as she trudges through this dreary stretch of countryside: 'for it could happen/ Even in this dull, ruinous landscape'. Inspiration, after all, is random and unpredictable. Ultimately the poet is 'ignorant' as to when she will be inspired and as to what form her inspiration might take. She decides to start walking, therefore, in a 'wary' or careful fashion, keeping alert for any sight or sound that might cause her to be inspired: 'At any rate, I now walk/ Wary'.

Even the rook 'Ordering' or tidying its feathers could act as a source of inspiration. It could 'seize' the poet's senses, so there is nothing else she could look at or think about. It could 'haul' her eyelids open, so that she would be unable to close her eyes or look away. Her experience of the rook would be heightened and it would seem to 'shine', to take on the burning glow associated with inspiration.

On this occasion, however, the poet is disappointed and no moment of inspiration occurs. Yet she remains hopeful for the future. She reminds herself that the miracle of inspiration does indeed occur from time to time: 'Miracles occur'. If she is lucky, inspiration will strike her sometime soon, allowing her to create a poem or story: 'With luck … I shall/ Patch together a content// Of sorts.' The poem concludes, then, with the poet waiting once more for the angel of inspiration to descend into her life: 'The wait's begun again,/ The long wait for the angel'.

FOCUS ON STYLE

The poem, it is important to note, has a 'hidden' rhyme scheme in which the first lines of each stanza rhyme or almost rhyme (there … fire … desire … chair) as do the second lines (rook … seek … backtalk … took … walk) and so on. It has been claimed that the poem's unusual structure contradicts its argument that the world is a random and chaotic place. It is possible, after all, that a hidden order lies behind the apparently chaotic and random events we see around us, just as there is a hidden pattern behind the arrangement of the poem's lines.

There are many poems where Plath creates what she described as 'psychic landscapes'. In this poem, the speaker's uninspired state of mind is reflected in the 'dull ruinous landscape' she trudges through, and in the dreary atmosphere that dominates the scene. This, she declares, is the 'season of fatigue'. This phrase describes the time of year – late autumn or winter – when nature itself is exhausted and winding down. Yet it also describes the poet's state of mind, how she is worn out from a period devoid of inspiration and creativity.

The poet, we sense, longs to be inspired by the natural world, like Wordsworth and the great poets of the Romantic tradition. Being inspired by nature, she suggests, is like hearing 'backtalk' from the sky. It's like being spoken to by God or the universe itself. The poet, however, has seldom been inspired by nature. For her, the sky has largely been 'mute' or silent. For the poet, inspiration has struck – when it has struck at all – in the context of domestic scenes, when she's sitting by the fire or performing some household task.

Plath presents this almost as a lesser form of inspiration, one that produces only a 'minor light'. The poet feels that she 'can't honestly complain' that she's tended to experience this lesser domestic sort of inspiration. We sense, however, that she still longs to be inspired by the natural world: 'I admit I desire,/ Occasionally, some backtalk/ From the mute sky'. It's as if she believes being a 'proper' poet means having profound experiences in forests and on mountain-tops.

THEMES

POETIC INSPIRATION

'Black Rook in Rainy Weather' presents an almost spiritual view of inspiration. Inspiration, as we've seen is associated with miracles, with mystical fire and with communication or 'backtalk' from the heavens above. In line 12, it is even personified as an angel that might 'Suddenly' descend from heaven and 'flare' beside the poet, appearing without warning in a burst of heavenly light. But the angel's appearances are described as 'random' as well as 'rare', reminding us that inspiration strikes in a haphazard and unpredictable way. We can't know in advance when it will strike. The poet must remain alert and hope she's lucky enough to be in the right place at the right time to be inspired.

But maybe the poet is overdoing this talk of angels and miracles? She concedes that not everyone will view inspiration in such a spiritual light: 'Miracles occur./ If you care to call those spasmodic/ Tricks of radiance/ Miracles'. The poet, as we have seen, believes that inspiration causes the world around her to blaze with light. But perhaps this effect is caused by 'spasmodic/ Tricks of radiance', by strange optical illusions that occur in a spasmodic or haphazard fashion.

The poet is aware that good writing requires perspiration as well as inspiration. Hard work will be required, then, if she is to turn a moment of inspiration into a finished poem. The poem, she declares, will have to be 'patched together', suggesting a process that involves false starts and redrafting. She will have to arrange and rearrange words like the rook adjusting its feathers.

MENTAL ANGUISH

The poet, as we noted above, has been going through an uninspired period. And Plath, we must remember, was someone who simply couldn't function unless she was writing; many of her diary entries and letters give the impression that literature mattered as much to her as friendship or family life. She is terrified, therefore, that if this lack of inspiration goes on too long it will plunge her into a state of 'total neutrality'; into a depressive limbo-like existence drained of passion and emotion. A moment of inspiration, however, would offer her 'respite' or relief from this fear.

ORDER AND CHAOS

'Black Rook in Rainy Weather' presents the world as a random and chaotic place. The leaves fall haphazardly, not according to some 'ceremony' or hidden pattern. The weather is described as 'desultory', which means without plan or purpose. Even inspiration occurs in a manner that is entirely haphazard and unpredictable.

The poet, we sense, longs to discern order amid this chaos (we get a sense of this, perhaps, when she refers to the rook 'Ordering its black feathers'). She is forced to conclude, however, that things seem to happen chaotically rather than according to some divine plan or higher purpose. Studying the leaves reveals no 'portent' – no sign of deeper meaning. There's no use looking for any purpose or 'design' in the weather or the natural world.

Morning Song

Plath with her first child, Frieda, in early 1961

LINE BY LINE

This poem was written in 1960, shortly after the birth of Plath's first child, Frieda. In a letter written to a friend a day after the birth, Plath wrote: 'Ted & I are happy to announce the birth of Frieda Rebecca Hughes. She was born at 5:45 a.m. yesterday morning, April 1st, weighing 7 pounds 4 ounces, 21 inches long & covered with white cream like a floured pastry. I am now sitting up in bed typing letters after the morning visit of the midwife who bathes me & the baby, eating yogurt and maple syrup & hardly able to take my eyes off the baby who has enormous blue eyes, a fluff of dark hair & seems to us extremely lovely: perfectly made.'

The watch

The poet, using a wonderful simile, compares her newborn child to an old style pocket watch, one that might be attached to a chain and displayed on a gentleman's jacket:

- Such a watch might be described as 'fat', reflecting its bulky, bulging design. The poet's child, similarly, might be described as 'fat', reflecting her natural, newborn chubbiness.
- Such a watch might be described as 'gold', reflecting its status as an expensive luxury item. The poet's child, similarly, might be described as 'gold', reflecting how precious she is to her parents.

- Such a watch, of course, would be a complex mechanism. The child's body, similarly, might be described as a complex biological mechanism, in which so many systems and organs interlock.
- Such an old-fashioned watch would be initiated or 'set going' by repeatedly turning its winding pin. The poet's newborn child, on the other hand, was initiated or 'set going' by the love-making between her parents: 'Love set you going like a fat gold watch'.

Remembering the birth

The poet focuses on the moments after her child's birth. She describes how the 'midwife slapped [her child's] footsoles' (such slapping, it was believed, encouraged newborns to inhale and to fill their lungs for the first time). She describes how her child took her very first breath and emitted her very first cry. The child has been tucked up safely inside the poet's own body. But now the child has been separated from her. The child and the child's cry are now just one more element or aspect of the wider world: 'your bald cry/ Took its place among the elements'.

The parents' reaction to the birth

The voices of the poet and her husband 'echo' that of their newborn child. We can imagine them leaning over the child's cot or crib, mimicking her cries and gurgles. By doing so, they magnify or amplify the sounds that accompany her arrival into this world: 'Our voices echo, magnifying your arrival'. The poet and her husband realise that their independence has been severely curtailed. For their naked, vulnerable child must always remain close to them. The child's 'nakedness' must 'shadow' or follow the 'safety' they provide: 'Your nakedness/ Shadows our safety'.

We expect the parents of a newborn to exhibit a kind of euphoric joy. But this of course isn't always the case. The poet describes how she and her husband respond 'blankly' to their child's birth. Overcome by shock, numbness and exhaustion, they exhibit little in the way of outward emotion. They are as inexpressive, she wittily declares, as bare undecorated walls: 'We stand round blankly as walls'.

The puddle and the cloud

The poet, using another memorable simile, compares herself to a cloud and her child to a puddle that has formed from the cloud's waters:

- The cloud 'distills' or produces rainfall that forms a puddle on the earth's surface. The poet, similarly, has produced her newborn child.
- The cloud is then effaced or erased, as the wind causes it to disintegrate. The poet, similarly, will be gradually effaced or erased by the processes of aging.
- The puddle functions like a mirror and reflects the cloud's 'effacement'. The poet's child, similarly, will reflect her 'own effacement', her gradual decline into exhaustion and old age. Perhaps the poet is suggesting that her child will survive and thrive at her own expense. It's as if the poet, by making every effort to ensure that her child grows and prospers, will leave herself mentally and physically exhausted.

The cloud, according to the poet, doesn't feel any particular attachment towards the puddle that formed from its waters. There are moments, during these first days of motherhood, when the poet, similarly, doesn't feel any particular attachment to her newborn child. There are moments when this tiny individual that has come bursting into her life seems remote, strange and unknowable.

Night-feeding

The poet describes her first night with her new child. The child sleeps on sheets that are decorated with pictures of roses (the roses, being two-dimensional, are described as 'flat'). The poet, it seems, is fascinated by the sound of her child's breathing and 'wakes' during the night just so that she can listen: 'I wake to listen'. She describes how her child's breathing 'flickers', suggesting a series of breaths that are short, shallow and irregular.

Throughout the night, the poet is highly alert to her baby's needs. No sooner has her child started crying than the poet 'stumble[s] from bed', puts on her floral nightgown, and heads towards the cot. Her child's mouth is open when she gets there, no doubt indicating a desire to be fed. The poet, it seems, stays up for hours with her baby until 'the window square// Whitens' with the dawn and the stars gradually disappear.

The poet, then, sits beside the crib, delighting in the babbling sounds her child produces. These sounds are described as notes, suggesting that they have a musical quality. They are also described as vowels, suggesting the repetitive series of 'o' and 'a' sounds commonly produced by infants.

FOCUS ON STYLE

Metaphor, Simile, Figures of Speech

'Morning Song' is a poem rich in metaphor and simile. In one of the poem's most cryptic metaphors, Plath compares her child to a 'New statue./ In a drafty museum'. These lines compare the child to an exhibit that would be examined and admired by various friends and relatives that come to see the new baby. The poet's house, then, is compared to a 'drafty museum' that houses this priceless newborn artefact.

The poet uses two fine metaphors to describe her child's breathing. The child, as we've seen, breathes in an irregular and 'flickering' pattern. For Plath, this calls to mind the irregular pulsing of a moth's wings as it flutters around the bedroom. The poet compares the sound of her child's breathing to a 'far sea', suggesting a repetitive series of hushing sounds that are both faint and soothing to the ear.

The poet uses a wonderful simile to describe how her child's sounds, like balloons, 'rise' upwards from the cot towards the ceiling. There is an element of synesthesia in this comparison, which, we remember, occurs when an experience associated with one sense is described in terms of another. In this instance, the child's sounds, associated with the sense of hearing, are described in terms of balloons, which we associate with the sense of vision. We imagine each note the child produces as a colourful, buoyant presence floating around the room.

Vivid and Unsettling Imagery

Plath's gift for vivid and unsettling imagery is evident in her depiction of the view from the bedroom window:
- The stars are described as 'dull' rather than glittering.
- The sunrise brings a rather sickly glow that 'Whitens' the world.
- The poet, in a startling and aggressive metaphor, describes how the stars, as they disappear from view, are swallowed by the 'window square'.

These images strike a note of dread and doubt, highlighting the poet's sense of foreboding at bringing a child into this troubled and uncertain world.

Verbal Music

The poem, as its title suggests, has a highly musical quality. The poem is especially rich in assonance, where repeated broad vowel sounds lend the lines a pleasant musical quality. We see this, for instance, with the repeated 'a' sounds in 'magnifying your arrival', or the repeated 'e' sounds in 'A far sea moves in my ear', or as well as in the 'o' and 'a' sounds in the poem's final line: 'The clear vowels rise like balloons'. There is an element of onomatopoeia in the opening two lines, where the repeated hard consonants lend the verse a stop-start quality reminiscent, perhaps, of the mid-wife striking the infant's footsoles.

THEMES

FEMININITY AND MOTHERHOOD

'Morning Song' is a brutally honest poem, one that addresses both the positive and negative emotions associated with becoming a mother for the first time.

- The poet is clearly fascinated by her child. She wakes during the night, for instance, just to listen to her child's breathing. She and her husband, as we've seen, lean over the crib, echoing and magnifying the child's cries and gurgles.
- The poet delights in her child's innocence. She describes her child's 'clean' mouth and the 'clear' sounds that rise from the crib, suggesting a pristine and newborn being that has yet to be sullied and corrupted by this all-too ugly world.
- The poet is clearly caring and attentive. She responds to her child's distress at the first sign of crying and stays up with her through the night. But the poet doesn't flinch from the negative emotions provoked by this major life transition.
- The poet describes herself as 'cow heavy', suggesting, perhaps, that she is none too happy about the changes pregnancy has wrought upon her body.
- The poet and her husband, like many parents, respond to the birth with an exhausted emotional blankness rather than the expected euphoria.
- The poet and her husband, like many first time parents, are overcome by a sense of responsibility, by the realisation that this naked vulnerable creature will 'shadow' them for years to come.

Perhaps the most striking feature of 'Morning Song' is the emotional distance experienced by the poet, now that her child has left her body and become just one more 'element' of the world. The poet, during these first few days, can't quite believe that she's actually her child's mother, that she created and is responsible for this tiny newborn being: 'I'm no more your mother'. Our sense of this distance is reinforced when the poet describes her child in non-human terms, as a moth, a cat, a statue and a watch. The poet, then, wonderfully captures the difficulties that can be involved with the adjustment to motherhood, how it can take days or even weeks for a new mother to settle into this most challenging role.

The poem, however, concludes on an optimistic note, with an image of the newborn baby cooing happily in its crib. There is a wonderful sense of freshness and experimentation in these lines, as the poet describes how her child seems to 'try' out different sounds. It's as if, even now, during these earliest days of life, her child was playing with language and taking the tentative first steps towards speech. The poem's title captures this optimistic tone. Perhaps the child's vowels are the morning song in question, a set of 'clear' and beautiful notes to greet the dawn. But the poem itself, of course, is also something of a morning song. It depicts not only an actual morning, but also the morning of her child's life, when the world is new and there is so much to be learned, explored and experienced for the very first time.

Mirror

LINE BY LINE

Like several of Plath's poems, 'Mirror' gives voice to an inanimate object. The mirror is silver (this may refer to a silver frame around its reflective surface. Alternatively, the reflective surface itself may be made from polished silver). It is square or rectangular in shape, being 'four-cornered'.

It hangs opposite a pink speckled wall. The mirror claims to stare continuously at this wall, 'meditating' upon it: 'I have looked at it so long'. Every night, it becomes too dark for it to see the wall opposite. Furthermore, people regularly check their reflections in the mirror's surface, blocking its view of the wall: 'Faces and darkness separate us over and over'.

The mirror has spent so long 'meditating' in this way that it now believes the pink wall is part of itself: 'I have looked at it so long/ I think is a part of my heart.' These lines are oddly touching. We get the impression that the mirror has somehow fallen in love with the speckled wall opposite it.

The mirror's accuracy

The mirror stresses how accurately it reflects anything that is put in front of it. It is 'exact' and 'truthful'. It shows each person and object 'Just as it is'. The mirror claims to 'swallow' all it sees. This is a metaphor for how mirrors create the illusion of depth. The reflection of a given object seems to be inside a double of the room we're standing in, as if it's been 'swallowed' or taken inside the mirror's world.

The mirror claims to have no feelings whatsoever towards those who examine themselves in its surface. It neither 'loves' nor 'dislikes' them, and has no biases or prejudices towards them: 'I have no preconceptions.' It doesn't blur or alter reflections in order to flatter those it likes or hurt the feelings of those it hates. Everything it shows is 'unmisted by love or dislike'.

Very often, people are disappointed by what they see when they look in the mirror. Most people want to look younger, thinner and sexier. The mirror, however, refuses to be blamed for any dismay or disappointment people might feel when they examine themselves in its surface. It is not 'cruel', having no interest in making them feel bad about themselves. It is simply being 'truthful', doing its job of reflecting the world as it really is: 'I am not cruel, only truthful'.

The mirror and its owner

Stanza 2 describes the relationship between the mirror and the woman who owns it. This woman seems to be mentally anguished. She is regularly gripped by fits of loneliness and despair that involve 'tears and an agitation of hands'. She spends a great deal of time staring in the mirror, gazing at her reflection in an attempt to understand herself.

We get the impression that the mirror looks forward to her daily visits, and would be lonely without them: 'Each morning it is her face that replaces the darkness'. The mirror acts almost like the woman's faithful servant, loyally continuing to reflect her back, even when she turns away from it: 'I see her back, and reflect it faithfully'.

The woman also needs the mirror: 'I am important to her'. The mirror is important to the woman in a casual, everyday sense (how else could she check her appearance before going out?). Yet it is also important to her in a psychological sense. She returns to the mirror again and again, gazing into it in an attempt to reach self-understanding – to find out 'what she really is'.

An unequal relationship

We get a sense, however, that the relationship between the mirror and the woman is an unequal one. While the mirror is confined to one place, the woman enjoys the freedom to move around: 'She comes and goes'.

The mirror describes the woman sitting in candlelight or gazing out of her window at the moon: 'Then she turns to those liars, the candles or the moon'. There is a sense in these lines that it is jealous of the candles and the moon, resentful of the fact that the woman is looking at them instead of into its own reflective glass. The mirror, it seems, feels hurt and betrayed when the woman turns away from it. Yet even when she does so, it remains faithful to her, loyally reflecting her back: 'I see her back, and reflect it faithfully'.

All the mirror gets in return for this loyalty is the opportunity to witness the woman's distress: 'She rewards me with tears'. According to several critics, the tone here is one of bitterness and sarcasm, as if the mirror feels the sight of the woman's tears isn't much of a 'reward' for its faithful service.

A terrible fish

The mirror compares itself to a lake. The comparison between the mirror and a lake is obvious. Like a lake, the mirror has a flat, reflective surface. It is possible, on a calm day, to study one's reflection in a lake just as it is in a mirror.

The mirror has recorded the slow ageing of the woman. When the woman looks at herself in the mirror, she can see traces of the child she once was. Those traces, however, become fainter and fainter as time goes on. The mirror uses a striking metaphor to describe this process, saying that the woman 'has drowned a young girl' in its depths.

Every day, the woman wakes up and looks in the mirror, and every day an older version of herself looks back. With each passing day she sees that the old woman she will one day become is closer and closer. Another powerful metaphor is used to depict this process, the mirror declaring that old age is a fish swimming out of the lake's depths and rising up towards her: 'in me an old woman/ Rises toward her day after day, like a terrible fish'.

FOCUS ON STYLE

Tone

An important feature of this poem is the shifts in tone it contains. At times, the mirror seems confident and assured. It is convinced of its accuracy and truthfulness, and it even thinks of itself as a kind of god that swallows all it sees. Yet there are also moments when the mirror's tone is one of need and sorrow. There is something almost pathetic about the way it seems to have fallen in love with the piece of wall opposite it. A similarly needy tone is evident in its jealousy of the candles and the moon and in how it remains faithful to the woman even when she turns away from it, loyally reflecting her back.

Metaphor, Simile, Figures of Speech

An interesting feature of 'Mirror' is its use of 'personification', where an inanimate object is given human characteristics. The mirror is presented as a 'thinking being', a character with thoughts, ideas and emotions. The poem endows the mirror with human traits such as truthfulness, faithfulness and jealousy. It even has a relationship, of sorts, with its owner, the rather disturbed woman on whose wall it hangs.

Form

The fact that the poem has two nine-line stanzas seems to reflect its title. There is a sense in which each stanza reflects, or mirrors, the other. Several critics have pointed out how the poem's opening stanza is like a child's riddle. If the poem was stripped of its title, it would be a challenge to work out what object was speaking.

Vivid and Unsettling Imagery

There are several metaphors and similes in this poem that exhibit Plath's customary invention. Using a fine metaphor, the mirror compares itself to the 'eye of a little god'. The mirror compares itself to a lake and the woman to someone on the lake shore staring into the water's murky depths.

The mirror uses a striking metaphor to describe the process of getting older, saying that the woman 'has drowned a young girl' in its depths. Another powerful metaphor is used to depict this process, the mirror declaring that an old woman is swimming out of the lake's depths and rising up towards her: 'in me an old woman/ Rises toward her day after day'. In a final striking simile, this swimming old woman is compared to a 'terrible fish'.

The mirror depicts itself as a kind of god: 'I am … The eye of a little god, four-cornered'. This comparison is not as strange as it might first sound – people, after all, pay an almost religious devotion to their reflections. We spend a great deal of time and energy in an effort to keep ourselves young and beautiful, to make sure the mirror is kind to us when we stare into it.

This description brings to mind the other meaning of the word 'exact', which is to demand payment. The mirror is a kind of god that exacts tribute or payment from those who worship it. The poem suggests that we are willing to pay a high price in sweat and money in order that the mirror will show us what we want to see: 'I am silver and exact'.

THEMES

MENTAL ANGUISH

The woman in the poem is gripped by a fit of loneliness or despair, examining herself in the looking glass as she cries and wrings her hands: 'She rewards me with tears and an agitation of hand'. We get a sense that much of the woman's turmoil stems from the fact that she has lost her way in life, has lost her sense of her own identity. She gazes into the mirror in an attempt to locate and reconnect with her true self. It's as if staring at her own reflection allows her to explore the depths of her own psyche and discover what really makes her who she is: 'Now I am a lake. A woman bends over me,/ Searching my reaches'.

Feelings of inadequacy and worthlessness are also explored in 'Mirror', where the speaker looks at her reflection with 'tears and an agitation of hands'. She turns away to the soft glow of candles and the moon, as if she does not like what she sees in the mirror. Perhaps she feels inadequate about her appearance, her personality or the way she is living her life. The notion of inadequacy brings to mind the depiction of the mirror as something threatening and menacing: as something that swallows all it sees, as an exacting god or as a lake with treacherous depths. Self-examination, the poem reminds us, can be a dangerous business, leading to all sorts of negative emotions.

FEMININITY AND MOTHERHOOD

It is also possible to read 'Mirror' as a comment on the pressure women feel to meet certain standards of beauty, pressure that comes from films, magazines and advertising (nowadays, it could be argued that men are also subject to such pressure – unlike when Plath wrote the poem). We see this in the depiction of the mirror as a kind of god that exacts tribute, or payment. Women, the poem suggests, will pay a high price in order that the mirror will be kind to them. The psychological dangers associated with this pressure are suggested by the description of the mirror having treacherous depths and swallowing all it sees.

POETIC INSPIRATION

Plath felt under pressure to conform to the ideal of the perfect 1950s American young woman: to marry, have children and be a successful mother and housewife. Yet, she also harboured the burning ambition to be a great writer. She worried that these two goals were incompatible, writing in her diary: 'Will I be a secretary – a self-rationalising housewife, secretly jealous of my husband's ability to grow intellectually and professionally while I am impeded – will I submerge my embarrassing desires and aspirations, refuse to face myself, and go either mad or become neurotic?'

'Mirror' depicts a situation where the front, or facade, of the perfect housewife is in danger of choking the artist within. The poem's speaker is in danger of forgetting about the artist she really is, and gazes into the mirror's depths in a desperate attempt to reconnect with her own creativity.

Plath felt that in order to be a true poet, one had to explore one's conscious mind, delving into the darkest depths of the psyche. 'Mirror' explores this theme. The woman looking into the mirror's depths can be taken as a metaphor for this kind of self-exploration.

Finisterre

LINE BY LINE

Finisterre, which means land's end, is the westernmost tip of Brittany, in north-west France. Plath visited Finisterre in 1960 with her husband, the poet Ted Hughes. Finisterre is a bleak and rugged headland frequently battered by high winds and stormy seas. The treacherous waters below it have caused so many shipwrecks and drownings that it is known as the bay of the dead.

The land

Finisterre is depicted as a 'gloomy' place: it is a headland of grim, black cliffs. These cliffs are described as 'admonitory', meaning they seem to warn those who see them to stay away. The only plant-life that grows on them are weak and withering 'trefoils', little three-leaved plants that are 'close to death'.

Rocky outcrops protrude from the water. They are worn and brittle, like the 'knuckled and rheumatic' fingers of an old man. Other large rocks lurk threateningly beneath the water's surface: they 'hide their grudges under the water'. Furthermore, many smaller rocks seem to have been 'dumped' into the ocean. These, too, contribute to the bay's gloominess: 'Now it is only gloomy, a dump of rocks'.

The sea

The ocean is presented as menacing and aggressive. It seems terrifyingly vast: 'With no bottom, or anything on the other side of it'. It is an 'exploding' force that 'cannons' into the coastline. It makes an endless and oppressive roaring sound – what Plath describes as a 'doom-noise'.

The ocean's erosion of the land is depicted as a military campaign. It slowly reduces the cliffs to little rocks that litter the seascape like corpses, casualties of its endless assault on the coastline: 'Leftover soldiers from old, messy wars'. The description of the sea 'cannoning' and 'exploding' reinforces our sense of it as a hostile military force.

The poem's opening statement, 'This was the land's end', can be read in two ways. On one level it refers to the fact that Finisterre is one of continental Europe's westernmost points. On another level, however, it can be read as stating that this was the end of the land's existence. The sea seems filled with such apocalyptic fury that it threatens to swallow the entire coastline.

The souls of the drowned

Plath is reminded of all the people who have drowned in the bay of the dead. She imagines that the souls of these poor people remain somehow trapped in the bay long after their bodies have passed away:

- She imagines their souls being imprisoned forever in these bleak waters, bobbing and tossing on its raging waves: 'rolled in the doom-noise of the sea'.
- She imagines that patches of white surf on the ocean's surface are the faces of these drowned people: 'Whitened by the faces of the drowned'.
- She imagines that the mist rising from the ocean is composed of these drowned souls.
- She imagines this mist of ghosts drifting sorrowfully, aimlessly and hopelessly around the bay: 'They go up without hope, like sighs'.
- When the poet walks into the mist, she imagines the ghosts wrapping themselves around her in a kind of cocoon and penetrating her mouth: 'they stuff my mouth with cotton'.
- When she walks out of the mist, she imagines the ghosts release her again: 'they free me'.

When she leaves the fog there are beads of water on her cheeks: 'I am beaded with tears'. This may simply be mist that has condensed on her face. However, it is also possible that the poet is actually crying, weeping out of pity for those who have drowned over the years off Finisterre's treacherous coast.

Our Lady of the Shipwrecked

The poet notices a pair of large marble statues near the cliff side. One depicts the Virgin Mary. She has a serene and holy smile on her face: 'Her lips sweet with divinity'. She is depicted wearing a windblown pink dress, and walking purposefully in the direction of the ocean: 'striding toward the horizon'.

The other statue depicts a sailor: 'A marble sailor kneels at her foot'. He is depicted kneeling before the Virgin and praying to her in a 'distracted' manner. In this instance, 'distractedly' probably means desperately and despairingly rather than casually and inattentively. A local woman has come to pray at the statues. However, she seems to focus her prayers more on the statue of the sailor than on the statue of the Virgin herself: 'A peasant woman in black/ Is praying to the monument of the sailor praying'.

The Virgin Mary is sometimes referred to as 'Our Lady of the Shipwrecked' because she is believed to help sailors and those who have been lost at sea. Plath, however, portrays the Virgin as ignoring the prayers of the sailor and the peasant woman: 'She does not hear what the sailor or the peasant is saying'. She is far more interested in admiring the ocean before her than in listening to such prayers: 'She is in love with the beautiful formlessness of the sea'.

Gifts and postcards

The locals also have stalls in the vicinity of the Finisterre headland, where they sell postcards and crêpes to tourists. They urge the poet to eat some freshly prepared crêpes before the sea wind cools them too much: 'These are our crêpes. Eat them before they blow cold'. It is not clear whether the locals are attempting to sell the poet crêpes or are offering them for free. They also sell little trinkets, which are made by beading seashells onto lengths of lace: 'pretty trinkets … necklaces and toy ladies'.

These shell-and-lace trinkets 'flap' in the stiff sea breeze and have to be weighed down with conches to stop them blowing away: 'Gull-colored laces flap in the sea drafts … The peasants anchor them with conches'. The peasants tell Plath about the shells used to manufacture these trinkets. They are found 'hidden' in the sea around Finisterre. However, they originate in a faraway, tropical sea: they come 'from another place, tropical and blue,/ We have never been to'. The poet marvels at the thought of the ocean carrying the shells thousands of miles from some tropical paradise to the bleak shores of western Brittany.

FOCUS ON STYLE

Psychic Landscapes

There are many poems where Plath creates what she described as 'psychic landscapes'. She uses a scene from nature or an element of the natural world in order to convey an inner state of mind. As we have seen, this tendency is evident in 'Finisterre'. The description of the bay can be taken to suggest a storm of emotional turmoil, a state of complete mental numbness or perhaps even both.

Vivid and Unsettling Imagery

Plath depicts the land and sea as being involved in an endless and brutal conflict: 'old messy wars'. The white surf on the sea's surface is compared to the faces of people who have drowned: 'Whitened by the faces of the drowned'. Rocky outcrops protruding from the water are described as fingers: 'the last fingers, knuckled and rheumatic,/ Cramped on nothing'. Smaller rocks are described as dead or wounded soldiers: 'Leftover soldiers from old messy wars'. The mist the poet walks into is compared to cotton: 'They stuff my mouth with cotton'.

Metaphor, Simile, Figures of Speech

There are several instances of personification in the poem. Personification occurs when we apply human qualities to inanimate objects or natural phenomena. In this poem, large rocks are described as having 'grudges'. The mists are depicted as human souls drifting mournfully around the bay. The description of the cliffs as 'admonitory', as issuing a warning, is arguably another instance of personification.

Personification also occurs in the depiction of the statues. The Virgin is depicted as a real person. She strides towards the ocean. She is capable of ignoring and of answering prayers. She is enthralled by the sea's formlessness. The statue of the sailor, too, is personified: it is depicted as praying 'distractedly' to the Virgin.

In line 4, Plath describes how the ocean has 'no bottom, or anything on the other side of it'. Of course, she isn't suggesting that the sea is literally bottomless or endless – rather, she uses hyperbole, or poetic exaggeration, to convey its enormity.

MENTAL ANGUISH

In 'Finisterre', the sea's violent fury is often taken to represent Plath's tumultuous mental state. The ocean is presented as a terrifyingly vast 'exploding' force that 'cannons' into the coastline, making an endless and oppressive roaring sound; a 'doom-noise'.

But some readers feel that 'Finisterre' expresses feelings of numbness rather than turmoil. The poem describes the ghosts of the drowned drifting eternally around the bay of the dead. They float endlessly and hopelessly: 'They go up without hope, like sighs'. Their grey, limbo-like existence suggests the mental limbo and emotional deadness that Plath so dreaded.

There are also several instances in Plath's poetry where she expresses what might be described as self-destructive thoughts or desires. Such desires are arguably expressed in 'Finisterre' when the poet describes herself walking into the sea-mist. She describes how this mist 'erases' the rocks and yet she enters it. It's as if on some level she herself desires to be erased from existence.

There is, however, a slight note of hope in 'Finisterre'. The peasants mention a peaceful place 'tropical and blue' far from the furious waters of the bay where they live. This suggests that the poet believes an end to her mental turmoil is possible, that she can enter a new and tranquil mental space. Yet as the poem concludes, we are left with the impression that such inner peace is a distant prospect, as distant as the faraway waters to which the peasants have 'never been'.

ORDER AND CHAOS

Many of Plath's poems deal with the notion of order and chaos. In this poem, the sea is associated with chaos. Perhaps its key feature is its 'formlessness'. It is presented as a vast, shapeless void churning chaotically. Order, on the other hand, is represented by the solidity and stability of the coastline.

The poem shows chaos slowly encroaching on order as the sea reduces the coastline to nothing. It breaks down the mighty cliffs of Finisterre until they are worn, rheumatic fingers, then little rocks, then only part of its formless drifting. Human beings, too, are reduced to nothing – or next to nothing – by the ocean. Those it drowns are left as wisps of fog, like lost, pathetic ghosts.

In a sense, this process is presented in a negative light. The poet seems horrified by the violence and menace of the raging sea's assault upon the land. Yet there is also a sense in which the poet finds the chaos represented by the ocean attractive and intoxicating. Its formlessness, after all, is described as a 'beautiful' formlessness. To Plath, then, chaos is simultaneously both horrific and attractive.

FEMININITY AND MOTHERHOOD

'Many of Plath's poems deal with the difficulties of motherhood and touch upon the idea of mothers failing their children. It is present in 'Finisterre' through the depiction of Our Lady of the Shipwrecked. Our Lady is often thought of as the 'mother' of the human race. Yet in this poem she is depicted as having failed her children. Despite her serene and beautiful smile, 'her lips sweet with divinity', she is cold, distant and uncaring. She no longer hears the pleas of those who pray to her, either of the despairing sailor or of the peasant woman. She is unmoved by the plight of the lost souls that drift around the place like mists (unlike the poet, who emerges from their fog 'beaded in tears').

POETIC INSPIRATION

To write poetry, Plath believed, it was necessary to explore the darkest recesses of the mind, to explore the deepest reaches of the soul. Plath felt probing the unconscious mind was a risky business, for it risked disturbing all kinds of inner demons. In this poem, the ocean is often taken as a metaphor for the unconscious mind. It is presented as a place of great danger, furious and treacherous, with 'no bottom, or anything on the other side of it'.

Yet just as the peasants venture into the ocean and extract little shells from it, so the true poet must venture into the depths of his or her own psyche. Just as the peasants produce little toys from the fruit of their explorations, so the poet might create a 'pretty trinket' from her own mental explorations – a trinket that would, of course, take the form of a poem.

In a postcard to her mother, written during a trip to Finisterre in 1961, Plath wrote: 'We are sitting in a little "crêperie" in Douarnenez, a lovely fishing port in Finisterre waiting for our crepes - a lacey thin pancake served with butter or jam or honey & cider to drink, for our Sunday supper. We have been swimming in clear Atlantic water, eating mussels, cockles, lobster & giant crayfish - 5 course dinners for less than $3 for the two of us'.

Pheasant

LINE BY LINE

Killing

The poet's husband, it seems, has been planning to kill the pheasant, no doubt convinced that it would make a fine dinner. He has had a particular day in mind for butchering the bird. And now that day has come: 'You said you would kill it this morning'. The poet herself, however, is having second thoughts about this plan and urges her husband to let the bird live: 'Do not kill it'.

Appearance

The bird, on this particular morning, is 'pacing' around a hill behind the house where an elm tree grows (this is the same tree that features in the poem 'Elm'). The poet watches it striding through the hill's 'uncut grass'.

The pheasant, according to the poet, has a most striking appearance. She describes how the pheasant's head 'juts' or jerks forward with every step it takes. Its head is a deep or 'dark' green in colour, which contrasts, no doubt, with its multi-coloured feathers. The term 'odd', meanwhile, captures how the features of certain species of fowl can exhibit an alien, almost reptilian, quality.

Living with an extraordinary sight all too often means taking it for granted. After a while, we don't even notice its splendour anymore. But this isn't true in the case of the poet and the pheasant. She is 'still' startled by the sight of this extraordinary

bird every time she sees it wandering around her garden: 'It startles me still'. It 'is something', the poet declares, 'to own a pheasant'. This, she suggests, is not a situation to be disregarded or taken lightly. In fact, it is a privilege to have such a creature present in one's home.

The phrase it 'is something … to be visited at all', meanwhile, hints at Plath's psychological state. It suggests the loneliness and isolation she might have experienced while living in the countryside, far from friends and acquaintances in London. It also hints, perhaps, at a sense of low self-esteem. Maybe the poet feels so down and lacking in confidence that she is surprised that anyone or anything would ever want to come and visit her.

Reasons

The poet engages in some self-analysis, trying to work out why she is so reluctant to see the bird slaughtered. The poet is adamant that she is not a 'mystical' person. She does not want to spare the pheasant because she believes it has a soul or 'spirit' of some kind.

Perhaps her reluctance stems from the fact that pheasants are 'rare' in the United Kingdom: 'Is it its rareness, then?' The poet, however, rejects this explanation. She imagines having a 'dozen' or even a 'hundred' pheasants. She feels that even in such circumstances she would be reluctant to lose a single bird: 'But a dozen would be worth having,/ A hundred, on that hill'. The bird, she concludes, simply has 'a right' to be here. This is 'its element', the setting in which it belongs. The poet in fact seems to feel that the pheasant has a greater right to be here than she and her husband do. She seems to suspect that the countryside belongs more to such creatures than it does to human beings like herself.

The pheasant, too, on some instinctive level, seems to realise that this is 'its element' and that it has a 'right' to be here. This causes it to exhibit a 'kingliness', a regal and commanding demeanour. It wanders around the garden, as if it were the true owner or ruler of the property. This sense of ownership is reinforced by the poet's recollections of the previous winter. It's as if the pheasant was marking its territory by dragging its tail through the snowfall. It stamped its 'big foot' on the fallen snow like a king stamping some royal declaration.

Plath's description of the property's courtyard as 'our court' further reinforces our impression of the bird's regal nature. The pheasant, we sense, is very much the king, while the poet and her husband are merely its courtiers (here Plath is playing on Court Green, which was the name of property in question).

The poet recalls a particular morning from the previous winter when the 'court' or courtyard of the property was covered in snow. She recalls how the footprints of 'sparrow and starling' had created a 'crosshatch' pattern on the snow fall. The traces left by the pheasant, however, stood out among those left by the other birds. She recalls noticing the 'print' of the pheasant's 'big foot'. She also recalls the 'track' left by its tail as it dragged through the 'pallor' or paleness of the fallen snow. This, according to the poet, was a sight that filled her with 'wonder'.

Back to beauty

The poet focuses once more on the bird's extraordinary appearance. Her simple declaration that the bird has 'such a good shape' wonderfully captures the pleasure she derives from studying this creature. Some aspects of the natural world, such as the pheasant, have a shape, a combination of contours, symmetry and proportion, that is 'good' to look at. They are simply pleasing to the eye in a manner that defies rational analysis.

The phrase 'so vivid', meanwhile, refers to its multi-coloured feathers and features. The pheasant, we remind ourselves, has coppery gold plumage, a dark green head and long, reddish-brown and black tail.

The poet uses a metaphor from Greek mythology, comparing the pheasant to a 'cornucopia', which was a horn-shaped vessel that over-flowed with fruits, flowers and other delights. The description of the pheasant as a 'little cornucopia', therefore, captures the abundance and variety of the colours it displays. The poet watches the pheasant 'sunning' itself in a patch of narcissus flowers. Then it 'unclaps' or opens its wings. It flaps its wings repeatedly, producing a 'loud' whirring sound, and flies up into one of the elm tree's branches. It settles there in what the poet describes a relaxed and 'easy' manner.

NATURE

This poem, like many by Plath, highlights the remarkable beauty of the natural world. The poet takes great pleasure in observing this creature, with its 'good shape' and 'vivid' colours, as it wanders around Court Green. She relishes everything from its 'odd, dark head' to its 'unclapped' wings, which, using a memorable simile, she compares to a brown 'leaf'. The poet enjoys watching it 'sunning' itself in summer and finds wonder in the tracks it leaves during the wintertime. The poem, therefore, concludes with a heartfelt plea that the pheasant be left alone rather than butchered and eaten: 'Let be, let be'.

This poem also highlights the complex nature of the relationship between humanity and the natural world. We human beings partition the countryside into properties and plots of land. We turn fields into gardens. We even kill the countryside's wildlife for food and sport.
But the countryside, the poem suggests, will never truly belong to us – it will always belong, instead, to the creatures of the natural world. The pheasant, therefore, representing all of nature, has a 'right' to be there and presides over the property as if it were its king or rightful owner. The poet herself, on the other hand, feels that she is trespassing as if she, as a human being, has no real right to own or occupy this land. She moves 'stupidly', suggesting that she, unlike the pheasant, is not in her natural 'element' here.

The poem seems to hint at a future in which humanity is no longer around, where we, through our short-sightedness and stupidity, have eliminated ourselves from the planet. We can imagine the grass, weeds and trees slowly reclaiming a property like Court Green. We can imagine the pheasant and other woodland creatures retaking their rightful place as the rulers of the countryside.

FOCUS ON STYLE

Vivid and Unsettling Imagery

'Pheasant' features several startling and memorable images:
- There is the image of the markings left by the various birds on the pristine coat of snow and the track produced by the pheasant's tail running across the 'crosshatch' left by the feet of smaller birds, such as sparrows and starlings.
- Another startling image occurs when the poet imagines dozens or even hundreds of pheasants 'Crossing and recrossing' the hill in a festival of colour.
- Equally memorable is the image of the pheasant rising from the narcissus flowers to settle in the elm tree.

The nature imagery in 'Pheasant', it should be noted, is elegant and uplifting and lacks the disturbing, violent quality found in other poems by Plath, such as 'Elm' or 'Finisterre'.

431

Elm

Plath with her children in Court Green in the summer of 1962

LINE BY LINE

In 1962 Plath was living, along with her husband Ted Hughes, in a house called Court Green in rural Devon. There was a large wych elm tree on a hill at the back of the property, which Plath found fascinating. The same tree, it should be noted, also features in the poem 'Pheasant'.

In this poem, Plath personifies the elm tree, imagining that it is capable of thought, speech dreams and emotions. The phrase 'she says' in the opening line indicates that the elm is expressing itself to the poet. The poet then relates its words to us, her readers.

The poem was written during the summer of 1962, which was a difficult period for the poet. It was becoming clear that Plath's marriage was in serious trouble and would not survive. This state of affairs filled Plath with mental and emotional anguish and the heartache she experienced is the subject of the elm's imagined speech or soliloquy.

The bottom

Plath imagines that the elm talks to her about 'the bottom'. Plath, as we have seen, is experiencing a psychological crisis. But she's terrified that things will become even worse, that she will reach what might be described as 'rock bottom', an extreme emotional state of utter loneliness and despair.

- The elm claims to know about Plath's fear of the bottom: 'It is what you fear'.
- The elm claims to have experienced the bottom itself, to have experienced utter loneliness and despair: 'I know the bottom, she says'.
- The elm, then, claims to have no fear of this extreme emotional state, having already experienced and survived it: 'I do not fear it: I have been there'.

There is a pun or play on words in these lines. The elm knows the bottom both psychologically, in the sense of loneliness and despair, and literally, in the sense that its main root or tap root has reached down through the soil to the very bedrock of the earth: 'I know the bottom, she says. I know it with my great tap root'.

The sounds made by the elm

Plath imagines that the elm is tormenting her in various different ways. The elm, for instance, claims that the wind in its branches will remind Plath of the sea. This, it seems, is a sound that Plath associates with sorrow and dissatisfaction: 'Is it the sea you hear in me,/ Its dissatisfactions?'

Indeed, Plath's poetry often presents the sea as a menacing presence, associated with 'formlessness' and destruction. It tends to represent the dissolution of order into chaos, meaning into meaninglessness, life into death (we see this, for example, in 'Finisterre').

The elm also claims that the wind in its branches will remind Plath of the 'voice of nothing'. This, it seems, is a sound that Plath associates with the bout of 'madness' she suffered during the 1950s. The elm suggests – or maybe threatens – that the sound of the wind passing through its branches will resemble a blank and relentless static hiss, reminding Plath of the terrible inner emptiness she endured during that period of mental ill-health. Plath imagines that elm comments on the failure of her marriage. It does so in a brutal and unsympathetic manner. 'Love', the elm declares, 'is a shadow' – a worthless and insubstantial fantasy. The elm mocks Plath's need for this illusion and her distress at being abandoned by her husband: 'How you lie and cry after it'.

The elm emphasises that Plath's relationship is at an end. Love, it declares, has left Plath's life like a prize racehorse that escapes and vanishes into the night: 'it has gone off, like a horse'. The elm will allow its branches to knock together, so that their sound resembles that of a galloping horse: 'these are its hooves'. This sound, it suggests, will torture Plath, reminding her of how she has been abandoned by her husband and by love itself.

The elm threatens to produce this percussive, repetitive sound all night long: 'All night I shall gallop thus, impetuously'. Plath will experience this sound as being incredibly loud, as if her pillow were the turf across which a horse is galloping. It's a sound that will utterly numb her mind, leaving her head feeling like a piece of stone: 'Till your head is a stone, your pillow a little turf'.

The tortures endured by the elm

Plath imagines that the elm is describing the various tortures it has suffered. The elm, for instance, claims to have experienced a bizarre form of acid rain. These toxic showers, the elm suggest, made 'the sound of poisons', causing an unpleasant sizzling noise when they fell upon the elm's leaves. They have caused the elm to produce poisonous berries that are a metallic white in colour: 'this is the fruit of it: tin-white, like arsenic'.

The elm claims to have endured sunsets that give off an unbearable and unnatural heat. It describes these sunsets as an 'atrocity', suggesting they are occasions of extraordinary suffering. These sunsets have 'Scorched' the entire elm, even its roots that lie buried in the ground. They have left the elm's filaments – its twigs and branches – red, dry and lifeless so that they resemble 'wires'.

The elm claims to have experienced a wind of extraordinary force and violence. This terrible gale tears off the elm's branches and sends them flying dangerously through the air: 'Now I break up in pieces that fly about like clubs'. In response to such an onslaught, the elm has no choice but to cry out in agony: 'A wind of such violence/ Will tolerate no bystanding: I must shriek'.

The elm claims to have been tormented by moon's brightness or 'radiance'. The moon's light 'scathes' or hurts the elm, as if it were a kind of laser beam that assaults the elm from above. The moon, the elm declares, is travelling on a low trajectory across the sky. It deliberately snags itself in the elm's branches. Then it continues moving, pulling and dragging the elm's branches as it does so. The moon, according to the elm, does so because it is jealous of the elm's fertility: 'She would drag me/ Cruelly, being barren'.

The elm, as we have seen, is presented as a female presence. The moon, too, is traditionally depicted as feminine. The moon, however, is an utterly 'barren' environment where nothing can grow. The elm, despite the tortures it has endured, retains fertility of a kind and manages to produce 'tin-white' fruit.

The elm, however, realises that it is the one at fault in this collision, having accidentally snared the moon in its branches: 'perhaps I have caught her'. The elm releases the moon and lets it continue on its nightly journey: 'I let her go, I let her go'. These lines represent a wonderful flight of fancy. We can imagine how Plath, looking out the window of Court Green, might have seen the moon framed against the elm tree. We can imagine how it might have looked to her that the moon was actually enmeshed in the elm's branches. We can imagine how her poetic imagination kicked in, allowing her to craft this bizarre but memorable confrontation.

The presence in the elm's branches

The elm claims that it is haunted by a 'dark' presence that dwells within its branches. In many respects this presence is bird-like. It is 'feathery' and has 'hooks' or talons. It rests each day and each night it 'flaps out' of the elm to hunt. The elm is desperately frightened by this presence: 'I am terrified by this dark thing'. She thinks of it as 'malign' or evil. She seems horrified by the thought of this presence sleeping within it: 'All day I feel its soft, feathery turnings, its malignity'.

The elm speaks about love

The elm studies the cloud formations in the night sky above and notes how individual clouds are rarely there for long. Some 'pass' across the sky and drift out of sight. Others 'disperse', dissolving in the wind. And once a given cloud formation breaks up it is 'irretrievable'; it can never be recovered or reformed. And love, according to the elm, is just as fleeting as these cloud formations: 'Are those the faces of love, those pale irretrievables?' Relationships, it declares, like clouds passing and dispersing, are destined to be transitory and short-lived.

Previously, the elm mocked the poet for caring about love, for allowing a failed relationship to distress her. Now, however, the elm admits that it too is troubled by love. The elm, like the poet, 'agitates [its] heart', torturing itself over some departed lover. It has allowed love, something no more substantial than a cloud or shadow, to bring it misery.

The elm seems to associate knowledge with suffering. At the beginning of the poem, the elm claims to 'know' the bottom, to have experienced the worst that can possibly be experienced. By the end of the poem, however, she seems to feel even more knowledge – even greater suffering – might lie in store. The elm declares itself 'incapable' of this knowledge, as if it is utterly exhausted from suffering and can endure no more suffering.

Conclusion

The elm focuses once more on the dark presence that dwells within its leaves. It describes how this creature might peer out from a 'strangle' or tangle of branches. The creature's face is described as 'murderous', suggesting that it has a violent and malevolent facial expression. Acid drips from its mouth, the droplets hissing or sizzling when they touch the ground: 'Its snaky acids hiss'. Merely looking at this face, the elm declares, freezes or 'petrifies the will'. Anyone who looks this creature in the eye will be utterly frozen with horror, incapable of thought or action.

FOCUS ON STYLE

Vivid and Unsettling Imagery

Plath's fears of a nuclear conflict between the USSR and United States greatly influenced the poem's imagery. The intense, blazing heat endured by the elm suggests less a normal sunset than the red sky caused by a nuclear explosion, which could, of course, be regarded as the 'sunset' of the world. Similarly, the unstoppably violent wind that tortures the elm calls to mind the force of a nuclear blast. The poisonous rain, meanwhile, suggests the aftermath of a nuclear disaster or of a comparable environmental catastrophe.

There are also several references to medical procedures in the poem. Lines 25 to 26, for instance, describe how the moon is left 'diminished and flat' as if it had been subjected to 'radical surgery'. This is surgery that involves the removal of a great deal of muscle tissue, or even an entire limb. In line 17, meanwhile, the description of the tree being 'scorched to the root' in line 17 was inspired by Plath's experiences of electro-convulsive therapy.

Plath's flair for bizarre and nightmarish imagery is also evident when the elm complains that it has somehow been experiencing the poet's 'bad dreams'. It's as if the poet's nightmares had been beamed, via some strange psychic link, into the elm's consciousness. Indeed, the elm complains that the poet's bad dreams 'possess it', suggesting that they take over its life and even its mind: 'How your bad dreams possess and endow me'. To endow someone, usually, is to offer them a gift of some kind. But the endowment offered by the speaker, in this case, is less a gift than a curse.

THEMES

MENTAL ANGUISH

'Elm' is a masterpiece of personification, one where Plath uses the figure of the elm tree to express her own mental anguish. The elm, as we've seen, suffers various torments: being lashed by poisonous rain, burned by the sun, whipped by the wind, then 'dragged' and 'scathed' by the moon. These torments serve as powerful metaphors for Plath's own mental ordeals, reflecting the tortured state of mind she experienced around the time of the poem's composition. 'Elm', it must be said, also offers a very beak depiction of romantic love. Love is presented as something transitory and insubstantial, like a shadow or a cloud. We are most foolish, the poem suggests, to 'agitate' our hearts for this illusion. But, of course, we can't stop ourselves from doing so.

The elm, as we've seen is 'inhabited' by a strange bird-like creature, just as Plath's mind is inhabited by depressive tendencies. Plath, then, sees her depression embodied in this creature. The creature's face as we've seen, 'petrifies the will' of those who look on it, making it impossible to think or act. Depression, similarly, compromises the will-power and enthusiasm of those who suffer from it. The creature's 'snaky acids', it must be said, powerfully represent how depression can corrode and dissolve our mental health.

The creature, according to the elm, is associated with 'faults', which suggests cracks or fault lines. We might imagine here fractures appearing on the surface of a piece of wood or pottery. These faults or cracks are described as 'isolate', suggesting that to begin with they are quite far apart from one another. They are also described as 'slow', suggesting that they only gradually expand. Eventually, however, the cracks spread and combine, causing the object to fall apart. These faults and cracks, of course, serve as another powerful metaphor for depression. The mental damage caused by depression, just like the physical damage caused by these cracks, can be 'slow' and 'isolate' at first, but over time it can lead to complete mental collapse.

The poem's dominant emotion, then, is that of terror. Plath, we sense, is grappling with a series of distinct but overlapping fears:

- She fears 'the bottom', a state of utter loneliness and despair.
- She fears returning to a state of madness with its terrifying 'voice of nothing'.
- She fears that her depressive tendencies will overwhelm her mind, petrifying her 'will' and leaving her incapable of action.
- She fears that her depressive tendencies will cause her very psyche to crack or fall apart.
- She fears that these faults, this slow but relentless cracking, might lead to self-harm or even suicidal tendencies: 'These are the isolate, slow faults/ That kill, that kill, that kill'. And Plath's fears, in this regard of course, were to prove tragically prophetic.

The Arrival of the Bee Box

LINE BY LINE

The poet has just received a 'clean wood box' that is full of bees. Tomorrow, she will release the bees into the hive she has prepared for them. Tonight, however, she must keep the box in her house: 'I have to live with it overnight'.

The box is square in shape ('square as a chair') and is quite heavy: 'almost too heavy to lift'. It is 'locked', and its only opening is a small grid, or grille, for ventilation: 'There are no windows … no exit'. The bees inside it produce a loud buzzing 'din'.

Reaction to the box

The poet reacts to the box with a feeling of dread and horror. She thinks of it as 'dangerous'. She seems to associate it with death, referring to it as a 'coffin'. We get a sense in the opening line that she is regretful or even somehow surprised that she purchased the bees in the first place.

Though the box horrifies the poet, it also fascinates her. She feels compelled to stay near it: 'I can't keep away from it'. She puts her 'eye to the grid', or grille, and attempts to peer into it. She lays her ear on its surface and listens to the bees buzzing within. The poet's reaction to the box, then, is complex and contradictory. It seems to repulse her and attract her at the same time.

Reaction to the bees

The box's interior is 'dark, dark', but when she looks through the grille she can just make out the bees scrambling and 'clambering' around within it. According to the poet, the bees look like the tiny shrunken hands of dead Africans. She finds the sound they make even more horrifying and upsetting than their appearance: 'It is the noise that appalls me most of all'. She compares their buzzing to a strange language full of 'unintelligible syllables'. She associates the bees with rage and anger, thinking of them 'as a box of maniacs'. They clamber 'angrily' and the sound they make is 'furious'.

The poet is highly conscious that a swarm of bees can pose a threat to a human being. In this regard, she compares the bees to a rioting crowd in ancient Roman times: 'It is like a Roman mob'. On his own, each member of a Roman mob was powerless; as a rioting group, however, they could threaten the stability of the entire city. Similarly, a single bee can do little harm to a human being. An entire swarm, however, could easily sting a person to death: 'Small, taken one by one, but my god, together!'.

The poet fears that once released, the bees will turn on her and overwhelm her: 'How can I let them out?' It took a powerful ruler like Caesar to master the mobs of Rome. Similarly, it will take a skilled and confident beekeeper to control the bees once they have been released from the box. The poet, however, feels she does not possess the qualities necessary to tame or control this raging swarm: 'I am not a Caesar'.

What will the poet do?

The poet considers her options with regard to the bees. First, she could return them to the shop she bought them from: 'They can be sent back'. Second, she could starve them and let them perish in their clean wood box: 'They can die, I need feed them nothing, I am the owner'. Finally, she could overcome her fear of the bees and release them in the morning as she had originally planned. She wonders if the bees are hungry enough to attack her should she decide to release them: 'I wonder how

hungry they are'. She feels there is little real chance of this attack occurring: 'I am no source of honey/ So why should they turn on me?'. The bees, in fact, will probably just ignore her if she sets them free: 'They might ignore me immediately'.

The poet has a god-like power over the bees – the power of life and death. She decides that tomorrow she will act like a 'sweet' or benevolent god. Instead of sending the bees back or letting them die, she will set them free. Having concluded that they pose little threat to her, she will release them into the garden: 'Tomorrow I will be sweet God, I will set them free.//
The box is only temporary.'

FOCUS ON STYLE

Vivid and Unsettling Imagery

This poem features vivid and unsettling imagery that is typical of Plath's poetry. We see this in her description of the box as 'the coffin of a midget/ Or a square baby'. On one level, of course, this description is outlandish and perhaps even slightly amusing. Yet there is also something unpleasant and unsettling about it. The description of the box as a coffin introduces the notion of death, and suggests the poet's desire for oblivion.

She uses a bizarre and somewhat unsettling metaphor to describe the bees, comparing them to the hands of dead African people that have been cut off, shrunken and exported back to Europe as souvenirs of the 'dark continent': 'African hands/ Minute and shrunk for export'. The image of thousands of tiny hands clambering around the box's dark interior is truly a disturbing one.

Metaphor, Simile, Figures of Speech

Plath uses a conceit or extended metaphor to describe the bees, comparing the swarm to a rioting mob in Roman times: 'It is like a Roman mob'. The sound of the bees' buzzing is likened to Latin, the now 'unintelligible' language spoken in Roman times. Just as it took a powerful ruler like Caesar to master the mobs of Rome, so it will take a skilled and confident beekeeper to control the bees once they have been released from the box.

Metaphor also features in line 31, where Plath compares a beekeeper's protective clothing to an astronaut's space suit. She also compares a beekeeper's protective face mesh to a veil worn by a dead woman at her funeral: 'in my moon suit and funeral veil'. These lines also feature a Classical reference, where the

poet imagines herself as Daphne, a doomed character from Greek myth who was transformed by the gods into a tree.

Verbal Music

We see cacophony in lines 13 to 15, where the repetition of hard 'b', 'r' and 't' sounds creates a harsh musical effect that is appropriate to the disturbing image the lines describe.

Euphony occurs in lines 32 to 36: the repeated broad-vowel sounds in 'source of honey', 'moon suit', 'funeral veil' and 'box is only' create a pleasant musical effect. So, too, do the repeated internal and external rhymes between 'honey', 'me', 'sweet', 'free', 'only' and 'temporary'. This pleasant verbal music is appropriate, as the poet imagines herself overcoming her fear and releasing the bees.

In a journal entry dated 10 June 1962, Plath wrote about going to collect a hive with her husband: 'Ted and I drove down to Charlie Pollard's about 9 tonight to collect our hive ... loaned us a bee-book. We loaded with our creaky old wooden hive. He said if we cleaned it and painted it over Whitsun, he'd order a swarm of docile bees. Had showed us his beautiful-red-gold Italian bee the day before, with her glossy green mark on the thorax, I think. He had made it. To see her better. The bees were bad-tempered, though. She would lay a lot of docile bees. We said: 'Docile, be sure now, & drove home'.

MENTAL ANGUISH

Like many of Plath's poems, 'The Arrival of the Bee Box' depicts mental turmoil. Plath, as we've seen, reacts to the bee box with horrified fascination. This is partly due to her finding the sights and sounds of the bees disgusting and unsettling. But it is also because the bee box represents her own anguished mental state. The bees buzz and vibrate inside the box just as anguished thoughts churn and agitate inside her troubled mind.

Plath, as we've seen, imagines releasing the bees into her garden. This seems to represent her belief that she might be able to free her mind from such negative and destructive thoughts. By releasing them, however, she will conquer her fear and empower herself. She will go from being powerless ('no Caesar') to being powerful ('sweet God'). If the poet can overcome this seemingly irrational fear of the bee box, perhaps she can also overcome the deeper mental turmoil that affects her. In Plath's case, however, this optimism was all too sadly ill-founded.

There are several instances in Plath's poetry where she expresses what might be described as self-destructive thoughts or desires. Many readers feel that these desires surface in 'The Arrival of the Bee Box'. When the poet imagines herself wearing the protective garments of a beekeeper, she describes the face covering as a 'funeral veil'. There is a sense here that she is anticipating her own demise, or on some level even desiring it. This tendency is perhaps also evident when she imagines herself being transformed into a tree: 'I wonder if they would forget me/ If I just undid the locks and stood back and turned into a tree'.

There is a sense in which Plath seems to desire this transformation, to leave behind the human condition, with all its trials and tribulations. She wants to give up human consciousness and become an unthinking but beautiful piece of plant life. A similar desire to be released from human consciousness is also present in 'Finisterre' and in 'Poppies in July'.

POETIC INSPIRATION

'The Arrival of the Bee Box' is often regarded as dealing with the theme of poetry and the unconscious. To write poetry, Plath believed, it was necessary to explore the darkest recesses of the mind, to explore the deepest reaches of the soul. Yet this, she felt, was a dangerous business, for it risked disturbing all kinds of inner demons: various traumas and negative emotions the mind has covered up.

The bee box, according to many readers, represents the hidden aspect of mind, the dark and mysterious parts the true poet must explore:

- Like the bee box, our unconscious mind is almost completely sealed: we cannot know what it contains until we begin to explore it.
- Just as the poet is terrified and disgusted by the bee box, so Plath was nervous about exploring her unconscious mind, and horrified by the demons that might lurk there.
- By opening up her unconscious, she will unleash her inner demons, just as the poet will release the bees.

Yet just as she can't stay away from the bee box, so Plath was drawn back again and again to probe around the edges of her unconscious, for she felt that only by exploring this hidden aspect of herself could she create great poetry.

ORDER AND CHAOS

Many of Plath's poems focus on the distinction between order and chaos. In this poem, the bees are a chaotic force, swarming hectically and frenziedly within their box. They are like a wild and disorderly mob. Only the box imposes order on them, containing their fury. Tellingly, the poem's opening lines associate the box with order: 'I ordered this, this clean wood box'. However, once the box is opened, order will be removed. The chaos represented by the bees will be free to make its way into the world.

The poet finds this an unpleasant and perhaps even frightening prospect: 'How can I let them go?'. In this poem, as in 'Finisterre', Plath seems to regard chaos with what can only be described as fear and horror. Yet also as in 'Finisterre', there is a sense in which chaos is presented as something alluring and attractive. We see this in the way the poet 'can't stay away' from the bees' frenzy, and in her decision at the end of the poem to release this 'box of maniacs' into the world.

Poppies in July

Plath with her husband and poet, Ted Hughes

LINE BY LINE

In 1962 Plath was living in rural Devon with her husband, poet Ted Hughes. In July of that year she discovered that Hughes was having an affair with another woman. 'Poppies in July' captures the great anguish, rage and pain that the poet experienced around this time, as she struggled to cope with the end of the relationship that had been so central to her life.

I

The poet is walking through the Devon countryside when she encounters a field of poppies. She imagines that these vivid red flowers are the flames of hell. Each 'little' flower resembles an individual tongue of flame. The poet describes how the poppies 'flicker', suggesting their slight, quick movements in the summer breeze. The term also suggests the flickering or unsteady movement of flames.

The poet expects these flames to be harmful. We get the impression, in fact, that she longs for them to burn her: 'I put my hands among the flames'. She is surprised and disappointed when 'Nothing burns', asking the poppies why they have failed to harm her: 'Do you do no harm?'

II

The poppies have a blood-red colour, which causes the poet to associate them with violence:

- She likens them to mouths that have been beaten and bloodied.
- She likens them to the skirts of women who are bleeding after some violent episode: 'Little bloody skirts!'

The poet, it seems, longs to experience such violence herself. She wants to be assaulted so that she bleeds: 'If I could bleed'.

She wants her own mouth to be beaten and bloodied: 'If my mouth could marry a hurt like that!'

III

The poet thinks of the 'opiates', drugs such as morphine, codeine and heroin that are obtained from the unripe seedpods of the poppy. These can be used as sedatives, inducing a deep slumber in those who take them. The poet longs to take such 'opiates' to dull the anguish she's experiencing.

She imagines that opiates are rising in 'fumes' from the flowers. But these are useless to her for she 'cannot touch' them. She longs, therefore, to harvest the seedpods or 'capsules' from which she will squeeze opiates in liquid form. This liquid is described as the poppies 'liquors', the flowers' potent, mind-altering beverage. It is also described as 'nauseous', reminding us that stomach upset is a common side-effect of such opiates.

The poet imagines drinking these 'liquors' and entering a state that can only be descrbed as suspended animation. She imagines the drug working its way through her system. She imagines it would have a 'Dulling and stilling' effect. The angish that she has been experiencing would start to dull and fade. Her agitated, highly strung body would gradually relax until she entered a state of oblivion.

The poet imagines her sedated body being placed in a 'glass capsule'. This capsule calls to mind the story of Snow White, where the title character, having eaten the enchanted apple, enters into a similar state of suspended animation and is placed in a glass coffin.

In the poem's final line, Plath repeats the word 'colorless'.
- This might refer to the liquid opiate, the greyish, milky sap or fluid drawn from the poppy seeds.
- Perhaps this repetition indicates the poet's desire to stop perceiving, at least for a little while. She wants to enter a deep slumber where she will no longer be exposed to the world's colours, shapes and sounds.
- But it might also be her own body that she wishes to become 'colorless'. As she enters a state of oblivion, she imagines the colour draining from her features, lending her a death-like hue.

FOCUS ON STYLE

Psychic Landscapes

Plath's use of seascapes and landscapes to represent or illustrate her inner feelings and psychological condition is one of the defining features of her poetry. 'Poppies in July', as we've outlined above, is less a portrait of an English summer landscape than a vivid representation of the poet's mental turmoil and anguish at this particular moment in her life.

Vivid and Unsettling Imagery

Like many of Plath's poems, 'Poppies in July' is rich in vivid and unsettling imagery. The flowers take on a disturbing and sinister appearance, resembling flames and bloodied faces. They seem to antagonise the poet, flickering endlessly before her in a manner that she finds exhausting.

Verbal Music

The poem consists of a series of short, snappy declarations that move from topic to topic in a jerking, almost unsettling manner, powerfully suggesting the poet's restless, agitated state of mind. This anguished state of mind is also suggested by the poet's use of cacophany. We see this in the 'r' and 'k' sounds in line 6 and the 'n' and 'p' sounds in line 10, where the hard, clashing vowel sounds create a grating verbal music.

Metaphor, Simile, Figures of Speech

This poem is a powerful example of apostrophe, which occurs when the speaker of a poem addresses an inanimate object. The poem is also distinguished by several memorable comparisons:
- The poem opens with a metaphor comparing each flower to a tongue of flame.
- Another metaphor compares the flowers to 'skirts'. We can imagine how the cup-like arrangement of each flowers' petals might be said to resemble a skirt.
- A fine simile, meanwhile, compares the individual petals to flaps of bloodied, wrinkled skin, such that we might find at the edge of a gash or wound.

MENTAL ANGUISH

The poet's agitated, anguished state of mind is evident in her response to the poppies. To most people, the sight of a field of poppies in summer would be a thing of great joy, a scene of beauty and inspiration. But to the poet, the flowers conjure up highly disturbing images of hellish fire and of mouths that have been beaten and bloodied.

The poet longs for two seemingly very different things: she wants to 'bleed' or she wants to 'sleep'. We can understand her desire to sleep, to ingest some sedative that would plunge her into a deep slumber that would allow her to escape her anguished state of mind.

But the poet's masochistic longing to experience pain, to be beaten and to 'bleed' is harder to fathom.
- Perhaps she feels that pain, like some form of shock therapy, might jolt her out of her anguised state of mind (Plath would have been familiar with such treatments, having undergone electroconvulsive therapy in 1953).
- Perhaps she feels that physical pain would be a welcome distraction from the mental pain she is currently experiencing.
- Or perhaps this desire comes from low self-esteem and feelings of self-loathing.

We can imagine how this particular July would have been a low point in Plath's life. Her marriage to Hughes, after all, had been central to her existence: 'My marriage is the center of my being. I have given everything to it without reserve'. Her discovery that he was having an affair, therefore, left her feeling worthless and rejected. Hughes, according to one of her letters, told her 'he was just waiting for a chance to get out, that he was bored and stifled by me, a hag in a world of beautiful women'.

Child

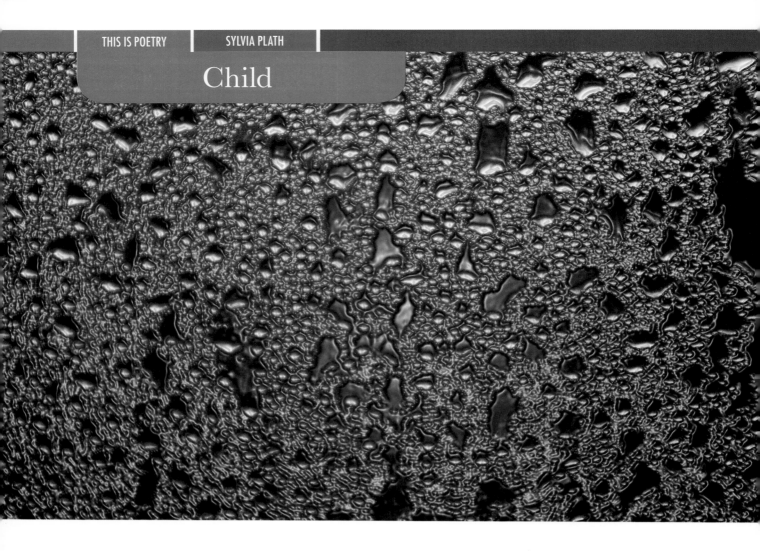

LINE BY LINE

In January 1962, Plath's second child, Nicholas, was born. The family were living in Devon at the time. In July 1962, Plath discovered that her husband, Ted Hughes, was having an affair with another woman and in September the couple separated. In December, Plath moved back to London with her two children (Nicholas, aged nine months, and Frieda, who was now two years old).

Plath rented a flat in Camden, only a few streets from the Chalcot Square flat she and Ted had shared when they moved to London in 1959. The winter of 1962 was one of the coldest on record; the pipes froze and the children were often sick. It was around this time that Plath's depression worsened and she experienced what one biographer has described as 'constant agitation, suicidal thoughts and an inability to cope with daily life'.

Despite her circumstances and illness, Plath experienced a great burst of creativity during this period, writing at least 26 of the poems that would be published posthumously in *Ariel*. One of these poems, 'Child', was written towards the end of January 1963, just two weeks before the poet took her own life.

I

The poet contemplates her child's eye, which she describes as 'clear', suggesting a number of things:
- The eye is unblemished or unmarked, the white of the eye pristine, the iris an intense shade of blue or green
- The child sees the world in a 'clear' manner, uninfluenced or biased by experience

Plath considers her child's eye to be the 'one absolutely beautiful thing'. To the poet, then, her child is perfect and she loves him unconditionally.

She wants the child to see objects that fill him with joy, wonder and happiness. The poet thinks of beautiful colours and cute animals that would delight a young child. These are the kinds of things she wants to be able to offer her child: 'I want to fill it with color and ducks'.

The child is eager to learn and ready to absorb the world that surrounds it. The poet wants to provide her child with experiences that are beautiful, positive and fun. The poet wants her child to experience the world in a joyful and positive manner. She wants his whole world to be a 'zoo of the new', a place full of objects and experiences that will fill the child with delight and wonder: 'The zoo of the new'.

The poet imagines showing her child images of flowers and plants and saying their names aloud: 'April snowdrop, Indian pipe'. The child would hear and begin to repeat these words over and over in an infantile babble. The poet compares this babbling to the chanting used in meditation: 'Whose names you meditate'.

II

The poet compares her child to a 'Pool'. We might imagine a reflecting pool that is a feature of certain buildings. The poet wants to create a stable and harmonious home for her child. Creating such a stable home environment is like constructing a beautiful, harmonious piece of architecture that will then be reflected in the pool's surface. Plath makes reference to 'grand and classical' images, to the architectural features – the columns and arches – that introduce a sense of balance and order to buildings.

III

But the poet is unable to show her child such harmony and stillness. Overcome with depression, she feels that she is denying her child the stable environment he needs, creating instead a home that troubled and problematic. Creating such a negative environment, she thinks, is like covering the pool with a 'dark/ Ceiling', so that it can reflect nothing at all, not even a single star'. The 'Pool', therefore, only reflects the dark ceiling and the sight of the poet wringing her hands in anguish.

THEMES

MENTAL ANGUISH

'Child' provides us with an insight into the terrible mental anguish that Plath was experiencing at this moment in her life. We get a sense of her feelings of inadequacy. She feels that she is failing her child, that she is not capable of offering it the things it needs to thrive and be happy.

We also get a sense of the depression that Plath was suffering. Her description of the 'dark/ Ceiling without a star' at the end of the poem captures her despair and lack of hope. The 'dark/ Ceiling' might be understood metaphorically as a description of the poet's psychological state or condition. To her the world seems bleak and without hope. She feels utterly trapped and alone. When she contemplates the future, it seems an endless vista of blackness, without a ray or shard of hope.

FEMININITY AND MOTHERHOOD

This poem, like 'Morning Song', documents the pressures that all mothers feel when it comes to taking care of their children. Every mother wants their child to experience only the beautiful and delightful aspects of the world and to shield them from all the horrors and ugliness that exist.

But no mother (or parent) ever thinks they are doing a perfect job – there is always the feeling that you are falling short of the ideal and that you could be a better parent. Yet most would believe that on balance they are doing the best they can and that they are providing their child with a positive environment in which to grow and thrive. In 'Child', however, we sense that Plath feels that she is utterly failing, that she has nothing positive and good to offer her child.

FOCUS ON STYLE

Vivid and Unsettling Imagery

At the heart of this poem is the contrast between the images that the poet wishes she could offer her child and images of the reality of her situation. The poem's first nine lines present us with images of colour, of fun and childlike wonder. Plath mentions 'ducks' and 'color'. She refers to beautiful flowers and exotic plants. The 'April snowdrop' is a white flower that blossoms late in spring. 'Indian pipe', meanwhile, is a plant native to the temperate regions of Asia and America. The mentioning of these plants suggests the beauty and richness of life, the idea that the world is full of fascinating detail.

But the poem concludes with images of confinement and darkness, or agitation and distress. The 'dark/ Ceiling without a star', as we mentioned above, represents the negative, troubled environment that the poet believes she has created for her child, a place devoid of all beauty, stability and harmony.

Metaphor, Simile, Figures of Speech

The poet uses a number of metaphors to capture her child's beauty and innocence. She compares her child to a pool of water that reflects its environment. She compares the child to a 'Stalk without wrinkle'. We might picture the stalk of a plant that has just sprouted, its stem perfectly smooth and spotless. Like the description of the 'clear eye' in the poem's opening line, this comparison suggests how pure and innocent a young child is, utterly unblemished by life and experience. Plath also uses the metaphor of the 'zoo' to convey how the world can be a fascinating and delightful place for a child, full of wonderful new experiences.

William Butler Yeats

Themes

Nature

Yeats is well-known for his celebrations of the natural world. We see this in 'The Wild Swans at Coole', which captures the unique qualities of an Irish autumn evening: a crisp path underfoot, a haunting stillness in the twilight sky, trees in their multi-coloured beauty. The poem provides an especially memorable portrait of the 'mysterious' and 'beautiful' swans that drift on the still water. It also highlights the explosive power and force they exhibit as they 'mount/ And scatter', their wings thumping with the piercing regularity of a bell.

'The Lake Isle of Innisfree' is another of Yeats' best-loved nature poems. The island is depicted as a place of sublime tranquillity. It's a place of silence, devoid of any man-made sound. Peace, we're told, 'comes dropping' slowly from the banks of mist that cover the island each morning, drenching the grasses where the crickets are busy about their song. Yeats longs for a retreat to Innisfree. He imagines building a primitive hut on the island and growing his own food. There he will be free from the stresses and strains of modern living. He will have no access to news or media, to devices or technology. He will be out of the rat-race that constitutes modern urban living. We sense, however, that such a solitary, self-sufficient existence is destined to remain a fantasy for the poet.

Yeats' poetry explores how the natural world is in a constant state of flux and change. We see this, for instance, in 'Easter 1916', which emphasises how the natural world changes 'minute by minute'. The poem describes a constantly shifting landscape, where a stream evolves like a 'living' thing as it pulses along its course, where clouds tumble through the sky, where horses' hooves thunder and splash. 'Sailing to Byzantium' is another poem that emphasises the shifting nature of the natural world. The poem views the natural world as a kind of system that cycles through phases of birth, death and renewal. Every living thing is part of this system. Every living thing is 'begotten' or conceived, born, reproduces and eventually dies.

In 'The Stare's Nest by My Window' Yeats looks to the natural world as a source of hope and guidance. The poem, written during the Civil War, highlights the bitterness that has taken root in the Irish heart and the violence and chaos that rage throughout the country. Each stanza concludes with a plea to the honeybees to 'Come build in the empty house of the stare'. We must look to nature's positivity, energy and creativity, the poem suggests, if we are to reverse the damage that has been done to the soul of the Irish nation. The challenge for the Irish people is to follow nature's example. They must turn away from the path of destruction and begin to rebuild their homes, their shattered country and their trust in one another.

Youth and Age

Many of Yeats' poems lament the negative effects of ageing. We see this in 'The Wild Swans at Coole, for instance, where the poet has started to exhibit not only physical weakness and psychological exhaustion, but also a lessening of his good-looks and sexual opportunities. His heart is 'sore' as he contemplates his decline. The poem centres on the contrast between the poet, whose life has endured such changes, and the swans, who are presented as being utterly changeless. The swans, as we have seen, are 'unwearied' in body and mind, as they pursue lives of unbounded passion and sexual adventure.

'Sailing to Byzantium' provides another moving portrayal of the ageing process. The poet feels disgusted and constrained by his own body. In a shocking memorable phrase, he describes his body as a 'dying animal' to which he has been 'shackled'. The poem highlights how the elderly often consider themselves 'paltry', as in feeble and insignificant, and how in a world obsessed with youth and beauty, they all too often feel unsightly and unwanted, ridiculous or even invisible.

The poem draws a powerful contrast between youth and age, specifically between the elderly poet and the young people he observes at the height of the Irish summer. The young people are sexually attractive in their sexual prime. The poet's body, on the other hand, has been left 'tattered' by the ageing process. The young people enjoy lives of sexual opportunity, wandering the streets 'in one another's arms'. The aged poet too experiences sexual desire. But for him, alas, such opportunities are a thing of the past.

'Politics' is similar in this regard. The poet is entranced by a beautiful woman, but knows he's now too old to ever win her affections. There is real emotion in the poem's final lines, when he wishes that he could somehow be young again and hold the beautiful woman he so desires in his arms. The tragic reality, of course, is that is there is no turning back the clock. The poet's desire for youth must remain forever thwarted.

'In Memory of Eva Gore-Booth and Con Markievicz' is yet another poem that deals with the changes, both mental and physical, that will be wreaked on us by time's relentless march. Time, Yeats reminds us, is the enemy not only of physical beauty but also of innocence: 'The innocent and the beautiful/ Have no enemy but time'. Its passage begins to leave us not only weakened and decrepit on a physical level but cynical and embittered on a mental level too. The ravages of time are memorably personified as a 'raving autumn' that shears off the flowers on the wreath of youth and beauty. It turns Eva from a creature of gazelle-like beauty and elegance into a 'withered' and 'skeleton-gaunt' old woman. And each of us, sadly but inevitably, must suffer a similar transformation.

'An Acre of Grass' takes a somewhat different approach to growing old. Here we find the poet more accepting of the ageing process and even celebrating certain advantages that accompany it. He is no longer distracted by sexual desire: 'My temptation is quiet'. His mind has grown more mindful and serene. He likens the aged body to 'an old house' that barely contains any life: 'an old house/ Where nothing stirs but a mouse'. The poet's mind is now free to gain insight or understanding that was unavailable to him when he was young. Yeats describes the aged man's mind in terms of an 'eagle': 'An old man's eagle mind'. The comparison not only suggests the sharpness of the older man's mind but also that it is capable of soaring and gaining a perspective on life that is not available to the young.

War, Violence and Social Upheaval

'September 1913' presents a rather romantic or idealistic view of war and violence. It celebrates the military achievements of the Wild Geese on the continents, and the almost foolhardy courage of soldiers like Robert Emmett and John O'Leary who led tiny revolts against a vast imperial power. The poem emphasises the noble side of warfare, the idealism and self-sacrifice displayed by soldiers in the service of a cause. But it downplays the horror and bloodshed of the battlefield.

It could be argued that 'An Irish Airman Foresees His Death' presents a rather romantic view of war and violence. Yeats was always a scholar rather than a soldier. But he exhibited a lifelong fascination with men of action, with those who, like the airman, had the bravery to enter the field of battle, putting their lives on the line as they fought, died and killed. No doubt Yeats also admires how the airman is a person apart. The airman, unlike his fellow soldiers, has no truck with the propaganda of public men and politicians. He is unmoved by the great wave of patriotism that has swept across the continent. Instead, as we have seen, he fights for his own reasons.

'Easter 1916', on the other hand, displays a more complex attitude towards war and violence. Yeats celebrates the heroism and sacrifice of these men who fought and died for the Irish cause, describing how they will be venerated forever 'wherever green is worn'. But Yeats is also horrified and terrified by what has happened. Though he once lamented the absence of such heroics in modern Ireland, now that heroes have re-emerged Yeats is fearful of what this means for the future. He is quick to realise that the celebration of those who died in the Rising will spur others on to do the same. War and violence, he fears or suspects, will engulf Irish society. The beauty of the leaders' sacrifice is a 'terrible beauty' indeed.

'The Stare's Nest by My Window' also explores the horrors of war and violence. The poem, written during the Irish Civil War, presents a community and a country that has been ravaged by war. For two weeks, the conflict has created a claustrophobic sense of isolation, leaving people 'closed in' as it traps them in their homes. It has created a great sense of dread and uncertainty among the populace, who are able to discern 'no clear fact' about what's going on in the country or what the future holds. Violence and terror stalk the land, as men are shot dead, houses are destroyed and acts of inhumanity, like the dragging of the dead soldier's corpse, are carried out.

'Politics' is another poem that registers the horror of war. It was written in 1938, just as the Second World War was poised to break out across the continent of Europe. As Yeats puts it, 'war's alarms' were ringing throughout the world. The 'travelled man' and the politician seem deeply concerned about the coming catastrophe. The poet, however, finds himself distracted by the presence of a beautiful young woman. For a moment, romantic longing overtakes his fear of the coming storm.

'The Second Coming' is probably Yeats' greatest statement on the topic of war, violence and social upheaval. The poem was written in 1919, during the chaotic aftermath of the First World War. To Yeats, it seems that the entire world is filled with confusion and disorder. It seems that everywhere the voices of reason and moderation are silenced, while those of intolerance and extremism shout ever louder. Evil men pursue their goals relentlessly, while the good stand idly by. Civilisation itself seems on the verge of being swept away by a tide of bloodshed. Furthermore, the poem predicts that even greater destruction is on its way, represented by the pitiless beast that 'slouches towards Bethlehem to be born'.

Art and the Role of the Artist

Yeats presents art as a continuous practice, a craft or trade that must be perfected throughout the artist's life. His most famous declaration of this belief comes in 'Under Ben Bulben'. Future Irish poets, Yeats decrees, must 'learn [their] trade'. These aspiring bards must understand that poetry involves more than ideas and inspiration, that it requires practice, patience and determination. They must approach poetry the way an apprentice carpenter approaches the work bench, realising that they have a great deal to learn and that only hard work will grant them the mastery they desire.

'Sailing to Byzantium' presents a similar view of creativity. Despite his old age, the poet is determined to keep developing his craft. If anything, the nearness of death makes him all the more eager to reach his full artistic potential. The poem stresses that such improvement can be made only by studying the great artists of the past. Yeats, then, despite being an accomplished, Nobel prize-winning poet, recognises that he must still attend 'singing-school' in order that his soul can express itself with ever-greater clarity and purpose.

'An Acre of Grass' also emphasises the need for an artist to keep developing despite old age. Yeats declares his admiration for artists like Michelangelo, Shakespeare and William Blake, who continued, even in old age, to strive for artistic perfection. Yeats clearly wants to emulate the passion and energy exhibited by these past masters, who kept changing and developing until the very end of their lives. The artist, Yeats believes, should never feel satisfied or content with what they have already achieved. It is the artist's duty, even in old age, to remain restless and to constantly seek new ways to explore and reveal the truth.

If poetry is a 'trade', then it must serve a useful function. Like carpentry and tailoring it must be necessary to society. Poetry's function, as Yeats presents it in 'Under Ben Bulben', is to 'cast [his or her] mind on other days', to remember and write about the past. Will Ireland become just another identical outpost of capitalism, just another banal node in an international network of technology? Only the poets, according to Yeats, can prevent this from happening. Only they can remind Ireland as a whole of what it once was and can be again. Through their words, they can spur us on to be 'indomitable' in the face of modernity, to create a future that resembles the best aspects of our past.

'Swift's Epitaph' also emphasises the public or political role of the poet in society. There is a sense in this poem that Yeats believes it is the writer's duty to respond to public events, to criticise society and its leaders for their various faults and failings. The poem challenges writers to 'imitate' Swift if they dare. It asks them to have the courage to criticise society in their work, even if they might suffer as a result of speaking out.

'September 1913' is one poem where Yeats follows Swift's example, using his platform as an established writer to attack the network of powerful businessmen that ran Dublin society. Yeats was responding to two public events – the Dublin Lockout and the controversy surrounding the Hugh Lane bequest. Here the poet uses ridicule and irony in a savage takedown of Dublin's leading captains of industry. 'Easter 1916' is another poem where Yeats presents the artist as having a public role. The leaders of the Rising, he insists, must be remembered by the Irish people. He uses his poetic skills to contribute to this process, writing a 'verse' that will help to keep the leaders' names alive.

'Politics' raises a number of important questions about the political role of the poet. Is it self-centred of Yeats as a writer to assign more significance to his private anguish than to the looming disaster of war? Is it wrong for the poet or artist to focus on his or her personal relationships and problems when there is so much evil and suffering in the world? On the other hand, however, it is possible to regard Yeats' involvement with themes of the heart as arising not from self-obsession but from a desire to write about universal human experiences.

The theme of achieving immortality through art is another that occurs throughout Yeats' poetry. In 'In Memory', for instance, Yeats imagines himself protecting innocence and beauty by destroying time itself. He longs to somehow put a match to time's very fabric, so it will be consumed in a great and climbing 'conflagration': 'Arise and bid me strike a match/ And strike another till time catch.' Yeats feels he can undo time's march by immortalising, in poetry, the beauty and innocence of the girls. A truly skilful artist, therefore, can defeat time by recovering an event or person lost in the past – an evening in Lissadell and two girls in silk kimonos, for instance – and preserving it in a piece of art to be enjoyed by future generations.

'Sailing to Byzantium' is perhaps Yeats' most profound statement on the idea of attaining immortality through art. The poet, we sense, would have little interest in prolonging the life of his body through some revolutionary scientific method. Nor does he show any interest in the type of immortality associated with the Christian concept of heaven. Nor, as we've seen, is he taken with reincarnation. Instead he focuses on the type of artistic immortality enjoyed by Michelangelo and Shakespeare. He is determined that he will live on in the 'artifice of eternity', through the poems, plays and texts he has created over the course of his life. This is represented by the poet's soul inhabiting the magnificent golden bird created by the Grecian goldsmiths all those centuries ago.

Yeats and Ireland

The Ascendency

Yeats, as we have noted, was a great admirer of the Anglo-Irish Ascendancy, the class that dominated Irish society between the 17th and 19th centuries, and of which he himself was a member. He especially valued the formal, orderly way in which life was conducted on the estates and in the mansions of these wealthy Protestant landowners. In 'The Second Coming', for instance, Yeats describes how the Anglo-Irish lifestyle was full of 'ceremony'. And such a civilised, ceremonial existence, he believed, produced people who were 'innocent', who were fundamentally decent and morally upright.

Meanwhile, in 'In Memory' he praises Lissadell, one of the famous 'big houses' associated with the Anglo-Irish. Yeats praises that 'old Georgian mansion' for its impressive architecture, for its 'great windows open to the South'. But it's worth noting that Lissadell, like other Anglo-Irish mansions, although luxurious, was also a little austere. The Anglo-Irish didn't really go in for 'bling', instead creating simple but elegant environments.

Yeats also admired Anglo-Irish society not only because it valued art and creativity but also because it was open to new ideas. Both of these trends are embodied in the 'silk kimonos' worn by the Gore-Booth sisters on that long-ago evening in Lissadell. These gowns, which might be considered art objects in themselves, reflect Anglo-Irish openness to fresh thinking and foreign cultures.

'Under Ben Bulben' also celebrates Anglo-Irish culture, looking back to its heyday in the 18th and 19th centuries. Yeats presents the Ireland of that period as a place of almost medieval simplicity. The 'lords and ladies' of the ascendancy resided in their 'gay' mansions or relaxed by 'hard-riding' through the countryside. The Catholic 'peasantry' worked the land and drank porter in the taverns, content with the noble simplicity of their lot. The monks, cooped-up in their monasteries, got on with being holy.

By the time Yeats was writing, however, the heyday of the Anglo-Irish was long since past. Their power had waned throughout the nineteenth century and all but disappeared in the new Catholic Ireland that emerged after independence from Britain. In 'The Second Coming', Yeats laments how the last influence of the Anglo-Irish seems to be disappearing, as the War of Independence against British rule in Ireland was getting into full swing. Everywhere Yeats looked, then, he saw the 'ceremony' of the aristocratic lifestyle being swept away amid the bloodshed of war and revolution: 'The blood-dimmed tide is loosed, and everywhere/ The ceremony of innocence is drowned'.

'In Memory' uses another striking metaphor to describe this decline. Yeats compares Anglo-Irish civilisation to a gazebo, a small roofed structure that is used for outdoor entertaining and dining. Gazebos are often ornamental and elaborately-designed, suggesting the emphasis Anglo-Irish society placed not only on hospitality but also on art and on beautiful objects. But gazebos are relatively flimsy structures, reflecting how the Anglo-Irish dominance of Irish life proved to be fragile and fleeting. In the early decades of independence, the great Anglo-Irish families, once so prominent in Irish life, drifted to its margins or disappeared altogether. Their civilisation was torn down as easily as one might dismantle a gazebo.

The Decline of Irish Society

'September 1913' is one of many poems where Yeats laments the decline of Irish society. This poem draws a stark contrast between Ireland's heroic past and the sad reality of what it has become. Yeats declares that Ireland was once a 'Romantic' country, a place that valued artistry and imagination. It was a place that exhibited community and self-sacrifice, and one that valued risk-taking and adventure. But this 'Romantic Ireland is dead and gone'. It has been replaced by a soulless, materialistic culture, as exemplified by the powerful businessmen Yeats criticises in the poem.

A similar point is made in 'Easter 1916'. Yeats admits that he believed Ireland to be a ridiculous place, one of 'casual comedy' inhabited by clowns and fools that might very well have been wearing the 'motley' of the traditional court jester. Ireland, he felt, could produce nothing serious, nothing beautiful and nothing heroic. The shock of the 1916 Rising, however, has revised his opinion of the country.

'Under Ben Bulben' features another lament about the state of Irish society. In 1939, when Yeats wrote the poem, Ireland was becoming a place dominated by science and technology, by industry and commerce. These changes, Yeats feels, have made the Irish of today a rather 'base' lot. The 'sort now growing up' are devoid of morality, are incapable of feeling and are even physically inferior. Yeats, then, looks back with affection to this golden time before modernity, when gentleman and peasant alike were uncorrupted by the grubby influences of capitalism and materialism. This was also a time before science came to dominate mankind's view of the world, a time that Yeats, a spiritualist rather than a scientist in outlook, harks back to with the greatest of nostalgia.

Patriotism and Revolt

Yeats' poetry is marked by a profound meditation on the nature of patriotism and revolt. In 'September 1913', for instance, Yeats declares that Ireland has lost its patriotic values. At one time, the country produced individuals like Robert Emmet and Wolfe Tone, who were prepared to sacrifice everything for the causes they believed in. The Ireland of 1913, Yeats believes, is incapable of understanding such self-sacrifice. The idealism exhibited by Emmet and Tone would strike contemporary Ireland as alien and incomprehensible. Yeats imagines the old heroes somehow coming back to life, only to be treated with scorn by the businessmen who currently lead the country.

A similar point is made at the beginning of 'Easter 1916'. Yeats describes how he used to laugh behind the backs of nationalists like Pearse and Connolly when he met them on the streets of Dublin. These men were fervently convinced that Ireland could be roused to rebel against British rule. Yeats, on the other hand, felt that Ireland was no longer capable of producing the self-sacrifice and heroism necessary for rebellion.

However, Yeats is forced to concede that he was wrong. The rebel leaders not only had a dream but they acted on that dream to make it a reality, paying the ultimate price as they did so. Yeats accepts that these men and women made the ultimate sacrifice for their country and will be remembered as heroes. Wherever Irish people gather, wherever 'green is worn', people will recount their deeds with awe and admiration. The Rising, in Yeats' memorable phrase, has unleashed a 'terrible beauty'. It is beautiful because it involves heroism, honour and self-sacrifice. It is terrible because it involves bloodshed and destruction. Yeats, as he contemplates the future, feel that the coming years will be shaped by both this terror and this beauty.

This mediation on patriotism and revolt continues in 'The Stare's Nest by My Window', which was written during the Irish Civil War. Here Yeats exhibits a much more sceptical attitude towards patriotism and revolt. We sense that the closer Yeats came to the grim realities of guerrilla warfare, the less time he had for the 'fantasies' of freedom and martyrdom. Disagreements over Irish freedom, he suggests, aren't worth such terror and destruction, such loss of life and property.

In 'September 1913', Yeats suggested that the Irish people had forgotten the ideas of freedom and martyrdom that motivated the heroes of the past. In this poem, written ten years later, he argues the opposite. The Irish people, he claims, have not only remembered these ideas but have become obsessed with them. And their obsession with these dangerous 'fantasies' has poisoned their psyches, turning their hearts 'brutal'.

The Lake Isle of Innisfree

LINE BY LINE

Stanza 1

The poem opens with a dramatic declaration of intent. It's as if the poet has suddenly made a decision. It's as if he's suddenly realised that he's had enough of modern living and that a change of direction is needed. And this new existence, he declares, will begin immediately, for he's going to stand up any minute now and embark on a new chapter in his life: 'I will arise and go now'. He even emphasises this intention by repeating it in Stanza 3.

Yeats declares his intention to go off and live on the island of Innisfree, a small uninhabited island on Lough Gill in County Sligo. He imagines he would live a very simple life once he gets there:

*   He would live 'alone' in a clearing or glade upon the island.
*   He would build his own cabin: 'And a small cabin build there'. This would be a very basic type of accommodation. It would be 'small'. It would be manufactured using the ancient 'wattle and daub' technique, which involves smearing mud over interwoven sticks and twigs.
*   He would even produce his own food, keeping bees for their honey and growing rows of beans: 'Nine bean-rows will I have there, a hive for the honey-bee'.

Yeats, then, seems to imagine living 'off the grid', going without the amenities and conveniences of his time. He imagines a life without telephones and telegraphs, with no newspapers or postal service, without the primitive gas and electrical services that were available in 1890s Dublin and London.

Stanza 2

The poet imagines the great beauty of Innisfree, taking us through a day on the island from dawn to dusk to midnight:

*   The poet would wake each day to the pleasant chirping sounds of crickets: 'where the cricket sings'.
*   He uses a wonderful metaphor to describe the banks of mist that drift across the island each morning, comparing them to 'veils' that drift and disperse, momentarily obscuring the island's beauty as they pass: 'the veils of the morning'.
*   Noon, too, is beautiful. Sunlight glitters on the heather that covers much of the island and gives it its name. ('Inis Fraoich', in Irish, means island of the heather). This glittering heather lends the whole place a 'purple glow'.
*   Evenings on Innisfree are 'full' of the sound made by linnets (small brown finches common in the west of Ireland) as they flit around the island: 'And evening full of the linnet's wings'.
*   Midnight, meanwhile, sees the starlight reflected on Lough Gill, so that its waters glitter and gleam: 'There midnight's all a glimmer'.

Stanza 3

The poet claims that the sound of Innisfree's beaches, of 'lake water lapping' on the island's shores, is always in his mind's ear. Like a catchy song he can't get out of his head, these 'low sounds' of water are 'always' present at the back of his mind.

They repeat over and over again, 'night and day'; we sense that the poet couldn't make them stop even if he wanted to.

These lines, then, emphasise the intensity of the poet's attachment to the little island. The lapping sound of its water echoes in the very 'core' of his heart, in the depths of his being or psyche. No matter where he goes, the sound of its waters is ever-present at the very centre of his mind, forming a kind of background music as he lives his life. But the thought of Innisfree, it seems, is especially important to the poet when he finds himself in an urban environment: 'While I stand on the roadway, or on the pavements grey'. We can imagine how the cold grey concrete makes him long for the island's beauty. We can imagine how the city's endless racket makes him long for that soothing, almost silent retreat.

Yeats, it's worth noting, was inspired to write the poem when he was living in London and was feeling homesick for his beloved Sligo. He was walking down Fleet Street, one of that city's busiest thoroughfares, when he saw a fountain in a shop window, which 'balanced a little ball upon its jet'. The trickling sound of the fountain reminded him of Innisfree's lapping waters and sparked the beginning of the poem.

FOCUS ON STYLE

Verbal Music

The poem contains many examples of assonance and alliteration. Assonance features in the second line, with its broad vowel sounds: 'a small cabin build there, of clay and wattles made'. It is also evident in line 7, where the repeated 'i' and 'o' sounds create a soft musical effect: 'midnight's all a glimmer, and noon a purple glow'. The repeated 'a' and 'o' sounds in line 10 have a similar musical quality: 'I hear lake water lapping with low sounds by the shore'. Combined with the alliteration of the 'l' sounds, these techniques make this line very pleasant to the ear.

Imagery

'The Lake Isle of Innisfree' is a poem of contrasting imagery. There is a stark difference between the imagery of the city and the imagery of Innisfree. The city is a drab and dull place, composed of roadways and 'pavements grey'. The island, in contrast, is alive with colour and sound. We can contrast the 'purple glow' of the heather with the 'pavements grey'. However, the city seems a very real place, while the island comes across as more of an imagined paradise.

Tone, Mood and Atmosphere

In his descriptions of Innisfree, Yeats creates a very peaceful, almost drowsy atmosphere. His days will be marked by the humming of bees and crickets. It is a place where 'peace comes dropping slow', where he can relax and be alone in nature. However, we also suspect that this is a highly idealised version of Innisfree. Were Yeats to actually go and try to live on the island by himself, the reality might be very different.

THEMES

NATURE

Nature's Beauty

This is one of Yeats' best-loved nature poems. Innisfree is depicted as a place of sublime tranquillity. It's a place of great silence, devoid of any man-made sound.

Innsisfree, then, is where the poet will discover the peace he so craves: 'And I shall have some peace there'. Yeats, in a wonderful turn of phrase, presents peace as a physical substance, 'dropping' in the form of dew to cover the entire island. Peace, we're told, 'comes dropping' slowly from the banks of mist that cover the island each morning, drenching the grasses where the crickets are busy about their song.

Getting Back to Nature

There are moments when each of us feels like escaping the 'rat race' that all-too-often constitutes modern living. We may feel, as Yeats suggests in Stanza 3, like trading in the cacophony of city living, with its endless traffic noise and car alarms, for a place of tranquillity where 'peace comes dropping slow'. We may feel, as Yeats does in this poem, that it's time to turn our backs on the stresses and strains of modern living, of exams and deadlines, and of career pressure and social obligations.

We may even fantasise about going off the grid completely, about living without media and devices, even without electricity. Some people even fantasise, as Yeats does here, about being completely self-sufficient, about growing their own food and building their own simple dwelling places.

Innisfree, as the poet describes it, is a place of fantasy, an idealised almost heavenly version of the actual island in County Sligo. It's a place where the poet can live out his dream of escape from modern life. But fantasy is the operative word. For we sense that Yeats, like most people, wouldn't last more than a week living alone and self-sufficiently upon Lough Gill. Think of the harsh winters, the difficulty of growing crops, the isolation, and the lack of warmth and electricity.

We sense, then, that the poet won't really follow through on this decision to 'arise and go'. We sense that this departure for Innsisfree won't happen now and probably never will, and we also sense that that the poet isn't quite prepared to leave the modern world behind and embrace what today we'd describe today as a hippy or New Age lifestyle. However, such fantasies can be important. For the poet, this dream of the simple life serves as a comfort or escape when times get tough. When the rat race proves too draining, when he tires of the grey city pavements, he can always daydream about his bean rows on the island of Innisfree.

September 1913

The Dublin Municipal Gallery, named in honour of Hugh Lane and his gift to the Irish nation

LINE BY LINE

This poem was inspired by two different controversies that raged throughout 1913. The first involved Hugh Lane who was a nephew of Yeats' great friend Lady Gregory. Lane had accumulated an important collection of priceless French paintings, which he was prepared to donate to the city of Dublin on condition that Dublin Corporation provided a suitable gallery. The businessmen who ran the corporation, led by Ireland's most prominent capitalist William Martin Murphy, proved unwilling to provide public money for the gallery. They were also unwilling to contribute to a private fund set up to cover the gallery's cost.

Yeats was disgusted at the small-minded attitude exhibited by Dublin's business leaders, and he was distraught that such a priceless collection would be lost to Ireland forever.

The second controversy is known to history as the 'Dublin Lockout'. This was a massive industrial dispute. On the one side were thousands of ordinary workers – dockers, carters, labourers, tram and railway workers. On the other side were a group of wealthy businessmen who controlled most of the employment in Dublin and the surrounding area. William Martin Murphy again played a central role, emerging as the de facto leader of the employers.

Yeats, as a relatively privileged descendant of the Protestant landowning class, had little in common with the dockers and factory workers of inner city Dublin. But he showed himself to be a man of the people, using his platform as a famous writer to support the workers and their struggle for better paying conditions. He complained, in particular about the police brutality experienced by the workers throughout this long and bitter dispute.

Stanza 1

'September 1913', then, is a very public and political poem. Yeats was determined that it would reach a wide audience and published it in The Irish Times. It can be viewed as a political satire, a poem in which the poet uses mockery, irony and exaggeration in order to attack his or her political opponents. Here Yeats sets out to criticise and ridicule William Martin Murphy and his fellow business leaders.

These businessmen, Yeats declares, have 'come to sense'. They have achieved a deep and total understanding of the world. They've realised that 'men were born pray and save', that the only important things in life are praying to God and accumulating wealth. If they save enough money, they will ensure that they are secure in this world. And if they pray enough, they will ensure that their souls are secure in the next world.

These opening lines, however, are dripping with irony and sarcasm. For Yeats doesn't really believe that these businessmen have life all figured out. In fact, he regards their view of life as being very much mistaken and far too limited.

Yeats accuses these businessmen of accumulating wealth in a miserable and miserly fashion. They are so mean that they don't let a single penny, or even a half-penny, slip through their fingers as they 'add the halfpence to the pence'.

Yeats accuses these businessmen of praying in a soulless and mechanical fashion, describing how they count their prayers the same way they count their money. Their approach to prayer, then, resembles a business negotiation rather than genuine spirituality. They seem to believe that when they've added enough prayers to their account, God will guarantee them a place in heaven.

Yeats, in a brilliant turn of phrase, describes the businessmen's prayers as 'shivering'. This suggests that all their praying is motivated by fear, either of priests in this life, or of hell in the next, rather than out of a genuine desire to communicate with God.

The phrase 'fumble in a greasy till' conjures up an especially vivid image. We imagine a greedy shopkeeper in his grubby, rundown little premises. We imagine him fumbling in his miserly haste to gather the last dirty little pennies from his till at the close of business.

The businessmen that Yeats is criticising were captains of industry. They wore the finest clothes, ate the finest foods and socialised in the finest hotels and gentlemen's clubs around Dublin. But their penny-pinching, small-minded ways, Yeats suggests, makes them no better than the grubby shopkeeper described above.

This comparison, then, is an especially devastating piece of criticism, one that very effectively takes these wealthy individuals down a peg or two.

Yeats feels that these businessmen have 'dried the marrow from the bone'. Their mean-spirited philosophy, in his opinion, sucks the goodness out of life and disregards everything that makes life worth living. Their emphasis on praying and saving doesn't leave space for art and heroism, beauty and love, things Yeats regarded as the highest aspects of human existence.

Stanza 2

In this stanza, Yeats refers to the patriots who fought and died for Irish freedom in the centuries leading up to 1913. He uses a wonderful simile to describe the fame achieved by these martyrs, declaring that their names have 'gone about the world like wind'. We can imagine the wind spreading stories of their courage to all four corners of the globe.

The businessmen of Dublin Corporation were children once. And during their childhood they looked up to these great historical figures. Yeats describes how they would stop playing whenever one of these patriots was mentioned by an adult. They would ask to hear more about the patriot in question, eager for tales of heroism and courage.

As adults, however, the businessmen have nothing in common with these patriots: 'Yet they were of a different kind'. For the patriots, unlike the businessmen, had little interest in money. Indeed, their lives were so consumed with the struggle for Irish freedom that they had no real opportunity to accumulate wealth: 'And what, God help us, could they save?' Nor were the patriot's interested in the grim, fearful brand of religion practised by the businessmen: 'But little time had they to pray'. Instead, their minds lay on higher things: heroism, honour and freedom.

Stanza 3

In this stanza, Yeats refers to several examples of heroism from Ireland's past:

* He mentions the 'Wild Geese'. These were soldiers who fought for Irish freedom in the 1690s. They were defeated and were forced into exile, where they served with great distinction in various European armies.
* He recalls Edward Fitzgerald and Wolfe Tone, who led a rebellion against British rule in 1798. Both died in prison while awaiting execution after the rebellion failed.
* He thinks of Robert Emmet who was executed after his own uprising failed in 1803.

The businessmen of Dublin Corporation, and other similar business leaders around the country, have created the new Ireland of 1913. And in doing so they have betrayed the legacy of patriots like Emmet and Fitzgerald. The businessmen, through their focus on praying and saving, have turned the country into a mean-spirited and materialistic place. This un-Romantic Ireland is not the Ireland the heroes fought and died to create: 'Was it … For this that all that blood was shed?'

Stana 4

In this stanza, Yeats wishes that he could 'turn the years again', that he could somehow reverse time's flow. By doing so, we could 'call' or summon Ireland's patriots from their graves. They would reappear just 'as they were' when they were alive, when they campaigned for Irish freedom all those years ago. What sort of reception, he wonders, would these patriots receive in the Ireland of 1913?

Yeats believes that the businessmen of Dublin Corporation would take a dim view of the resurrected patriots. They would look at the assembled heroes and come to the conclusion that every single one of them ('every mother's son') was utterly insane. The businessmen would claim that the patriots had been driven mad by their love of Ireland, just as a man might be driven mad by love for a beautiful woman: 'You'd cry, 'Some woman's yellow hair/ Has maddened every mother's son'.

The patriots, Yeats points out, willingly laid down their lives. Indeed, they did not think of their own lives as especially valuable or important: 'They weighed so lightly what they gave'. For they believed in a cause far greater than themselves. It's as if, having weighed their lives against their values and beliefs, they had concluded that their lives were less important. The heroes, therefore, don't belong in the Ireland of 1913, which is dominated by the businessmen of Dublin Corporation and others like them. This new Ireland is an individualistic and materialistic place, one incapable of appreciating the patriots' extraordinary self-sacrifice. The patriots, were they somehow to return, would only be mocked and misunderstood. Yeats concludes, therefore, that it's better to let the heroes rest in peace: 'But let them be, they're dead and gone/ They're with O'Leary in the grave'.

THEMES

YEATS AND IRELAND

In this poet Yeats laments the decline of Irish society. Yeats feels that the Ireland of 1913 is being shaped by the values of Murphy and his cronies in the Dublin Corporation, and by other materialistic business leaders throughout the land.

This poem draws a stark contrast between Ireland's heroic past and the sad reality of what it has become. Yeats declares that Ireland was once a 'Romantic' country. The word Romantic, as used here, suggests several different things:

- It suggests that Ireland was once a place that valued artistry and imagination, where images, songs and stories were valued by the people.
- It suggests that Ireland was once an idealistic place, one that exhibited community and self-sacrifice rather than miserly focus on self-enrichment.
- It suggests that Ireland was once a place that valued risk-taking and adventure. Now, however, it is a place where people play it safe, focusing on their prayer books and their bank accounts.

For Yeats, the values of Romantic Ireland were especially embodied by the great Irish patriot John O'Leary, who fought in the 1848 rebellion against British rule in Ireland. After this rising, he continued to campaign for Irish freedom, which led to him spending years in prison and in exile. He returned to Dublin in 1885, becoming a great friend and mentor to the young Yeats. But now O'Leary is 'dead and gone', having passed away in 1907. The Romantic Ireland he represented has passed away as well. It has been replaced by a soulless, materialistic culture, as exemplified by Murphy and his fellow business leaders.

The poem also tackles the theme of patriotism and revolution. There was a time when Ireland produced revolutionary patriots like Tone and Emmet. These were men who dreamed big and gave everything to make their dreams a reality. They were prepared to sacrifice everything for the causes they believed in – their wealth, their wellbeing and even their lives.

The Ireland of 1913, Yeats believes, is incapable of understanding such self-sacrifice. The idealism exhibited by Emmet and Tone would strike contemporary Ireland as alien and incomprehensible. Yeats imagines the old heroes somehow coming back to life, only to be treated with scorn by the businessmen who currently lead the country. But Yeats recognises that there was also something tragic about these men's lives. Their lives, he suggests, were marked by 'pain', as they invested year after thankless year into the impossible project of Irish freedom. 'Loneliness', too, was their lot. They were 'exiles' not only when sent abroad after defeat, but also in their own land, because their passionate beliefs alienated them from society at large.

Yeats stresses that the patriots were almost destined to fail, with the odds being stacked overwhelmingly against them. In a memorable turn of phrase, he describes how 'the hangman's rope was spun' for these heroes, as if their defeat and execution were pre-determined. There was almost suicidal element, therefore, about the patriots' efforts. They knew that failure and death were almost inevitable. But they fought anyway.

The middle classes are criticised for failing to understand the patriots' bravery, for regarding them as simply insane. But perhaps Yeats himself can't help suspecting that these heroes had been 'maddened' by their love for Ireland. Yeats says that the heroes 'weighed so lightly what they gave', referring to their patriotic willingness to lay down their lives for their cause. But is there a sense in which he believes that the heroes were a little too willing to die, that they weighed their lives too lightly?

ENERGY, PASSION, VITALITY

This poem celebrates the passion and conviction of certain heroic figures from Irish history, men such as Wolfe Tone and Robert Emmet who gave their lives in the pursuit of Irish independence. These men possessed a number of qualities that Yeats greatly admired. These were men who followed their own principles and instincts. They believed deeply in the idea that Ireland should be free of English rule and devoted their lives to bringing this about. They were not guided by the opinion of the masses and did not try to conform to anyone else's idea of what their lives ought to be. Instead, they let their principles and instincts guide them, believing in something greater than themselves.

These men were reckless, casually risking their lives for what they believed in. Though they knew that they were fated to die, that the odds were greatly stacked against them, they fought on regardless. As Yeats says, from the moment they began to fight, the 'hangman's rope was spun'. But these men seemed to place little stock in their own individual lives, believing that their causes and principles were worth dying for: 'They weighed so lightly what they gave'.

WAR, VIOLENCE AND SOCIAL UPHEAVEL

'September 1913' acknowledges the suffering endured by the patriots of Ireland's past. Many of them, as he notes, endured the loneliness and pain of being sent into exile. Many others suffered execution by the 'hangman's rope'. Overall, however, the poem presents a rather romantic or idealistic view of war and violence. It celebrates the military achievements of the Wild Geese on the continents, the almost foolhardy courage of soldiers like Robert Emmet and John O'Leary who led tiny revolts against a vast imperial power.

The poem emphasises the noble side of warfare, the idealism and self-sacrifice displayed by soldiers in the service of a cause. But it downplays the horror and bloodshed of the battlefield. In this regard, it can be contrasted with 'Easter 1916', which takes a less idealistic view of patriotic violence. It can also be contrasted with 'The Stare's Nest by My Window', where Yeats comes face to face with the terror and confusion of reality in a war zone.

The Wild Swans at Coole

LINE BY LINE

A walk in Coole Park

The poem is set in Coole Park, Co. Galway, which was the private estate and home of Lady Augusta Gregory. Lady Gregory was a major figure in Yeats' life. She helped him in discovering Ireland's heritage of myth and folklore. She collaborated with him on various projects, such as the founding of the Abbey Theatre, and she also provided the frequently cash-strapped poet with financial support. Yeats was a regular visitor to Coole Park, a place he found conducive to his writing.

This poem was written during one such visit to the estate. It is an October evening:

- The evening, according to the poet, is exceptionally 'still'. We imagine an evening without a puff of wind, the clouds static in the twilight sky,
- The woodland paths, according to the poet, are 'dry', which suggests a period of crisp, fine weather. We can imagine the pleasant crunching sound made by the poet's footsteps as he makes his way through the grounds.
- The trees in the park exhibit the beauty of autumn. We can imagine a multi-coloured array of browns, yellows and reds.

The poet comes to one of Coole Park's lakes. The evening is so still that the lake's surface is utterly un-rippled. Its surface resembles a mirror that perfectly reflects the twilight sky above. The lake is described as 'brimming', which suggests that gentle wavelets lap onto the stones around its edges.

The poet back then

As we mentioned above, the poet has been coming to Coole Park on a regular basis. Each time he visits, he takes the same walk around the estate's exquisite grounds, his route taking him past this lake 'among the stones'. He always pauses by this particular lake to count the swans that swim upon its surface. The poet remembers his 'first time' standing on the lake's rocky shore. It was 19 years ago, during his very first visit to Coole Park. That was the first time he attempted to count the swans on the lake's surface: 'The nineteenth autumn has come upon me/ Since I first made my count'.

On that occasion, however, the swans scattered and flew away before he could finish counting them. The poet still recalls the sound of the swans' wings as they circled above him in the 'twilight' nineteen years ago. The noise they produced was rhythmical and powerful, like the regular chiming of a bell: 'The bell-beat of their wings above my head'.

The poet now

Now we move back to the present day. The poet has come once more to the lake 'among the stones'. He pauses, as usual, to count the swans upon its surface. He manages, on this occasion, to complete his count, coming to a grand total of 59. The poet refers to the swans as 'brilliant'. The adjective 'brilliant' suggest that the swans are creatures of exceptional beauty. But it also suggests the extraordinary whiteness of their feathers. Watching these 'brilliant creatures', however, fills the poet with sorrow: 'And now my heart is sore'.

He finds himself thinking about the great changes that have occurred in the 19 years since he stood on this very lake shore and counted the swans for the very first time. And these changes, we sense, have not been for the better:

- The poet has aged physically. He is slower and weaker than he was on that first visit 19 years ago.
- The poet has grown psychologically exhausted over the past 19 years. He has been involved in any number of personal, political and financial struggles, enduring great disappointment and frustration.
- The poet has been unlucky in love. Yeats was famously infatuated with the great beauty Maud Gonne. But his pursuit of her proved unsuccessful. Now, as he enters middle age, he finds himself childless and unmarried.
- The poet's good looks have diminished. He no longer feels himself to be handsome or sexually attractive.

The poet describes how his footsteps were 'lighter' on that first visit to Coole Park. This of course suggests the physical changes the poet has experienced. He's now nearly two decades older and walks in a slower, more deliberate fashion. But it also suggests the psychological changes the poet has experienced. For over the past nineteen years he has become burdened by cares, regrets and disappointments. In the phrase 'All's changed', then, we hear the sigh of a man who fears that his best years are behind him.

The setting seems to correspond with the poet's feelings about his life. It is autumn, meaning the splendours of summer are passed and the bitterness of winter lies in wait. The poet, similarly, has entered the 'autumn' of his life. The splendours of youth are a distant memory and old age is fast approaching. Even the dryness of the woodland paths suggests the physical decline that accompanies the ageing process.

Contrast between the poet and the swans

The poet draws a sharp contrast between himself and the swans. The swans are 'Unwearied still'. They exhibit none of the physical decline that has affected the poet. They still have the strength to 'climb the air', to launch themselves skyward in a powerful and majestic fashion.

The swans are also 'Unwearied' in a psychological sense. 'Their hearts', unlike the heart of the poet, 'have not grown old'. They experience none of the mental exhaustion that has affected the poet, and they are unburdened by the cares and disappointments that weigh him down.

The swans, according to the poet, experience a rich and varied love life. A swan, he suggests, will have a passionate affair with one companion before moving on to the next. Each new affair will begin with flirtation and seduction, followed by a moment of sexual conquest. Each relationship is filled with passion and affection.

In this regard, the contrast between the poet and the swans couldn't be sharper. The swans exist in waters that are 'companionable', each swimming contentedly beside its current partner. The poet, in contrast, has no lover, wife or family. The swans enjoy lives of endless sexual opportunity. No matter where they go, they will experience passion and conquest: 'Passion or conquest, wander where they will,/ Attend upon them still'. The poet, by contrast, feels that his opportunities for love and passion have passed him by.

Will the swans depart?

The poet continues to watch the swans gliding on the lake's surface. He relishes this sight, emphasising its mystery and beauty: 'But now they drift on the still water,/ Mysterious, beautiful'. But he realises that the swans will not always be here. Sooner or later the colony will depart for some new home, leaving Coole Park behind forever. He imagines the swans arriving at some faraway 'lake' or 'pool', where they will build new nests for themselves among the rushes at the water's edge: 'Among what rushes will they build [?]'

The poet imagines some future visit to Coole Park. He imagines walking by the lake only to discover that the swans have departed. He will no longer be able to enjoy the sight of these magnificent creatures. That privilege will now fall to others, those who live beside the swans' new home.

FOCUS ON STYLE

Form

This is a lyrical poem, comprising of five six-line stanzas. Each stanza follows the same rhyming scheme ABCBDD.

Verbal Music

There are several places where assonance and alliteration create a pleasant musical effect, reflecting the stillness of this fine October evening. We see this with the repeated 'i' sounds in 'drift on the still water' and 'Mirrors a still sky'.

A similar musical effect is created by the repeated 'a' and 'u' sounds in the poem's opening lines: 'autumn beauty' and 'woodland paths'.

There is an element of cacophony in the second stanza, where the clashing 't', 'k' and 'l' sounds suggest the rackett produced by the swans as they scatter screeching into the sky. Finally, the repeated broad vowel sounds in 'trod with a lighter tread' slow the pace of the verse, suggesting the poet's plodding, laborious gait.

Imagery

This poem is redolent with imagery of the natural world. Especially vivid is the image of the swans suddenly taking flight. Each mounts the air as though it were a horseman preparing to ride into battle. Yeats brilliantly captures the circular flight-path of the swans as they spiral upwards: 'scatter wheeling in great broken rings'.

The poem also features a memorable instance of personification. Personification occurs when an abstract concept is presented as if it were a person. In this instance, passion and conquest are presented as attendants or servants that follow the swans wherever they go: 'Passion or conquest, wander where they will,/ Attend upon them still'.

THEMES

NATURE

This is one of Yeats' best-loved nature poems. The poet captures the unique qualities of an Irish autumn evening: a crisp path underfoot, a haunting stillness in the twilight sky, trees in their multi-coloured beauty.

The poem especially celebrates swans, those most mysterious and beautiful creatures. Yeats shows us the swans in two very different states. He highlights their grace and serenity as they drift on the still water, and he also highlights the explosive power and force they exhibit as they 'mount/ And scatter', their wings thumping with the piercing regularity of a bell.

YOUTH AND AGE

The poet, as we've seen, laments the beginnings of middle age. He has started to exhibit not only physical weakness and psychological exhaustion, but also a lessening of his good looks and sexual opportunities. His heart is 'sore' as he contemplates his decline.

The poem centres on the contrast between the poet, whose life has endured such changes, and the swans, who are presented as being utterly changeless. The swans, as we have seen, are 'unwearied' in body and mind, as they pursue lives of unbounded passion and sexual adventure.

The end of the poem is almost unbearably sad. The poet, as we've seen, imagines that the swans will someday leave behind Coole Park. The park, then, will be deserted by the swans just as the poet will be deserted by the last of his vitality and good looks. The swans will be enjoyed by other people in the far-away places where they build their homes. Similarly, youth and vitality will be the preserve of the younger generation, as the poet sinks into old age.

An Irish Airman Foresees His Death

LINE BY LINE

This is an example of a 'persona poem'. In such poems, the poet speaks not as him or herself, but takes on the voice of someone completely different. In this instance, Yeats speaks in the voice of an Irish pilot serving with the British armed forces in World War 1.

The poem was inspired by Major Robert Gregory, an Irish friend of Yeats who fought with the British Royal Flying Corps. He was shot down and killed in 1918, just before the end of that terrible conflict. Robert was the son of Lady Augusta Gregory, Yeats' great friend, supporter and collaborator. Yeats was a frequent visitor to the Gregory estate in Coole Park, Co. Galway, which inspired his famous poem 'The Wild Swans at Coole'.

The airman somehow knows in advance that he will die in battle: 'I know that I shall meet my fate'. He knows that his plane will be shot down 'Somewhere among the clouds above'. Despite this premonition, however, he still volunteers to fight. Why does he make this seemingly suicidal choice?

The airman claims that he has no affection for either side in the First World War, which saw Britain and her allies ranged against Germany and the other central powers. As a member of the Flying Corps, the airman flies on many missions against German forces, attacking enemy planes and ground positions. But he doesn't do so because he hates the German people: 'Those that I fight I do not hate'. His job as a member of the Flying Corps is to protect Britain and her interests in the world, especially to 'guard' the island of Britain itself from possible invasion. The airman carries out this task, flying in mission after mission aimed at making Britain more secure. But he does not do so out of any special love of the British people: 'Those that I guard I do not love'.

Nor did the airman volunteer in order to help his own people, the poor folk of Kiltartan in Co. Galway: 'My country is Kiltartan Cross,/ My countrymen Kiltartan's poor'. He knows that the result of the war will make no difference to them and to the rest of the Irish nation. The conflict – no matter how it ends – won't leave them any 'happier'. Nor will it bring them any great 'loss'.

He doesn't serve because he is required to do so by 'law'. Though Ireland was under British rule during the First World War, Irish people like the airman were not legally obliged to serve in the British army. Nor did he volunteer out of a sense of 'duty'. As an Irish person, he doesn't feel morally obliged to fight for Britain and her interests on the continent.

He is motivated neither by the speeches of politicians nor by by the cheers of the crowds that listened to them: 'Nor public men, nor cheering crowds'. We might think here of images and footage from the beginning of the war, which show a wave of patriotism sweeping across Europe. In London, Paris, Berlin and Vienna, thousands would gather to hear their leaders speak, each 'cheering crowd' convinced that right was on their country's side and that victory would be theirs. The airman, however, is unmoved by this mass patriotic hysteria.

So why does the airman fight? Why does he journey again and again into that 'tumult in the clouds', into the noise and confusion of aerial combat? Why did he volunteer, of his own free will, when he anticipates that doing so will lead to his death?

The airman describes how he was driven to volunteer by an 'impulse', by a strong and almost irresistible urge. According to the airman, the impulse driving him is one of 'delight':

- There's the delight that comes from the act of flying itself, from handling this magnificent piece of hardware and making it respond to one's slightest touch.
- There's the delight that comes from being so far above the world, from experiencing what might be described as a God's-eye view of creation. For the airman, operating at the dawn of aviation, such excitement must have been even more pronounced. For he was experiencing something few other humans ever had.
- There's the adrenaline rush that comes with all sport and competition, as the airman engages his German opponents in move and counter-move, in a noisy and chaotic game of three-dimensional chess.
- There's the thrill that comes from putting your life on the line. Again and again, soldiers and emergency responders report how they never feel more alive than in those moments when their deaths are a real possibility.

We often think that people who act on impulse behave in an unreflective and irrational manner. The airman, however, is adamant that he has not acted in such a way. He claims that he has assessed his life calmly and rationally, weighing up its every aspect: 'I balanced all, brought all to mind'. The conclusion he draws from this assessment is a bleak one. He regards his life up to this point as utterly pointless. All the years he's lived through were no more than a waste of time and energy: 'A waste of breath the years behind'. The years remaining to him seem equally futile: 'The years to come seemed waste of breath'. To the airman, then, life is a meaningless affair.

The airman views death in aerial combat as a fitting or appropriate end to the life he has lived: 'In balance with this life, this death'. This line is open to a number of interpretations. Perhaps the airman is simply suggesting that death offers him an escape from a life he finds pointless, dreary and depressing. Or perhaps he feels that going down in one final blaze of glory will 'balance out' or make up for the pointless waste of breath that was his life. It is also possible that the airman wants to die in aerial combat because that was the only place in which he truly feels alive. Such a death, therefore, would be a 'balanced' or appropriate conclusion to his life.

FOCUS ON STYLE

The poem is marked by a strong, propulsive rhythm. Repetition, too, features strongly, with repeated patterns of phrasing in lines 3 and 4 ('Those that... Those that...') as well as in lines 5 and 6 ('My country...My countrymen...') Similarly, the last four lines feature the repetition of 'all', 'balance', 'the years' and 'waste of 'breath'.

Rhythm, rhyme and repetition combine to lend the poem a relentless, driving music, one that echoes, perhaps, the sound of the airman's propellers rotating, or that evokes the thoughts swirling around and around his mind as he prepares for his final journey into battle.

THEMES

WAR, VIOLENCE AND SOCIAL UPHEAVAL

The poem was written at a time of extraordinary violence, when Europe witnessed the bloodiest and most destructive war it had ever seen. Yeats was always a scholar rather than a soldier. But he exhibited a lifelong fascination with men of action, with those who, like the airman, had the bravery to enter the field of battle, putting their lives on the line as they fought, died and killed.

No doubt Yeats also admires how the airman is a person apart. The airman, unlike his fellow soldiers, has no truck with the propaganda of public men and politicians. He is unmoved by the great wave of patriotism that has swept across the continent. Instead, as we have seen, he fights for his own reasons.

DEATH

Yeats, we sense, admires the airman's vitality and energy. The airman exhibits a reckless abandon, plunging almost joyfully into the terrifying melee of aerial combat, risking his life again and again in the chaotic 'tumult' of engagements with the enemy. There's a sense, then, in which the airman comes across as what today we would call a thrill-seeker or an adrenaline junkie, being someone who lives for the adventure of flight and the exhilaration of aerial combat. Like participants in various extreme sports, the airman takes 'delight' and pleasure in risking his life. We sense he only feels alive when he is involved in the chaos and 'tumult' of battle above the clouds. To the airman, life is only worth living when it's at its most intense.

But the airman, it must be noted, also exhibits a terrifying 'nihilism', which is the belief that everything in life is utterly pointless and without meaning. It is not surprising that he describes himself as being driven by a 'lonely impulse', given his depressing outlook on life. Many readers have taken issue with what might be described as the airman's 'suicidal tendencies' or 'death wish'. They also question his contemptuous disdain for everyday life. Can we endorse the airman's verdict that these things represent no more than a 'waste of breath'? Or can we reject his view of life as that of a 'lonely' individual whose only relief from depression comes in the thick of aerial combat?

Easter 1916

LINE BY LINE

The Easter Rising took place in Dublin between Monday 24 April and Saturday 29 April 1916. It was a rebellion against British rule in Ireland and was defeated after a swift British military response.

The Rising was planned in secret by seven men, mostly of the Irish Republican Brotherhood (IRB), who had formed a 'Military Council' to this end just after the outbreak of the First World War.

Yeats was absent from Dublin for the Rising but his response to it was intense: "I had no idea that any public event could so deeply move me," he wrote to Lady Gregory, "and I am very despondent about the future".

Section 1

Yeats recalls how he sometimes encountered the revolutionaries when walking through Dublin. He would run into them late in the afternoon, as they emerged from their various places of work around the city: 'I have met them at close of day/ Coming ... From counter or desk'.

These young men would have been barmen and shopkeepers, teachers and clerks. But they would have also been members of illegal organisations such as the IRB. They would

meet regularly to discuss and plan the possibility of Irish independence being achieved by means of violent revolution. The passion and enthusiasm for their cause would be written on their faces, which the poet describes as 'vivid'.

Yeats would have known some of these people through their involvement in the theatre world or the arts. Others, he would have known just to see, perhaps from frequenting their shops or offices. He, like many people in Dublin, would have known that they were radicals, members of illegal organisations committed to revolution.

The poet would have been sympathetic to the revolutionaries' ultimate goal – Irish independence from Britain – but he did not believe that violence was the best means to achieve this. Although Yeats had in his youth flirted with the idea of revolution, he later came to believe that independence was best achieved through political means. And the possibility of this happening was very real. The Home Rule Act, intended to provide home rule for Ireland, had been passed by the British Parliament in 1914, but the implementation of it was postponed with the outbreak of the First World War. Home Rule would not have meant complete freedom from Britain, but it would have been a significant step towards this.

As such, Yeats believed that the 1916 rebels were misguided. But, more than this, he considered them to be naïve and foolish in their outlook and beliefs. What, he must have wondered, did they really think they were going to achieve? Ireland had been under British rule for over 800 years. The very buildings that the revolutionaries worked in were built by the British: 'grey nineteenth century houses'. The British empire at the time was the biggest empire the world had ever seen. There had been a number of attempts at violent revolution over the years, and every single one had utterly failed – both in terms of advancing the Irish cause and in terms of convincing the Irish public that violence was the best means of achieving independence.

Yeats never imagined that the revolutionaries he encountered on the streets would ever do or achieve anything of significance. He was quite sure that their talk of revolution was just that – talk. And if they ever did manage to organise a revolt, it would surely be a pathetic and embarrassing failure. He regarded the rebels as fools and clowns, who played at revolution but lacked the ability to make it a reality. He was sure that Ireland had become a place where 'motley', the colours of the jester, were worn.

The poet's contempt for the revolutionaries can be partly explained by the differences in their backgrounds. Yeats' family were members of the Protestant ascendancy, the landowning class that had dominated Ireland until the early 20th century. Although times were changing and the poet was by no means a wealthy man, Yeats' outlook and opinion of who he was were still defined in terms of this background.

Yeats had inherited enough money that he did not need to work. He socialised in the Gentlemen's clubs in Dublin, private clubs whose members would have all shared similar backgrounds to Yeats. The revolutionaries, in turn, were descendants of Irish Catholics, the very people whose land the Protestants had taken and held for centuries. These were men who had to work for a living and would socialise in the pubs around Dublin.

The poet could never imagine that the future political leaders of Ireland would come from the Catholic middle classes – he did not think they had the necessary qualities and intellect. Ireland's political leadership, both intellectual and political, would surely come only from the Protestant land-owning class as it always had. The idea that political power would come to rest in the hands of the shopkeepers and clerks who spoke excitedly about rising up against the British struck the poet as ridiculous.

And so, when the poet encountered these men as they came from their shops and offices after work, he would barely give them the time of day. More often than not, he would simply pass them with a 'nod of the head' or say something civil and perfunctory as they went by: 'polite meaningless words'. Occasionally, the poet would stop out of courtesy and have a brief chat. But again, nothing significant would be said apart from 'Polite meaningless words'. While he was chatting to them, he would be thinking about how he would later speak with scorn and ridicule of the encounter to some friend at a social club: 'a mocking tale or a gibe/ To please a companion/ Around the fire at the club'.

But then the Easter Rising took place and changed everything: 'All changed, changed utterly'. On Monday 24 April, the insurgents proclaimed an Irish Republic with Pearse as President and Connolly as commander in chief. They occupied positions around Dublin at the General Post Office, the Four Courts, the South Dublin Union, Boland's Mill, Stephen's Green and Jacobs' biscuit factory. Over the following week, the British deployed over 16,000 troops, artillery and naval gunboats in the city to suppress the Rising. In the week's fighting, about 450 people were killed and over 2,000 wounded. Sixteen of the rebel leaders were later executed.

Suddenly, therefore, the very people that Yeats had mocked and disparaged had acted with courage and conviction, risking and sacrificing their lives for the cause of Irish independence. They had staged an event that was momentous, that had earned the support and the sympathies of the Irish public. This forced the poet to re-evaluate and question many of his beliefs and convictions.

Yeats had to respect the manner in which these revolutionaries had put their lives on the line for their beliefs, but the whole idea of blood sacrifice and glorification of violence as a means of achieving political ends made him anxious and fearful for the future. The rebels had done something heroic and revealed a form of 'beauty' in dying for their cause, but the idea that an independent Ireland would be founded on violent insurrection was also 'terrible' and terrifying.

Section 2

Yeats was especially shocked and moved by the Rising because he knew some of those who were involved personally. He describes some of them, outlining what they did and how he felt about them prior to the Rising.

He begins with Constance Gore-Booth, someone that Yeats knew when she was a young lady. In 1894, the poet stayed at Lissadell, the home of the aristocratic Gore-Booth family in Sligo. He became friends with Constance and her sister Eva, and he greatly admired their beauty. Yeats recalls how 'beautiful' Constance looked when she was out riding with the hunt: 'When, young and beautiful,/ She rode to harriers'. He also remembers how delightful her voice sounded back then: 'What voice more sweet than hers'.

But when Constance later became involved in politics, Yeats was scornful and critical of her involvement. He believed that a beautiful, aristocratic lady such as Constance had no business involving herself in the grubby world of politics. Her intentions might have been good, but Yeats had little regard for her grasp of politics: 'That woman's days were spent/ In ignorant good-will'. Her involvement in politics, he believed, rendered her ugly. Her once 'sweet' voice 'grew shrill' when she engaged in political debates and arguments: 'Her nights in argument/ Until her voice grew shrill'.

Yeats describes two of the leaders of the rebellion, Pádraig Pearse and Thomas MacDonagh. Pearse had started his own school for boys in 1908: 'This man had kept a school'. Here the students were taught in English as well as Irish. Yeats also alludes to the fact that Pearse was poet, saying that he 'rode our winged horse' (Pegasus, a creature from Greek mythology, was a winged horse and a symbol of poetic inspiration).

Thomas MacDonagh was a friend of Pearse's and assisted him in running the school: 'This other his helper and friend'. MacDonagh was also a poet and dramatist and Yeats felt that he had real potential as a writer. He was 'coming into his force'. Yeats speculates that 'He might have won fame in the end' for his writing. He is described as 'sensitive' and his thoughts as 'so daring and sweet'.

Finally, Yeats describes Major John MacBride. In 1903 ,MacBride had married Maud Gonne, the lady that Yeats had loved and considered his muse. The marriage failed and there were accusations that MacBride had abused Maud Gonne and molested her daughter from a previous marriage. Yeats despised MacBride. He describes him as aggressive, drunken, and vain: 'A drunken, vainglorious lout', someone who had 'done most bitter wrong' to people that Yeats held dearly.

But that is who these people were and what the poet thought of them prior to their involvement in the Easter Rising. Now they have become heroes, and in the case of Pearse, MacDonagh and MacBride, martyrs for the cause of Irish independence. They have, therefore, 'been changed' and 'Transformed utterly'. It does not matter what Yeats once thought about these people – he might as well have 'dreamed' that MacBride was a 'lout' – the reality is that they will forever be remembered for their roles in the Rising. They are no longer part of the 'casual comedy' of Irish life; they have become detached from this petty world and have been elevated to the ranks of Wolfe Tone and Robert Emmet.

Section 3

Yeats considers the determination of the revolutionaries and the manner in which they were willing and able to devote their lives to a single cause: 'Hearts with one purpose alone'. Such steadfast commitment to a single cause strikes the poet as unnatural. How can people devote themselves to 'one purpose alone' in a world that is constantly transforming and changing?

Yeats compares life to a stream that is constantly flowing and, therefore, changing: 'the living stream'. He paints a picture of the surrounding landscape, which is also changing 'minute by minute'. The scene that the poet describes is full of movement and flux:

- A horse and rider come 'from the road' to cross the stream. When the horse enters the stream, it kicks and splashes the water as it crosses.
- Birds fly in different directions across the sky, through clouds that are 'tumbling' and changing and casting shadows on the ground that constantly shift and change.

- 'long-legged moor-hens dive' from the sky towards the stream and call out to the moorcocks.

It is a dynamic scene full of life and energy: 'Minute by minute they live'. But those who commit themselves and devote their entire lives to a single cause seem to be at odds with a world that is constantly moving and changing. It is as if they have been put under a spell that renders them oblivious and impervious to what is going on around them: 'Hearts with one purpose alone/ Through summer and winter seem/ Enchanted to a stone'.

Section 4

Yeats greatly fears that the Rising might instigate a new period in Irish history, one marked and defined by violent upheaval. He worries not only about the ensuing loss of life but also the toll that years of war, fighting and bloodshed will take on people. There can come a point when people stop caring, when they are no longer appalled at the notion of individuals sacrificing themselves for a cause: 'Too long a sacrifice/ Can make a stone of the heart'. And what amount of sacrifice is sufficient, the poet wonders, to achieve a goal such as Irish independence: 'O when may it suffice?'

The poet wonders if those who lost and sacrificed their lives in the Rising did so needlessly: 'Was it needless death after all'. As we mentioned above, the Home Rule Act had been passed by the British Parliament in 1914, but the implementation of it was postponed with the outbreak of the First World War. In 1916, this war still raged and many doubted that the bill would ever be implemented. But Yeats considers the possibility that England would keep its word. If this was to be the case, then the Rising would have been for nothing: 'Was it needless death after all?/ For England may keep faith'.

Yeats also considers the possibility that the rebels acted in a crazy, irrational manner, that they were 'bewildered' by their great love for Ireland and that this led them to take foolhardy action: 'what if excess of love/ Bewildered them till they died?' But ultimately he does not see any point in such reservation or surmise. It is impossible to know now what would have happened had the Rising not taken place, and it seems pointless to speculate whether the rebels acted rationally or irrationally. It is enough to know that they had a dream Ireland would be a sovereign country and they gave their lives to bring this about: 'enough/ To know they dreamed and are dead'.

Yeats knows that he is not in a position to say when or if such a sacrifice will lead to Irish independence. As a poet, all he can do is chronicle what has happened and record the names of those who selflessly sacrificed their lives for this cause: 'our part to murmur name upon name'. There is something soothing and loving about this act. Yeats likens the rebels to children who have been out running 'wild' and have now fallen asleep: 'When sleep at last has come/ On limbs that had run wild'. Those who recite the names of the rebels are likened to the mother who lovingly speaks the child's name as she soothes it

Dublin's General Post Office on fire after the 1916 Easter Rising

to sleep: 'To murmur name upon name,/ As a mother names her child'.

And so Yeats rounds the poem off by writing the names of some of those who died 'out in a verse': 'MacDonagh and MacBride/ And Connolly and Pearse'. He knows that, no matter what happens after, these individuals have become part of Irish history and will be remembered by Irish people all over the world: 'Wherever green is worn'. Their partaking in the Rising has transformed them into heroes and martyrs: 'Are changed, changed utterly'. By emulating the great Irish heroes of the past and sacrificing their lives for their country, these men have done something noble. Their actions, the poet knows, will inspire others to do the same: 'A terrible beauty is born'.

FOCUS ON STYLE

Form

The poem is composed of four stanzas: two comprising 16 lines and two comprising 24 lines. The rhyme scheme is made up of four-line rhyme units, i.e. ABAB CDCD EFEF etc. The poem's form and structure are deliberately symbolic, as the Easter Rising took place on the 24th day of the fourth month of 1916.

Metaphor, Simile, Figures of Speech

In stanza 3, Yeats uses the metaphor of the stream to represent life and the manner in which it is constantly moving and changing. He uses the metaphor of the stone to represent the revolutionaries' unwavering commitment to their cause: 'Hearts with one purpose alone … seem/ Enchanted to a stone'. The revolutionaries' hearts are like stones because they remain unaffected by the changes that are happening in the world around them, just as a stone lodged in a stream remains static and unchanged by the water's flow. Instead, it is the stone that affects the water, causing the stream to flow around it: 'To trouble the living stream.' This suggests the ripple effect that the revolutionaries' actions and courage had on the entire population.

In an effort to soften the tragedy of the revolutionaries' deaths, Yeats uses the metaphor of sleep: 'What is it but nightfall?' But he quickly dismisses the analogy, suggesting that there is no way to diminish the impact or the stark reality of what has happened.

Three of the poem's four stanzas end with the line, 'A terrible beauty is born', a refrain that captures the poet's conflicted feelings about what has happened. The phrase 'terrible beauty' is an oxymoron because it consists of two terms that we would normally consider contradictory. How can something be both beautiful and terrible? But for Yeats, the Rising and the manner in which the revolutionaries sacrificed their lives was a thing of beauty. There is something noble and heroic about the rebels' actions, and the poet believes that it signals the re-emergence of these qualities in a country that he had written off as shallow and farcical. However, their sacrifice is also 'terrible' because it involves violence and death, and Yeats fears that the Rising will provoke more bloodshed in the future.

YEATS AND IRELAND

This is another poem in which Yeats talks about the decline of Irish society. Yeats believed that Ireland was a ridiculous place, one of 'casual comedy' that was inhabited by clowns and fools that might very well have been wearing the 'motley' of the traditional court jester. Yeats, as he indicated in 'September 1913', believed that Ireland had become a crass and materialistic culture. Ireland, he felt, could produce nothing serious, nothing beautiful and nothing heroic.

This poem also continues Yeats' meditation on patriotism and revolt. At the beginning of the poem, Yeats describes how he used to laugh behind the backs of nationalists like Pearse and Connolly when he met them on the streets of Dublin. These men were fervently convinced that Ireland could be roused to rebel against British rule. Yeats, on the other hand, felt that Ireland was no longer capable of producing the self-sacrifice and heroism necessary for rebellion (we see this in 'September 1913' where Yeats lamented that 'Romantic Ireland is dead and gone').

But Yeats is forced to concede that he was wrong. The rebel leaders not only had a dream, but they acted on that dream to make it a reality, paying the ultimate price as they did so: 'We know their dream; enough/ To know they dreamed and are dead'. They persuaded a small army to seize the centre of Dublin in defiance of the world's greatest empire, and in doing so utterly changed Ireland's political situation.

However, Yeats' undoubted admiration for the Rising leaders is tempered by a sense of unease:

*   Perhaps the leaders were overly patriotic, experiencing an 'excess of love' for their country that drove them to extreme measures.
*   He presents them as obsessives, who focused completely on 'one purpose alone'. Even when walking home from work, they had the 'vivid faces' of men on a mission, of people fired-up to make their 'one purpose' a reality.
*   Many of the rebels had sacrificed a great deal in the years leading up to the Rising, devoting all their time and energy to the project of revolt. This sacrifice, Yeats believed, changed them as people, leaving them ruthless and unfeeling: 'Too long a sacrifice/ Can make a stone of the heart'.
*   Yeats also suggests that their sacrifice might have all been for nothing. For Ireland might have gained a measure of independence anyway, without the Rising and all its attendant bloodshed and destruction: 'Was it needless death after all?'

Ultimately, however, Yeats accepts that these men and women have made the ultimate sacrifice for their country and will be remembered as heroes. Wherever Irish people gather, wherever 'green is worn', people will recount their deeds with an awe

and admiration. It is the duty of Irish people, Yeats suggests, to keep their names alive, so that the story of their deeds is passed down to future generations.

The Rising, in Yeats' memorable phrase, has unleashed a 'terrible beauty'. It is beautiful because it involves heroism, honour and self-sacrifice. It is terrible because it involves bloodshed and destruction. Yeats, as he contemplates the future, feel that the coming years will be shaped by both this terror and this beauty.

NATURE

In the third section of the poem, Yeats describes how the world is in a constant state of flux, forever changing 'minute by minute'. He compares life to a 'stream' that is constantly moving and, therefore, changing: 'the living stream'. Yeats also captures the dramatic vibrancy of the natural world by describing a landscape that is constantly shifting. The different elements in the scene he describes impact on each other:

*   The horses' hooves 'plashes' the water of the stream.
*   The clouds tumble through the sky and create different, shifting shadows on the landscape below.

The poet contrasts this constant change with the singular commitment of the revolutionaries to their cause. He describes how 'Hearts with one purpose alone' are immune or oblivious to the fact that the world is constantly shifting and changing around them. He compares them to stones that lodge themselves in the stream and stubbornly refuse to move or change. In this regard, the revolutionaries strike the poet as unnatural. Ironically, however, the revolutionaries' singular commitment to their cause brings about great change in the world. By remaining immune to change and sticking to their purpose, they end up greatly disturbing or troubling 'the living stream'.

ART AND THE ROLE OF THE ARTIST

This is another poem where Yeats presents the artist as having a public role. The leaders of the Rising, he insists, must be remembered by the Irish people. He uses his poetic skills to contribute to this process, writing a 'verse' that will help to keep the leaders' names alive.

The Second Coming

LINE BY LINE

Anarchy loosed

Yeats wrote 'The Second Coming' in 1919, which was a time of chaos and uncertainty across Europe. The Great War, which had just ended, had torn the continent apart, leaving unprecedented disorder in its wake:

- Vast tracts of central Europe were left with no government, or with several competing governments, as old empires collapsed and new states arose from the ashes of war.
- In many cases, vital services provided by the state (such as policing, law and the provision of medical assistance) simply disappeared.
- Post-war food shortages put an end to the normal buying and selling of goods.
- Communist revolution added to political and social instability, most famously in Russia, but also in Germany, Hungary, Italy and elsewhere.
- To make matters worse, a vicious flu epidemic was raging across the continent, claiming millions of lives.

To Yeats, then, it seems like 'Things fall apart', that the entire structure of society is falling to pieces. The continent, he feels, has been plunged into 'anarchy', a state of complete disorder. In a brilliant turn of phrase, Yeats describes how anarchy has been 'loosed' or released, as if it were a pack of dogs that's now free to ravage the entire continent: 'Mere anarchy is loosed upon the world'.

The poet is also greatly troubled by what he sees as the rise of extremism. We often think of moderate political views as the 'centre'. More extreme or radical views, meanwhile, are associated with the left or the right. When Yeats looks at the world, he sees reasonable or sensible opinion giving way: 'the centre cannot hold'. Meanwhile, views he regards as worryingly extreme, or even dangerously crazy, seem to be gaining ground.

Yeats uses a metaphor from the sport of falconry to represent this chaos. In falconry a sportsman, known as a falconer, uses a trained falcon to hunt small animals and birds. Yeats depicts a falcon that has been released by its falconer and goes soaring into the air.

The bird's flight path forms the shape of a 'gyre', or upside-down cone, as it spirals upwards and outwards away from its master's hand: 'Turning and turning in the widening gyre'. Usually, the falconer controls the falcon by means of verbal commands. But on this occasion, the falcon has wheeled so far into the sky that it can no longer hear him: 'The falcon cannot hear the falconer'. The bird is out of control now, flying where it will.

The spiralling falcon serves as a powerful metaphor for current events. Just as the falconer has lost control of his falcon, so the voices of moderation have lost control of Europe's political scene. It seems to Yeats that there are no longer sensible people in charge; there are no longer rational people steering the governments of the world. Events, it seems to him, are quickly spinning out of control.

The bloody tide

1919 was also a time of great violence. The unprecedented slaughter of World War One was barely over when several terrible civil wars broke out across the continent. There were bloody conflicts in Russia, Greece and Germany for instance. Many other countries experienced lesser bouts of violence associated with riot, revolution and counter-revolution. Ireland, too, was wracked by the trauma of warfare, as the IRA fought for independence from British rule.

As he considers these events, Yeats feels that Europe is about to become an extremely violent place, a nightmarish zone of eternal war where once unimaginable bloodshed is now the norm. He uses a wonderfully vivid metaphor to describe this descent into butchery:

- He pictures a sea into which an enormous quantity of blood has flown.
- This blood had functioned as a kind of dye, so that the ocean's usually transparent waters have been dulled or dimmed.
- He imagines this gory ocean thrusting and sweeping forward in a great tidal wave to engulf the continent, or maybe the entire world: 'The blood-dimmed tide is loosed'.

Yeats' final complaint is that evil men seem to be full of strength, energy, and a sense of purpose. Good men, on the other hand, lack these qualities: 'The best lack all conviction, while the worst/ Are full of passionate intensity'.

Apocolypse and visions

Yeats, then, is greatly perturbed by the violence and chaos that characterise current events in Europe, from Dublin all the way to Moscow. But these disturbances, terrible as they are, strike him as mere omens of 'the Second Coming'; they seem to signal an event of even greater and more terrible consequence. 'Surely the Second Coming is at hand'. He imagines that the continent will soon face a disaster of truly apocalyptic

proportions, a cataclysm that will make even the recently concluded First World War seem tame in comparison.

Throughout his life, Yeats was a great believer in mysticism and the occult. He was convinced that certain individuals, under the right conditions, were capable of extraordinary supernatural visions in which they witnessed past, present and future. We might think of these visions, often experienced during a trance-like state, as 'revelations' because they 'reveal' deep truths about the universe and the world.

'Spiritus Mundi' is a Latin term that literally means, 'world spirit'. We might think of it as a vast soul or consciousness that, according to Yeats, contains the memories of the entire universe. Mystics and prophets could at times 'tap into' Spiritus Mundi, especially when they entered a trance-like state. Artists, too, could commune with this 'world soul' when they permitted themselves to be guided by their unconscious rather than their conscious minds. To Yeats, Spiritus Mundi is the source of all images and symbols, 'a universal memory and a 'muse' of sorts that provides inspiration to the poet or writer'.

As he considers the dark direction of European society, Yeats feels that he himself is about to experience such a visionary moment: 'Surely some revelation is at hand'. Indeed, no sooner has Yeats considered this 'Second Coming' than his longed-for vision commences: 'The Second Coming! Hardly are those words out'. It's as if contemplating Europe's doom somehow triggers a supernatural capacity that has always lain dormant within him. The vision he experiences, however, is a not a pleasant one. For in this moment of revelation he witnesses a 'vast' entity, a creature that disturbs him greatly, that, as he puts it in a typically inventive turn of phrase, 'Troubles [his] sight'.

The beast

Yeats goes into some detail about the beast that dominates his vision. The phrase 'stony sleep' suggests that the beast is made out of stone, that it resembles a vast statue slowly coming to life. In many respects, it seems to resemble the statue of the sphinx at Giza in Egypt:

- It exists in a bleak desert landscape and is a grotesque mixture of man and animal: 'in sands of the desert/ A shape with lion body and the head of a man'.
- The expression on its all-too-human face is terrifying, suggesting that it is utterly incapable of any form of empathy or kindness: a 'gaze blank and pitiless as the sun'.
- The beast has been sleeping for 'twenty centuries' or two thousand years. But now its rest becomes 'vexed' or disturbed by a 'rocking cradle'. The cradle in question is almost certainly the world itself, which has been 'rocked' by the various upheavals referred to in the opening lines.
- It's as if the still-slumbering beast senses these dark happenings on an unconscious level and realises they serve as omens of its birth, that the time is quickly approaching when it must awaken and re-enter the world.

- The beast, having had its slumber disturbed in this fashion, experiences a state of nightmarish agitated sleep before finally awaking.
- The adjective 'rough' describes not only its harsh and unforgiving nature but also its stone surface, which has been left pock-marked, eroded and uneven by its two-thousand-year slumber in the desert.

The beast's thighs are described as 'slow', suggesting the difficulty with which its vast limbs (composed perhaps of granite or some other hard-wearing rock) creak into motion after such a long period of dormancy. It 'slouches' towards Bethlehem, suggesting that, after its long slumber, it's still moving in a rather stiff and ungainly fashion.

The beast's motion disturbs the 'desert birds' that have been roosting on its stony surface. The startled birds 'reel' away into the sky, outraged or 'indignant' that their resting place has suddenly started moving under them.

The end of the vision
Yeats believed that it's only in moments of revelation, like the one described in this poem, that we really see the universe for what it is. To Yeats, therefore, the end of his vision is like passing from light into darkness: 'The darkness drops again'. It's like a curtain has fallen across the great stage of the universe, obscuring his view of its mysteries.

The poet, however, has seen enough to learn something profound about the future: 'But now I know'. He knows that the beast's two-thousand-year-long slumber is at an end. He knows its time is coming: 'its hour come round at last'. According to Yeats, the beast will be 'born' in Bethlehem: 'what rough beast…/ Slouches towards Bethlehem to be born?'

Yeats was partial to occult and outlandish ideas. But not even he believed that an actual lion with the head of a man was going to suddenly appear in Bethlehem. Nor did he believe that this creature would be incarnated or born in the form of a human being. To him, the beast is instead a symbol, representing a wave of 'laughing, ecstatic destruction' that would soon be visited upon the world.

FOCUS ON STYLE

Metaphor, Simile, Figures of Speech
The falcon spinning out of control serves as a powerful metaphor for the chaotic nature of current events. Equally vivid is the metaphor of the 'blood-dimmed tide'. This tidal wave of blood-polluted water represents the violence Yeats sees 'everywhere' in 1919 and the even greater violence he believed was on the horizon.

A wonderful simile, meanwhile, is used to describe the creature's demeanour and facial expression. Yeats declares that it has a 'gaze blank and pitiless as the sun'. We can imagine the monster's face being as cruel and impassive as the scorching sun of the desert.

Imagery
The poem is dominated by the unforgettable 'vast image' of the sphinx-like creature awakening in the depths of the desert. We can visualise this enormous stone creature slowly stirring and flexing its stiff limbs before it 'slouches' off towards Bethlehem, its ultimate destination.

Equally vivid is the image of the birds that have been startled by the beast's awakening. 'all about it/ Reel shadows of the indignant desert birds'. The word 'Reel' suggests that there is something violent and frenzied about their movement. We can imagine the din of their angry cawing as they recoil through the air.

Personal Symbolism
The slow awakening of the 'vast' stone monster in 'sands of the desert' serves as a powerful personal symbol for the poet, representing the apocalyptic wave of destruction he believed the world would soon experience.

Verbal Music
'The Second Coming' has been compared to a dirge, which is a mournful, discordant song. Many of the lines in 'The Second Coming' are examples of cacophony, which is a grating mixture of sounds. A good example is the opening line, with its harsh, repeated 'i' sounds and the heavy stresses: 'Turning and turning in the widening gyre'. This discordant verbal music contributes to the sense of turmoil in the opening lines, with its description of the 'anarchy' that is consuming the world.

There is a change in the second stanza. The lines become more musical, the 's' alliteration has a calming effect, and the use of repetition slows down the frantic pace somewhat: 'Surely some revelation is at hand;/ Surely the Second Coming is at hand.' Lines 13 to 20, however, slowly build towards the poem's cacophonous ending: 'And what rough beast, its hour come round at last,/ Slouches towards Bethlehem to be born?' The harsh vowels of 'rough beast' and 'Slouches', as well as the heavy 'b' alliteration, brings the poem full circle and back to the turmoil of stanza 1.

Tone, Mood and Atmosphere
The poet's tone is full of urgency and conviction as Yeats tries to impress on the reader the dire state of the world: 'Things fall apart; the centre cannot hold'. There is a strong sense of menace and foreboding to lines such as 'The blood-dimmed tide is loosed'. With its use of the present tense – 'Mere anarchy is loosed upon the world' – the poem asserts that it is too late to reverse or undo the terrible future that awaits us.

WAR, VIOLENCE AND SOCIAL UPHEAVAL

'The Second Coming' is Yeats' appalled and powerful reaction to a time of violence and chaos. To him it seems that the entire world is filled with confusion and disorder. It seems that everywhere the voices of reason and moderation are silenced, while those of intolerance and extremism shout ever louder. Evil men pursue their goals relentlessly, while the good stand idly by. Civilisation itself seems on the verge of being swept away by a tide of bloodshed. Furthermore, the poem predicts that even greater destruction is on its way, represented by the pitiless beast that 'Slouches toward Bethlehem to be born'.

'The Second Coming', though written in 1919, is a poem for our times. For in our age, too, it seems that 'things fall apart', that chaos and anarchy are everywhere. Each day the newspapers are so full of reports from 'small wars' around the world that it's easy to think we're drowning in a 'blood-dimmed tide'. Watch Sky News for even an hour and it's quite clear that evil is triumphing while good men do nothing. The worst are still 'full of passionate intensity', while the best, unfortunately, still lack all conviction. Given the state of the world today it's easy to think, sometimes, that some great beast of destruction is still out there waiting to be born, and that even now its hour is coming around.

Yeats' attitude to the impending catastrophe is somewhat unclear. He certainly presents the beast as being very unpleasant. As we've seen, he's appalled by the violence of 1919 and 'troubled' by the further upheaval the beast represents. But there's also a sense in which he seems fascinated and even excited by what this terrible creature promises.

Yeats was very unhappy with the current state of what he described as our 'scientific, democratic, fact-accumulating civilisation'. He believed that the 'laughing, ecstatic destruction' represented by the beast would change things forever. It would sweep away our tired, worn-out civilisation and give birth to a new era. Yeats looked forward to this new age. It would, he felt, be more in keeping with his own ideal society, being spiritual rather than scientific and aristocratic rather than democratic.

'The Second Coming', as we noted above, is greatly informed by Yeats' occult beliefs, especially by the ideas expounded in *A Vision*. This was a book Yeats wrote in response to his wife Georgie Hyde-Lees' automatic writing. Georgie would lapse into a trance and write page after page of mysterious statements, which she claimed were dictated to her by various spirit guides.

- In *A Vision*, Yeats outlines the occult notion that human history was divided into eras, each lasting roughly two thousand years.
- Our present era, which began with the birth of Chirst two thousand years ago, is soon due to expire.

- It will end, like all the eras before it, in a cataclysm of violence and destruction.
- This apocalypse is represented by the beast, with its terrible 'pitiless' gaze.
- This orgy of destruction, however, will clear the way for a new form of civilisation to arise, one that, as we noted, would be more in keeping with Yeats' ideal society.

Yeats' choice of Bethlehem as the beast's birthplace is highly symbolic. Just as Bethlehem was the place where the Christian era began with the birth of Christ, so it is the place where that era will end, with the coming of the beast. This almost blasphemous inversion of the Christmas nativity tale gives the conclusion of the poem real power, real shock value. Many early readers of the poem were horrified at the image of this rough, slouching monstrosity defiling the holy place of Christ's birth.

YEATS AND IRELAND

Yeats, as we have noted, was a great admirer of the Anglo-Irish Ascendancy, the class that dominated Irish society between the 17th and 19th centuries, and of which he himself was a member. He especially valued the formal, orderly way in which life was conducted on the estates and in the mansions of these wealthy Protestant landowners. To Yeats, then, this was a lifestyle full of 'ceremony'. And such a civilised, ceremonial existence, he believed, produced people who were 'innocent', fundamentally decent and morally upright.

In 1919, however, as Yeats was writing this poem, the War of Independence against British rule in Ireland was gaining traction. This war, and the Free State it produced, would greatly diminish the status of the Ascendancy class, which had already seen much of its influence evaporate over the preceding century.

Elsewhere in Europe, too, it seemed that the aristocratic way of life favoured by Yeats was under threat. The aristocracies of Germany and Russia, for instance, had all but vanished amid the chaos of the First World War. The new post-war world of democracy (not to mention socialism, communism and fascism) had little regard for such an existence. Everywhere Yeats looked, then, he saw the 'ceremony' of the aristocratic lifestyle being swept away amid the bloodshed of war and revolution: 'The blood-dimmed tide is loosed, and everywhere/ The ceremony of innocence is drowned'.

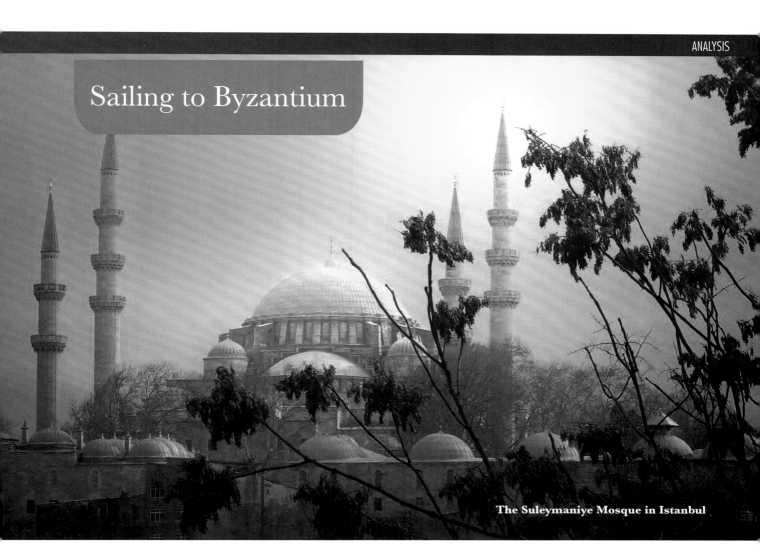

Sailing to Byzantium

The Suleymaniye Mosque in Istanbul

LINE BY LINE

The cycle of birth and death

This poem's opening stanza is all about the cycle of birth and death. This cycle applies to everything in nature. It encompasses mammals, or creatures of the 'flesh'. It encompasses birds, or 'fowl'. It encompasses the 'fish' that fill the seas. Every one of these creatures is 'begotten' or conceived through sexual activity. Then it is 'born'. Then, eventually, it 'dies'.

It is summer, a time when the 'begetting' phase of this cycle seems especially prominent. Every where the poet looks, he sees creatures of various types engaging in sexual activity:

- The 'birds in the trees' sing out their mating calls, their sweet tunes of flirtation and seduction.
- The seas are 'crowded' with throngs of mackerel that have gathered in their mating grounds at various points off the Irish coast.
- Salmon, too, are engaged in their mating season. They will then swim up river, leaping over falls and currents along the way, before spawning the next generation of their species.
- Summer, the poet suggests, is also the mating season for human beings. Everywhere he looks he sees young people in 'one another's arms', as they kiss, flirt or simply hold

hands. Here the poet refers to the ancient (though perhaps unscientific) idea that human beings are more sexually active in the summer time.

All of nature, it seems to the poet, has been sexually active 'all summer long'. He has witnessed a festival of begetting, in which entire new generations of 'fish, flesh [and] fowl' have been conceived. Every creature, it seems to the poet, engages joyfully and willingly in sexual activity. And by doing so, they 'commend' or celebrate the cycle of birth and death, of which sexual activity is a crucial part.

The poet's attitude to this cycle

The poet himself, however, cannot 'commend' or celebrate this cycle of birth and death. There are several reasons for this.

- The poet is keenly aware that the cycle ends in the extinction of every creature. Each new generation is a 'dying generation'. No sooner is each creature conceived than the countdown to its death begins.
- Because the poet is an elderly man, moving gradually towards the end of his own life, this awareness of death is amplified.

- Because the poet is an elderly man, he is no longer sexually desirable. He could not, even if he wanted to, participate in the summer-long festival of begetting. The business of sexual reproduction, he suggests, must be left to the young: 'That is no country for old men'.

The poet, at this stage of his life, wants to focus on art rather than on sexuality. He especially wants to focus on the great artworks of the past, which he refers to as 'Monuments of unageing intellect'. This phrase suggests that great artworks, like monuments, are publicly available. Many artworks, after all, can be viewed by anyone who cares to do so. It suggests that great artworks, like monuments, are commemorative because when we engage with a great artwork, we remember its creator.

The frenzy of procreation described in the opening stanza is compared to a symphony or chorus. Each procreating creature is like one of the performers in this symphony. These creatures, Yeats suggests, are 'caught' or lost in the music they create; they are so absorbed in the pleasure and pursuit of sexuality that they forget about everything else.

It also suggests that great artworks, like monuments, are large and noticeable. Many great artworks exhibit a psychological vastness rather than a physical vastness. We might think of a play by Shakespeare or a miniature painting by Rembrandt, which doesn't take up much physical space, but reveals entire psychological worlds.

These artworks – whether they are films or poems, statues or songs – are described as 'unageing' because their ability to inspire us never grows old. Each individual artwork, Yeats suggests, possesses an 'intellect' of its own, a unique personality or intelligence. When we study a particular artwork then we engage with its 'intellect'. We develop our own conversation or relationship with the artwork in question. We need only think here of the intense bonds that people tend to form with their favourite songs, books or movies.

The poet's tattered body

Each human being, the poet believes, is composed of two distinct parts: a physical body and a non-physical soul. The body is doomed to waste away and die. The soul, on the other hand, is immortal. Our souls, according to tradition, are housed within our bodies. Each soul, Yeats suggests, wears its body like a 'mortal dress', a temporary garment it will cast off at the moment of death.

The poet laments how the ageing process has affected his own body, his own 'mortal dress'. Old age, he declares, has robbed his body of both its physical vigour and its good looks. The poet, in a striking turn of phrase, compares himself to a scarecrow: 'a tattered coat upon a stick'. This is a most revealing comparison:

- His body is 'tattered', its flesh, bones and sinews damaged by the ageing process.

- His body is withered to the point where it is stick-thin.
- His body, he feels, has come to resemble a scarecrow; it is both grotesque and ridiculous-looking.

The poet, therefore, is faced with the 'paltriness' of old age. He is faced with being physically 'paltry', with being pitiful or pathetic. He is faced with being socially 'paltry', with being negligible and insignificant. He is faced with being a 'thing', rather than a proper human being. For who, in a world dominated by youth and beauty, really cares about or even notices the old?

Focusing on the soul

Old age, then, is only bearable if we focus on the soul rather than the body.

- The soul, Yeats declares, must 'clap its hands and sing'. For Yeats, no doubt, this singing of the soul involves artistic expression: the creation of poems, plays and other texts.
- Our souls, Yeats says, must sing 'louder' as we approach death. This reflects Yeats' determination to keep improving his artistic practice. He wants to become better and better at writing as death approaches. He wants to create texts that explore the human condition with ever greater clarity and profundity, texts that will truly stand the test of time.
- The soul, Yeats insists, must attend 'singing school'; it must study and practice so it can sing with greater clarity and volume. This reflects Yeats' belief that artistic improvement can only be achieved by studying great artworks of the past. The word 'but', as used in line 7, means 'apart from', leading us to read the lines as follows: 'there is no singing school [apart from] studying [the great artworks of the past]'.

They poet, therefore, decides to make the long sea voyage to the ancient city of Byzantium. Given its imperial past, Byzantium is absolutely filled with extraordinary artworks, each one a monument to the 'magnificence' of the human soul that created it.

Byzantium is an old name for Istanbul, the capital of Turkey. In medieval times, Byzantium was a great military power and the centre of a Christian empire that lasted for nearly a thousand years. It was also an extraordinary centre of learning, one that inherited the wisdom of both Ancient Greece and the Roman Empire. It was especially famed for the skill of its artists and craftsmen, who created everything from enormous cathedrals to tiny but ingeniously crafted ornaments.

The mosaic

The poet has finally reached Byzantium and stands before one of the city's many extraordinary mosaics (a 'mosaic' is an image made from assembling small pieces of coloured glass and stone). This particular mosaic decorates a 'wall' somewhere in the city, perhaps in one of Byzantium's many palaces and cathedrals. It is hundreds of years old. Yeats describes how it shimmers with a 'gold' effect, suggesting the brightly coloured materials that were used in its construction.

The mosaic depicts 'sages' or men of great wisdom. God's presence surrounds the sages, taking the form of golden flames: they are 'standing in God's holy fire'. This miraculous blaze, however, doesn't harm the sages in any way. Instead, it fills them with vigour and intensity as if they were somehow sharing in the energy of God himself (it's been suggested that Yeats was inspired by a Byzantine mosaic depicting Moses and Elijah, two great sages or prophets from the Bible).

Yeats, as we noted above, believed that every great artwork had its own 'intellect' or personality. And the poet, it seems, is captivated by the intellect of this particular mosaic. He develops an extraordinary connection with this golden image. We can imagine him spending hours before the mosaic, returning to visit it again and again during his visit to Byzantium.

Yeats' connection with the mosaic is so powerful that the sages seem almost alive to him. He imagines that the sages could come to life and step out of the mosaic: 'Come from the holy fire'. He imagines that the sages could act as his mentors or instructors: 'be the singing-masters of my soul'. Under their guidance, Yeats' soul will learn to 'sing' better than it ever has done before. They would help him to create extraordinary texts that capture profound truths about time, reality and human existence.

Yeats had a number of occult beliefs, which he detailed in his prose book *A Vision*. He believed that time is a stream that spirals in a 'gyre' or clockwise direction. He imagines the sages 'perning' or moving in a counter-clockwise direction, as if they were swimming against time's current. Eventually, the sages will make it all the way to the twentieth century and stand before the poet as alive as they ever were.

Yeats, of course, doesn't believe that such time travel is possible, nor does he expect the sages will literally step from the mosaic. But this metaphor powerfully captures the intensity of the poet's relationship with the mosaic. It highlights how real the sages seem to him as he spends hours contemplating their golden forms.

Body and soul

Yeats calls on the sages to burn away his body using their 'holy fire'.

- He memorably refers to his body as a 'dying animal', suggesting that it is subhuman, disgusting and beneath contempt. He longs for this wretched, scarecrow-like body to be utterly burned up, utterly consumed away by the sages' miraculous flames.
- In particular, he wants the sages to eliminate his 'heart'. This refers not only to the organ itself, but to all bodily systems associated with love and sexuality. Yeats' heart is filled with sexual longing. But these are desires that he as an old man can't satisfy or act on. This preponderance of unsatisfied desire has left the heart 'sick' or dysfunctional. Yeats is, therefore, happy for it, along with the rest of his body, to be consumed away.

- Yeats' soul, then, would be liberated from the failing body in which it is currently confined.
- Yeats calls on the sages to 'gather' or carry his newly liberated soul and transport it into the 'artifice of eternity'.

Let's take a moment to unpack this phrase. The word 'artifice' refers to expert workmanship. It also refers to something that has been cunningly or skilfully designed. Yeats, then, has in mind here great artworks like the *Mona Lisa* and Michelangelo's *David*, which exhibit such extraordinary workmanship and design. These works are eternal in that they speak to people century after century.

The poet, then, longs for his soul to be gathered into one of these eternal artworks. It would reside forever within in some exquisite and unageing piece of craftsmanship.

The bird

The poet would like his soul to inhabit one such object in particular, a mechanical bird he has seen during his visit to Byzantium.

- The bird is hundreds of years old and was constructed during the heyday of the Byzantine Empire.
- The bird is made of gold that has been 'hammered' into shape by the gifted goldsmiths that constructed it. The goldsmiths are described as 'Grecian' because Byzantium was a Greek-speaking civilisation.
- The bird has been further decorated with gold varnish or 'enamelling'.
- The bird's body contains a carefully concealed set of pipes. Whenever the breeze passed through these pipes, it produced a sound like that of birdsong.

Yeats clearly takes great delight in this ingeniously constructed object that was created so long ago. He imagines a courtier placing it on an artificial golden branch, an extraordinary ornament that must have brought great joy and wonder to the 'lords and ladies' of the Byzantine court.

Or perhaps the bird was a gift for the emperor himself. Yeats imagines this precious object taking a place of honour beside the emperor's throne. It would serve as an amusement and a distraction from the cares of state. Its mechanical singing would serve to rouse the emperor if he started to doze off on a hot Byzantine afternoon.

THEMES

NATURE

The poem views the natural world as a kind of system that passes through phases of birth, death and renewal. Every living thing, be it fish, flesh or fowl, is part of this system. Every living thing is 'begotten' or conceived, born, reproduces and eventually dies. The bustling sexual activity of summer conducted by birds, fish and youthful human beings seems to 'commend' or celebrate this cycle. The poet has come to view this process of birth and death in a very negative way, for his own personal cycle is nearing its end.

The poet draws a sharp contrast between art and nature. Birds, animals and human beings are subject to the cycles of nature described above. They are temporary; they change and they die. Great works of art on the other hand are subject to no such cycle. These 'unageing' objects never change or decline. These great songs, paintings, poems and films – collectively referred to as the 'artifice of eternity' – last forever, speaking to generation after generation.

YOUTH AND AGE

This poem, then, draws a powerful contrast between youth and age, specifically between the elderly poet and the young people he observes at the height of the Irish summer.

- These young people are presented as sexually attractive. The aged poet, on the other hand, feels like he has lost his good looks. He thinks of himself as a wizened and grotesque scarecrow.
- The young people are in their physical prime. The poet's body, on the other hand, has been left tattered by the ageing process.
- The young people enjoy lives of sexual opportunity, wandering the streets 'in one another's arms'. The aged poet too experiences sexual desire. But for him, alas, such opportunities are a thing of the past. His heart is 'sick with desire' that he cannot satisfy.
- The lives of the young seem relaxed and carefree. Their only concern is love, romance and flirtation. The elderly poet on the other hand seems preoccupied with thoughts of mortality, ageing and decay.
- The ageing poet finds himself focusing more and more on 'monuments of unageing intellect', on the great artworks of the past. The young people, preoccupied with the 'sensual music' of procreation, care little about great works by past masters such as Shakespeare, Blake and Michelangelo.

The poem, then, provides a moving portrayal of the ageing process. It highlights how the elderly often consider themselves 'paltry', as in feeble and insignificant, how in a world obsessed with youth and beauty, they all too often feel unsightly and unwanted, ridiculous or even invisible.

The poet feels disgusted and constrained by his own body. In a shocking memorable phrase, he describes his body as a 'dying animal' to which he has been 'shackled'.

ART AND THE ROLE OF THE ARTIST

This is another poem in which Yeats presents art as a continuous practice, a craft or trade that must be perfected throughout the artist's life. Despite his old age, the poet is determined to keep growing as an artist. If anything, the nearness of death makes him all the more eager to reach his full artistic potential. The poem stresses that such improvement can be made only by studying the great artists of the past. Yeats, then, despite being an accomplished, Nobel prize-winning poet, recognises that he must still attend 'singing-school' in order that his soul can express itself with ever-greater clarity and purpose.

'Sailing to Byzantium' is also Yeats' most profound statement on the idea of attaining immortality through art. The poet, then, considers two different concepts of immortality. One is a form of reincarnation such as that envisaged by Buddhism and other Eastern religions. The soul would leave behind the body and the earthly plane of existence. It would be temporarily 'out of nature'. It would then rejoin the natural world, housing itself within some new person, bird or animal.

Yeats, however, rejects this form of immortality. The poet will not be re-born as any 'natural thing'. He is determined that his soul, 'once out of nature', will never rejoin the natural world. He will never again be subject to the cycles of birth and death that govern the natural world. His soul will never again be attached to such a 'dying animal'.

The poet instead is focused on the type of artistic immortality enjoyed by Michelangelo and Shakespeare. He uses an extraordinary set of metaphors to describe the process by which such immortality might be attained.

- The artist of today can only achieve greatness by studying the masterpieces of the past. This is represented by the sages stepping out of the mosaic to act as Yeats' mentors or 'singing-masters'.
- The artist must focus on the soul rather than the body. This is represented by the sages consuming the poet's body with their holy flame.
- The distractions of sex and sexuality in particular must be overcome. This is represented by the sages consuming away the poet's heart.
- The poet will live on through the poems, plays and texts he has created over the course of his life. This is represented by the poet's soul inhabiting the magnificent golden bird created by the Grecian goldsmiths all those centuries ago.

The poet would have little interest, we sense, in prolonging the life of his body through some revolutionary scientific method. Nor does he show any interest in the type of immortality associated with the Christian concept of heaven. Furthermore, as we've seen, he is not taken with reincarnation. Instead, he goes all-in on achieving the 'artifice of eternity'. And maybe he has succeeded. After all, we are still reading his works today.

The Stare's Nest by My Window

LINE BY LINE

This poem was written during the Irish Civil War of 1922 to 1923. This was an especially bitter conflict as former comrades turned against one another. Men who had fought the British side by side in the earlier War of Independence now took up arms to fight each other. Towns, villages and even families were split down the middle, as some took the 'pro-Treaty' side, associated in the popular imagination with Michael Collins, and some took the 'anti-Treaty' side, associated with Eamon de Valera.

When the civil war broke out, Yeats was staying at Thoor Ballylee, a 15th Century Norman tower in County Galway that he and his wife had recently renovated and moved into. For a time, Yeats was isolated by the guerrilla warfare that raged in the countryside around him and made travel impossible. This isolation was made worse when the anti-Treaty forces blew up the bridges and blocked the roads in the surrounding area.

Stanza 1

Yeats begins by considering the state of Thoor Ballylee. The mortar that binds its stone walls together has started to crumble: 'My wall is loosening'. If you pushed at one of the walls' stone components it might jiggle a little. Gaps have even begun to appear between one stone and the next.

Bees have colonised some of these cracks or 'crevices', using them as safe locations in which to construct their hives: 'The bees build in the crevices/ Of loosening masonry'. Other gaps have been used by birds as convenient nesting places. Their chicks have hatched, and the 'mother birds' bring food back to the tower for their young: 'and there/ The mother birds bring grubs and flies'.

One of the nests in the tower wall has been abandoned. Once a starling (a 'stare') had raised its young there. Now, however, this family of birds has moved on, leaving its 'house' or nest empty. Yeats wants a colony of bees to inhabit this gap in his tower wall, to build their hive and honeycomb in this empty crevice where the stare once nested: 'honey-bees,/ Come build in the empty house of the stare'.

Stanzas 2 and 3

Yeats considers the state of County Galway, gripped as it is by civil war. This bitter conflict has been raging for two weeks now: 'Some fourteen days of civil war'. During this time, the people of Galway have effectively become prisoners in their own homes: 'We are closed in'. They are afraid to stray very far, terrified of the violence that grips the countryside. Many roads have been closed off with 'A barricade of stone or of wood', making travel even more of an impossibility.

The civil war has visited death and destruction upon the countryside: men have been killed and houses burned down. There have been other even more brutal acts. One young soldier was beaten to death and had his bloody corpse dragged or 'trundled' down the road like a sack of grain: 'Last night they trundled down the road/ That dead young soldier in his blood'. These lines were inspired by an actual incident that took place near Yeats' home: a young soldier was beaten so badly that his mother could only recover his disembodied head for burial.

Nowadays, we get news updates from social media, from internet news sites, from television or from radio. At the time this poem was written, however, none of these things existed. There were only newspapers. Nor were there mobile phones, landlines or social media. People communicated by letters and by telegram.

The civil war, then, has brought the people of Galway great dread and great uncertainty: 'the key is turned/ On our uncertainty'. With the roads closed, the people of Galway had no newspapers, no letters and no clue about what was going on around the country.

They hear vague rumours about terrible events that are taking place: 'somewhere/ A man is killed, or a house burned'. But they have no solid and definite information, either about events in County Galway or in the country as a whole: 'no clear fact to be discerned'.

They didn't know what was happening up the road in Galway City, never mind in Wexford or Athlone. They didn't know if their friends and relatives around the country were still alive. They didn't know which side was winning the war, or was in control of the government in Dublin.

They didn't know how many farmhouses and villages were being burned down, or whose household would be next. We can imagine, then, how this 'uncertainty', and the swirl of rumour that accompanied it, added to the terror experienced by the people of Galway as the war raged on around them.

The walls of Yeats' home aren't as stable or secure as they once were, a fact that's emphasised through the repetition of 'loosening' in lines 2 and 3. The walls that protect him from the outside world, then, become increasingly insecure as their masonry crumbles. Surprisingly, however, Yeats seems to welcome this 'loosening' of his defences. He seems happy that nature's creatures have made their homes among the walls' gaps. He chooses not to fill in the crevice where the stare once nested, instead hoping that bees will use it to construct their hive.

Perhaps this loosening of walls represents a loosening of attitudes. The minds of the Irish people have allowed their minds to be 'closed in' by certainties, by the conviction that their understanding of Irish freedom is the proper one. They have allowed their minds to be straitjacketed by the fantasies and obsessions outlined above.

The Irish people must now relax and loosen these narrow-minded attitudes that have led them to a bloody civil war. If they do so, there is the possibility that a new attitude of forgiveness will slip into the national psyche just as the bees might slip into the tower wall. Forgiveness, the poem suggests, is as sweet as the honeycomb the bees construct, and it will serve as an antidote to the sour attitudes of hatred that have so gripped the national psyche.

Stanza 4

Yeats considers the state of the Irish psyche in the years leading up to the civil war. During this period, he suggests, the Irish people became obsessed with questions of nationhood, with what an independent Ireland meant and how it should be achieved. Ideas of freedom and martyrdom, of killing and dying for one's country came to predominate.

But these ideas, Yeats maintains, are mere 'fantasies'. 'Freedom' and 'martyrdom' can be considered fantasies in several different senses:

- They're abstract ideas rather than real things. When Yeats looks out from his tower, he sees the reality of everyday life: of real people in real homes trying to get on with real existence. But he also sees real terror, real violence and real destruction as people are shot to death and burned out of their homes. In light of such stark reality, notions like political freedom begin to seem very abstract, unreal and unimportant.
- 'Freedom' and 'martyrdom' are fantasies in the sense that they're obsessive preoccupations, goals or desires that the Irish people dwell on and return to again and again.
- The term 'fantasies' also suggests how the Irish people had developed an idealised concept of what 'freedom' and 'martyrdom' actually involved. They'd developed an idealised, almost comic book understanding of warfare, one that involved daring deeds and noble sacrifice, a million miles away from the grim reality of burning farmhouses and corpses 'trundled' down roads.

Yeats uses the strange but vivid metaphor of 'feeding the heart' to describe the country's obsession with these dangerous fantasies. To obsess about something, as Yeats puts it, is to feed it to your heart. In this instance, the Irish people have become obsessed with 'fantasies' of freedom and martyrdom and have fed their hearts with these dangerous notions: 'We had fed the heart on fantasies'.

The 'fare' or diet of fantasies has made the hearts of the Irish people 'brutal'. We might imagine here an organ that's become putrid and diseased, pumping bitter bile rather than life-giving blood. This is a powerful metaphor for the nation's corrupted psyche. A constant obsession has poisoned the minds of the Irish people, leaving them uncompromising and inflexible regarding what an independent Ireland would mean and how it should be achieved.

Corrupted hearts can now only find 'substance' or nourishment in hatred rather than in love: 'More substance in our enmities/ Than in our love'. This wonderfully suggests how the Irish people are now motivated more by hatred of their enemies than by love of their family and friends. It's as if they need enemies in order to thrive. And now, with the British gone, they've found the enmity they need in the form of antipathy to other Irish people, specifically those who have a different understanding of what Irish freedom means.

FOCUS ON STYLE

Imagery

'The Stare's Nest by My Window' can be described as a dialogue between images. On the one hand we have the beautiful, life-giving images of the building bees and the nesting birds. On the other, we have the horrific image of the dead solider 'trundled' down the road. The image of the 'loosening' tower walls serves as a symbol of reconciliation, as a bridge between the present horror of the civil war and a more positive future.

Verbal Music

A notable feature of this poem's soundscape is its use of repetition. Each stanza concludes with the same haunting refrain, as Yeats calls again and again on the bees to build in the starling's deserted nest. Each stanza broadens the horizons of the poet's meditation once more, from his tower home in stanza one, to his neighbours in County Galway in stanzas two and three, to the Irish people as a whole in stanza four.

At the end of each stanza, however, Yeats focuses in once more on his crumbling walls and the starling's empty nest, where he wants the bees to build. It's this image of hive-building, with all its sweetness and creativity, that he sees as an antidote to the poisonous and destructive mentality that has gripped the Irish people.

THEMES

WAR, VIOLENCE AND SOCIAL UPHEAVAL

'The Stare's Nest by My Window' presents a community and a country that has been ravaged by the horrors of war. For two weeks, the conflict has created a claustrophobic sense of isolation, leaving people 'closed in' as it traps them in their homes. It has created a great sense of dread and uncertainty among the populace, who are able to discern 'no clear fact' about what's going on in the country or what the future holds.

Violence and terror stalk the land, as men are shot dead, houses are destroyed and acts of inhumanity, like the dragging of the dead soldier's corpse, are carried out. The horror is amplified by that fact that Irish people are committing these acts against other Irish people, against neighbours and former friends, against people who had been close comrades in the struggle against British rule.

YEATS AND IRELAND

This poem continues Yeats' meditation on patriotism and revolt. 'September 1913' and 'Easter 1916' saw Yeats praise, in a cautious and qualified manner, those who fought and died for Ireland. In this poem, however, he has little time for the violence committed in Ireland's name. We sense that the closer Yeats came to the grim realities of guerrilla warfare, the less time he had for the 'fantasies' of freedom and martyrdom. Disagreements over Irish freedom, he suggests, aren't worth such terror and destruction, such loss of life and property.

In 'September 1913', Yeats suggested that the Irish people had forgotten the ideas of freedom and martyrdom that motivated the heroes of the past. In this poem, written ten years later, he argues the opposite. The Irish people, he claims, have not only remembered these ideas but have become obsessed with them. And their obsession with these dangerous 'fantasies' has poisoned their psyches, turning their hearts 'brutal'.

Now the notion of freedom means more to them than family, friendship or life itself. Many Irish people are willing to die to defend a particular concept of Irish freedom and are willing to kill those, including their former friends and comrades, who believe in a different concept. Now enmity and conflict nourish their souls rather than love, community and friendship.

NATURE

This poem, then, highlights the bitterness that has taken root in the Irish heart and the violence and chaos that rage throughout the country. Yet each stanza concludes with a plea to the honeybees to 'Come build in the empty house of the stare'. We must look to nature, the poem suggests, if we are to reverse the damage that has been done to the soul of the Irish nation:

- The sweetness of the bees' honey contrasts with the bitterness that has filled the hearts of the Irish people.
- Whereas the Irish people have become dedicated to destruction, the birds and bees that dwell in the tower walls are dedicated to building and creation.
- The Irish people willfully destroy life. The birds and bees, on the other hand, are dedicated to bringing new life into the world. They create nests and hives for their young to be born into and the mother birds bring food to keep their chicks alive.

The poem, then, celebrates the natural world, emphasising its positivity, energy and creativity. The challenge for the Irish people is to follow nature's example. They must turn away from the path of destruction and begin to rebuild their homes, their shattered country and their trust in one another.

In Memory of Eva Gore-Booth and Con Markievicz

LINE BY LINE

In 1894 Yeats stayed at Lissadell, the beautiful mansion of the aristocratic Gore-Booth family in Sligo. During his visit, Yeats became friendly with the daughters of the house, Constance and Eva. Yeats was greatly taken with these two fine-looking young women, especially Eva. For a while, he even considered asking for Eva's hand in marriage.

Yeats always looked back on his time at Lissadell with great affection. In 1916, twenty years after his stay, he wrote to Eva: 'Your sister and yourself, two beautiful girls among the great trees of Lissadell, are among the dear memories of my youth'. This poem was written in 1927, just months after the death of Constance. Eva had died the previous year.

A memory of Lissadell

Yeats fondly recalls a summer's evening spent with the sisters in their beautiful home. He recalls how the drawing room's 'Great windows' were open to the warmth: 'Great windows open to the south'. We can imagine how the 'light of evening' poured through these windows in fantastic golden shafts (these large sash windows can still be seen today and are south-facing to maximise their exposure to the sunlight).

He also, of course, has fond memories of the sisters themselves, remembering how both were 'beautiful'. Though Yeats recognised the beauty of both girls, he admired Eva in particular. He describes her as 'a gazelle', a small antelope famous for the graceful way it moves.

Yeats noted that both sisters wore silken Japanese dresses: 'Two girls in silk kimonos'. Such garments would have been extremely rare in the Ireland of the day. The girls' fondness for kimonos suggests not only that the girls were stylish but also that they were open to different cultures.

The girls' youthful beauty could not last, however. That summer, like all summers, inevitably gave way to autumn, causing the blooms and flowers to wither away. Similarly, the girls' youth gave way to middle age and then old age, causing their beauty to wither away. Yeats argues that their involvement with politics contributed to the decline of their good looks. Similarly, just as autumn strips away the foliage of summer, so the passage of time stripped away the sisters' beauty.

Constance's political campaigns

Constance was a member of the Irish Citizen Army and fought in the 1916 Rising, serving as a commander of the forces that occupied Stephen's Green. After the rebels' surrender, she was 'condemned to death' by the British authorities. However, the military court, reluctant to execute a woman, 'pardoned' her, commuting her sentence to life imprisonment. Constance, along with other rebel leaders, was released as part of an amnesty in 1917.

Yeats focuses on Constance's later years, between the end of the Irish Civil War in 1923 and her death in 1927. Constance had taken the losing anti-Treaty side in that terrible conflict and never quite made her peace with the Free State that emerged in its wake. In the years after the Civil War, she remained active in politics and vigorously opposed to the new regime, which in her opinion betrayed the ideals of the 1916 Rising.

Yeats takes a dim view of Constance's activities during this period. She spent her time, he says, 'conspiring', hatching various plots and plans with other opponents of the new Irish state. But in his opinion her fellow conspirators were 'ignorant' men and women, whose plots were destined never to get off the ground. Perhaps he thinks of them as being blinded by an extreme form of idealism. Or maybe, in his view, they were simply too stupid to get with the programme and accept the reality of the new Irish state.

Constance's final years, Yeats suggests, were 'lonely' ones. The implication is that her trenchant political views left her marginalised. She had, after all, fallen out with so many former friends and colleagues, regarding them as traitors for accepting the new Irish state. Where once she had been at the centre of Irish political life, now she occupied its fringes, pointlessly conspiring with a few fellow diehards. According to Yeats, Constance 'dragged out' these last few isolated years, as if they were a dull but necessary chore, as if, deep down, she couldn't wait for them to be over.

Eva's political campaigns

Eva, the younger Gore-Booth sister, also became active in the politics of her day. She settled in England and for twenty years was at the forefront of what became for her two overlapping struggles: the campaign for workers' rights and the struggle to win the right to vote for women. She was also committed to social work and spent much of her time voluntarily helping the poor workers of northern England.

Yeats, however, regards Eva as a hopeless idealist who dreams of bringing about a 'utopia', a perfect society that in practice can never be achieved. Yeats suggests that Eva and her fellow campaigners are very 'vague' about what their ideal society would actually be like. Theirs is a project, he suggests, that's long on ideals but short on detail. In fact, Yeats is so dismissive of Eva's political ideals that he doesn't even bother to engage with them or learn about them properly: 'I know not what the younger dreams–/ Some vague Utopia'.

Yeats considers Eva's appearance near the end of her life, when she seemed not only 'old' and 'withered' but also gaunt as a skeleton. Her shrivelled appearance, he says, was an 'image' of her political beliefs. This might suggest that Eva's devotion to her political struggle has 'withered' her gazelle-like beauty, leaving her gaunt and exhausted.

But it might also suggest Yeats' view of Eva's political beliefs. Perhaps Yeats viewed socialism and 'feminism' as withered belief systems. Once these ideas were powerful political forces, but now they're only shrivelled versions of their former selves, ideas that are irrelevant to the modern world and attract few new adherents.

Regrets

Many years have passed since that glorious summer's evening in Lisadell. There were many occasions over the intervening period when Yeats considered reaching out to one of the Gore-Booth sisters: 'Many a time I think to seek/ One or the other out'. He would have loved to arrange a meeting, to sit down with either Constance or Eva and talk about long ago times in Lisadell: 'and speak/ Of that old Georgian mansion'. However, we get the impression that he never quite got around to having this wonderful nostalgic conversation with the Gore-Booth sisters. Now, alas, both sisters have passed away and his chance is gone.

Yeats returns to the image of the beautiful girls in their silk kimonos, as lines 19 to 20 repeat lines 3 to 4 exactly. We read the same words and experience the same image. Now we see it differently, however, influenced by our knowledge of all that has happened: the sisters' decline and death as well as Yeats' failure to 'seek one or the other out' before they passed. The first time we encountered these lines they were energetic and celebratory. But now they reverberate with sadness.

'Dear Shadows'

In lines 21 to 30, Yeats speaks to the dead sisters directly. He addresses them as 'Dear Shadows' because he views them as shades or spirits residing in the afterlife. Now that they've passed on, he says, the sisters have realised the terrible mistake or 'folly' they committed while alive: 'Dear Shadows, now you know it all,/ All the folly'.

Their foolishness, Yeats maintains, was to involve themselves in political struggles and campaigns. They should never, he believes, have embroiled themselves in such a 'fight' against what they regarded as great 'wrongs' but that their opponents, naturally, regarded as right and appropriate: 'All the folly of a fight/ With a common wrong or right.'

Yeats seems to be playing on three separate meanings of the word 'common' here. He may be suggesting that political battles are 'common' because they affect the entire community. He may also be suggesting that the world of politics is 'common' in the sense that it is coarse and vulgar and quite unsuited to these beautiful aristocratic women. Finally, he may be suggesting that such political struggles are 'common' because they become commonplace in the lives of those who engage in them. They become everyday, gruelling struggles that suck up all the campaigner's time and energy.

Yeats regards the Gore-Booth sisters as paragons of innocence and beauty. Such people, he says, have only one adversary: 'The innocent and the beautiful/ Have no enemy but time'. For it is only the passage of time itself that can rob them of their fine qualities, of the virtues that set them apart from the rest of us. All their energies, therefore, should be devoted to their personal battle with time, towards retaining their innocence and beauty. Anything else, like the political campaigning undertaken by the Gore-Booth sisters for instance, is a mere distraction from this all-important struggle.

Indeed, involvement in political life, with all its exhausting and bitter conflicts, will only make the destructive work of time easier. Eva's efforts leave her utterly drained and withered like a skeleton. Constance, meanwhile, is reduced to a lonely, ignorant conspirator. It would be far better for the innocent and beautiful to avoid such communal battles and focus instead on staving off time's ravages for as long as they possibly can.

Setting time alight

Yeats concludes the poem by expressing an extraordinary desire. He wishes to do no less than destroy time itself and thereby prevent it from doing further damage to the innocence and beauty he so values. Specifically, he wants to set time on fire. He envisages striking match after match until the fabric of time itself somehow catches fire: 'Arise and bid me strike a match/ And strike another till time catch'.

Yeats imagines that this blaze or 'conflagration' will 'climb', rising the way fire does, laying waste to time as it goes. If this happens, if Yeats is successful in his mission to make time no more, he wants the sisters' shades to go running through the afterlife, spreading the good news.

Specifically, he wants them to inform the 'sages' of his staggering achievement. The term 'sages' refers to the spirits of the great thinkers and artists Yeats admired (included in their number, no doubt, are Michelangelo and William Blake, both mentioned in 'An Acre of Grass'). Yeats, it seems, imagines these great minds gathering in the afterlife, celebrating the Irish poet who'd put an end to time itself.

FOCUS ON STYLE

Verbal Music

The music of the poem's opening lines reflects the serenity and grandeur of that long-ago evening in Lissadell. Yeats uses assonance to achieve this. In lines 1 and 3, for example, the repetition of the 'i' sound creates a pleasant, euphonious effect: 'The light of evening Lissadell … two girls in silk kimonos'. A similar word music is generated in line 2, with its repeated broad-vowel sounds: 'Great windows open to the south'.

The slow, stately pace of line 2, courtesy of the proliferation of broad-vowel sounds, suggests the majesty and dignity of the Georgian mansion. Lines 5 to 6, however, shatter this pleasant music. Just as summer gives way to autumn, so the soothing music of lines 1 to 4 gives way to the harsh combination of sounds in lines 5 to 6. The words 'raving' and 'shears', in particular, contribute to this jarring effect.

Imagery

Yeats depicts the two sisters very vividly in this poem. He depicts them as wearing 'silk kimonos', traditional Japanese garments that would have been a rare sight in the Ireland of the early 20th century. This suggests that the sisters were stylish and perhaps a little eccentric. Yeats asserts that they were 'both/ Beautiful' and that Eva was particularly elegant: 'one a gazelle.'

However, Yeats depicts their political thinking as ruining their youthful beauty and innocence. Con is depicted as a lonely figure after participating in the 1916 Rising, with only 'the ignorant' for company. Eva, who had idealistic left-wing views that Yeats dismisses as dreaming of a 'vague Utopia', becomes old and haggard: 'withered old and skeleton-gaunt,/ An image of such politics.' In the second stanza, he laments the effects of time on the sisters: 'The innocent and the beautiful/ Have no enemy but time'.

Personal Symbolism

Yeats uses the image of a 'great gazebo' to describe Ireland. He, Eva and Con were all members of the Anglo-Irish ascendancy. They grew up in a society that believed Ireland to be a mere offshoot of Britain, the way a gazebo is an offshoot of a large house. He ruefully notes that it is families like theirs that built this idea of Ireland as a flimsy 'gazebo', unable to stand on its own: 'We the great gazebo built'.

Despite the fact that he, Eva and Con were nationalists, Yeats suggests they will get little thanks for it because of their privileged Anglo-Irish backgrounds. In fact, they will be seen as being complicit in the oppression of Ireland by Britain: 'They convicted us of guilt'. By the ordinary people of Ireland, they are seen as a relic of the past, something to be forgotten about, even destroyed. Yeats alludes to the destruction of Anglo-Irish mansions in the 1920s in the final line: 'Bid me strike a match and blow.'

YEATS AND IRELAND

Yeats was a great admirer of the Anglo-Irish aristocracy, the Protestant land-owning class that dominated Irish society between the 18th and 20th centuries. In this poem he praises Lissadell, one of the famous 'big houses' associated with that class. Yeats praises that 'old Georgian mansion' for its impressive architecture, for its 'great windows open to the South'. But it's worth noting that Lissadell, like other Anglo-Irish mansions, although luxurious, was also a little austere. The Anglo-Irish didn't really go in for 'bling', instead creating simple but elegant environments.

Yeats also admired Anglo-Irish society not only because it valued art and creativity but because it was open to new ideas. Both of these trends are embodied in the 'silk kimonos' worn by the Gore-Booth sisters on that long-ago evening in Lissadell. These gowns, which might be considered art objects in themselves, reflect Anglo-Irish openness to fresh thinking and foreign cultures.

The poet, then, laments the passing of this cultured way of life. By the time Yeats wrote this poem, the heyday of the Anglo-Irish had long since past. Their power had waned throughout the nineteenth century and all but disappeared in the new Catholic Ireland that emerged after independence from Britain.

Yeats uses a most unusual metaphor to describe this passing, comparing Anglo-Irish civilisation to a gazebo, a small roofed structure that is used for outdoor entertaining and dining. Gazebos are often ornamental and elaborately-designed, suggesting the emphasis Anglo-Irish society placed not only on hospitality but also on art and on beautiful objects.

But gazebos are relatively flimsy structures, reflecting how the Anglo-Irish dominance of Irish life proved to be fragile and fleeting. During the struggle for independence, for instance, many Anglo-Irish mansions were burned down by the IRA. The Catholic middle classes, the dominant force in the newly-independent Ireland, 'convicted' the Anglo-Irish, regarding them as little more than collaborators with British oppression: 'They convicted us of guilt'. In the early decades of independence, the great Anglo-Irish families, once so prominent in Irish life, drifted to its margins or disappeared altogether. Their civilisation was torn down as easily as one might dismantle a gazebo.

YOUTH AND AGE

'In Memory' is a masterpiece of nostalgia in which Yeats deftly recreates a golden memory from his youth: two beautiful young women, a splendid mansion, the light of a summer's evening. There is something very moving about the poet's declaration that he often thought of 'seeking out' the sisters to reminisce with them about that long-ago time. Sadly, however, it seems that Yeats left it too late to meet up with the sisters and 'recall/

That table and the talk of youth'. Like many of us, he was simply too busy to find the time for chatting with old friends.

'In Memory', then, is another poem in which Yeats confronts the changes, both mental and physical, that will be wreaked on us by time's relentless march. Time, Yeats reminds us, is the enemy not only of physical beauty but also of innocence: 'The innocent and the beautiful/ Have no enemy but time'. Its passage begins to leave us not only weakened and decrepit on a physical level but also cynical and embittered on a mental one.

The ravages of time are memorably personified as a 'raving Autumn' that shears off the flowers on the wreath of youth and beauty. It turns Eva from a creature of gazelle-like beauty and elegance into a 'withered' and 'skeleton-gaunt' old woman. And each of us, sadly but inevitably, must suffer a similar transformation.

ART AND THE ROLE OF THE ARTIST

In this poem, just as in 'Sailing to Byzantium', Yeats considers the possibility of achieving immortality through art. Yeats imagines himself protecting innocence and beauty by destroying time itself. He longs to somehow put a match to time's very fabric, so it will be consumed in a great and climbing 'conflagration': 'Arise and bid me strike a match/ And strike another till time catch.'

Yeats, of course, doesn't think he can literally set time on fire. The act of putting a match to time is a metaphor for overcoming time's destruction through the power of art. Yeats feels he can undo time's march by immortalising, in poetry, the beauty and innocence of the girls. A truly skilful artist, therefore, can defeat time by recovering an event or person lost in the past – an evening in Lissadell and two girls in silk kimonos, for instance – and preserving it in a piece of art to be enjoyed by future generations.

Not surprisingly, many critics find Yeats' atitude to the sisters' political activity more than a little sexist. Yeats values women like the Gore-Booths for their physical appearance and their 'innocence' rather than for their abilities and achievements. He celebrates Constance's prettiness as a young girl rather than her courage in the 1916 rising, or her achievement in becoming one of the world's first female government ministers. He celebrates Eva's gazelle-like beauty, but not the selfless work she did on behalf of London's poor.

Critics argue that not only does Yeats make the sexist claim that beautiful, aristocratic women have no business in politics, but that he also unfairly devalues the sisters' social and political energy. He dismisses their political beliefs as the striving for 'Some vague Utopia' and an 'ignorant conspiracy'. By doing so, he shows his own ignorance of the good the sisters achieved. He also ignores their independence of mind and their selfless dedication to the various causes they supported.

Swift's Epitaph

A scene from *Gulliver's Travels*, a work by Swift that has
inspired artists and writers for hundreds of years

LINE BY LINE

Jonathan Swift (1667–1745) was a writer, a Protestant
clergyman and, eventually, Dean of St Patrick's Cathedral in
Dublin. Swift was born in Dublin, but his parents were English.
Following his education at Trinity College, he spent a lot of
time in England, where he moved in the world of the upper
classes. He settled permanently in Dublin in 1714.

Like Yeats, Swift had a complex relationship with Ireland. He
claimed to hate the country, but devoted a lot of his writing
to defending Ireland. In particular, he defended the Irish
economy, which was being unfairly exploited by the London
government. He was also extremely generous to Dublin's poor,
to whom he contributed one third of his own small income.

Swift is famous for the novel *Gulliver's Travels*, but he was also
a poet and one of the greatest prose satirists in the English
language. His other well-known works are *The Drapier Letters*
and *A Modest Proposal*, a satire in which Swift argues (ironically)
that it would make good economic sense for the children of the
poor Irish to be raised on farms for consumption on the dinner
tables of their English masters.

Swift implies that this would be no more difficult to justify than
the economic system that allowed England to exploit Irish
labour and trade. Swift is buried in St Patrick's Cathedral,
where his epitaph is in Latin. Yeats' poem loosely translates the
inscription into English.

The opening line tells us that Swift has gone to his rest and
reward in the next life, after the struggles of this earthly
existence. There, in the next world, he will be relieved from the
righteous anger, the 'savage indignation' that prompted him to
consistently speak out against the ills of society. His frustration
and anger will no longer torment him – in effect, it will no
longer cut his heart to pieces ('lacerate his breast').

In lines 4 and 5, Yeats addresses the reader directly, whom he
describes as 'World-besotted traveller'. We are 'world-besotted'
because we are obsessed with the things of this life, for example
money, sex, and success. The word 'traveller' reminds us that
we are not here forever. It reminds us that we are on a journey
through life, a journey that will end when we, like Swift, have
sailed into our rest.

Yeats concludes this short poem with a challenge to the
reader, to us world-besotted travellers. He challenges us to
imitate Swift: 'Imitate him if you dare … he/ Served human
liberty'. Yeats implies that serving human liberty, as Swift did
in his writings, is a risky business. Serving the cause of liberty,
Yeats seems to suggest, may bring you only anger, frustration,
ingratitude and the misunderstanding of the public. It will
probably leave you with a lacerated breast!

An Acre of Grass

LINE BY LINE

The poem was written towards the end of the poet's life. Yeats had recently moved into Riversdale, an 18th-century farmhouse in Rathfarnham, a village near Dublin. The house came with a small plot of land, an 'acre of green grass'. Remarking on the move in a letter to a friend, Yeats wrote: 'At first I was unhappy, for everything made me remember the great rooms and the great trees of Coole, my home for nearly forty years, but now that the pictures are up I feel more content'.

The poet takes stock of his life

It is late at night and the poet seems to be sitting by himself, perhaps unable to sleep. He describes the stillness and quietness of the house. The only movement that the poet detects is that of a 'mouse': 'Where nothing stirs but a mouse'.

The poet takes stock of his life and what he is left with at this late stage. There is a sense that his life has been whittled down, and that very little now remains:

- This is someone who was a frequent guest at the grand houses and estates of the Irish Ascendency class. He is accustomed to 'great rooms' and vast private lands. Now his life is confined and restricted to an 'acre of grass'.
- This is someone who is well travelled, a world-famous poet and recipient of the Nobel Prize for Literature, someone who has played a prominent role in Irish cultural and political affairs. Now, all he has are his memories and framed pictures – only the 'picture' remains.
- This is a man who has devoted his entire life to his craft, who has spent countless hours labouring to produce poems that would stand the test of time. Now, his life's work is held or contained between the covers of a book. We can imagine the poet looking at a single hard-backed copy of his collected works and having a sense that his work is done.

The poet's body is also weakening: 'strength of body goes'. He no longer has the physical desires or appetites that he had as a younger man: 'My temptation is quiet'. The description of the house in which he now resides seems to serve as a perfect symbol or metaphor for his physical body. Like the house, the poet is 'old'. Nothing much now 'stirs' within him.

But the poet is not lamenting his lack of material wealth. There is a sense of acceptance that this is what he has. In

ART AND THE ROLE OF THE ARTIST

'Swift's Epitaph' emphasises the public or political role of the poet in society. This poem is Yeats' tribute to Swift. In middle age, Yeats began to regard Swift as one of his most important influences. Yeats admired not only Swift's skill as a writer, but also the courage and tenacity with which his writing opposed greed, stupidity and exploitation.

There is a sense in this poem that Yeats believes it is the writer's duty to respond to public events, to criticise society and its leaders for their various faults and failings. The poem challenges writers to 'imitate' Swift if they dare. It asks them to have the courage to criticise society in their work, even if they might suffer as a result of speaking out.

Yeats admires Swift because Swift was a man of conviction. He stood up for these beliefs even when it cost him dearly to do so. Swift acted as if he didn't care what others thought about him. Like the airman in 'An Irish Airman', he seemed to weigh very lightly the personal consequences of his actions. He acted because he was compelled to do so and did not let fear or failure or ridicule stand in his way. Yeats also admires the passion that Swift exhibited in his life and work. Swift's writing, even when it dealt with serious matters, was always marked by zest, energy and humour.

fact, we could say that he has all he needs to live comfortably and continue to work as a poet. The 'acre of grass' is ideal for getting fresh air and taking the exercise that the poet needs.

Nor does Yeats dwell on or lament the the fact that his body no longer affords him any pleasure. He is primarily concerned with creativity and his ongoing work as an artist. Rather than feeling proud and content about what he has achieved, the poet seems to be dissatisfied.

Making the 'truth known'

Yeats' desire or objective as a poet is to gain profound insight into the meaning of life, to achieve a deep understanding of the world. There is a sense in which he feels that his work, despite having devoted his life to it, has not yet achieved this.

Yeats hopes before he dies to arrive at some profound understanding of the world and to 'make the truth known'. He has traditionally used two different methods to fuel his poetic enterprise:

• He gives free reign to his thoughts, using what he calls

Timon was an Ancient Greek philosopher who died in 399 BC. Shakespeare, in his play Timon of Athens, presents him as someone who devoted his life to his city, only to end up an outcast in his later years. The experience resulted in him acquiring a bitter understanding of life and humanity. Lear is the titular character from Shakespeare's King Lear. When he relinquishes control of his kingdom, dividing it up amongst his daughters, he suddenly realises what it is to be without power and respect. He wanders out into the world, goes insane and gains an insight into the sufferings of humanity.

'loose imagination', in the hope that some interesting idea will arise.
• He meditates on the information that his mind receives each day, processing it and shaping it in such a way that it might lead to a poem. Yeats compares his mind to a 'mill' that processes the rough material it receives, the 'rag and bone' of daily life.

However, the poet feels that he needs something more than this if he is going to make the 'truth known' in the time that he has left.

The poet's appeal

Yeats considers the possibility that he will succumb to some form of frenzy or madness in his old age. He makes an appeal, perhaps to God, to allow this to happen: 'Grant me an old man's frenzy'. In this frenzied state, his mind will be greatly disturbed, and this will lead to profound understanding or insight. Yeats refers to two Shakespearean characters who experienced something like what he has in mind: Timon of Athens and Lear.

But the poet cannot be sure if he will be granted such a 'frenzy'. Therefore, he must take it upon himself to bring about the change that he needs to achieve the understanding he desires.

Through a great effort of will, he must somehow 'remake' or refashion himself so that he becomes the kind of person he believes capable of gaining such profound insight or accessing such truth: 'Myself must I remake'.

Here Yeats cites the examples of William Blake and Michelangelo, two artists renowned for their ability to create great works even in old age. Yeats presents Blake as someone who kept pushing and pushing until he achieved the understanding he desired: 'beat upon the wall/ Till truth obeyed his call'. Michelangelo is described as having a brilliant, piercing mind that is capable of of penetrating insight and understanding: 'A mind Michel Angelo knew/ That can pierce the clouds'.

Yeats is hoping that in the time remaining he can somehow emulate Blake and Michelangelo and achieve the understanding he requires. There is a real sense of urgency in these closing lines. The poet knows that he cannot afford to be patient and complacent. He needs to get angry, to experience a rage that will disturb his mind and shake things up.

The poet believes that being old should not prevent this from happening. Rather, now that he is no longer distracted by physical desire or by any social duties, he is free to devote himself to this pursuit. Yeats compares the aged mind to an 'eagle', suggesting that the mind in old age is free to soar and gain a view or understanding of the world that is not possible to achieve when you are younger.

FOCUS ON STYLE

Yeats refers to the information that is received through the senses as the 'rag and bone' of the mind. Rag and bone is a term used to describe scraps or discarded items that someone would collect and try to sell for cash. Rag and bone men would spend their days searching for such scraps, in the hope that they might come across something valuable.

In a similar manner, the poet processes the day-to-day information that his mind receives, hoping to be inspired by it and convert it into a poem. Yeats compares the mind to a 'mill' or factory that processes and sorts the information it receives: 'the mill of the mind'.

The description of the 'old house' in which the poet lives is a metaphor for the poet's own decrepit body: 'an old house/ Where nothing stirs but a mouse.'

Yeats also uses the image of the eagle to represent the aged mind: 'An old man's eagle mind'. An eagle can soar into the air, gaining a wide perspective of the world. But it can also focus with extraordinary sharpness on any given object. An old man's mind, according to Yeats, can see life with a similarly broad perspective. Old people, after all, have lived and experienced more than younger people. An old man's mind also exhibits an eagle-like sharpness of focus because it is undistracted by the sexual desire and other fivilous concerns of youth.

THEMES

YOUTH AND AGE

Many of Yeats' poems lament the negative effects of ageing. 'An Acre of Grass', however, takes a different approach. The poet is accepting of the ageing process and even celebrates certain advantages that come with growing older. He is no longer distracted by sexual desire: 'My temptation is quiet'. His mind has grown more mindful and serene. He likens the aged body to 'an old house' that barely contains any life: 'an old house/ Where nothing stirs but a mouse'.

The poet's mind is now free to gain insight or understanding that was unavailable to him when he was young. Yeats describes the aged man's mind in terms of an 'eagle': 'An old man's eagle mind'. The comparison not only suggests the sharpness of the older man's mind but also that it is capable of soaring and gaining a perspective on life that is not available to the young.

ART AND THE ROLE OF THE ARTIST

This is another poem in which Yeats presents art as a continuous practice, a craft or trade that must be perfected throughout the artist's life. He admires artists like Michelangelo, William Shakespeare (who created the characters of Lear and Timon), and William Blake, who continued, even in old age, to strive for artistic perfection. Yeats clearly wants to emulate the passion and energy exhibited by these past masters, who kept changing and developing until the very end of their lives. The artist, Yeats believes, should never feel satisfied or content with what they have already achieved. It is the artist's duty, even in old age, to remain restless and to constantly seek new ways to explore and reveal the truth.

Yeats also presents the artist as a truth-seeker, someone who works to gain a profound understanding of the world, to break through the normal limits of the mind. Yeats compares such limits to walls or clouds that need to be somehow broken down, transgressed or pierced.

Yeats presents Blake as someone who kept pushing and pushing until he achieved the understanding he desired: 'beat upon the wall/ Till truth obeyed his call'. Michelangelo is described as having a brilliant, piercing mind that is capable of penetrating insight and understanding: 'A mind Michel Angelo knew/ That can pierce the clouds'.

from Under Ben Bulben

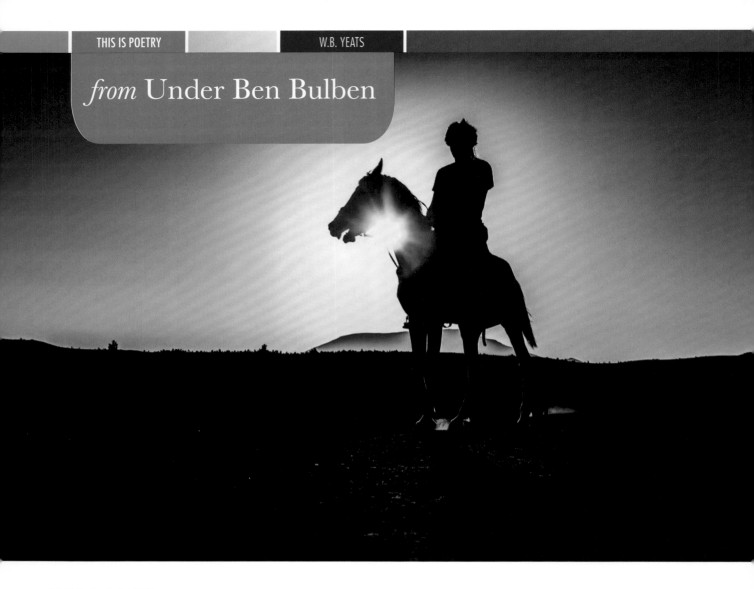

LINE BY LINE

In this poem, Yeats addresses future Irish poets and offers them advice. Yeats presents poetry as a 'trade' that one must 'learn'. Poetry, according to this view, has much in common with other trades like carpentry, plumbing or silver-smithing.

Poetry, like all these professions, involves a particular set of skills and techniques, which are passed on from one generation of poets to the next. A poet, like any tradesman, must serve an apprenticeship, during which time he acquires these skills, methods and trade secrets.

The sort now growing up

Yeats is unimpressed at the direction that Irish society is taking. The population, in his view, is becoming increasingly 'base'.

- This term implies that the Irish people, increasingly, are devoid of morality and honour. Their hearts are 'unremembering' as if they no longer recall what decency and virtue actually are.
- The phrase 'unremembering hearts' also implies a different form of baseness, suggesting that they're incapable of subtle and complex emotions, the feelings involved, for instance, in contemplating Swift's poetry or Byzantine art.

- But their baseness also lies in their 'unremembering heads'. They have forgotten their country's heritage and traditions, its literature, its stories and its songs.
- We might even read the term 'base' as suggesting that the population is becoming physically inferior, as if these 'base' people are somehow ugly or deformed.

The Irish, then, are getting 'out of shape from toe to top', becoming more and more physically, intellectually and morally unfit.

Yeats suggests that these base qualities are growing more widespread with every passing generation because 'base' parents generate offspring who inherit their negative characteristics. With each generation, then, there are more and more of these ill-begotten children, these 'Base-born products of base beds'. Yeats cautions aspiring poets to avoid these base characters who form an increasingly large segment of the Irish population: 'Scorn the sort now growing up'. These 'out of shape' individuals, he advises, should never be used as a subject matter for poetry. But there's also a suggestion that poets should avoid associating with these 'base-born' masses, for fear, perhaps, that their negative qualities might rub off.

Proper sources of inspiration

Aspiring poets, Yeats advises, should stick to a specific range of subject matters, confining themselves to 'whatever is well made'. Poems should be inspired by beautiful objects, like the sculpted bird in 'Sailing to Byzantium', that have been 'well made' by gifted craftsmen. Or they should celebrate elements of the natural world, like birds, bees and flowers, that have been 'well made' by nature's processes. Or they should find inspiration in beautiful and noble people who have been 'well made' by a combination of genetics and upbringing.

In this regard, Yeats suggests the 'peasantry' as a fit subject matter for poetry. This refers to Ireland's poor farmers, especially those in the west of the country. These small farmers endured extreme poverty: living in tiny cottages without electricity, making their own clothes, working the same few stony acres for generation after generation, producing just enough to get by.

Another fit subject, according to Yeats, would be 'Hard-riding country gentlemen'. Here we imagine wealthy landowners dressed in the finest equestrian gear, powering through the countryside on thoroughbred steeds. Ireland's up-and-coming poets, Yeats suggests, should let themselves be inspired by such riders, by the force and motion they exhibit as they gallop through the countryside, by the grace and elegance of their prize animals.

Poets, according to Yeats, should also be inspired by Ireland's monks, taking inspiration from the 'holiness' and spirituality of their lives. Yeats, though by no means a conventional Christian, greatly admired how monks live in a way that is focused, disciplined and completely devoid of materialism. And he also venerated the learning and artistry associated with the monasteries of Ireland's past, which produced annals, chalices and fantastically illustrated volumes like The Book of Kells.

But poets can also find inspiration in less spiritual places, in the country's pubs for instance. Yeats, perhaps surprisingly, suggests a 'porter drinker' as a fitting subject matter: 'Porter drinker's randy laughter'. We might imagine here an exuberant and entertaining companion, someone full of life and energy, of laughter and talk, of stories and sexual desire.

The aristocrats of Ireland's past are another appropriate source of inspiration. Yeats describes these 'lords and ladies' as 'gay', which in this instance suggests that they were jovial and carefree. These aristocrats lived and died in a way that was energetic, exuberant and joyful. The term 'gay' also has connotations of vividness and bright colours, suggesting how these aristocrats valued art, design and beauty.

But these lords and ladies were also fierce warriors, commanding armies in a 'heroic' resistance to English rule in Ireland. Their struggle continued for 'seven centuries', from the 12th century to the 20th century. Time after time, these 'lords and ladies' were crushed and defeated, were 'beaten into the clay' by English oppression. But their descendants would always rise up again, continuing the struggle for generation after generation, so that their country might finally be free.

Looking to the past

Yeats concludes his advice to up-and-coming poets by urging them to look to history for inspiration: 'Cast your mind on other days'. For the things he values as sources of inspiration are increasingly things of the past. The peasantry, the gentlemen, the monks, the lord and ladies were rare in 1939 when Yeats wrote the poem and are even rarer in the Ireland of today.

The present and future, meanwhile, seem increasingly the province of the 'base' with their 'unremembering hearts and heads', who, as pointed out above, are under no circumstances to be considered fit subject matter for poetry.

Yeats' grave

Yeats imagines a time after his own death. He writes in the third person, as if he were an unnamed speaker contemplating the grave in which he has been laid (note how the speaker refers to the poet in the third person, using terms like 'Yeats' and 'his'). This anonymous onlooker describes Yeats' burial as a kind of homecoming:

- He has been buried in his beloved County Sligo, specifically under Ben Bulben, the famously distinctive mountain that from childhood haunted his imagination: 'Under bare Ben Bulben's head...Yeats is laid'.
- He has been buried in the grounds of a church with which he has a family connection. At some time in the past, one of his relatives worked as a minister in this very chapel: 'An ancestor was rector there/ Long years ago'.
- He has been buried near 'an ancient Cross', which symbolises his deep engagement with Ireland's history, heritage and mythology.
- His gravestone is manufactured from locally-sourced Sligo limestone, from 'limestone quarried near the spot'. Yeats has chosen this over marble, which was the material typically used in such monuments: 'No marble'.

Gravestones are typically carved with expressions like 'beloved uncle' or 'rest in peace' or 'here lies with God'. According to the speaker, however, Yeats' gravestone is marked with no such ordinary or 'conventional phrase'. The speaker describes how instead

Unlike marble, a hard-wearing material that can last for decades or even centuries, limestone erodes relatively quickly. It's as if Yeats' choice of limestone reflects his desire to become one with the Sligo landscape. His headstone, he imagines, will be washed away by the rain, draining into the soil of the county he so loved.

Yeats requested that his monument be carved with a mysterious three-line poem: 'By his command these words are cut'.

FOCUS ON STYLE

Imagery

'Under Ben Bulben', like the best of Yeats' poetry, combines a powerful, logical argument with memorable images. In part V, the images flash by like a deck of cards being flicked at one corner: the monks, the hard-riding gentlemen, the porter drinkers, the lords and ladies. Part VI, in contrast, lingers on the single image of Yeats' burial place. The camera pans across every detail, from Ben Bulben in the distance to the cross by the roadside. The poem closes, fittingly for one of Yeats' final poetic statements, with the haunting image of the horseman.

Tone, Mood and Atmosphere

The poem's tone shifts between the sections. The tone in part V is premonitory and commanding, almost angry at times, as it issues decrees and condemnations. In part VI, however, the tone is one of calmness and detachment. There is a matter-of-factness to these lines that is in keeping with the lack of sentimentality that the poet urges us to have in our attitudes to life and death.

THEMES

ART AND THE ROLE OF THE ARTIST

This is another poem in which Yeats presents art as a continuous practice, a craft or trade that must be perfected throughout the artist's life. Future Irish poets, Yeats decrees, must 'learn [their] trade'. These aspiring bards must understand that poetry involves more than ideas and inspiration, that it requires practice, patience and determination. They must approach poetry the way an apprentice carpenter approaches the work bench, realising that they have a great deal to learn and that only hard work will grant them the mastery they desire.

'Under Ben Bulben' also explores the public or political role of the poet in society. If poetry is a 'trade', then it must serve a useful function. Like carpentry and tailoring it must be necessary to society. Poetry's function, as Yeats presents it here, is to 'cast [his or her] mind on other days', to remember and write about the past.

For seven centuries the 'Irishry' resisted English rule, proving themselves 'indomitable', impossible to overcome. But now they're in danger of succumbing to a new and more subtle foe, that of modernity. Will Ireland become just another identical outpost of capitalism, just another banal node in an international network of technology?

Only the poets, according to Yeats, can prevent this from happening. Only they can remind Ireland as a whole of what it once was and can be again. Through their words, they can spur us on to be 'indomitable' in the face of modernity, to create a future that resembles the best aspects of our past.

Many readers, perhaps understandably, have taken issue with Yeats' decrees about the appropriate subject matter for poetry. After all, why should a poet write about only what's 'well made'? Why can't she be inspired by things that are badly made, by images of horror and disgust? And who's to say what's well made anyway? Why can't we view soccer matches and computer terminals as fitting poetic material, instead of peasants and monks? Can we look to the future instead of always being stuck in the past?

YEATS AND IRELAND

This is another poem in which Yeats laments what he saw as the decline of Irish society. In 1939, when Yeats wrote the poem, Ireland was becoming a place dominated by science and technology, industry and commerce. These changes, Yeats feels, have made the Irish of today a rather 'base' lot. The 'sort now growing up' are devoid of morality, incapable of feeling, and even physically inferior.

Yeats, then, looks back with affection to this golden time before modernity, when gentleman and peasant alike were uncorrupted by the grubby influences of capitalism and materialism. This was also a time before science came to dominate mankind's view of the world, a time that Yeats, a spiritualist rather than a scientist in outlook, harks back to with the greatest of nostalgia.

This is also a poem in which Yeats celebrates the revolutionary patriotism of Ireland's past. We see this in his mention of the lords and ladies who rose up again and again to challenge English rule over centuries of resistance.

The mention of the 'hard-riding country gentleman' reminds us of the Anglo-Irish, the Protestant landowners who dominated Irish life between the 17th and 20th centuries. Yeats felt great affection for this class, relishing the restrained and tasteful elegance of their mansions, admiring the formal, almost ceremonial, nature of their lifestyle and appreciating their devotion to art and culture.

The poem looks back to the heyday of the Anglo-Irish, long before his own time, in the 18th and early 19th centuries. Yeats presents the Ireland of that period as a place of almost medieval simplicity. The 'lords and ladies' of the ascendancy resided in their 'gay' mansions or relaxed by 'hard-riding' through the countryside. The Catholic 'peasantry' worked the land and drank porter in the taverns, content with the noble simplicity of their lot. The monks, cooped up in their monasteries, got on with being holy.

By the time Yeats wrote this poem, the heyday of the Anglo-Irish was long since past. Their power had waned throughout the nineteenth century and all but disappeared in the new Catholic Ireland that emerged after independence from Britain.

DEATH

Each of us who reads Yeats' famously enigmatic three-line inscription, whether on his headstone in Drumcliffe Churchyard or on the printed page, is a kind of horseman, a traveller on a journey through life. For all we can do is 'pass by' as we make our way from moment to moment, from year to year, and ultimately from the mysterious state before birth to the even more mysterious one that awaits us at our journey's end. The horse of time that carries us forward, relentlessly forward, will permit no pausing.

Yeats urges us to 'cast a cold eye' on this journey. We must assess our lives and the sum of our experience in a calm and coldly rational manner. We must be equally 'cold' about the reality of our own impending deaths, accepting that death, whether we like it or not, is our ultimate destination. For in such coldness, in such a purging of emotion, lies emotional freedom, an utter release from anxieties about life's failures and death's inevitability. We might even find ourselves laughing at the whole beautiful, ridiculous journey.

Politics

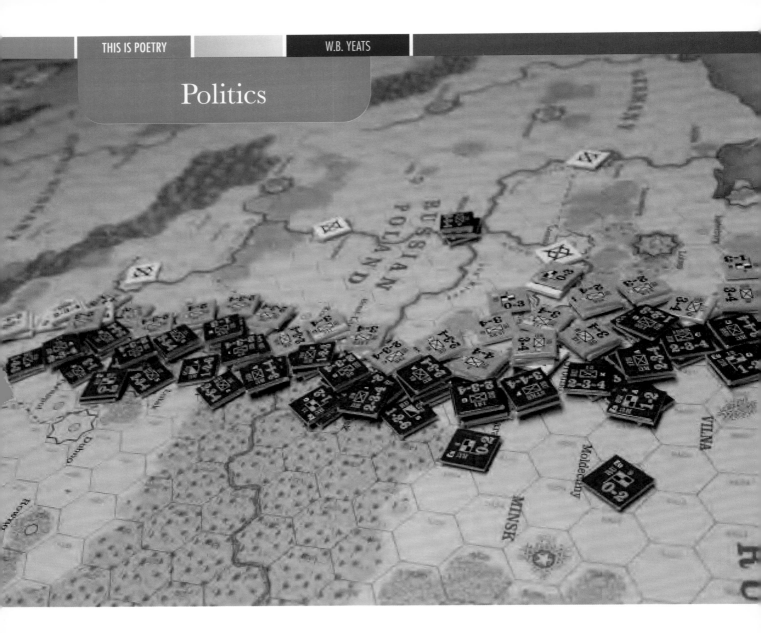

LINE BY LINE

Yeats is in conversation with two wise, well-informed people:

- The first is a man who has travelled extensively throughout the world and, therefore, has a good understanding of the political and social affairs in different countries. Yeats says that this man speaks from experience, that he 'knows/ What he talks about'.
- The second is an experienced politician. Yeats says that the politician is 'learned', suggesting that he not only knows much about political affairs, but that he is a well-educated man who likely has a broad understanding of the world.

The conversation focuses on the political situation in Italy, Russia and Spain. In 1938, when Yeats wrote the poem, the situation in each of these countries was very grave as Europe was sliding towards World War Two. Russia was under the brutal rule of Stalin, who in 1938 was attempting to purge the country of all those he deemed a threat to his rule. Italy was ruled by fascist dictator Mussolini, while Spain was gradually

being taken over by far-right forces led by General Franco. While all this was happening, Hitler, having just annexed Austria, was now pushing to take control of Czechoslovakia.

It is unsurprising, therefore, that the conversation between the poet, his well-travelled friend and the 'learned' politician centres around events in these countries and the growing possibility of war in Europe.

The poet knows that the men with whom he converses are knowledgeable and that their opinions are to be respected. He accepts that their predictions of approaching war are probably accurate: 'And maybe what they say is true/ Of war and war's alarms'.

Yet the poet cannot focus or 'fix his attention' on these urgent matters. All the while that they are talking, the poet is distracted by a beautiful young girl who is standing close by. He wishes he was young once again, so that he could be her lover: 'But O that I were young again/ And held her in my arms!'

THEMES

YOUTH AND AGE

Like many of Yeats' poems, 'Politics' laments the tragedy of old age. The poet is entranced by a beautiful woman, but knows he's now too old to ever win her affections. 'Politics', then, like 'Sailing to Byzantium' and 'An Acre of Grass', movingly depicts the restrictions and frustrations that come with growing older.

There is real emotion in the poem's final lines, when he wishes that he could somehow be young again and hold the beautiful woman he so desires in his arms. The tragic reality, of course, is that is there is no turning back the clock. The poet's desire for youth, and for this beautiful girl, must remain forever thwarted. This nostalgic lament for a vanished youth echoes both 'The Wild Swans at Coole' and 'In Memory of Eva Gore-Booth and Con Markiewicz'. All three poems find the poet yearning nostalgically for an earlier stage of his existence.

WAR, VIOLENCE AND SOCIAL UPHEAVAL

Yeats wrote this poem in 1938, a very dark time in the history of Europe. The Second World War was poised to break out over the continent like a terrible storm. As Yeats puts it, 'war's alarms' were ringing throughout the world. There is, then, a certain sense of dread in this poem. The 'travelled man' and the politician seem deeply concerned about the coming catastrophe. The poet, however, finds himself distracted by the presence of a beautiful young woman. For a moment romantic longing overtakes his fear of the coming storm. In this regard, 'Politics' is not unlike 'The Second Coming' and 'The Stare's Nest by My Window'. All three poems register a dread of the great violence, war and upheaval that marred the world during the last years of Yeats' life.

ART THE ROLE OF THE ARTIST

'Politics' is another poem that explores the public or political role of the poet in society. 'Politics' was inspired by an article by the writer Archibald MacLeish that criticised Yeats for failing to comment on political issues in his work. The poem contrasts a public catastrophe with private suffering. The public catastrophe is that of the impending war. The private suffering is that of the poet, as he endures the anguish of old age and the frustration of thwarted desire.

The poem suggests that this private tragedy is of more significance to Yeats as an artist than the public tragedy of war. He is unable to shift his attention from the beauty of the girl to important political matters. The poem seems to answer MacLeish by suggesting that poets are not obliged to write about 'public' matters of national importance. Instead, they should be free to deal with 'private' matters that will eventually affect us all, such as the delight and torture of romance and the decay and indignity of old age.

Therefore, although 'Politics' is a relatively simple poem, it raises a number of important questions. Is it self-centred of Yeats as a writer to assign more significance to his private anguish than to the looming disaster of war? Is it wrong for the poet or artist to focus on his or her personal relationships and problems when there is so much evil and suffering in the world? On the other hand, however, it is possible to regard Yeats' involvement with themes of the heart as arising not from self-obsession but from a desire to write about universal human experiences.

FOCUS ON STYLE

Form

The poem consists of twelve lines with no stanza breaks. It follows an ABCB DEFE GHIH rhyme scheme.

Tone, Mood and Atmosphere

Unusually for Yeats, the tone of 'Politics' is quite humorous, self-deprecating and tongue-in-cheek. Despite the fact that the poem references much of the political unrest in Europe at the time, Yeats insists he can't possibly focus on such serious issues when there is a beautiful girl standing in front of him: 'How can I, that girl standing there,/ My attention fix/ On … politics'.

There is also a wistful note to this poem. Whereas in 'The Stare's Nest by My Window' he praises the ability of the older man to focus on the serious issues in life, here he wants nothing more than to return to his youth: 'But O that I were young again/ And held her in my arms.'

How to Answer the Poetry Questions

I've been asked to write an essay in response to the following statement: 'I like (or do not like) to read the poetry of Sylvia Plath'.

STAGE 1: PLANNING THE ANSWER

ESTABLISH A POINT OF VIEW

First, I'm going to decide what my point of view is. I'm going to declare that I like the poetry of Sylvia Plath for the following reasons:

- It is emotionally intense, and it deals with the darker aspects of the human psyche.
- Her vivid and violent imagery lingers in the mind long after we have read the poems.

This is one of the most important steps in the whole process. I have decided a point of view. I will not be rambling on vaguely about my attitude to Plath's poetry. Everything in my answer will now relate to this point of view.

DECIDE WHICH POEMS TO TALK ABOUT

I am now going to decide which poems to talk about. It's good to talk about four to six poems in an answer. I'm going to talk about six: 'Elm', 'Poppies in July', 'The Arrival of the Bee Box', 'Morning Song', 'Black Rook in Rainy Weather' and 'Child'. I'm going to quickly jot down the titles of these poems along with a couple of quotations from each poem that will relate to my point of view.

STRUCTURE THE ESSAY

Now I'm going to structure my essay. I'm going to write six paragraphs.

- The first paragraph, the introduction, will clearly state my point of view.
- The second paragraph will deal with 'Elm' and 'The Arrival of the Bee Box'. I will be discussing Plath's inner turmoil as exhibited in these poems.
- The third paragraph will discuss 'Black Rook in Rainy Weather' and 'Poppies in July'. I will discuss feelings of numbness or mental neutrality as exhibited in these poems.
- My fourth paragraph will discuss 'Child' and 'Morning Song'. I will discuss the feelings of inadequacy as a mother as exhibited in these poems.
- My fifth paragraph will discuss vivid and memorable images in Plath's poetry. I will refer to a number of the poems mentioned above.
- The final paragraph will be the conclusion.

STAGE 2: WRITING THE ESSAY

WRITING THE INTRODUCTION

I'm going to write my introduction. The first one or two sentences of my introduction will simply state the point of view I came up with in the planning stage:

> I really admire the poetry of Sylvia Plath because it is emotionally intense and it deals with the darker aspects of the human psyche. I also like how her vivid and violent imagery lingers in the mind long after we have read the poems.

I am now going to flesh this out in a few more sentences. It is good to make these sentences personal, if possible, to describe the impact the work had on you. In this instance, I am going to emphasise the impact Plath had on me by contrasting her with the other poets I have studied:

> I really admire the poetry of Sylvia Plath because it is emotionally intense and it deals with the darker aspects of the human psyche. I also like how the vivid and violent imagery she uses lingers in the mind long after we have read the poems. Throughout my life I have always found poetry to be dull, boring and intellectual. The poets I read never really connected with me. However, this was definitely not the case with Sylvia Plath. This is poetry that came from the heart as much as from the head. Her work spoke to me immediately due to its raw and intense emotional content and its unforgettably violent imagery.

It is obvious that the five sentences I have added here flesh out my
point of view. The sentences are personal and show that I have really engaged with the work of the poet.

WRITING THE BODY PARAGRAPHS

I see from my plan that my first body paragraph will deal with the inner turmoil expressed in 'Elm' and 'The Arrival of the Bee Box'. So I'm going to start the paragraph with a topic sentence, declaring what the paragraph is going to be about.

Every other sentence in this paragraph is going to relate to or expand on this topic sentence. If I find myself writing something that does not relate directly to this topic sentence, I know I've gone wrong. To complete this paragraph I am going to write a couple of sentences about 'Elm' and 'The Arrival of the Bee Box':

> In 'Elm' and 'The Arrival of the Bee Box' we see Plath expressing intense inner turmoil. 'Elm' depicts a mind at the end of its tether. The poet is tormented by the dark emotions that dwell within her psyche: 'I'm terrified by this dark thing/ That sleeps in me'. The elm tree has been 'scorched' by the 'atrocity' of 'sunsets', has been lashed by poisonous rain and blasted by 'wind of such violence'. Yet we feel that these terrible sufferings are a metaphor for the mental turmoil the poet endures. 'The Arrival of the Bee Box' is another poem that deals with mental turmoil. The bee box has thrown the poet into a state of confusion and distress. She is both frightened and fascinated by this object: 'The box is locked, it is dangerous./ I have to live with it overnight/ And I can't keep away from it'. She is disgusted by the sight of the bees through the box's grill: 'Black on black, angrily clambering.' She is even more upset by the sounds that are coming from the box: 'it is the noise that appals me most of all'. As in 'Elm', we feel that there is an element of metaphor to this poem. The box serves as a symbol for the darker side of the poet's psyche, for the feelings of fear and inadequacy that she keeps locked inside her and that she fears will destroy her should she set them free.

Note how every sentence I have written relates to my topic sentence. I don't wander off the point by talking about Plath's marriage or about life in the 1950s when she wrote the poem.

Note also how I don't fall into the trap of paraphrasing the poems, of telling the examiner everything that happened in each of them. I simply take two or three aspects that are relevant to my topic sentence.

Note also how I back up every point with a quote. The golden rule here is 'Always be quoting!'

Finally, note how at the end of my paragraph I link the two poems it discusses. This is a skill that can be acquired with practice.

I see that my next paragraph is going to deal with feelings of numbness or mental neutrality as exhibited in 'Black Rook in Rainy Weather' and 'Poppies in July'. Once again, I start off with a simple topic sentence.

Also, as before, I am going to write a number of sentences that relate to this topic sentence. I'm going to make sure that nothing I write strays away from this topic.

> 'Black Rook in Rainy Weather' and 'Poppies in July' display a desperate state of mental neutrality and numbness. In 'Black Rook in Rainy Weather', the poet expresses her 'fear/ Of total neutrality'. In one sense, this suggests her fear of writer's block, the fear that she will never again be visited by 'the angel' of inspiration, by that 'rare, random descent'. However, the mention of 'total neutrality' calls to mind the intense numbness or emptiness experienced by those suffering from depression. The grey, desolate landscape in which the poem is set serves as a metaphor for this state of 'total neutrality'. The 'desultory weather' and the 'season/ Of fatigue' calls to mind the dead inner emptiness the poet fears. In 'Poppies in July', this fear seems to have been realised. The poet is gripped by a feeling of numbness and emptiness. She longs for physical pain just so she can feel something: 'if I could bleed, or sleep! –/ If my mouth could marry a hurt like that!' She wishes the 'flames' of the poppies could burn her in order to return some sensation of feeling to her life.

Note again how every sentence I have written relates to my topic sentence.

I don't fall into the trap of paraphrasing the poems, of telling the examiner everything that happened in each of them. I simply take two or three aspects that are relevant to my topic sentence.

I back up every point with a quote.

The remainder of the body paragraphs will follow the same format outlined above.

WRITING THE CONCLUSION

The idea here is to sum up what I have said in the essay without repeating myself too much. I am going to bring the point of view I established in the introduction back in again. I am going to try and get personal. The first thing I am going to do is rewrite my point of view in slightly different language.

> For me, then, Plath's poetry stands out because of its sheer emotional power.

Now I am going to add a sentence that contains a phrase like 'In the poems discussed above' or 'As I have outlined above' or 'As I have discussed'. This sentence will refer back to the essay I have just written.

> For me, then, Plath's poetry stands out because of its sheer emotional power. In poems like those discussed above, there is an emotional intensity like nothing else I have come across in poetry.

Now I am going to add two or three more sentences that flesh out this point. I am going to try to make these as personal as possible.

> For me, then, Plath's poetry stands out because of its sheer emotional power. In poems like those discussed above, there is an emotional intensity like nothing else I have come across in poetry. Reading Plath's poetry, I felt she was really talking to me, that she was describing dark emotional states that I and every other human being will experience at some point. The powerful imagery, like that of the elm, the bee box and the disturbing field of poppies, will remain with me for the rest of my life.

If you are good at English, it can be good to finish with a flourish. This might involve using a memorable phrase, a quote from a famous writer or the poet under discussion, or some poetic sentence of your own.

THE SEVEN GOLDEN RULES

1. **Read the question carefully.** This sounds obvious but I can't stress how important it is.

2. **Establish a point of view.** Do this at the beginning of your planning stage. Remember that every sentence in your essay will relate to this point of view.

3. **Structure the essay carefully.** Determine what every paragraph is going to be about before you commence writing.

4. **Begin each paragraph with a topic sentence.** Every other sentence in the paragraph will relate to this sentence.

5. **Don't paraphrase.** Don't retell the story or the action of the poem – the examiner already knows this. Just identify the two or three elements of the poem that relate to your topic.

6. **Always be quoting.**

7. **Be aware of genre.** Are you being asked to write a straightforward essay or are you being asked to do something else like write a letter or give a short talk? If you are being asked to write a letter or a short talk, then the introduction and the conclusion of your piece will need to reflect this.

SEE NEXT PAGE FOR THE FULL ESSAY

SAMPLE ANSWER

Write an essay outlining the reasons why you like or dislike the poetry of Sylvia Plath

I really admire the poetry of Sylvia Plath because it is emotionally intense and it deals with the darker aspects of the human psyche. I also like how the vivid and violent imagery she uses lingers in the mind long after we have read the poems. Throughout my life, I have always found poetry to be dull, boring and intellectual. The poets I have read have never really connected with me. However, this was definitely not the case with Sylvia Plath. This is poetry that came from the heart as much as from the head. Her work spoke to me immediately due to its raw and intense emotional content and its unforgettably violent imagery.

In 'Elm' and 'The Arrival of the Bee Box' we see Plath expressing intense inner turmoil. 'Elm' depicts a mind at the end of its tether. The poet is tormented by the dark emotions that dwell within her psyche: 'I'm terrified by this dark thing/ That sleeps in me'. The elm tree has been 'scorched' by the 'atrocity' of 'sunsets', has been lashed by poisonous rain and blasted by 'wind of such violence'. Yet we feel that these terrible sufferings are a metaphor for the mental turmoil the poet endures. 'The Arrival of the Bee Box' is another poem that deals with mental turmoil. The bee box has thrown the poet into a state of confusion and distress. She is both frightened and fascinated by this object: 'The box is locked, it is dangerous./ I have to live with it overnight/ And I can't keep away from it'. She is disgusted by the sight of the bees through the box's grill: 'Black on black, angrily clambering'. She is even more upset by the sounds that are coming from the box: 'It is the noise that appals me most of all'. As in 'Elm', we feel that there is an element of metaphor to this poem. The box serves as a symbol for the darker side of the poet's psyche, for the feelings of fear and inadequacy that she keeps locked inside her and that she fears will destroy her should she set them free.

'Black Rook in Rainy Weather' and 'Poppies in July' display a desperate state of mental neutrality and numbness. In 'Black Rook in Rainy Weather', the poet expresses her 'fear/ Of total neutrality'. In one sense, this suggests her fear of writer's block, the fear that she will never again be visited by 'the angel' of inspiration, by that 'rare, random descent'. However, the mention of 'total neutrality' calls to mind the intense numbness or emptiness experienced by those suffering from depression. The grey, desolate landscape in which the poem is set serves as a metaphor for this state of 'total neutrality'. The 'desultory weather' and the 'season/ Of fatigue' calls to mind the dead inner emptiness the poet fears. In 'Poppies in July', this fear seems to have been realised. The poet is gripped by a feeling of numbness and emptiness. She longs for physical pain just so she can feel something: 'If I could bleed, or sleep! –/ If my mouth could marry a hurt like that!' She wishes the 'flames' of the poppies could burn her in order to return some sensation of feeling to her life.

This feeling of numbness surfaces again in a poem that Plath wrote about the birth of her child, called 'Morning Song'. Standing before the newborn child, the poet and her husband seem empty, devoid of the feelings we expect of parents: 'We stand round blankly as walls.' Plath's honesty here is admirable, and I really respect her for the way she writes about her feelings of inadequacy as a mother. Becoming a mother is a daunting and overwhelming experience, and Plath struggles in the role, feeling that she lacks what it takes to be an effective parent: 'I'm no more your mother/ Than the cloud that distils a mirror to reflect its own slow/ Effacement at the wind's hand.' A similar feeling of inadequacy is evident in 'Child' where the poet describes a desperate desire to fill her child's world with beauty and wonder but is unable to do so because of her struggle with depression. It is heartbreaking to read of her 'troublous/ Wringing of hands, this dark/ Ceiling without a star.'

The images of the 'Wringing of hands' and the 'dark/ Ceiling without a star' perfectly illustrate Plath's genius for creating vivid and startling images in the minds of those who read her poems. In three short lines at the close of 'Child' she perfectly captures the horror of depression. Each of her poems is full of such memorable imagery. In 'Poppies in July', she startles us with the comparison she makes between the colour of the poppies and 'the skin of a mouth// A mouth just bloodied./ Little bloody skirts!' 'Elm' is rich with powerful and unforgettable imagery. In this poem, Plath describes the moon as being 'Diminished and flat, as after radical surgery', and speaks of branches of trees being 'a hand of wires'. Just like the bird in 'Pheasant', these images startle me still.

For me, then, Plath's poetry stands out because of its sheer emotional power. In poems like those discussed above, there is an emotional intensity like nothing else I have come across in poetry. Reading Plath's poetry, I felt she was really talking to me, that she was describing dark emotional states that I and every other human being will experience at some time. The powerful imagery, like that of the elm, the bee box and the disturbing field of poppies, will remain with me for the rest of my life.

UNSEEN POEM: SAMPLE ANSWER

Back Yard

by Carl Sandburg

Shine on, O moon of summer.
Shine to the leaves of grass, catalpa and oak,
All silver under your rain to-night.

An Italian boy is sending songs to you to-night from an accordion.
A Polish boy is out with his best girl; they marry next month;   [5]
    to-night they are throwing you kisses.

An old man next door is dreaming over a sheen that sits in a
    cherry tree in his back yard.

The clocks say I must go—I stay here sitting on the back porch drinking
    white thoughts you rain down.   [10]

    Shine on, O moon,
Shake out more and more silver changes.

Answer either Question 1 or Question 2

1. (a) Do you like the world that the poet describes in this poem? Give reasons for your answer supporting them
    by reference to the text. (10)

  (b) Choose a line or two that you find particularly appealing and explain why. (10)

OR

2. Write a personal response to the poem 'Back Yard'. (20)

(a) Do you like the world that the poet describes in this poem? Give reasons for your answer supporting them by reference to the text. (10)

I love the world that the poet presents in this poem. It is a magical and rather fantastical world, all coated in 'silver': 'All silver under your rain to-night'. Everything seems to have taken on a special glow or 'sheen' in the moon's light. The 'grass, catalpa and oak' and the 'cherry tree' in the neighbour's backyard are cast in a special light by the moon, beautifully transformed and altered. The poet's mood is also affected by the moon. He seems to be in a blissful state of mind, perfectly content and happy 'drinking white thoughts' that the moon inspires. Though he knows it is late, he cannot bring himself to leave this wonderful moment.

The world of the poem is also perfectly romantic. The poet thinks of others who may be appreciating the moon's special glow on this night. He imagines 'An Italian boy is sending songs to' the moon tonight 'from an accordion'. He also pictures a 'Polish boy' on a date with 'his best girl'. This couple will 'marry next month' but tonight they are out 'throwing' kisses to the moon. It seems that the world is unified on this night in its appreciation of the moon.

(b) Choose a line or two that you find particularly appealing and explain why. (10)

I like the lines: 'The clocks say I must go – I stay here sitting on the back porch/ drinking white thoughts you rain down'. The poet sets the world of convention and propriety against the romantic world of dreams and freedom. The 'clocks' seem to represent the restricted, ordered world of responsibility whereas the poet 'sitting on the back porch' seems to have entered a place free of duty and care. The line begins with the blunt demand of the 'clocks': 'The clocks say I must go'. The terse and matter-of-fact statement is set in stark contrast against the more poetic and gentle words that follow: 'I stay here sitting on the back porch/ drinking white thoughts you rain down'. The dash in the line neatly separates the two worlds and the way that the words 'I stay' stand alongside 'I must go' makes the poet's decision all the more bold and satisfying: 'I must go – I stay'.

The poet suggests that the moon is inspiring him, feeding him 'thoughts' that are pure and joyous. It is as though the moon's rays are an intoxicating liquor that is making the poet tipsy. The image of him 'drinking white thoughts' calls to mind the term 'moonshine' that is used to describe certain illegally produced spirits. The poet by staying out upon his back porch seems to be rebelling against what is expected of him. It is late and he should be in bed, but he does not wish to act according to convention tonight.

Write a personal response to the poem 'Back Yard'. (20)

This is an inspiring and romantic poem that made me feel good when I read it. The poet conjures up a magical world that is all coated in the 'silver' light of the moon: 'the leaves of grass, catalpa and oak,/ All silver under your rain tonight'. It is a world of wonder and romance peopled with lovers and dreamers. The poet mentions an Italian accordion player, a young Polish couple and an elderly neighbour, each enthralled by the moon on this summer's night. The world of the poem seems to be blissfully innocent and good, devoid of troubles.

The poem contains some lovely imagery. The poet describes the effect of the moon's soft light upon his neighbour's cherry tree: 'a sheen/ that sits in a cherry tree in his back yard'. The soft sibilant 's' and 'ch' sounds correspond with the tranquil atmosphere of the night. I also loved the way the poet introduces images of people in other countries far away who are sharing his pleasure on this night. The 'Italian boy' and the 'Polish boy' who 'is out with his best girl' introduce a wonderful international dimension to the poem.

I especially liked the lines 'The clocks say I must go – I stay sitting on the back porch/ drinking white thoughts you rain down'. The 'clocks' seem to represent the dull and tedious world of work and responsibility. Such a world stands in opposition to the world of romance and dreams that the poet is part of on this summer's night. He knows that he ought to get to bed but he cannot resist the beauty of the moon's light and wishes to savour the moment for as long as he can. The moon's rays are like an intoxicating drink that the poet wants to keep on 'drinking'. They inspire sweet and pure thoughts ('white thoughts') that give the poet great pleasure.

SAMPLE ANSWER 2

I Want to Write

by Margaret Walker

I want to write
I want to write the songs of my people.
I want to hear them singing melodies in the dark.
I want to catch the last floating strains from their sob-torn

throats.   [5]

I want to frame their dreams into words; their souls into

notes.

I want to catch their sunshine laughter in a bowl;
fling dark hands to a darker sky
and fill them full of stars   [10]
then crush and mix such lights till they become
a mirrored pool of brilliance in the dawn.

Answer either Question 1 or Question 2

1. Write a response to the above poem, highlighting the impact it makes on you. (20)

OR

2 (a) Write down one phrase from the poem that shows how the poet feels about her people. Say why you
have chosen this phrase. (10)

2 (b) Does this poem make you feel hopeful or not hopeful? Briefly explain why. (10)

1. Write a response to the above poem, highlighting the impact it makes on you. (20)

This poem had a powerful impact on me. It reminded me forcefully of the suffering and hardship endured by the African American community throughout the ages, bringing home the fact that the ancestors of modern African Americans were stolen from Africa and forced to endure centuries of slavery and discrimination. The poet's mention of the 'sob-torn/ throats' of African Americans powerfully makes this point. We can imagine these people sobbing until their throats are sore, ravaged and exhausted. The references to darkness also suggest this history of suffering; the poet's people sing 'in the dark' and a 'darker sky' hangs over them. It's as if this darkness becomes a symbol for the suffering of her people.

The skillful way the poet writes about the art of writing itself also made an impact on me. The repetition of the phrase 'I want to write' at the beginning of the poem powerfully captures the poet's bursting, uncontainable desire to record the history of the African American community: 'I want to write the songs of my people'. Of course, the fact that the poem is entitled 'I want to write' also emphasises this desire.

I particularly enjoyed the fine metaphors the poet used to describe this process. She describes recording the laughter of her people as catching 'their sunshine laughter in a bowl'. The comparison of a poem to a bowl really works for me because it perfectlydescribes how a poem can catch, store and preserve a people's qualities so that they will not be forgotten by future generations.

In another fine metaphor, she describes her desire to write a poem that will shine like a beacon throughout the ages. She brilliantly describes this poem she longs to create as a 'mirrored pool of brilliance in the dawn'. This poem will remember and celebrate the African American people of which she is a part. For this reason, she imagines the 'pool of brilliance' being formed from stars African American hands have snatched from the heavens: 'fling dark hands to a darker sky/ and fill them full of stars'.

2 (a) Write down one phrase from the poem that shows how the poet feels about her people. Say why you have chosen this phrase. (10)

For me the phrase that best sums up the poet's feelings about her people is 'their sunshine laughter', as I believe this phrase seems to work on several different levels. First, it is an excellent metaphor. The comparison of laughter to sunshine is extremely clever, capturing the brightness, energy and cheerfulness we associate with the simple human act of laughing. Laughter and sunshine are, after all, linked in our imaginations.

I also like how this phrase captures the indomitable spirit and resilience of the African American people. These people have endured incredible and unimaginable suffering since they were first enslaved in Africa all those centuries ago. Walker wonderfully and succinctly captures this grim history with her reference to the 'sob-torn/ throats' of her people. Her people have cried out in suffering until their throats are sore and torn from doing so. The mention of 'sunshine laughter', therefore, wonderfully captures the spirit and resilience of the African American people. They have somehow retained their golden sense of humour in spite of all the suffering they have endured.

The phrase also introduced an element of symbolism to the poem. The brightness of this African American laughter is contrasted to the darkness that surrounds them. The sunshine of their laughter contrasts with the darkness in which they sing and the 'darker sky' that hangs over them.' It's as if their sunshine laughter represents their inner strength and resilience while the darkness represents the endless suffering that strives to wear their resistance down.

2 (b) Does this poem make you feel hopeful or not hopeful? Briefly explain why. (10)

This poem made me feel hopeful about the African American people. I would argue that it contains a great deal of optimism, optimism that the poet successfully conveys to the reader. The poem skillfully conveys the suffering endured by the African American race throughout history. It does so in a single well-chosen phrase: 'their sob-torn/ throats'. Here we can envisage the cries and lamentations of African American people throughout the centuries, as they were so cruelly taken from their African homeland and forced to endure centuries of slavery and hardship in America. We powerfully imagine their 'throats' being wracked or torn with the effort of so much sobbing.

Yet despite this powerful reference to hardship, the poem retains an optimistic outlook. The African American people have not lost their pride. We sense the poet's pride in her African American heritage when she writes: 'I want to write/ I want to write the songs of my people'. The African American people have not lost their wit and brightness, nor their ability to laugh: 'their sunshine laughter'. The African American have not forgotten their traditional songs or where they came from. The poem's last image of African American hands catching stars from the night sky and forming a 'mirrored pool of brilliance' indicates that this proud people that has endured so much will have a bright and shining future.

PAST EXAM QUESTIONS

EMILY DICKINSON

2016: "Dickinson's use of an innovative style to explore intense experiences can both intrigue and confuse." Discuss this statement, supporting your answer with reference to the poetry of Emily Dickinson on your course.

2014: "The dramatic aspects of Dickinson's poetry can both disturb and delight readers." To what extent do you agree or disagree with the above statement? Support your answer with reference to both the themes and language found in the poetry of Emily Dickinson on your course.

JOHN DONNE

2006: Write an introduction to the poetry of John Donne for new readers. Your introduction should cover the following: - The ideas that were most important to him. - How you responded to his use of language and imagery. Refer to the poems by John Donne that you have studied.

2008: "John Donne uses startling imagery and wit in his exploration of relationships." Give your response to the poetry of John Donne in light of this statement. Support your points with the aid of suitable reference to the poems you have studied.

SEAMUS HEANEY

2003: Dear Seamus Heaney … Write a letter to Seamus Heaney telling him how you responded to some of his poems on your course. Support the points you make by detailed reference to the poems you choose to write about.

GERARD MANLEY HOPKINS

2004: "There are many reasons why the poetry of Gerard Manley Hopkins appeals to his readers." In response to the above statement, write an essay on the poetry of Hopkins. Your essay should focus clearly on the reasons why the poetry is appealing and should refer to the poetry on your course.

2013: "Hopkins' innovative style displays his struggle with what he believes to be fundamental truths." In your opinion, is this a fair assessment of his poetry? Support your answer with suitable reference to the poetry of Gerard Manley Hopkins on your course.

EILÉAN NÍ CHUILLEANÁIN

2015: "Ní Chuilleanáin's demanding subject matter and formidable style can prove challenging." Discuss this statement, supporting your answer with reference to the poetry of Eiléan Ní Chuilleanáin on your course.

2018: "Eiléan Ní Chuilleanáin tells fascinating stories, often examining themes that are relevant to contemporary Ireland, in a style that is both beautiful and mysterious." To what extent do you agree or disagree with this statement? Support your answer with reference to the poetry of Eiléan Ní Chuilleanáin on your course.

SYLVIA PLATH

2014: "Plath makes effective use of language to explore her personal experiences of suffering and to provide occasional glimpses of the redemptive power of love." Discuss this statement, supporting your answer with reference to both the themes and language found in the poetry of Sylvia Plath on your course.

2019: Discuss how effectively Plath uses a range of images to develop her themes and add drama to her poetry. Develop your response with reference to the poems by Sylvia Plath on your course.

WILLIAM BUTLER YEATS

2014: "Yeats uses evocative language to create poetry that includes both personal reflection and public commentary." Discuss this statement, supporting your answer with reference to both the themes and language found in the poetry of W. B. Yeats on your course.

2019: "Yeats's poetry is both intellectually stimulating and emotionally charged." Discuss the extent to which you agree or disagree with the above statement. Develop your response with reference to the themes and language evident in the poems by W. B. Yeats on your course.